# THE OTHER HONG KONG REPORT 1993

Related Titles Already Published

*The Other Hong Kong Report* (for 1989)
Edited by T. L. Tsim and Bernard H. K. Luk

*The Other Hong Kong Report 1990*
Edited by Richard Y. C. Wong and Joseph Y. S. Cheng

*The Other Hong Kong Report 1991*
Edited by Sung Yun-wing and Lee Ming-kwan

*The Other Hong Kong Report 1992*
Edited by Joseph Y. S. Cheng and Paul C. K. Kwong

# THE OTHER
# HONG KONG REPORT
## 1993

Edited by Choi Po-king ▪ Ho Lok-sang

The Chinese University Press

ISBN 962–201–600–6


The Chinese University Press
The Chinese University of Hong Kong
Shatin, New Territories
Hong Kong

ACKNOWLEDGEMENTS

To Mr. Chan Kai-cheung for the map on page 456.

To Bank of China for illustration on page 424.

To Government Information Services for illustrations on pages xxxiv, 402.

To Hospital Authority for illustration on page 220.

To Hong Kong Council of Social Service for Figure 1 of Chapter 14 on page 243.

To Hong Kong Professional Teachers' Union for illustration on page 192.

To Land Development Corporation for illustration on page 176.

To Radio Television Hong Kong for illustration on page 24.

To *South China Morning Post* for illustrations on the cover and on pages 14, 38, 56,
74, 94, 128, 148, 236, 264, 298, 326, 344, 360, 370.

To Trade Development Council for illustration on page 110.

Printed in Hong Kong by Magnum (Offset) Printing Co., Ltd.

# Contents

## ILLUSTRATIONS

# Calendar of Events in 1992–1993

1.7.1992    The government rejects calls to make the Legal Aid Department independent.

2.7.1992    China Motor Bus Company accepts cut of 26 routes in new two-year franchise.

3.7.1992    Lord Wilson quits post in an emotional farewell and is warmly praised by the Chief Secretary for strong leadership.

3.7.1992    Sino-British talks on airport financing between Sir John Coles and Mr. Chen Ziying begin on an unpromising note in Beijing.

8.7.1992    Legco approves motion supporting unconditional renewal of China's most-favoured-nation (MFN) status after heated debate.

9.7.1992    Chris Patten arrives to assume post of Governor of Hong Kong and vows to stand up for the people of the colony and build mutual trust with China.

9.7.1992    Legislators call for direct emergency link between Daya Bay nuclear power plant and Hong Kong.

9.7.1992    The Housing Authority promises to provide homes for "sandwich class" within three years.

12.7.1992   Patten intervenes in confrontation with husbands petitioning Government House over non-admission of wives from China.

13.7.1992   Hongkong and Shanghai Banking Corporation sells entire holding of Cathay Pacific Airways shares to China interests for HK$3.39 billion.

15.7.1992   The Financial Secretary, Hamish Macleod, discloses Exchange Fund of HK$236 billion on eve of JLG (Joint Liaison Group) Airport Committee talks on airport financing.

20.7.1992   Executive Council (Exco) members volunteer to step down to let Patten appoint members of his own choice.

23.7.1992   Patten declines to accept the invitation of Lu Ping, Director of the State Council's Hong Kong and Macau Affairs Office, to visit Beijing before maiden address to the Legislative Council (Legco) in October.

2.8.1992    International Commission of Jurists proposes local group to monitor human rights in Hong Kong after 1997.

5.8.1992    U.S.–H.K. Policy Act is approved by House Foreign Affairs Committee in Washington despite Chinese allegations of interference.

12.8.1992   Patten says polluters must pay to clean up the environment.

13.8.1992   The police round up 140 illegal immigrants and express concern about the escalation of inflow.

20.8.1992    Zhou Nan, Director of New China News Agency (NCNA), warns Patten to converge with the Basic Law at their first meeting at Government House.

21.8.1992    The Hong Kong government rejects Beijing's request for extradition of Shenzhen Public Security defector Gao Peiqi.

25.8.1992    Patten starts new round of meetings with political groups.

27.8.1992    Lu Ping warns that China will dissolve Legco in 1997 if it does not comply with the Basic Law.

30.8.1992    The Transport Complaints Unit reports 36 per cent increase in complaints against taxi drivers as against 1991.

31.8.1992    China wants the Hong Kong government to put more money into new airport and reduce callable equity.

1.9.1992     Lu Ping warns that failure to align Hong Kong political reforms with the Basic Law will breach the Sino-British Joint Declaration.

7.9.1992     Hong Kong Chinese Civil Servants Union presses Alastair Goodlad, Minister of State at the Foreign and Commonwealth Office, for HK$15 billion provident fund to cover pensions after 1997.

9.9.1992     The Immigration Department decides to create a 100-strong new task force to cope with illegal immigration.

11.9.1992    David Li Kwok-po criticizes the Cooperative Resources Centre (CRC) for switching allegiance from Britain to China.

14.9.1992    The Local Police Inspectors' Association says the pace of localization is too slow.

17.9.1992    The Hong Kong government tries to break airport deadlock by offering HK$40 billion land sale input to reduce borrowings.

18.9.1992    China alleges that Hong Kong's airport financing proposals are in breach of the Joint Declaration and the Memorandum of Understanding on the new airport.

22.9.1992    The Environmental Protection Department defends the use of Clearwater Bay Country Park as a rubbish landfill.

22.9.1992    Teacher shortage is likely as enrolment at teacher training colleges has dropped 30 per cent over two years.

25.9.1992    Chinese armed militia board Hong Kong Marine Police launch in British waters and threaten crew.

25.9.1992    Lu Ping says the Basic Law cannot be amended before 1997.

29.9.1992    China apologizes for armed incursion on 25 September.

1.10.1992    NCNA urges Patten to appoint China experts to Exco and make all policies conform with the spirit of the three Sino-British agreements on the future of Hong Kong.

1.10.1992    The Housing Authority lowers flat prices for failed scheme for sitting tenants to 30 per cent of assessed market value.

3.10.1992    Lord MacLehose, in Hong Kong for award of honorary degree, condemns Martin Lee and the United Democrats of Hong Kong (UDHK) for pushing for democracy but blames himself for not pushing for a new airport when he was governor.

6.10.1992    NCNA's Zhang Junsheng warns that in tabling electoral arrangements for 1994 and 1995 without China's blessing Patten will be breaching the principle of convergence and hampering Sino-British cooperation.

7.10.1992    Patten unveils his constitutional package to enfranchise about half of Hong Kong citizens and enrages China.

11.10.1992    Cheung Man-yee, Director of Broadcasting, pleads for end to seven-year delay on corporatization of Radio Television Hong Kong (RTHK).

12.10.1992    NCNA accuses Patten of masquerading as "a saviour" in offering to democratize Hong Kong and go it alone on the airport.

14.10.1992    Legco backs motion moved by legislator Jimmy McGregor in support of an Election Committee to elect ten seats in 1995 but comprised of elected members of District Boards.

16.10.1992    Chinese Premier Li Peng blasts Patten and Chinese side of JLG calls unprecedented press conference to demand changes in British funding proposals for the new airport.

19.10.1992    China's Xiao Weiyun says there will be no "through train" for the Hong Kong government's policy secretaries and Executive Councillors and Beijing will vet them prior to change of sovereignty.

19.10.1992    The Accident Insurance Association of Hong Kong reports staggering increase in unrecovered stolen luxury cars over 1991.

21.10.1992    A total of 500 contract expatriate police officers fear non-renewal of contract under localization policy.

22.10.1992    Local civil service unions are fearful of the consequences for them of Patten's confrontation with Beijing.

23.10.1992    Lu Ping calls Beijing press conference to say that China will form the Special Administrative Region (SAR) legislature, judiciary and government unilaterally if Britain reneges on its previous commitments to converge with the Basic Law.

26.10.1992    Former Executive Councillor, now Beijing-appointed Hong Kong Affairs

Adviser, Sir S. Y. Chung, supports China's objections to Patten's alleged deviation from convergence policy.

28.10.1992  British Foreign Office jumps the gun on Beijing by releasing the Hurd–Qian correspondence of 1990 on electoral arrangements for 1995.

1.11.1992  *Sunday Morning Post* poll of 452 residents of Shenzhen and Guangzhou indicates that Governor Patten is better-known and has higher performance ratings than his provincial equivalents.

5.11.1992  Former Chief Secretary Sir David Akers-Jones criticizes Patten's policy of "divergence" in interview with *Wah Kiu Yat Po*.

6.11.1992  NCNA's Zhou Nan accuses Patten of seeking political independence for Hong Kong and perpetuating "colonial rule".

9.11.1992  Former U.S. Consul General in Hong Kong, Burton Levin, and Australia's Foreign Minister, Gareth Evans, both publicly back Patten's proposed political reforms for Hong Kong.

9.11.1992  The Education Department asks the Social Welfare Department and the Hong Kong Council of Social Service jointly to investigate causes of spate of student suicides.

10.11.1992  Shiu Sin-por, Hong Kong Delegate for China's National People's Congress (NPC), says that every Hong Kong citizen should disassociate himself or herself from the UDHK because of their assistance to Chinese dissidents fleeing China after June Fourth crackdown.

16.11.1992  British Foreign Secretary Douglas Hurd gives full backing to Patten in London whose constitutional proposals, he says, were fully discussed in the British Cabinet before they were announced by the Governor.

16.11.1992  China attacks Patten for meeting with Taiwan's Central Standing Committee Member, Hsu Sheng-fa, in Hong Kong on 3 November.

17.11.1992  Hang Seng Index drops 206 points on report that China's Zhu Rongji said, in London, that if Patten pushes ahead with his political programme for Hong Kong, China might as well abandon the Joint Declaration.

20.11.1992  *People's Daily*, overseas edition, mounts another "blistering" attack on Patten alleging conspiracy with foreign powers to destabilize Hong Kong and China.

27.11.1992  The Finance Committee of Legco, after five and a half hours' meeting and filibustering by CRC members, approves HK$6.69 billion for airport site formation contract by a majority of two votes.

28.11.1992  Chinese Ambassador to London, Ma Yuzhen and NCNA representative are summoned by British diplomats and warned against any further attacks on Container Terminal No. 9 contract.

30.11.1992 China threatens to invalidate all current and future Hong Kong government contracts which extend beyond 1 July 1997 if these contracts are not previously validated by China.

1.12.1992 Hang Seng Index falls 308.92 points on fears of worsening Sino-British relations.

2.12.1992 Double robbery shoot-out with armed gangs in Tsuen Wan and To Kwa Wan leaves 2 dead, 11 injured and Hong Kong stunned.

3.12.1992 Hang Seng Index drops 433.44 points but unfazed Patten denies responsibility. However, Sir Percy Cradock on BBC Television avers that Beijing would rather ruin Hong Kong's economy than give up struggle against Patten to block democratic reform.

10.12.1992 Chinese JLG team leader, Guo Fengmin, expresses doubts on the worth of JLG meetings if Patten does not abandon his political plans. He also accuses Britain of having a negative attitude towards funding civil service pensions.

12.12.1992 Senior expatriate civil servants consider using Human Rights Bill to contest the government's localization policy.

14.12.1992 Lee Kuan-yew, at The University of Hong Kong, warns against trying to fight China for more democracy for Hong Kong but is barracked by students on Singapore government's record on human rights.

14.12.1992 Ms. Liu Yiu-chu abandons earlier resolve not to serve on the NPC and agrees to be nominated for another five-year term in order "not to be arrogant".

18.12.1992 Cathay Pacific Airways threatens to take hard line against cabin crew refusing to work down as strike action looms.

21.12.1992 Over 250 labour and community organizations denounce Patten's reforms in advertisements in Chinese language newspapers.

22.12.1992 Hong Kong Bar Council issues statement questioning the propriety and legality of China's comments, made on 30 November, that contracts leases and agreements straddling 1997 which were entered into by the Hong Kong government needed to be specifically validated by China.

22.12.1992 U.S. President Bill Clinton hints at link between China's favourable balance of trade with the U.S. and Hong Kong's unfavourable prospects of freedom under Chinese sovereignty in the future.

31.12.1992 Twenty revellers die in Lan Kwai Fong midnight stampede.

4.1.1993 Country Parks Ordinance is under review after public complaints over Shalotung golf course and Clearwater Bay landfill.

10.1.1993    Beijing attacks RTHK, through *Wen Wei Po*, for alleged instigation of subversion against China.

10.1.1993    Chairperson of Hong Kong Bar Association, Jaqueline Leung, at opening of the Legal Year, denounces China's threat to set up its own judicial system in Hong Kong.

13.1.1993    Legislator Philip Wong's move to block introduction of Patten's electoral bill is heavily defeated by 35 votes to 2 in motion debate.

14.1.1993    Cathay Pacific Flight Attendants Union strike causes chaos at Kai Tak Airport.

14.1.1993    The Secretary for Recreation and Culture, James So, is accused of bad faith and continued prevarication over corporatization of RTHK.

15.1.1993    ICAC (Independent Commission Against Corruption) report links triads, professional touts and solicitors clerks in widespread malpractice in the legal profession.

18.1.1993    Housing Authority members' declarations of interest reveal extensive involvement in property, property consultation and engineering businesses.

26.1.1993    Continuing Cathay Pacific Airways strike raises fundamental questions about the adequacy of Hong Kong industrial law and protection for striking workers.

27.1.1993    China mounts personal attack on the Secretary for Economic Services, Anson Chan, over Container Terminal No. 9 and for "defending the British acts of violating the Joint Declaration and misleading international investors".

29.1.1993    Cathay Pacific cabin crew strike ends after Legco intervenes on the Labour Department's failure to implement prescribed conciliation procedure.

1.2.1993     Zhou Nan at NCNA Spring Reception again attacks Britain and vows that China will never "barter away principles" and Zhang Junsheng refutes Hurd's London statement of 19 January that Hong Kong people must be involved in the discussions on their future.

6.2.1993     Beijing's Hong Kong Affairs Adviser and former Secretary for Home Affairs, Donald Liao, is reported as saying that Hong Kong government officials who publicly back Patten's constitutional package will be putting their careers at risk.

7.2.1993     Allen Rogers, Chairman of the Localization Committee of the Association of Expatriate Civil Servants, says they "may embark on campaigns that may embarrass the Government" if it does not allay their fears of localization.

16.2.1993    Hong Kong Amateur Sports Federation backs Beijing's bid for Olympics 2000.

16.2.1993    Exco defers decision on gazetting of electoral bill.

18.2.1993    The Secretary for Recreation and Culture, James So, tells Legco Panel that the proposal to corporatize RTHK has been "shelved for the moment" because of the unfavourable political climate.

18.2.1993    Government spokesmen confirm that if Sino-British talks on the 1994 and 1995 elections do take place the British team will be led by Ambassador, Sir Robin MacLaren; the Political Adviser and the Secretary for Constitutional Affairs will be on the team.

26.2.1993    NCNA's Zhang Junsheng says that neither Exco nor Legco have any right to a say on the electoral arrangements for 1995 and arouses further concern over the possibility of a secret Sino-British deal.

26.2.1993    Eight hundred Laguna City residents demonstrate at Legco Building to protest against provision of facilities for ex-psychiatric patients.

27.2.1993    British Foreign Secretary Douglas Hurd gives unambiguous pledge that Britain will never again enter into a secret deal with China on Hong Kong.

28.2.1993    CRC, reformed as the new Liberal Party, holds first meeting under Chairman, Allen Lee Peng-fei.

2.3.1993     Surprise retirement by the Secretary for Education and Manpower, John Chan Cho-chak, at 50, triggers reshuffle of policy portfolios.

3.3.1993     The Financial Secretary's low-tax, high-spending budget sets pattern for annual deficits up to 1996–1997 but projects reserves of HK$78.4 billion for the SAR government.

3.3.1993     Tung Tau Estate residents confront the police in an attempt to stop the construction work of a resource centre for the mentally handicapped.

5.3.1993     Patten explains delays in gazetting electoral bill, for the fourth time, in question and answer session in Legco and lifts Hang Seng Index.

6.3.1993     Horse Trainer Brian Kan Ping-chee gives up reliance on the Hong Kong Commissioner of Police and gets back his stolen Mercedes Benz from China, promptly, by phoning Public Security contacts in Shenzhen and Guangdong. Kan commented "that's what friends are for".

7.3.1993     Two thousand public housing tenants demonstrate in Chater Garden and outside Central Government Offices against Housing Authority's double-rent policy for better-off households.

9.3.1993     Legco's Security Panel told that only 1 in 1,827 formal complaints against the police in 1992 had been substantiated after investigation.

12.3.1993    Patten gazettes electoral bill after China declines to fix a date for talks on electoral arrangements.

15.3.1993    Chinese Premier Li Peng, in work report to NPC at 8th Congress, launches unprecedented and ferocious attack on Patten's "perfidious and unilaterally crafted proposals to violate previous Sino-British Agreements", and knocks 315.79 points off the Hang Seng Index.

17.3.1993    Lu Ping tells Beijing Press Conference that Patten will be condemned by history as "a man of guilt" and warns that China will set up its own "stove".

18.3.1993    The Court of Appeal reviews suspended sentence passed on former legislator Tai Chin-wah for forged credentials and jails him for nine months.

19.3.1993    The Association of Expatriate Civil Servants, after unsatisfactory meeting with the Secretary for the Civil Service, Barrie Wiggham, vows to challenge the localization policy in the courts.

21.3.1993    Zhou Nan says that China's "new stove" for Hong Kong will consist of Hong Kong Affairs Advisers and Chinese experts and will "converge" with the 1996 Preparatory Committee. It will work under the guidance of the Hong Kong and Macau Affairs Office and meet in Beijing.

29.3.1993    Beijing releases names of second batch of 49 Hong Kong Affairs Advisers including the only non-Asian and former Chief Secretary, Sir David Akers-Jones. First batch of 44 was appointed on 11 March 1992.

1.4.1993     Hong Kong Affairs Advisers are mobbed by student protesters at Kai Tak Airport on their way to inauguration ceremony in Beijing.

2.4.1993     Hong Kong businesspersons urge Hong Kong and Macau Affairs Office to separate economics from politics in their current dispute with Patten and free infrastructure projects connected with the airport.

6.4.1993     Patten at Royal Institute of International Affairs, in London, appeals to China to begin dialogue on electoral arrangements for 1995 and gets warm support from audience of officials, politicians and academics.

6.4.1993     Beijing Hong Kong Development Company withdraws equity participation from New China Hong Kong Group after Lu Ping denies accusations by Legislative Councillor Martin Lee Chu-ming that Mainland officials were playing the stock market on inside information. Lu Ping admitted that there was "a small linkage" since former deputy department head in the Beijing office Yu Dapeng was founder of the company.

7.4.1993     New Territories Heung Yee Kuk objects to an amendment to the New Territories Ordinance to allow women the right to inherit land.

13.4.1993    Surprise announcement by China and Britain to start talks on electoral arrangements is described by Patten as "a victory for common sense" and lifts Hang Seng Index 371 points in record one-day rise.

15.4.1993 China says it will reserve right to veto legislators returned in 1995 elections and refuses to issue permits to reporters to cover talks in Beijing starting on 22 April.

18.4.1993 A substantial fall in car thefts suggests that joint action by Hong Kong and Guangdong police in combatting cross-border crime is taking effect.

23.4.1993 Legislators rumble financially self-serving fiddle over new post of Commissioner for Economic and Trade Affairs in Washington to be filled by Barrie Wiggham but fail to force the government to back down.

27.4.1993 Beijing-affiliated business groups sweep the board in elections for the General Committee of the Hong Kong General Chamber of Commerce, also ousting Jardine & Matheson (China)'s Chairman, Martin Barrow.

29.4.1993 The government declines to reveal progress in discussions with Chinese authorities on contingency plans for an accident at Daya Bay nuclear power plant when pressed by Legco's Environmental Affairs Panel.

30.4.1993 Legislative Councillors threaten to invoke Powers and Privileges Bill to break government silence on the causes and costs to taxpayers of the resignation of Provisional Airport Authority's Chief Executive, Richard Allen.

2.5.1993 Over 1,000 Laguna City residents march to Central Government Offices to protest at government secrecy over plans for facilities there for ex-psychiatric patients.

6.5.1993 NCNA's Zhang Xianglin tells a Public Administration Association Seminar that the appointments and promotions of Hong Kong's senior civil servants after 1997 might be affected if they go too far in supporting the British government's policies and names the Secretary for Constitutional Affairs as a case in point.

12.5.1993 Sino-British Land Commission's approval of the release of 127.8 hectares of land for development lift Hang Seng Index 263.37 points since 11 May and through the 7,000-point barrier.

12.5.1993 The Financial Secretary in face of heavy pressure from legislators makes partial disclosure of the Allen case but refuses to explain the basis of calculation for the golden boot of HK$5.5 million.

19.5.1993 Business and Professional Federation's HK$5 million report *Hong Kong 21* predicts a prosperous future for Hong Kong but ignores political problems and dangers of loss of autonomy.

20.5.1993 China unexpectedly endorses issue of Wharf Cable 12-year Pay-TV licence, the Scheme of Control for Hong Kong Electric and New Territories West Landfill contract at JLG meeting.

23.5.1993    Sir Percy Cradock arrives in Hong Kong on the way to Beijing to meet Vice Foreign Minister Jiang Enzhu and warns that a confrontatioanl approach with China will achieve nothing and that if Patten pushes reforms unilaterally they will last "no more than a couple of years".

26.5.1993    Legco passes Boundaries and Electoral Commission Bill and supports a motion calling for disclosure of agenda and progress at each round of Sino-British talks.

27.5 1993    China criticizes "unilateral" passing of Boundaries and Electoral Commission Bill by Legco as creating new obstacle to Sino-British talks on electoral arrangements.

31.5.1993    Hong Kong Monetary Authority moves to stop reckless borrowing for purchase of stock as happened with Denning Investment flotation in February in which HK$240 billion was tied up.

31.5.1993    Thai survivors of disastrous fire at Kadar International (Thailand) factory in Bangkok come to Hong Kong to seek compensation from parent company.

1.6.1993     Former Legislative Councillor, Gilbert Leung Kam-ho, is jailed for three years for trying to buy votes.

1.6.1993     The House of Common Foreign Affairs Committee decides to visit Hong Kong, China and Taiwan to investigate Sino-British relations.

2.6.1993     Twelve workers die in fatal lift plunge at worksite in Quarry Bay.

4.6.1993     In spite of heavy rain, over 12,000 persons attend candlelight vigil in Victoria Park to commemorate June Fourth crackdown in Beijing.

7.6.1993     NCNA's Zhang Junsheng criticizes Britain for "playing little tricks" and describes Legco as "an advisory body" of the Governor that has "downgraded" itself to "a city forum".

9.6.1993     Legco delegation in London to lobby British Ministers and Members of Parliament on behalf of potentially stateless ethnic minorities in Hong Kong gets the British government to make a major concession to holders of BDTC (British Dependent Territory Citizenship) passport holders applying for BNO (British National [Overseas]) passports.

13.6.1993    Local Crown Counsels say the Legal Department's localization scheme is a failure and demand more opportunities to "act" in senior posts.

16.6.1993    British Prime Minister John Major calls summit meeting on Hong Kong in London on 1 July because of slow progress in Sino-British talks.

18.6.1993    China eases stalemate over airport development by approving franchise for West Harbour Crossing at meeting of the JLG Airport Committee.

19.6.1993    Historic Memorandum of Regulatory Cooperation to pave way for listing of yuan-denominated shares is signed in Beijing by officials of state and commercial regulatory organizations from Beijing, Shanghai, Shenzhen and Hong Kong.

22.6.1993   China releases names of working group or "second stove" of 27 Mainland officials and 30 Hong Kong citizens chaired by Chinese Foreign Minister, Qian Qichen, to pave the way for the 1996 Preparatory Committee.

23.6.1993   JLG meeting in Hong Kong ends in frustration whilst, in Beijing, the Sixth Round of Sino-British talks on electoral arrangements opens with expression of good intent.

24.6.1993   Moody's Investor Services analysis gives Hong Kong high credit rating but expects China to interfere in Hong Kong's internal affairs after 1997.

# Preface

Like its predecessors, *The Other Hong Kong Report 1993* is a complement to the official *Hong Kong 1993*, in that it contains the critical assessment of events and developments that occurred within the year — from July 1992 through June 1993 — by scholars, veteran journalists, commentators, and professionals in their areas of specialty. Like its predecessors, apart from the standard chapters that match with chapters in the official report, *The Other Hong Kong Report 1993* contains special feature chapters that cover topics of interest and importance. This year the special topics span the political, sociological, economic, and historical dimensions. Frank Ching wrote lucidly on politics, politicians, and political parties — all of which have assumed new meaning in today's Hong Kong. Paul Kwong carefully documented and commented on the internationalization of population and the globalization of families, a subject most pertinent to the stability of the economy and having far-reaching implications on the fabric of Hong Kong society. Lai Wai-chung studied the operation of the Land Development Corporation, whose urban redevelopment projects have always been controversial and criticized in particular by affected residents of blocks acquired for redevelopment purposes. Tsang Shu-ki studied income distribution, and found worrying developments that deserve public and official attention. Choi Po-king gave a detailed report on women-related issues, again a subject of recurrent interest. Robert Chung wrote on public opinion, which appears to assume increasing sway in the course of public policy development. George Shen did a thorough study on China's investment in Hong Kong. His effort in gathering information that is often scattered and certainly not easily accessible deserves to be commended. Finally, Chan Kai-cheung gave a new perspective on Hong Kong's historical past. This perspective, as readers will surely agree, is timely in this final hour of transition to Chinese sovereignty.

The more traditional chapters of this volume continue to benefit from the painstaking work of many veteran authors and professionals whose pens wrote with both authority and insight. John Walden, a long-time friend of *The Other Hong Kong Report*, prepared the Calendar of Events and wrote on the implementation of the Sino-British Joint Declaration. Norman Miners wrote the chapter on constitution and administration; Margaret Ng reviewed the legal system. Developments in law and order were covered by John Ho. Henry Ho, Y. C. Jao, Li Kui-wai and Kenneth Lo, and Chau Leung-chuen wrote the chapters on the economy, monetary and financial affairs, trade and industry, and the labour market.

We have tried to enlist new authors to give a fresh point of view on traditional topics. Lee Wai-man's chapter on education is not only illustrated with traditional Chinese mythology, but he also discussed at length the interface between postmodernism and education. Leung Man-fuk's chapter on medical and health is written from the vantage point of a medical practitioner. Cecilia Chan's chapter on social welfare was written with much conviction. Leung Wai-tung's chapter on housing and Stephen Tang's on transportation have two things in common. They are both rich in details, with the earlier drafts requiring considerable trimming in favour of space. Both chapters present a clear stand and are unusually advocative. Man Si-wai and Simon Davies wrote respectively the chapters on the environment and Hong Kong broadcasting.

We thank the authors for the tremendous effort they have made in meeting deadlines and in researching their articles. We also thank The Chinese University Press for the professional support given us throughout the preparation of this volume. In particular, Fung Wai-kit has served this onerous project well with his profound patience and meticulousness, and Patrick Kwong has proved most encouraging and inspiring throughout. We hope the combined effort of our team of dedicated authors and profes-sionals will prove worthwhile for our readers, and make this volume a useful reference and source of insight for many years to come.

Ho Lok-sang
Choi Po-king
*October 1993*

# Introduction

Choi Po-king

In the year of 1888, the Cantonese scholar-bureaucrat Huang Zunxian 黃遵憲 wrote a poem about the British colony of Hong Kong, as he stopped over in the territory on home leave from San Francisco, where he worked as Consul General. The poem goes like this:

> *The waters of Yao flows while the sun of Xia prevails*, (he was referring to the early, legendary Han rulers)
> *Doubtless the attire here is also properly Han*;
> *Ascending the storeys I see land of our own all around*,
> *But there is no Yellow Dragon* (the Yellow Dragon was the national flag under the Qing) *insignia to be found*.

水是堯時日夏時，衣冠又是漢官儀。
登樓四望真吾土，不見黃龍上大旗。

A hundred and five years has passed since Huang wrote this little piece, and the Yellow Dragon flag has already been superseded by two others: the "Blue Sky, White Sun and the Red Land" (the Nationalist flag), and the "Five Stars" (the Communist flag), both of which are still flying, in Taiwan and the Mainland respectively. Yet the misgiving he harboured, namely, Chinese people and customs under foreign rule, is still very much alive and is indeed an issue placed at centre stage today.

## ☐ Not Properly Chinese?

There has been much talk about Hong Kong being a meeting place of the

---

Choi Po-king is a lecturer in the Department of Educational Administration and Policy, The Chinese University of Hong Kong.

East and West, with the implication that the Chinese in Hong Kong have been westernized to a certain extent. This, coupled with the fact that the territory has been under British rule for more than a century, gives rise to much disdain on the part of ethnic and cultural purists. This disdain is undoubtedly fed by the Confucian insistence on *zhengtong* 正統 , approximately translated as "the orthodox way", and is now linked to its modern version, namely, a restrictive kind of nationalism and a related anti-foreignism.

Such disdain is evident in many instances. Film-makers and critics from the Mainland and Taiwan, for example, would talk *past* their counterparts from Hong Kong at conferences. In official accounts of the Chinese film industry, too, Hong Kong's role would usually be glossed over. This is despite the territory's importance in the history of Chinese film-making, and the fact that it is largely Hong Kong films instead of Mainland Chinese or Taiwanese ones which have made a significant impact internationally.[1] Similarly, there is talk of eliminating all traces of colonial influences from school contents and implementing a kind of "nationalist education" after 1997.

A wariness of such purists' disdain and restrictive nationalism underlies some of our contributions in this year's edition of *The Other Hong Kong Report*. Paul Kwong, for example, ends his chapter on "Internationalization of Population and Globalization of Families" with a number of queries, among others:

> Will this internationalized populace [of Hong Kong] be gradually cleansed in favour of the Han race? And will Putonghua, actually a dialect originating from Hebei province, be utilized as an linguistic agent to cleanse the Cantonese dialect out of all major formal discourses in town? Will formal Chinese documentation (*gongwen*) practically replace English as the official written language? What about the filing system?

While Kwong is explicit about his worries over the exacerbation of what he calls "Han-race chauvinism" in this late transition period before 1997, Frank Ching, in his chapter on "Politics, Politicians and Political Parties", coolly outlines the positions of the various political parties regarding the ethnic make-up of the Legislative Council (Legco) of the future Special Administrative Region (SAR). He noted with a tinge of irony that it

---

[1] See Lam Lei, "The Two Banks and the Three Territories — The Marginalisation of Hong Kong Films", *Hong Kong Economic Journal*, 23 July 1992.

is two of the three liberal groups, namely, Meeting Point and the Hong Kong Association for Democracy and People's Livelihood (HKADPL) which have made the most restrictive proposal. This is, namely, "that foreign passport holders be barred altogether from membership in Legco".

Purists' disdain notwithstanding, Hong Kong, in fact, remains very much a Chinese society in terms of its cultural make-up. Indeed, more detached observers, like the late anthropologist Barbara Ward, have remarked on the paradoxical fact that Hong Kong, under foreign rule and rapid modernization, preserves more of Chinese customs and rituals than in the Mainland itself.[2]

This seemingly improbable situation comes about largely because this territory has been spared the interventionist social and cultural policies and upheavals implemented or caused by modern party-rulers. Of course, Hong Kong has also not experienced the social revolution which had taken place in the Mainland, and which effectively shattered the social order that had been the bedrock of so many traditional customs and rituals.

The "Chineseness" of Hong Kong people was, in fact, evident in some of the popular reactions to the worsening of Sino-British relationships in the past year. Since Governor Chris Patten presented his constitutional reform proposals in October 1992, there has been no lack of commentators who, in one way or another, attribute the deteriorating relationships to Patten's unfamiliarity with Chinese ways.

What exactly are "Chinese ways" is not clear, but to many people, they include at least the avoidance of outright confrontation. This is where Patten differs most from his predecessor, Lord Wilson, who is well known for his diplomatic and accommodating style in dealing with the Beijing government.

While John Walden, author of the chapter on "The Implementation of the Sino-British Joint Declaration", regards such a style as manifesting capitulation to the Beijing government and a shameful sell-out of the people of Hong Kong, others tend to look on it rather more favourably in retrospect. Prolonged unfriendly Sino-British exchanges in the past year, coupled with the unfavourable effects these had on the stock exchange, were depressing to many in Hong Kong. Some of them then began to see the dispute as having arisen from fundamental cultural differences between

---

[2] See Barbara Ward and Joan Law, *Chinese Festivals in Hong Kong* (Hong Kong: The Guidebook Co. Ltd., 1993).

the Chinese and British, and as mentioned, to Patten's unfamiliarity with Chinese ways.

While the cultural explanation cannot substitute for the complex configuration of political and economic factors behind the Sino-British dispute, it is nevertheless important in one's assessment of what Hong Kong society is like. Robert Chung, in his chapter on "Public Opinion", offers an interesting observation in this regard. His public opinion polls indicate that, from late December 1992 to early July 1993, Patten's popularity went up when he took a relatively low profile at the Sino-British dispute. Otherwise, it went down. This seems to show that Hong Kong people do tend to view confrontation unfavourably. If one takes this tendency to be a Chinese trait, then Hong Kong people at large can be said to be very Chinese.

## ☐ A Different Look at Hong Kong's History

If one is to take seriously the Chineseness of Hong Kong society and people, then one would have to dig deeper than its westernized facade would allow us to see. Chan Kai-cheung, author of the chapter on "History", suggests a way of doing this.

Chan's thesis is a historiographic one, namely, that Hong Kong history to date has been flawed by a blindness to the geo-political importance of the territory in the Chinese dynastic histories in the past. This blindness, he says, has been induced by a colonial paradigm which effectively treats Hong Kong's pre-colonial history as virtually non-existent. Following his argument, the study of the history of Hong Kong would now have to undergo a total revamping. One would have to get out of the colonial straitjacket which has restricted one's view to no further back than the mid-nineteenth century. Such a move is indispensable to a better comprehension of how the present situation of Hong Kong has come about, as well as to a more accurate assessment of its future possibilities.

## ☐ Keeping Each Other at Arm's Length

There is of course no simple answer to the question of how westernized or Chinese in character the society and people of Hong Kong is. My own observation is that Hong Kong has never achieved a balanced and thorough integration of cultures, East and West, or more specifically, Chinese and Anglo-Saxon. The dispute between local and expatriate civil servants, which was still brewing at the time of writing, serves to underline very clearly the long-existing distance and mistrust between the two communities that had lived in close proximity with each other for more than a century.

The Hong Kong Chinese community is very cosmopolitan in business and related transactions, but it nevertheless keeps a wide social and cultural distance from the expatriates. In the consumption of cultural products such as leisure reading, films, popular songs and so on, the Chinese community also manifests a distinct centripetal tendency. The British, at the same time, have also kept to themselves, much in the same way as the Chinese have done, for the past century and a half. The sense of superiority as colonialists and as white people obviously did not help them mix freely and easily with the Chinese.

Perhaps the New Year tragedy in Lan Kwai Fong, which claimed the lives of twenty-one youths, is an ominous sign of the insurmountable difficulty of cultural integration. Significantly, Lan Kwai Fong is located at the juncture of the historical Western (largely British), Indian and Chinese business settlements dating back to the late nineteenth century. Since the late 1980s, for some fortuitous reasons, it has turned itself into an entertainment spot, largely for expatriates, but increasingly attracting local Chinese youths and westernized "yuppies". In the past one or two years, Lan Kwai Fong has evolved its own festivals and occasions, and it might have become a unique and rare cultural phenomenon of East–West integration. That is, if not for the New Year tragedy of 1993, which unfortunately sets its development back for at least some time to come.

Perhaps it was not only the precipitous gradient and the slippery road surface which had caused the tragedy to happen in Lan Kwai Fong? Perhaps it was also for the lack of mutually binding norms that characterize a truly integrated community?

These are wild speculations indeed. One thing for sure, however, is that cultural integration on a concrete, day-to-day basis, would have to find its ways apart from, or despite, Lan Kwai Fong.

## ☐ The Common Hero

If Lan Kwai Fong serves to underline the lack of East–West integration, another tragic accident in 1993 illustrates very well the high level of cultural integration and maturation within the Hong Kong Chinese community itself.

For many Chinese schoolchildren and youths in Hong Kong, the beginning of the summer vacation in 1993 was sadly marred by the death of thirty-year-old Wong Ka-kui, lead singer of a local Canto-rock band, BEYOND. Falling from a height in a TV studio in Tokyo while shooting a show, Wong sank into coma and died a few days later.

Prior to Wong's fatal accident, BEYOND had already been in Tokyo for some months, trying, as some Hong Kong pop singers have done, to make inroads into the competitive Japanese pop music market. BEYOND's endeavour, though tragically curtailed by Wong's premature death, nevertheless stands as good testimony to the strength and potential of Hong Kong's popular culture. Compared to other Hong Kong artistes who have made good overseas, BEYOND distinguish themselves by their originality. They are, for example, among the very few who write their own music and lyrics. The fatal detraction of their number is undoubtedly a great loss to the development of local popular culture, as well as to the on-going process of its internationalization.

Wong's death brings to light more than the potential of Hong Kong culture, however. Anyone who has been to his memorial concert in the neighbourhood Ko Shan Theatre in Kowloon could feel the strong sense of common bond in the grief for the artiste.

One could, of course, argue that such a common bond is characteristic of rock concerts the world over, not to say a memorial concert attended essentially by devoted fans. Yet, what is peculiar about the memorial concert of Wong Ka-kui, and indeed, society's reaction to his death, is that the grief and, at least, the sense of loss, cuts across the age spectrum and across social class.

The fact about Hong Kong's popular culture is that, instead of being a counter-culture posed against the mainstream, middle-class, adult generation, it is a widely shared and very MOR (middle-of-the-road) entity. This homogeneity, or absence of social divisiveness, is perhaps typical of a newly emergent culture, such as that of Hong Kong. Of course, the rise to stardom of Wong Ka-kui from very humble origins is also something which many Hong Kong people, adult and youth alike, can easily identify with. This undoubtedly adds to his attraction as a common hero for all.

## ☐ Emergence of a Public Forum

Hong Kong, like Taiwan, may be a very Chinese society. Yet it is definitely not a traditional one, just as Taiwan is not either. Among other things, what sets Hong Kong, and perhaps also Taiwan, apart from traditional societies is the growth of an increasingly visible public forum. The emergence of this public forum is very much evident in the various chapters of this edition.

Robert Chung traces the recent development of opinion polls as the medium of public expression, prompted by the first direct elections held in 1991, and more recently, the arrival of Chris Patten, a political heavyweight and a rather outgoing character. "As society becomes more open, and the voice of the people needs more often to be heard, opinion polls will have an increasingly important role to play," Chung observes.

Indeed, the voice of the people comes through in many other ways, not only through opinion polls but also through the media, political representation, and even collective action. Furthermore, as the public forum expands, the traditional, closed decision-making structure, together with its associated rules of the game, is also forced to change. Government policies become more contestable, and, for the first time in the colony's history, legislators feel it necessary to respond more to their constituencies rather than to the administration.

These developments, as reflected in the constitutional structure and administration of the territory, are well delineated by Norman Miners in his chapter. Though it might appear that many of the changes he discusses (for example, the end to overlapping of membership of the Executive and Legislative Councils, hence the considerable weakening of the former) were introduced by Chris Patten on his assumption of office, it could be argued that they are, in fact, consequences of more subtle socio-political developments that have been going on for at least the past decade.

The emergence of the public forum and its impact is indeed evident in many aspects of local life. Cecilia Chan, in her chapter on "Social Welfare", for example, raises the issue of the "politicization of welfare". In the year under review, such politicization manifested itself, among other things, in the heated debate between residents' group on the one hand, and "client groups, welfare agencies, parents' organizations together with the Joint Council for the Physically and Mentally Disabled" on the other, over the establishment of resource and rehabilitation centres for the mentally handicapped and mentally ill persons respectively.

Cecilia Chan is concerned about the disastrous possibility of "political concerns", i.e. the concern on the part of individual political groups and politicians to curry favour with their constituencies (the residents' groups in this case) overriding the principles of social equity. Is this threat not an inevitable price to pay for a more open and participatory society?

Perhaps this price could be ameliorated through society's proper recognition of the rights of the individual, regardless of his or her sex, race, status, or state of health. At the time of writing, Anna Wu Hung-yuk, appointed Legco member, is actively seeking to enact comprehensive anti-discrimination legislation, through the tabling of a private members' bill if necessary. Her effort has been prompted by the openly discriminatory actions of residents' groups against mentally handicapped and ill persons in the past year. Yet it is also warmly welcomed by the women's front, which has been gathering force in the past few years, as reviewed in the chapter on "Women" written by myself.

Demands for the widening of public discussion and participation are often precipitated by concerns over one's own interests, which, at the same time, arouses debates over one's legitimate rights. These may be the rights of a resident of a housing estate in which a resource centre for parents of mentally handicapped children is built or, conversely, a parent of a mentally handicapped child, or a resident of a public housing estate required to pay double-rent, an owner of property included in urban redevelopment schemes, or fisherfolk whose catch is affected by extensive dredging or dumping, just to name a few categories discussed in our various chapters. These debates are often confusing, not to say heated and even emotionally charged, especially for those intimately concerned. Yet, taken together, these debates would ultimately contribute to a more thorough and sophisticated understanding and, hopefully, acceptance of the workings of an open and fair society.

## ☐ Policy as Choice

Among other things, debates such as the ones outlined above would make more transparent the fact that government policy entails a choice of some sort. Seeing policy as choice, one would not take policy as an incontestable "given", but rather, as a deliberate favouring on the part of decision-makers of one option or principle over another.

Several authors in this edition contribute to this perception by contesting the principles underlying given policies, or choices, made by the government in recent years.

Lai Wai-chung, for example, challenges government-led urban renewal in the name of better and more efficient land use, undertaken by the Land Development Corporation (LDC). He warns of possible economic and political destabilization which might result from the

LDC's violation of private property rights in the process of land resumption.

In the related field of housing, Leung Wai-tung criticizes with vigour the various forms of public housing subsidies for their deviation from the principle of social equity. Upholding the basic criterion of subsidization based on need, Leung Wai-tung expresses serious misgivings over recent housing policies. These policies seem to her to serve the purpose of appeasing the advantaged sectors, thereby promoting stability of some sort, rather than fair distribution of public resources.

## ☐ Professionals and the Public Forum

In the extension of the public forum, professionals as distinct social groups may find themselves involved in crucial yet ambivalent ways. As groups with relatively easy access to abstract concepts as well as information for evaluating policies, professionals could often play an important role in facilitating public discussions on various matters. On the other hand, the entrenched power of individual professional groups which hold virtual monopoly of expertise in certain fields might inhibit public participation and discussion, particularly on the grassroots level.

Medical practitioners are a case in point. Leung Man-fuk, himself a medical consultant, discusses in his chapter on "Medical and Health" the recent debate on patients' rights. This debate, which he says has arisen from accusations of doctors' deliberate mystification of medical matters, overcharging by private medical practitioners, and increasing awareness of individual rights among an educated public, is basically a human rights' issue:

> Patients' rights should be an extension of basic human rights which implies equality of all human beings. In this sense, the traditional relationship between the medical practitioner in a superior position to their patients should be changed.

Medical practitioners may well be experts, comparatively speaking, in matters of health. Yet it is clear from Leung Man-fuk's discourse that they may not be better judges than other citizens regarding a related and equally important issue. This is, namely, the issue of "the mode of health care delivery", including, in Leung's words, "the goals and targets of health care provision", and a "proper integration between private and public health care systems".

While it seems necessary to debunk the power of an over-mystified body of experts in the field of health, Man Si-wai argues for a reinforcement of the "legal, financial, academic, political, organizational, and operational resources" of local Green Groups in order to meet the challenge of their newfound role in policy-making. In short, Green Groups have to be more professional, in the sense that they should strengthen their theoretical and legal grounding in environmental issues, as well as mobilization capabilities.

Of course, what Man Si-wai is advocating is not a professionalization in the direction of what the medical practitioners have achieved, namely, a strong interest group jealously guarding their turf. Rather, what she is arguing for is the nurturing of a broad-based, environmentalist forum. This forum might be led by more informed activist groups, but basically these groups are poised to "empower ... other citizens' groups including other NGOs [non-governmental organizations], political parties, ... etc."

## ☐ Towards a More Open Society?

As Leung Man-fuk points out in his chapter, the broadening of the public forum is premised on the emergence of a more educated public. Yet the opening up of the forum is not a smooth, automatic process. On the contrary, it is one fraught with innumerable struggles and setbacks. One major obstacle is the unavailability of information to the public. This is raised by at least two authors of this edition.

One of these authors, Tsang Shu-ki, concludes his chapter on income distribution with the following complaint:

> Taxation and expenditure policies need to be guided at least partly by these [redistributive] objectives, and as a start, much better data and information on income and wealth distribution should be collected and made available to the public. The present degree of data availability is bordering on the absurd.

While writing on women as a social group, I myself share Tsang's concern about the dearth of statistics necessary for objective assessments of the situation. This gap in information is, I think, detrimental to Hong Kong's evolution towards a more open society, and should therefore top our agenda in discussions for reforms.

# ☐ Hong Kong as a Chinese City

Living in a world very much different from that of our poet and scholar-bureaucrat Huang Zunxian, we naturally have things on our minds which he would not have understood, let alone share. Public representation and participation are examples of these.

As for Huang's concern about Chinese people under foreign rule, the added twist now is how Hong Kong society is going to readjust to its renewed ties with the Mainland, and vice versa. This issue has not arisen from British colonialism alone, but has been complicated by social revolutions on the Mainland, as well as drastic economic and social changes on both sides of the Shenzhen border over these decades.

The economists among our authors all agree on one fact, and that is, Hong Kong and China are intricately linked by numerous commercial, financial and industrial ties. George Shen, for example, gives an impressive account of China's extensive investments in Hong Kong, made by various tiers and sectors of the Chinese bureaucracy.

The existence of close ties, however, does not mean that the two societies would necessarily be well-adjusted to each other, now and after the Chinese communist government resumes sovereignty in 1997. This is a grave concern indeed, and one which is discussed at length in many of our chapters, particularly the ones on the political and legal aspects.

On the cultural front, it is clear that Hong Kong is Chinese in many ways: in the practice of time-worn Chinese rituals and customs, and probably as Robert Chung would agree, in the manifestations of certain Chinese traits. Yet it is also evident that Hong Kong, having moved along its own path apart from that of China, has developed its unique identity and culture. Whether this identity and culture is basically Chinese is an interesting issue. It calls into question one's understanding of Chinese culture itself, and of one's appreciation of its inherent lines of cleavage: official versus folk, mainland versus regional, north versus south, Confucian versus Taoist, and so on.

The year 1997 has prompted a lot of discussions on economic, political and legal issues. Perhaps it is time we began our deliberations on the social and cultural fronts too.

# 1

# Constitution and Administration

Norman J. Miners

Since the new Governor, Chris Patten, addressed the Legislative Council (Legco) for the first time on 7 October 1992, the main focus of public attention has been on his proposals for the conduct of the 1995 elections, and the reactions of the Chinese government. But the changes in the constitutional structure and administration of the territory which were made public at the same time are of equal or greater significance. As the first politician to govern Hong Kong since Sir John Pope Hennessey left in 1882, he has attempted to reshape the colonial system of government more boldly than any of his predecessors.

## ☐ The Executive Council

When Chris Patten arrived in July 1992 he found that all the unofficial members of the Executive Council had been appointed by Lord Wilson for two-year terms which did not expire until September 1993. This was quite contrary to precedent: when Sir Edward Youde took over from Sir Murray MacLehose, the Executive Council unofficials had only three months to serve, which made it possible for the new governor to remodel the Executive Council, if he wished to do so. Fortunately for Chris Patten the senior unofficial on the Executive Council, Baroness Dunn, took the lead in offering her resignation, and so persuaded the other unofficials to follow her example. This allowed Chris Patten to carry through the most drastic

Norman J. Miners is a reader in the Department of Politics and Public Administration, The University of Hong Kong.

reorganization of the Executive Council that there has ever been. Seven of the nine unofficials found to their surprise that their offers of resignation were accepted and at the same time one official member, Barrie Wiggham, and the Commander British Forces were informed that their services would no longer be required. Only five of the fourteen members of Lord Wilson's Executive Council were left in place. If Patten had not carried out this purge, it is doubtful whether he would have been able to secure the support of a majority of the Executive Council for his reform programme, judging by the opinions that they had expressed in public before his arrival.

The Commander British Forces had been an *ex-officio* member of the Executive Council since 1844. Until 1902 he was normally the official deputy to the Governor and acted as Governor during his absence. His role on the Council was to give advice on defence matters and on the security implications of internal policy. Patten decided that his presence on the Council was no longer appropriate. It might also give an undesirable precedent for the Commander of the Chinese Army garrison to serve on the Executive Council after 1997. The removal of the Commander required an amendment of the Royal Instructions, which was not completed until February 1993. During the interim period General Foley remained formally a member of the Executive Council, but did not attend any meetings.

The Chief Secretary, the Financial Secretary and the Attorney General, all *ex-officio* members and all expatriate, were left undisturbed. They were now joined by three Chinese administrative officers, the heads of policy branches in the Secretariat, Anson Chan, John Chan and Michael Sze. They were promoted over the heads of Chinese colleagues who had greater seniority, and seemed to be marked out for the highest positions in the civil service before 1997. The increase in the number of official members from four to six reversed the steady decline in the representation of the civil service on the Council which had taken place since 1948.

In his address to the Legislative Council, Patten announced that in future the non-official membership of the Executive and Legislative Councils would be entirely separated. This gave a plausible explanation for dropping six Legislative Councillors from the Executive Council, and requiring two of the new Executive Council members who were already appointed members of the Legislative Council to resign their seats. (The *ex-officio* members, the Chief Secretary, the Financial Secretary and the Attorney General remained members of both Councils). This was a complete reversal of normal British colonial policy. When two unofficial members were first added to the Executive Council in 1896, the Secretary of

State indicated to the Governor that it was obviously desirable that they should as a rule be chosen from among the unofficial members of the Legislative Council. In accordance with this directive only five Executive Councillors over the past 96 years (Sharp, Morse, Sandberg, Purves and Wang Gungwu) have not been members of the Legislative Council at the time of their appointment. After a period of service on the Executive Council, members have normally been permitted to give up their Legislative Council seats, but (apart from the period 1916–1920) there have always been some members who sat on both Councils.

The advantage of this overlapping membership was that it normally ensured a consensus between the two Councils. Executive Councillors could normally predict the likely reactions of their colleagues in the Legislative Council, and so could avoid approving the introduction of draft legislation which Legislative Councillors might consider objectionable. The system occasionally broke down, as occurred over the Crown Leases Renewal Bill 1972, but such clashes were very rare. After 1985, when the government could no longer rely on the votes of the official members to give it a majority, the senior members of the Legislative Council who also sat on the Executive Council were expected to keep the appointed members in line to vote in support of government measures. From the government's point of view this system was very successful: between 1985 and 1991 no government measure was defeated.

However, after the 1991 election this method of controlling the Legislative Council through the influence exerted by the Executive Councillors was no longer effective. The appointed members knew that their seats would be abolished in 1995 so they could not hope that their membership would be renewed for another term even if they always loyally voted as the government wished. Executive Councillors might be obliged by collective responsibility to vote in favour of Executive Council decisions in the Legislative Council, but they were unable to mobilize support for unpopular measures, since elected members, and those appointed members who might seek election in 1995, were more responsive to the views of their constituents than the needs of the government. This was made clear by the decision on 4 December 1991 when a motion objecting to the Sino-British agreement on the composition of the Court of Final Appeal was passed by 34 votes to 11. This was the first time that the colonial government had ever been defeated in a division in the Legislative Council. There had been occasions when the government voluntarily withdrew a measure after it had been criticized, or when the official members were instructed to abstain from voting, or allowed to vote according to their consciences, but never before had government policy been defeated when the officials all voted together to support it.

Faced with this situation, Patten had two alternative courses of action if the overlapping membership of the two Councils was to be maintained. One possibility would have been to appoint leading members of the United Democrats of Hong Kong and Meeting Point to the Executive Council, making Martin Lee effectively the head of the government. This would have been in accordance with British policy elsewhere in the colonial empire, since his party had won an overwhelming victory in the directly elected seats. However, such a government could not have commanded a majority in the Legislative Council (since Lord Wilson had filled all the appointed seats with conservatives), and it would have provoked vehement and unpredictable reactions from China.

The second alternative would have been to include members of both the United Democrats and the Cooperative Resources Centre in the Executive Council. But it would be difficult for such a coalition to reach agreement on policy. Even if a consensus could be reached and all Executive Councillors accepted the rule of collective responsibility and supported it in the Legislative Council, there could be no guarantee that their followers would similarly feel bound to vote for it, if they thought the Executive Council decision was contrary to party policy or the interests of their constituency.

Since neither alternative appeared to be viable, Patten decided to separate the non-official membership of the Executive and Legislative Councils, following the American rather than the British model of democratic development. To provide a channel of liaison between the administration and legislators he proposed the formation of a new Government-Legco Committee which would discuss the handling of the legislative programme. But this suggestion has not been implemented since the twenty or more legislators who are independent of any party affiliation could not agree on who should represent them on such a committee.

The effect of the separation of the two Councils has been to diminish the authority and importance of the Executive Council. Though individual members may have had distinguished careers none of them except Baroness Dunn are well-known and respected public figures. None has ever won an election, and most of them owe their position entirely to the Governor. Though the Executive Council formally remains the highest decision-making body in Hong Kong it seems unlikely that its current membership will be able to act as an effective check upon the plans of the Governor.

As a gesture of conciliation to China, one of Patten's new Executive Councillors is an official Adviser to the Chinese government. Councillors are bound by an oath to keep all the proceedings confidential, but the Governor is now unlikely to inform the Council of any matter which needs to be kept secret from China. So the effect of this appointment will be to restrict the range of issues which come before the Executive Council for decision.

The separation of the Executive and Legislative Councils puts an end to any hope of the institution of a ministerial system of government. In other British colonies leading members of the political party which won the election have been appointed to Executive Council where they took over responsibility for various departments of government, and explained and defended the policies of their departments in the Legislative Council. This paved the way for the development of responsible party government, with the Executive Council being transformed into a cabinet presided over by an elected Prime Minister. The possibility of any development along these lines has now been ruled out. It would certainly be contrary to the system of government envisaged by the Basic Law. So it seems that in the final years of British rule the system of government will more closely resemble that of the United States, where the executive is always liable to be frustrated by a legislature which has the power to refuse to grant it the money or the laws which it needs, but is unable to turn it out of office, or compel it to follow the policies which the majority of the legislature prefers.

There was only one British colony where overlapping membership of the Executive and Legislative Councils was explicitly prohibited. This was the crown colony of Ceylon (now called Sri Lanka) under the constitution of 1923. The result of this was that the Executive Council became eclipsed in importance by the Finance Committee of the Legislative Council. When the constitution was next revised in 1931 the Executive Council was abolished completely and policy-making effectively passed into the hands of the committees of the legislature. Nothing like this can occur in Hong Kong, since the Basic Law forbids it. But what happened in Ceylon lends support to the fears expressed by China that Patten's proposals could lead to the demise of executive-led government.

## ☐ The Legislative Council

The changes in the constitution of the Legislative Council which the Governor announced in October 1992 were not so great as those made to the

Executive Council. In his words, they were intended to strengthen the effective development of the legislature as an independent check on the government.

In February 1993 the Royal Instructions were amended to replace the Governor as President of the Legislative Council by a member elected by the 57 non-official members from among themselves. John Swaine, who had presided over the Council since October 1991 as Deputy President appointed by the Governor, was now unanimously elected as President. Elsie Tu was elected Deputy President at the same time. This change was in any case required by the Basic Law, and it had been expected that it would take place in 1995. But Patten decided to make the change much earlier. It serves to emphasize that the Legislative Council is now completely independent of the executive and free to arrange its own rules and procedures. Swaine's election was uncontroversial, but there may be more difficulty in finding an impartial President acceptable to all members and parties after the 1995 elections. All members will then be elected, so Swaine, an appointed member, is unlikely to be available to fill this position.

Patten's other innovation was to institute Governor's question time. For one hour each month he comes to the Legislative Council chamber to answer without preparation any questions on government business which members may wish to ask him. The intention is to demonstrate publicly that he considers himself accountable to the legislature, and that he is fully informed on all areas of government activity. The Governor has given an impressive performance, as he has done at other public forums which he has conducted. But this period of questioning does have its drawbacks. Since many members wish to pose a question to the Governor there is no time for supplementaries, which would allow the Governor's reply to be probed in detail before he moved on to answer the next question. Questioners are generally polite, if not deferential, to the Governor. He does not have to face the rough and tumble of debate and repartee which mark Prime Minister's question time in the House of Commons.

On 8 July 1992 the Legislative Council voted to amend its Standing Orders in order to reshape its committee system. The issues had been hotly debated by members over the previous six months, but the final result did little more than rationalize and formalize the existing system. Liberal members had wished to set up a system of permanent standing committees each of which would monitor a particular area of government policy and conduct the detailed examination and amendment of all bills which fell into its policy area. Such committees would be similar to the Standing Committees of the United States Congress. This plan was opposed by the Cooperative Resources Centre and others who were apparently influenced by the fears expressed by China that such a reorganization would make the Legislative Council too powerful and lead to the end of executive-led government. In the event the Council voted to transform the informal in-house meeting of all unofficial members into a House Committee which would be responsible for deciding on the arrangements for the detailed consideration of bills after they had been introduced by the official member in charge of the bill at the Second Reading Debate.

In the past controversial bills had been examined by an *ad hoc* committee set up by the in-house meeting. Under the revised Standing Orders, a bill will be referred by the House Committee to a new Bills Committee. These Bills Committees are like the old *ad hoc* committees in all but name. They do not have a permanent existence: once the bill has been examined and returns to the Legislative Council for the resumed Second Reading debate the Bills Committee is dissolved, and the expertise accumulated during the consideration of the bill is lost. Though the Bills Committee is an official committee of the Legislative Council, it does not have the right to require the attendance of any person and the production of any document which it may need for its deliberations. These powers under the Legislative Council (Powers and Privileges) Ordinance may only be exercised with the agreement of the full Council. Though this diminishes the status of the Bills Committees, it is not likely in practice to cause members great inconvenience. The policy secretary in charge of a bill is normally eager to supply the committee with detailed briefing papers and to appear before the committee to explain why the bill in its present form is as near perfect as can be as a result of the exhaustive consultations conducted by the department concerned. Spokespersons for pressure groups are equally anxious to brief the committee on the particular aspects of the bill which they find objectionable. Normally members of a Bills Committee find themselves faced with too much information rather than too little. The new Standing Orders provide that sittings of the Bills Committee are to be held in public, unless the chairperson decides otherwise.

The sixteen panels set up by the House Committee to consider various policy areas remain formally unchanged. They were not made official committees of the Legislative Council. The convenors and deputy convenors are chosen by the House Committee as previously. Members may attend any panel meeting when they please. The only recent change follows the separation of the Executive and Legislative Councils: Executive

Councillors no longer take part in the panels, since they are not now members of OMELCO (Office of the Members of the Executive and Legislative Councils). However, over the past year the conduct of panel meetings has altered considerably. Instead of providing an opportunity for an intimate briefing by policy secretaries and heads of departments on the developments in their sectors, panel meetings are now often held in public. Civil servants may be subjected to rigorous questioning over any recent problems in their departments and can be compelled to defend their actions or omissions. Panel meetings have now become an additional means by which members can call officials to account and expose their failures to public view. This usefully supplements the traditional procedure of questions and debates at meetings of the full Council.

In his October speech the Governor proposed that OMELCO should be reorganized to give it greater autonomy. It has now been renamed the Legislative Council Secretariat and will become a public corporation. In October 1992 about two-thirds of the staff were on secondment to OMELCO from government departments, most of whom were executive officers and clerical staff. The rest of the staff were directly engaged on contract terms. The intention is that in future the entire staff will be independently recruited to avoid any problem of divided loyalties. In addition to the staff of the Legislative Council Secretariat which serves the committees and panels and provides translation services for the Council as a whole, members have hired their own personal secretaries, researchers and office assistants. The government provides some office space for members in nearby government accommodation and a monthly expenses allowance. This was increased from $32,700 to $73,000 in May 1993. These improvements in the research assistance available to members should enable them to make a more critical evaluation of the information provided by officials and argue with them on more equal terms.

The most important changes in the way the Legislative Council operates have come about not as a result of the alterations in its constitution and internal arrangements but as a consequence of the arrival of a new Governor whose attitudes and policy preferences are completely contrary to those of his predecessor, Lord Wilson. Chris Patten is a party politician who believes passionately in democracy and the maximum feasible participation of the people in the government. The policies which he announced in his October speech incorporated many proposals already made by the United Democrats, such as the abolition of appointed members on the District Boards and Urban and Regional Councils, and an increase in the number of directly elected members in the 1995 legislature. In the 1991–1992 session of the Council motions in support of these policies had been voted down by a majority largely made up of the members appointed to the Council by Lord Wilson. The change of Governor in July 1992 was the Hong Kong equivalent of the replacement of a British Prime Minister by the Leader of the Opposition. This was made clear when Chris Patten dismissed the four members of the Cooperative Resources Centre from his Executive Council.

However, it was not so easy to secure a majority for his policies in the Legislative Council. The 18 members nominated by Lord Wilson in 1991 had been appointed for the full four-year term of the legislature, and they saw no reason to follow the example set by the unofficial members of the Executive Council and offer their resignations. The Governor has the right to dissolve the Legislative Council and hold fresh elections, in which case the appointed members would all automatically lose their seats, but Chris Patten had no reasonable excuse for exercising this power at the beginning of his term of office. But he was able to make some marginal changes to increase the number of his supporters. Two of the new Executive Council-lors were already appointed members of the legislature. Under Patten's new system of separating the two Councils, they were obliged to resign their seats in the Legislative Council, enabling him to fill the vacancies with new members who supported his policies. A further seat was unexpectedly made available when Rita Fan impulsively resigned from the Legislative Council as soon as she was informed that her presence on the Executive Council was no longer required. These changes enabled the Governor to secure a majority of 32 votes to 21 when his proposals for the 1995 elections were debated on 11 November 1992. The members of the Cooperative Resources Centre and most of the functional constituency members voted against the Governor's proposals, but three of the members appointed by Lord Wilson were persuaded to vote for Patten's proposals as well as the members he had appointed, and the officials. Five members were absent or abstained from voting.

The administration has not been able to rely on this majority to support all the decisions made by the Executive Council. The United Democrats and other liberal legislators have been successful in reversing two decisions: on 25 November 1992 the Legislative Council voted by 23 votes to 20 to cancel an increase in the fees for the Labour Tribunal and on 24 February 1993 members voted by 19 votes to 11 to reduce the tunnel charge from $6 to $5. These defeats both took place on motions to amend govern-ment regulations. All government bills introduced into the Legislative

Council have been passed. This is mainly the result of intensive lobbying of the Bills Committees by policy secretaries, and their readiness to accept minor amendments when necessary to secure the passage of the bill as a whole. The Financial Secretary engaged in intensive consultations with legislators before preparing his budget and so ensured that the 1993 Appropriation Bill was approved without significant opposition.

Government policies such as the double-rent policy in housing estates and the refusal to set up a Central Provident Fund have been severely criticized and defeated during debates on motions moved by members, but this has had little or no practical effect. Officials promise to consider carefully the points made in the debate and to keep the matter under review. But in most cases the policy approved by the Executive Council continues unchanged, or at most minor modifications have been made to show that the Executive Council takes some account of the views expressed in the legislature. Such incidents underline the inherent weakness of the Legislative Council as at present constituted: it has the power to refuse requests for money and can refuse to approve draft legislation which the administration puts before it, but it cannot dictate to the executive what policy it should follow. If a single political party or a coalition of like-minded parties with a disciplined membership controlled an overall majority of the seats in the Legislative Council, it would be in a position to bring the whole government to a halt and compel the executive to follow its instructions. But at present the Legislative Council is composed of at least five political parties and more than twenty independent members. This makes it possible for the administration to cobble together the majority it needs on most important issues which come before the Council, and to accept defeat in other debates without suffering any serious inconvenience.

This situation would not be significantly altered if the Government-Legco Committee proposed by the Governor were to be established. The problem is not caused by the failure of the two Councils to establish channels for liaison, but by the absence of a stable party with an overall majority in the Legislative Council. This situation is likely to continue so long as the Council is composed of an incoherent mixture of directly elected members, indirectly elected members, and appointed members or members chosen by an electoral college.

## ☐ The Civil Service

The changes introduced in the civil service during the past year have been less dramatic than those affecting the Executive and Legislative Councils. They are developments of existing policies rather than radical new departures.

The administration has always been concerned with maximizing the efficiency and effectiveness of the civil service to secure the best value for taxpayers' money. In May 1992 a new Efficiency Unit was established within the Civil Service Branch to promote better management of the administration's human and material resources. In May 1993 this was upgraded to become the Management Services Agency as a new department. In his October speech Chris Patten announced the aim of establishing a new Culture of Service within the administration. All government departments providing services directly to the public would be required to publish performance pledges setting out the standards of service which the public could expect on such matters as how many days before a reply would be sent to a letter, and how many minutes an applicant would have to wait when renewing a vehicle licence. A number of departments have now published their pledges, and their performance is being monitored by user committees attached to each department.

A number of new departments and agencies were established during the past year. A new Monetary Authority was set up to perform some of the functions in managing the government's reserves and regulating the exchange value of the Hong Kong dollar which in other countries are carried out by a central bank. The Post Office gave birth to a new Telecommunications Authority. The Insolvency Service Department, the Land Registration Department and the Companies Registration Department were established as independent offices. The last two are to manage their own trading funds and operate like a business firm financing their work by the fees they receive and deciding what staff to employ to meet the demands of their clients. The idea of a trading fund has also been applied to the workshops of the Electrical and Mechanical Services Department which are now run on commercial principles, charging other departments for the services they provide.

Where it seems that a service provided by the government can be more efficiently conducted by a business firm, the government has been ready to privatize the operation. The management of the Aberdeen Tunnel was let out on contract in 1991. In 1993 similar arrangements were made for the tunnels at Lion Rock, Shing Mun and Tseung Kwan O. However, the proposal to transform Radio Television Hong Kong from a government department into a public corporation seems to have been abandoned. This is partly because of objections from government staff to the redundancies and salary reductions which might follow, but mainly because China has made known her strong disapproval of any diminution of direct government control over any part of the Government Information Services.

# 2

# The Legal System:
# Turbulence and Shadows

## Margaret Ng

In her speech for the opening of the legal year on 11 January 1993, the Chairman of the Hong Kong Bar Association described 1992 as a "turbulent year" for Hong Kong, and predicted that 1993 would only be more so.

She was referring to the threat to the rule of law and the future of the judiciary posed by an official statement made by Lu Ping, Director of the State Council's Hong Kong and Macau Affairs Office, following the visit of the new Governor of Hong Kong, Chris Patten, to Beijing. If Patten did not take China's views into account, Lu said, then, "When the time comes we will form the first Legislative Council, the first government and the first judicial organizations of the Special Administrative Region". This was followed soon after by China's declaration that the government land grant for Container Terminal No. 9 was in breach of the Sino-British Joint Declaration and the Basic Law. For good measure, all government contracts beyond 1997 were declared to be without effect and would not be recognized by China. The Bar had responded in a strongly worded statement which drew instant abuse in the pro-China press.

## ☐ Fusion

But 1993 was to be turbulent also in another way: it stirred up a great controversy within the legal profession itself, in a subject called "fusion". This was touched on in the speech of the Chairman of the Law Society of

---

Margaret Ng is a writer and a practising barrister.

Hong Kong on the same occasion, but the full force was to come later, in a pamphlet called "The future of the legal profession in Hong Kong", in which fusion was strongly advocated, in language scarcely disguising the Law Society's scant respect for the Bar.

Similar to the practice in the United Kingdom, the legal profession is divided in Hong Kong into two branches: solicitors to whom the general public has direct access, and barristers who may only be instructed through solicitors. "Fusion" is the proposal that the two branches be combined into one. Innocuous enough to the general public, within the profession it is a highly charged subject for many. For, under the proposal of fusion, the Law Society launched its criticism against the Bar for enjoying the privilege of audience in the High Court and Court of Appeal to the exclusion of solicitors, and occupying a senior position in the perception of the public without justification. In resisting fusion, the Bar sees its jealously guarded independence threatened, and its traditional areas of practice encroached upon. In spite of the Law Society's claim, in its pamphlet, that the aim of the proposals in it was to rid the legal profession of its out-moded practices and restrictions, and to deliver better and cheaper legal services to the public, many members of the Bar, and not a few solicitors, saw the attempt as motivated by the self-interest and ambition of the more powerful firms of solicitors.

Nevertheless, the promises held out by the Law Society were attractive ones, particularly the promise of lower costs and more accessible services to the general public. For it has long and frequently been a complaint that legal fees are too high, and that the law and lawyers are so full of mystique that the consumer is virtually helpless before the charges demanded of them.

Yet in at least one area the public's hopes are misguided. The largest number of complaints comes from complaints about fees charged on property transactions, particularly about scale fees. These have nothing to do with fusion, for here the monopoly is the Law Society's, and there is no sign that the Law Society is either giving it up or cutting the costs down. In other areas the problems are far more complex and serious, and directly implicates the reputation of practitioners in both branches.

The cost of litigation is one of them. Touting is another. As education standard and the quality of life improve in Hong Kong, people have in-evitably resorted to the law more readily to settle their disputes and, in that sense, become more litigious. However, over the past few years, complaints are increasingly bitter about the high and often uncontrollable cost of litigation. This partly lies in the system itself, resulting in long trials with numerous delays and complications, of which more will be said below. But it also lies in charges being excessive in some cases. In many others cases, the method and reason of charging were not fully explained beforehand or fully justified afterwards, resulting in the consumer feeling aggrieved and dissatisfied.

The problem of touting is particularly widespread in criminal proceedings. Unqualified "clerks" or touts with little or no knowledge of the law or legal procedures prey among those who are charged with criminal offences and their families. They induce them to pay, frequently quite unjustifiable sums, for legal representation based on unfounded assurances or threats. For example, they may be encouraged to believe that they will be able to "get off" if they are willing to pay large sums of money for the services of some superior counsel, when in fact there can be little merit in a defence. Yet others may be told that they may count on being sentenced to a long imprisonment unless they hire some clever lawyer to plead for them in mitigation, while in fact a prison sentence is only a remote possibility in the circumstances of the offence.

Touts cheat people in vulnerable position of their money and put their rights and interest at risk. It is widespread and deeply rooted in the system, and brings disrepute to the legal profession as well as the legal system as a whole.

Touting has troubled the legal profession for many years. The Bar Association and the Law Society have long deliberated separately and together on it. They have failed, as yet, to come up with a solution. Criminalization of touting having been rejected at an earlier stage, they are now still in the process of setting up a system of internal policing or inspection. There is no time to lose, for public confidence is being fast eroded by a state of affairs which cannot be concealed.

Especially damaging to the public's faith in the legal profession was the disclosure, at the beginning of the year, that the Independent Commission Against Corruption (ICAC) is investigating a number of lawyers, including solicitors and barristers for, among other things, paying commission. The ICAC has refused to name names. While this is going on, a shadow is cast upon the entire profession. Mutual recriminations between the Law Society and the Bar cannot add to the public's respect for either branch.

Moreover, with the sudden expansion of legal education in the universities and polytechnics, a larger-than-ever crop of law graduates were produced in the summer of 1992. Many of these failed to find places in law firms as articled clerks. This expansion raised the question of quality among the profession as well as from the public. To the new graduate, the far more pressing problem is whether they have a future in their chosen career.

## ☐ Localization

The legal system had been under attack from a number of directions. One major underlying worry, already voiced in a regrettably inconclusive speech of the Chief Justice, Sir Ti-liang Yang at the opening of the legal year in 1991, was whether the common law will have taken root by the time of the change of sovereignty in 1997. There are two aspects to this question. One is how far is the common law system understood and supported by the local community. The other is how well local legal personnel, including the legal profession and the judiciary, are able to carry on the common law tradition.

There is every fear that, after some 150 years' practice, the common law system has remained alien to the vast majority of the population which is Chinese. Up to five years ago, all the statutes were written in English. Up to two years ago, the language of the court was exclusively English. The hundreds of thousands of local Chinese who were tried or gave evidence relied on interpretation. To the language barrier is added the mystique of the law, the technicalities of theory and practice, of substance and procedure. Many of the fundamental concepts such as the presumption of innocence, the right of silence, the very peculiarly English sense of "fair play" and natural justice, the adversarial system itself, the umpire nature of the role of the judge, were all more or less exotic to the traditional Chinese mind. Thus the common law system, though readily understandable to the minority of the deeply westernized, is far from so to the ordinary person in the street.

Following the signing of the Joint Declaration, there was tremendous enthusiasm to "localize" the law, by adopting relevant English law into Hong Kong's statutes, by translating existing statutes, by adopting bilingual legislation, and by promoting the use of "*punti*" (local Cantonese) in the lower courts in which the overwhelming majority of defendants are tried.

Yet experience proves that practice is far more difficult than the enthusiasts have imagined. As the former Attorney General recently said in a speech to the American Chamber of Commerce, while nearly half of the 532 existing Ordinances have been translated since 1989, most of them have not yet been scrutinized or approved by the Bilingual Law Advisory

Committee. Only six have been declared authentic texts. The Chief Justice regretted that he had not been as determined as he wished about insisting on the use of Cantonese in court. Following his renewed determination, Cantonese became more frequently chosen in magistrates courts for cases like traffic offences, hawkers' summonses and petty crimes. But this only hides an unresolved problem: the language of the record of the court is still English, because there is no possibility, in the foreseeable future, for Chinese to become the language of the High Court or Court of Appeal as almost all legal texts and authorities, and certainly the entirety of the case law, are in English and will remain so for a long time. So what has happened is that magistrates are simply acting as unqualified interpreters when they record their hearings in English. It is only a matter of time for a case to come along where the argument turns on the record of what a defendant or a witness is supposed to have said, for the new practice to be challenged and get into trouble.

Localization of the language of the statutes and the language of the court presupposes the localization of practitioners, magistrates and judges. In the Legal Department, the word has long become weary with repetition. Yet few believe that there is any chance of real success, in terms of quantity or quality, particularly in that while there is no lack of local officers on the junior levels, the top ranks are still expatriate-heavy.

While discrimination may have a part to play, at the root of the problem is the late start of a local law school. The first, the Law Faculty of The University of Hong Kong, had its first intake only in 1969. Before that, Hong Kong had happily relied on expatriate practitioners and on law schools in England to which locals were sent for legal training. The policy of quickly increasing local training facilities that repentance brought, has resulted in a bottom-heavy local legal profession which will need time — and some hard thinking — to sort itself out.

Meantime, the problem of the local roots of the common law system remains a matter for concern which increases with 1997 drawing nearer and no relief in sight.

## ☐ The judiciary

The problem of localization is an even greater concern in the judiciary. There again, the root of the problem appears to be the familiar "too little, too late". In the view of the Chairman of the Bar Association, significant achievement was made in the last decade or so, especially in the last seven years in recruiting judiciary personnel from the local Bar. A total of 16 members of the Bar have been appointed to the ranks of the Court of Appeal, the High Court and the District Court since 1973, of whom 12 were appointed within the last seven years. In addition, a further 12 have been appointed as magistrates over the same seven-year period. If the achievement is not greater, in her view, it was because the government has never been really determined. But again, success is, significantly, more with the recruitment of magistrates than for the High Court bench. And this is not just because the remuneration is not comparable to the fees a successful practitioner of the relevant standing may expect to earn, but more so because of the political uncertainty that one has to face in committing oneself to a career on the bench in the next 20 years. What is more, the problem of localization has another grave dimension to it, and that is the ultimate strength of the judiciary.

With the retirement last year of three of the most respected justices of appeal, the higher ranks of the judiciary is looking depleted. Recruiting is no longer an easy matter. The pressure to recruit locally is matched only by the reluctance of local practitioners of the right calibre and standing. At the same time, overseas judges and practitioners clearly cannot count on a long and stable career here, given the exceeding reluctance to increase or even maintain the proportion of overseas judges.

The most immediate problem is the court list. With the shortage of judges at every level, the waiting time for cases to be tried is reaching intolerable lengths. In certain cases the law's delay has resulted in the miscarriage of justice. The judiciary's efforts to mend appearances have not always been meaningful or successful. For example, by constantly reserving several district court judges as deputy judges to sit in the High Court cases the glut is simply pushed one level down; and by listing a larger number of cases for the day than a court can realistically hope to hear most of them have to be re-fixed for another date. This, coupled with the fact that cases are becoming longer and longer, is making litigation a hazardous and prohibitively costly way to settle disputes.

Rather than providing funds to recruit more judges, the government chooses to see the problem primarily as one of administrative efficiency. A Judicial Administrator's post is being established at a senior level to assist the Chief Justice to take care of the administration and budgetary aspects of the judiciary. How well this is going to work, and whether an Administrator accountable to the Legislative Council will encroach upon the independence of the judiciary, remains to be seen.

However, the long-term consequence of the recruitment problem is, inevitably, the weakening of the very foundation of the rule of law, namely the strength and the independence of the judiciary. It goes without saying that the rule of law is to any degree assured only if the judiciary is not made an instrument of the executive but remains firmly and uncompromisingly independent. But the independence of the judiciary has no other protection than the respect it commands by its sheer excellence and fearlessness. Not every judge is bright or uncompromising. Indeed, the thick-headed, drunk and pro-establishment judge is a standard caricature of the English legal tradition. But every age has been vindicated by upright judges, and isolated examples apart, the tradition of independence has been upheld. It has also to be admitted that the tradition of respect for the independence of the judiciary has helped. Where the separation of power is accepted as a fundamental principle, the executive abhors being seen as interfering with the judiciary. That also is Hong Kong's tradition. But facing up to the change of sovereignty is a formidable test by vast unknown elements. If the future judiciary is to be supported in its independence, then it has to have command of the world's respect — a world which is becoming more and more sophisticated in its knowledge of law and justice. If Hong Kong fails to recruit judges of the highest calibre and integrity and keep them, then the independence of the judiciary will be no more than a forlorn hope.

In itself a problem, the difficulty of recruitment at higher level makes even more acute yet another problem: the problem of succession. More than ever, Hong Kong needs a strong Chief Justice to head the judiciary. This person has to be of a calibre and standing to command the respect of the legal profession. His or her integrity and determination to withstand any encroachment on judiciary independence has to be beyond doubt. Above all strong support from fellow judges is indispensable. In the hands of the ambitious or the weak, the independence of the judiciary in Hong Kong will be gravely endangered.

But the future Chief Justice must be sought among locals, if not necessarily among the local ethnic Chinese, according to the Basic Law. The question increasingly whispered along the corridors of justice, among practitioners and judges is: Will the ideal candidate emerge on time?

## ☐ The Office of the Attorney General

The problem of succession is not only with the judiciary but also with the Attorney General's Chambers. No question is more obvious than: Who is going to be the first local Attorney General? Here the importance of getting the right person is just as great, and the difficulty, if possible, even greater. For the outstanding legal practitioner is not always a sound administrator. But the Attorney General has to be both a sound administrator and a person of vision. The Attorney General is not just head of a government department providing legal expertise as and when required by any other government departments. He is the principal advisor of the government, particularly on matters of international, public and constitutional law. He has the prerogative to prosecute or not to prosecute, and he makes the decision personally in important criminal cases.

If Hong Kong people fear that the law may one day be made a weapon in the hand of the government against the people, the Attorney General will be the person they have to fear most directly. From a totally different point of view, if Hong Kong were to have and maintain a healthy and efficient system of law to meet adequately the demands of an increasingly sophisticated metropolis, then the foresight and forethought of the Attorney General must be dependable.

As the present incumbent continues into his fifth year of office, it has long ceased to be fashionable for various enterprising members of the legal profession or the public to call for his resignation. But the question is not thereby becoming less pressing, indeed it has become more so: Where is the local lawyer to succeed him?

## ☐ The Court of Final Appeal

In 1991, the public's reaction to the agreement reached in the Sino-British Joint Liaison Group on the composition of the Court of Final Appeal was so hostile as to stop the government from any attempt to implement the agreement by legislation. The matter is therefore held in abeyance. In the meantime no efforts have been made — at least, none that the public knows of — to reopen negotiations with China. However, the question is being mooted again, no doubt by prime movers in the government, for the Court of Final Appeal to be set up as soon as possible, albeit along these imperfect lines. "The perfect has been made the enemy of the good," quotes one formidable orator. His doing so no doubt makes the idea attractive to many.

The government's law draftsmen are certainly going to begin work before long. It probably has to do so if only to avoid being attacked by China for going back on the agreement reached in the Joint Liaison Group. Going ahead, however, will require sacrificing the ideal composition, which will prove not a small sacrifice. It is to give way on a basic principle: that it must conform with the Joint Declaration and not erode the promises given under it. In practice, then, the advantage of an early set-up, say by 1996, or even 1995 will be minimal.

# 3

# Politics, Politicians and Political Parties

Frank Ching

Politics in its true sense came to Hong Kong in mid-1992 with the arrival on 9 July of the new Governor, Chris Patten, a senior British politician whose last job was to serve as chairman of the Conservative Party. Patten, a politician down to his fingertips, gave Hong Kong a taste of politics that it had never before experienced.

The new Governor and his family took Hong Kong by storm. He eschewed the traditional gubernatorial uniform, which was topped off by a pith helmet with ostrich feathers, and settled for a business suit for his inauguration. He also eschewed the knighthood which, since the colony's early years, always went along with the job of being governor.

Patten's informality quickly won him acceptance in Hong Kong. Sometimes, he acted like he was campaigning for office, picking up children to hug and kiss. (Subsequently, a Chinese official upbraided the Governor, saying he was not running for office in Hong Kong.)

Even before his arrival, Patten had made it clear that he was different from his predecessor, Sir David Wilson, who was elevated to the House of Lords prior to his return to the United Kingdom. Instead of repeating the standard formula of wanting to preserve Hong Kong's "prosperity and stability", Patten pointedly added that he wanted to preserve the territory's freedom as well.

However, the new Governor did not have a free hand. A decade of negotiations between Britain and China had resulted in a slew of

---

Frank Ching writes a weekly political column in the *Far Eastern Economic Review*.

agreements that could not be easily overturned. In particular, the Basic Law, promulgated by the National People's Congress of China in April 1990, stipulated how Hong Kong's post-1997 executive and legislature would be produced. Patten also knew, although the Hong Kong public did not, that the British government had indicated to Beijing its acceptance of the limitations on democratic development even before the Basic Law was promulgated.

## ☐ The Exco Reshuffle

One of the pressing issues the new Governor had to address was membership of the Executive Council (Exco). Although the United Democrats of Hong Kong (UDHK) had swept the 1991 elections, Governor Wilson had not appointed any of its members to Exco for fear of offending China. Instead, there were four members in Exco who belonged to the conservative Cooperative Resources Centre (CRC), a grouping of conservative Legislative Council (Legco) members none of whom had been directly elected. Members of the CRC often voted *en bloc* in the legislature in support of the government during the Wilson administration, while the UDHK constituted the opposition. Naturally, Patten came under pressure from liberal groups to appoint members of the UDHK into Exco. Privately, the UDHK indicated that they wanted four seats, to match the number held by the CRC. At the same time, the Chinese government made it known that they would consider it unacceptable for such leaders of the UDHK as Martin Lee and Szeto Wah to sit in Exco. China also made it clear that any attempt to increase the number of popularly-elected seats in Legco beyond the numbers laid down in the Basic Law would be unacceptable.

Thus, the Governor's room for manoeuvre was severely circumscribed. He spent the first three months in office meeting people and getting a better feel of Hong Kong, and avoided making policy statements. His position on key issues, he said, would be disclosed when he made the Governor's annual address to Legco in October 1992. Before that, the members of Exco, in a move designed to allow the new Governor to pick his own advisers, jointly offered to resign. Patten called that "a generous offer" but did not indicate if their resignations would be accepted.

In October, Governor Patten showed his hand. He accepted the resignations from Exco of all four members of the CRC — Allen Lee, Selina Chow, Edward Ho and Rita Fan. At the same time, he announced a new policy of ending overlapping membership of Exco and Legco, so that no one could serve on both Councils at the same time. This new policy was his way of justifying not appointing UDHK members onto Exco, without seeming to be giving in to Chinese demands. This move also led logically to the dismantling of OMELCO — the Office of the Members of the Executive and Legislative Councils — which had served as a secretariat for the two bodies and had provided for an interface between them. Severing of ties between Exco and Legco was presented as a move towards greater separation of powers between the executive and the legislature. However, in a situation where Legco at least was partially elected, the ending of dual membership meant that Exco became a body none of whose members was elected. Exco thus became in a sense less accountable and, indeed, somewhat isolated from the political process. This would return to haunt Exco in the following months.

## ☐ The Patten Reform Package

In his address to Legco in 1992, the Governor unveiled his proposals for greater democracy in Hong Kong. The Basic Law provides for a 60-seat legislature in 1997, with 20 seats filled by direct elections, 30 by functional constituencies and 10 by an election committee. While technically adhering to the Basic Law's stipulations, he widened the franchise significantly by proposing that every working person should have a vote in a functional constituency. This he did by creating nine new functional constituencies, which embraced the entire workforce. The effect was to make these nine seats scarcely distinguishable from the twenty directly elected seats. He also proposed the total phasing out of appointments to District Boards, and proposed that the election committee be made up of directly elected District Board members.

The rest of the Patten package had to do with such things as lowering the voting age from 21 to 18, the setting up of a Legco Committee to liaise with the executive and a widening of the franchise in some of the existing twenty-one functional constituencies. But the most controversial proposals were the ones relating to the nine new functional constituencies and the make-up of the election committee. These were widely seen as a thinly disguised attempt to increase the number of directly elected seats from the twenty laid down in the Basic Law to a total of thirty-nine legislators who would be elected more or less democratically.

Immediately after his proposals were made public, the Governor engaged in a whirlwind of activities to explain his proposals to the public and to win its support. He held an unprecedented series of town hall meetings, where anyone could attend and ask him questions. He went on radio phone-in programmes. He went on television to answer questions from a panel of people, including a number of hostile questioners, such as the editor of the pro-communist newspaper *Wen Wei Po*, and James Tien, a former appointee of the Wilson era.

Patten made himself accessible in a way that no governor had ever done before. In addition to giving an incredible number of interviews to the print and electronic media, both local and overseas, he met with representatives of political groups, some of whom told him he had gone too far, while others said he had not gone far enough. The Governor himself insisted that he had found a "point of balance" that was just about right.

Another new thing Patten instituted was a Governor's "Question Time" in Legco, when he would go to the legislature and answer any questions that legislators might wish to ask him. This became instituted as a monthly affair. The Governor also gave up his position as President of Legco. This position of President was filled by John Swaine, who had previously served as acting president. Swaine became the first legislator to be elected president by his colleagues in the chamber. Elsie Tu was chosen as his deputy.

## ☐ The Sino-British Squabble

The initial response to the Governor's proposals were overwhelmingly positive. He appeared to have found a way to satisfy demands for greater democracy while remaining within the confines of the Basic Law. This situation changed, however, when Beijing made clear its strong opposition. When the Governor went to Beijing to explain his proposals, he was snubbed by not being granted an audience with any senior members of the leadership. His meetings with Lu Ping, Director of the Hong Kong and Macau Affairs Office under the State Council, did not go well. In fact, within minutes of the Governor's departure from Beijing, Lu held a press conference in which he vehemently denounced the Governor's proposals and threatened that China would, if necessary, "build a second stove", or create its own governmental structure for Hong Kong. He also said that if the British went ahead and built the new airport without Chinese approval, planes using that airport would not be allowed to fly over Mainland territory. This was a strange threat since the airport is not scheduled to be completed until 1997, when Hong Kong would have become part of China.

Lu and other Chinese officials were careful to focus their attacks on Patten in the hope of driving a wedge between him and the British government in London. The Governor, on his part, publicly declared that he and the British Prime Minister John Major were so close that there was not even room for anyone to put a piece of tissue paper between them. In any event, the Governor continued to enjoy the support not only of the Prime Minister but also of Foreign Secretary Douglas Hurd, even after an embarrassing series of letters exchanged between Hurd and his Chinese counterpart, Foreign Minister Qian Qichen, were made public.

This came about as a result of Chinese disclosures that, in addition to the Sino-British Joint Declaration and the Basic Law, there were "other relevant agreements and understandings" between London and Beijing regarding Hong Kong that had to be honoured. An outcry arose in Hong Kong calling for such letters to be made public. After a period of prevarication, seven letters were eventually made public by both sides. These letters, exchanged in early 1990 before the final adoption of the Basic Law, showed that contrary to the public British position of pressing China to give Hong Kong as much democracy as possible, the British were actually asking for much less than what Hong Kong wanted, and eventually settled for even less than that. In 1989, the turmoil in Beijing that led up to the Tiananmen military crackdown had resulted in all the unofficial members of the Executive and Legislative Councils agreeing on what was called the "OMELCO Consensus", which called for thirty seats, or 50 per cent of Legco, to be directly elected in 1995 and a fully directly elected Legco by 2003. From the letters, however, it was obvious that Hurd, at least by early 1990, was asking for only 24 seats to be directly elected in 1995. Even this he failed to get, and ultimately settled for 20 seats. This was then incorporated into the Basic Law.

In the letters, Hurd also said he agreed "in principle" that the Basic Law's provision for the election committee of 1999 would be put into effect in Hong Kong in 1995. The Patten proposals, therefore, seemed to the Chinese to be reneging on a previous understanding.

## ☐ Political Realignment

The Patten proposals had a curious effect on the political groupings in Hong Kong. The UDHK, which during the Wilson era was firmly in the opposition, warmed to Patten. While saying that he did not go far enough, the UDHK was clearly pleased by his reform plans. But the CRC, which during the Wilson era was strongly pro-government, turned in effect into an opposition party. A reversal in Britain's attitudes towards China had resulted in a reversal of roles on the part of the two major political groupings in Hong Kong.

The period under review also saw a strong surge in the development of political parties. A pro-Beijing political party, the Democratic Alliance for Betterment of Hong Kong (DABHK), was inaugurated the day after Patten's arrival in Hong Kong. Its chairman was Tsang Yok-sing, principal of what used to be known as a "patriotic" school. The party's 56 founding members included Vice Chairman Tam Yiu-chung, a serving Legislative Councillor, as well as Cheng Kai-nam and Chan Yuen-han, candidates in the 1991 Legislative Council elections, both of whom served on the seven-member standing committee.

The new party issued a strong warning against outside interference in Hong Kong's political affairs. Tsang described the party as both "pro-China and pro-Hong Kong". He said: "We support China's policy towards Hong Kong. But such a stand would never stop us from serving Hong Kong's interest."

Although the new party permitted dual membership, one of its members, Elsie Leung, announced that she had withdrawn from another pro-Beijing grouping, the New Hong Kong Alliance, which was set up in 1989 by T. S. Lo, a former member of the Executive and Legislative Councils. The alliance itself expanded greatly in 1992, increasing its membership from fewer than 40 to about 630 in a six-month period. Its founders included many influential businesspersons and professionals who had been members of the Basic Law Consultative Committee. The alliance adopted a low profile after the promulgation of the Basic Law in 1990 and the candidates it supported for the 1991 elections, like those of the like-minded Liberal Democratic Federation (LDF), had been roundly defeated. The lackluster LDF, in an attempt at revitalization, invited Maria Tam, who had been appointed a Hong Kong adviser by China, to play a leading role. Both the alliance and the LDF were to some extent eclipsed by the DABHK after its creation, since the DABHK had a popular base not enjoyed by either of the other two groupings.

Another stronghold of conservative business interests, the Business and Professional Federation (BPF) which is headed by Vincent Lo and whose members include most of the territory's major hongs, decided late in the year not to convert itself into a political party, but the BPF did come out strongly against Patten's political blueprint. Some members made it clear that they preferred the BPF to remain an organization that was not involved in politics. Subsequently, the Hong Kong General Chamber of Commerce pulled out of the BPF to maintain its position as a purely business body. (Ironically, the chamber itself became politicized some months later when five pro-China figures were elected onto the board of directors and the Jardine representative thrown out.)

The weakness of the New Hong Kong Alliance, at least within the legislature, was made clear when Philip Wong, its only member in Legco who was elected by the Chinese Chamber of Commerce, sponsored a motion debate in December 1992 that called on the Governor to withdraw his reform proposals. That motion was roundly defeated, attracting only one vote in support from Tam Yiu-chung, besides that of Wong himself. The defeat of Wong's motion marked the third time when Legco had indicated support for the Governor's package. Before that, a motion debate seeking endorsement of the composition of the 1995 Election Committee similar to the one suggested by Patten, and a motion seeking general support for the Patten proposals, were passed with overwhelming majorities.

Meanwhile, the CRC was trying to turn itself into a political party. The situation was unusual because all the members of the group, led by appointed member Allen Lee, were legislators. The group had little grassroots support. An opinion survey published in August 1992 showed that only 11 per cent of the public supported the CRC, 24 points behind the liberal grouping led by Martin Lee, the UDHK. The total support for liberal groups, including Meeting Point and the Hong Kong Association for Democracy and People's Livelihood (HKADPL), stood at 49 per cent, while that of conservative and pro-Beijing groups was 20 per cent.

Despite such poll findings, however, the UDHK lost the by-election held on 30 August 1992 to fill the Legco seat left vacant by the death of Stephen Ng Ming-yum. The UDHK's vice president, Albert Ho, was soundly trounced by Tang Siu-tong, a conservative with no affiliation to any political group. It was known, however, that pro-China individuals and organizations had given their support to Tang. The defeat also strained ties between the UDHK and another liberal group, the HKADPL, whose offer of assistance during the campaign had been turned down. Further signs of disarray within the liberal ranks emerged when a legislator, Leong Che-hung, who helped to found the Hong Kong Democratic Foundation in 1990, resigned to join Meeting Point when it officially turned itself into a political party in mid-September 1992, thereby increasing the group's representation in the legislature to four. The formal setting up of Meeting Point, a group formed in 1983, as a fully-fledged political party also led to the withdrawal of two prominent members, Lee Chik-yuet and Lo Chi-kin, from the UDHK in a bid to end overlapping membership.

Meeting Point's move meant the HKADPL was the only major liberal grouping that had not turned itself into a political party. Plans to do so were made in late 1992, along with the opening of three service centres across the territory, but they were put in abeyance because of the Sino-British row over Hong Kong's political development. Frederick Fung, the HKADPL's only member in Legco, announced that its resources had been stretched thin because of the need to study the various political reform proposals. He predicted that the group would be a political party by 1995, when the last round of elections to the legislature under British administration would be held.

The UDHK, formed in April 1990, was by far the largest of the liberal groupings, with 600 members. However, because its principal leaders had been targeted by Beijing, and the group itself had in effect been blacklisted by Chinese officials, it had great difficulty in expanding its membership and in raising funds. UDHK efforts to establish a dialogue with Chinese officials in Beijing and with the New China News Agency (Xinhua News Agency) in Hong Kong were rebuffed. A letter to the New China News Agency asking for a meeting with Director Zhou Nan was rejected out of hand, with Vice Director Zhang Junsheng saying that any such meeting would be fruitless unless the group thoroughly changed its stance. "The public stance of a handful of UDHK leaders in opposing the Basic Law and adopting a hostile attitude towards the Chinese government is widely known," Zhang said.

The UDHK's dilemma was that if it continued on a confrontational course with Beijing, it would continue to be treated like a pariah by people fearful of bringing down China's wrath on Hong Kong. On the other hand, a conciliatory attitude towards Beijing would risk charges that the group was abandoning its principles and result in an erosion of its core supporters. The public's identification of the group with an anti-China stance was strengthened by the fact that many of the UDHK's leaders, such as Martin Lee, Szeto Wah, Lau Chin-shek, Cheung Man-kwong and Lee Wing-tat, were also leaders of the Hong Kong Alliance in Support of the Patriotic Democratic Movement in China, which had helped finance the democratic movement in Beijing and assisted in the escape of several Chinese democratic leaders to the West via Hong Kong.

The UDHK constantly found itself torn between wanting to support the more assertive British line represented by Governor Patten and fear of being branded a pro-government party. It was also torn between a desire to support proposals that, because they originated from the British, seemed more feasible than plans opposed by both Britain and China, and a desire to go even further, as was its natural inclination. It called for a referendum on political development, postponed and then renewed the call, only to have the motion defeated as it came to a vote on the eve of the opening of formal Sino-British negotiations in Beijing on the 1994–1995 elections. Similarly, it found itself in an awkward position on the issue of whether the United States should continue to give most-favoured-nation (MFN) trade status to China. It realized, as did the majority of people in Hong Kong, that the withdrawal of MFN status from China would hurt the Hong Kong economy. At the same time, it did not want to appear to condone the human rights situation in China by calling for the unconditional extension of Beijing's MFN trading status.

Perhaps ironically, the emergence and consolidation of political groupings led to the defeat of one of Governor Patten's key proposals, the setting up of a Government-Legco Committee to provide better communications between the executive and the legislature. The proposal had been made in the aftermath of the separation of Exco and Legco. All the various groupings in Legco, as well as the independent members, wanted to be represented on the committee and it was impossible to leave anyone out. This meant, in effect, that short of including the whole legislature, it was not possible to set up a committee. In the end, the proposal was dropped, though the government made clear that it could be revived if Legco should ever be interested in doing so.

## ☐ Bureaucratic Blunders

The severance of ties between Exco and Legco was followed by several controversies that led to charges that Exco was, as a result, cut off from the sentiments of the legislature and of the Hong Kong public. One issue was that of replacing British Dependent Territory Citizenship (BDTC) passports with British National (Overseas) (BNO) passports. The Hong Kong government insisted, with Exco's blessing, on a strict phased timetable for people of various age groups to apply for the new passports, beginning in 1993. Failure to apply before certain cutoff dates would result in the forfeiture of a person's right to acquire the new passport. Legco revolted, pointing out that the Joint Declaration had said that Hong Kong people would be able to keep their BDTC passports until 1997, when they would have the option of applying for a new passport, namely the BNO. Forcing people to give up their BDTC passports, Legco members said, was inconsistent with the Joint Declaration. Legco proposed that if people had to apply for BNO passports before 1997, then they should be allowed to keep their BDTC passports at the same time. Exco was embarrassed when the British government accepted Legco's arguments and agreed that Hong Kong people could hold two passports at the same time.

Another issue was the treatment of expatriate officers within the Hong Kong government. Under pressure from expatriate officers, the government agreed, again with Exco's endorsement, that expatriate officers would be allowed to give up their expatriate status, under which they enjoyed more favourable terms than their local counterparts, and be allowed to keep their jobs on local terms after the expiry of their overseas contracts. At the time this chapter was being written, the issue was heating up and it appeared likely that the government would end up antagonizing both local officers and expatriates by trying to please first one group and then the other.

## ☐ The Liberal Party and the Liberals

The CRC, in the months leading up to its transformation into a political party, laid the groundwork by building up its public image. It sent delegations to London and Beijing, whose members met with the British Prime Minister John Major and the Chinese Premier Li Peng. The CRC was thus able to present itself as a group with access to both governments, and one that was trying to get the two sides to sit down together and talk things out.

The arrival of 1993 saw the three liberal groups — the UDHK, Meeting Point and the HKADPL — holding sporadic meetings in an attempt to reach a consensus on the Patten proposals. But such a consensus was elusive. Even members of one group often could not agree on a common position. Eventually, three founding members of Meeting Point resigned in protest when the party endorsed the Patten proposals.

Meanwhile, over in the conservative camp, the CRC continued its work to set up a political party. It put out a position paper at the beginning of 1993 calling for a smooth transition in 1997. It called on Britain and China to hold negotiations and proposed serious amendments to the Patten proposals, in effect supporting the Chinese position on the Election

Committee and the nine new functional constituencies. The paper, *A New Vision for a Better Future*, spelled out five principal objectives:

1.  To safeguard the people of Hong Kong by protecting their interests and upholding individual rights and liberties;
2.  To maintain and improve the quality of life of the people of Hong Kong;
3.  To preserve and enhance the social, economic, legal and political systems that have created Hong Kong's prosperity and stability;
4.  To ensure a smooth transfer of sovereignty in 1997 and a smooth transition through 1997; and
5.  To participate in the governing of Hong Kong in the achievement of those objectives.

After many months of agonizing, including abortive plans for a merger with the LDF, the CRC finally metamorphosed into the Liberal Party, a name that was the butt of numerous jokes, since the party's founders were known for their conservatism. (The name of the party created problems for headline writers, since Liberals, with a capital "L", referred to the conservatives and "liberals", with a small "l", referred to the democrats. The fact that the leaders of the two parties were both surnamed Lee made matters worse.) The LDF, which turned down a merger with the Liberal Party, was to suffer a severe drop in membership as some of its leading figures, including Peter Wong, Ngai Shiu-kit and James Tien, defected to the new party. Even the UDHK was affected when Sha Tin District Board member Cheng Yuk-choi left its ranks to join the Liberal Party, claiming it was more democratic.

The Liberal Party was the first political grouping in Hong Kong to use the word "party" in its name, a sign that the age of political parties had really dawned in Hong Kong. It was known that the New China News Agency had agreed to the name.

At the end of February, Allen Lee announced the formation of a 44-member Preparatory Committee, consisting mainly of professionals and businesspersons, for the setting up of the new Liberal Party. Lee, who had not previously held an elected office, signalled a determination to plunge into electoral politics. He said the new party would contest seats in the forthcoming elections, including that for chief executive of the future Special Administrative Region. "We believe the success of a political party rests on active political participation by having enough seats in the various councils and the support of the people," Lee said.

The nascent Liberal Party sponsored a visit to Beijing to present their views to Chinese officials. The fact that their visit was approved, while a similar visit proposed by Meeting Point was turned down, indicated that the conservative grouping enjoyed China's favour, certainly to a greater extent than any of the genuinely liberal political groupings in Hong Kong. But Meeting Point's chairman, Anthony Cheung, did secure a meeting with the Director of the Hong Kong and Macau Affairs Office, Lu Ping, in mid-March 1993 and had a private conversation with him on Hong Kong's transitional arrangements.

## ☐ Storm over the "Second Stove"

The decision in March by the Governor to gazette his political reform proposals, following the failure of the talks-about-talks in Beijing to bear fruit, showed the division within Hong Kong's political groupings. Chairman Tsang Yok-sing of the pro-Beijing DABHK deplored the move, saying it would "only further toughen China's stance". Allen Lee, too, wondered what the Governor hoped to achieve by his controversial move, though he tempered his remarks by voicing disappointment at China's opposition to Hong Kong government officials taking part in any Sino-British talks. However, Martin Lee of the UDHK voiced strong support for Patten's move.

Meanwhile, Chinese officials in February 1993 again threatened to set up a "second stove" in Hong Kong if Legco should go ahead and approve the Patten package. These threats were repeated in March, immediately after Governor Patten gazetted his reform proposals, by Lu Ping, who dubbed the Governor a "man of guilt". Lu said: "If Mr. Patten sticks to his plan and insists on confrontation with the Chinese side, we have no other choice but to take corresponding measures. So, starting from now, we have to make preparations in all areas because we don't have much time left." Although the Patten proposals only related to the legislature, Lu indicated that if they were implemented, China in 1997 would reject not only the Hong Kong legislature but the executive and judiciary as well.

The creation of a "second stove" was interpreted by many as in effect setting up a shadow government. While the "second stove", formally known as the preliminary working committee for the future Preparatory Committee of the Special Administrative Region, was not set up by the National People's Congress until July, China did name a second batch of Hong Kong advisers in March. Forty-nine prominent local residents were appointed. The new batch, mostly conservative politicians, businesspersons and academics, joined an earlier group of advisers chosen in 1992. Political figures chosen included Allen Lee and Stephen Cheong of the yet-to-be-established Liberal Party as well as Tsang Yok-sing and Tam Yiu-chung of the pro-Beijing DABHK. No liberal politicians were appointed, though the Chinese authorities left the door open for such appointments in the future. Martin Lee, commenting on the absence of UDHK members from the Chinese list, termed it an "honour" for his party that no members were chosen, a remark that showed the ambivalence of the party, which was hoping, unsuccessfully, for a dialogue with Chinese officials.

DABHK chairman Tsang Yok-sing, one of those appointed, sought to calm fears of a shadow government by saying of the working party: "It is not a decision-making body and not a shadow government. It makes proposals and suggestions to the National People's Congress and the future preparatory committee."

Others appointed included members of the Liberal Party, the Liberal Democratic Federation, the New Hong Kong Alliance and the Business and Professional Federation. Again, no members of the UDHK or other liberal groups were appointed.

## ☐ Party Blueprints for the Future

The Liberal Party's draft manifesto, made public in May 1993, created controversy by calling for the setting up of a ministerial system. Various former members of the Basic Law Drafting Committee denounced the proposal as being inconsistent with the Basic Law. However, Selina Chow, a member of the party's preparatory committee, insisted there was enough flexibility in the Basic Law to accommodate a ministerial system. "Basically," she said, "the proposal we are now putting forward will not be in fundamental breach of the Basic Law. There is a lot of room for development." The draft manifesto also proposed that foreign passport holders be banned from standing for direct elections and in functional constituencies, except for two proposed new seats for non-Chinese and foreign chambers of commerce. The manifesto suggested that, these exceptions aside, foreign passport holders should only join Legco if chosen by the Election Committee.

The manifesto was by no means a totally conservative document. It called for a "wholly elected government, including a democratically elected chief executive", after 2007, since the Basic Law has already laid down specific provisions for the period before 2007. In the manifesto, the Liberal Party also asserted that it would always put the interests of Hong Kong first. In case of disagreement between Hong Kong and China, it said, the party will "seek to persuade China to respect the desires of Hong Kong people".

Meanwhile, another pro-China group, the Federation for the Stability of Hong Kong, whose leadership has been dominated by prominent rural and pro-Beijing figures, disclosed plans to set up a political party. The main personalities included Legislative Councillor Lau Wong-fat, chairman of the Heung Yee Kuk, and Cheung Yan-lung, Chan Yat-sun and Kan Fook-yee, all of whom were serving as China's Hong Kong advisers.

As the summer wore on, many political groups were busy drafting their proposals for the transition in 1997 from a British colony to a Chinese special administrative region. One problem was the Basic Law's stipulation that people holding foreign passports or who had the right of abode in foreign countries could not hold more than 20 per cent of the seats in Legco. The DABHK suggested, among other things, that the provision be observed by the drawing of lots whenever the quota of 12 in the 60-member chamber is exceeded. It suggested that not more than six of the 30 seats returned by functional constituencies, four of the 20 by direct polls and two of the 10 by Election Committee be allocated to foreign passport holders.

The LDF proposed that the foreign-passport-holder issue be dealt with by allowing foreign passport holders to run in only 12 functional con-stituencies. Executive committee member Maria Tam explained that under the LDF's proposals foreign passport holders could not be elected by the Election Committee or take part in direct elections. The LDF's proposal for the formation of the Election Committee was identical to that proposed by the DABHK, which was to adopt the model described in the Basic Law. It said the nine new functional constituencies should come mostly from the business sector.

Perhaps surprisingly, two liberal groups, in their proposals, took an even more extreme position than that of pro-Beijing bodies. Both Meeting Point and the HKADPL proposed that foreign passport holders be barred altogether from membership in Legco. Frederick Fung, chairman of the HKADPL, said allowing foreign nationals to sit in the legislature would compromise Chinese sovereignty over Hong Kong. He called for the Basic Law to be amended so as to bar all foreign nationals.

# 4

# The Implementation of the Sino-British Joint Declaration

## John Walden

In December 1989, when the originators of *The Other Hong Kong Report* launched their first volume in the series, the work of implementing the Sino-British Joint Declaration had already been going on, in secret, for more than four years, under the control of the Sino-British Joint Liaison Group (JLG) at meetings held in London, Beijing and Hong Kong. Fourteen such meetings of the JLG had already taken place, without Hong Kong being formally represented. The thirteenth meeting of the JLG was postponed from July to September 1989 because of the military crackdown on Chinese student demonstrators in Beijing on 3 and 4 June.

## ☐ Foreign Affairs Committee Inquiry

Long before the tragic incidents in Tiananmen Square put the people of Hong Kong into a state of deep shock and fear for their future, the Foreign Affairs Committee (FAC) of the House of Commons, at Westminster, had become aware of mounting discontent in Hong Kong over the slow pace of constitutional reform. Such was the concern that, in February 1989, the FAC invited public representations on the matter in pursuance of a formal inquiry, which would include a visit to Hong Kong to hear evidence.

One of the many written submissions put to the FAC prior to its arrival in Hong Kong described the dramatic decline of public confidence in

---

John Walden joined the Colonial Administrative Service in 1950 and served with the Hong Kong government for thirty years, retiring in 1981 as Director of Home Affairs.

the Joint Declaration since its signing in December 1984 and suggested possible causes:

> When implementation began following ratification on 27 May 1985 the attitude of the public and the media was one of confidence in the Joint Declaration and respect and gratitude to Britain and China for the achievement. At the time of writing, less than four years later, that attitude has changed to one of disillusionment with the Joint Declaration and deep distrust and resentment towards both signatories and a sense that they have been betrayed by Britain. This submission will not discuss the causes of this change of heart but if the Committee wishes to understand the reasons for it, it may wish to consider the following possibilities:
>
> (1) that initial official over-confidence in the acceptability of the Joint Declaration to the people of Hong Kong, bearing in mind their deep distrust of the Communist Party of China, led to;
>
> (2) lack of appreciation of the essential fragility of the agreement as a means of dispelling peoples' fears at the coming change of sovereignty, giving rise to;
>
> (3) failure to realise that if the public were to perceive that Britain was in breach of any sensitive provision, the agreement as a whole would be seen to be flawed, as exemplified by;
>
> (4) Britain's action in yielding to Chinese demands to discuss constitutional reforms at the second meeting of the Joint Liaison Group in November 1985 when it was agreed to tailor these to conform with the future Basic Law and Britain's subsequent denials that this had happened, and
>
> (5) the impression given by Sir David Wilson that, since taking up his appointment as Governor of Hong Kong, he has not been willing to take the side of the people of Hong Kong in issues arising from the Joint Declaration when the Peking Government or its agents appear to be deviating from the terms of the Joint Declaration, or going back on their assurances not to interfere in the affairs of Hong Kong either before or after 1997.
>
> Whatever reasons may finally be adduced to account for this loss of public confidence in the Joint Declaration and British assurances of a safe future under Chinese sovereignty, it is an inescapable fact of Hong Kong political life that there has been serious slippage in Britain's own plans for political reform to achieve truly representative government before 1997. It is unrealistic to suppose that the form of government Parliament had in mind for Hong Kong people in 1984 can be realised by 1997.
>
> — Foreign Affairs Committee, Session 1988–89,
> *Second Report — Hong Kong*, Volume II, pp. 431–32

## ☐ Hong Kong's Concerns

After hearing evidence in Hong Kong between 17 and 22 April and returning to London, via Beijing, just five weeks before the June Fourth crackdown there, the FAC rushed out its report on 28 June. The report's 472 pages and 500,000 words records a wide range of Hong Kong's concerns from loss of nationality, fear for human rights, the Basic Law and its interpretation to the long-standing problem of the Vietnamese boat people. But underlying and exacerbating these various concerns was the belief that the Hong Kong government had not taken the initiative in developing a more representative system of government as provided for in the Joint Declaration. Quite apart from the many individual submissions which complained of this procrastination, representatives of more than 20 professional and other bodies who gave oral or written evidence criticized the Hong Kong government for not fulfilling public expectations of political reform.

The report of the FAC's inquiry and its recommendations fully and fairly reflected Hong Kong's concerns. These were germane to the question of whether the people of the territory would be granted the institutional capability to manage their own internal affairs, with a high degree of autonomy, as intended by Parliament, and as repeatedly promised by the Beijing government in the lead-up to the signing of the Joint Declaration in 1984. As Hong Kong's right to enjoy this capability has become the bone of contention in the current Sino-British deadlock over electoral arrangements for 1995, I make no apologies for quoting the relevant section of the FAC report in full:

**Administration to 1997**

3.4 It is most important that in the day-to-day administration of Hong Kong prior to 1997 the Hong Kong Government is seen to be governing Hong Kong in accordance with the wishes and interests of the Hong Kong people and not in response to the perceived wishes of the Beijing Government or even of the British Government. We were told that in the past there has sometimes been a perception that that seemed not to be the case. A particular example, and one which was frequently mentioned to us, was the 1987 review of the development of representative government which culminated in the 1988 White Paper. We do not believe that there is anything to be gained from a detailed re-examination of these events, but the mistrust of the Hong Kong Government which was caused among a significant proportion of Hong Kong people during that time persists and should not be underestimated.

3.5 During our evidence session on 12 June with Sir David Wilson we asked whether he still believed in "mirror-imaging" the arrangements established in Hong Kong before 1997 with what was expected to be provided in the Basic Law. In March, Sir David had told us that "mirror-imaging" had the objective of providing the continuity of the legislature through 1997 which demanded that "whatever is the percentage of direct elections laid down in the Basic Law [would be the percentage] in our final election under British administration." We were disappointed that he still argued in June that, particularly with regard to developing representative government, "people in Hong Kong will also be looking at the question of how they can be sure … what they are trying to set up goes on after 1997." We fully recognise the importance of carrying China with the developments instituted in Hong Kong, but we do not see the situation in this way. We believe that this approach can be damaging to confidence in Hong Kong. The Hong Kong Government remains responsible for the administration of Hong Kong to 30 June 1997. It must carry out that duty in accordance with the needs and demands of Hong Kong itself, particularly now that negotiations with the Chinese have been so disrupted. Although there is a risk that the Chinese Government will be unwilling to accept the consequent developments in Hong Kong, at the worst, by refusing to incorporate them in the Basic Law, we believe that far greater are the risks to confidence and stability associated with appearing to wait upon Chinese approval before taking action in Hong Kong prior to 1997. **Indeed we believe that the Hong Kong Government must take this opportunity to seize the initiative so as to establish in Hong Kong in advance of 1997 the institutions and systems best designed to guarantee Hong Kong's future autonomy and stability within the terms of the Joint Declaration.** [original emphasis]

— Foreign Affairs Committee, Session 1988–89,
*Second Report — Hong Kong*, Volume I, p. xii

## ☐ Must Try Harder

It was against this alarming evidence of the British government's ambivalence in developing the political rights granted to the people of Hong Kong in the Joint Declaration that Chapter 3 of *The Other Hong Kong Report* (1989) was written. Not surprisingly it took both the British and Hong Kong governments severely to task for conspiring with China to hold back political reform in Hong Kong until the Basic Law Drafting Committee had devised a model for Hong Kong to "converge" with. British performance overall in implementing the Joint Declaration for the first third of the 12-year run-up to the British handover to China was summed up as follows:

> If any lesson is to be learned from this sad saga of poor political judgment, wishful thinking, broken promises, lack of determination and deliberate misrepresentation, it is this. Implementation of the Joint Declaration should not be resumed until the British and Hong Kong Governments have agreed on ways of ensuring that whatever is done from now on is in the best interests of the people of Hong Kong, that it does not derogate from their rights under the Joint Declaration, and that it is done with their participation and general consent wherever possible. It cannot be right that the future well-being of the six million people of Hong Kong should continue to be entrusted to a small team of British officials, operating in strict confidence, who do not have to live with the future they are laying down for all those people, and who are not directly accountable to them.

If the political ground lost in the first four years of the transition period is to be won back in the eight short years still remaining; if the proposals made by the Foreign Affairs Committee for faster constitutional reform and improved protection for human rights in the Basic Law are accepted by the British Government and are to be implemented; if the Hong Kong Government is not to be intimidated by China and is to be seen by its people to be firm in rightfully claiming what it was promised under the Joint Declaration, a much stronger Hong Kong front will have to be presented to China when implementation of the Joint Declaration is resumed.

Until Hong Kong has had time to develop representative local leaders with broad-based support, that front will have to be organized and led by the Governor of Hong Kong. If public confidence in the future of Hong Kong is going to be restored that Governor will have to be perceived as the strongest Governor of Hong Kong that the people have ever had, and not as the most cooperative Governor of Hong Kong that China has ever had....

The choice facing the Foreign Secretary and the Governor of Hong Kong is either to go all out for what Hong Kong people were promised under the Joint Declaration, knowing that this will have international support, and incur the risk of confrontation with the Beijing Government or, to avoid all risk of confrontation by making the kinds of compromises that were made in the first stage of implementation, in the certain knowledge Hong Kong people will get only those rights and conditions written into the Joint Declaration which China deems fit to grant them. It is a choice between uniting to wage a righteous fight for survival and freedom with a good chance of coming through bruised but alive and victorious; or offering no resistance to the Beijing Government's attempts to claw-back power and suffering certain death by slow strangulation.

There is little doubt that the people of Hong Kong owe it to themselves, to their children and to the future well-being of China to encourage and support the British Government and the Governor of Hong Kong in taking the former road in spite of the risk it entails. What is in doubt is whether Sir David Wilson is the right Governor of Hong Kong to lead them along that road....

But if the present Governor is to be replaced by someone with appropriate leadership qualities who is it to be? The candidate is certainly not to be found in Hong Kong. The task is difficult and it is time consuming. It requires a style of leadership rare in career civil servants and unlikely to be found in anyone from the British Foreign Office. It needs someone with a sense of mission and with the sure touch that comes from competence backed by an unassailable social and political pedigree. It has to be someone with unquestionable authority and the gift of being able to bring together in support of the common cause powerful Hong Kong interest groups with divergent or opposed objectives.

*— The Other Hong Kong Report* [1989], pp. 55–62

It might well be imagined that in the fall of 1989, after Parliament's most prestigious select committee had presented the Thatcher government with overwhelming proof of its failure to sustain the confidence of the people of Hong Kong in the viability of the Joint Declaration and made strong recommendations on how to redress the lack of progress in political development, her government would have moved swiftly and decisively to honour the undertakings given by the government to Parliament on constitutional changes in Hong Kong in the transitional period. After all, if those undertakings had not been given during the Parliamentary debates on the Joint Declaration in 1984, and at the time of the passing of the Hong Kong Bill, in January 1985, Parliament would not have given its consent to the government's unprecedented proposal to deny the people of Hong Kong the right of self-determination and hand them over involuntarily to a communist state.

## ☐ Britain's Moral Imperative

To put it in another way, if the Chinese government would not countenance the grant of the right of self-determination to the people of Hong Kong and the British people would not allow the British government to grant Hong Kong people the option of right of abode in the United Kingdom, then the Thatcher government was obliged to help them develop a system of government, sufficiently democratic and autonomous, to ensure that their free lifestyle would not be put in jeopardy after 1997. This, after all, was the quintessence of Mrs. Thatcher's vow, at the time of her visit to Hong Kong in September 1982, after opening discussions with Deng Xiaoping in Beijing on the future of Hong Kong.

Speaking at a press conference in the Legislative Council Chamber on 27 September, the British Prime Minister was adamant on the matter:

> I have been at pains to stress that the British Government has a clear responsibility for the people of Hong Kong. As leader of that Government, what matters to me is that we discharge our moral duty to them.

Questioned by reporter Jesse Wong of the *Asian Wall Street Journal* about Britain's interests, aside from the moral obligation, Mrs. Thatcher's tart response reflected the strength of her personal convictions:

> Well, you say "aside from the moral obligation — it's quite a big aside!" I mean, that is our main commitment and responsibility and that's what comes first with us.

## ☐ Still No New Initiative

However, there is nothing in the brief official communiqués of the nine plenary meetings of the JLG held between March 1990 and June 1992 (the last to be held before Chris Patten replaced Lord Wilson as Governor of Hong Kong) to suggest that the British government had responded at the speed and in the way hoped for by the FAC. Nor do the annual reports laid before Parliament for 1990 and 1991 indicate a new initiative. On the contrary, it seems that the diplomatic stint on the Hong Kong front, three years on from the trauma of 4 June 1989, was much the same as before. The same tired team of decent British chaps wilting under the relentless pressure of their tough Chinese counterparts, getting nowhere and having to give in on such fundamental issues as the Memorandum of Understanding Concerning the Construction of the New Airport in Hong Kong and Related Questions (dealt with by Margaret Ng in the 1991 report in this series) and the setting up of a Court of Final Appeal in Hong Kong before 1997 (covered by Frank Ching in the 1992 report). The outcome in the first case was a codicil to the Joint Declaration that turns it into the last in a long line of "unequal" treaties but the first to be decisively to China's advantage. It is now being used by Beijing to get a stranglehold over the Hong Kong government in the last few years of British administration. In the second case the agreed decision of the JLG was a bilateral contravention of the Joint Declaration and the Basic Law.

## ☐ Mission of the International Commission of Jurists

If these unfavourable impressions of the performance of the Chinese, British and Hong Kong governments in carrying out their prescribed responsibilities under the Joint Declaration are thought to lack objectivity, the reader should take note of the summary of the conclusions and recommendations of the International Commission of Jurists (ICJ) in the Appendix to this chapter. The ICJ is the first independent body to conduct a formal inquiry into the implementation of the Joint Declaration and visited Hong Kong in April 1991 to receive written and oral evidence. Its views on the crucial question of whether the Basic Law of the Hong Kong Special Administrative Region correctly reflects the spirit and letter of the Joint Declaration are as follows:

> It is therefore our conclusion that the Basic Law is inconsistent, in twelve respects, with the obligations which the PRC accepted by its signature and ratification of the Joint Declaration. Having regard to the number and importance of these inconsistencies, the Basic Law has to be seen as a deliberate attempt by the PRC to renege on its obligations. To take only the most important points, Hong Kong will not,

even after 2007, have a democratically elected legislature or Chief Executive. Its courts will not have the power of final adjudication on the constitutional validity of its own laws or on the interpretation of the Basic Law. Its executive will not have the sole power to decide when a state of emergency exists and will be required to prohibit whatever the Standing Committee considers to be "subversion". Its legislature will be unable to legislate without the consent of a Chief Executive who is not elected by a democratic process.

All this casts grave doubts on the commitment of the Government of the PRC to fulfil its obligation to allow genuine autonomy to Hong Kong after 1997.

Meanwhile, the attitude of the British Government to the promulgation of the Basic Law has, at least in public, been one of supine acquiescence. This is typified by the statement of a spokesman for the United Kingdom (Mr. Beamish) to the U.N. Human Rights Commission on 4 April 1991 that "the Government of the United Kingdom had satisfied itself that the Basic Law was on the whole consistent with the basic principles enshrined in the Joint Declaration and corresponded with its intention to resume the continued application of the Covenant beyond 1997". The accuracy of that view can be judged in the light of our own analysis of the Basic Law.

— "Countdown to 1997", *Report of a Mission to Hong Kong on behalf of the International Commission of Jurists* (1992), pp. 114 and 115.

## ☐ Parliament's Sovereignty Flouted?

The period of implementation reviewed thus far in this chapter runs from the first meeting of the JLG, in London, in July 1985 and ends with the twenty-third meeting held in Beijing in June 1992, exactly seven years later. If the measure of the performance is to be the degree of success in achieving the long-term objectives of the Joint Declaration, as defined by British Ministers from time to time, such as to guarantee "to provide a secure future for all Hong Kong residents — one in which they can feel confident and can continue to prosper" (Lord Glenarthur, House of Lords, 20 January 1986) or "to build up a firmly-based, democratic administration in Hong Kong in the years between now and 1997" (Richard Luce, House of Commons, 5 December 1984) it is clear that implementation of the Joint Declaration has failed abysmally and that those responsible may have usurped the sovereignty of Parliament by secretly collaborating with China in denying Hong Kong the means to attain a high degree of autonomy in the conduct of its internal affairs. This is not a matter that can be shrugged off simply because it is now all behind us and China is on the verge of taking over. In Britain, as this book goes to press, a public inquiry by Lord Chief Justice Scott into British arms sales to Iran is revealing disturbing evidence that officials working behind the scenes unilaterally modified a ban on sales without informing Parliament. There is a remarkable similarity between those events and the introduction of the "convergence" policy in 1985.

The parallel opens up a rich lode for speculation, particularly over the peremptory removal of Lord Wilson as Governor and his replacement by a politician, Chris Patten, who immediately reversed British tactics in dealing with the Beijing government on implementing the political provisions of the Joint Declaration. There has to be a very high probability that by 1991 the British Cabinet had come to realize that the decline in the authority of the Hong Kong government and the steadily mounting tension in local politics had come about because unsound advice had been fed to ministers by a small circle of career diplomats occupying key posts in Whitehall, Beijing and Hong Kong. It would seem that the nub of that unsound advice was that it made no sense to run the risk of invoking the wrath of Beijing by resisting its demands to set the agenda for political reform in Hong Kong in the transitional period because, in the end, not letting China have its way would make it worse for the people of Hong Kong.

## ☐ So Wrong So Long

What is so extraordinary about the implementation of the Joint Declaration is not that it began to go wrong almost from the outset but that it was allowed to go on going wrong for seven years, or almost two-thirds of the transitional period, before a decision was made at cabinet level to try to put things right. Unfortunately, unlike the events leading up to the signing of the Joint Declaration, which are admirably chronicled in Robert Cottrell's *The End of Hong Kong*, there is no reliable account in the public domain of the inside story of the implementation. Nor is an objective account likely to be forthcoming in the near future, for those responsible for such an inglorious episode in British history will not be raring to go public on their performance, except in self-serving personal memoirs.

## ☐ The February 1984 Protocol

Nonetheless, Cottrell's book, which was warmly commended for "broad accuracy" by Sir Percy Cradock, Mrs. Thatcher's former *éminence grise* of the Sino-British interface, has a useful account of the origins of the JLG which helps to throw light on how the "convergence" policy came to be thrust on the British side in late 1985. He reports on page 143 *et seq.*, that in February 1984, when the form of the Sino-British agreement was under discussion, the Chinese side unexpectedly tabled a protocol. Its central element was a Sino-British joint commission to oversee all major aspects of Hong Kong's administration in the final years of British rule. This appears to have been Deng Xiaoping's own stratagem for preventing the British from plundering the wealthy colony before they pulled out. This protocol was much disliked by the British negotiators and even more bitterly opposed by Hong Kong's Executive Council. But at the last major breakthrough in the negotiations, on 28 July 1984, a modified form of Deng's much-favoured "joint commission" (the present supposedly "powerless" JLG) was accepted by the British for inclusion in the Joint Declaration, in return for China agreeing to treat the Joint Declaration and its Annexes as one, single, binding agreement.

It now begins to look as if the Chinese negotiators accepted substantial British modifications to Deng's original supervisory commission, to make sure that it was included in the final draft of the Joint Declaration, but all along they intended to make the JLG serve Deng's aim of keeping an eye on the Hong Kong government and when necessary enable them to put pressure on the British, in private, to stop the Hong Kong government doing things which China did not want.

## ☐ Deng's Veto and Political Convergence

There is much evidence to suggest that the veto was first used at the second meeting of the JLG in November 1985 to call a halt to any further unilateral development of representative government in accordance with the Hong Kong government's 1984 White Paper. It was from around this time that the Hong Kong government adopted the practice of outwardly encouraging public participation in the electoral process while secretly preparing to discourage the idea of holding direct elections to the Legislative Council in 1988. An account of how the survey of public reactions to the 1987 Green Paper was manipulated, to justify a decision to defer direct elections until 1991, is to be found in Chapter 2 of a memorandum submitted to the FAC on behalf of "1997 Concerns", on pages 196–99 of Volume II of the 1989 report. It is difficult to believe that the British and Hong Kong officials involved in this duplicitous process of restraining political development on orders from China could have failed to realize that the outcome might be a gradual buildup of political frustration and tension as 1997 drew closer.

## ☐ Patten's Last Stand

It only remains to assess the significance of the appearance on the stage where the drama of the survival of Hugh Baker's endangered species "Hong Kong Man" is being played out, of a *deus ex machina* in the improbable form of Chris Patten, the last British Governor of Hong Kong. From the outset he has made no secret of what he is attempting to do within the overall British objective of upholding the Joint Declaration. He has given more publicity to his plans and generated more public debate about them than any of his predecessors.

In considering his impact on the future of Hong Kong only the political core of his agenda, the constitutional package, really matters. The other elements of his programme, though important in other respects in their various ways, are peripheral to the question of whether Hong Kong, the place Mr. Patten rightly described as one of the Wonders of the World, is to survive as we know and love it, beyond 1997 and into the twenty-first century. The constitutional implications of his political initiative are fully dealt with by Norman Miners in Chapter 1 and its political consequences by Frank Ching in Chapter 3. That ground will not be gone over again here, suffice it to say that Patten has injected more political adrenalin into Hong Kong in one year of colonial rule than his forebears did in the previous one and a half centuries. If only 50 per cent of his effort had been invested in the political development of Hong Kong in 1979 or 1985, who can say how different Hong Kong's future might look today?

## ☐ Losing the Battle for Democracy but ...

Not unexpectedly so much political initiative so late in the day has brought the Governor into a seemingly perilous confrontation with the Beijing government which, prior to his appointment, had skilfully edged itself to within five years of assuming sovereignty over Hong Kong very much on its own terms. Driven by a historical imperative that overrides any deal they have had to make to get the British to disgorge this last bit of the Motherland still in foreign hands, Beijing officials are still quivering with suppressed rage at Patten's challenge to their sacred patriotic mission.

It seems unlikely that China's present leaders will be persuaded to make any significant compromise with Mr. Patten over his constitutional package. To the Chinese, this package violates their basic premise that no political changes made by the British in Hong Kong in the transitional period are acceptable unless they have been specifically endorsed by China in advance. The current state of play will become clearer when the Governor delivers his second annual address to the Legislative Council on 6 October 1993 but good news from the political frontline is most improbable.

## ☐ Winning the War for Autonomy?

What really matters for Hong Kong is not whether Mr. Patten wins or loses the battle he started last year to claw back for Hong Kong people some of the political power granted to them in the Joint Declaration but surrendered to China in accordance with the convergence policy. It is whether he can win the war for their right to exercise some degree of autonomy in the management of their internal affairs under the government of the Hong Kong Special Administrative Region.

Patten's row with Beijing over the political rights of Hong Kong's six million people has already shifted Hong Kong and its problems from the wings of international affairs and closer to centre stage. Unwelcome as it is to China, this internationalization of local concern that Hong Kong should continue to be governed according to the principles of freedom within the rule of law, is likely to prove more effective as a deterrent to arbitrary surrogate rule by Beijing, after 1997, than the implementation of Patten's constitutional package.

## ☐ The Verdict on Patten

In 1988, the late David Bonavia, former Beijing correspondent of *The Times*, wrote in a perceptive foreword to *Basic Law, Basic Questions* (Ed. W. McGurn, Review Publishing Co., Ltd.), that while Britain's attempts to bestow on her colonies what was best in her own institutional heritage had not always been successful, at least she had tried to do the right thing. Not so in Hong Kong where the British have failed to live up to their own ideals.

The results of Chris Patten's late bid to redress that failure, to borrow Bonavia's words, "may be tolerable, or may be terrible", but at least he will go down in history as "having been seen to have tried harder". That is something, surprisingly enough, that both Sun Yat-sen and Lee Kuan-yew would recognize as being in China's long-term interests.

**APPENDIX**
**Report of a Mission to Hong Kong**
**on behalf of**
**The International Commission of Jurists**
**Geneva, Switzerland**
**by**
**Sir William Goodhart, Q.C., UK (Chairman)**
**Y.M. Raja Aziz Addruse, Malaysia**
**The Hon. John Dowd, A.O., Q.C., Australia**
**Prof. Hans-Heiner Kuehne, Germany**
**1992**

## Terms of Reference

1.  The nature and extent of the rights to self-determination of the people of Hong Kong before or upon the termination of the colonial status of Hong Kong under international law, as evidenced in the United Nations Charter, International Human Rights Covenants and relevant resolutions of the United Nations General Assembly, and the extent to which the United Kingdom has fulfilled its obligations to implement such rights;

2.  The extent to which after the transfer of sovereignty over Hong Kong from the United Kingdom to the Peoples' [People's] Republic of China in 1997 the Joint Declaration, agreed between the United Kingdom and the Peoples' [People's] Republic of China and the Basic Law enacted by the National Peoples' [People's] Congress of the Peoples' [People's] Republic of China, adequately protect the rule of law and the fundamental human rights of the people of Hong Kong as recognised by international law;

3.  The extent to which the draft Hong Kong Bill of Rights Ordinance adequately protects the rule of law and the fundamental human rights of the people of Hong Kong as recognised by international law, including the extent to which the Ordinance conforms to international human rights law;

4.  The steps, if any, that are necessary to ensure:
    (a)  that any default in complying with international law, including international human rights law, is rectified before the transfer of sovereignty over Hong Kong is effected in 1997; and
    (b)  that the observance of human rights in Hong Kong, including of the

relevant human rights instruments is monitored after the transfer of sovereignty is effected in 1997; and
5.  Any other related matter.

## *Chapter XV*

*Conclusions and Recommendations*

(1) The Joint Declaration, though creditable in other respects, is seriously defective in failing to ensure that the Chief Executive will be democratically elected by and democratically accountable to the people of Hong Kong.

(2) The decision of the National People's Congress on the establishment of the SAR should be clarified urgently by the publication of the map to which it refers, to eliminate the possibility that some or all of the New Territories may be excluded from the SAR.

(3) There are serious doubts as to the validity of the "one country — two systems" principle under the Constitution of the PRC as it now exists; these doubts can only be removed by amendment of the PRC Constitution.

(4) The people of Hong Kong are entitled to the right of self-determination under international law.

(5) The British Government should have obtained the authority of a referendum of the people of Hong Kong both before entering into the negotiations which led up to the Joint Declaration, and before signing the Joint Declaration.

(6) The people of Hong Kong have not been allowed to exercise the right to self-determination.

(7) In present circumstances a meaningful exercise of the right of self-determination is impracticable.

(8) The only way in which the United Kingdom can now compensate BDTCs in Hong Kong for the loss of the right to self-determination is by the provision of rights of residence in the UK itself or acceptable third countries.

(9) Whatever the practical problems may be the United Kingdom has an obligation in principle to provide rights of abode in the UK, or in third countries acceptable to them, for all Hong Kong BDTCs.

(10) Immediate British citizenship and a right of abode in the UK should be granted to Hong Kong BDTCs of non-Chinese descent with no

right of abode outside Hong Kong, and to Hong Kong BDTCs under 18 who would have been British citizens if born on or after the 1st [of] January 1983.

(11) For other Hong Kong BDTCs, the UK should grant a right of abode but would be entitled to impose a reasonable quota system for admission. Those who became BDTCs by naturalisation after the date of signature of the Joint Declaration (19th December 1984) would have a lower priority.

(12) Hong Kong BDTCs (except those given immediate citizenship) should be required to exercise their right to take up an abode outside Hong Kong before a date about six years after the transfer, subject to any further delay imposed by the quota system.

(13) The Legislative Council to be elected in 1995 should be elected solely from geographical constituencies.

(14) Functional constituencies, since they do not provide for universal and equal suffrage, involve a breach of Article 21 of the Hong Kong Bill of Rights, notwithstanding the exception in section [Section] 13 of the Bill of Rights Ordinance. Since no challenge was made before their election, the present members should however be allowed to remain in office until 1995.

(15) The term of office of the 18 appointed members should be brought to an end in 1993, when they should be replaced by further elections in the 18 geographical constituencies.

(16) The "through train" will be of little benefit to Hong Kong and does not justify a refusal to hold fully democratic elections in 1995.

(17) The provisions of the Basic Law relating to the appointment of the Chief Executive should be replaced by provisions ensuring the direct popular election of the Chief Executive, or an alternative system ensuring that the Chief Executive or Government is selected by a democratic process.

(18) The Chief Executive should report to but should not be made accountable to the Government of the PRC, and the Chief Executive's accountability to the legislature of the SAR should be clarified and strengthened.

(19) Article 19 of the Basic Law should be modified so as to limit the exclusion of the jurisdiction of the Hong Kong courts to defence and foreign affairs only.

(20) The power of interpreting the Basic Law in its application to the SAR and the power of deciding whether existing laws contravene the Basic

Law should be transferred from the Standing Committee of the National People's Congress to the courts of Hong Kong.

(21) The Judicial Services Commission should be restored to its previous form, but with selection by five affirmative votes.

(22) The maintenance of an independent judiciary in Hong Kong after 1997 is of the highest importance both for the preservation of business confidence and for the protection of human rights.

(23) There is an urgent need to recruit local lawyers of ability and integrity to the bench and reduce the dependence of the bench on expatriate lawyers.

(24) Judges of the superior courts should be appointed with tenure to retiring age rather than fixed-term contracts.

(25) Terms of service of the judiciary (particularly in relation to housing) should be improved and judges should be allowed to return to practice after resignation from the bench.

(26) A formal system of appointing local lawyers to serve as part-time Recorders or Deputy Judges should be adopted.

(27) The agreement reached by the Joint Liaison Group on the composition of the Court of Final Appeal is contrary to the Joint Declaration and the Basic Law and is constitutionally invalid; the Court of Final Appeal itself should be allowed to determine the number and identity of foreign judges to sit as temporary members.

(28) Articles 18 and 158 of the Basic Law should be amended to confer on the Government of the SAR the exclusive power to declare a state of emergency in the SAR.

(29) The Basic Law should be amended to make it clear that permanent residents of the SAR are not subject to conscription.

(30) Section 5 of the Bill of Rights Ordinance should be amended to restrict the power of derogation to emergencies which threaten the life of Hong Kong.

(31) The power to extend the exemption of certain Ordinances from the Bill of Rights Ordinance for a second year should not be exercised.

(32) The permanent reservations in Sections 9 to 13 of the Bill of Rights Ordinance should be repealed and the UK should withdraw its corresponding reservations to the ICCPR.

(33) Immediate steps should be taken to identify and expressly repeal or amend existing Ordinances which are wholly or in part inconsistent with the Bill of Rights Ordinance.

(34) The Bill of Rights Ordinance is consistent with the Basic Law and its

repeal or restriction after 1997 would involve a breach of the undertakings given by the Government of the PRC in the Joint Declaration.

(35) The Ordinance is likely to have a significant effect on the application of human rights in Hong Kong and will be vigorously [rigorously] applied by the judiciary up to 1997.

(36) The value of the Ordinance for the protection of human rights after 1997 will depend on

   (i)   the continuance of an independent judiciary

   (ii)  the willingness of the Government of the SAR to abide by the decisions of the courts and

   (iii) the development of a human rights culture in Hong Kong.

(37) A strong Human Rights Commission should be set up for the purposes of

   (i)   informing and educating the public on human rights issues

   (ii)  advising and assisting claimants or potential claimants for redress under the Bill of Rights Ordinance and

   (iii) bringing proceedings in their own name under the Ordinance.

(38) The independence of the Legal Aid Department must be ensured.

(39) The Government of the PRC will be obliged by the Joint Declaration to report to the UN Human Rights Committee under Article 40 of the ICCPR on human rights in Hong Kong after 1997.

(40) The foregoing obligation can only be implemented if the PRC ratifies the ICCPR, at least in relation to Hong Kong.

(41) An independent body should be set up as soon as possible, either by the ICJ or by a consortium of human rights organisations, to monitor human rights developments in Hong Kong.

(42) The United Kingdom should accept on behalf of Hong Kong the Optional Protocol to the ICCPR.

(43) The Basic Law in inconsistent in many important respects with the obligations accepted by the PRC by its signature and ratification of the Joint Declaration; in the case of the method of election of the Chief Executive, although not inconsistent with the Joint Declaration, the Basic Law fails to provide an acceptable system.

(44) The PRC should modify the Basic Law accordingly.

(45) The Government of the United Kingdom, as the other party to the Joint Declaration, should use all means within its power to press the PRC to make the necessary amendments to the Basic Law.

# 5

# Law and Order

## John D. Ho

On his way to visit Beijing in the summer of 1993, the British Foreign Secretary Douglas Hurd characterized Hong Kong as a "political city". That description is a far cry from the conventional view of the territory as a community interested in nothing but the generation of wealth, and apathetic to and ignorant of politics. Whether one agrees with that assessment, there is no doubt that Hong Kong is going through a period of rapid and fundamental changes as its scheduled reversion of sovereignty to China in 1997 approaches.

Regarding law and order, it has its share of problems, just like any other major city in the world: robberies, drugs, prostitution, illegal immigration, white-collar crime, etc. While crimes committed with heavy weaponry, including grenades, automatic rifles and AK47's, do happen once in a while, in terms of crime statistics and in comparison with other major cities, the situation is by no means the most violent or worrisome. As a matter of fact, thanks to its economic, cultural, social and ethnic background, Hong Kong is probably still one of the world's safer cities.

But the transition brings its own problems, the nature of which must be understood within the context and perspective of its unique position in time and space. Although under the principle of "one country, two systems", most of the existing laws will be preserved and — as provided by Article 5 of the Basic Law — the capitalist system and way of life shall remain unchanged for fifty years after 1997, the transition entails a process of

John D. Ho is a university lecturer in the Department of Law, City Polytechnic of Hong Kong.

decolonization and changes in its institutions. At the same time, integration with China — especially economic integration — has already begun, and interaction with China has been increasing at an exponential rate. As Hong Kong approaches the end of its colonial era, the solutions to problems that these changes bring can be found only with the understanding and cooperation of China, its giant neighbour and future suzerain, which is going through some fundamental and rapid changes of its own.

## ☐ The Judiciary

### *The Court of Final Appeal*

At present, appeals lie from the Court of Appeal to the Judicial Committee of the Privy Council in London. The future highest appellate court is provided by Article 82 of the Basic Law, which says: "The power of final adjudication of the Hong Kong Special Administrative Region shall be vested in the Court of Final Appeal of the Region, which may as required invite judges from other common law jurisdictions to sit on the Court of Final Appeal."

An agreement on the Court of Final Appeal had been reached by the Sino-British Joint Liaison Group and the Court was originally scheduled for introduction at the end of 1993. But since it was revealed in 1991 that the Court would allow only one optional overseas judge on the panel of five, the agreement has met with intense opposition from the Legislative Council and the legal profession. The agreement was voted down in an unprecedented Legislative Council debate in December 1991, when legislators called for more flexibility to invite foreign judges.

The impasse remains and its consequences will no doubt become increasingly critical as 1997 approaches.

### *Judicial Personnel*

The prospective retirement of 9 out of 10 Appeal Court judges by 1997, and 15 out of 23 High Court judges within the decade will add to the burden of the judicial system. For some years now, it has been obvious that local barristers are reluctant to join the judiciary, and this reluctance may have been exacerbated by the impending political changes. But bringing judges from other common law jurisdictions would run counter to the policy of localization and the process of decolonization.

## Delays in Courts

Trials in Hong Kong are taking longer than necessary, partly because judges have to take their own notes. The lack of equipment and resources to produce full and accurate transcripts of proceedings has caused fear of miscarriage of justice as appeal judges have to rely on incomplete notes kept by magistrates or lower court judges. As judges have to take notes during a trial, it is difficult for them to observe the reactions and demeanour of witnesses.

The average waiting time for trials and hearings at Hong Kong's courts and tribunals continues to grow, despite the judiciary's undertaking a year ago to cut "unacceptable delays". There has been a fourfold increase since 1985 in the time it takes to bring a criminal case before the High Court.

For the High Court, the average waiting period for civil and criminal cases is about eight months, two to three times the performance target set by the judiciary. The long waiting time could allow defendants to apply for a stay of prosecutions pursuant to the Bill of Rights.

## The Jury System

A defendant was found not guilty of trafficking 59 grams of drugs and of an alternative count of possession. But immediately after leaving the court, five jurors returned to complain that the foreman had returned a verdict on the alternative charge without allowing them to deliberate it.

The problem may have arisen due to the jurors' standard of English or educational background. It has been suggested that in future foremen should record the jury's verdict on a piece of paper prepared during the trial to avoid any miscarriage of justice. However, no changes in the procedure have been implemented, and there is no assurance that a similar situation will not recur.

## ☐ Witness Protection

A bungled murder trial of a Vietnamese asylum seeker in which the principal Crown witness refused to testify because the authorities could not guarantee sufficient protection to him and his family caused the case to collapse. The then presiding judge, Justice Sears, described the outcome as an outrage. No evidence was offered in *R v Nguyen Van-bau* (High Court Criminal Case No. 291 of 1991). On 30 May 1991 Nguyen Manh-cuong was killed at the Whitehead Detention Centre for Vietnamese. Nguyen Van-bau was charged with murder, on the basis of a witness statement given by Bui Van-xuan, a cousin of the deceased. Bui expressed concern for the safety of himself and family if he gave evidence implicating the accused. The hearing was adjourned several times by the Judge for arrangements to be made to allay his anxieties. However, no arrangements satisfactory to Bui, upon whose testimony the prosecution depended, were made. He declined to give evidence. Finally the Crown elected to offer no evidence, nor did it enter a *nolle prosequi*, resulting in the formal acquittal of the accused.

The current witness protection procedures only focus on the safety of the witness during court hearings. There is not much thought given to what may happen to him or her once the case is finished and protection lifted. The police deals with witness protection on a case-by-case basis and there is little coordination with other government departments.

The Commission of Inquiry into Witness Protection recommended that a centralized Witness Protection Authority be established, to be chaired by a Deputy Secretary for Security. Other members of the authority would include representatives from the police, the Correctional Services Department, the Immigration Department, and the Attorney General's Chambers. Under the plan the Attorney General's Chambers would be responsible for considering whether the assistance of the authority should be sought, while the Security Branch would serve as the Secretariat. It also recommended that a memorandum of understanding should be reached between the witness and the authority setting out what protection and provision would be afforded and what would be required of the witness in return. These may include the continued provision of safe accommodation, armed guards during and after the trial, a change in the identity of the witness, and relocation or a new address in Hong Kong or overseas.

## ☐ The Police

### *Extended Role*

The police are expected to take on an extended role as the British Garrison continues to withdraw from the territory in preparation for 1997. Already the Army has relinquished its border guard role, with three police units now on the front line in the New Territories. Only one unit of soldiers remains as backup and they will be replaced before the end of 1993 by another squad of 170 police officers. The Army has also scaled down duties in typhoon emergencies and clean-up operations, offering only a backup service to the civilian operation. Bomb disposal skills are one of the remaining training tasks for the Army. The transfer of security skills has continued with three police dog handlers and their canine companions being trained in arms and explosives search tactics by the Royal Veterinary Corps' Defence Animal Support Unit in the New Territories. They are the first policemen to have bomb squad skills, in preparation for a role which had previously been the sole responsibility of the Army. The Navy advises the police on search and rescue tactics and anti-smuggling methods.

## Police Gambling

The Local Inspectors' Association, a major police group, called for an internal police inquiry into officers frequenting all-night gambling "schools" in a Kowloon restaurant, to ensure police were not breaking laws or regulations at their gambling sessions. The chairman of the Association called for restraint by police who gambled to ensure they did not fall heavily into debt and leave themselves open to "temptations". It was said that police officers would meet at the end of each month, often on pay days, and gamble the night away. According to one newspaper report, 60 uniform and plain-clothes police officers once gambled between midnight and dawn in games of mahjong, *pai kau* and cards in a Kowloon seafood restaurant, with more than $100,000 changing hands. The activities started after a meal, with the policemen locking themselves away in function rooms. Senior police said they did not believe the session was illegal as the gamblers were not playing against a fixed bank and there was no charging of commissions or entry fees. But police involved might have breached a Police General Order which requires prior notification of any plans to hold a social function involving gambling.

Senior police sources say gambling has long been a serious problem, affecting morale, work attitudes and the image of the police force. Officers heavily in debt become security risks because they might visit loansharks, many of whom triad-related, to help pay their debts.

In one case, five loansharks, charged with detaining and assaulting a Hong Kong police officer, were sentenced to jail by the Macau District Tribunal. The policeman had lost money at a Macau casino and had got a loan of $10,000. After losing the $10,000, the policeman borrowed another $10,000 but lost that as well. He was taken to a defendant's home, where he was threatened and beaten. He was ordered to call his family in Hong Kong and was released only after they deposited money into his bank account.

Sources also claim hefty gambling debts are one of the main reasons behind a spate of police suicides.

## Complaints against Police

Despite repeated calls by some members of the Legislative Council for an independent body to monitor complaints against police, the Police Complaints Committee (PCC) has decided against setting up an independent body to investigate public complaints against police. Instead, it continues to support the present system where it is left to the police to investigate complaints made against them through the Complaints Against Police Office (CAPO). The PCC, an independent non-statutory committee appointed by the Governor, is made up of a chairman, two vice-chairmen and eight members drawn from a pool of active Justices of the Peace. The PCC has a staff of twenty while the CAPO employs more than 200 full-time investigators. The PCC, which has been described as a "virtually toothless watchdog", bases reviews on written reports submitted by the CAPO. It has no power to re-investigate a particular case.

In arguing for the CAPO's retention the PCC believes that the police are well-equipped to probe complaints internally. The PCC has also warned that setting up an independent agency to replace the CAPO may seriously undermine the authority of the Commissioner of Police and damage the morale of the Police Force.

There was a total of 3,250 complaints made against police in 1992. However, only 0.7 per cent were substantiated. To the public, this rate seems astonishingly low and suggests that the police may not be the most impartial investigators when it comes to probing their own. Although the PCC found no evidence to substantiate the perception that justice is not being done, it does acknowledge that there is room for improvement and that with more checks and balance justice will be seen to be done.

The PCC proposes that it be given statutory powers so that anyone who feels their grievance has not been properly investigated would be able to seek judicial review. Armed with such statutory teeth, the PCC would have the right to interview witnesses or sit in as observers while police investigators interview witnesses in connection with complaints. By having direct access to witnesses, the PCC could help clarify any ambiguities or discrepancies and help minimize the risk that statements might be influenced by the way in which CAPO officers asked their questions.

### Police Liaison Officers from China

Two Mainland Interpol officers have arrived in Hong Kong to take up a one-year term as China's first police liaison officers in the territory. They work closely with their counterparts in Hong Kong to ensure the maintenance of law and order in the territory in the run-up to the 1997 handover of sovereignty. They have kept a low profile, and, despite attempts by members of the Legislative Council to find out more about their operations in the Territory, information has not been forthcoming from either themselves or the Hong Kong police.

## ☐ Cross-border Crime

The open door policy of China has made it easier for criminals to commit cross-border crime. Concern has been expressed by members of the judiciary and the Legislative Council about the escalating crime committed by Mainlanders and their relatively easy access to guns, grenades and ammunition.

It has been necessary and is proving effective to establish stronger Sino-Hong Kong links to fight violent crime. Police figures show a more than 46 per cent fall in the number of robberies involving firearms and an almost 30 per cent drop in offences involving pistol-like objects compared with the first half of 1992. There was an average of 689 crimes per 100,000 people, a drop of 1.6 per cent from the first half of last year.

### Car Thefts

Hong Kong continues to be plagued by the problem of car thefts, which has led to the imposition of car-theft surcharges by the Accident Insurance Association of Hong Kong. Many stolen cars are smuggled to Mainland China, and some to other neighbouring countries, including Singapore, Malaysia, India and Thailand. The surcharge is still in place despite a 7 per cent drop in the total value of car thefts insured with members of the Association in the first two quarters, from $227 million in 1992 to $211 million in 1993. The drop was attributed to vigorous action by the police and their counterparts in Guangdong. The police have arrested more than

90 people connected with car smuggling and seized at least eighteen *tai fei*'s or high-powered speedboats this year. From time to time, batches of stolen vehicles have been returned by the Guangdong Public Security Bureau.

This year also saw a change in the mode of car smuggling. While there were no cases of land smuggling discovered at the crossings last year, and vehicles were usually recovered on high-speed boats or in containers to be loaded on cargo ships, smugglers now take advantage of the busy traffic at land border crossings to smuggle cars stolen from Hong Kong into the Mainland after a crackdown on marine smuggling. At the Lok Ma Chau checkpoint alone, officers have to deal with more than 11,000 vehicles every day, making it impossible for officers to closely inspect all the lorries.

Similarly, the neighbouring city of Shenzhen had 1,300 car thefts in 1992 — and many veteran "teachers" of the crime were reportedly from Hong Kong.

### *Robberies*

Villages on the island of Lantau have formed their own armed vigilante groups to protect themselves against robbers arriving by sea — many suspected to be from the Mainland — to raid their homes in the middle of the night. The raiders prey on small villages under the cover of darkness and in some cases have threatened residents with violence should they resist or report the robberies to the police. Those villages which border on Chinese territorial waters have been the worst hit.

### *Extradition*

The lack of an extradition treaty between China and Hong Kong has added to the difficulty of law enforcement. This difficulty is unlikely to be solved until the transfer of sovereignty in 1997. While China has recently responded to pleas from Hong Kong police and sent over the border an unprecedented number of suspects wanted in Hong Kong, such cooperation is done only on an *ad hoc* basis. Similarly, some suspects facing investigation in China flee to the territory.

## ☐ Legal Aid

Pressure is mounting on the government to establish an independent legal aid authority. The Law Society of Hong Kong and the Hong Kong Bar

Association have taken the position that independent legal aid is an integral part of the justice system, as civil servants working in legal aid may be discouraged from granting services to someone in a legal action against the government.

In a consultation paper on legal aid, the government has estimated that the establishment of a non-government authority for the day-to-day administration of publicly-funded legal aid services would cost $80 million. The government suggested retaining the Legal Aid Department and setting up a council to advise on matters relating to the operation of the system and the delivery of services.

The Law Society has criticized the proposals, saying it would only bring cosmetic changes to the system. Citing the case of the former Director of Legal Aid Patrick Moss, in which it was widely speculated that he lost his job for granting legal aid in cases against government interest, legislators said they wanted a statutory legal aid authority that was outside the government "not just in name but in substance". Simon Ip, the legal representative in the Legislative Council, said the integrity of the administration of justice would be gravely impaired should the doubts about possible political or executive influence over legal aid not be cleared.

However, the Chief Secretary Sir David Ford reiterated that there would be "considerable disruption" and additional costs incurred if the Legal Aid Department was to be made independent. He also said there was no question of the department being interfered with by the executive and that the non-renewal of the former Director's contract was only the result of the policy of localization.

## ☐ The Public Order Ordinance

While Security Branch officials wanted to hurry overdue changes to the Public Order Ordinance, which has been described as "a classic piece of colonial legislation", ironically it was fears of protests from China that have delayed the introduction of a more liberal public order law.

It was reported that Governor Chris Patten intervened to avoid complaints from China that it had not been informed, as he did not want to risk damaging Sino-British talks. At the least, China was expected to accuse Britain of further undermining China's position while extending Britain's colonial influence.

The changes will, if implemented, make it easier to stage protests and demonstrations and drastically weaken the powers of the Commissioner of

Police in suppressing uprisings, in an attempt to bring Hong Kong in line with the International Covenant on Civil and Political Rights and the Bill of Rights. Under the existing ordinance, the Commissioner has wide discretionary power to refuse a licence for public processions or to impose conditions on them, and does not have to make his reasons known. Under the proposed changes, the Commissioner will have to make public his reasons for refusing demonstrations. Any applicant will have the right of public appeal to the Governor or head of the post-1997 administration. Other changes include increasing the ceiling on the number of people allowed to gather publicly without notifying the police from 30 to 50, free use of loudhailers and sound amplification equipment, and easing of the licence procedure.

# ☐ Corruption

## *Public Perception*

As the annual report on the activities of the Independent Commission Against Corruption (ICAC) for 1992 observes, the secretive and insidious nature of corruption, and often the absence of an aggrieved party, prevents the use of statistics alone to reveal the extent of corruption in any society. But there is a perception that corruption will worsen in the run-up to 1997, according to surveys conducted by the ICAC. Some 62 per cent of this year's respondents felt corruption had worsened, compared with 37 per cent in 1991 and 21 per cent in 1990.

## *Trends*

Reported corruption within the Police Force rose 42 per cent in the first quarter of 1993 compared with the same period last year, although that figure could be misleading because last year's figures were unusually low. Claims involving government departments increased by 27 per cent on the same quarter last year. There was a 25 per cent rise in reported corruption cases in public bodies; in the ICAC's largest area of investigation, the private sector, there was an 18 per cent increase. In the first quarter of this year, the ICAC arrested and charged 93 people over corruption allegations — a rise of 33 per cent compared with the first quarter of last year.

There is a disturbing rise in corruption within the immigration, customs and police departments. Recent clampdowns have led to arrests of immigration and customs officers, including a senior customs inspector involved with a cross-border smuggling ring for arranging the unimpeded clearance of vehicles containing unmanifested goods at the Man Kam To and Lok Ma Chau checkpoints.

## Passport Schemes

Demand for foreign passports remains high, and allegations of corruption against both Hong Kong immigration officials and consulates based in the territory have escalated, prompting warnings of caution in investing in "official" passport or citizen schemes. According to the ICAC the number of complaints against consular staff based in Hong Kong has almost doubled from just 45 between 1983 and 1987, to 86 between 1988 and 1992. The complaints involved allegations that consular staff took bribes or other favours in return for facilitating the issue of passports, citizenship or visas. The figures also show a corresponding rise in the number of complaints to the ICAC involving Hong Kong immigration authorities. The allegations ranged from the supply of false passports for the illegal movement of people to other countries. Between 1988 and 1992 the number of complaints more than doubled from 16 to 43, and 19 similar complaints had been made in the first six months of 1993.

## Political Elections

Changes in the political system and the introduction of political elections are also expected to add to the complaints. One member of the Legislative Council, Gilbert Leung Kam-ho, was jailed for three years for trying to buy votes in the 1991 election.

## Relations with China

With the increase in the number of Chinese enterprises in Hong Kong, there is concern that for political reasons the ICAC may not pursue cases related to Chinese enterprises with as much vigour as Hong Kong companies. However, when asked by a member of the Legislative Council if the Commission would charge government-linked Chinese enterprises operating in Hong Kong during a Legislative Council Security Panel meeting, the then Acting Commissioner for ICAC Jim Buckle disclosed that several Chinese state-owned enterprises were under investigation.

The ICAC has commissioned a research project into problems which

Hong Kong businesspersons are facing in operating their business in China, in response to the business community's concern for the differences between anti-bribery regulations in Hong Kong and China. Citing the need to protect confidentiality, however, the ICAC would release only the report's main findings, and not the report itself, to provide advice to businesspersons engaged in trade with China on what activities could be criminal offences in Hong Kong. According to a 1991 survey by the ICAC, cash and gifts paid to Mainland Chinese to facilitate business transactions in China added between 3 to 5 per cent to business operating costs.

More than 1,000 Mainland businesspersons and ten Chinese government officials will come to Hong Kong for training provided by the ICAC this year. They will learn about the ICAC, local laws and possibly prevention methods. About ten officials from the Guangdong People's Provincial Procurate and the Hainan Supervision Bureau would also serve brief attachments with the ICAC's community relations and corruption prevention departments.

## ☐ Triad Societies

Triad societies remain strong and are growing. One authority on triads said he feared the powerful Sun Yee On would spread "beyond the scope" of police control. With membership at 45,000 members in 1988, the Sun Yee On is now estimated to have about 65,000 members. Membership of the Sun Yee On triad society would reach 100,000 within five years if police anti-triad efforts failed. It is believed to be moving into the professions with the aim of spreading its influence in the upper echelons of society. The 14K triad society is reported to have nearly 100,000 members, but is said to be loosely knit, and thus less powerful than the Sun Yee On.

### *Triads in Schools*

A survey conducted by the Association of Heads of Secondary Schools on the influence of triad societies in secondary schools showed that about one-fifth of the students in Tsuen Wan, Kwai Chung and Tsing Yi have been harassed by triads. It also showed that out of a total of 6,947 students interviewed in 42 secondary schools, about 4 per cent of the respondents were "triad students" — students who had formally joined a triad (49), paid a membership fee (47), or had a triad "big brother" or "sworn brother" (179). The survey found that intimidation and extortion were the commonest forms of harassment. Some 27.1 per cent of the respondents said they would not make a report to the authorities for fear of retaliation. The most common reason students gave for joining a triad was the protection it offered against bullies. The second most common reason was curiosity. A total of 23.2 per cent of students were not aware that it was an offence to claim membership in a triad society.

The police were concerned about a "disturbing trend" of drug syndicates using schoolchildren as couriers, equipping them with pagers. During the investigation, the police discovered the Wo Sing Yee triad group targeted youths mostly in video game arcades.

In an attempt to halt the spread of triad influence in schools, special postage-paid crime information forms were circulated to students in Wong Tai Sin and in Hong Kong Island's Western District in a six-month pilot programme to enable students who have information on triad gangs or other crime to report it to the police without revealing their own identities. There has not been a single arrest in the first four months the scheme has been operating. Most complaints were anonymous, and found to be malicious complaints against teachers or fellow students.

### Triads in Housing Estates

Like schools, housing estates are a favourite target of triad activities. Residents in Tsing Yi, Tuen Mun, Tsuen Wan and Sham Shui Po housing estates were forced by gangs of triad youths to buy medicinal ointments at three to five times the usual market prices. Gangs of two to seven youths would roam public housing blocks every week or two, going from flat to flat and hammering on doors to intimidate residents into buying ointments from them. If a resident refused, a gang member would shout out the flat number and ask an accomplice to write it down.

Triads posing as decorators threatened tenants of two new housing estates in Sham Shui Po and creamed off hundreds of thousands of dollars in contract work.

### Triads and Hawker Control

Municipal staff from the Urban Services Department and Regional Services Department carrying out raids against illegal hawkers faced increasing threats from triads members controlling the hawking business.

## *Loan-Sharking*

Loansharks often tout business by distributing business cards into mailboxes or lifts, with only a paging number and no company or individuals' names on the cards. Borrowers are assured of prompt loans but are not told until a week later of the interest rates, which can be up to 100 per cent a month. Debt collectors usually resort to life-threatening means, including arson attacks, to terrorize borrowers and their relatives or neighbours if the money is not repaid.

After a series of arson attacks by loansharks Tsing Yi Island residents resorted to hanging rope-ladders from windows, leaving their doors unlocked (for easy escape in case of arson) and hoarding buckets of sand. Concern groups have accused the police of playing down the problem and said they had heard of more than 100 loanshark-related intimidation cases last year — about six times the police figure.

In one case a borrower reported the matter to the police after excrement was left on his door, only to be told to come forward more quickly next time.

According to a police spokesperson, most loanshark cases originated in Macau where Hong Kong operators sent people to lend money to gamblers, and police investigation was sometimes hindered by the victims' unwillingness to report the cases.

Loansharks have gone high-tech in data protection. A notorious syndicate was being investigated and the police had the details of how the group operated its business in and around a number of housing estates in Tuen Mun. A police raid was conducted. When officers barged into the hidden loan office, a suspect pulled the plug on the office computers. The police were unable to gain access to the computer system, which was protected by a coding device, to obtain more relevant data.

Under existing laws, a person creating or holding such data is not obliged to help the police in making the material readable. A proposed Organized and Serious Crimes Bill seeks to make it compulsory for witnesses to produce relevant information, thus breaking the "wall of silence".

## *Overseas Connections*

Widespread emigration from Hong Kong has given many triad members familial links overseas, allowing them to emigrate under family reunion programmes to Britain, Australia, Canada and the United States.

Triads have also spread their influence into at least two of China's special economic zones. The gangs have set up small companies or restaurants in both Shenzhen and Zhuhai as fronts for unlawful activities. One report said they had been financing Mainland gangsters and using them to bribe Chinese frontier guards. Armed with the privilege of being able to enter and leave the Mainland without harassment, triad members smuggle drugs and firearms out of China into Hong Kong and Macau. Local triads have also been recruiting Mainland gangsters to operate prostitution syndicates. These make quick cash from Hong Kong people travelling to the two zones. Recently, several Hong Kong and Macau residents who were arrested in connection with drugs and arms smuggling cases were put on trial and executed in Shenzhen and Zhuhai.

## Future Status?

Police detectives believe a number of senior triad members, who have made substantial sums from their illegal activities, want to distance themselves from their pasts and become "legitimate" businesspersons in the local mainstream society. They are also reported to have established links with China and invested heavily there.

Police sources predict that triad infiltration at the District Board, Urban Council and Legislative Council levels will increase substantially in the 1994–1995 elections. A Security Branch triad report revealed that a District Board member was a protector of a Sun Yee On office-bearer, helping him in a range of illegal activities, including loan-sharking, extortion and book-making.

A confidential Royal Hong Kong Police Force document is reported to claim that covert links between Mainland public security forces and Hong Kong's ruling triads have been initiated by China for financial gain. The police assessment was compiled more than a year ago by the Organized Crime and Triad Bureau and was based on extensive investigations into the Sun Yee On. "The lead-up to 1997 and after will see an increase in triad influence," the report is quoted as saying.

Triad societies are illegal under current Hong Kong law. But whether they will remain so in the Special Administrative Region was brought into question by remarks made by China's Minister of Public Security Tao Siju. Tao is reported to have said that China is happy to unite with triads provided they were patriotic and concerned with the stability and prosperity of Hong Kong, and that while China "vehemently opposed any of these organizations engaging in crimes such as murder, arson and looting, ... one must also agree that some members or some organizations have renounced past wrongdoings and started to do good things."

Despite subsequent insistence by a Chinese spokesman that Tao was misunderstood, police officers fear that they will lose informers and witnesses will refuse to give evidence against triads in the run-up to 1997 following the reported comments, and that anti-triad efforts will suffer because of fear of retaliation after 1997.

## ☐ Maritime Security

There have been reports of pirate attacks from the South China Sea to the Straits of Malacca against shipping into and out of Hong Kong, threatening the lives of seamen as well as the reputation of Hong Kong as a safe port.

Efforts by the Hong Kong and Chinese governments to clamp down on smuggling have forced pirates to target fisherfolk. The situation is made worse by local fisherfolk being forced to fish further away from the territory because of increasing pollution. Many boats are now going farther out of Hong Kong waters and into Chinese and international waters. There was at least one report of a Hong Kong fisherman shot and killed when pirates attacked his boat.

There were also attacks by people in Chinese security personnel uniforms. Marine Department and shipping industry officials fear some aborted official raids could also be reported as piracy.

Another source for concern is confrontations between Hong Kong's Marine Police and Chinese Public Security Bureau personnel. In one case, armed Chinese security officers boarded a Marine Police vessel near Wagland Island within Hong Kong waters and threatened the local officers with an AK47 assault rifle, demanding the camera with which a constable had taken photographs of the incident. The camera was handed over and the film ripped out and thrown into the sea. The policy of photographing Chinese officials during incursions into Hong Kong waters by Chinese vessels is now said to be under review. Local officers had always photographed their Mainland counterparts with extreme reluctance, fearing that they might provoke violence and possibly suffer retaliation after 1997.

At an OMELCO (Office of the Members of the Executive and Legislative Councils) Security Panel meeting, Acting Deputy Secretary for Security Alasdair Sinclair said China had repeatedly insisted that it was not its policy to exercise its jurisdiction within Hong Kong waters. But he also added that it would be difficult to prevent such incidents because of the large number of Chinese vessels, by and large small vessels commanded by junior personnel, operating near Hong Kong waters.

In any incident involving armed attack on the seas, the issue arises whether it occurred within Hong Kong waters, whether those involved were officials or pirates posing as officials, and whether they were carrying out official anti-smuggling duties. According to legal opinions obtained by the Security Branch, piracy can be committed only by private individuals, and a report presented in May 1993 by the Marine Department at a United Nations International Maritime Organization adopted that position.

In early August this year, the Guangdong Public Security Bureau is reported to have issued a directive forbidding anti-smuggling enforcement in the territorial waters of Hong Kong, Macau and Taiwan, as well as the interception or detention of Hong Kong, Macau, Taiwan and foreign-registered ships without accurate intelligence and sufficient evidence. Personnel found participating in smuggling, or robbery committed in the name of anti-smuggling enforcement, would be held criminally liable.

But China has also accused "overseas smuggling groups" of manipulating the Hong Kong media in a bid to slander the "good name" of its security forces. The official newspaper *Legal Daily* claimed that the Shenzhen Public Security Bureau and Border Defence Bureau had been perfectly justified in raiding ships off Hong Kong which were believed to be smuggling luxury cars. It maintained that all of the twenty-two ships seized between August 1992 and June this year had been proven to be engaged in smuggling.

## □ Concluding Remarks

The maintenance of stability and prosperity for Hong Kong, both before and after 1997, is a delicate balancing act. Uncertainties associated with the political transition bring inevitable fears and apprehensions. Whether a framework of law and order — one that is accepted and trusted by the population — can be maintained will have far-reaching consequences for the continuous success of Hong Kong as one of the world's finest business centres, as well as the fate of China and its development into an economic superpower.

The 1993-94 Budget
Speech by the Financial Secretary, moving the
Second Reading of the Appropriation Bill, 1993

Introduction to the
Estimates
1993-94

# 6

# The State of the Economy

## Henry C. Y. Ho

This chapter highlights the important features of the economy in 1992 and the first half of 1993 and puts them in perspective. It also discusses the major economic policies which have been proposed or implemented. In discussing economic policy, it is important to note that conflicting objectives are often involved and the trade-offs among them cannot be determined according to any objective criterion. Even for a given objective, it is often impossible to arrive at a consensus as to what it should actually involve.

## ☐ The Economy in 1992

### *Economic Growth*

In 1992, total gross domestic product (GDP) in Hong Kong increased by 5 per cent in real terms[1] and per capita real GDP by 4 per cent. At current market prices, per capita GDP was $127,778 which was close to that in the United Kingdom (U.K.) and Australia and above that in Spain and New Zealand. The favourable growth rates experienced in Hong Kong in 1992 were a continuation of the upward trend since 1989 when the real growth rates for total and per capita GDP dropped to 2.8 and 1.8 per cent

---

Henry C. Y. Ho is a senior lecturer in the School of Economics and Finance, The University of Hong Kong.

[1] Unless otherwise indicated, all statistics quoted in this chapter are from government publications.

respectively as a result of the impact on the local economy of the Tiananmen incident in China. Since 1989, revival has been rather gradual, with total GDP registering real growth rates of 3.2 per cent in 1990 and 4.2 per cent in 1991 while per capita real GDP grew by 2.9 per cent in 1990 and 3.3 per cent in 1991. The growth rates achieved in 1992 were still below the average real growth rates of 6.5 per cent and 5.4 per cent for total and per capita GDP for the ten-year period from 1982 to 1992.

Improvements in Hong Kong's economic performance since 1989 have been due largely to the continuation of the open door policy in China and the acceleration of its economic reform. In January 1992 Deng Xiaoping and President Yang Shangkun made well-publicized trips to the frontier boom towns of Guangdong province, giving a boost to the open door policy and the reform programme in general. Deng warned that his reform and open door policies were the only way out for China and those who opposed them would have to step down. Within Hong Kong itself, a favourable factor for economic growth has been the reduction in interest rates in accordance with the world trend and especially in keeping with interest rate movements in the United States (U.S.) because of the linked exchange rate between the Hong Kong dollar and the U.S. dollar. In 1992 local interest rates were reduced three times, with the best lending rate falling from 8.5 per cent to 6.5 per cent and savings deposit interest rate from 3.5 per cent to 1.5 per cent. These interest rate cuts occurred even when the economy was at full employment and inflation at around 9 to 10 per cent. Another factor stimulating economic growth in 1992 was public spending on the projects related to the new airport as a result of the Memorandum of Understanding on the Port and Airport Development Strategy between Britain and China signed in September 1991. For the financial year 1992–1993, government expenditure on the ten Airport Core Programme (ACP) projects amounted to $5,348 million[2] or 22.5 per cent of total government capital expenditure.

Offsetting the above-mentioned favourable factors for economic growth in 1992, there were other factors which had a dampening effect. Early in the year, there was some uncertainty as to the renewal of China's most-favoured-nation (MFN) status in the U.S. in 1992. In February, the U.S. Senate passed a bill setting conditions for the renewal. Though this was vetoed by the U.S. President, the veto could be overridden by the

---

[2] *The Foundation*, March 1993.

House of Representatives and Senate. Eventually the Senate failed to override it, and it was only in June that the U.S. President formally notified Congress of his intention to renew China's MFN status unconditionally for another year. Again in September another bill was passed attaching conditions on the renewal of China's MFN status in 1993. This was vetoed by the President and the veto was sustained by the Senate. Failure to renew China's MFN status in the U.S. would have been detrimental to Hong Kong's economy. It has been estimated that the loss of China's MFN status could mean the loss of up to 70,000 jobs in Hong Kong and a reduction of up to three percentage points in annual GDP growth.

Apart from the question of China's MFN status, trade prospects were also threatened by the dispute between the U.S. and China regarding market access to China. In August 1992, it was announced that the U.S. and China failed to reach an agreement on the market access issue under Section 301 of the U.S. Trade Act. Subsequently, the U.S. published a list of export items from China which might be subject to U.S. retaliatory tariff under the Section 301 provisions. Later, it was reported that China was also contemplating retaliation against U.S. imports. Finally, in October the two countries reached an agreement on this issue and a trade war was avoided.

Internally, the curbing of speculation in the property market had its effect on economic activity. The anti-speculation measures introduced by the government and the banks in late 1991 also affected end-users. Though the upward price trend was maintained in the first half of 1992, the rate of price increase slowed down in the third quarter, and in the fourth quarter property prices in general fell by 2 to 4 per cent.

Another factor having a deflationary impact was the 1992–1993 budget. This budget provided for a sizeable surplus of $7.6 billion (which would be higher if the share of land revenue going to the future government of the Hong Kong Special Administrative Region was included) and raised the corporate profits tax from 16.5 per cent to 17.5 per cent together with other tax increases. Even without tax increases, the budget could yield a surplus of $4 billion. However, in budgeting for a huge surplus, the Financial Secretary did not intend to use the budget as a tool of macroeconomic policy. He was only concerned about maintaining adequate reserves against the contingencies of the next five years.

Hong Kong's economic growth in 1992 can be elaborated by examining the growth performance of the components of GDP. Since total production equals total expenditure,

$$GDP = C_p + C_g + I + X_D + X_R + X_S + S - M_g - M_S$$

where  $C_p$  = private consumption expenditure,
     $C_g$  = government consumption expenditure,
     $I$  = gross domestic fixed capital formation,
     $X_D$  = domestic exports,
     $X_R$  = re-exports,
     $X_S$  = export of services,
     $S$  = changes in stocks,
     $M_g$  = imports of goods, and
     $M_S$  = imports of services.

In simple terms, GDP, being the total value of final goods and services produced in an economy, equals the sum of consumption, investment, exports, and increase in stocks less imports. Table 1 shows the real values of these components as percentages of GDP in 1992 and their real growth rates. Except for increase in stocks, which is a minor component of GDP, re-exports scored the highest growth rate, followed by investment in machinery and equipment, while consumption expenditure, a major component of GDP, also experienced good growth. Almost zero growth was registered by domestic exports, which are an important component of GDP, and a low growth rate was found for construction. In fact, domestic exports have been stagnant since 1989 while construction expenditure has barely recovered from the slight decline in 1991.

Table 1.  Components of GDP, 1992

|  | % of GDP | Real growth (%) |
|---|---|---|
| Private consumption expenditure | 66.6 | 8.2 |
| Government consumption expenditure | 7.0 | 8.2 |
| Gross domestic fixed capital formation | 29.4 | 10.3 |
| of which: construction | 8.0 | 0.7 |
| machinery and equipment | 14.1 | 22.9 |
| Domestic exports | 49.6 | 0.3 |
| Re-exports | 132.1 | 28.2 |
| Exports of services | 22.0 | 10.7 |
| Increase in stocks | 2.0 | 89.8 |
| Imports of goods | 190.3 | 22.3 |
| Imports of services | 18.2 | 6.2 |

The GDP components of consumption, investment and exports constitute total final demand in the economy and their contribution to GDP growth depends not only on their magnitude but also on their import content. Thus, for re-exports which had the highest growth rate and exceeded GDP almost by one-third, their import content is quite large and therefore their direct contribution to the overall growth of the economy will be much smaller. However, apart from their direct contribution, re-exports also contribute indirectly to GDP growth through their demand for supporting services, thus generating additional consumption and investment. This indirect contribution can be seen most clearly in the processing of products carried out in China for Hong Kong firms, which accounted for the greater part of the growth of re-exports. In 1992 about 46 per cent of Hong Kong's re-exports to China were for outward-processing purposes and for Hong Kong's domestic exports to China the corresponding figure was about 74 per cent. Although outward processing reduces value-added in Hong Kong, this loss is more than offset by the increased demand for related business services and the additional profits and income generated.

Because of the large volume of capital flowing into and out of Hong Kong, foreign investors receive income in Hong Kong while local investors also get returns from their investment overseas. GDP is only a measure of income generated within Hong Kong, even though some of it may accrue to foreigners, and it does not include income from abroad accruing to Hong Kong residents. In order to take this into account, we have to calculate gross national product (GNP) for Hong Kong. GNP equals GDP plus net factor income from abroad. Thus GNP is a better measure from the point of view of the welfare of the Hong Kong people, though GDP serves its purpose well as a measure of production and resource utilization. The compilation of GNP in Hong Kong is difficult because of the lack of data. For Hong Kong, GNP is probably greater than GDP because Hong Kong is a net exporter of capital, as seen from the persistent surplus of exports over imports of goods and services over the last nine years, so that there is a net inflow of factor payments.

## *Inflation*

Apart from economic growth, inflation is a matter of great concern in Hong Kong. Since double-digit inflation appeared in 1989, inflation as indicated by the annual rates of increase of consumer price indexes and the GDP deflator has hovered around 10 per cent in recent years. Although consumer price increases eased somewhat from 12 per cent in 1991 to 9.4 per cent in 1992, the GDP deflator rose by about 10 per cent, almost the same rate as in the previous year. Among consumer prices, housing charges registered the highest increase, followed by the prices of food and services. These items are major components of household expenditure. In fact, the increases in food prices and housing charges each accounted for one-third of the increase in the composite consumer price index.

As for the GDP components, the highest rate of increase was maintained by the deflator for government consumption expenditure which increased by 9.1 per cent in 1992. This is to be expected because the government sector is engaged mainly in the provision of services and the greater part of its consumption expenditure consists of wages and salaries. Private expenditure, on the other hand, includes a larger proportion of goods the prices of which can benefit from productivity increases. The greater price increases faced by the government means that the same level of public services can only be maintained with rising expenditure unless productivity improves.

The deflator for exports, an important component of GDP, has been rather stable in recent years, rising by only 1.4 per cent in 1992. This has enabled Hong Kong exports to remain competitive in foreign markets. Similarly, import prices have risen very slowly, showing a rate of increase of 0.2 per cent in 1992. Hong Kong's inflation, therefore, cannot be attributed to import prices.

Much has been written on the causes of inflation in Hong Kong and it is only necessary to outline them here. Inflation arises from the special circumstances of Hong Kong. The first is the opportunity taken by Hong Kong manufacturers to carry out part of their production process in China to take advantage of the low cost of labour and land there. The result is the transformation of the Hong Kong economy into one which is dominated by the service sector. Since service sector is more labour-intensive the demand for labour is increased at a time when Hong Kong is experiencing a slowdown in the growth of the labour force. Rising profits from outward processing in China drive up prices and wages further. As long as production costs remain low in China, this process continues and internal price increases in Hong Kong can do little to restrain demand.

The other special circumstance in Hong Kong giving rise to inflation is the linked exchange rate of the Hong Kong dollar. Because the government is committed to maintaining the current exchange rate of the Hong Kong dollar with the U.S. dollar, the curbing of foreign demand for Hong Kong products by exchange rate appreciation is ruled out. Also, interest rates have to follow those in the U.S. and this is why interest rates were reduced thrice in 1992 even in an inflationary situation. According to Sir Alan Walters who has been referred to as the architect of Hong Kong's linked exchange rate, an appreciation of the Hong Kong dollar to HK$7.10 = US$1 could get inflation down to five per cent. He even suggested that this could probably be achieved with a revaluation of four per cent to HK$7.50 = US$1.[3] However, a firm commitment to the current pegged rate is justified by the need to protect the Hong Kong currency from speculation against it if there is any political disturbance undermining confidence in Hong Kong. It should be remembered that the linked exchange rate system was established in 1983 as a result of the currency crisis triggered by political uncertainties at that time. Without a firm commitment to the pegged rate, any political disturbance in China or severe disagreement between China and Britain over the future of Hong Kong can bring pressure on the Hong Kong dollar. Thus, in his first annual address to the Legislative Council in October 1992, the new Governor, Chris Patten, said, "The political risks of tampering with the link would be enormous. The risks to our economic stability would be equally daunting. The link must and will remain".[4] Acceptance of this policy means that an effective tool for curbing inflation cannot be used and it has to be dealt with by other less effective methods. In fact, inflation is the price for maintaining general economic stability in an uncertain political environment.

Popular discussions of inflation usually centre around rising prices and wages. Surely, these are symptoms rather than causes of inflation. Essentially, these discussions say that all price increases can be passed on and consumers can demand higher wages which in turn produce higher prices, setting off a cost-price spiral. For this to happen, the price increases must be sustained by rising income or growth in money supply. As discussed above, rising income is generated by the prosperity from the outward-processing trade with China and a fixed exchange rate while money supply is determined by the link with the U.S. dollar. These are the special circumstances mentioned above responsible for inflation in Hong Kong.

---

[3] *Sunday Morning Post*, 14 March 1993.

[4] Hong Kong Legislative Council, *Official Record of Proceedings*, 7 October 1992.

If one deals only with the symptoms of inflation and not its causes one can be led to the wrong policies. Thus, the popular policy recommendations are that the government should restrain increases in prices and wages under its control and should not increase or levy indirect taxes. Restraining prices in some sectors would lead to reduction and deterioration in the quantity and quality of output in these sectors and greater price increases in other sectors. As for the recommendation regarding indirect taxation, one has to consider the alternatives. If indirect taxes are not to be used, the government must either reduce its expenditure, or finance it by direct taxes, loans or fiscal reserves. Each alternative has its own impact on inflation which, together with its other economic effects, should be compared with those of indirect taxes. In fact, the plea to restrain price and tax increases is often motivated by the desire to relieve the burden on the lower-income groups. This motive should not be confused with that for using price restraints to curb inflation.

Apart from restraining prices and wages, another popular policy recommendation is to urge the government to increase the supply of resources and their productivity. The government is certainly taking steps in this direction. Within the government sector, productivity is to be increased through the setting up of an Efficiency Unit. Labour supply is to be increased through the labour importation scheme and the Employee Retraining Scheme. However, in practice these measures have some limitations. Efforts to improve productivity cannot guarantee that productivity will actually increase. Labour importation has to overcome the opposition of the workers and retraining has to be financed. Besides increasing labour supply, the government is also urged to increase land supply. This is impractical as land supply is limited by the Sino-British Joint Declaration. Even if it is not limited in this way, land production in Hong Kong requires resources and thus adds to the inflationary pressure. Leaving aside the above practical issues, one still has to ask why the government should satisfy the insatiable demand for resources by profit-seeking entrepreneurs when full employment has been reached. Efforts to improve labour skills and develop land and infrastructure are required for future growth. Although there is high income and employment now, Hong Kong could be overtaken by its neighbours if she does not invest for the future. Thus, the purpose of increasing the supply and quality of resources is to sustain growth rather than to curb inflation. However, a careful balance should be maintained between growth and stability.

### *Earnings and Wages*

In spite of inflation, economic growth in 1992 has produced some increase in real income for the working class. The median monthly employment earnings of employed persons in the fourth quarter of 1992 increased by 12 per cent over the same quarter in 1991. With an increase of 9.4 per cent in consumer prices, the real increase in earnings was only about 2.4 per cent. This is low compared with the 4 per cent increase in real GDP per capita during the year. Probably, it would even be lower if comparison is made with real GNP growth in view of the amount of factor income that Hong Kong derives from abroad. It appears therefore that the economic gain in 1992 had not been spread evenly, with the working class getting a smaller share.

Though real earnings have increased, real wages have been rather stagnant. The overall real wage index for September 1992 increased only slightly by 0.3 per cent compared with the same period in 1991. Since this index fell by 1 per cent in 1991, real wages in 1992 were still slightly below those in 1990. Table 2 shows that over the two-year period, 1990–1992, real wages increased only in the trade and transport sectors and declined in all other sectors. Also, real salaries for middle-level managerial and professional employees remained almost stationary for the last three years. This phenomenon of stagnant and even declining real wages and salaries occurred despite full employment and economic growth.

### ☐ 1993 Economic Prospects and Developments

According to government forecasts, real GDP will grow by 5.5 per cent in 1993 and, on a per capita basis, it will increase by 4.8 per cent. These growth rates are better than those achieved in 1992. At the forecast rate of

Table 2. Rates of Change in Real Wages (Percentages)

|  | September 92/ September 91 | September 91/ September 90 |
|---|---|---|
| Manufacturing | 0 | −1 |
| Banks, insurance and business services | 0 | −1 |
| Wholesale, retail and import/export trades | 3 | −1 |
| Restaurants and hotels | −2 | −1 |
| Transport services | 2 | 2 |

growth, GDP per capita in Hong Kong can easily overtake that in the U.K. and Australia.

The official GDP forecast is in general agreement with those by other researchers though some more optimistic forecasts have been made, such as that of 6 per cent by the Asian Development Bank.[5] The impetus to growth will be from the Asia-Pacific region which is expected to maintain its growth momentum, except for Japan, which is expected to attain only modest growth. In particular, Hong Kong will continue to benefit from its trade and other economic relations with China which had its open door policy and market economy reaffirmed. In fact, in October 1992, the Chinese Communist Party in its 14th National Congress endorsed the notion "socialist market economy" and the Party Secretary-General pledged to continue with economic reform and open door policy.

The favourable GDP forecasts are not without qualifications. First, they are dependent on the renewal of China's MFN status in the U.S. after mid-1993. It was mentioned previously that the loss of China's MFN status would reduce Hong Kong's real GDP growth rate by up to three percentage points. This problem is more serious this year given President Clinton's stance on the issue. It was only late in May 1993 that the U.S. renewed China's MFN status for another year but extension beyond June 1994 will depend on progress in China's human rights record.

The second qualification of the favourable growth forecasts is the satisfactory resolution of the Sino-British dispute regarding the Governor's proposals for elections to the Legislative Council in 1995. This dispute aggravates the prolonged disagreement between Britain and China over the construction of the new airport and jeopardizes anything which requires cooperation and consultation with China. According to the estimates of the Hang Seng Bank, if the political issue is not resolved quickly, it will hold up consumption and investment plans and the forecast GDP growth rate for 1993 will fall from 5.5 per cent to 4.1 per cent.[6] People have become more optimistic since Britain and China started negotiations in April on Hong Kong's 1994–1995 elections. However, by late June no concrete results have been reached on this issue and the airport financing scheme.

Another threat to Hong Kong's economic performance in 1993 is that China's economic growth has been too rapid, bringing about inflation and

---

[5] *Wah Kiu Yat Po*, 17 April 1993.

[6] *Hang Seng Economic Monthly*, December 1992.

other problems. Many fear that any drastic measures to curb growth in China may also affect Hong Kong's economy.

As for inflation, the government's forecast is that both the Consumer Price Index (A) and the GDP deflator will increase by 9.5 per cent in 1993. This was generally regarded as somewhat too optimistic at the time of the forecast in view of the 1993–1994 budget which entails a deficit of $3.4 billion and a big increase in expenditure. However, for the first few months of the year, the rate of increase of consumer prices slowed down. An important factor contributing to the moderation of price increases has been the depreciation of the Renminbi.

According to the official *First Quarter Economic Report 1993*, the real GDP growth rate in the first quarter of 1993 was probably in the region of 5 to 5.5 per cent and the Consumer Price Index (A) rose by 8.8 per cent compared with the same period last year. For the first half of the year, it seems that the economy has developed in accordance with the government's forecasts. Performance in the second half of the year will depend crucially on the outcome of the Sino-British negotiations on Hong Kong issues and developments in the Chinese economy.

## □ The New Governor's Economic Agenda, 1992–1997

Although Hong Kong is an open economy dependent very much on external influences, its economic policy can determine to a significant extent its economic performance. The new Governor, Chris Patten, in his first annual address to the Legislative Council in October 1992, set out the government's agenda for the remaining years of British administration in Hong Kong. The agenda covered different aspects of the Hong Kong society but the following discussion is confined to economic matters only.

Of the economic objectives of growth, stability and equity, the Governor put growth first because "the success of the economy is central to all our hopes".[7] His recipe for economic success is a continuation of the policy which Hong Kong has adopted for decades and which was characterized by him as "minimum interference and maximum support" for business. Minimum interference requires low and predictable taxes and government spending to follow and not outpace economic growth. Although in the

---

[7] All quotations in this section are from the Governor's address.

Governor's address there were a number of proposals to increase spending on various key programmes, such expenditure will grow by slightly less than the predicted rate of GDP growth and will be financed by accumulated budget surpluses and revenue growth so that there is no need to raise taxes. Minimum interference also means that "businessmen not politicians or officials make the best commercial decisions". Thus, a Governor's Business Council would be set up, comprising distinguished members of the business community, to advise the Governor on the promotion of trade and industry and the impact of government policies on business. A first task of the Council would be to develop a comprehensive competition policy since competition is essential for business efficiency and consumer protection.

As for maximum support to business, the government would continue investment in physical and human capital. Over the period 1992–1997, government spending on infrastructure would be 44 per cent higher than in the previous five years. This increase in expenditure would be in addition to the ACP projects and environmental protection programmes. The employee retraining fund would be increased by government contribution to enable more workers to be retrained for new skills. The quality of education would be improved by increasing the number of teachers and reducing class size. Funds for research in tertiary education institutions would also be increased.

With regard to stability, the Governor stressed the importance of maintaining the linked exchange rate and therefore recognized the constraints on policy in combatting inflation. The government's role in containing inflation would be limited to improving efficiency, restraining public expenditure growth so as not to outpace economic growth and increasing spending on labour retraining. Although a Hong Kong Monetary Authority was to be established, this would simply be brought about by merging the existing Office of the Exchange Fund with the Office of the Commissioner of Banking and no new central banking functions were to be performed by the Authority. In the private sector, competition was said to be "our best defence against inflation" and the competition policy to be developed by the Governor's Business Council would contribute to increased efficiency and lowering prices.

For the equity objective, the government would make an immediate fund allocation to meet the key targets set out in the White Paper on social welfare and the Green Paper on rehabilitation and to undertake a thorough overhaul of the social security system. This would increase recurrent spending on social welfare by 26 per cent in real terms between 1992 and 1997.

Spending on health care would also increase by 22 per cent in real terms over the same period. Housing would continue to be a significant component of government spending. A new middle-income housing scheme for the "sandwich class" would be introduced. "Sandwich class" refers to the group of people who are above the income limits for public housing but are unable to afford a flat on the private market. By 1997, this scheme would benefit about 13,000 families. Since the new housing units from this scheme would not be available until 1995–1996, in the meantime the government proposed to buy flats from the private sector to sell to the sandwich class at affordable prices. This proposal was later dropped in favour of a low-interest loan scheme for qualified families.

## ☐ The 1993–1994 Budget

The implementation of the Governor's economic agenda requires public funds. Thus, the provisions of the 1993–1994 budget and its forecast of the government's financial situation in the next few years are important.

Before an account of the 1993–1994 budget and its forecasts is given, it should be pointed out that in the Financial Secretary's budget speech, the figure of $132.5 billion for total government spending requires some explanation and it will be shown that it is inconsistent with the budgeted deficit of $3.4 billion. According to him, the amount of $132.5 billion of total government spending excluded payments from the Capital Investment Fund. This fund is used to finance the government's capital investments in public bodies, such as equity injection in the Mass Transit Railway Corporation, capital investment in the Hong Kong Housing Authority and advances to the Provisional Airport Authority. Ordinarily such payments are not regarded as expenditure. For 1993–1994, the budgeted payments from the Capital Investment Fund amount to $19.7 billion which was excluded from the above quoted figure of total government spending. However, the Financial Secretary failed to mention another exclusion of $1.2 billion for the repayment of government bonds from the Capital Works Reserve Fund. With the inclusion of these two amounts, total government spending would be $153.4 billion in 1993–1994.

As for the much-publicized budget deficit of $3.4 billion, since the budget speech did not give the figure for total government revenue it is natural for anyone to think that this deficit is derived from the total government spending of $132.5 billion, exclusive of the two items of spending mentioned previously. However, detailed figures in the appendix to the budget speech show that the deficit is arrived at by including these two items of spending as expenditure. If these are excluded so that total expenditure is only $132.5 billion, there will be a surplus of $17.5 billion. Though it is true that the way in which the budget balance is defined depends on the purpose of analysis, it must be consistent with total revenue and expenditure. Thus, when the Financial Secretary said that total government spending would be $132.5 billion, then the budget should be in surplus to the amount of $17.5 billion. On the other hand, when he said that the budget would show a deficit of $3.4 billion, then total spending should be $153.4 billion, inclusive of the expenditure from the Capital Investment Fund and the repayment of government bonds.

With this clarification the main features of the budget and its forecasts can now be given. The budget speech was entitled "Building on Success". This means that because of the excellent state of Hong Kong's public finances as reflected in the higher-than-expected surpluses of the last two years the 1993–1994 budget was able to make proposals which, for the period up to 1997, would reduce tax payments, increase government spending and add to the reserves. This view is a reflection of the approach adopted by the Governor in his address to the Legislative Council mentioned earlier, in which he referred to the unexpectedly good revenue situation in the recent past and his expectation of this to continue. Later, in reply to questions from Legislative Councillors, he again mentioned the use of this windfall to finance his programmes without the need to raise taxes and at the same time leave substantial reserves in future.

With regard to expenditure, the 1993–1994 budget not only provided funds to achieve the goals set for 1993–1994 in respect of those programmes announced by the Governor, but also included a considerable number of new expenditure initiatives involving both recurrent and capital expenditure. Recurrent expenditure would be increased for the expansion of the Kindergarten Fee Remission Scheme and the introduction of a mortgage-interest subsidy scheme to provide housing benefits for staff in aided schools and subvented social welfare and health organizations. Capital expenditure would be increased for the improvement of public health, environmental protection, housing, manpower training, promotion of cultural activities, support for trade, industry and tourism, and road building.

As for government revenue, the budget increased salaries tax allowances substantially and widened its tax bands. Estate duty and stamp duty on stock transfers were lowered. The duty on cosmetics and the tax on entrance to race meetings were abolished. Tax concessions in transport were introduced for the benefit of the disabled and the elderly. The duties on fuel, alcohol and tobacco were increased to keep up with inflation. Similar adjustments would be made in the course of the year for government fees and charges.

As usual, the budget was criticized from all viewpoints ranging from left to right. The main issues are discussed below.

## Growth of Government Expenditure

Compared with the revised estimate of the previous year, budgeted expenditure for 1993–1994 increases by 33.3 per cent or 21.5 per cent depending on whether one adopts the broad or narrow concept of expenditure discussed above. Even after an adjustment for inflation, these rates of increase are far above the forecast GDP growth rate. This violates the government's own guideline that public spending must not grow faster than the economy. However, this guideline cannot be applied on a year-by-year basis but is meant to hold only over a period of time. Moreover, the government considers it more meaningful when applied to public expenditure as a whole. Public expenditure, as defined by the government, equals the narrow concept of government expenditure plus expenditure of the Hong Kong Housing Authority and the Urban and Regional Councils and payments from the Lotteries Fund. The government's capital investment such as that in the Mass Transit Railway Corporation and advances to the Provisional Airport Authority are considered irrelevant, the reason given being that they do not reflect the actual consumption of resources by the government, though this reasoning is debatable. This limitation must be borne in mind when one examines the government's forecasts of public expenditure growth. For the period up to 1997, real public expenditure is forecast to grow by 12.5 per cent in 1993–1994, 5.6 per cent in 1994–1995 and 6.4 per cent in 1995–1996 and to drop by 0.4 per cent in 1996–1997. With an assumed trend of GDP growth rate of 5 per cent, public expenditure will increase from 18.5 per cent of GDP in 1993–1994 to a peak of 19.4 per cent in 1995–1996 before falling to 18.7 per cent in 1996–1997. Even with this levelling off, this ratio is still higher than that of 17.1 per cent in 1992–1993.

Great concern has been expressed about the growth of government expenditure but it is difficult to see what the concern is all about. Perhaps the government's own commitment to minimum interference and efficiency would require a small public sector. However, this must be balanced against the government's other objectives of maximum support to business and protection of the disadvantaged. The optimal size of the public sector depends on society's relative preference for the various objectives. Since people have different preferences, there is no such thing as social preference. It is often argued that even though we do not know what the optimum is, it is bound to be less than the actual size. The reason is that pressure groups are able to secure government spending in their favour at the expense of the whole society. To substantiate this view would require an examination of the composition of government expenditure.

## *Inflation*

With full employment, an increase in government expenditure diverts resources from private use. The impact on prices depends on the way by which the expenditure is financed. Deficit finance involving the use of reserves is more inflationary than increasing taxes. Given the current inflation situation, many people have criticized the budget for its inflationary impact but few have considered the alternatives. To eliminate the deficit, there would have to be either a reduction in expenditure and tax concessions or tax increases. For each alternative course of action, there would be numerous choices as to which expenditure or tax is to be changed. As an example of the possibilities, the elimination of the two major tax concessions in respect of salaries tax and stamp duty would offset the deficit but the question is whether these concessions should be given up for the purpose of containing inflation. Another course of action is to reduce expenditure. It was mentioned previously that the budget should be in surplus with the exclusion of payments from the Capital Investment Fund. If such payments were reduced, the budget could be balanced. For 1993–1994, major payments from the fund include equity subscription to the Mass Transit Railway Corporation for the construction of the airport railway and advance to the Provisional Airport Authority. A reduction in payments from the Fund means that these organizations have to reduce their expenditure or finance it by other means.

Another viewpoint should be briefly mentioned. Some economists argue that the macroeconomic effect of an increase in government expenditure is the same irrespective of the method of finance. If it is financed by debt instead of tax, people will expect that future taxes have to be raised to repay the debt and so they save enough to pay for the future taxes. If the deficit is financed by increasing the money supply, or running down reserves, the erosion of the real value of money balances would also lead to an increase in savings to offset this inflation tax. Thus the effects of using tax, debt and reserves are the same. It is doubtful whether people do behave in this way.

## *Equity*

The sandwich class seems to benefit more from the budget than other groups because of the new housing scheme for them and the salaries tax concessions. However, it should be noted that the housing programme for the lower-income groups under the Housing Authority is being continued at a rapid pace though this was not mentioned in the budget because it is an independent public body financed indirectly through the Capital Investment Fund. Moreover, the increase in income support payments to the needy under the new Comprehensive Social Security Assistance Scheme by 19 to 22 per cent is comparable to the revisions of the salaries tax.

## *Narrowing of the Tax Base*

The salaries tax concessions introduced by the 1993–1994 budget have the effect of exempting 260,000 existing taxpayers from the tax and reducing the tax liability of 1.23 million taxpayers. These concessions have therefore been criticized for narrowing further the tax base which has a limited coverage. The problem of a narrow tax base was brought up by the former Financial Secretary, Sir Piers Jacobs, who argued that a wider and more stable tax base is necessary. However, revenue stability depends more on the existence of different types of taxes than the number of taxpayers of a particular tax. Also, any broadening of the tax base will involve a consideration of the distribution of the tax burden, i.e. equity.

## *Resource Allocation*

Some people have criticized the budget for spending too much on welfare services and too little on those promoting economic growth. The dividing line between these two types of expenditure is not always clear and the incomplete data can be interpreted in different ways. Table 3 shows a breakdown of public expenditure in 1993–1994 and the real growth rates of the various components. It was pointed out before that the expenditure of some public organizations financed by the Capital Investment Fund is not

Table 3.  Components of Public Expenditure, 1993–1994

|  | % of total expenditure | | Real rates of increase (%) | |
| --- | --- | --- | --- | --- |
| Security | 11.6 | | 1.6 | |
| Support | 13.9 | | 23.7 | |
| Community and external affairs | 5.9 | | 13.9 | |
| Social services | 17.1 | | 12.2 | |
| Social welfare | | 6.1 | | 9.2 |
| Health | | 11.0 | | 13.9 |
| Housing | 11.5 | | 12.8 | |
| Education | 16.2 | | 4.7 | |
| Environment | 2.6 | | 14.1 | |
| Infrastructure | 15.8 | | 25.2 | |
| Transport | | 6.1 | | 52.7 |
| Land and building | | 7.1 | | 16.1 |
| Water supply | | 2.6 | | 3.2 |
| Economic | 5.4 | | 1.6 | |
| Total | 100.0 | | 12.5 | |

regarded as public expenditure. On the basis of such incomplete data, it can be seen from Table 3 that spending on infrastructure, which can be regarded as growth-promoting, has the highest rate of increase which is about twice those for social services and housing. However, in terms of their share in total expenditure, social services and housing are more important than infrastructure.

## *Reserves*

The question of fiscal reserves has always been a sensitive issue. Many people believe that the fiscal reserves will be transferred from Hong Kong and somehow become the property of the British government. China also seems to suspect that it is to the advantage of the Hong Kong government to spend all the reserves by 1997 and leave nothing to the future Hong Kong Special Administrative Region (SAR).

The budgeted deficit for 1993–1994 and forecasts of even larger deficits for the next three years mean that fiscal reserves will be reduced from $119.6 billion in March 1993 to $78.4 billion in March 1997, a reduction of more than one-third. This raises some alarm. The Financial Secretary pointed out that his 1993–1994 budget actually increases the reserves in 1996–1997 as compared with the forecast of his previous budget. Instead of being concerned about its adequacy, he said he did not regard the reserves as excessive. In fact, the amount is much larger than the minimum of $25 billion required by the Sino-British Memorandum of Understanding on the Port and Airport Development Strategy. An indication of the adequacy of reserves is that by 31 March 1997, the amount of reserves will be equal to about 40 per cent of total government spending in 1996–1997.

The forecasts of reserves are based on an assumed real GDP growth rate of 5 per cent per annum, an average annual inflation of 8.5 per cent, maintaining the real yield from fees, charges and duties, and adjustments of the various tax thresholds in the light of inflation. These assumptions appear reasonable but some concern has been expressed about the future inflation rate. Should it be at a higher rate, expenditure would be higher and reserves lower than the forecasts. However, in addition to the forecast reserves of $78.4 billion, the Hong Kong Special Administrative Region Government Land Fund will be available to the future SAR government. This fund already reached $33.7 billion in late 1992 and will be increased by its share of land sales revenue and interest earnings. The Land Fund and the forecast reserves will together cover more than half of government expenditure in 1996–1997. Since the forecasts have taken into consideration the government's commitments on the airport project, the reserves should provide an adequate cushion against unforeseen shortfalls in revenue or increases in expenditure.

# 7

# Monetary and Financial Affairs

## Y. C. Jao

The year 1992–1993 has been another eventful year for Hong Kong's monetary and financial sectors. Among the highlights were the formal establishment of the Hong Kong Monetary Authority, the authorization of the Bank of China to issue legal tender notes, the disclosure of the Exchange Fund, the rise of the Hang Seng index of stock prices to record highs, and the further development of Hong Kong as an international financial centre.

## ☐ Establishment of the Hong Kong Monetary Authority

From the point of view of the institutional framework for monetary management, the most important event during the past year was undoubtedly the formal establishment of the Hong Kong Monetary Authority (HKMA) on 1 April 1993. The intention to form such a body had been discussed for some time, and was first publicly announced in Governor Chris Patten's address to the Legislative Council in October 1992. In any case, the HKMA was formed by the merger of the Exchange Fund Office and the Banking Commissioner's Office, both of which were formerly constituent parts of the Monetary Affairs Branch. The Monetary Affairs Branch itself has been renamed Financial Services Branch, whose jurisdiction is now confined to non-bank financial intermediaries (such as

Y. C. Jao is a reader in the School of Economics and Finance, The University of Hong Kong.

insurance companies, mutual funds, and unit trusts) and financial markets other than the foreign exchange market.

The government claims that by giving an autonomous status to the HKMA, outside the civil service, professionals can be employed to manage the Exchange Fund more effectively. It has been suggested that a mere one percentage point improvement in the rate of return on the Exchange Fund's assets can more than offset the increase in emoluments of the officials of the HKMA. Whether this will be the case remains to be seen. For the time being, however, the reorganization has resulted in a larger bureaucracy and greater public expenditure in the monetary sector.

More importantly, the formation of the HKMA has inevitably also led to considerable debates about two related but separate issues. One is whether the HKMA has become a *de facto* Central Bank; the other is whether a formal Central Bank should be established in Hong Kong. Undoubtedly, a wide range of views exist with respect to these two questions. My own considered view is that the answer to both questions should be negative.

Concerning the first question, it is true that during the past decade, the Exchange Fund has been assuming an increasingly high profile in respect of perhaps the most important central banking function, namely the well-known "lender of last resort" (LLR). For example, during the banking crisis of 1982–1986, the securities market crisis of 1987, and the BCCI crisis of 1991, the Exchange Fund played a pivotal role in organizing bailouts for collapsing institutions, and injecting liquidity into the whole financial system. In some extreme cases, the Exchange Fund even took over directly the ownership and management of insolvent banks. By contrast, the two note-issuing banks, the Hongkong and Shanghai Banking Corporation (HSBC) and the Standard Chartered Bank, which used to play this role prominently in the banking crisis of the 1960s, receded into the background.

Since the HKMA also comprises the former Banking Commissioner's Office, it may be said that it assumes not only the LLR function, but also another key central banking function, namely the prudential supervision of all depository institutions. It is also true that in recent years, certain institutional changes, such as the Accounting Arrangements between the Exchange Fund and the HSBC in 1988, the issuance of Exchange Fund Bills starting from 1990, and the inauguration of the Liquidity Adjustment Facility in 1992, have increased considerably the HKMA's control of interbank liquidity, as well as its open market operations capability.

However, unlike other fully-fledged central banks, the HKMA does not issue fiat money (legal tender banknotes); it does not have the power to require depository institutions to keep non-interest-bearing reserves with it; and it also does not perform the role of the banker to the government, particularly on the retail side. It cannot control therefore the monetary base (usually defined as the sum of legal tender currency and depository institutions' reserves with the central bank). All it can control at its discretion is the balance on the HSBC's account with the Exchange Fund under the Accounting Arrangements. But this amount is trivial relative to the monetary base.

Concerning the second question, there is a naive and simplistic view in some quarters which tends to treat the Central Bank as a panacea for all monetary and banking problems. This view arises perhaps because of the lack of a formal and fully-fledged Central Bank in Hong Kong. However, standard central banking functions still exist in Hong Kong: the only difference with most other countries is that they are shared in this territory by both public and private-sector institutions. This division of labour is, in my opinion, in the long-term interests of Hong Kong. In the matter of currency issue, for instance, there is a mechanism of automatic checks and balances between the private sector and the government. The note-issuing banks cannot issue banknotes without first paying 100 per cent U.S. dollar backing to the government's Exchange Fund; the Exchange Fund, moreover, cannot squander away the foreign exchange reserves, since the banks can always return the Hong Kong dollar notes and the Certificates of Indebtedness to it in order to redeem their U.S. dollars. This system precludes any irresponsible over-issue of currency. If however the currency issue is monopolized by a government-owned Central Bank, the mechanism of checks and balances will be lost. The danger of the Central Bank becoming a printing press and an instrument for interfering with the working of a market economy can hardly be overemphasized. The sharp fall of the Renminbi (RMB) during the past year is a timely reminder of what will happen to a currency if it has no formal legal backing, and is issued by a Central Bank not independent of political pressures.

## ☐ The Third Note-issuing Bank — The Bank of China

In early 1993, the Hong Kong government approved the application of the Bank of China (BOC) to issue legal tender notes in Hong Kong. The BOC first broached the idea of issuing Hong Kong currency in June 1992, and it is remarkable that the process of application and approval took only seven months. According to press announcements, the BOC undertakes to observe all the rules and regulations governing the currency issue. These include not only prior payment of 100 per cent U.S. dollar cover to the Exchange Fund, but also other technical conditions pertaining to printing, circulation, distribution, cancellation, etc. The BOC plans to issue currency amounting to $6 billion in 1994, gradually increasing it to $10 billion in 1996. By that time, the BOC will have become the second largest note-issuing bank, accounting for about 10 to 15 per cent of the total currency in circulation.

The BOC was founded in 1905 under the Qing Dynasty as the Treasury Bank. Both the National Government of China (1927–1949) and the Central People's Government (since 1949) designated it as a bank with special responsibility for foreign exchange and international trade. According to the authoritative monthly, *The Banker* of London, the BOC ranked sixteenth among the top 1,000 commercial banks of the world in 1991, in terms of a weighted criterion comprising such factors as assets, deposits, profitability, etc.

The authorization of the BOC as a note-issuing bank is pregnant with political and economic significance. Immediately after the news that the BOC would issue notes was released, the two existing note-issuing banks, the HSBC and the Standard Chartered Bank, welcomed it and pledged their support. They also announced plans to withdraw from circulation their notes bearing words or designs incompatible with Hong Kong's post-colonial status. The quick approval by the government, and the friendly response of the two British banks, show clearly that the bitter dispute between China and Britain on political reform in Hong Kong has fortunately not affected the normal functioning and evolution of the monetary sector.

Economically, the BOC's new status has also been widely welcomed for three reasons. The first is of course the BOC's pledge to observe the "rules of the game" in Hong Kong. The second is that the international standing and prestige of the BOC augurs well for the soundness of the Hong Kong dollar. Last but not least, by becoming a note-issuing bank, the BOC also assumes responsibility for maintaining Hong Kong's macroeconomic stability. The BOC recognized this when in its statement it pledged full cooperation with the monetary authorities and the existing note-issuing banks.

There is a school of thought — the "Free Banking School" — which argues that all private banks should be allowed to issue notes, and that free competition would ensure that no bank could over-issue without jeopard-izing its own position. Although the idea is intuitively attractive, in the special circumstances of Hong Kong, it is hard to imagine how this ideal can be implemented. Indeed, no country or territory to date has adopted even partially the "free-banking" prescription. Hong Kong is one of the very few territories where commercial banks still issue legal tender cur-rency. In principle, though, there is no reason why in future, other qualified banks which are able and willing to observe strictly the rules and regulations governing the note-issue should not be authorized to issue legal tender notes.

## ☐ The Disclosure of the Exchange Fund and Land Fund

Since the Exchange Fund was created in December 1935 after Hong Kong followed China in abandoning the silver standard, the government had published every year a very simple statement of the fund's assets and liabilities between 1937 and 1940. This practice was however interrupted by the Japanese Occupation.

After the end of the Second World War, the government had for various unknown reasons steadfastly refused to disclose the Exchange Fund. In recent years, however, this policy had come increasingly under attack. First, it was clearly inconsistent with the growing worldwide trend towards more "transparency" on the part of the administration. Second, it also smacked of "double standard" when the Hong Kong government itself, in tightening up its prudential supervision of the financial sector, increasingly demanded fuller disclosure by all financial institutions of their business and financial activities. Third, the policy also hampered Hong Kong's credit standing when the territory wanted to tap international capital markets to finance its huge infrastructural projects for meeting the needs of a rapidly growing economy.

These were powerful criticisms, to which the government finally bowed. In July 1992, the government published for the first time in fifty-two years the annual accounts of the Exchange Fund for the period 1986–1991. Then in July 1993, the government released the account for 1992. The figures are reproduced in Table 1.

As may be seen from Table 1, at the end of 1992, total assets of the Fund amounted to HK$287 billion (US$37.14 billion). Of these, foreign currency assets amounted to HK$275 billion (US$35.9 billion). The pub-lished foreign exchange reserve figure was higher than generally expected.

Table 1. Assets and Liabilities of the Exchange Fund (in HK$ million)

| | 1986 | 1987 | 1988 | 1989 | 1990 | 1991 | 1992 |
|---|---|---|---|---|---|---|---|
| *Assets* | | | | | | | |
| Foreign currency assets | 84,715 | 113,089 | 127,089 | 149,152 | 192,322 | 225,333 | 274,948 |
| Hong Kong dollar assets | 3,876 | 5,746 | 5,962 | 9,625 | 3,874 | 10,788 | 12,546 |
| Total | 88,591 | 118,835 | 133,051 | 158,777 | 196,197 | 236,121 | 287,494 |
| *Liabilities* | | | | | | | |
| Certificate of indebtedness | 20,531 | 26,831 | 31,731 | 37,191 | 40,791 | 46,410 | 58,130 |
| Transfers of fiscal reserves | 23,359 | 32,557 | 38,269 | 52,546 | 63,226 | 69,802 | 96,145 |
| Coins in circulation | 1,441 | 1,470 | 1,890 | 2,012 | 2,003 | 2,299 | 2,559 |
| Exchange Fund bills | — | — | — | — | 6,671 | 13,624 | 19,324 |
| Other liabilities | 4,103 | 4,453 | 2,554 | 1,603 | 391 | 4,834 | 3,220 |
| Balance of banking system | — | — | 860 | 978 | 480 | 500 | 1,480 |
| Total | 49,434 | 65,311 | 75,304 | 94,330 | 113,562 | 137,469 | 180,858 |
| *Accumulated earnings* | 39,157 | 53,524 | 57,747 | 64,447 | 82,635 | 98,652 | 106,636 |

Source: Office of the Exchange Fund.

Indeed, Hong Kong's per capita foreign exchange reserve at the end of 1992 stood at US$5,972, the second highest in the world, next only to Singapore.

In November 1992, the Chinese government also published the accounts of the Land Fund of the Special Administrative Region for the six-year period ended 31 March 1992. The accounts show that the Land Fund had total assets of HK$33.7 billion at the end of March 1992, of which HK$22.5 billion were denominated in foreign currencies. Taken together, the two funds at the end of 1992 had total assets of about HK$321 billion, of which foreign currency assets amounted to HK$297.5 billion (US$38.4 billion). Barring any catastrophe (such as a major war in the region), these financial resources should be adequate, under prudent management, to see Hong Kong through the transition period to 1997 and beyond.

## ☐ Currency Substitution

One interesting and important monetary phenomenon in recent years has been currency substitution, which may be briefly defined as the steady rise over time in the foreign currency components of bank deposits and monetary aggregates. The raw statistics released by the Hong Kong government present however two problems. One is that since all relevant figures are denominated in Hong Kong dollars, the fluctuations in exchange rates may overstate or understate the true extent of currency substitution. This distortion is known as the "valuation effect". The other is that "swap deposits" are classified under "foreign currency deposits". Since they are repayable in Hong Kong dollars, it is more appropriate to treat them as Hong Kong dollar deposits. Both the "valuation effect" and the "swap effects" can be eliminated by suitable statistical means.

The adjusted foreign currency components of bank deposits and monetary aggregates are summarized in Table 2. It may be readily seen that for the narrow monetary aggregate M1 (currency outside the monetary sector plus demand deposits), the foreign currency proportion was not only modest, but also trendless. However, for the broader monetary aggregates M2 (sum of M1 and savings and time deposits with licensed banks) and M3 (sum of M2 and time deposits with other depository institutions), and total deposits in all depository institutions, their foreign currency components all showed a rising trend. Moreover, there was a significant "quantum jump" in 1982, the year when a "confidence crisis" erupted after China and Britain began their formal negotiations on the future of Hong Kong.

Table 2. Adjusted Foreign Currency Components of Bank Deposits and Monetary Aggregates

| End of year | M1 Amount (HK$ m) | M1 % of total | M2 Amount (HK$ m) | M2 % of total | M3 Amount (HK$ m) | M3 % of total | Total deposits Amount (HK$ m) | Total deposits % of total |
|---|---|---|---|---|---|---|---|---|
| 1980 | 1,122 | 4.64 | 10,755 | 11.18 | 11,232 | 8.09 | 10,642 | 8.26 |
| 1981 | 1,408 | 5.59 | 13,760 | 11.78 | 21,081 | 11.92 | 19,504 | 11.90 |
| 1982 | 1,270 | 4.62 | 67,029 | 32.43 | 78,909 | 31.53 | 78,909 | 31.53 |
| 1983 | 2,028 | 6.56 | 78,487 | 30.45 | 91,734 | 29.89 | 91,734 | 29.89 |
| 1984 | 2,812 | 7.64 | 99,249 | 31.60 | 119,751 | 31.89 | 119,751 | 31.94 |
| 1985 | 3,068 | 6.78 | 151,820 | 38.90 | 172,286 | 39.99 | 172,286 | 39.99 |
| 1986 | 3,791 | 6.75 | 212,646 | 41.04 | 239,080 | 41.06 | 239,080 | 41.06 |
| 1987 | 6,547 | 7.99 | 279,661 | 41.31 | 307,527 | 41.37 | 307,527 | 41.37 |
| 1988 | 7,460 | 8.40 | 331,738 | 40.23 | 358,768 | 40.16 | 358,768 | 40.16 |
| 1989 | 7,657 | 8.07 | 412,886 | 41.75 | 445,318 | 42.00 | 445,318 | 42.00 |
| 1990 | 13,104 | 12.19 | 560,173 | 46.29 | 598,970 | 46.50 | 598,970 | 46.50 |
| 1991 | 14,016 | 10.91 | 615,790 | 44.92 | 651,212 | 45.31 | 651,212 | 45.31 |
| 1992 | 14,109 | 9.07 | 694,832 | 45.75 | 723,092 | 45.93 | 723,092 | 45.93 |

Source: Underlying data from *Hong Kong Monthly Digest of Statistics*.

Several observations may be made on the trend in currency substitution. First, it is primarily undertaken for performing the "store of value" function rather than the "medium of exchange" function. Second, it is strongly influenced by political uncertainty, though other factors, such as interest rate differential, and exchange rate expectations, may also play some role. Because of the space constraint, we will not go into detail here. But the most important observation is that, whereas under the floating rate regime, currency substitution led to the unprecedented currency crisis of 1982–1983, the continuation of currency substitution since the establishment of the linked exchange rate system in October 1983 has not caused any similar panic.

It is also noticeable that while the Hong Kong dollar is the passive object of substitution inside Hong Kong, outside the territory, the Hong Kong dollar actively displaces the Renminbi in South China and the Portuguese patacas in Macau. No similar phenomenon has ever existed in other countries or territories. It is this aspect that distinguishes currency substitution in Hong Kong most conspicuously from those in other developing countries, especially Latin America.

## ☐ The Inflation Problem

The rate of inflation, as measured by the weighted average of the three consumer price indexes (CPIs), eased from 11.8 per cent in 1991 to 9.5 per cent in 1992. In the first four months of 1993, there was a further slight easing of the CPI inflation, but this improvement would be most unlikely to continue, as the lagged effects of fiscal deficit, higher consumer spending, increases in government and public utilities fees and charges etc. would make themselves increasingly felt in the second half of the year. For the year as a whole, the weighted CPI inflation rate would most probably remain at around 9.5 per cent.

Most economists agree that Hong Kong's inflation in recent years has been predominantly structural rather than monetary or imported. This new type of inflation is characterized by (1) a chronic labour shortage, as exemplified by a very low rate of unemployment (averaging only 2 per cent in the past three years); (2) a much higher rate of increase in consumer prices than those of tradables; (3) a much higher rate of increase in prices of services than those of other goods.

It is well known that against such a new type of inflation, the traditional monetary policy will be useless, especially as Hong Kong adopts a form of fixed exchange rate regime operating under almost perfect capital mobility. For example, in May 1991, the authorities jacked up the interest rates in an attempt to curb inflation. But as the interest rate differential between Hong Kong and the United States widened, a rapid inflow of capital ensued, forcing the authorities to lower interest rates again barely one month later.

A more effective and feasible anti-inflationary strategy should therefore consist mainly of a tight fiscal policy, supplemented by a suitable combination of labour policy, land policy, and incomes policy.

Given Hong Kong's special circumstances, it is therefore puzzling and disturbing to note that the government has opted for an expansionary fiscal policy for the 1993–1994 fiscal year. Even though the projected deficit of HK$3.4 billion is relatively small, it is difficult to see how deficit financing under conditions of full employment can be anything other than being inflationary.

## ☐ Hong Kong Dollar and Renminbi

With the increasing integration of the Hong Kong and Chinese economies, the relationship between the Hong Kong dollar and the Renminbi, and their circulation in each other's territory, has attracted considerable attention during the past year.

The circulation of Hong Kong dollar in South China has a long history, and can be traced back at least to the turn of the century. In the first thirty years of the People's Republic of China, the circulation and holding of the Hong Kong currency was officially prohibited, but after China launched its open door and economic reform policies in 1979, the desirable properties of Hong Kong dollar as a monetary asset could no longer be suppressed. In the "Special Economic Zones", especially Shenzhen, the Hong Kong dollar has become not only the preferred "abode of purchasing power", but also the preferred medium of exchange or means of payment.

There are no official statistics on the outstanding amount of Hong Kong currency circulating in South China, but private estimates have put it at between HK$11 and $14 billion in 1991. It is often claimed in banking circles that a substantial part of this currency has been recycled back into Hong Kong's banking system via the China-owned banks. As a result, net liabilities of the Hong Kong banking system to banks in China had increased sharply, and stood at HK$42 billion at the end of 1992. It is also alleged that such recycling has been a main cause of the steady rise in the loan/deposit ratio to over 100 per cent in recent years.

While the recycling is certainly one of the many possible channels through which China builds up its financial claims on Hong Kong, the fundamental cause is China's persistent balance of payments surplus against Hong Kong. It is entirely legitimate for China to keep or invest a part of such surplus in Hong Kong, a financial and commercial centre of world stature. However, China should also do well not to endanger Hong Kong's financial stability when deploying its huge holdings of Hong Kong dollars.

By contrast, the Renminbi was not allowed to circulate outside China until 1 March 1993, when the Chinese authorities allowed residents and visitors to bring in or out of the country Chinese currency up to a limit of 6,000 yuan. Because the number of Chinese tourists to Hong Kong had steadily increased to about one million in 1992, many shops have begun to accept Renminbi in payment, and most money-changers and some banks have also begun buying and selling Renminbi in cash. It is to be noted that, following the abolition of the Foreign Currency (Prohibition) Ordinance in 1985, the Renminbi, like any other foreign currency, can freely circulate in Hong Kong, but it is *not* a legal tender.

The sharp fall in the external value of Renminbi in 1993 has caused concern whether the circulation of the Renminbi will exacerbate Hong Kong's inflation. Our view is that, as long as the Renminbi is not a legal tender in Hong Kong, its adverse effect should be minimal. This is because Hong Kong residents have little or no incentive to hold Renminbi either as medium of exchange, or as store of value in Hong Kong. Whatever Renminbi balances they keep are for use inside China only. Even if the Chinese authorities further relax the limit on cash which Chinese citizens can bring out of China, any large influx of Renminbi can only result in a precipitous fall in the exchange value of Renminbi. The proportion of outstanding Renminbi to Hong Kong's total money supply should therefore be quite trivial.

The important thing is that Hong Kong should jealously safeguard its monetary independence by insisting that only the Hong Kong dollar is the legal tender. This is implicitly, though not explicitly, acknowledged in both the Sino-British Joint Declaration and the Basic Law.

## ☐ The Stock Market and the China Factor

The stock market during the past year has been characterized by two major trends. One is the pronounced fluctuations of stock prices along a rising trend. The other is the growing influence and importance of the "China Factor".

The bull market which began in mid-1991 generally continued, albeit with frequent interruptions. The Hang Seng index of stock prices, which began the year 1992 at around 4,300, surged over a span of 17 months to a record high of 7,529 in late May 1993. Subsequently, a correction phase set in, and at the time of writing (late July 1993), stocks were consolidating within the range of 6,700–6,900. Still, a rise of 60 per cent over a period of only 18 months made the Hong Kong market one of the best performers in the world. The average daily turnover also shot up from $960 million in 1990 to $2,802 million in 1992.

The importance of the "China Factor" manifested itself in the fact that the bull market of 1981–1983 was mainly China-driven, in the sense that political and economic developments in China had a disproportionate influence on market sentiments and price trends. The bull market began in July 1991, when China and Britain signed the Memorandum of Understanding on Hong Kong's new airport and when both the Chinese and Hong Kong economies had recovered from the shock of the Tiananmen incident. This trend was further stimulated in early 1992 by Deng Xiaoping's famous visit to South China, during which he urged an acceleration of the open door and market-oriented reform programme.

Hong Kong could not remain unaffected, of course, by the euphoria generated by Deng's policy directive, since at least in the economic sense, it virtually took Hong Kong as the model for China. Moreover, the relatively low price/earning ratios of good quality Hong Kong stocks, and the vast prospect of the China market, attracted considerable international interest in the local market. The Hang Seng index therefore rose continuously from 4,300 in early January to 6,447 in November 1992. At that point, however, the increasingly bitter dispute between China and Britain on Governor Patten's political reform proposals caused a sharp reversal in sentiments, and the Hang Seng index fell about 25 per cent to 4,978 in early December. A slow recovery then took place, but it was not until 13 April 1993, when China and Britain agreed to open formal negotiations on electoral arrangements for Hong Kong, that the market again took off to a new high at the end of May. However, starting from June, numerous signs have emerged on the difficulties confronting the overheated Chinese economy: accelerating inflation, sharp fall in the external value of the Renminbi, peasant unrest, etc. The decision of the Chinese government to dismiss the Governor of the People's Bank, and to launch a much-awaited austerity programme, again caused a setback to the Hong Kong market. At the time of writing, stocks were trading cautiously within the range of 6,800–6,900.

The influence of the "China Factor" is not however confined to stock prices. The growing prominence of "Red Chips" — a portmanteau term that comprises Hong Kong companies with large exposure to China, "shell companies" taken over by Chinese interests, and listed state-owned enterprises — has also been a salient feature of the stock market during the past year. At least before the recent clampdown on the overheated economy by the Chinese authorities, the investing public in Hong Kong (including non-resident investors) seemed to be seized by a speculative craze for the "Red Chips". The most spectacular example is the case of Denway Investment Company, a China-owned enterprise which offered its shares to the Hong Kong public in February 1993. By the time the offer was closed, the shares had been over-subscribed by 659 times. Funds totalling some $240 billion (equal approximately to 5 times the total currency in circulation, or about 40 per cent of the gross domestic product in 1991) were frozen during the subscription period, a record not only for Hong Kong, but perhaps also of the whole world. Prior to Denway, four other issues of Chinese enterprises were also heavily over-subscribed. At the time of writing, preparations were being made for the listing of another nine state-owned enterprises in Hong Kong.

On the positive side, the listing and trading of Chinese enterprises is mutually beneficial to both China and Hong Kong. China can raise much-needed capital for its economic development and modernization, while Hong Kong is able to consolidate its position as the financial centre par excellence for Greater China, as well as a leading financial centre for the whole Asian-Pacific Basin.

The mushrooming of China-related stocks, however, has also raised thorny issues for the regulatory authorities. There is still a wide gap between Hong Kong and China in respect of legal protection of shareholders, transparency of listed companies, accounting and auditing standards, etc. The signing of a memorandum of understanding for mutual cooperation between the regulatory authorities and stock exchanges in China and Hong Kong on 19 June 1993 is therefore a major step in the right direction for mutually beneficial and healthy development of securities markets. Given the rapid changes in technology and the proliferation of financial innovations in the global financial markets, however, the accord by itself will not prevent abuses and irregularities if it is not effectively enforced and constantly updated. For example, "backdoor listing" through the acquisition of "shell companies" in Hong Kong, which became quite rampant in the first half of 1993, may pose a potential threat to the soundness of the market. Perhaps the most insidious problem is "insider trading", which was bad enough even before the invasion of China-owned or related companies. Unlike some other industrialized countries, "insider trading" is not a criminal offence in Hong Kong. Insiders have virtually a free hand in abusing their privileged position. The influx of China-owned enterprises is likely to exacerbate the problem.

In short, the integrity and credibility of Hong Kong's regulatory authorities will be put to a severe test during the transition to 1997 and beyond.

# 8

# Trade and Industry

Li Kui-wai and Kenneth W. K. Lo

On the trade front, the Hong Kong economy in 1992 was characterized by a continuation of trade expansion with Mainland China. Deng Xiaoping's visit to Guangdong and other parts of southern China in early 1992 had led to renewed confidence in China's reform. Both investment from Hong Kong to China and trade with China reached new peaks. China has become Hong Kong's number-one trading partner. At the same time, efforts to maintain trade links with the West have also been made. In addition to various trade lobbying activities organized by Hong Kong businesses and government officials, the Hong Kong government announced in the first quarter of 1993 that the position for the Commissioner for Economic and Trade Affairs in Washington will be upgraded from its original D4 rating to D8. The proposed remuneration, which includes the benefit of accommodation in a HK$12 million house, raised some eyebrows among legislators.[1] Meanwhile, renewed confidence in China has also led to renewed business confidence in Hong Kong. One sign of this renewed confidence is that between 1991 and 1992 businesses choosing Hong Kong as the site of their regional headquarters rose by 53 per cent.[2] External relationships and regional cooperation have also increased. For example, Hong Kong joined

Li Kui-wai is a university senior lecturer in the Department of Economics and Finance, City Polytechnic of Hong Kong.

Kenneth W. K. Lo is a demonstrator in the Department of Economics and Finance, City Polytechnic of Hong Kong.

[1] *South China Morning Post*, 31 March 1993.

[2] *South China Morning Post*, 28 April 1993.

the Asia-Pacific Economic Cooperation (APEC) forum in November 1991. The major aims of APEC are to strengthen the multilateral trading system, to increase prospects for trade and investment flows within the Asia-Pacific region and to identify common economic interests in the region. Hong Kong also became a full member of the Pacific Economic Cooperation Conference (PECC) in May 1991. PECC, which is not affiliated to any government, comprises a tripartite membership drawn from the academia, private business, and the public sector. Its aim is to develop closer cooperation on trade and economic policy issues within the Asia-Pacific region.

On the industry front, low labour and land costs in Guangdong and other parts of southern China are the major pull factor explaining the migration of Hong Kong investment. Industrial reallocation to China is reflected in the fall in the Hong Kong industrial production index by 7.32 per cent between 1990 and 1991.[3] The decline in the industrial sector, however, has been accompanied by new emphasis on the role of technology. The survival of Hong Kong industries depends also on the changing economic structure. The tertiary industry has become the dominant economic sector. Continued growth of major service industries such as finance and tourism is indispensable to the territory's future economic success.

## ☐ Bilateral Trade Flows with China

By 1992, China had become Hong Kong's largest trading partner. One can see from Table 1 that China is Hong Kong's largest source of imports and destination of re-exports. Although the United States (U.S.) still is the largest buyer of Hong Kong's exports, the growth rate of exports to the U.S. is far lower than that to China. By 1992, Hong Kong's exports to China had grown to 95.9 per cent of its exports to the U.S. from 71.5 per cent only two years earlier. If the rates of growth between 1990 and 1992 continues, exports to China will exceed those to the U.S. in 1993. In addition, re-exports have grown by nearly 40 per cent since 1990. While most of the re-export trade with China consists of outward-processing activities, with rising income and the expanding consumer market in China, growth in

---

[3] Census and Statistics Department, *Hong Kong in Figures* (Hong Kong: Government Printer, 1992).

Table 1. Hong Kong's External Trade (HK$ million)

| Country | 1990 | 1991 | 1992 | % change (92/91) |
|---|---|---|---|---|
| *Imports* | | | | |
| China | 236,134 | 293,356 | 354,348 | +20.8 |
| Japan | 103,362 | 127,402 | 166,191 | +30.4 |
| U.S. | 51,788 | 58,837 | 70,594 | +20.0 |
| Germany | 14,828 | 16,641 | 21,911 | +31.7 |
| *Exports* | | | | |
| U.S. | 66,370 | 62,870 | 64,600 | +2.8 |
| China | 47,470 | 54,404 | 61,959 | +13.9 |
| Japan | 12,079 | 11,666 | 10,997 | −5.7 |
| Germany | 17,991 | 19,318 | 15,956 | −17.4 |
| *Re-exports* | | | | |
| China | 110,908 | 153,318 | 212,105 | +38.3 |
| U.S. | 87,752 | 110,802 | 148,500 | +34.0 |
| Japan | 24,376 | 29,574 | 37,465 | +26.7 |
| Germany | 23,406 | 32,073 | 33,103 | +3.2 |

Source: *Hong Kong 1993* (Hong Kong: Government Printer, 1993).

exports and re-exports to China as the final destination is expected to remain high.

The picture from the China side is no different, as Table 2 suggests. China's total trade with Hong Kong far exceeded that with other major trading partners in the first three quarters of 1992. In the case of exports, the highest yearly percentage change in the first three quarters is the U.S., while Japan is highest in the case of imports. The U.S. is China's largest export market, Japan is China's largest source of imports. Hong Kong is China's foremost destination for re-exports.

Table 2. China's Major Trading Partners (Jan.–Sept. 1992)
(US$ million)

| Country | Total trade | Exports | Imports |
|---|---|---|---|
| Hong Kong | 40.1 (36.4) | 25.8 [17.1] | 14.1 [17.0] |
| Japan | 16.6 (15.0) | 7.8 [14.1] | 8.6 [31.8] |
| U.S. | 11.8 (10.7) | 5.5 [36.6] | 6.2 [16.1] |
| Germany | 4.0 (3.6) | 1.6 [−2.4] | 2.4 [14.7] |
| Taiwan | 4.0 (3.6) | 0.4 [15.2] | 3.5 [49.2] |

Note:    ( ) = percent of total. [ ] = yearly percentage change.
Source: *China Customs Statistics*, Beijing.

Rapid economic development in Guangdong works as a bridge between China and Hong Kong's trade and investment. Exports from Guangdong and the Pearl River Delta are expanding. Between 1990 and 1991, exports from Guangdong have increased by nearly 30 per cent. In 1990, exports from the Pearl River Delta alone amounted to 67 per cent of total export from Guangdong.[4]

Much higher labour and land costs in Hong Kong than those in Guangdong provide the impetus for Hong Kong's industrial investment in the province. Between 1979 and 1990, Guangdong absorbed US$120 billion in foreign direct investment, 80 per cent of which came from Hong Kong, according to the former Governor of Hong Kong, Lord David Wilson.[5] Liu, Wong, Sung and Lau (1992) report that actual foreign investment in Guangdong between 1979 and 1991 was US$83.97 billion, some 36.5 per cent of the national total. Major forms of foreign investment are wholly foreign-owned, equity joint venture, cooperative joint venture and compensation trade. Foreign investment in the processing of imported raw materials in the Pearl River Delta accounted for the largest share of Guangdong's exports. In 1990, this amounted to 52.4 per cent. Most industries in the Pearl River Delta are labour-intensive light industries. Economic growth in the Guangdong province is much higher than the rest of China. The average annual growth rate of Guangdong's share of gross national product (GNP) was 12.5 per cent from 1985 to 1990, compared to 7.6 per cent for China's total GNP. Guangdong, with only 6 per cent of China's total population, accounts for 15.4 per cent of China's exports.[6] Major manufacturing industries are toys, textile and clothing, electrical and electronics, chemical, paper and printing. Geographical proximity,

---

[4] Liu Pak-wai, Richard Wong, Sung Yun-wing and Lau Pui-king, *China's Open Door Economic Reform and Economic Development in the Pearl River Delta* (Hong Kong: Nanyang Commercial Bank Ltd., 1992), p. 3.4.

[5] Lu Ping, "The Economic-Technological Cooperation between Pearl River Delta and Hong Kong: A Retrospect and Prospects," in *Economic Development of the Pearl River Delta* (Guangzhou: Zhongshan University, Research Centre of Pearl River Delta Economic Development and Management, 1992), pp. 141–50.

[6] *Beijing Review*, 33.51 (17 December 1990), p. 27; and Swada Yukari, "Guangdong's Reforms and Their Impact on Society," *China Newsletter*, JETRO, No. 97 (March–April 1992), pp. 6–12.

attractive investment environment, and abundant supplies of cheap labour and land are Guangdong's absolute advantages.

Table 3 shows that Hong Kong is the largest direct foreign investor in China both in terms of number and total value of contracts, followed by Taiwan. Japan ranks third in terms of value and the U.S. is third in terms of numbers. In the first half of 1992, a total of 8,358 Hong Kong contracts were entered into with a total value of US$9,703 million, over seven times that from Taiwan. The rapid rise in investment, however, has generated some problems such as soaring prices of land, unreliable quality of workers, shortages of engineers and managerial professionals which have been exacerbated by insufficient infrastructure and confusing legislation and regulations.

Moreover, the rising property market in China has attracted much attention from Hong Kong developers in recent years. Statistics from Guangzhou report that in the first three months of 1992, 58 per cent of the foreign investment contracts valued at more than US$5 million were real estate projects.[7] In 1992, Hong Kong's largest fifteen publicly owned companies have invested HK$10 billion in real estate projects in China.

Table 3.  Foreign Direct Investment in China

|  | 1990 | 1991 | 1992 (1st half) |
|---|---|---|---|
|  | Number of contracts | | |
| Hong Kong | 4,751  (17) | 8,502  (79) | 8,358 |
| Taiwan | 1,103 (105) | 1,735  (57) | 1,702 |
| Japan | 341  (16) | 599  (76) | 571 |
| Germany | 13  (32) | 24  (85) | 33 |
| U.S. | 357  (29) | 694  (94) | 815 |
|  | Total value (US$ million) | | |
| Hong Kong | 3,833  (21) | 7,215  (88) | 9,703 |
| Taiwan | 900 (106) | 1,389  (54) | 1,320 |
| Japan | 457  (4) | 812  (78) | 826 |
| Germany | 46  (69) | 558 (1,113) | 36 |
| U.S. | 358  (44) | 548  (53) | 809 |

Note:   Figures in parentheses represent the percentage change from the previous year.
Source:  Ministry of Foreign Economic Relations and Trade, Beijing.

---

[7] *China Market*, No. 3 (1993).

These include residential and commercial buildings and industrial warehouses. Even though China's property market is still at an early stage of development, investors expect returns of up to 40 per cent, or even as high as 100 to 250 per cent. Such lucrative profit opportunities are attracting sizeable capital flows from Hong Kong into China's property market.

## ☐ China's Investment in Hong Kong

China has become a big player in both direct and portfolio investment in Hong Kong. China's investment covers a broad spectrum of areas including trading, utilities, manufacturing, travel, transport, banking and finance, and property development.

China is Hong Kong's second largest market for domestic exports and is also Hong Kong's largest re-export trade partner. Hong Kong, moreover, can provide various means to facilitate China's trade in the world market. All of China's provinces, districts and towns have offices or companies in Hong Kong to represent their provinces or units' economic interests, handle trade matters, and facilitate investment opportunities in the territory or overseas. The role of Hong Kong as an entrepôt has become increasingly significant, benefiting the two economies mutually. For example, the China International Trust and Investment Corporation (CITIC), a prominent state-owned enterprise, is a major shareholder in some of the most successful Hong Kong firms.

According to the *Survey of Overseas Investment in Hong Kong's Manufacturing Industries* published by the Industry Department in 1992, China is the third largest investor in manufacturing industries. Industries with Chinese representation include transport equipment, electronics, textiles and clothing, electrical and chemical products. Investments are either wholly owned, joint venture without a local interest or joint venture with a local interest. Most of the investment falls into the third category. This contrasts with American and Japanese investments in Hong Kong which are mostly wholly owned. Table 4 shows the value of China's investment in Hong Kong. Total investment at book value and at original cost have increased by 20 per cent and 26.9 per cent respectively between 1989 and 1992, reflecting China's direct economic influence in the territory.

China's portfolio investment in Hong Kong has also been very active, making use of Hong Kong's position as a important international financial centre. Direct investment in Hong Kong's banking and financial markets serves various purposes: facilitate inward investment to China and provide

Table 4.  Total Value of China's Investment (HK$ million)

|                                              | 1989  | 1990  | 1992  |
| -------------------------------------------- | ----- | ----- | ----- |
| Gross addition to fixed assets               | 526   | 317   | 244   |
| Stock of fixed assets at book value (a)      | 1,363 | 1,914 | 1,660 |
| Stock of fixed assets at original cost (b)   | 3,090 | 2,655 | 2,736 |
| Working capital (c)                          | 863   | 523   | 1,011 |
| Total investment at book value (a + c)       | 2,226 | 2,437 | 2,671 |
| Total investment at original cost (b + c)    | 2,953 | 3,178 | 3,747 |

Source:  Industry Department, *Survey of Overseas Investment In Hong Kong's
         Manufacturing Industries* (Hong Kong: Government Printer), various issues.

channels for external borrowing in the international capital market. This is
vital for China's economic development in the long run. The Bank of China
(BOC) Group is the second largest banking group after the Hongkong Bank
group. The BOC Group can make use of Hong Kong's financial facilities to
raise offshore funds for China.

## ☐ The Industrial Performance

The export-led nature of the Hong Kong economy has meant that manufactured outputs are mainly geared to the export market. The level of industrial
export reflects the size of output in the industrial sector. The larger
manufactured export items include articles of apparel and clothing accessories, textile yarn, fabrics, made-up articles and related products, watches
and clocks, telecommunication equipment, baby carriages, toys, games
and sporting goods, jewellery, goldsmiths and silversmiths' wares, manu-
factures of metal, automatic data-processing machines and units, and
household-type electrical and non-electrical equipment.

Table 5 shows the domestic exports of industrial products. As a result
of the reclassification of industrial products in 1992, the 1992 figures in
Table 5 may not be comparable to the 1991 figures. Most industrial exports
experienced continuous growth up to 1991. The worst performers were
baby carriages, toys, games and sporting goods, and household-type electrical and non-electrical equipment. Watches and clocks, jewellery and
telecommunication equipment faced a negative growth rate in 1991. Industrial export performance in 1992, moreover, was disappointing. With the
exception of apparel and clothing accessories which experienced a small
growth, all other industrial export items experienced a negative growth rate
in 1992.

Table 5.  Domestic Export of Industrial Products, 1988–1992 (HK$ million)

| Industries | 1988 | 1989 | 1990 | 1991 | 1992* |
|---|---|---|---|---|---|
| Articles of apparel and clothing accessories | 67,309 (3.0) | 71,874 (6.8) | 72,165 (0.4) | 75,834 (5.1) | 77,156 (1.8) |
| Textile yarn, fabrics, made-up articles and related products | 15,551 (−2.8) | 16,814 (8.1) | 16,906 (0.6) | 17,630 (4.3) | 17,226 (−2.3) |
| Plastics in primary and non-primary forms | 2,617 (94.7) | 3,586 (37.0) | 4,567 (27.4) | 4,928 (7.9) | 4,659 (−5.5) |
| Manufactures of metal | 5,659 (25.5) | 5,317 (−6.0) | 4,523 (−14.9) | 4,929 (9.0) | 4,659 (−2.9) |
| Watches and clocks | 16,588 (23.9) | 16,344 (−1.5) | 18,319 (12.1) | 15,855 (−13.5) | 15,476 (−2.4) |
| Jewellery, goldsmith and silversmiths' wares | 6,229 (21.7) | 6,577 (5.6) | 6,881 (4.6) | 6,533 (−5.1) | 5,047 (−22.7) |
| Automatic data-processing machines and units thereof | 3,722 (98.7) | 3,949 (6.1) | 3,660 (−7.3) | 3,821 (4.4) | 3,370 (−11.8) |
| Household-type electrical and non-electrical equipment | 5,479 (−3.3) | 4,252 (−22.4) | 3,376 (−20.6) | 3,207 (−5.0) | 3,078 (−40.4) |
| Telecommunication equipment | 11,092 (38.7) | 11,840 (6.7) | 12,683 (7.1) | 11,483 (−9.5) | 10,991 (−4.3) |
| Baby carriages, toys, games and sporting goods | 10,233 (−19.0) | 7,155 (−30.1) | 5,452 (−23.8) | 4,895 (−10.2) | 4,159 (−15.0) |

Notes:  1.  Figures in parentheses represent the percentage change from the previous year.
2.  * = The Third Revision of the Standard International Trade Classification (SITC R3) has been adopted in 1992.
Source:  Census and Statistics Department, *Hong Kong Monthly Digest of Statistics* (Hong Kong: Government Printer, April 1993).

The decline in industrial exports is reflected in the decline in the number of employees and establishments in major industries. Table 6 shows that both employment and the number of manufacturing industrial establishments have declined since the mid-1980s. The 1992 export decline was not incidental, but reflected the changing structure of the manufacturing sector in Hong Kong.

## ☐ The Industrial Structure

The manufacturing sector, which used to be Hong Kong's largest employment sector, lost its dominant position in the 1980s. Employment in the manufacturing sector fell from 41.7 per cent (904,709) of total employment in 1984 to 23.3 per cent (571,181) in 1992. Similarly, the manufacturing sector's contribution to gross domestic product (GDP) has declined from 24.1 per cent in 1984 to 15.5 per cent in 1991. Despite the decline, manufacturing is still Hong Kong's second largest employer, and the third largest contributor to GDP, following financial and business services. In 1992, there were 41,937 manufacturing establishments, 86.75 per cent of which were of small scale employing fewer than 20 persons, and 95.09 per cent fewer than 50 persons. The largest 2,055 establishments account for more than half Hong Kong's total industrial employment.[8] Many small establishments, however, work as subcontractors to larger factories. This is often regarded as reflecting Hong Kong's flexible industrial character.

The flexibility of Hong Kong's industries has contributed greatly to the territory's economic success in the past. The question is whether Hong Kong's industries can face up to the challenge of the future. Several major changes are taking place. Industrial migration has resulted in work displacement. Developments in technology suggest that small firms are unlikely to enjoy the economies of scale and scope in the application of technology. Emigration of Hong Kong citizens to the West has caused capital to be transferred to other destinations. In view of these new challenges, the industrial structure that had contributed to flexibility may become very fragile.

One suggested alternative is industrial amalgamation, where several indigenous firms join together and become a large corporation. The amalgamated firm will have a greater capital asset, part of which can be invested

---

[8] *Hong Kong 1993* (Hong Kong: Government Printer, 1993).

Table 6. Number of Employees and Establishments in Manufacturing Industries, 1950–1991

| Industries | 1950 | 1960 | 1970 | 1980 | 1986 | 1987 | 1988 | 1989 | 1990 | 1991 |
|---|---|---|---|---|---|---|---|---|---|---|
| Garments | 1,944 | 51,918 | 158,025 | 275,818 | 299,932 | 298,377 | 286,659 | 274,732 | 251,746 | 224,925 |
| | (41) | (970) | (3,491) | (9,499) | (10,392) | (10,556) | (10,412) | (9,672) | (9,746) | (8,837) |
| Electronics | — | 183 | 38,454 | 93,005 | 103,796 | 106,835 | 109,677 | 99,455 | 85,169 | 71,466 |
| | | (4) | (230) | (1,316) | (1,823) | (1,949) | (1,939) | (2,009) | (1,815) | (1,633) |
| Watches & | — | 2,433 | 9,773 | 49,454 | 32,805 | 31,629 | 31,180 | 30,091 | 27,154 | 23,936 |
| clocks | | (61) | (229) | (1,509) | (1,633) | (1,648) | (1,729) | (1,845) | (1,690) | (1,707) |
| Textiles | 24,975 | 54,759 | 77,057 | 88,812 | 70,714 | 75,118 | 71,967 | 73,504 | 68,638 | 62,004 |
| | (421) | (589) | (1,149) | (3,645) | (3,195) | (3,522) | (3,543) | (3,555) | (3,786) | (3,611) |
| Plastic | 231 | 18,131 | 70,958 | 86,314 | 89,447 | 83,829 | 72,412 | 63,557 | 53,137 | 41,522 |
| products | (8) | (544) | (2,756) | (4,816) | (5,460) | (5,718) | (5,572) | (5,621) | (5,263) | (4,377) |
| Toys | — | 7,430 | 39,473 | 55,644 | 56,164 | 49,034 | 39,684 | — | 24,734 | 18,715 |
| | | (204) | (1,137) | (2,128) | (2,264) | (2,151) | (2,003) | | (1,735) | (1,431) |
| Jewellery | — | 853 | 2,573 | 10,889 | 14,868 | 18,270 | 19,551 | — | 17,457 | 16,204 |
| | | (42) | (161) | (1,031) | (1,196) | (1,430) | (1,493) | | (1,506) | (1,522) |
| Metal | 14,361 | 18,515 | 35,565 | 62,751 | 50,277 | 49,699 | 49,317 | 45,751 | 41,780 | 38,995 |
| | (218) | (500) | (2,336) | (6,786) | (5,843) | (5,992) | (5,957) | (5,798) | (5,677) | (5,379) |

Note:    Figures in parentheses show the number of the establishments.
Source:  Industry Department, *Hong Kong Manufacturing Industries, 1991* (Hong Kong: Government Printer, August 1992).

in China, or overseas, while the base remains in Hong Kong. Large corporations may have a greater chance of applying modern technology. Employees working in large corporations tend to have better job security in terms of employment and training. Furthermore, today's amalgamated firms may be the multinationals of tomorrow. Obviously, the major obstacle to industrial amalgamation lies with its implementation, namely, how to create a suitable atmosphere among indigenous industrialists and make them aware of the economic benefits derived from amalgamation. The Hong Kong government will not intervene actively in the industrial structure. The traditional sole-proprietorship management attitude of Hong Kong businesses is not conducive to amalgamation unless it is replaced by a corporate attitude of industrial ownership and management. However, ultimately it is the industrialists themselves who must take the initiative to pursue industrial amalgamation.

## ☐ Government Involvement and Technological Upgrading

Unlike other Asian countries where active government intervention in industries and technology has been common, the Ministry of International Trade and Industry (MITI) in Japan being a case in point, the Hong Kong government plays a rather passive role in promoting industrial development. The significant contributions have been limited to the areas of infrastructure and educational development. To maintain Hong Kong's competitiveness, the government provides a free port, an efficient transport network, an efficient and open financial market and a sound legal system. The government also contributes to the accumulation of human capital through the compulsory nine-year free education and the expansion of tertiary education. The inflow of foreign direct investment and the maintenance of Hong Kong as the regional headquarters of many multinational corporations provide testimony to the success of this strategy.

More recently, structural changes in the manufacturing sector have forced the government to reconsider her role in industrial development. First, the government has expanded the tertiary education sector. By 1992, about 20 per cent of the 17–20 age group can receive tertiary education, compared with only 5 per cent ten years ago. In order to maintain industries' international competitiveness, the Research Grants Council was established in 1991. By 1992, the Council disbursed $122 million in earmarked grants. Promoting university research in the areas of engineering, physical science, biology, humanities and social science can strengthen local academic standard and international linkage, and enhance industrial connection and product upgrading. The Precision Tooling Training Centre was set up in 1990 under the agreement of both the Hong Kong and Japanese governments. Its aim is to transfer precision sheet metal technology to local industries. In June 1991, the New Technology Training Scheme was launched. The government provided financial support to employers to train managers and technologists in areas associated with industrial, technological and economic developments in Hong Kong.

Academics from the local tertiary institutions have also contributed to technological upgrading of industries. For example, a consultancy firm called the "CPHK Enterprises" has been established in the City Polytechnic of Hong Kong. The goal is to maximize the use of experts in the Polytechnic participating in the industrial community. The five tertiary education institutions produced a research report in 1991 known as the *Technology Road Maps for Hong Kong*, which is an in-depth study of four technology areas. They are information technology, biotechnology, materials technology and environmental technology. The report provides a comprehensive analysis and shows the various opportunities of developing the new technology industries. The tertiary educational institutions are ready to provide technical assistance.

In addition, the government established an Industry and Technology Development Council (ITDC) in early 1992. Its aim is to advise the government on the overall development of industry and technology in the territory. In its first meeting held on 18 March 1992, a \$200 million scheme for applied research and development was discussed. In 1991, the Industry Department carried out a survey on overseas investment in Hong Kong's manufacturing industries: 58 per cent of the sample firms reported the use of advanced technology ranging from production planning and control to office information systems. In 1992, the Department studied the pace of industrial automation in textiles and clothing, and metals and light engineering industries. The possible establishment of a Science Park in Hong Kong was also investigated in the same year. The two industrial estates, the Tai Po Industrial Estate and Yuen Long Industrial Estate, have provided industrial land for the application of advanced technology in manufacturing industries. The third industrial estate at Tseung Kwan O will provide a total of 68 hectares of industrial land when construction is completed in 1995. The Hong Kong Productivity Council (HKPC) regularly holds training courses for various industries. For example, it hosted the 32nd Workshop Meeting of Heads of National Productivity Organizations in 1992, which provided a forum for the discussion of numerous issues on industrial development.

Whether government intervention in industrial development does promote growth is debatable. In the future, Hong Kong's manufacturing industries will become more integrated with Mainland China. To maintain high standards of international competitiveness, investment in human capital in Hong Kong is of utmost importance in order to produce technical expertise and managerial skills.

## ☐ New Dimension of Industry Policy

The manufacturing sector in Hong Kong has dominated the economy since the 1950s. Industrial development has led the Hong Kong government in the past to set up the Industry Department to look into all aspects of the industrial and manufacturing sector. Since the 1980s, however, the tertiary sector has emerged as the largest industrial sector in Hong Kong. The percentage share of the service or tertiary sector in GDP at current prices in 1991 was about 58.1 per cent, compared with 54.5 per cent in the previous year. Major industries in the service sector are: wholesale, retail and import/export trades; restaurant and hotels; transport, storage and communication; and financing, insurance, real estate and business services.

The financing, insurance, real estate and business services group has experienced a high growth rate in the last few years. The favourable geographical location of Hong Kong provides a viaduct between the East and the West. Together with its solid tie with Mainland China, Hong Kong has made herself one of the most important international business centres in the world. Table 7 shows that the number of establishments and the persons engaged in the financing, insurance, real estate and business services sector have increased by 46.14 per cent and 25.89 per cent

Table 7. Number of Establishments and Persons Engaged in Financing, Insurance, Real Estate and Business Services

| Year | No. of establishments | Persons engaged |
|------|----------------------|-----------------|
| as at March 1992 | 37,654 | 303,422 |
| as at March 1990 | 29,212 | 263,335 |
| as at March 1989 | 25,766 | 241,015 |

Source: Employment and Earnings Statistics Section, Census and Statistics Department, Hong Kong.

respectively between 1989 and 1992. Even though the sector creates thousands of jobs each year, there were 10,242 vacancies in 1992. As the expansion of tertiary education continues, more and more recent graduates are expected to be employed in business-oriented industries.

As an international banking centre, Hong Kong provides a worldwide banking and financing network including the existence of foreign banks. By 1992, some 79 of the top 100 banks in the world had representative offices or branches operating in Hong Kong. As of March 1992, there were 1,706 banking establishments (including branches) in operation and about 67,567 people employed. These banks are licensed banks, restricted licensed banks and the representative offices of foreign banks. This means that the banking network can facilitate all kinds of tailor-made services from daily operation, trade finance, loans and mortgages, foreign exchange to international banking services and transactions. Moreover, international capital flows of investment and savings through the syndication of loans and fund management consolidate Hong Kong's leading role as an important financial centre in the Far East.

Fifty-four companies with a total amount of HK$9,084 million were newly listed in the stock market in 1992. The market capitalization was over HK$35,000 million. Because of the economic interdependence between Hong Kong and China, more and more international funds have flowed into Hong Kong *en route* to China. State-owned Chinese companies have considered the Hong Kong stock market as a potential source of funds. The increasing role of Hong Kong as a Far East financial centre, with special trade and corporate finance linkage with China, continues unchallenged.

Tourism is one of the largest service industries in Hong Kong. It is actually the third largest earner of foreign exchange. Despite the fall in the hotel occupancy rate in 1991 due to the global recession and the Gulf War crisis, there was a new record figure of seven million visitors coming to Hong Kong in 1992, an increase of 15.5 per cent over the previous year. An increasing number of tourists comes from Mainland China and Taiwan. Owing to increasing economic ties between China and Taiwan, Hong Kong serves as a transit destination for Taiwanese going to the Mainland, since there is no direct flight between the two places. Unlike European visitors, Taiwanese (as well as other Southeast Asian tourists) have short stopovers in Hong Kong and demand less lavish hotel services with middle-rate hotels being favoured. In 1992, six such hotels were opened.

The Hong Kong government has noted the rapid expansion in the tertiary industrial sector, but has not reacted by setting up an official department to look into the various aspects of the tertiary sector. Indeed, the tertiary sector is composed of three different types of service industries. One relates to the external aspect of the Hong Kong economy. Typical examples are the financial market and tourism. The other two types relate purely to the local economy. One is generally known as public utilities such as taxi transport. The third type is services consumed by private individuals, examples being estate management, car parks, and hair-dressing industries. As far as the financial sector is concerned, the Hong Kong government has been trying to provide a favourable environment with various regulations to ensure sound business and trading standards. The Commissioner of Banking, the Office of the Commission of Insurance are institutional examples showing the government's will to enhance the various activities of the financial sector. Public utilities in Hong Kong have been regulated by the government constantly. Price increases, for example, have to be approved by various government agents.

The type of service industries which has escaped the government's attention are those services provided for private consumption. In general, it is difficult for manufactured products to escape competition, but not so for service industries. Because of various locational factors, service industries tend to have a lower degree of market competition than manufactured industrial goods. Car parks (a consumer service goods), for example, can raise their fees much more easily than suppliers of motor cars (a manufactured goods) or taxis (a public service goods). Since the tertiary sector has become the largest industrial sector in Hong Kong, economic changes in the tertiary sector can have significant welfare impact on the economy. Table 8 shows that between 1992 and 1993, the monthly inflation rate in the service sector, as indicated by the three Consumer Service Price Indexes (CSPI(A), CSPI(B), and the Hang Seng CSPI), is constantly higher than the overall inflation rate, as indicated by the three Consumer Price Indexes (CPI(A), CPI(B), and the Hang Seng CPI). Increase in the price of services has contributed more to inflation than that of other components.

It is time for the Hong Kong government to consider the establishment of a Department for Service Industries to look into the economic and business activities of services in the private sector. Unlike, for example, the Monopoly Commission in other developed countries which considers the monopolistic element of a single firm, a Department for Service Industries can look into the extent of competition in different service industries. In the initial stage, resources within the Industry Department should be made available for studying the different aspects of the service sector and for

Table 8. Inflation Rate (% Change of Index Over 12 Months)

| Year/ Month | CPI(A) | CSPI(A) | CPI(B) | CSPI(B) | Hang Seng CPI | Hang Seng CSPI |
|---|---|---|---|---|---|---|
| 1992/6 | 9.3 | 10.8 | 9.6 | 11.3 | 10.0 | 10.6 |
| 1992/7 | 8.8 | 11.0 | 9.3 | 11.6 | 10.1 | 10.6 |
| 1992/8 | 8.3 | 10.8 | 9.1 | 11.6 | 9.8 | 10.8 |
| 1992/9 | 9.9 | 12.0 | 10.2 | 12.4 | 10.2 | 10.7 |
| 1992/10 | 9.5 | 12.3 | 10.0 | 12.8 | 9.5 | 10.9 |
| 1992/11 | 9.2 | 12.2 | 9.6 | 12.7 | 9.5 | 11.1 |
| 1992/12 | 9.4 | 12.6 | 9.7 | 12.7 | 9.7 | 11.5 |
| 1993/1 | 10.1 | 12.7 | 10.3 | 13.0 | 10.1 | 12.1 |
| 1993/2 | 8.6 | 11.8 | 9.1 | 12.0 | 9.1 | 11.5 |
| 1993/3 | 7.8 | 11.1 | 8.5 | 11.6 | 9.2 | 11.2 |
| 1993/4 | 7.7 | 11.0 | 8.5 | 11.6 | 9.5 | 11.3 |
| 1993/5 | 8.5 | 10.6 | 8.8 | 11.2 | 9.8 | 11.2 |

Note: The CSPI occupies 39.26 per cent of the weighting of the official CPI(A), 43.05 per cent of CPI(B), and 50.65 per cent of the Hang Seng CPI.

Source: The Hong Kong General Chamber of Commerce, *Hong Kong Coalition of Service Industries*, June 1993.

classifying various types of service industries. The second stage would be the formal establishment of a Department for Service Industries.

## ☐ Conclusion

To a large extent, the economies of Hong Kong and China have been integrated. Economic activities in both Hong Kong and China move together. In 1992, import and export trade with China contributed 37.1 per cent and 27.6 per cent respectively to Hong Kong's total import and export trade. In terms of re-exports, as classified by final destination, China's share of total re-exports was about 30.7 per cent. Moreover, the most-favoured-nation (MFN) trading status granted to China by the U.S. government is expected to give an additional 35 to 47 per cent rise in Hong Kong's re-exports. Figure 1 shows that since 1989, income growth rates of Hong Kong and China have experienced a similar trend. China and Hong Kong have enjoyed higher income growth rates than the U.S., which traditionally was Hong Kong's leading trade partner, as well as Japan and Germany.

Figure 1.  GDP Growth Rate, 1987–1992

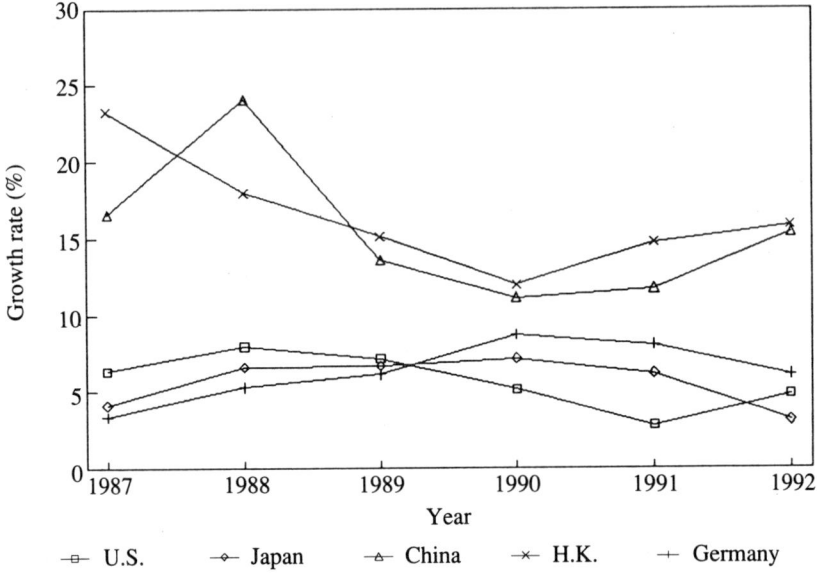

Note:     GNP data is used in the case of China.
Sources: International Monetary Fund, Washington, *International Financial Statistics*,
          various issues; Census and Statistics Department, Hong Kong government,
          *Hong Kong Monthly Digest*, various issues; Asian Development Bank,
          Manila, *Key Indicators of Developing Asian and Pacific Countries*, Volume
          23 (1992).

The basic element that permits integration to take place is economic complementarity between Hong Kong and China, or Guangdong in particular. Typically, Hong Kong entrepreneurs look after the financing, marketing, technology know-how, sales and management aspects of production, while the cheap land and labour resources in southern China support the manufacturing arm. Such an "office-factory" relationship seems to have worked well both for Hong Kong and China. Given that Hong Kong lacks natural resources, economic integration with southern China offers the prospect of a prolonged period of economic growth.

# 9

# Labour and Employment

Chau Leung-chuen

## ☐ Introduction

In every part of the world, from the most advanced countries to the least developed economies, the main, if not the only, economic concern has been a shortage of jobs. The average rate of unemployment among the 19 member countries of the Organization for Economic Cooperation and Development in Europe will hit 11 per cent in 1993. In the summit meeting of the seven richest industrialized countries just completed in Tokyo at the time of writing, it was decided that a high-level meeting in autumn to deal exclusively with the unemployment problem would be convened.

In Hong Kong, the employment "problem" since 1987 has been a shortage of workers. From Table 1 we note that unemployment rate fell below 2 per cent in 1987, and has more or less stayed there ever since. From 1991 onwards, the market showed signs of easing, but both the unemployment and underemployment rates stayed close to the 2 per cent mark throughout 1992 and during the first half of 1993. Labour shortage has remained the centrepiece of discussion on policy issues and in assessing the performance of the economy.

Hong Kong's economy grew by 5 per cent in 1992. This is low by historical standards and labour constraint becomes a handy explanation. Yet it is not clear how it can account for the slow growth of per capita income, which was much lower than that achieved in 1988, when the unemployment

Chau Leung-chuen is a senior lecturer in the School of Economics and Finance, The University of Hong Kong.

## Table 1. Labour Supply and Unemployment

| Year/Month | Mid-year population, aged 15 & over (1,000) | Labour force participation rate (%) | Labour force (1,000) | Unemployment rate, seasonally adjusted (%) |
|---|---|---|---|---|
| 1980 March |  | 62.8 | 2,276.0 | 3.2 |
| 1981 March | 3,906.1 (2,987.9) | 66.8 | 2,456.3 | 4.1 |
| 1982 March |  | 64.7 | 2,477.7 | 3.5 |
| 1983 March |  | 63.8 | 2,497.8 | 5.1 |
| 1984 March |  | 64.9 | 2,539.8 | 4.0 |
| 1985 March |  | 64.8 | 2,598.5 | 3.3 |
| 1986 March | 4,250.9 (3,372.2) | 64.6 | 2,656.0 | 3.2 |
| 1987 March |  | 64.2 | 2,662.0 | 2.1 |
| Sept. |  | 65.2 | 2,752.0 | 1.8 |
| 1988 March | 4,381.8 | 64.4 | 2,739.0 | 1.6 |
| Sept. |  | 65.0 | 2,775.0 | 1.6 |
| 1989 March | 4,445.7 | 64.1 | 2,761.0 | 1.3 |
| Sept. |  | 63.7 | 2,743.0 | 1.4 |
| 1990 March | 4,478.2 | 63.4 | 2,743.0 | 1.7 |
| Sept. |  | 63.1 | 2,736.0 | 1.7 |
| 1991 March | 4,550.4 | 63.5 | 2,782.0 | 1.8 |
| Sept. | (3,620.2) | 63.4 | 2,796.0 | 2.1 |
| 1992 March | 4,620.0 | 62.4 | 2,780.0 | 2.4 |
| Sept. |  | 61.9 | 2,768.0 | 1.9 |
| 1993 March |  | 62.6 | 2,845.0 | 2.3 |

Note: Figures in parentheses are for those aged 15–64.
Source: Census & Statistics Department, *Hong Kong Annual Digest of Statistics*, various issues.

rate was even lower. Inflation rate remained at close to 10 per cent, and is not expected to come down significantly in the near future. Again, wage spiral is widely cited as a main contributing factor. Debate on whether labour shortage exists has continued, but the government has chosen to expand the labour importation scheme. In January 1992 it was decided to double the import quota of skilled and semi-skilled workers to 25,000 (inclusive of already admitted workers). Unlike previous arrangement, the additional quota is not pre-assigned to specific sectors, allowing more flexibility to better accommodate up-to-date conditions. Response to the scheme was overwhelming, with employers applying to recruit 92,600 workers, against an *available* quota of 12,000. In addition, 13,859 professional, managerial, or technical personnel, as well as an additional 16,563 domestic helpers were admitted for employment in 1992. A large number of emigrants also returned to Hong Kong from Canada and Australia due to the poor employment prospect of those countries.[1] These factors have contributed to a 2.16 per cent annual growth in labour force in March 1993, the steepest increase, by far, since 1988.

There were few initiatives on the legislature or policy front during 1992. The process of legislating mandatory retirement protection is still in progress. A consultation paper on *A Community-wide Retirement Protection System* was issued in November 1992.

The Employee Retraining Scheme initiated in 1991 and financed by a levy on employers of imported workers came into operation during the year. At the end of March 1993 a total of 397 workers completed training under various pilot projects. With an overall placement rate of about 85 per cent, the Scheme has gained initial success. Despite the widely publicized strike by the cabin crew of Cathay Pacific Airways, industrial peace prevailed, in general. There were no other major disputes and there was no large-scale layoff. A total of 3,496 working days were lost to work stoppage, at the same level of 1989 and 1990, though much higher than that in 1991. The number of disputes between employees and employers heard by the Labour Tribunal fell 20 per cent. In view of the extensive relocation of workers among industrial sector and the high labour turnover, this is a gratifying outcome. The number of occupational accidents has been steadily falling since 1988, probably because more and more workers are employed in the tertiary sector which are less accident-prone. A particularly steep fall of 14 per cent was achieved in 1992. Regrettably, there was no fall in the number of fatality.

## ☐ Analysis of Labour Shortage

Labour has been in short supply since 1987. After some easing in 1991, the labour market tightened up again in the latter part of 1992. The main causes

---

[1] For example, it was estimated by the International Business Week that during the twelve-month period prior to September 1992, about 30,000 people returned from Canada. See *Hong Kong Economic Journal*, 4 October 1992.

of this prolonged shortage are not difficult to identify. As noted in last year's *The Other Hong Kong Report*, the labour force ceased to grow in recent years. This trend persisted in 1992. From Table 1 we see that there was practically no change in the size of labour force over a five-year period between September 1987, when unemployment rate dropped below 2 per cent for the first time, and September 1992.

The change in labour force depends on three factors: population growth, its demographic structure, and labour force participation rates. The growth of working-age population slowed down progressively over the decade due to steadily falling fertility rate from late 1960s onwards. It grew by 8.8 per cent between 1981 and 1986, already a low rate by historical standards. During 1986 to 1991 it slowed down to 7 per cent. For the prime age group of 20–64, it dropped from 13 per cent to 7 per cent. On top of that, the overall labour force participation rate fell sharply, from 65 per cent in 1986 to 62 per cent in 1992. Using census data we can analyse the source of this change in participation and measure its impact on the supply of labour.

Participation rate by broad age and sex group for selected years of census is presented in Table 2. Along with a change in the population pyramid, it caused a systematic change on labour supply. Three outstanding trends in participation rates are noteworthy. Participation rate of those aged 15–24 fell substantively. For male, this has been going on over the entire decade of 1980s, but for female, it became noticeable only after 1986. For the next age group, participation of males was very high and stable, but participation rate of females went up sharply, which is perhaps the most important and interesting change. Surprisingly, there was practically no increase in the participation rate of women aged 35–54, at a relatively low rate of about 50 per cent. Finally, participation of those aged 55 and over, irrespective of sex, fell sharply throughout the decade.

The direction of these changes are not difficult to explain. With rising affluence and increasing opportunities for post-secondary education, more and more young people continue their study beyond the secondary level, resulting in falling participation rate of the age group 15–24. The postponement of marriage and the continued fall in fertility have boosted the participation rate of young women. Inflows of domestic helpers produced the same result. Both factors should have contributed to raising the participation rate of women aged 35–54. But it did not materialize. During these years, the economic structure of Hong Kong was changing rapidly. Manufacturing jobs were relocated massively across the border, while employment in trade and services increased rapidly. It is more difficult for

Table 2.  Composition of Population and Labour Force Participation Rate by Age and Sex, 1981, 1986 and 1991 (%)

| | 15–24 | | | 25–34 | | | 35–54 | | | 55 and over | | | Total | | |
|---|---|---|---|---|---|---|---|---|---|---|---|---|---|---|---|
| | M | F | Total | M | F | Total | M | F | Total | M | F | Total | M | F | Total |
| Age-Sex composition of population aged 15 and over | | | | | | | | | | | | | | | |
| 1981 | 16.0 | 14.6 | 30.6 | 12.7 | 10.8 | 23.5 | 14.7 | 12.0 | 26.7 | 8.9 | 10.3 | 19.2 | 52.3 | 47.7 | 100.0 |
| 1986 | 12.5 | 11.9 | 24.4 | 13.7 | 12.8 | 26.5 | 15.2 | 13.3 | 28.5 | 9.8 | 10.9 | 20.6 | 51.2 | 48.8 | 100.0 |
| 1991 | 9.8 | 9.3 | 19.1 | 13.3 | 13.5 | 26.8 | 16.6 | 15.4 | 32.0 | 10.6 | 11.5 | 22.1 | 50.3 | 49.7 | 100.0 |
| Labour force participation rate | | | | | | | | | | | | | | | |
| 1981 | 69.3 | 61.5 | 65.6 | 98.5 | 55.9 | 78.5 | 97.1 | 49.9 | 75.6 | 59.5 | 23.8 | 40.0 | 82.5 | 49.0 | 66.3 |
| 1986 | 63.9 | 61.4 | 62.7 | 98.6 | 64.2 | 82.1 | 97.1 | 50.5 | 75.9 | 50.5 | 17.9 | 33.1 | 80.5 | 48.9 | 65.1 |
| 1991 | 56.9 | 55.2 | 56.0 | 98.2 | 69.1 | 83.4 | 97.3 | 50.9 | 75.5 | 46.4 | 13.7 | 29.4 | 78.8 | 47.8 | 63.4 |

Sources: Standard Chartered, *Hong Kong Economic Indicator* (April 1993); Census & Statistics Department, *Annual Digest of Statistics 1992*.

older workers to switch to a new occupation. At the same time, with rising affluence many of them could afford to withdraw from the labour force.

As can be seen from Table 2, the demographic structure of the labour force also changed over the years. Most notably, the sex ratio has become more balanced over the decade. Between 1986 and 1991, there was a sharp decrease in the proportion of population aged 15–24, a sharp increase of those aged 35–54, and a moderate increase of the senior group. As participation rates are normally quite different between these broad age groups, this shift in age composition itself will affect the overall participation rate. The different impacts of changes in participation rates and demographic composition can be separately identified. If the 1986 participation rates had applied to the 1991 population the labour force would have been noticeably larger than the one actually observed. Thus the change in labour force participation by different age-sex groups over 1986–1991 had a significant negative impact on the supply of labour. It accounted for about 60 per cent of the observed decline in the overall participation rate. The residual is due to changes in demographic composition of the working age population. In sum, all three factors: population growth, changes in demographic composition, and changes in labour force participation rates, all worked to lower the labour supply over 1986–1991.

The stagnant labour force since 1987 was confronted by shifting and rising demand for labour. The general situation is reflected in the sectoral composition of employment over the period, as presented in Table 3. From 1988 onwards, employment in manufacturing started to fall absolutely due to continued relocation of labour-intensive production process across the border. And the rate of decline has also accelerated. Workers released from manufacturing were mostly absorbed by the sectors of finance and trade. By 1991, trade and commerce overtook manufacturing as the largest sector in terms of employment. By the end of 1992, employment in finance was more than half as large as that of manufacturing employment. Employment in restaurants and hotels also increased rapidly. The combined employment of these three tertiary sectors in 1992 was twice as large as the combined employment in manufacturing and construction. Indications are that this trend of tertiarization of the economy has continued.

We now come to the topical and important issue of whether labour shortage is easing, or if it still exists. There are four important indicators on the tightness of labour market: unemployment rates, vacancy rates, labour turnover, and wage changes. The unemployment rate is, of course, the most direct measure. From Table 1 we note that there was practically no change

Table 3. Employment by Major Sectors (in Thousands)

| | September of | | | | | | December 1992 | |
| --- | --- | --- | --- | --- | --- | --- | --- | --- |
| | 1987 | 1988 | 1989 | 1990 | 1991 | 1992 | Employment | Year-on-year growth (%) |
| Manufacturing | 875 | 845 | 803 | 730 | 655 | 571 | 565 | –10 |
| Finance, insurance, real estates & business services | 210 | 231 | 249 | 273 | 289 | 308 | 315 | 6 |
| Wholesale, retail & import/export trade | 466 | 512 | 557 | 602 | 657 | 673 | 680 | 5 |
| Restaurants & hotels | 182 | 186 | 201 | 213 | 224 | 233 | 235 | 6 |
| Construction | 71 | 73 | 68 | 71 | 64 | 63 | 59 | 0 |
| Civil service | 182 | 185 | 187 | 190 | 191 | 183 | 182 | 0 |
| Total | 2,702 | 2,735 | 2,710 | 2,695 | 2,742 | 2,722 | 2,763 | 2.3 |

Note:    The total number of employment is inclusive of other sectors.
Source:  Census & Statistics Department, *First Quarterly Economic Report 1993*.

in the overall rate of unemployment compared with a year earlier. However, we should consider this rate in conjunction with the growth of employment. Here some important changes have taken place.

In last year's *The Other Hong Kong Report* we noted that total employment fell absolutely between March 1991 and March 1992 (p. 200). The drop was proportionately small to be sure, but, against a stagnant labour force and rising unemployment rate, it reveals a weakening labour market. In sharp contrast, the March 1993 employment registers a year-on-year growth of 2.2 per cent, which represents the largest growth, by far, since 1988. It did not raise the unemployment rate only because the additional workers were largely recruited from outside. In other words, the large increase in labour supply was created by a strong demand. Significantly, the rate of underemployment has been falling steadily, from 2.2 per cent in March 1982 to 1.9 per cent in September 1992, and 1.6 per cent in March 1993. The rate of vacancy also went up moderately in 1992 for the three expanding sectors: trade, restaurants and hotels, and transport. It fell for manufacturing, but at 3 per cent, it was still well above the unemployment rate. However, for reasons elucidated below, wages do not respond readily to labour shortage. And basic wage rate is that part of the package of employee remuneration that tends to be most sticky. Changes in wage rates are therefore not a good indicator of contemporary market condition.

Finally, labour mobility is an unequivocal indicator of market situation. In a tight labour market jobs are plentiful, and wage differentials widen across firms and industries. Workers are more ready to seek out better jobs, so labour mobility is high. High labour turnover has become a common complaint of employers. Information on turnover rate is sporadic. But perhaps we can look at a proxy. There was a noticeable increase in the number of pages devoted to advertising job openings in newspapers and magazines. A couple of specialized weeklies targeted to people contemplating job changes were launched during the year, one of them being distributed free in Mass Transit Railway stations. Aside from reflecting the abundance of job openings, such wide dissipation of job information can only help to promote labour mobility. All things considered, the labour market remained very tight in 1992.

Labour shortage is expected to persist in the near future. The continued economic boom in south China, and the accumulated affluence from a decade of high growth will fuel further expansion of Hong Kong's tertiary sector. For example, the number of visitors from China went up by 22 per cent in 1992. Economic strength and potential of the neighbouring region continued to attract recognition and publicity. In particular, the economy of Vietnam is poised to take off, following the recent normalization of its relationship with the United States. And Hong Kong managed to retain its favourable position as a regional headquarters for multinationals.[2]

When the PADS (Port and Airport Development Strategy) projects finally get underway, many more jobs will be created. The recent boom in hotel, office, and commercial properties is a reflection of this potential. On the supply side the net increase of new entrants to the labour force will continue to be small given the population pyramid. The contraction of manufacturing employment is likely to continue. But with a much narrower base, the number of workers released will be smaller. Also, workers most suitable for relocating have probably done so already. To add to the problem, the number of local residents working in China will increase sharply, now that Hong Kong-based companies have extended their investment in China from manufacturing to the tertiary sector, and from Guangdong to inland cities. To alleviate shortage, Hong Kong will have to bring in more workers from outside and to arrest the declining trend of participation rate of its working-age population.

## □ Adverse Impacts of Labour Shortage

It is the belief of the business community that a prolonged state of labour shortage is detrimental to growth performance and smooth operation of the economy. It stunts economic growth in several ways. Most directly, exports are reduced because the required workforce is not forthcoming, because manufacturers dare not accept order with short notice under a very tight labour market, or because high wage costs have eroded Hong Kong's competitiveness. What is more, when shortages are developed in strategic areas, it becomes a bottleneck to the rest of the economy. Shortage stimulates labour mobility. High rate of labour turnover is costly. A tight labour market and high mobility tend to erode work ethics and workplace discipline. It lowers the quality of work and incentive to do training as workers are less committed to their jobs. Recent experience with our service industries seems to bear this out. A less stable and reliable workforce, and a

---

[2] According to recent surveys Hong Kong is the top destination for foreign and investment among countries in the region. See *South China Morning Post*, 23 March 1993 and 22 June 1993.

less predictable wage bill increase the risk of business and discourage the start of new enterprises, particularly those by direct foreign investment. Eventually, the overall business environment deteriorates, leading to the relocation of local business. This will undermine the long-term growth prospect of the economy. It is generally believed that labour shortage leads to rapidly rising wages which fuels inflation. As a matter of fact, sellers tend to justify their price increases with rising costs, particularly wages. And inflation rate accelerated in 1988 after labour shortage became widespread in 1987.

Wage increases will not solve the shortage problem for particular sectors, according to this argument, as the shortage is "absolute", or because certain jobs are shunned by local workers. They advocate labour importation as the only solution. This view is strongly contested by unionist and liberals. They deny that labour supply is not responsive to higher wages. Shortage persists in some sectors only because wages are held down. Particularly, during recession years of mid-1970s and early 1980s the market mechanism worked to restore full employment through cutting real wages. It follows that the price mechanism of a competitive labour market can also effectively and efficiently allocate the scarce labour to its most productive use in boom time. Labour importation then deprives the right of workers to enjoy the good time after they have suffered in the bad time. The government has taken a compromised stance. A restricted scheme of labour importation has been in operation since 1989. The scheme seems to have met with the approval of neither the workers, the business community, nor the academicians. And the debate on the needs and wisdom of importing labour goes on. The crux of the issue appears to be the extent to which flexible wages can be, and have been, used to handle labour shortage in Hong Kong. It is an empirical as well as analytical issue.

## ☐ Wage Rigidity and Labour Shortage

In a market economy, when a commodity is in short supply relative to demand, its price rises sharply. Labour is no exception.

When employers compete for workers, they bid up the wage rates. Historically, this was true in Hong Kong. In the 1950s, labour was in surplus, wages for unskilled labour were flat. When supply tightened up towards the end of the decade, wages started to rise sharply in 1960. Throughout the 1960s unemployment was kept at a low level, and real wages rose at an annual rate of 7.9 per cent, broadly in line with per capita income. Wage growth slowed down markedly after 1973. Manufacturing wages were growing at a compound annual rate of only 2.3 per cent over 1973–1982. Particularly, the recent spell of labour shortage was not manifested in rapidly rising wages. Indices of wages and labour income by sectors are presented in Table 4. In general, the increases in real wages or labour income since 1987, when the present spell of labour shortage began, were sluggish. For manufacturing, payroll per person increased by a total of 18 per cent between September 1987 and September 1992, or an annual growth of 3.3 per cent. Over this five-year period, real wage rates was up by a mere 3 per cent. To some extent, this may be accounted for by the fact that manufacturing employment was shrinking. But the increases in wages and labour income in other sectors fared only slightly better. The compound annual growth rate of real wage indices in the rapidly expanding sectors of trade, finance, and services over these five years (1987–1992) ranged from 1.64 for wholesale trade to 5.38 for retail trade. Even for the banking sector, the growth rate was only 4.14 per cent. Only in construction did wages increased at a rate faster than that in the 1960s, and only over a three-year period. Between 1987 and 1990 real wages of construction workers went up at an annual rate of 8.8 per cent. But since then construction wages have stagnated.

As for payroll per person, data for workers of non-manufacturing sectors were not available before 1990. The average real growth over 1990–1992 for various sectors is presented in the same table. There is no discernible pattern between the wage increases and growth in payroll. Also, the year-on-year changes in payroll growth (not shown) for different sectors are highly erratic. In addition to wage rates payroll depends on the occupational and skill composition of the labour force, as well as degree of employment. Thus the sharp increase in unit payroll for manufacturing in spite of stagnant wage rate is probably related to the elimination of unskilled jobs through outward processing. But it can also be caused by more overtime employment. Particularly, data observed for a single month are highly sensitive to cyclical as well as seasonal factors. Given the short time series, it is not possible to make a generalization. On the other hand, it is clearly indicated by the wage statistics that, in spite of sustained labour shortage, wage increases in recent years were sluggish by historical standards, and tend to lag behind income growth.

How do we interpret or explain this unexpected wage rigidity? A straightforward interpretation is that the labour market in Hong Kong has ceased to be competitive. Wage rates are administered, or the annual

Table 4. Indexes of Wages and Payrolls by Sectors

| Industrial sector | Real wage index: compound rate of annual growth, 1987–92 (%) | Real index of payroll per person: average annual growth, 1990–92 (%) | Nominal wage index, September (March 1982 = 100) | | | Ratio of nominal wage index | |
|---|---|---|---|---|---|---|---|
| | | | 1985 | 1988 | 1991 | 1988/85 | 1991/86 |
| Manufacturing | 0.43 | 8.5 | 125.3 | 156.5 | 215.3 | 1.249 | 1.376 |
| Trade, restaurants & hotels | 1.46 | 3.1 | 120.8 | 159.6 | 221.7 | 1.321 | 1.389 |
| Wholesale | 1.64 | 3.8 | 136.6 | 187.8 | 251.6 | 1.381 | 1.340 |
| Retail | 5.38 | 5.9 | 132.8 | 215.5 | 323.8 | 1.623 | 1.502 |
| Hotels | 3.26 | 7.3 | 132.2 | 180.2 | 266.8 | 1.363 | 1.481 |
| Transport, storage & communication | 4.51 | 7.6 | 136.4 | 184.2 | 288.5 | 1.350 | 1.566 |
| Finance, insurance, real estates & business services | 4.45 | −0.8 | 130.3 | 182.3 | 280.2 | 1.399 | 1.537 |
| Community, social & personal services | 4.58 | 7.1 | 124.5 | 169.7 | 248.2 | 1.363 | 1.462 |
| Construction | 4.85 | n.a. | 685 | 1,130 | 1,741 | 1.650 | 1.541 |
| Consumer Price Index (A), Oct. 89–Sept. 90 = 100 | | | 72.6 | 84.6 | 114.5 | 1.165 | 1.353 |

Note:    For construction wage rate, January 1970 = 100.
Sources: Census & Statistics Department, *Annual Digest of Statistics; Monthly Digest of Statistics.*

increase in wages is orchestrated by formal or informal associations of employers, a view advanced by Turner that has been in circulation for some time.[3] As a large number of small employers predominate in the trade and service sectors, this view is not that persuasive. We need to consider other explanations. The accelerating rate of inflation can be an important factor.

The rate of inflation averaged to 4.7 per cent during 1955–1988, it went up to 10.3 per cent in 1989–1992. Money illusion may affect both employers and workers in their wage negotiations. Aside from that, as wage increases are geared to inflation the previous year, wage increases tend to lag in periods of rising inflation. The behaviour of nominal wages in Table 4 lends support to this conjecture. There is a certain stickiness in the magnitude of nominal wage increase between the two sub-periods, in spite of worsening inflation. The three-year increases range between 35 to about 55 per cent, or about 10 to 15 per cent per annum. One may conjecture that the 10 per cent mark represents a common threshold for both parties. Secondly, the extents of price increases differ among sectors. Employers in some sectors cannot afford to match their wage increases with inflation. Manufacturers, for example, are selling their products in the highly competitive world market. Often they cannot pass on the cost of wage increase to overseas buyers. Their excess demand for labour manifests not so much in rising wages as in rising vacancies.

Wage adjustments are also constrained by the existing wage structure. When shortage exists primarily for particular grades of workers doing certain types of jobs, it is not practical for the employers to raise their pay much above the going rate, for it will upset the existing hierarchy, resulting in widespread resentment among other employees. For example, the falls in fertility and labour force participation rates have greatly reduced the supply of young job seekers with secondary education qualifications or below. It has resulted in an acute shortage of messengers. To eliminate the shortage, it may entail paying them more than other white-collar workers with much better education and greater seniority. Instead, employers may choose to attract workers with a good job title (messengers are now known as office assistants) and other fringe benefits that do not show up in wage statistics. In this connection, a distinction can be drawn between the rapid expansion

---

[3] See H. A. Turner, *et al.*, *The Last Colony: But Whose?* (Cambridge: Cambridge University Press, 1980), p. 153.

of manufacturing employment in the 1960s and the growth of tertiary employment in the 1980s. Much of the growth in industrial jobs in the 1960s were created by new industries: plastics, wig, electronics. The entrepreneurs there were making big profits and they were not constrained by an existing pay structure. Generally, this is not so with the growth of the tertiary sector in recent years, where the expansion is in the existing lines of businesses or even the existing firms. It is not practical for them to pay new recruits much more than what they are paying their existing labour force. Also they are less obliged to fill quick orders from overseas buyers, or to race against time lest the fad products they produce become out of fashion. So wages are more sticky.

Employers have other reasons to prefer adjusting fringe benefits rather than basic wages as a means for attracting workers during a tight labour market situation. It is more flexible. It is easier to trim fringe benefits than to cut basic wages. It is less likely to evoke hard feelings from other employers competing for workers, particularly the former employers of the workers concerned. The enactment of the long-service payment regulation in 1986 provides another reason for employers to opt for non-wage adjustments. When the employee retires, or becomes redundant, he is entitled to a long-service payment of up to a year's salary based on his last month's wages. Employers thus have a strong incentive to hold down the rate of wage increases, by adjusting other components of the pay package, including working conditions.

Wage rigidity for the various reasons suggested above is not inconsistent with a competitive labour market. Competition prevails if adjustment is made through atomistic, rational actions. Clearly, labour market contracting is much more complicated than transaction in commodity market. Institutional factors are important. Personal feelings are involved. The textbook competitive model is too much a simplification. For example, according to this model only two variables are involved: price and quantity. In reality, price involves much more than the basic wage rate, but a composite package of remuneration. Theoretically, each small employer is a price taker. If she pays her workers less than the market-clearing, equilibrium wage, which is supposedly known to all, her entire workforce will desert her. In reality, the equilibrium price is more like a hazy band, differentiated with fringe benefits and working conditions, not readily known to individual workers. When an employer pays less than the "going price", many of her workers will stay, at least in the short run, because the cost-benefit of relocating is different among her workers. Inertia, ignorance, personal attachment to work team, accessibility of workplace, and job prospect, perceived or real, all have a role to play.

With wage rigidity, labour shortage in a competitive labour market setting can be given a more definite interpretation. The general situation is depicted in Figure 1. It applies to the entire local labour market, or to an individual sub-market.[4] Unemployment will not be zero at any time because of frictions. Given the demand and supply as depicted, and the underlying labour market institution, $\overline{EE}$ represents the locus of all feasible employment (realized employment). At a given wage rate unemployment is then the difference between labour supply and this realized employment,

Figure 1.  Unemployment and Vacancies

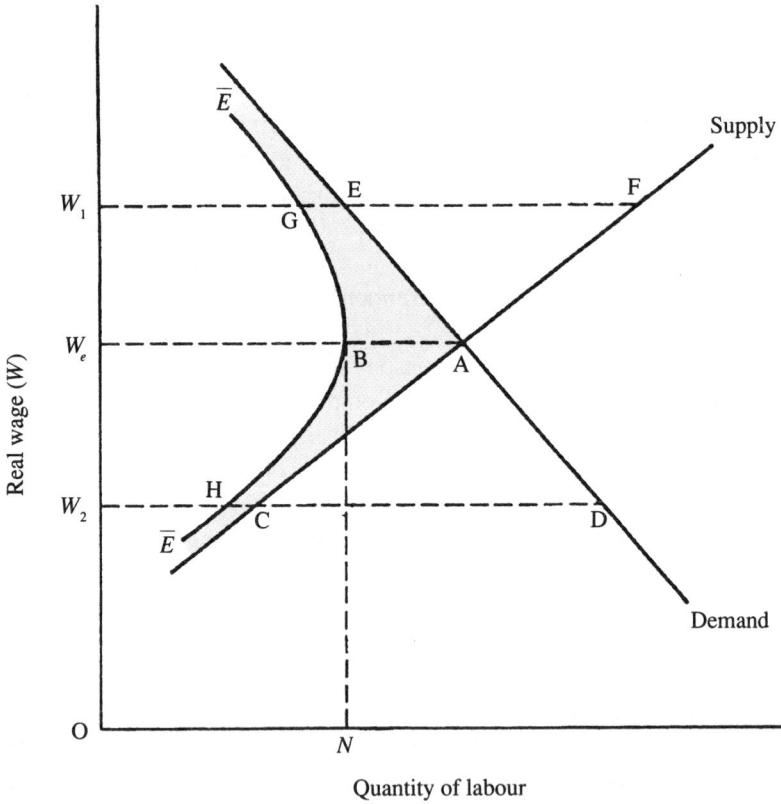

Quantity of labour

---

[4] The analysis is taken from C. Hasluck, *Urban Unemployment* (London: Longman, 1987), pp. 108–11.

and unfilled vacancies is the difference between demand and realized employment. The shaded area represents frictional unemployment. When the wage rate is set at the equilibrium level ($W_e$), unemployment is equal to vacancies, and is all frictional. With changing demand and supply conditions the existing wages may deviate from the equilibrium level. Particularly, in a period when demand has been steadily increasing, or supply falling, wages tend to lag behind due to various frictions. And this could be the situation in Hong Kong in recent years. Diagrammatically, wage rates in some markets are set at $W_2$, lower than the equilibrium wage $W_e$, then vacancies (HD) exceeds unemployment (HC), and a condition of labour shortage exists. The disequilibrium can be short-run due to cyclical or other transitional changes in demand. Otherwise, the wages tend to gravitate towards the equilibrium level, but the process can take a long time.

## ☐ Implications on Some Major Policy Issues

We have discussed and documented the following salient features of Hong Kong's labour market and its operation: (1) labour shortage has existed since 1987, and is expected to prevail in the near future; (2) labour shortage notwithstanding, the labour force participation rate of female population aged 35–54 has not increased, and participation by those aged 55 and over has fallen sharply; and (3) sustained labour shortage has not resulted in steep increase in overall wages; even in rapidly expanding sectors, the rise in wages was moderate.

The third outcome is most significant for policy considerations. It means that wage adjustment were not used widely to attract or to retain workers. We have discussed why this is so from institutional and managerial point of view; and why it may represent rational behaviour on the part of employers. Practically, when the supply is inelastic, wage increases will not be effective in inducing supply. A good example is the construction industry. Between 1986 and 1989, nominal wages went up by 85 per cent, compared with a 40 per cent gain for other sectors, yet total employment in construction changed very little. It implies that the supply of construction workers is very inelastic. This is because local workers do not want to enter the industry. Another important example is domestic helpers. In the years before large-scale importation, the pay for household maids had been increasing much faster than income of factory workers, yet their number had also been shrinking rapidly. With rising affluence, young women simply refused to take up employment as domestic helpers because of its long hours of work and, at that time, class stigma. The supply will also be rigid if the required skills or experience takes time to acquire. Finally, highly flexible wages may not be efficient. If wages are very fluid, adjusting freely and rapidly to any change in demand and supply, wage rates and wage structure become highly unstable. It results in high labour turnover. But high mobility is costly to both workers and employers. That is why most pay packages are designed to foster workers' loyalty and a stable labour force. And workers tend to prefer job security. It increases the risk of doing business, causes great inconvenience to consumers, and probably contributes to fluctuating prices. In sum, even in a highly competitive labour market as that in Hong Kong, flexible wages are not observed, and they may not be effective or efficient. As a result, shortage, in the sense that at the going wages, demand exceeds supply by a wide margin, can persist in some sectors, while in other sectors, workers are underemployed.

These findings have significant implications on some important policy issues, particularly labour importation and government-sponsored retraining scheme.

## ☐ Labour Importation

The recent debates on the appropriateness of importing labour may give the impression that labour importation is a novel or important departure from existing policy. This is not the case. With little fanfare, professional, managerial, and technical personnel have been routinely admitted for employment for many decades. Since the 1970s domestic helpers have been recruited from overseas without any quota constraint. In the postwar years, Hong Kong have received several waves of large influx of immigrants from Mainland China. Before the 1950s, we had an open border with Guangdong. While receiving immigrants is normal for cities, for obvious reasons, the geographically confined and overpopulated Hong Kong cannot afford this luxury. Importation of workers must be justified on economic and social grounds.

The empirical and analytic results of our analysis lend support to labour importation, in principle at least. Consider first its impact on income and growth. As wage adjustments are not operative, workers will not be relocated by rapidly rising wages to the expanding sectors, and shortages will persist. The various short-term and long-term impacts noted earlier will materialize. Under this circumstance, labour imported at the going wages will not displace any local workers. They only add to output. Obviously they add more to output than their wages due to producers' and consumers' surplus, as well as on consideration of the external costs of prolonged shortage. In cases where the vacancies cannot be filled locally through wage adjustment, because the required skills are not there, or because local workers reject those jobs, labour importation becomes the only alternative to income loss. The importation of domestic helpers provides an excellent illustration. Their presence has released many female workers from household work so that they can participate more fully in the labour force. Many experienced and highly trained wives and mothers can now devote themselves to more remunerative and pleasant jobs. Both these families and the community at large have gained tremendously from this import, in which the basic trade principle of comparative advantage is at work. However, we should also bear in mind the external costs imposed by imported guest workers on the community at large, which justifies a levy on labour importation.

Equity is a legitimate concern with labour importation. Most important, if the vacancies will not be filled by local workers in the absence of labour importation, local workers will not be made worse off. Secondly, the importation should not depress local wages. In principle at least, these issues have been addressed by existing schemes. It also means that careful administrative design and device will be needed to administer the system. This can be justified as we expect shortages to persist. Also, given the large difference between our wage rates and prevailing wages in the sources of our labour import, the parties concerned can be made to bear the administrative expenses.

## ☐ Assistance to Employee Retraining

In 1991 the government initiated an Employee Retraining Scheme which is to be financed by a levy on employers of imported workers. Some pilot projects have been put into operation. The principle of publicly funding the retraining of workers have been questioned on efficiency grounds. The main argument is that the benefits of retraining accrued almost entirely to the employees or employers. If benefits from a specific retraining outweigh the costs, either party, or a third party vendor, will undertake, or organize such retraining. The results of our analysis can be used to counter this line of argument. Firstly, the benefits of filling a vacancy through retraining do not accrue entirely to employers and employees because of taxes and external benefits. Secondly, given wage lag in a period of rising demand, the wages offered by employers will be smaller than the net benefits accruing to them, so it fails to convey to employees the full value of retraining. Thirdly, our data show that labour participation rates of those aged 55 and over are falling steeply while the relatively low participation rate of females aged 35–54 has failed to increase. Given the general availability of jobs, and the sharp decrease in manufacturing employment, they reveal that many displaced workers in that age group have failed to be relocated. So in addition to a labour shortage problem, we may also have a redundancy and skill obsolescence problems among our older workers. This argues for government-sponsored retraining programmes on both economic and social grounds.

# 10

# Internationalization of Population and Globalization of Families

## Paul C. K. Kwong

For over a century, Hong Kong has been a stepping stone for all sorts of "foreign devils" (*Gwailos*) to venture into China. Sadly too, Hong Kong has long been a heart-breaking halfway house for the best and the brightest of China's children, from Dr. Sun Yat-sen to the post-June Fourth dissidents, who are forced to leave that vast motherland of theirs. This chapter on the demographics of Hong Kong is dedicated to the "immigration role" of Hong Kong in both directions. Two of the sensitive issues touched upon in the following pages are (1) the internationalization of the population of Hong Kong, and (2) the rise of "anti-foreign" sentiments in certain quarters of Hong Kong society.

Over the past year, the booming economy of the People's Republic of China (P.R.C.) has attracted thousands of foreign companies to set up beachhead operations in Hong Kong. Still larger in number are existing operations that have extended their reach into China. Along with these movements of companies came thousands of professionals and entrepreneurs from all over the world. Interestingly, many former overseas students from China who, as permanent residents of their former host countries, are taking up professional jobs in Hong Kong. The territory has become the most internationalized city in East Asia.

Globalization of Chinese families proceeds conveniently through Hong Kong. Officially, emigration from Hong Kong has in 1992 reached a

Paul C. K. Kwong is a lecturer in the Department of Sociology, The Chinese University of Hong Kong.

historical high of 66,000 people. Largely unnoticed have been scores of thousands of P.R.C. citizens who passed through Hong Kong to emigrate abroad. Hundreds of thousands of these emigrants have since secured foreign passports, contributing to the spread of the Chinese diaspora (overseas Chinese communities). Finally, thousands of *nouveau riche* Mainland Chinese in Hong Kong, for complex reasons, are also setting their sights on lands far away.

The picture of the identities of the Chinese in Hong Kong is a confusing one. Three controversies over the definitions of nationality and citizenship are intensifying. First, the Britishness of a "British" passport for Hong Kong-born Chinese. Second, the localization of jobs in the civil service. Third, the very definition of a Chinese "national". In all of these, the smell of discrimination (reverse?) is getting stronger in the air. At stake is not just the fate of the varieties of passports for the six million Hong Kong people. At stake too are the rights of employment, schooling, investment, consulate protection and permanent residency in Hong Kong for the tens of millions of "overseas Chinese" who may want to stay in Hong Kong in future.

## ☐ Internationalization

### *People on the Move*

Hong Kong's population is always on the move, to and from all corners of the earth. Her immigration policy freely allows the inhabitants to study overseas, do business abroad, acquire foreign citizenship and return to settle with no questions asked. At the same time, some 77 million people travel through this city of 5.5 million people in 1992. At the time of the 1991 census, a total of 151,833 Hong Kong residents were temporarily away from Hong Kong. The total population was estimated at 5,522,281 persons which did not include the 151,833 absentees, the transients and the Vietnamese migrants. This amounts to almost three absentees for every 100 who stayed on that day of 15 March 1991. This absentee ratio is much higher in the summer. In a typical Lunar New Year, over one million residents would leave the territory, representing close to one-fifth of all residents.

### *Expatriates in Hong Kong*

Former residents of Hong Kong with new foreign passports or permanent residence profoundly determine the nationality make-up of the population and the social character of Hong Kong. I shall call these former residents the "returnees". Many if not most of the returnees do not register with their respective consulate offices. So the figures supplied by the Immigration Department of Hong Kong (see Table 1) do not sufficiently account for all the foreigners in Hong Kong. As of October 1992, the top nine countries with the largest number of expatriates in Hong Kong have a total of 231,100 of their citizens reported. Compared to the year-end figure for 1991 of 195,000, there has been a big jump of 18.5 per cent in ten months.

To what extent was this rapid rise of foreigners caused by the returnees as opposed to the foreign-born nationals? Stanford Miller, Managing Director of KPMG Management Consultants, attributed the rapid growth of the foreign community in Hong Kong to the large crop of foreign companies that have been set up in Hong Kong in the past year. A case in point is that the number of American firms here has increased almost 30 per cent in two years, from 700 to 900 by the end of 1992. He further estimated that only "10 to 15 per cent of the foreign population [in Hong Kong] were emigrants returning to Hong Kong after finding that overseas markets were less attractive." (*South China Morning Post*, 29 December 1992)

Table 1.  Expatriates in Hong Kong by Country, 1980, 1991, 1992

|                  |          |          |          | % change between | |
|------------------|----------|----------|----------|------------------------|------------------------|
| Country          | Oct. 1992 | Dec. 1991 | Jan. 1980 | Dec. 1991–Oct. 1992 | Jan. 1980–Oct. 1992 |
| Philippines      | 90,700   | 72,000   | 10,290   | 26.0   | 881.4  |
| United States    | 24,600   | 21,000   | 10,880   | 17.1   | 226.1  |
| United Kingdom   | 19,200   | 16,000   | 23,490   | 20.0   | −18.3  |
| Thailand         | 19,200   | 17,000   | 6,520    | 12.9   | 294.5  |
| India            | 18,800   | 18,000   | 13,940   | 4.4    | 134.9  |
| Canada           | 17,200   | 15,000   | 3,050    | 14.7   | 563.9  |
| Australia        | 15,000   | 13,000   | 7,600    | 15.4   | 197.4  |
| Japan            | 13,800   | 11,000   | 7,460    | 25.5   | 185.0  |
| Malaysia         | 12,600   | 12,000   | 8,480    | 5.0    | 148.6  |
| Total of above   | 231,100  | 195,000  | 91,710   | 18.5   | 252.0  |

Source:  *South China Morning Post*, 29 December 1992.

## *Place of Birth*

Data from the 1991 census concerning the place of birth of Hong Kong residents show clearly that the population of Hong Kong is rapidly internationalizing. The 1981 census recorded 3.2 per cent of her population (158,100 persons) whose place of birth was outside Hong Kong, China and Macau; the comparable 1991 figures are 60 per cent higher — 4.6 per cent or 255,200 persons (Hong Kong 1991 Population Census, *Main Report*, p. 28). The largest increase has come from the 25–64 adult working-age group, rising from a share of 4.8 per cent to 6.3 per cent of the total population (Hong Kong 1991 Population Census, *Graphic Guide*, p. 31).

One should note that most of this growth can be accounted for by the domestic helpers from Southeast Asian countries; however, in recent years "returnees" have also contributed significantly to this dramatic growth (see Table 1).

## ☐ Reverse Migration (*Wui-lau* or *Hui-liu*)

Increasingly, reverse migration or the return of former emigrants has contributed to the internationalization of the Hong Kong population. To be an emigrant, a Hong Kong resident must have "landed" in a foreign country as a permanent resident. After a length of stay there, from a day to a few years, he or she may return to Hong Kong with or without a foreign passport. As pointed out in an editorial of *South China Morning Post*, the proportion of emigrants willing to return would not be large. The IPM (Institute of Personnel Management) survey in 1990 had found that only 17 per cent Hong Kong migrants with Canadian passports would be "willing" to return (*South China Morning Post*, 13 July 1992).

## *Definition*

If the term "migration" implies an *intention* to stay in a foreign country for good, then the so-called "reverse migration" is a misnomer because the commitment of the returnees to stay in Hong Kong permanently (*regardless* of the developments of the 1997 turnover) is impossible to establish. If further, the term requires giving up the citizenship that the migrants have acquired abroad, then few returnees would irrevocably do so at present. By this harsh definition, hardly anyone would qualify. The word "returnees" as used here is a liberal one: they are simply former Hong Kong emigrants and students who return to Hong Kong and stay indefinitely.

## Numbers and Trends

Contrary to the supposedly big flood of return migration, the actual documented cases of foreigners "leaving to live in Hong Kong" have been minimal. For example, *South China Morning Post* reported that in the year ending July 1992, 252 Australians moved to Hong Kong; and a further 302 arrived between July and September in the same year (*South China Morning Post*, 14 January 1993). Perhaps these are Australia-born Australians. It seems then the order of magnitude of the inflow from Australia, Canada, the United States (U.S.) and the United Kingdom (U.K.) numbers only in the thousands, certainly not hundreds of thousands.

Regarding the number of returnees, the direct evidence comes from two territory-wide surveys conducted by the government. The General Household Survey (GHS) conducted during the first quarter of 1992 found that an estimated 43,000 persons have returned from overseas between 1982 and 1991. An earlier survey for the first quarter of 1990 established an estimated level of only 24,000 for 1980–1989 (*Hong Kong Standard*, 5 March 1993; *Wah Kiu Yat Po*, same day). Obviously, these numbers pale in the face of the cumulative number of emigrants from 1980 to 1992: 450,300. Furthermore, many overseas Hong Kong students, who are not counted in the above figure, became emigrants after completion of study. The 1992 GHS survey found that merely "200 [persons] have returned over the last two years" (translated from *Wah Kiu Yat Po*, 5 March 1993).

It is not known what proportion of the respondents in the GHS are foreign *passport* holders (citizens) as opposed to permanent residents. So it would be misleading to report a "returning rate" *per se*, as did some local newspapers and magazines. For example, pro-China daily *Wen Wei Po* reported on 20 May 1993 a "70 per cent rise" of returning rate of Hong Kong emigrants. It is common knowledge that most of the people who come back to Hong Kong are returning students, not "reverse migrants" by the definition stated above. In any case, the apparently rising number of returnees has not reversed the trend of emigration.

Other than the GHS surveys, the other source of data on returnees has been the annual poll of companies by the IPM. The 1992 survey of 135 large companies (half of which employing over 200 persons) found that between January and June 1992, 430 employees (out of a total of 80,000) left their jobs for emigration purpose. Conversely, returnees totalled only 63 persons, giving thus a ratio of 14.7 returnees per 100 emigrants. The earlier figures for 1987 and 1988 (see *The Other Hong Kong Report 1990*, p. 326) were 8.2 and 8.5 respectively (*Wah Kiu Yat Po*, 5 April 1993; *Hong Kong Economic Times*, 20 May 1993).

This higher ratio of 14.7 confirms the general impression that more professionals are returning to Hong Kong in recent years. One of the largest moving company in Hong Kong and the most popular one among the Chinese migrants, Asian Express Packing Company, revealed that inbound business has increased about 50 per cent since 1991. By April 1992, 12 containers (representing 220 to 250 customers) per month are arriving from overseas. Most of the customers are emigrants to Canada and Australia under the independent and business categories (*Pai Shing Newsweek*, 30 April 1993, p. 26). If the firm's market share is one half of the returnee-moving business, then an annual total of 6,000 Hong Kong Chinese families would be on the way back to Hong Kong. From the same company it has been revealed that the outbound business has stayed at about 600 orders (families) a month. Assuming a market share of 70 per cent, then about 10,000 Chinese families (not including the "mere landing" im-migrants who keep their household effects in Hong Kong) are packing to leave this year. Roughly then, the inbound-outbound ratio would be six to ten for the year of 1993.

The absolute number of returnees is clearly rising. Does this imply a halt of emigration tide in Hong Kong? The answer is no. Apart from the outbound estimates just noted, the IPM survey found that the annual rate of emigration for 1992 had *gone up* 16 per cent in a year: from 0.91 emigrating employees per 100 staff members in 1991 to 1.06 in 1992. In contrast, the figure for the year of 1989 was 0.8. This means that the emigration rate of employees three years after 1989 was actually 33 per cent higher. IPM's trend of the emigration ratio shows that it rose 100 per cent in the year after June Fourth, dropped in 1991, and then rose again in 1992. Among the 20,000 turnovers in 1992, the share of emigrants was 4.23 per cent, a slight decrease from 4.51 a year ago. Compared to the share of 3.30 per cent in 1989, the 1992 share was 28 per cent higher.

According to the Principal Investigator of the IPM survey, Sara Tang, a more worrisome trend was the fact that more than 50 per cent of those departed were experienced managers and professionals. This is a level higher than either 1990 or 1991 (*Hong Kong Standard*, 20 May 1993). My interpretation is that when previously junior staffers have been made "senior", some too would emigrate soon after.

What all these figures mean is that emigration of better-qualified staff in larger firms has continued to rise, amidst a quicker pace of overall staff turnover. The threat of massive emigration has remained real. This threat has not been lessened substantially by the rising flow of returnees.

## *Reasons for Returning to Hong Kong*

Employment and racism are the two main "push" factors that underlie the rise of returnees. Economic opportunities in China and Hong Kong are the "pull" factors, in spite of the unsettled political situation. Sustained recession in North America, Australia and the U.K. has made life very hard for many hopeful Hong Kong immigrants. A survey in March and April of 1992 in Toronto (sample size being 400 of which 280 were Hong Kong migrants) by the Chinese Information and Community Services (CICS) found that 40 per cent of new Hong Kong immigrants were out of a job for one or more years; 45 per cent were jobless for six to twelve months. Among those who arrived after 1989, 24 per cent were still unemployed at the time of the survey. The overall unemployment rate of the Chinese community in metropolitan Toronto was much lower, at 13 per cent. Finally, three quarters of those who got work were "stuck" in "ethnic jobs".

The reasons for the dismal prospects are many: racial discrimination disguised as cultural differences, jealousy of wealthy immigrants, over-qualification, unrecognized qualifications, and little demand for their skills due to recession. Perhaps the most absurd reason was that Hong Kong immigrants were "workaholics", as reported by Robyn Iredale of the University of Wollongong based on findings of a survey of 55 Australian firms (*South China Morning Post*, 7 October 1992). Adverse employment conditions accorded just 80 per cent of the CICS respondents with full-time jobs and 20 per cent part-time jobs. Some 20 per cent of those surveyed worked in all-Chinese speaking firms while two-thirds were engaged in fields "totally different from ... [what they had] done before". Fully 60 per cent settled for jobs of lower status. The take-home pay after tax was low in comparison with Hong Kong families: HK$9,600 a month among a quarter of all those surveyed.

The bright side was that the respondents who had jobs said they were happy with the working environment and with their co-workers (*South*

*China Morning Post*, 23 October 1992). Many who had no jobs or had unsatisfying jobs were unhappy and longed to return to Hong Kong. They were in a bind because they realized that returning to Asia alone would be at the expense of family life; yet if they returned as a family, the cost would be very high. A large number of them do take the plunge and have returned.

## Stability

How "stable" are the returnees? What impact would they exert if they all leave Hong Kong suddenly? This sensitive question has been analysed in my chapter on emigration in *The Other Hong Kong Report 1990* (especially pp. 316–28). In the last three years, scattered reports in magazines and newspapers have conveyed an impression that the situation will be volatile in the next few years. Anecdotal evidence suggests that (1) people in business are more likely to return than professionals; that (2) married males in their prime years typically return alone and commute across the oceans to meet family members; that (3) wives and children stay abroad; that (4) they most likely would keep their spacious home abroad; and that (5) most of them would give themselves three to four years to accomplish one mission: "Make as much money as possible, and then either stay after 1997 to make more money or pull out from Hong Kong and China." A closer exploration of the psychological state of two ideal types of returnees is in order: those who returned alone are called "lonely cowboys" and those who returned with families are the "returning swallows".

### Lonely Cowboys

As mature returnees in their thirties and forties, few returnees regain their former positions and salary levels after they come back. Many change careers outright. Among those who choose to start afresh, the pattern of change has been towards careers in finance, real estate, marketing and China trade. Their careers are to be built on both sides of the China–Hong Kong border. Under pressure to make it again at middle age (35 being considered to be the onset age), they would be willing to venture far afield. They would labour hard to make good use of their experience and connections gained abroad. Being around or slightly off the peak, they would begin by "following the trail" set by their friends who did not emigrate or who did emigrate but returned long time ago. The more ambitious among the pack look forward to amassing sufficient capital and expertise to launch their own ventures some time in future.

Risky and exciting as these ventures may be, the toll exacted from these lonely venturers is high. As an "executive recruiter" (head-hunter) guessed it, "one tenth of the returnees with families overseas" ended having a divorce (*Hong Kong Standard*, 27 January 1993). Figuratively speaking, the "astronauts" could be blown into pieces in the family space.

*Returning Swallows*

Like the seasonal birds travelling in family formation, these relatively young returnees come back as a family whole. The heads of family are demographically similar to the "lonely cowboys" characterized in the preceding section. The scenarios are by and large similar. Although they enjoy an emotional cushion provided by the close family, the stress upon them is no less great. Many returning families have suffered enormous financial losses resulting from the migration cycle. A four-way jeopardy has been described: selling their former Hong Kong flats at a low price, buying houses abroad at a high price, selling or renting them out at loss before returning to Hong Kong, and now finding themselves not being able to afford the astronomically high real estate prices in Hong Kong. A loss of three quarters of their pre-emigration wealth has been confided (*Pai Shing Newsweek*, 30 April 1993, p. 32).

Education for children is a big hurdle to overcome. The older kids usually cannot get back to the public schools because of the language barrier — for, among other deficiencies, they cannot compose Chinese essays anymore. Neither are they competitive anymore *vis-à-vis* their local classmates who have been conditioned to study hard and take gruelling competitive examinations. In terms of financial capital and human capital, many a returnee are resigned to a reality that they have suffered losses on both fronts. Confronted with bottom lines like these, not too many settled immigrants would, or could afford to, move the whole family over. Relatively small total enrolment in the International Schools in Hong Kong testifies to the extent of this "educational constraint". A case in point is the Canadian International School (CIS) which was established in 1987 by the Chinese Canadian Association (H.K.) Limited. The membership of the Association in 1993 was "200 to 300" and the school enrolment was "more than 200". Of these, 65 per cent were Canadians and the rest were from 12 countries (*Hong Kong Standard*, 28 January 1993). This suggests that roughly 150 Canadian kids were enrolled in CIS. If the situation in other International Schools is similar, then the number of the offsprings of returned migrants would total approximately in the thousands for the whole territory. Granted some youngsters do manage to return to "mainstream" public schools, their whole lot would still be dwarfed by the 1.2 million locals under 20 years of age who are studying full-time (*Hong Kong Population Census*, Main Tables B4).

*Allegiance*

If, over the next few years, the redeeming value of making fast money does not compensate for the burden of losing face, lowering living standard, or breaking up a family, then the propensity to leave Hong Kong would rise naturally. Much like "hot financial capital" on the flow, Hong Kong professionals are "hot human capital" that collectively recognizes no sovereignty boundaries. The political allegiance of Hong Kong immigrants to Australia, Canada, the U.S. and the U.K. is a pragmatic one. Although they support human rights causes and although they identify with China's current reforms, they have no illusion about the political system in China to change fundamentally any time soon. Passports in hand and links "back home" maintained, making deals is the order of the day, not local politics or patriotic involvements.

## ☐ Emigration

The importance of Hong Kong emigrants to the world could be easily understated. The role of Shanghainese entrepreneurs in the post-1949 development of Hong Kong has given us a valuable clue about this importance. In the present age of information, says microelectronics journalist George Gilder (Fellow at Harvard's Kennedy School of Government), "As the [semiconductor] chip reorganizes industry and commerce, so also will it reorganize the powers of states and nations.... The great liberator in the quantum economy is the mobility of mind.... A key to competition in the global economy will be who wins the hundreds of thousands of skilled workers and entrepreneurs now leaving Hong Kong." (p. 370 of his 1989 book *Microcosm*)

The three main developments affecting emigration from Hong Kong during 1992–1993 were (1) the implementation of the British Nationality

(Hong Kong) Act; (2) the decrease of intake of immigrants by Canada and Australia; and (3) the low responses to the business immigration schemes offered by foreign countries. During the year there was also a growing trend of "emigration" of Hong Kong residents to Mainland China.

## The British Passports

After the world-tormenting events in June 1989 in China, the U.K. hastily formulated a measure to keep the "key personnel" in Hong Kong by promising them full British passports and right of abode, whether or not they would settle in Britain after 1997. At the time of the announcement of the British Nationality (Hong Kong) Act of 1990, the British and Hong Kong governments hinted that "up to 225,000" full British passports for Hong Kong people would be issued. The only hard figure printed on the legislation was "50,000 heads of households". An average family size of 4.5 persons was imputed in that Act. By the end of 1992 when the statistics of the first batch of successful British Nationality (Hong Kong) passports are compiled, the actual family size of each application was 2.8 which was only 62 per cent of 4.5. This prompted the Chairman of the Legco Subcommittee on Nationality, Legislative Councillor Emily Lau Wai-hing, to accuse the U.K. of cheating Hong Kong people. She said, "Hong Kong [is] sold sadly short over passports." (*South China Morning Post*, 1 January 1993 and *Ming Pao*, 30 December 1992)

Family size figures aside, suspicion arose when it was reported that the British and Hong Kong governments somehow managed to register only 16,270 heads of households by the end of February 1993. This poor interim result fulfilled only 41 per cent of the planned quota of 39,400 for Phase I which will end in December 1993. The success rate was low. In fact the rejected cases outnumbered successfully registered cases by a ratio of three to two. The statistics by the end of 26 February 1993 stood as follows: 24 per cent of the 66,511 applicants have registered, and two more per cent are waiting to do so. Some 30 per cent have been interviewed but not yet "recommended" while another 4 per cent are the borderline cases. Some 40 per cent of all applicants failed — 37 per cent being rejected and 3 per cent invalid or withdrawn (*Hong Kong Economic Journal*, 26 February 1993).

Confronted by the poor response to the scheme, Hong Kong government officials patched up by encouraging those rejected in the first instance to try again. The government offered that in Phase II it would reallocate the quotas and readjust the requirements in order to take in more qualified people (*Hong Kong Standard*, 21 August 1992). But as Emily Lau eloquently charged, racism of U.K. politicians had to be blamed for giving so few passports in the first place. Besides, the U.K. should not have treated non-ethnic-Chinese Hong Kong residents so cruelly by excluding them from the scheme, she said (*South China Morning Post*, 3 January 1993 and *Ming Pao*, 30 December 1992).

Judging from the declared objectives of the 1990 British Nationality (Hong Kong) Act, I would say that so far the scheme has been a flop and a face-losing débâcle at that. First, the volume of applications was much smaller then expected. The cumbersome procedures give prospective applicants an "unfriendly" feeling. A complex and complicated application form has been widely blamed for the low rate of form submission. Second, many highly qualified applicants that the British government might have wanted to attract did not bother to apply. For example the category "Managers" was 16 per cent undersubscribed (*Hong Kong Standard*, 1 January 1993). Third, a good proportion of those applicants who succeeded probably already have other foreign passports available to them or to their close kin members anyway. Fourth and consequent to the third, because of the (deliberately?) long period of implementation, the scheme's avowed original purpose of stabilizing Hong Kong people would have been defeated.

The sentiment of the local people, polled four years ago, was that the U.K. had been the least desired English-speaking country for emigration. This sentiment is still prevalent. In social occasions when emigration is mentioned, a full British passport (not the British Dependent Territory Citizenship, BDTC or British National (Overseas), BNO) holder might remark that, "It is just a backup passport." His or her true destination remains to be Australia, Canada, or the U.S. Scathing remarks about "the Brits" abound these days, surprisingly out of the mouths of the sons and daughters of the colony now made good on their own hard-earned merits. Having amassed wealth and turned cosmopolitan, these young and middle-aged professionals and entrepreneurs can afford to be "reverse snobs". When the chips are down, the U.K., in the hands of over-calculating politicians, will lose out in the post-1997 era. Not only will the U.K. miss out on the Hong Kong talents and their money, but also their hearts and minds. By then the former colonists would have few "grateful" allies in the civil service and the private sector.

## *Emigration to Canada, Australia and the United States*

Confusing statistics of emigration are difficult to interpret. A study by a historian from the University of British Columbia documented that 14,500 immigration applications were filed in 1991 by people who had Hong Kong identity cards, of whom 16 per cent had lodged the applications in places outside Hong Kong. In other words, for every five Hong Kong residents who applied in Hong Kong to emigrate to Canada, there was one who filed somewhere else on the globe. A popular route to Canada was via the U.S. (*Ming Pao*, 16 December 1992). The point is that, quite a large number of Hong Kong travellers end up being immigrants abroad. To get a fuller picture of Hong Kong's emigration, therefore, the emigration figures announced by the Hong Kong government must be adjusted upward.

### *Canada*

Arrivals at Canadian ports for 1991 numbered 22,147 persons, down 24 per cent from 1990. The great majority of the recent immigrants has been family reunion and independent cases. For 1991, only 3,583 (16 per cent) were entrepreneurs while 246 (11 per cent) were investor migrants (*South China Morning Post*, 8 August 1992).

If one subtracts the 22,147 arrivals from the 26,647 visas issued in 1991, then the difference of 4,500 are "unused" visas which reflects the degree of immigrants' hesitation to "land" before the validity of the immigration visa expires. Although most visa holders will eventually land, the time lag will be influenced principally by the economic prospects on the two coasts of the Pacific Basin. Because of recession in Canada and the booming Hong Kong–China region, immigration applications to Canada had fallen by 40 per cent for the first five months of 1992 (*Ming Pao*, 8 June 1992).

### *Australia*

A 50 per cent fall was also reported for Australia in the third quarter of 1992. For the year 1991–1992 the number of Hong Kong emigrants to Australia was 13,339, down 23.6 per cent from the peak of 17,451 in 1990–1991. The projected decline was much higher for 1992–1993: only 5,266 visas which roughly equal the 1986–1987 level (Australian Consulate General, Hong Kong).

## The United States

The "safety net" scheme which was announced in 1990 would allow Hong Kong employees working in American firms in the U.S. (not Hong Kong) to get American permanent residence. The response has been lukewarm. By December 1992 less than one half of the 36,000 quota has been filled (*Hong Kong Standard*, 4 December 1992). Nevertheless, it is expected that many more applications under this scheme will be filed during 1993 when the U.S. economy recovers and more U.S. firms do business in China.

## Other Countries

Between 1987 and 1992, New Zealand saw a thirty-fold rise in immigration from Hong Kong, from 188 "resident visa" for the year ending March 1987 to 5,411 in the 12-month period ending March 1992. South Africa became a more popular destination for immigrants from Hong Kong and Taiwan. That country took in 37 households in 1989, 617 in 1991, and 800 for the first nine months of 1992 (*South China Morning Post*, 4 August 1992). Although fewer scandals about passport-for-sale have been publicized in the last year, it is doubtful that such shadowy operations in Hong Kong have been eradicated. Current wisdom is that many of them have by now coagulated into an international network. In addition to the 66,000 persons who physically left Hong Kong, an unknown number of people who have gotten immigration visas or right of abode, like the U.S. and U.K. schemes described above, have chosen to stay in Hong Kong for the moment. Some of the early receivers of the U.K. scheme did "land" in the U.K. during 1992–1993. Most of the significant increase is, however, probably due to emigration to other countries.

## Business Migrants

From February 1993, any business immigrant to Canada must invest at least a quarter of a million Canadian dollars (C$100,000 more than in 1992) in a pre-selected province and be willing to stay there longer than before. The invested funds must be frozen for five years, two years longer than under the old regulations (*South China Morning Post*, 3 January 1993). These added restrictions were precipitated by many complaints about abuses of the business immigration scheme. For instance, an official survey in 1992 discovered that 85 per cent of the investment schemes failed. Five investment funds patronized by Hong Kong and Taiwan businessmen folded and were under investigation by the Manitoba government (*Ming Pao*, 18 January 1993).

Similar abuses have also been reported in Australia and New Zealand. Tightened requirements practically stopped the Australian intake of entrepreneurs. For the year 1989–1990, some 6,389 business persons from Hong Kong, Taiwan, and Macau qualified under the old regulations; but by November of 1992 only 42 persons had been approved under the new regulations (*South China Morning Post*, 15 November 1992). New Zealand had 581 business migrant cases in the second half of 1991 but only 59 during the next six months (*South China Morning Post*, 4 August 1992).

As for the U.S., a new scheme targeting at wealthy Hong Kong businesspersons turned out to be almost a complete failure. It offered a quota of 10,000 wealthy people, investing US$1,000,000 each, to have the "green cards". The scheme only attracted twelve applications from Hong Kong by November 1992. According to the U.S. Immigration and Naturalization Service just one application had been approved by mid-November 1992.

*Moratorium*

Many "immigration consultancy" companies closed for lack of business during 1992–1993. Industry commentators speculate that as 1997 approaches, their business would pick up again, perhaps in 1995 and 1996 (*South China Morning Post*, 15 November 1992). The current lull in the volume of emigration reflects a moratorium rather than cessation of outflow of the determined emigrants. Fragmentary evidences render partial support to this scenario. Take the case of Australia. Although immigration applications plummeted, the number of visitors from Hong Kong and Macau has jumped 35 per cent from 41,302 to 55,750 in 1987–1992. It should be noted that the visitor category excludes students, other temporary residents, and travellers in transit. Many visitors could well be making use of the trips to prepare for emigration later; for example, to buy a house for investment. A certain degree of a "substitution effect" could be reasonably assumed to be operating, for instance, as a global diversification strategy among members of a family. In this context, then, the number of visitors would be a leading indicator of chain migration in future years.

## ☐ Students as Potential Migrants

### *Visas for Overseas Studies*

I have discussed the concept of potential migrants in *The Other Hong Kong Report 1990*. It suffices here to update some statistics (see Table 2).

The total number of Hong Kong students leaving for overseas studies had reached a peak of 21,000 in 1990 and then steadily declined to 16,000 in 1992. These levels represent a very high level of exodus of Hong Kong high school students because, by comparison, only 10,570 full-time degree places were available in Hong Kong in 1991. Coinciding with the decline of overseas visas, enrolment in Form Six and Form Seven increased from 36,370 in 1990 to 47,560 in 1992. The two main reasons for this development are: (1) there had been a rapid expansion of tertiary education in Hong Kong, and (2) it is much cheaper to go to college here than abroad. Besides, most local students probably enjoy the colourful lifestyle and the family ties in Hong Kong.

Britain's Right of Abode scheme will bring more local students to study in the U.K. for the next few years. Most of the successful applicants are heads of households in the childrearing age group. It is projected that many such parents will send their young children to boarding schools in the U.K. ahead of 1997.

### *Returned Students as Potential Migrants*

At the crossroads of "staying or leaving" in the next four years are a huge number of former overseas students aged in the mid-twenties through mid-thirties. Many were too young to emigrate in the mid-1980s when

Table 2. Number of Hong Kong Student Visas for Overseas Study, 1990–1992

|  | 1990 | 1991 | 1992 |
|---|---|---|---|
| United Kingdom | 4,349 | 4,428 | 4,408 |
| United States | 5,840 | 5,866 | 5,410 |
| Canada | 5,681 | 4,541 | 3,583 |
| Australia | 5,108 | 3,591 | 2,866 |
| Total | 20,978 | 18,426 | 16,267 |

Source: Australian Education Centre, *Country Report*, 1993.

the first wave of "1997 emigrants" appeared. By 1991, many were unqualified for the British Nationality Scheme primarily because of the dismal number of quotas and the tight requirements of age and experience. Unmarried and ambitious, these are the Cantonese-speaking, bilingual, young professionals who find themselves suddenly amidst the whirlwind of the post-June Fourth economic bonanza in South China. Replacing their older and more senior colleagues who vacated their posts due to emigration, these young and coming returnees have become indispensable work horses in countless joint ventures in China. Their drive and stamina make up for the lack of experience. These young warriors take heart from the lessons of the many war stories told to them by the older, seasoned China traders. With sharp eyes and quick minds, these are the younger generation of entrepreneurs who are tempered to suit the volatile market of China today.

It is hard to guess how many of them would emigrate because they are highly differentiated in personal and political orientations, e.g. their views on democratization in Hong Kong and China. Having marched in the June Fourth rallies at a more tender age, and having cried anti-corruption and anti-authoritarianism slogans from the bottom of their hearts, many of these uncommitted but quickly maturing youths have remained idealistic (innocent) and democratic at heart. The ideals that they might have cherished are subdued but not dashed. Being restless, many change jobs frequently. After a few years, some would settle down to start a family. Most would hesitate to have children.

After 1997 if the situation turns nasty (e.g. being squeezed out by the P.R.C. interests or forced to be intolerably corrupt in order to survive), then with enough money and connections abroad, they too would beat retreat and ride the waves overseas. In short, the number of the returned students who may emigrate depends not only on the future economy *per se*, but also on the business and social environment of the future Special Administrative Region (SAR) society.

## ☐ Emigration — Mainland Bound

Seeing the inevitable merging of Hong Kong with China, big flocks of Hong Kong professionals have opted for an "Early Bird" strategy. "*Shun-lau*, follow the flow" is a recent Cantonese vernacular designating an emergent migratory trend — heading north into Mainland China to live and work there. For decades the dominant direction of flow has been southbound: from China to Hong Kong. Nowadays, many Hong Kong residents are flowing in an opposite direction. Complex forces have been at work:

1. **Political Forces**
    i.  Stepped up involvement of China's state and collective enterprises in Hong Kong's real estate and security markets, thereby causing increased two-way flow of personnel;
    ii. Lax control of Hong Kong entrepreneurs in China many of whom (have been forced to) bribe their way to exploit business opportunities in untapped markets hitherto inaccessible to outsiders.

2. **Economic Forces**
    i.   Rising demand for Hong Kong professionals, managers, and designers to run businesses in China's fast-growing cities as well as in the slower but newly opened interior regions;
    ii.  Moving of labour-intensive manufacturing away from Hong Kong to China in order to make use of the lower factor costs inland;
    iii. Improving infrastructure in China such as telecommunications, transport and banking, thereby facilitating efficient exchange of goods, funds, information and personnel.

3. **Social and Demographic Factors**
    i.   Ageing of the Hong Kong population and the "home-coming" of retired workers from Hong Kong to China because of lower health cost in China, especially for chronic diseases and long-term care;
    ii.  Surging supply of houses in China at a fraction of Hong Hong's exorbitant prices, attracting middle and lower-middle class families to diversify their real estate portfolio;
    iii. Relaxed travel restrictions on Chinese citizens to Hong Kong, leading to renewal of contact among relatives and friends, and to instrumental ties for joint ventures;
    iv.  Shortage of marriage partners and high cost of "entertainment (read sex)" in Hong Kong and abundant low-cost supply of such in China;
    v.   Increasing job-related trips to China by Hong Kong workers who stay there for a long period of time, thereby breeding new forms of "*yi-nai* (concubine)" homesteads across the border.

## *Work, Get Married, and Have Kids in China*

To illustrate the last development sketched in the preceding paragraph, let
me summarize the results of three enquiries about workers who work and
marry in China. The 1988 GHS carried out from October to December 1988
found that there were 52,300 Hong Kong residents aged 15 and above who
had ever worked in China during the past twelve months. The group
represented 1.9 per cent of the labour force. The percentage was higher for
males than females, 2.6 per cent versus 0.5 per cent. Of the 52,300 persons,
42,300 (81 per cent) were still working in China at the time of the survey,
representing 1.5 per cent of the labour force. Some 77 per cent were
employees, the rest being employers or self-employed; 43 per cent were
production and transport workers, 26 per cent professionals and managers,
20 per cent sales, and the rest clerical and service workers. Half of these
respondents started working in China in 1987 or later. Six-tenths of the
workers visited China ten times or more over the last twelve months, staying for a median period of three days (GHS Special Topic Report No. 6).

A similar GHS survey was conducted in 1989. After a year there were
proportionally more employers than employees who worked in China.
There was a higher percentage of workers in the sales occupation and
personnel in the tertiary sector. In terms of pattern of visit and stay, the 1989
survey found the respondents visiting China more frequently than before —
65 per cent versus 60 per cent having been to China ten times or more. They
were staying longer too — 3.4 days versus 3.0 days as the median (GHS
Special Topic Report No. 7).

In order to find out the number of people in Hong Kong who have
spouses in China and the fertility of these families, the Census and Statistics
Department initiated a special topic about these in its GHS of April to June
1991. This representative sample yielded an estimate of 95,200 Hong Kong
residents who had married in China and had their spouse living there. Most
were older persons who came to Hong Kong many years ago; 6 per cent
were under the age of 30, and 29 per cent were aged between 30 and 39.
Some 93 per cent were men.

There has been a rising tide of "China brides". Whereas 12.3 per
cent and 14.7 per cent of the 95,200 persons were respectively married
during 1976–1980 and 1981–1985, many more (27.5 per cent) did so
between 1986 and the first half of 1991. Most of the grooms (56 per cent)
have had attained primary school education, while only 3 per cent had
post-secondary and university education.

## Fertility

The average number of children that these 95,200 persons have had was 2.1 and about four-fifths of these children are still living in China. Many couples who live together in Hong Kong have their children residing in China. It is estimated that 149,500 Hong Kong residents have 310,200 children living in China; their median age was 25. Some 10 per cent are under five years of age, 10 per cent are 5–9, 9 per cent are 10–14, and 11 per cent are 15–19. Altogether, a total of 12,450 children and youths with parent(s) in Hong Kong are residing in approximately 10,000 households all over China (GHS Special Topic Report No. 8).

## Cohabitation

The foregoing summary of the GHS results pertain to long-term relations that have been entered into mainly by Hong Kong working-class people through matchmakers. The children and spouses they have, if legitimate, are entitled to enter Hong Kong after 1997. The opening of China since the early 1980s has since sprouted an unknown number of sexual deals that have been struck between willing partners. "*Ah-yi*", literally "The Number Two" (concubine), phenomenon is well known in Hong Kong. Many transport and manufacturing workers operating in China who cannot afford high-price prostitutes and who do not want to be caught by the Chinese police, simply set up secret households by renting flats (units) in small towns near the main highways and sea ports. The cost is low. At HK$2,000–3,000 a month, many a pseudo-husband are supporting young women from inland China.

The pattern of alternative nesting of professionals and managers has not been blatantly portrayed in the press, though extramarital and commercial sex are known to be widespread. No one knows how many of these relationships, open or not, would be maintained after 1997. It is conceivable that a considerable number of them might solidify into permanent households inside China. Fleeing the high cost of living and the stressful "Animal Farm" life-world in future Hong Kong society, quantities of locals and returnees alike might bail out and move to live in China. For, beckoning inland is a seducing chance for a new lease of life in business and family.

If one looks farther into the future, the possibility of a kind of "population swapping" does exist. Underlying this movement of population are the following assumptions: one-party politics would dominate in the SAR government of Hong Kong; the rule of common law would deteriorate; the immigration of the rich and the powerful from China would not be stopped; inflation due to wealth effects would run unabated; and finally, social development in the SAR would be such that life in "Special" Administrative Region (Hong Kong) will be no more special than life in a Mainland city.

Applying the sociological theory of "Relative Deprivation" one would expect that the middle and the lower-class people in Hong Kong would find themselves worse-off *vis-à-vis* the new mainland immigrants whose mentality would be: "It's our turn now after the Brits have gone." The theory would also envisage that the ego and well-being of Hong Kong residents would be boosted significantly if they "return home" to live and do business in China. For sure, though, the great majority would stay in Hong Kong. In fact, many former servants of the colonists will cope quite well. In the future SAR society (Animal Farm?), playing the new rules of the game would improve their lots tremendously.

## ☐ Immigration

### *Vietnamese Boat People*

The most significant development in the year has been the sharp drop in the arrivals of Vietnamese boat people (VBP) and the consolidation of a successful repatriation programme. Whereas the first half of 1991 saw the arrival of over 11,000 VBP, merely seven VBP entered Hong Kong in the same period of 1992 (*Ming Pao*, 20 June 1992). By mid-1992 the total population of VBP in Hong Kong had dropped to a four-year low, at under 50,000. Claiming that the voluntary repatriation programme was working, the head of UNHCR (United Nations High Commissioner for Refugees) office in Hong Kong, Robert van Leeuwen, said that he was confident that all VBP would be repatriated within three years (*Wah Kiu Yat Po*, 22 July 1992 and *South China Morning Post*, 5 July 1992).

### *Illegal Immigrants from China*

At the same time when VBP arrivals by sea seemed to have totally ceased, there had been a rapid rise of illegal immigrants (IIs) from China, primarily construction workers and craftsmen from coastal counties of Guangdong such as Haifeng and Taishan. A significant number of the IIs were IIs into China from northern Guangdong where many Vietnamese have been held in farms. In the first four months of 1993, some 12,400 arrests were made, 45 per cent more than in 1992 for the same period. The 1992 level was doubled. What was worrisome was that many of the arrested persons were repeated offenders: 60 per cent have been arrested once or more, and among them fully one half have been arrested three times or more! The Hong Kong police conceded that the policy of immediate repatriation of IIs had failed to deter them (*Hong Kong Economic Daily*, 10 May 1993 and *Ming Pao*, 1 June 1992). Consequently, prisons in Hong Kong are overcrowded by some 20 per cent, and 36 per cent of the prisons have been filled by IIs (*South China Morning Post*, 2 June 1992 and *Hong Kong Standard*, 31 December 1992).

Risking humiliation and physical harm, the IIs are arriving by sea and land roughly half and half. They are siphoned by well-organized criminal networks to labour in construction sites, factories, and service industry establishments like eateries. Some who cannot find jobs or who fail to adjust to the hard work and fast pace in Hong Kong sneak back to China. Many have been caught *en route* — 643 between January and April 1992, three times more arrests than in the same period of 1991 (*Ming Pao*, 4 June 1992).

While scenes of II raids have become a familiar feature in Hong Kong television news, a largely unnoticed undercurrent has been a huge rise of P.R.C. visitors who overstayed. There were 22,566 such cases in 1991 which mean that 5 per cent of the 440,000 P.R.C. visitors for that year, about 1,880 persons per month. However, since the warnings of stiff fines (HK$5,000 and a two-year prison term), the rate has declined to about 400 persons a month.

Many female overstayers had one goal in mind — to give birth in Hong Kong so that their children would be Hong Kong residents. There were 1,746 births of this kind in 1990; in 1991 there were 2,750; and in the first ten months of 1992, the number reached 3,527 (*Wah Kiu Yat Po*, 11 May 1993). Since the present immigration regulations allow only the babies to stay in Hong Kong but not the mothers, they must sadly go home in China. The braver ones go into hiding and hope for a periodic amnesty. A conservative estimate of such "immigration mothers" is 5,000 (*Ming Pao*, 8 July 1992).

The Immigration Department estimated that altogether approximately 300,000 dependents (mostly spouses and children) of Hong Kong residents are in the P.R.C. After 1997 they would be entitled to reunite with their Hong Kong family members, according to the Basic Law. Some commentators doubt whether they could all come to Hong Kong within a short period of time (*South China Morning Post*, 19 August 1992).

A subject under discussion by Britain and China is how to release the immigration pressure exerted by these people on the SAR government and society after 1997. One proposal has been to increase the daily quota of intake of "one-way" P.R.C. passengers from 75 a day, to say, 100. Furthermore, the theory of chain migration predicts that the "eventual" volume of arrival will be many times more than the initial number of immigrants.

## *Immigration of P.R.C. Professionals*

A final source of P.R.C. immigration is intriguing — they are from North America, Europe, and Australia. These are P.R.C. students who have obtained professional qualifications and stayed abroad long enough to have a permanent residence or citizenship. The Hong Kong Immigration Department has imposed stringent requirements besides skill and experience in order to limit the number of entry of such people, such as being forbidden to work in the civil service, allowing no studies in local institutions, and no job changes other than renewing their original employment contracts. They must have a valid travel document and a reentry visa to those Western countries where they came from (*Ta Kung Pao*, 1 April 1993).

The population of these newcomers is probably in the low thousands. Working in tertiary institutions of learning, the "hongs", and the professions, these much needed talents in Hong Kong will be eligible to become Hong Kong permanent residents in seven years' time. Early cohorts among them would start working in the SAR after September 1997 because relevant regulations were promulgated in September 1990. Having learnt about how Hong Kong works, a number of these early batches of P.R.C.'s overseas students during Deng Xiaoping's open policy era will take over the running of some sectors of Hong Kong society just in time. Also, they will be just in place because some of them are well connected with high places in the P.R.C. and with heavyweights of international capital. In our present context, I would say that these young hopefuls will play the dual roles of internationalization and Sinicization of Hong Kong.

## □ Globalization of Families

In the final analysis, to maintain Hong Kong as an international city, the rule of law and fair play in business and social life must prevail. Important too are public security and a safe physical environment. In the eyes of most of the family heads of the returnees including those from the P.R.C., one way or another, their long-term fate has been basically charted if not sealed. Businesspersons and professionals alike, their families will be globalized. Lingering uncertainties would have prompted them to diversify their family capital (children and wealth), and keep the foreign passports at hand. If their families manage to withstand the trying 1990s and remain intact beyond year 2000, then most of them would eventually settle overseas for good. By that time though, their grown-up children would probably have "globalized" into a confederation of conjugal nuclear families that would be strategically networked in different parts of the world including, of course, Mainland China.

After all, globalization of the family is an acceptable tradition that harks back to the Ming Dynasty six hundred years ago when populations of Guangdong and Fujian emigrated to Southeast Asia and Taiwan *en masse*. Deng and other prominent P.R.C. "Families" (*jiazu*), plus almost all the Hong Kong advisers and planners, have done in various forms and styles too? Namely, to send close kins abroad to get foreign passports or permanent residence, "just in case … "?

## ☐ Conclusion

The door of Hong Kong, though a colony, has always been open to goods, ideas and people, enabling her to prosper by leaps and bounds to become what now she is, a proud, buzzing international city endowed with an internationalized population. In the years leading to 1997 and into the next century, questions that loom large are: Will this internationalized populace be gradually cleansed in favour of the Han race? And will Putonghua, actually a dialect originating from Hebei province, be utilized as an linguistic agent to cleanse the Cantonese dialect out of all major formal discourses in town? Will formal Chinese documentation (*gongwen*) practically replace English as the official written language? What about the filing system?

In short, will there be some disguised forms of "ethnic cleansing" in a broad socio-linguistic sense? Simply, will "two" be purified into "one"? (Ref. the "one country, two systems" promise.)

One wonders whether the door of Hong Kong will remain open to all 24 hours a day? Or will its opening hours depend on the efficiency of the legions of "Ethnicity Inspectors" — akin to their political cousins the

"Through Train Inspectors" — whose job will be enforcing new sets of immigration laws and employment "guidelines"? Will such new laws and guidelines be imposed by powerful organs in Beijing for the purpose of deterring undesirable visitors and forbidding the return of unwelcomed former residents?

By mid-1993 the writing is already on the wall. The deciphered message implies that a gentle form of cleansing is in the making. In a series of exchanges in the press, noted commentator Qi Xin (Mr. Li Yi) and an official of the Security Branch argued over the definition of a "local person", the nationality of Hong Kong residents, and the validity of existing British passports (BNO, BDTC and British Overseas Citizens [BOC]) (*Hong Kong Economic Journal*, 26 April, 2 May, 17 May and 30 May 1993).

The gist of the debate boils down to this. If the post-1997 immigration regulations and localization policies are distinctively racist and linguistically biased, then they would very probably transform "Fragrant Harbour" (Hong Kong) into "Flagrant Harbour". An atmosphere of inhospitality could then remind foreigners of China's former national airline, CAAC. The "new" regulations could be so anachronistic — much more restrictive than the present colonial ones — that they could make the future SAR government a laughing stock the world over.

Parochialization could replace internationalization. The harbingers are those norms and behaviour in society which discriminate people according to (1) racial features and blood relations (*xuetong* or *xueyuan*), (2) languages and dialects, (3) political party affiliation, and (4) vacuous oaths. Concrete examples of (reverse) discrimination are: People who will have an advantage in the SAR will be those who (1) have Han-race Chinese parentage; (2) speak Putonghua, read and write formal documents better in Chinese than in English; (3) are members or close associates of a pro-China political party, and (4) have the audacity to declare sole and exclusive permanent residence in Hong Kong, i.e. having no residence elsewhere.

The threat of such discriminatory regulations to the institutions in society may not be obvious at first thought. For it is entirely possible that the racial and linguistic criteria of screening and dividing Hong Kong people could diffuse to wider spheres of life. Demagogues could agitate concentric waves of "ethnic cleansing" of sorts, starting with the public institutions, then the subvented (government-subsidized) agencies, and then ... By that time the refined criterion of Chinese language proficiency could probably be distinctly in favour of the southbound cadres (*nan-xia ganbu*) from the P.R.C. to take over key positions in government much like the British colonists have been commanding. Local Hong Kong civil servants, though having been promoted as a result of localization now, could be practically replaced for reasons such as failure in an oral Putonghua test, or in a written test on formal Chinese documents (*gongwen*), such as keeping Chinese minutes and following Beijing's filing system.

As the Chinese saying about how to survive in winter goes, "If your lips are severed, your teeth will be chilled." Once the expatriates and those Chinese civil servants who are suspected to be British "residuals" are dealt with, the next rounds of cleansing could start in subvented organizations, and later to all those who are on the payroll of government funds.

Of course there always exists an upbeat scenario which would see post-Deng Chinese political and economic stability being restored after minor and short-lived conflicts involving only the top echelons of the P.R.C. government but not any massive protracted regional rivalries bordering on economic warlordism. Confidence would be restored and the stock markets in Hong Kong and China would roar and sustain themselves in the stratosphere. Beijing interference of Hong Kong affairs would be kept to a minimum. Happy days would be maintained and Hong Kong would become inhabitable to all: Communist cadres, patriotic capitalists, Cantonese-speaking local commoners, overseas Chinese and even *Gwailos* of all colours and stripes. Corruption would be low in Hong Kong and in fact her Independent Commission Against Corruption (ICAC) would be emulated all over China, effectively controlling corruption that infests China today. In just a few decades the vast China market would mature and turn healthier each day, and the Greater China (Economic) Region will radiate the hope of the new millennium.

That hope hinges (1) upon keeping Hong Kong's population internationalized, non-racist and non-discriminatory in both immigration, employment and business-related policies; (2) upon removing the last vintage of British colonialism but not instilling a new colonialism with "Chinese characteristics"; (3) upon bringing democracy to the common masses; and (4) upon containing ferments of Han-race chauvinism. Before that kind of millennium is attained, however, transitional problems must be pragmatically handled in order to avert the spectre that minor post-1997 rumblings in Hong Kong would invite rash decisions from Beijing. The group of Beijing-appointed Hong Kong Affairs Advisers and the SAR planners for the future SAR government therefore must devote themselves selflessly for a couple of years to untangle the Gordian knot of internationalization. The danger looms large that Beijing, overpowered by the fear of subversion, would be misled by self-serving Hong Kong politicians and corporate representatives and tragically repeat those Sino-centric and anti-foreign (*pai-wai*) mistakes that had been made in the liberation of Shanghai.

Which path would the two best-known Shanghainese nowadays, Jiang Zemin and Zhu Rongji, be prepared to take Hong Kong? Would it be along the path of further internationalization, or a path of regression to anti-foreignism which will certainly bring the loss of yet another internationalized city, "Paris of the East," *deja vu*?

# 11

# Urban Renewal and the Land Development Corporation

Lai Wai-chung

It has become popular to think that whenever something in the economy goes wrong, or is alleged to have gone wrong, the government should step in and "do the right thing". This may refer to adopting new administrative measures, having better-coordinated policies and, better still, introducing new legislation. Indeed, it is due to this way of thinking, within and without government, that the public sector has become more interventionist and departed from its *laissez-faire* role as an umpire regulating competition in a free market built on private property rights. Government intervention may alter existing contractual rights and obligations between the government and citizens. It is obvious that unless the implications of such alterations are carefully considered, urban renewal schemes may run the risk of destabilizing society both politically and economically, although in principle they may promote environmentally and economically sound policies.

Government intervention in the land market is a case in point. "Urban renewal", in particular, has led to major legislative initiatives cumulating in the Land Development Corporation Ordinance of 1988, which confers on the Land Development Corporation the power to resort to the Crown Land Resumption Ordinance when necessary to acquire private land for profit-seeking development. This chapter gives an overview of the economic nature of urban renewal in general, the past and present urban renewal efforts of the government, and some private property rights issues that pertain to the Land Development Corporation.

Lai Wai-chung is a lecturer in the Department of Surveying, The University of Hong Kong.

## ☐ The Economic Nature of Urban Renewal

Urban renewal or urban redevelopment is a key concept in the specialized disciplines of "urban economics" and "urban planning". In the United States and Western Europe, this concept stands for attempts to rejuvenate derelict urban cores replete with social problems like crime, depopulation, business decline and racial segregation, i.e. the problem of "urban decay". In the so-called "Less Developed Countries", abbreviated "LDC" by development economists, urban renewal may be a euphemism for forceful and massive clearance of urban and sub-urban slums.

Rapid and sustained economic growth and development, the tolerant social culture of Hong Kong and the lack of rigid zoning regulations render "urban decay" in the American or "Less Developed Countries" sense of the word totally irrelevant. In the urban cores of Hong Kong are a high concentration of population and viable business activities which have in the past decade witnessed chronic labour shortages. Admittedly, there are problems of poverty but poverty is fundamentally relative in nature. The problems have been dealt with by well-funded social welfare programmes of the government. Crime rates and social problems in urban Hong Kong are no worse than those in most great cities of the world. In this context, the real object of urban renewal in Hong Kong cannot be regarded as a vehicle to deal with "urban decay" or the phenomena of poverty, but to speed up the rate of redevelopment in order to capture the unexploited development potential permitted under the Building Regulations.

Such a redevelopment process is simply the result of a rational maximization behaviour in land economics. From the point of view of physical environment, this process would inevitably bring to society more and better designed buildings and associated environmental improvements, notably, better street layout, modern transport interchanges and open space. In fact, one of the major reasons for urban renewal is that it can produce comprehensively planned buildings which are compatible with land use structure and are well supported by infrastructure and public facilities. However, it seems that the advocates for urban renewal tend to downplay the real economic incentive for this process. Perhaps, they are afraid that if they openly discuss the economic benefits of urban renewal, they will be criticized politically for "making money". It is therefore not surprising that planning reports on urban renewal always stress the environmental benefits that urban renewal schemes could bring. The reader will be easily persuaded to consider that environmental benefits "explain" the fact of urban renewal. In fact, such benefits are only consequences of urban renewal rather than its cause, which is really floor-space maximization subject to planning and building regulation constraints. The suppression of economic articulation contributes to the neglect of property rights issues.

The land market, like any other markets, is not able to feel the professional "reasons" or "justifications" but only obeys the laws of demand and supply, i.e. financial returns. Why, then, is there the need to seek justification for urban renewal?

The real estate market has in fact always been conducting urban renewal. However, in professional and academic articulation, the received view is that urban renewal means government or government-led duty. Some people believe that the government is better able to carry out urban renewal on two main grounds, namely: (1) urban renewal carried out by the market has a lot of "imperfections" and difficulties; and (2) the government is benevolent and has legal authority — the market is cruel and is not as powerful. "Imperfections", due to the greed for profit, refer to (1) the neglect of social needs (say rehousing needs), and (2) lack of comprehensive design. The difficulties referred to above include (1) fragmented ownership, (2) unclear ownership, and (3) the huge time and financial costs of negotiation in a context of multiple ownership.

So the reasons run: as the government is the spring of justice and the source of social welfare, well endowed with professional expertise and with supreme power in land resumption, government intervention must be the solution to market failure. More sophisticated commentators would add to this line of interventionist thought a host of political and administrative constraints, such as "public consultation" and "political scrutiny" by elected politicians, to make sure that the agencies involved in urban renewal are fair, effective and accountable to the public. Urban renewal then becomes characterized as compulsory urban renewal led by the government. The notion of compulsion in the Less Developed Countries may suggest a scenario of the military and police paving the way for bulldozers. In Hong Kong, which has been governed by "consensus" and consultation, compulsory urban renewal refers to the ultimate resort to legislative and administrative authority, observing always the due process of law, to interfere with or to supersede the private property rights of property owners in designated urban renewal areas.

As soon as the onus of urban renewal is taken up by the public sector, the government becomes bound, as a matter of duty and political expediency, to justify or give reasons for its behaviour. Hence, resources are expended to carry out detailed planning studies to support urban renewal schemes. In the reports of these studies, a few local economic issues (like low income) and social issues (ageing, concentration of singletons, and lack of community facilities) are canvassed. One big question arises: if upon implementation, the inhabitants or shop owners who are found to have suffered from the above economic and social problems, are not the direct beneficiaries of the schemes, then in terms of equity, the renewal schemes can hardly be justified in terms of their espoused social objectives. Compulsory urban renewal schemes as such, very sound and solidly based planning studies and design inputs notwithstanding, are in social terms not much different from urban renewal by the "imperfect" market. Other questions follow: Is government-led urban renewal necessarily more effective than private market solutions? How should effectiveness be measured? How could politicians effectively monitor the renewal agencies? How could professional bodies measure their contribution? Here, we may get some insights from the writings of Ronald Coase, the 1991 Nobel Laureate in Economics.

Coase's "Nature of the Firm" (1937) argues that the firm is an organization that serves to avoid the transaction costs of using the market. Such costs include the costs of the establishment and maintenance of a system of private property rights, costs of information, searching, negotiation, contract formation and enforcement. A government can be seen as a special kind of firm which reduces the transaction costs in the land market. Therefore, a government-led urban renewal scheme which is explicable in terms of Coasian economic reasoning is one which can save more costs than the alternative of allowing private sector to carry out urban renewal, which is predicated on the voluntary participation of property owners. However, whether the particular types of transaction costs of the markets saved are sufficient to offset the transaction costs specific to government bureaucracy, like the time costs absorbed in lobbying, public relations management, public and internal consultation, etc., is a decisive question. If the transaction costs of using the government are smaller than those of using the market, then there are economic grounds for government-led urban renewal. However, as pointed out in Coase's "The problem of Social Cost" (1960), government interventionists tend to ignore the comparative advantages and disadvantages of the market *vis-à-vis* the government. Instead, they presume that government intervention must be more effective. Their general way of thinking is like this:

1.  define socially desirable objectives;
2.  identify the problems of existing institutions (like the market) in meeting the above objectives; and
3.  suggest interventionist measures to solve the above problems.

Whether the costs of the interventionist measures are greater or smaller than those involved in the status quo, whether the same results can be better achieved by a relaxation of existing regulatory measures are seldom considered. It is plainly true that government intervention may be in some circumstances be more cost-effective than market solutions. As far as urban renewal is concerned, the use of resumption power is definitely more cost-effective. Besides, it would be difficult to resist on economic and planning grounds renewal proposals which could convert obsolete, four to five-storey tenement houses to modern 30 to 40-storey and comprehensively designed office or residential complexes. The issue is really that the use of resumption power for profit-making urban renewal ventures violates private property rights. That such violation is justified on economic grounds does not mean that it can be ignored, because private property rights is the pillar of the market economy.

Coase's analysis of market transactions in his "The Problem of Social Cost", as pointed out by Professor Steven N. S. Cheung, presupposes the existence of private property rights. Coase's paper "Nature of the Firm" about the emergence of the firm can also be regarded as an exposition of the evolution of the private property rights system. The costs of endangering the structure of an economic system could be greater than the gain in individual projects. There is a great danger in paying attention to project planning and finance on the one hand but ignoring its implications for the system of private property rights on the other.

The existing literature on Hong Kong's urban renewal, with their recent focus on the Land Development Corporation's performance, is either convivial, if not paternalistic, ultra-radical or fundamentally historio-descriptive, focusing on procedural details, progress matters or the question of natural justice. Rarely are matters of some theoretical substance or analytical rigour invoked. Government-led urban renewal could actually have been evaluated in terms of a whole array of positive and normative factors, including:

1.  tackling of externalities or neighbourhood effects;
2.  provision of more and/or better public goods;
3.  wealth transfer effects and equity issues;

4. financial gain and cost to government;
5. maximization of development potential;
6. the contractual nature of the implementation agency; and
7. impact on private property rights.

"Externalities" or "neighbourhood effects" and "public goods" referred to above are welfare economics concepts. In simple terms, the former concept refers to the spillover effects of a run-down urban area, whereas the latter refers to community services or facilities, which are considered to be better provided by the government due to the lack of profit incentive.

In the following section, the official version of urban renewal efforts as described in the government publication *Town Planning in Hong Kong* (Buildings and Lands Department, 1988) is rewritten and reinterpreted in terms of the above factors. This would set the context for evaluating the economic role and performance of the Land Development Corporation in its attempt to foster urban renewal.

## ☐ The History of Urban Renewal

In 1884 and 1909, the government initiated "slum clearance schemes" in the Tai Ping Shan, Lower Lascar Row and Kau U Fong areas in the aftermath of a plague in these tenement areas. These schemes were epitomes of government solution to the "neighbourhood effects" of congested living environment and public health problems. Few people, however, would question the scientific wisdom of such "aftercare" which understandably was a reaction to major disasters. Indeed, if a preemptive clearance approach had been taken, most of the tenement areas in Hong Kong which were slums in terms of physical appearance by Western standards would have required massive clearance.

In 1959, a layout plan (LH 6/9/IC) for part of Tai Hang Village was prepared combining small lots, realigning lot boundaries and providing other facilities such as a market complex, schools and open space. As a result of strong objections from local residents because of their loss of development rights, the plan was superseded by the Causeway Bay Outline Zoning Plan (LH 6/24B) in which the majority of the original environmental improvement proposals were deleted. The concept of the Tai Hang Village attempt represented a typical physical planning approach to perceived urban problems. In addition to physical means to tackle neighbourhood effects and public goods provision by zoning, a property boundary readjustment proposal was made to provide a framework for zoning. Such an approach was attempted again in the early 1960s with legislative backup for implementation.

In 1964, the Governor appointed a Working Party on Slum Clearance. In 1965, the Working Party recommended the designation of Sheung Wan as an Urban Renewal District within which a specific area was identified as a Pilot Scheme Area. The Town Planning Board was directed to prepare a statutory plan for the Urban Renewal District and the government was given the power of resumption in the implementation of the scheme. A layout plan (LH 3/38) for the Pilot Scheme Area was later completed and adopted in 1970 with a view to upgrading the living environment, improving the traffic circulation of the area and providing necessary local facilities. However, apart from the concern with neighbourhood effects and public goods, the scheme also had an economic motive: to generate revenue through resale of publicly acquired land. Ignoring the effect of wealth distribution, this new dimension can be regarded as socially beneficial, as society would obtain more usable floor space. However, the issue of the infringement of private property rights was left unnoticed.

Acquisition was planned to be carried out in four phases. The first phase was to concentrate on sites required for road-widening and the later phases on the consolidation of land for resale to private developments for commercial/residential development.

Because of the lack of adequate funds, the implementation of the programme took longer than scheduled. The whole project has taken more than a decade to complete. During the process of implementation, the physical as well as the socioeconomic character of the area has changed due to natural out-migration. It is concluded by the government that "while the sociological implications of the project can be a subject for further study, on a physical and environmental basis, the Pilot Scheme Area has generally achieved its objectives." The issue of private property rights has seldom been articulated in the vast academic or professional literature on this scheme.

Following the designation of Sheung Wan as an Urban Renewal District, consideration was given to designate other such areas. However, the concept of "Environmental Improvement Area" (EIA) was introduced to take cognizance of the renewal on financial grounds. Its main objective was to upgrade the environment by providing more land for government and community facilities. Several areas including the former Urban Renewal District outside of the Pilot Scheme Area, Wan Chai, Yau Ma Tei, Shek Kip

Mei, Tai Kok Tsui, Cheung Sha Wan and Kennedy Town were designated as EIAs. In 1973, the overall coordination and programming of EIAs was assumed by the Urban Renewal and Environmental Improvement Coordinating Committee. Resumption powers remained in the background but were under the policy restricted to acquire land for public goods provision. Open space development is the typical example. This restrictive approach is more supportive of private property rights. However, the pendulum began to swing again very soon.

Several years later, the government made another attempt to implement comprehensive renewal schemes by introducing Comprehensive Redevelopment Area (CRA) in selective urban areas, but this time with participation from private owners instead of through government resumption. CRA became known as Comprehensive Development Area (CDA) in the mid-1980s. An example of CDA is the Tsim Sha Tsui "Four Streets" case. The implications of this zoning upon private property rights on land are discussed in the next section.

Almost all the land of the "Four Streets" areas was held on non-renewable leases whose terms were about to expire. Contractually, the government was perfectly entitled to re-enter the land. However, owners of the land were invited to participate in its comprehensive development according to a master layout plan. In spite of this, owners were divided on their individual claims to cost and benefit-sharing. There were also problems on vacant possession because some tenants were unwilling to accept cash compensation where owners were not required to provide them with alternative accommodation. As a result, there has been little progress in the redevelopment.

Another example of the CDA is the redevelopment of the old industrial, storage and godown areas along the waterfront in North Point. As the sites are all owned by single owners, the redevelopment of the sites into residential purposes encountered little difficulties as far as land ownership was concerned, in contrast to the "Four Streets" case. The development, such as Provident Centre, City Garden, Harbour Heights etc. have been developed according to their master layout plans approved by the Town Planning Board.

Almost at the same time when the Environmental Improvement Area Scheme was proposed, the Executive Council agreed to provide financial support to an Urban Improvement Scheme proposed by the Hong Kong Housing Society. The scheme was commenced in 1974 with a view to improve the environment of old districts by redeveloping properties with fragmented or absentee ownership, selling flats produced by the scheme to affected families at discounted prices, and retaining the strong community ties which exist in old districts.

Projects providing over 2,000 flats have been completed under the scheme at Mei Sun Lau, Lai Yan Lau, Oi Kwan Court, Po Man Street, Western Garden, "Six Streets" at Yau Ma Tei, Hollywood Road/Shing Wong Street, Yuk Ming Tower at Third Street and Lascar Court at Lok Ku Road. Ancillary community and recreational facilities are provided in some of these projects. The scheme is ongoing and more projects are expected to be completed in the years to come. However, most projects were piecemeal and fell short of the scale and design of the CDAs.

One of the major problems identified by the government is site assembly. Many potential sites are small and often each site has a large number of owners. Some of these owners are residing aboard, in other cases there are succession problems. As such bargaining with the owner of the last title can prove a formidable obstacle.

Another problem identified is the social concern for rehousing. Many of the older areas are overcrowded and on redevelopment the population in the area may often not increase and in some cases may decrease. The residents have in many cases lived in the area for many years. Their jobs, schools for their children and their family and social ties are mostly located in the same area. Unless rehousing can be arranged in a nearby area, there is understandably strong resistance to any idea of moving out of the existing accommodation even though the present living environment may be unsatisfactory. Equally difficult is the relocation of "incompatible uses" such as service trades and small-scale industries. In many cases, it is not possible to find appropriate sites nearby to accommodate such uses which usually have been seen as creating bad neighbourhood effects on their residential neighbours.

The financial cost of resumption and rehousing is high as sites are often located in urban areas where land prices are high. This inhibits the use of substantial areas of the land for community purposes since these uses have to meet the full costs of land assembly and clearance.

Despite the opportunities offered for substantial profit on redevelopment, owners are often unable to agree upon and implement a redevelopment scheme, sometimes through lack of expertise, often due to their inability to agree on the sharing of costs and profits. The process of resumption is also a cause for delay in the realization of urban renewal schemes. Negotiations over compensation are usually time-consuming.

It is considered by the government that the lack of a single agency able to fund and implement a scheme has meant delays, inflated costs and has unduly complicated and lengthened the implementation process. This led to a consultancy study supervised by the Town Planning Office to look for a new institution to undertake urban renewal more effectively. The proposed Land Development Corporation (officially abbreviated LDC, which is to be distinguished from the abbreviation for "Less Developed Countries") recommended by the study was accepted in principle by the Executive Council in 1985. A provisional Board of Directors was formed in 1987. The legislation for the Corporation was enacted later in the same year. This was followed by the appointment of the formal Board of Directors in early 1988.

The government had expected that the LDC would perform the role of a development agency as a business concern. Its functions would include the selection of suitable areas for redevelopment and cooperation with the government to produce planning briefs for these areas. It would acquire land or property through negotiation with the owners and would, where necessary, seek government assistance to resume properties. Once the development scheme had been agreed and the acquisition negotiated, the LDC would set up a subsidiary company to develop the area. This subsidiary company would raise its own finance from private sources, undertake the development and disposal of the property once development was completed. The LDC would assume responsibility for management and the subsidiary company would be wound up. Clearance would be part of the initial development process and the LDC would be responsible for rehousing and resettling those affected by the development.

Before the formal establishment of the LDC, the Town Planning Office had been responsible for preparing urban renewal plans. A methodology had been devised and a survey carried out to collect relevant data. On the basis of these data, sites suitable for urban redevelopment had been identified. The redevelopment potential of these areas had also been evaluated in terms of their rehousing commitment, ease of implementation, constraints and demographic characteristics. These studies provided information for the LDC in determining initial development priorities. The Town Planning Office, which became the Planning Department in January 1989, has been involved in the planning of the procedural aspects of the Land Development Corporation Ordinance. The Coordinating Urban Renewal Team (now the Coordinating Urban Renewal Section in the Planning Department) was also set up in early 1988, as a special task force in the

Office to coordinate urban renewal matters between the LDC and the government. Studies had been carried out to identify other areas which need to be redeveloped and to ensure that the redevelopment will fit in with the overall renewal planning. The Planning Department would also assess redevelopment schemes submitted by the LDC to the Town Planning Board for approval. Most of the schemes would attract CDA zoning.

Since the inception of the LDC, three development schemes in Hong Kong (Jubilee Street, Wing Lok Street, Queen Street) and two schemes in Kowloon (Argyle Street/Shanghai Street, Shamchun Street) were approved by the Town Planning Board and subsequently gazetted under the Town Planning Ordinance.

Both the Jubilee Street and Wing Lok Street Schemes in Central District are to be redeveloped comprehensively with provision for high-quality office/commercial buildings, open space at prominent locations and associated government/institution/community or "GIC" facilities. The Jubilee Street Scheme was the first LDC development scheme approved by the Executive Council (in May 1991), to be followed by the Wing Lok Street Scheme. The Queen Street Scheme, which is located in Sheung Wan District and will make provisions for a purpose-designed social welfare building, together with commercial and residential development, was gazetted in March 1991.

The redevelopment schemes in Argyle Street/Shanghai Street and Shamchun Street in Kowloon were approved by the Town Planning Board and gazetted in March and May 1991 respectively. The Argyle Street/Shanghai Street Scheme aims to redevelop the area into a commercial centre with a mixture of office, hotel, retail uses, and a landscaped local open space at the hub of Mong Kok. The Shamchun Street Scheme offers opportunities to redevelop the existing Mong Kok Market in site together with a new area community centre, and to resettle the bird stall operators from the existing Hong Lok Street as they will be affected by the Argyle Street/Shanghai Street redevelopment scheme. The Scheme has, however, been abandoned due to successful planning objection.

It is evident that the experience of the government in urban renewal has convinced the policy-makers that the CDA zoning approach, which has proven to be successful in several private-sector schemes, is professionally indispensable. They are also convinced that unitary ownership of land is the prerequisite of success. With most built-up land under multiple ownership, resumption is the ultimate solution. Other than the establishment of a statutory body, which involves itself in redevelopment, and CDA zoning, the LDC concept is not much different from the Sheung Wan Scheme as far as land rights are concerned.

## ☐ Land Development Corporation and Private Property Rights

According to the Land Development Corporation Ordinance, the LDC must be run on the basis of "prudent commercial principles". This legal stipulation has led to a popular feeling that the LDC is but another government initiative towards privatization and is a profit-seeking public corporation in the same position as the Mass Transit Railway Corporation or the Kowloon–Canton Railway Corporation. This idea is not convincing. Firstly, policy or legislation intent is one thing, its viability is quite another. Secondly, the LDC is *not* a private enterprise. A private enterprise has three essential characteristics: (1) freedom in the use of resources; (2) freedom in the acquisition, accumulation and distribution of profits; and (3) freedom in the alienation, acquisition, subdivision and agglomeration of ownership rights. Apart from greater freedom in the use of resources in comparison with an ordinary government department, the LDC has no equivalent freedom in profit distribution or transfer of ownership rights. Thus, its economic behaviour is more properly interpreted as that of a state trading company. This characterization of the LDC might lead to interesting academic research on its cost-effectiveness, and maximization behaviour. The focus here, however, is the savings in transaction costs incurred otherwise by private-sector urban renewal on the one hand and the impact of the LDC urban renewal schemes upon private property rights on land on the other.

The potential economic contribution of the LDC is that it could substantially reduce the transaction costs in land assembly for comprehensive redevelopment, which is better able to capture the unexploited development potential under the constraints of the Building Regulations. The existence of unexploited development potential is a result of the characteristics of the prevailing statutory building regulations: plot ratio control is not uniformly applied to building sites — the larger the site and the more accessible it is, the greater would be the legally permissible Gross Floor Area (GFA). The maximum amount of GFA is achievable for "Class C" sites and the least for "Class A" sites. Because of the piecemeal nature of many of the existing office, commercial and residential development, not too many of them fall within the Class A category. As a result, society has forgone a great amount of achievable GFA. This is often regarded as an "economic waste". This can be shown by examining the development potential of the Central Business District of Hong Kong, Central.

In Central, there is at present a total office GFA of 1,688,200 square metres. In other words, the existing office GFA is only about 59 per cent of the legal maximum. The opportunity cost of this loss is huge. Given a monthly rent for Grade A office of $483.6 per month (average 1992 rental), the lost stream of income would be in the region of $577 million per month. Given this consideration, one would wonder whether there is a genuine need to establish new office centres, which in any case have not been faring well in terms of rent generation. The answer to this question is that the "economic waste" of unexploited plot ratios must be seen as a result of maximization behaviour of developers subject to the constraints of transaction costs. Such costs include not only the costs of building construction but also the costs of land assembly. As market would not be so irrational to forgo a huge amount of uncaptured rent, the reason why there is no massive redevelopment in the form of Class C sites must be because of prohibitive transaction costs for land assembly. That the LDC is able to capture the unexploited plot ratios must be seen in the light that it has statutory power of compulsory acquisition of land. This attempt, however, creates other types of transaction costs. The costs of political interaction between the aggrieved owners and the developers operating in commercial joint venture with the LDC are the commonly discussed types of costs. Above all, there exists the costs of threatening private property rights over land and the more profound issue of the concept of government by consent.

Land in Hong Kong has been allocated in the form of leasehold for private use by auction and competitive tender. Before the advent of statutory zoning control, the lessee thereby acquired private property rights during tenancy period of (1) freedom in land use, subject to the terms against nuisance and obnoxious trades; (2) freedom to derive income from the most profitable use of land; and (3) freedom to alienate, transfer, subdivide and combine interests in land. In return, the lessee pays the "land price", Crown rents and rates, and observes the lease terms.

The lease is a civil contract between the government and the proprietor. Either party may renegotiate the user clauses, tenancy period or premium involved in lease modification. Consent is the basis of such land contracts. To the extent that the leaseholds are allocated in accordance with a pre-specified street layout block plan, an embryonic element of planning is involved. Thus we may conceive the land disposal and management system that has evolved since 1842 as a kind of planning by contract or consent.

The land contract, of course, is subject to the ultimate judgement about the collective good or public interest of society. Such interest naturally covers defence matters, public health and community uses. The government is justified in going back on its promises on land if public interest so dictates. Thus, the government has introduced the Crown Land Resumption Ordinance which enables itself to retake land before the lease naturally expires. In other countries, where freehold is the dominant land tenure, this provision is called eminent domain. However, in respect of private property rights, the government would only resort to resumption where: (1) as a last resort there is no better alternative; (2) the purpose is "public" as interpreted by the law; and (3) due compensation is paid to the party affected.

As far as compensation is concerned, the so-called Pointe Gourde Rule is followed. The rule is that compensation is to be assessed on the basis of the value of the existing use but not the most profitable alternative use (the full opportunity cost of the land). The economic merit of this approach is open to dispute. However, from the stance that the government is not using the land retaken for private purpose, we may argue in terms of social contract theory that the public must be deemed to have consent to this arrangement.

The above model of planning by contract or consent based on Crown leases has in time been undermined by the inception of planning legislation. Planning by consent based on market forces has become superseded by planning by design based on professional judgement. Freedom in land use, and consequentially in deriving maximum income or utility has become constrained by statutory land use zoning. In the extreme case where private land is zoned open space for GIC uses, resumption is lurking in the background. Such infringement of private property rights could of course be justified analytically using externalities or public goods arguments.

Besides, the permissiveness of the zones, with a lot of "always permitted uses" and uses which may be permitted on application to the Town Planning Board, and the toleration of "existing uses" mean that in substance the statutory planning constraint over lease terms is minimal for existing lessees. Above all, statutory control over land use was often introduced at the same time that plot ratio control over the intensity of use was relaxed. However, increasingly, the permissiveness of statutory planning control is tightened by two innovations: (1) the introduction of plot ratio control in town planning zones which are more restrictive than those permissible under the Building Regulations (the lowering of industrial plot ratios in Tsuen Wan in 1991 is a case in point); and (2) the removal of the private property rights of use, subdivision and agglomeration of land rights by the CDA zoning. LDC's use of CDA zoning backed by resumption powers is a serious threat to the institution of private property rights over land.

The use of CDA zoning and the application of resumption power are infringing the private property rights of the proprietors. LDC's schemes in this light are contentious not so much because of the infringement *per se*, which might be justified on the same welfare economics grounds supporting planning by design but because of the facts that (1) they involve the use of the Pointe Gourde Rule in a context where the LDC and her joint venture private-sector partners are intending to reap profits; and (2) the rehousing issue has not been satisfactorily resolved.

That "public purpose" has been explicitly declared by the Land Development Corporation Ordinance to cover urban renewal and that the Pointe Gourde Rule is applicable for such schemes (untested) do not prevent us from holding that the law can be bad on economic grounds! The LDC in their public relations exercises have often resorted to the pathetic argument that they have to (1) subsidize schemes that are not financially viable; and (2) bear business risk and hence there is no guarantee of a profit that could be shared with the proprietors. These excuses beg the question of the global financial credibility of urban renewal by a corporation which is supposedly able to utilize the best of the two worlds: justice of the public sector and profit of the private sector. Would the argument be stronger that the LDC should not run non-viable schemes (like the luxury of the Western Market renovation project) before profits are made? Besides, it is not due to the fault of the proprietors, but for LDC's attempts, to run the business risks of the renewal schemes. Above all, it is difficult to dismiss the alternative of allowing the affected Crown lessees to have shares in the redevelopment gain denominated in terms of floor-space entitlement (this can avoid the fluctuations in profit shares and can be traded in the open market as future options).

One must however agree that the LDC is attempting to observe the Paretian efficiency criterion: that affected lessees are left "not worse off" by being compensated in cash by an amount which may buy or rent a similar alternative accommodation in the same district. This approach, however, is hardly consistent with the espoused objective stated in the LDC's planning reports that the renewal schemes will benefit the occupants. Nor can this approach be seen in the best possible light without a reference to private property rights of the occupants. As far as rehousing is concerned, which is particularly relevant to those sub-lessees with a lesser degree of private property rights, the situation is even more pathetic. There is no undertaking by the government, the Housing Authority, the Housing Society or the LDC to automatically rehouse the affected lessees or sub-lessees. There are only a few small-scale rehousing schemes which have been completed by the LDC. These projects are located at Third Street and Li Chit Street on the Hong Kong Island and Soy Street in Kowloon. The scale of this rehousing is however too restrictive compared with the scale of the redevelopment areas. This is very odd in the light of the following legal provisions and public policies:

1. statutory security of tenure for private housing tenancies;
2. huge injection of *ex gratia* payment and rehousing benefits for Kowloon Walled City clearees, who have no land rights at all; and
3. privileges of public housing tenants to acquire subsidized home-ownership units on a preferential basis.

If the LDC's schemes do, as their planning reports suggest, have a social dimension, then the present state of affairs can hardly be regarded as desirable.

The LDC has recently announced that the proprietors affected by their schemes would be given an opportunity to participate in the redevelopment schemes. It remains to be seen if the "no worse" rule adopted by the LDC for the early batches of schemes would be genuinely modified to pay some respect to the private property rights of the lessees. It also remains to be seen whether the general presumption against rehousing would be replaced by measures which tally with the social intent of the government to cater for the "housing needs" of the citizens.

# 12

# Education

---

Lee Wai-man

---

## ☐ The Revival of *Hundun* — A Higgledy-Piggledy Year

In an editorial that summarized last years' events, the publisher of *Teacher Plus*, a glossy magazine not particularly well-liked by local teachers, wrote unfavourably about how the governing polity played hazard with its ruling policies including educational ones. The year 1992 had indeed brought forward a chaotic and boisterous year, not only in the political arena, but also in the educational community. Unwittingly, the publisher's penetrating exposition has revived a *zeitgeist* — the reign of the Emperor *Hundun*.

One can best find out about the Emperor *Hundun* by referring to one of the most witty parables recorded in *Zhuangzi*, a book attributed to a Chinese philosopher of the same name. The parable goes something like this:

> The emperor of the Southern Sea was called *Shu* (literally, brief), the emperor of the Northern Sea was called *Hu* (literally, sudden), and the emperor of the Centre was called *Hundun. Shu* and *Hu* often met in *Hundun*'s land. The two were always well treated by him. They decided to repay his kindness. "All humans," they said, "have seven openings so they can see, hear, eat, and breathe. *Hundun* alone has none. Let's bore him some!" Every day they bored one hole, and on the seventh day *Hundun* died.

Since *Zhuangzi* recorded this fable some two thousand years ago, there have been copious interpretations by both his admirers and critics, ranging

---

Lee Wai-man is a doctoral candidate in The University of Hong Kong.

from a Taoist nostalgia for primal spontaneity and the transforming power of chaos to the compulsion to distinguish disorder (*Hundun*) from man-made absolute order (*Shu* and *Hu*). It is not the intention here to initiate another round of hermeneutic interpretation on this ever-charming moral story. Suffice it to say that *Hundun* (literally, chaos, facelessness; in daily language, the term is generally used to denote the condition of matter before separation and submission into the phenomena of hierarchy and regulation) may not have died after all. Soon after *Shu* and *Hu* carved two eyes and other five openings which composed a human face, the boisterous human world had immediately put him into a coma. *Hundun* closed his eyes for a long period, till the publisher of *Teacher Plus* made his latest call. *Hundun* decided to find out why on earth someone would mention his name.

To his surprise, *Hundun* woke up to discover that Hong Kong is no longer a piece of barren rock in the Southern Sea, as he remembered it when he first visited with *Shu* years ago. The skyline of the city is now decorated with several eye-catching architecturally-designed tall buildings towering the waterfront with polyhedral-shaped apexes and antenna-like spires.

Out of curiosity, *Hundun* wanted to know more about these strange new edifices in order to satisfy his utter innocence (*Hundun* is said to have a pure heart of a new-born baby with outright gullibility). He put his newly acquired ears, gifts from *Shu* and *Hu*, close to the tallest antenna shooting up through the skyline, as if he wanted to receive some signals from the microwave-drenched sky. Here he heard a whisper of the word "post-modernity" that came from nowhere.

*Hundun* took a good look around the city from his vantage point. Though not so sure what exactly this word may mean, he immediately found that "postmodernity" is in vogue these days, judging by the fact that the majority of the latest super structures in the skyline all have a polyhedral apex. Through the keen eyes that also were given to him by the two over-enthusiastic heavenly gods *Shu* and *Hu*, the impression led him to conclude that this so-called postmodern design is in fact an eclectic style, a diverse melange of classical ornaments and modern technology, mixing intimate classical details with modern functionalism, which give the local architecture a new articulation.

Hundun admitted that this current trend of postmodernity may not be only a vogue but in fact a *zeitgeist*, because he observed that these postmodern conditions are not confined to the architectural design but have expanded to every walk of life in the city. For instance, the current educational reform and innovations are one of more higgledy-piggledy than cynicism or mistrust, though the latter are also abundant.

If the 1970s can be perceived as a decade of expansion in local education, the 1980s as a decade of concern with quality issues, however little has been achieved, then the 1990s could perhaps be perceived as a decade of pandemonium. With the pledge of a rosy garden wilfully planted in the local educational field, part of the agenda envisioned by Governor Chris Patten during his first policy address in October 1992, the arrival of this higgledy-piggledy state of affairs has been officially declared.

One well-known example is the classroom size issue. Just as it became a strong point of attack by local educators at the beginning of 1992 when the Education Department planned to increase the number of pupils in a class from 38 to 40, a few months later, Patten promised that he would like to see it reduced to 35. With a chronic shortage and a high turnover of teachers, such a dramatic wavering in policy could not be anything but disastrous. As Au Pak-kuen, Vice-President of the Hong Kong Professional Teachers' Union, put it, "The Government seems to draw lines arbitrarily to fit in with expansion for the sake of expansion — there is poor planning." (*South China Morning Post* [*SCMP*], 7 September 1992).

Notwithstanding the disquieting chronic issues of the quality of education, the language of instruction, marginalized students, professionalization of teaching practice, etc., the real worry is that educational policies have become a means to rally popular support for the Governor first, whereas benefits for the majority only comes second.

## ☐ Polyhedral Apex and Spire: The Arrival of Postmodernity

Mass and compulsory public schooling in Hong Kong, an achievement of the modern era in the 1970s, involves the coming together of a number of developments associated with the rise of the so-called progressive society. It takes on the problems of socializing and disciplining young minds and bodies through production ideology and school organization. This mass compulsory schooling most often advances a non-reflective form of pedagogy and individual achievement, as the term "compulsory" implies, focusing on the instilling of external norms as part of the discipline of the "selves". Mass schooling promotes social and political conformity by producing intelligent but acquiescent citizens, obedient children for worried parents, and productive workers for the capitalist economy. The discovery of new possibilities is miniaturized to problem-solving along existing lines.

The pervasiveness of technicality and rationality in the received modes of thinking has denied authenticity to groups outside the mainstream. With the production ideology which emphasizes efficiency, rationality, and objectivity, terms like "accountability" and "effectiveness" have been used as an aegis of legitimacy for bureaucratic control, as the delineation of the teaching profession by the Education Commission Report No. 5 (ECR5), released in June 1992, proves.

Social progress, including mass education as designed by the modernists, has dehumanized students, rendering them as objects, as automatons to be made more productive, and as deviants subject to control and surveillance. The classification of students and schools into "bands", the decline of literacy and numeracy, drug abuse, juvenile delinquency, suicides, and the misbehaviour of marginalized students have all worked to debunk the comfortable, liberal myth of the modernists that mass public education has served primarily democratic interests and promoted equality of opportunity, therefore a better quality of life. The cracking of such make-believe indicates that modernism seems to have run out of steam and has, at least temporarily, exhausted its potential.

Postmodernity may mean different things to different people. At times, the term postmodernity is used to designate a particular style of living — buildings towering insolently or shopping mall-loitering as a past-time, as the skyline and the mushrooming of large-scale shopping malls since the 1980s in Hong Kong testifies. It may stand for a social condition, a historical juncture that is said to capture the currently fractured world, as the next section in this chapter will explain. It may mean a licence in a certain language game, such as the political flimflam and its counterpart the *mo-lei-tau* (literally, non-logical, out-of-the-blue) subculture that consumed the young generation just a couple of years ago — a subculture that talks about anything that does not add up to ordinary logic and does not take anything one says and/or does too seriously, as reflected in the catch phrase which has now become almost a cliché but still has wit: "Are you talking?" Postmodernity may also point to the lightning pace of change with which moods succeed one another, so that one can hardly remember what has happened just a moment ago (Do you still remember the *mo-lei-tau* subculture?).

At other times postmodernity may designate a particular mode of critique or analysis. It is a state of mind compatible with institutionalized pluralism, absence of universally obliged authority, particularism instead of universalism, constant change, and ambivalence. In the era of postmodernism, one is left with a world defined by fragmentation, indeterminacy, and partiality. These features of postmodernity can be seen as modernity liberated from false consciousness, perhaps as an indirect result of the June Fourth incident and the current dispute over political reforms. Postmodernity in its prime can help alert people to the hegemony and oppression of the technical, Weberian type of formal rationality, and to the need to become sensitive to the "others", including the alienated and marginalized young generation.

## ☐ A Fragmented-self Generation Plagued by Drugs, Delinquency, and Suicide

Although the arrival of postmodernity in Hong Kong brought with it a new look, yet it has scored tragedies and casualties. The varieties of cultural products, be they material or spiritual, from both the East and the West, are so overwhelming that they have grown beyond the assimilating capacity of both the old and the young. In a *zeitgeist* that dramatizes diversity, societies like Hong Kong which lack a tradition of respect of "otherness" may easily become sceptical and cynical, show less mutual trust and a clear-cut cohesiveness. Such a society tries to do without standards, moral ones included, and becomes normless. Yet morality in its best sense is a functional necessity of a world with an intrinsic completeness and definiteness of choices and alternatives. It requires its practitioner to weigh the ethical implications of her or his action and behaviour. The current postmodern society of Hong Kong has gone beyond, if it ever reached, such a world. This state of normlessness, difficult to describe but certainly self-constituting, self-propelling, determined by nothing but one's own impulse and not subject to any guiding standards, has become the emergent worldview (life attitude) for the local young generation.

It is this new postmodern worldview and experiences that has shaped the young generation in Hong Kong throughout the 1980s and the early 1990s. This last decade has seen the rise of a mobile and multi-faceted society on the one hand, and the transmutation of the nature of human self on the other. Under such a fast-changing pace, self-concepts of Hong Kong people have become volatile too. Questions of unity of the self and of self-presentation thus become crucial, including the propensity to adapt to short-term relationships, be they human or consuming products.

These transmutations make the sense of self in Hong Kong people problematic at least in the area of human relationships, if not the deeper structure of life: that parents and their children, teachers and their students *do not know* each other. They are always surprised by the different assumed identities of their fellow "others" at the other end of the relationship. Self-disclosure is conditional, not only among and between adults (including both the parents and the teachers) and the youth, even among peers too. Discovering hollowness in human and social relationships and discovering the "real" self becomes a painful task in the social life of the young generation in Hong Kong. Phrases like "loneliness", "sadness", "separation", and "void" which flood the contents of local popular songs seem to testify to the existence of such a psychological state.

## □ The Unbearable Heaviness of the Fragmented Self

In spite of the fact that Hong Kong is proud of itself as a meeting point of, or a potpourri for, things East and West, remnants of the old tradition, nevertheless, share the field with current postmodern perplexities. The two virtually mount a psychological warfare. The possibility of dissonance and a resultant fragmentation of the self is always imminent. While this fragmented self is no longer regarded as exceptional and threatening but part of the "normal" course of life, the breakdown of a unified self nevertheless makes the life of alienated persons unbearable.

This fragmented self repudiates the traditional Chinese dialectical unification of the *dawo* (the Great Self) with the *xiaowo* (the Little Self) — a unity of selves which includes the individual self and his or her society. The fragmented selves in this postmodern era demand special effort to maintain the continuity of the traditional Chinese selves (*dawo* and *xiaowo*), and to harmonize with the lately acquired "selves" with a Western individualistic touch. This is difficult enough for any person, yet more so throughout the vicissitudes of adolescent life.

Families in Hong Kong have changed too in composition and nature in the modern and postmodern eras. With an increasing rate of divorce and a high rate of remarriage among divorcees, the impact of single-parents and living with a stepfamily on the psychological make-up of the young generation can be tremendous. Studies from the 1960s to the early 1980s have already indicated that the nuclear family as a basic network for social support and need fulfilment is on the decline in this fast-changing society. Members of nuclear families have to rely increasingly on their own or on other social institutions such as the school rather than their kin.

With the arrival of the sub-nuclear (single-parent) and multi-nuclear (stepfamily) familial structure, this reliance on social institutions may even be intensified. Together with increasing division of labour in a "modernized" society, some conventional functions of the family, like protection, socialization, and social control, have more or less been taken over by other institutions such as schools, police and the Youth Charter. The provision of a sense of acceptance, intimacy, security, and mutual support by parents, including teachers who play the role of *loco parentis*, has been thinned out in local society.

In this postmodern era, people have been subjected to a variety of standards. However, it is the adults, parents and teachers included, who often "get away" from these multiple standards while trying to enforce norms of which some of them may have doubts. Discrepancies in norms or between spoken norms and actual behaviour are intentionally and/or unintentionally transmitted to the young generation.

Under such circumstances, interpersonal conflict arises when it involves persons in positions which do not permit them to retaliate directly against those who aggrieve or frustrate them. After several unsuccessful attempts at gaining others' understanding, some youth choose to abandon the traditional forms of communication — speaking to their significant others — in order to seek attention and make themselves understood. This lack of self-confidence, together with pent-up frustration, once triggered by an unexpected precipitating factor, be it disappointing academic performance, a broken heart, wrongful accusation by an adult or a peer, may be released with devastating effects. This may result in an increase of misbehaviour among the youth. One lethal choice is ending their own lives, the very act which tells the world that at least they have one thing at their command — the ability to dispense with their own life. Other less dramatic actions include anti-social behaviour such as drug abuse and delinquency. This tragic waste of life is a formidable challenge which local society is not yet ready to meet.

## ☐ Misbehaviour: Drug Abuse, Delinquency, and Suicide

Since the beginning of the 1990s, there has been an increasing number of misbehaviour among students in Hong Kong. The number of cases involving drug abuse (Figure 1), delinquency (Figure 2), and suicides (Figure 3) are all on the rise.

Suicide continues to be the single largest cause of death, other than those from natural causes, in the last few years in Hong Kong. The year

Figure 1. Newly Reported Drug-abusers under 20 Years Old, 1983–1992

Number of cases

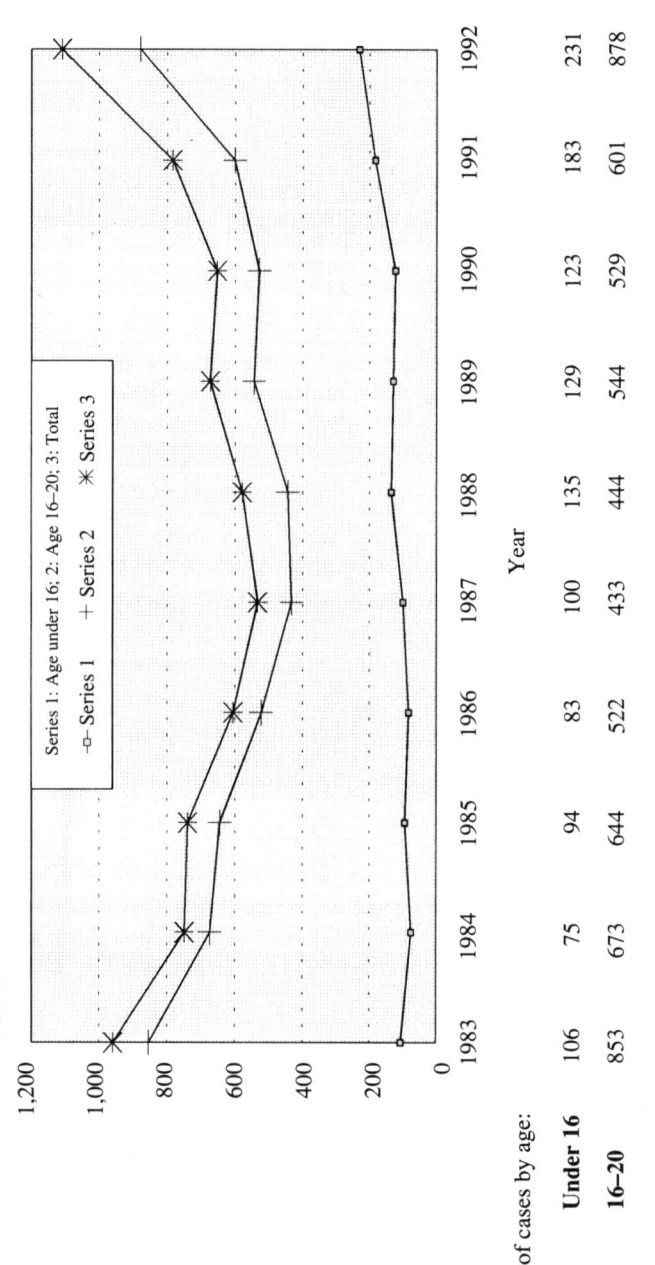

No. of cases by age:

| | 1983 | 1984 | 1985 | 1986 | 1987 | 1988 | 1989 | 1990 | 1991 | 1992 |
|---|---|---|---|---|---|---|---|---|---|---|
| **Under 16** | 106 | 75 | 94 | 83 | 100 | 135 | 129 | 123 | 183 | 231 |
| **16–20** | 853 | 673 | 644 | 522 | 433 | 444 | 544 | 529 | 601 | 878 |

Source: Narcotics Division, Government Secretariat, *Central Registry of Drug Abuse, Thirty-First Report (1983–1992)* (Hong Kong: Hong Kong Government, 1993).

Figure 2. Persons Under Age 16 Arrested/Prosecuted, 1987–1991

Number of persons (1,000)

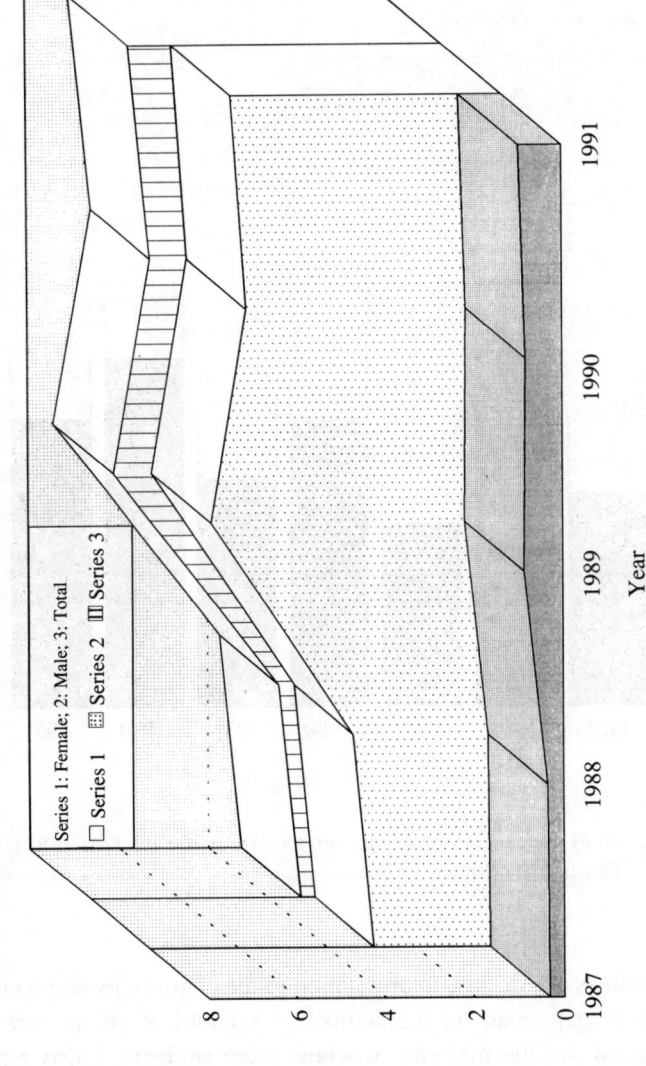

Source: *Royal Hong Kong Police Force Review, 1987–1991* (Hong Kong: Government Printer).

Figure 3.  Number of Suicides, Age 0–19, 1985–1992

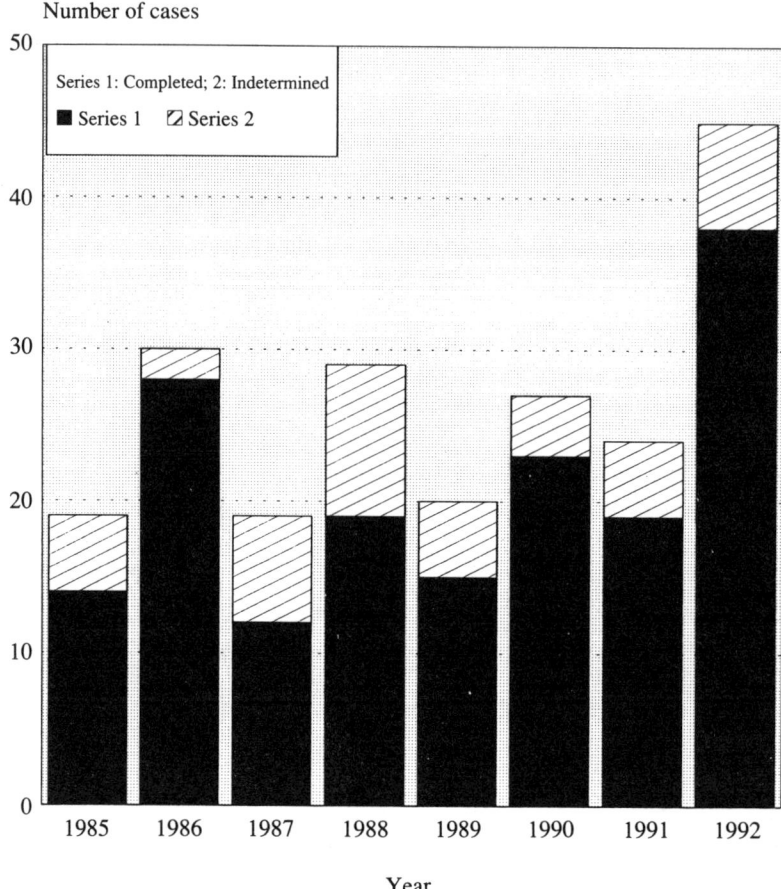

Source:  H. M. Sinclair, *Hong Kong Coroners Report for the Year 1992* (Hong Kong:
Government Printer, 1993).

1992 witnessed, despite interpretation to the contrary by some empiricists, an alarming increase in the number of suicides of young persons under the age of 20, the majority of whom were students. Thirty-eight young persons, 23 of whom were students, terminated their lives by various means, while more than 50 failed attempts have also been recorded. In addition, an unknown number of cases for milder self-destructive behaviour which were not recorded in the official tally took place. This significant jump (19 cases in 1991 and 38 cases in 1992, an increase of 100 per cent) in the number of suicides of youngsters is not reflected in other age groups. A similar upward trend is observed in 1993. In the first two weeks of this year, eight youngsters took their own lives by various means. The results of a review conducted by the Advisory Committee on School Guidance and Support Service on the 21 fatal suicide cases recorded by the Education Department in the academic year 1991–1992 indicated that a majority of them were pupils aged between 11 and 13.

The phenomenon has caused tremendous concern, including the chief Coroner, H. M. Sinclair, who discussed at length the matter in his 1992 annual report. While Sinclair tried to write off the problems in bureaucratic tone by saying that "the motivating factors continue to be, for the most part, failing to achieve or disappointed love in the younger grouping", in reality suicide may involve rather complex determinants, including failure in parenting, social pressures, insensitive schoolteachers, high academic demands, pressures from school (even the "traditional" rote-learning, too much pointless homework and cramming are said to be factors that "could ruin young lives" [see *SCMP*, 21 May 1993]), heavy homework loads (some pointed out that this may not be the only cause, as a few of those who committed suicide had good academic records), the desire to kill oneself, aggression towards others, an appeal for pity and succour, a form of amelioration, an effective weapon against parent and teacher, an indirect form of revenge against their provokers, the copycat epidemic effect, the 1997 complex, and whatnot. In most cases the motives are mixed. In a frenzied attempt to find a quick-fix and to account for the tragedies, the local schools in particular have been portrayed as "pressure-cookers", and are a "mental health hazard to children, making unreasonable demands on students and being insensitive to their needs" (*SCMP*, 6 January 1993).

## ☐ Stigmatization and Marginalization: The Labelling Game

When educators discuss children who have difficulty in school, they often place the child's school problems in the context of the child's family and/or social background. Linking family background to school performance has also become a new feature of the local educational discourse — policy, research, practice, and the current emphasis on reform.

Take school-home relations as an example. For many families in Hong Kong both parents have full-time jobs in order to make a "decent" living.

However, this knowledge about the socioeconomic background of families is socially constructed and used to single out low-income and/or single-parent families as groups that have difficulty facilitating its children's development in relation to educational goals. The tone of communication between school and home, to use the words of the ECR5, "may inadvertently make parents feel that they are being called to account for the failings of their children." In a sense, the current practice affirms the normative ordering held by middle-class families, constructing some families, low-income (including double-income) and single-parent families among them, as educational, if not social, defects. The same can be observed when the Education Department deals with the so-called band-five students and their schools.

### *The Bottom 10 Per Cent — The Band-five Student*

In spite of the abolition of the Secondary School Entrance Examination in the late 1970s, a move considered by liberals as a step towards equality of opportunity in education, the selection mechanism of the local school system has not changed much in essence. While a few prestigious schools, to their own merit perhaps, still remain elitist, quite a number of others are considered as band-five schools, with a considerable proportion of so-called band-five students (see Table 1).

A school-based remedial support programme, as recommended in the Education Commission Report No. 4 (ECR4) and to be implemented soon, is designed with the intention to ameliorate inequality through schooling. This move of developing a basis for supplementary funding to band-five schools is perhaps one of the significant shifts in educational policy in the 1990s. The differential funding was intended to offset, at least partially, the "disadvantaged" position of children from a poor social background. One may begin to appreciate how precarious it can be in that such criteria reflect the labelling effect upon the students, the teaching and administrative staff, the school, and even the community at large.

The Education Department plans to pump extra resources into the "band five schools" because the students are viewed as being at the risk of academic failure. They are often perceived as "culturally deprived" and "academically low achievers", terms currently adopted by the Education Department. In a circular (No. 111/93) distributed to local schools, the Education Department described the academic performance of this group of students as "the bottom 10 per cent". For teachers of these schools, courses

Table 1.  Form One Band-five Students and Their Numbers in
Schools, 1992

| No. of schools | No. of Form One Band-five students | No. of schools | No. of Form One Band-five students |
|---|---|---|---|
| 23 | 1–5 | 1 | 136–140 |
| 14 | 6–10 | 3 | 141–145 |
| 9 | 11–15 | 2 | 146–150 |
| 6 | 16–20 | 3 | 151–155 |
| 6 | 21–25 | 5 | 156–160 |
| 5 | 26–30 | 2 | 161–165 |
| 7 | 31–35 | 3 | 166–170 |
| 5 | 36–40 | 3 | 171–175 |
| 3 | 41–45 | 3 | 176–180 |
| 4 | 46–50 | 1 | 181–185 |
| 2 | 51–55 | 1 | 186–190 |
| 5 | 56–60 | 2 | 191–195 |
| 3 | 61–65 | 2 | 196–200 |
| 5 | 66–70 | 1 | 201–205 |
| 3 | 71–75 | 1 | 206–210 |
| 6 | 76–80 | 1 | 211–215 |
| 3 | 81–85 | 2 | 221–225 |
| 1 | 86–90 | 3 | 231–235 |
| 5 | 91–95 | 1 | 256–260 |
| 1 | 96–100 | 1 | 276–280 |
| 2 | 101–105 | 1 | 281–285 |
| 1 | 106–110 | 1 | 286–290 |
| 5 | 111–115 | 1 | 306–310 |
| 6 | 116–120 | 1 | 361–365 |
| 4 | 121–125 | 1 | 381–385 |
| 3 | 126–130 | 1 | 386–390 |
| 5 | 131–135 | 1 | 531–535 |
| | Total: | 190 | 17,032 |

Source:  *Sing Tao Jih Pao*, 12 February 1993.

of "classroom management and management of behaviour problems commonly associated with these students will be introduced". However, the results of a study published in May 1993 indicate that there is no statistically significant difference in school behaviour between band-one and band-five students. For band-five students, it is doubtful whether the differential resource allocation programme will offset the damage of the labelling effect.

## *The New Town Youth: Victims of Marginalization*

Massive emigration from Hong Kong in the last decade has become part of the reality in local life. Several bodies from the helping service sectors even provide counselling services and organize seminars for these high-flying "refugees", and published academic articles to show their concern. While such concern may have its reasons, it is sad to note that less has been done on internal migration within the city. Indeed, there has been mass internal migration taking place in Hong Kong in the last two decades. Some two million people have migrated from the urban core to new towns in the New Territories under a deliberate decentralization policy.

One justification for developing new towns in the New Territories was to solve problems such as poor living conditions, traffic congestion, insufficient public facilities which were associated with high density urban development, to supply manpower to the industrial parks, and perhaps to give new town-dwellers a better living environment. Yet with the collapse of the plan for self-contained and balanced communities, these new towns on the urban fringe fail to provide residents with the conveniences of life. Many residents still need to depend on the mother city for various facilities, services, and employment opportunities. With the exception of Tsuen Wan, a fair proportion of the population work outside the new towns. Parents journey to work and children journey to school in other districts. These migrants are a population spillover from the urban core, and they become marginalized because of the disutilities or the inadequacy in the provision of recreational facilities and supporting services. The sense of being uprooted is keenly felt by the youth.

Misbehaviour is frequent where social cohesion is low and mobility high, where the links of common beliefs, activity and aspiration binding individuals to the community in which they live are loosened. Suicide is a case in point. As early as 1958 when the first systematic study of suicide in Hong Kong was conducted, one significant conclusion was that the breakdown of primary group support and the substitution of "modern" values for the traditional had led to an increase in suicide.

The concept of "social disorganization" — disruption of functional relations among persons to a degree that interferes with the normal functioning of the group — had been used to account for the findings of the then higher rate of suicide in the urban ghetto. Various processes contributing to such disorganization has its psychological consequences. The failure of the individual to adjust to social change may lead to so-called anomic suicide. Such indeed is the situation of those youth who have moved to new towns in the New Territories where many live in isolation and anonymity. Unlike the trends in the 1950s, where the urban (Hong Kong Island, Kowloon and New Kowloon) suicide rate was higher than the suburban rate (the New Territories and Islands), the data in Figure 4 indicate that this trend has been reversed in the 1990s. The significantly higher rate of suicide in the New Territories is perhaps indicative of this marginalizing effect.

## ☐ Curriculum Innovations: Hot Potatoes Half-baked, Half-Digested Half-heartedly

Though Hong Kong has changed a lot since the introduction of nine-year compulsory education fifteen years ago, the educational community has not developed a corresponding change in school curriculum and teaching

Figure 4.  Number of Suicide by District of Residence, Aged 10–19,  1989–1992

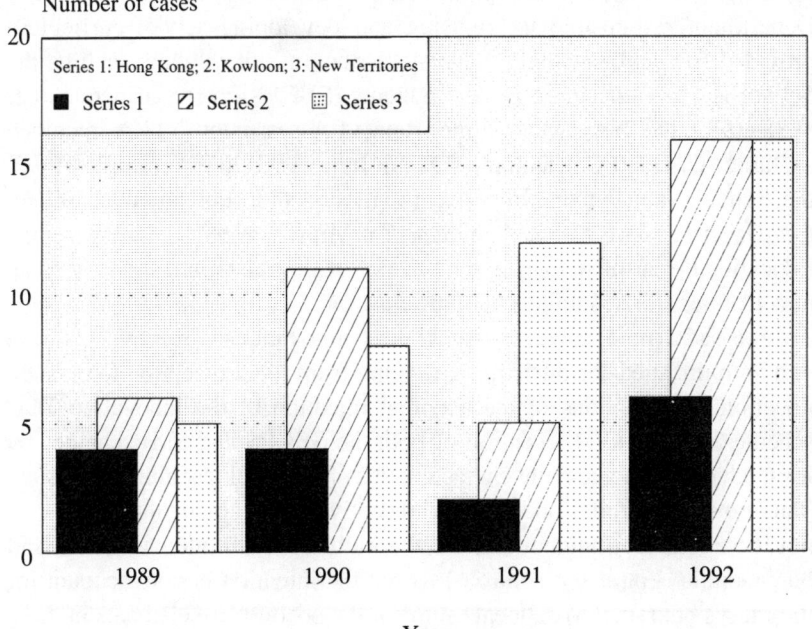

Number of cases

Series 1: Hong Kong; 2: Kowloon; 3: New Territories

■ Series 1    ▨ Series 2    ▦ Series 3

Year

Source:  H. M. Sinclair, *Hong Kong Coroners Report for the Year 1992* (Hong Kong: Government Printer, 1993).

methods. In the past few decades, it has become relatively common for both local policy-makers and teaching practitioners to regard curriculum development as solely technical or procedural questions, to be answered by appeal to centralized curriculum guidelines, textbooks materials, or presumed experts outside the schools. For a long time, teachers in Hong Kong have got used to this top-down or periphery-to-centre approach, and to teaching their students with centrally prescribed syllabi. These prescribed syllabi have been criticized for being too centralized, out of touch with social realities as well as site-specific problems such as juvenile delinquency and distress in schools. It also fails to give students life skills to cope with such distress. "We hear too often complaints from teachers about the declining academic standards of students and the impossibility of keeping order in class." Tik Chi-yuen, a Legislative Councillor and now chairperson of the Committee on Home-School Cooperation, explained, "Meanwhile, students are complaining about the boredom of school life." (*SCMP*, 10 May 1992)

Curriculum development has lately become the task of the Curriculum Development Institute (CDI), a central agency within the Education Department responsible for revising and developing school curriculum provided for public schools. Several curriculum innovations, such as the School-Based Curriculum Project Scheme (SBCPS) in the academic year 1988–1989, the Targets and Target-Related Assessment (TTRA, renamed as Target-Oriented Curriculum, TOC, in June 1993) in the spring of 1993, the School Management Initiative (SMI) and the publication of *School Education in Hong Kong: A Statement of Aims*, are recent moves by the Education Department to avert the practice of centralization, and to open up new frontiers for school/teacher participation.

It is sad to note, however, that all these innovations in recent years were met with uncalled-for difficulties, ranging from tepid reception to outright rejection. Explanations of the apparent rejection of the innovative TOC scheme and the stolid reception of both the SBCPS and SMI schemes by local educators include: the characteristics of the local teaching profession, practitioners' attitudes and level of receptivity, the practicality of the in-novations, the institutional climate, the indifferent attitude of parents, and bureaucratic centralized control. It is not the intention here to account for the causes but rather to delineate some of the postmodern elements in these innovations and their weaknesses.

The purposes of these curriculum innovations perhaps include meeting the individual need of students, asking teachers "to play a more active role in curriculum development" (ECR5), and providing a forum in which teachers can discuss how to meet the changing needs of society. The attempt to implement these innovations indicates that policy-makers at least have noted that the centralized curriculum may not be able to meet the varied needs of students and schools with different contingencies.

However, the introduction of such innovations as the SBCPS, SMI, and TOC, laudable as they are, may not be all. These programmes were carried out haplessly in piecemeal fashion without an explicit concerted effort. Throughout the modern and postmodern era, there has been a lack of "a joint enterprise" spirit but sizeable mistrust within the local education community. Under such circumstances and within the existing highly centralized and bureaucratic mechanisms of decision-making and resource allocation, the successful implementation of any less centralized curriculum innovation, which requires active participation and joint endeavour among policy-making bodies, schools, and teaching practitioners, can easily become a facade for a political score rather than ensuring implementation.

Yet the difficulties encountered by all these recent curriculum innovations may imply that the foci of change is institution-wide, rather than site-specific, as innovations have not yet become a readily acceptable alternative in the local educational community. There has been little overall progression since the early 1980s when reform and innovations became cliché, as the United Nations Educational, Scientific, and Cultural Organization described it, as "a centralized curriculum with a non-organized implementation structure". Reforms have been half-baked half-heartedly by policy-makers, and half-digested half-heartedly by the practitioners.

Take the SBCPS as an example. It was implemented under the condition that the prevailing forms of assessment, as administered by the Hong Kong Examinations Authority (HKEA), remained. As a result, projects were confined mainly to the junior secondary or primary levels and were not public examination-related. Similarly, the TOC that was planned to be implemented in the current academic year is not accompanied by corresponding changes in the existing school class structure.

The current selective innovations in curriculum will thus continue generally to weaken non-dominant groups in the system — teachers and students alike. Teaching practitioners continue to feel disenfranchised and helpless even in this "new" site-specific curriculum innovating process. In a critique of the new Secure Hong Kong Attainment Tests planned to be implemented for the first time in December 1993, Gregory Lam Shu-wing, president of the Association of Lecturers at Colleges of Education, put it succinctly, that "schooling would suffer because subjects not included in the territory-wide tests would be ignored in the quest for the best results in English, Chinese and mathematics." In spite of its changes, the curriculum on the whole still remains examination-driven and pupils will not enjoy an all-round development. A similar reasoning may be applied to other current curriculum reform programmes.

In curriculum innovation the crucial questions are what knowledge is most worthwhile and what forms of experience to students are most worth having. These fundamental questions are ethical, political, and cultural inquiries that take educators well beyond the classroom. For example, educators must consider the relationship between what is included and excluded in the current curriculum and how this is related to the social dynamics of power, influence, and domination; how events, such as the notorious Opium War in modern Chinese history, are portrayed and interpreted in textbooks that lend credibility to certain points of view at the expense of others (e.g. the success of colonial rule); how the very form of curriculum materials (such as English first, Chinese second) affects students' perceptions of themselves as well as their peers and teachers, knowledge, and education itself (e.g. overemphasis on academic success and the stigmatization of academic failure); how the curriculum as it actually unfolds in a classroom assists or retards personal development. Finally, they must consider the extent to which different forms of language (such as one that incorporates the dominant male consciousness) and systems of value (e.g. band-five and special students and other school labels) infiltrate the processes of creating and enacting the curriculum, and so on.

Few of these questions are touched upon in the current deliberation of curriculum innovations in Hong Kong. Because of its self-evidently worthwhile goals, the rhetoric of education reform and curriculum innovation has become an attractive political platform. Despite the adoption of a liberal, progressive oratory which emphasizes participation, democracy, and student-centred approach, the practice of various policy-making bodies, school administrations, and even practitioners themselves act otherwise. The discourse has been used to develop platitudes that mainly emphasize accountability, conformity, and self-interest. For example, one of the stated aims of the SMI is "to provide for greater participation of teachers, parents and *past* [emphasis added] students in school management" (Circular No. 28/93). The absence of involving incumbent students is conspicuous, as if the initiatives of students are "naturally" not important in school management.

Questions of curriculum deliberation are unavoidably normative in character, charged with cultural, social, and moral choices that require our most penetrating interpretation, our deepest commitment to beneficial social relationships, and our most thoughtful and heart-felt moral imaginations. There are commitments in curriculum deliberation, explicitly or implicitly, regarding the kind of people the educators want their students to be and become: how they will act with others, form their identities, shoulder social responsibilities, and exercise as well as act on their own choices. These commitments need to be witnessed first and foremost by the practitioners themselves and to be instilled in their students through their own behaviour and example. Today, educators in Hong Kong have before them a plethora of challenges that require not only critical reflection but also analyses of present school inequities, and a real consideration of what types of knowledge, experiences, and dispositions are most educationally valuable for the young generation of Hong Kong. These challenges may yet be too serious for local educators, for whom both intellectual engagement and transformative practice are imperative.

Local practitioners need not espouse the technicist's approach of the modern era and see the educational system as something given. In the postmodern view, educators not only create the system, they are the system. Education systems exist in a continuous process of bargaining and negotiation rather than in a state of homeostasis and stability. Groups, including policy-makers, administrators, parents, practitioners, and to the surprise of many, students, are different actors who divide power and allocate resources in ways that appear most beneficial to them. Both parents and the community at large are known to put a high value on educational success which can open a narrow door to higher education and a prosperous career and bright future for their children and society. The important and critical question would be: is our society willing to abandon its production and meritocratic ideology to save young people from the risks of suicide, delinquency, and drug abuse? If not, the very fixation with merits and high examination scores to the neglect of an all-rounded development will remain a debilitating feature of Hong Kong school life. Local teachers who take up a critical approach regard the current realities of schooling as important but not defining features of what the preparation of students might include. These teachers themselves take a moral stand on how the best interests of students, parents, and members in the community are to be served. The choices they make will, in important respects, affect the kinds of students we will have in our schools, and the kinds of citizens we will have in our society. In curriculum innovations, emphasis may then be put on the development of life skills, including critical reflection, and a view of learning as a moral calling.

## ☐ Professionalization without Professionalism: A New Control Mechanism

The term "professionalization" is alluring. It has become a catch phrase among local educators. Teacher unions even have this term in their organizational names. Unlike the four previous reports by the Education Commission, ECR5 dealt with only one single subject and adopted "The Teaching Profession" for its title. This reflected, as the then Secretary for Education and Manpower, John Chan, put it, "both the size of the problem and the importance of the proposed reforms".

Professional expertise and progressive educational reform arise hand in hand with the appearance of the corporate state in the modern era. Professionalization of local teaching practices has been perceived as a sacrosanct, unproblematic pursuit. The pioneering work of progress in the local mass and compulsory schooling have been delegated to professional educators of various ranks. This perception yet tends to overlook the very real limitations of the pursuit, blind spots which in turn lead to unfortunate pedagogical consequences. Professionalization of the teaching practice may be inconsistent with its status if not properly carried out. It can be harmful unless its nature and functions are appreciated.

Government-initiated reform designed to professionalize the local teaching practice calls for the specification of teacher training courses and the requirement for certification in teacher education. However, these policies of professionalization are more malleable to central direction and top-down implementation rather than the other way round. Furthermore, this dominant discourse on teaching professionalism is designed, ironically, to control both the teachers and the students through the rationalization of their work — teachers are encouraged to think of themselves as more professional because they have access to a good deal of technical knowledge about student testing, "effective" lesson planning formats, various skill-based curricular programmes, and assertive discipline techniques for classroom control.

The notion of forming a professional body can be, and has been, used by local authoritative individuals (such as some union leaders) and groups (such as several self-claimed professional bodies) to assimilate differences among people and to homogenize alternative perceptions, ideas, and feelings in a manner that protects their power and interests rather than for the beneficial interests of their practice and their clients. Any movements towards pluralism that will support difference by altering structures of power threatens the established interest of the "professional" leaders in the field. In a truly democratic community of educators, personal and social conditions need to be continually created, re-created, and reinforced in ways that will encourage, respect, and value expressions of difference.

A new kind of protectionism is in fact emerging in the local scene. There is an increasing tendency to make the process of education policy-making a major battlefield of politicking for established interests and power sharing. Some teacher unions have evolved to become essentially bureaucratic and politicking bodies. When the government launched an overseas recruitment drive to recruit 780 additional non-graduate teachers to work by September 1993, at least two local unions — the Hong Kong Professional Teachers' Union and the Union of Government Primary School Headmasters and Headmistresses, put up a demand that the government must be very strict with the regulations in recruitment.

Several scholars have argued that professionalism of local teachers is low. Several factors have been suggested: little autonomy in decision-making, small percentage of professionally qualified teachers in its ranks, a heavy workload which consumes much of their time and energy, a lack of altruistic attitudes towards their clients, and last but not least, a paucity of commitment that goes hand in hand with an ethics of caring. The first two factors may have their own merit; the third one is hardly convincing as other professionals too have a heavy workload.

A low level of professionalism manifests itself in apathy towards reforms. During the initial stage of implementation of the SBCPS, extrinsic rewards through copyright in designing new curriculum project schemes became one major attraction for some participants. Most of the other teachers, however, developed a self-protective indifference with a highly sceptical wait-and-see attitude.

Teachers face numerous dilemmas each day that compel them to make critical choices that are either beneficial or detrimental to students. As discussed above, if morality implies that at least one has to act responsively towards self and others, then teaching is a moral activity that requires educators to do the same. Teaching behaviour and curriculum decisions must be grounded in an "ethics of caring". Educators as organic and transformative intellectuals — a concept often used by the "popularists" in postmodernism — set up linkages and organic connections and establish relationships among various relevant groups in society, and play a significant role in social change. These educators may be performing an important role by attempting to look beyond the politics of fragmentation and cynicism to a new philosophy of caring. With this authentic professional spirit, teaching is oriented towards sustaining a relationship that cares about genuine dialogue, the needs of individual students, curriculum innovations, and the dialectic interplay between teaching and learning. The educators may help students to minimize the tension that arises from atomization of city life, thus cultivating a sense of community. Such are the ideals of teaching and learning complementing each other — the essence of the Confucian philosophy of education.

These commitments have to be given concrete rather than merely abstract meaning in the current historical juncture. Educators need to be engaged continuously in creating and re-creating the meaning of the practice of teaching and learning complementing each other. This principle, which finds its parallel in the critical curriculum approach in the West, includes the support for the enhancement of individual and institutional freedom (in conjunction with the principle of the right of individuals and groups to receive equal treatment without discrimination), participation within bureaucratic institutions, quality education that empowers both students and teachers, helping them develop their full potential. Simply put, it embodies authenticity, equity, and liberty in its spirit. At times, these principles have been articulated within the framework of politically conservative discourse as well as social movement. However, platitudes about professionalization and professionalism will never make up for the lack of commitment for an ethics of caring. Such a commitment will involve challenging powerful interest groups and established worldviews. This requires local educators who are committed to the task to make sure that no serious voices are left out of the great dialogue that shapes our curriculum and education system.

## ☐ Research

With all these ostensibly bleak scenarios in the local educational field one may wonder whether there is anything educators can do. One logical answer would be to carry out an investigation to find out where the problems are. The failure to illuminate those issues that are neglected or deliberately omitted from the agenda by the established circle in the educational field needs to be noted. As established bodies, educators have interests of their own to defend. Under such circumstances, it seems very unlikely the type of research envisioned in the ECR5 or the University and Polytechnic Grants Committee (UPGC) would run counter to the interests of established groups. One can expect that those researchers who adhere to official guidelines and are "pragmatic" in their research aims would be privileged in resource allocation, including research grants. Applicants would frame their grant application forms around narrowly pre-defined competencies, rewrite proposals with bureaucratic jargon in the language of official rules, and arm themselves with the conventional empiricist discourse (full of "scientific" and "statistical" banality) of education. Any research project that is not up to the expectations of the central bureaucracy would hardly be approved through the multi-level decision-making mechanism of granting bodies. The effect would be a narrowing of academic freedom and curriculum diversity through the unseen hand of "market demand".

Given the lack of an independent research base and/or resources of its own, there would be little room for educators and researchers to conduct investigations or to carry out innovative projects that are counter to the received view. The guidelines for application for SBCPS grants which "encouraged" applicants to submit proposals that focused on pre-defined issues are a good example of this new "pragmatism" in the postmodern era. This by itself poses a serious question: What kinds of approaches will be helpful for local educators and researchers to reach a better understanding of the situation?

This practice of "pragmatism" reminds one of the vulgar pragmatism of the dominant positivist paradigm in education that has tyrannized the modern era. This vulgar pragmatism fails to look beyond a narrow technical-rational, means-ends approach to understand education and their relevant groups.

Take educational psychology as an example. In the modern era, professional "expert" knowledge in educational psychology has served in teacher education courses to construct concerns with control and discipline of students in terms of individual student adjustment. In fact these concerns are related to the role the schools assume in socializing students for docility and conformity to expected roles as workers, citizens, and family members. The perennial concern of educational psychology has been the study of "underdevelopment" among students, especially marginalized ones, which put fault in the individual and orient educational reform towards normalizing the "deviant" populations in classrooms. By focusing the teacher education curriculum on psychological explanations for control problems, the received discourse also depoliticizes and dehistoricizes conflicts in schools and classrooms.

In the local educational setting, the worst lies yet in the fact that the majority of these theories are imposed from without. Many local researchers attempt to use concepts and instruments originated in the West, mainly North America, to study behaviour in a predominantly Chinese cultural setting, and these are assumed to be a valid basis for studying local phenomena. Many cross-cultural studies in the last two decades have demonstrated the serious fallacy of such assumptions. Take the concepts of intelligence and personality, two of the hottest topics for educational psychologists, as examples. Cross-cultural investigations have demonstrated that the indigenous conceptions of intelligence and personality of many national groups around the world differ significantly from the Western (North American) view of intelligence as quick, analytic and purely cognitive. Many national groups also do not perceive personality as a cluster of individualistic traits, again a socially constructed concept from the Western societies.

One can easily see how dangerous it can be if one adopts these imposed Western concepts of intelligence and personality to assess the ability of non-Western children, such as the majority of students in Hong Kong. Unfortunately, these imposed concepts have been used by many researchers to study the intelligence and personality of local students. Thus in the early 1980s the indiscriminate applications of the MMPI (the Minnesota Multiphasic Personality Inventory, a very popular personality instruments originating from the United States) to assess the personality of Chinese students had "found" that these students have a relatively high tendency to lie! The development of a Chinese version of MMPI, called the Chinese Multiphasic Personality Inventory (CMPI), by a group of researchers both in Hong Kong and in Mainland China, is hopefully a step in the correct direction removed from using the imposed approach. Any theory that attempts to explain the educational phenomena in the local setting must arise out of the process of inquiry itself and be well grounded in the data which it seeks to describe, explain or predict.

Another conventional practice of many local researchers is the adoption of the empirical approach in their investigations. Take another example from educational psychology, the study of misbehaviour of marginalized youth. To say that misbehaviour appears because it only happens within marginalized youth is of course to some extent tautological. It is necessary to explain why such misbehaviour appears, to begin with, and here one should be aware of falling into an intellectual trap of trying to interpret the motivations and personality of the marginalized group. A comprehensive examination of the aetiology of misbehaviour of students, such as juvenile delinquency, drug abuse, and suicide requires more than statistics and clinical observations. The precise meanings of such statistical correlations or clinical observations remain elusive. Both the statistical and clinical approaches to the problem of, for example suicide, have been subjected to criticism for advancing little our understanding of the suicidal phenomenon. A more extensive approach may help rescue discussion of these problematics from the dangers of oversimplification.

Local research practices at the current level of sophistication are ill-equipped to handle the multifarious features of local daily educational life in this postmodern era. Conventional educational theories, especially the functionalist theory under the aegis of empiricism, may not be refined enough to reveal the rich multiplicity of life in its full cultural and historical context. The postmodern worldview when concretized in conducting research would, on the other hand, entail the dissipation of "objectivity", and emphasize the subjective involvement, viz. the active participation of both the researcher and his/her subjects throughout the process of research (the so-called Participatory Action Research, PAR).

Postmodernism, especially those schools related to phenomenology, advocates a presupposition-free philosophy which sees the social world in terms of reality constituted in the minds of both the actors and the researchers in their daily lives. One prominent feature along this line is the rejection of the definition of truth and meaning by those who are out of context or "extraterritorial". The kind of actions required for significant change through research must be guided by genuinely dialogic social relations — conditions under which previously silenced voices can be expressed and be heard. It seeks to abolish power differentials that deny the authenticity of the "other", be they students, parents, educators, professionals or non-professionals, researchers or subjects in the research process. This kind of research action enables society to interpret better the basic problems that it presents for various groups, including educators and social workers in the helping services, parents, even the students themselves as well as members in the community at large in order to tackle their problems.

Instead of the traditional epistemological conception of social reality that builds upon an either/or logic and speaks of one being set contrastively against the "other" (the logic of differentiation), a logic of both/and (the logic of complement), which has been part of the traditional way of Chinese thinking, and now being promoted by the interpretive approach in the West, sees all "otherness" in the human ecosystem not as one of opposition but only of differences. Local researchers may consider breaking with the conventional ontological and epistemological premises of opposite dualism of both modernity and postmodernity, and a return to the *hundun* state of affairs in which things are not necessarily opposite to one another but can be complementary. A *hundun* kind of chaos may not be that bad after all.

## □ Final Remarks: The Submission of *Hundun*

If the conception of educators as transformative agents educating the young generation to become citizens of the global village holds, this implies a reform of culture, of worldview, and of intellectual stance. Going over the educational policies in Hong Kong since the beginning of the 1990s, and in particular last year, *Hundun* came up with several questions. They are: how do schools, teachers, and students participate in the construction of knowledge and power in ways that advance a liberating and egalitarian worldview in the local educational sites? How can curriculum and teaching methods be innovated to empower students in general and those who, for one reason or another, have been marginalized in particular — the so-labelled band-five students? How do issues of the essence of both the Chinese and the Western traditions such as *ren* (humanity), life purposes, social justice, ethics, currently being repressed or ignored within education-al discourse be returned to the educative process? The accurate description and interpretation of the existing discourse and practice will illuminate what type of response might be in order to advance a new educational project that is beneficial to the majority of its members.

Like modernism, postmodernism has its limitations too. It makes it difficult to create a sense of community in order to put forth coherent political and moral stances, and to examine the educational terrain for the ways it bestows benefits and injuries. The dialectic deliberations cannot be carried out in isolation, especially if local educators hope to resist the powerful influences of the received practices that seek to bring students and their practitioners into even greater conformity with corporate interests and the agenda of the neo-conservative during the decolonization period. Yet if the tolerance of otherness precludes the search for some common good that can induce solidarity, the society will be left with a hullabaloo that disallows political and social action that is ethically and educationally compelling. The recognition of otherness that transcends the usual search for commonality becomes an imperative. Such a recognition makes possible the fact of mutuality even while differences are not only tolerated but protected and celebrated.

In the process of building a genuine, liberating educational movement for change in Hong Kong, *Hundun* submits that the community need not abandon the modernist empiricist ideals, nor digest postmodernity half-heartedly. Instead what the local community needs is to reconstruct and reappropriate them in terms of the advancement of the proper values and ethical commitments of both the East and the West (as discussed in last section), and integrate them into a liberating educational movement. It also needs to reappropriate notions of schooling rather than dismiss them because of their historical interpretations and limitations, as seen in the deschooling proposition suggested in the 1970s. The community also needs to articulate and link various dialectical social dynamics around a new liberating discourse of education. It will need to forge some sense of common or public interests that most Hong Kong people can unite behind if it is to successfully challenge received practices. The movement should be grounded on a number of organizing principles that define a public interest and that articulate the concerns and interests of various groups around a common agenda. One possible organizing principle is that it is difficult to be a good person (ethically speaking) in the absence of a good society — one that is committed to the beneficial advancement of certain ethical ideals: an interdependent prosperity that counteracts predatory relations among individuals and groups, and enables everyone to participate in the economic, political, and educational decisions for the good of individuals as well as society.

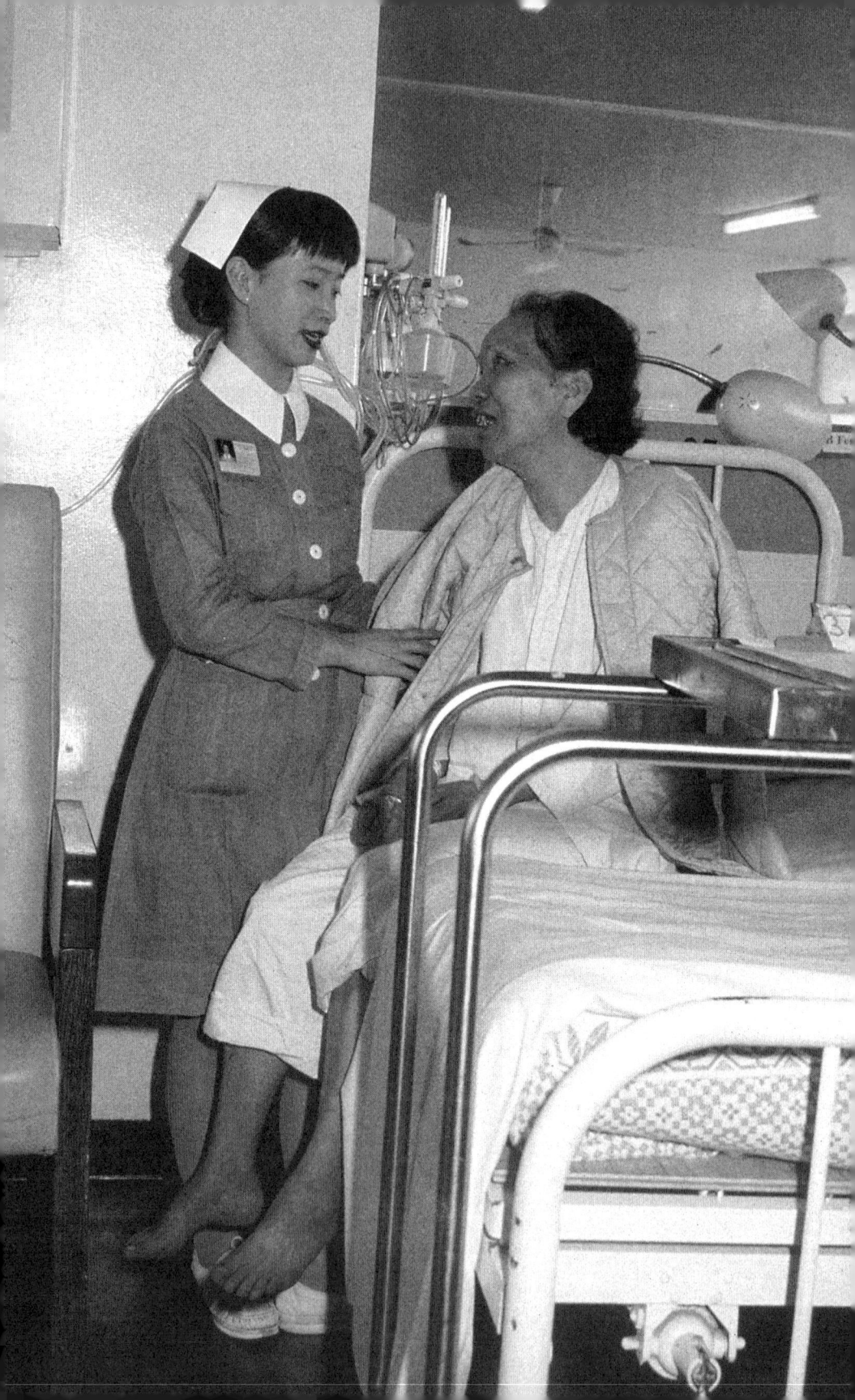

# 13

# Medical and Health

Leung Man-fuk

## □ Introduction

People of Hong Kong should be proud of their health care system. It has demonstrated a high standard of health indexes on a worldwide basis. Long life expectancy (81 for females and 75 for males) and low infant mortality rate (less than seven per 1,000 live births) is evident from Table 1. The contributing factors are: good public health, wide spectrum of medical and health care facilities, and most important of all, increasing affluence of the people.

Table 1.  Comparison of Health Indicators

|  | Hong Kong 1991 | U.S. 1990 | U.K. 1990 | Japan 1989 | Singapore 1990 |
|---|---|---|---|---|---|
| Expectation of life at birth | | | | | |
| Male | 75.1 | 72.1 | 72.9 | 75.9 | 72.1 |
| Female | 80.6 | 79.0 | 78.5 | 81.8 | 76.8 |
| Infant mortality rate (deaths per 1,000 live births) | 6.4 | 9.7* | 7.9 | 4.6 | 6.7 |

Note:    The figure with an asterisk (*) is for the year 1989.
Source:  *Towards Better Health: A Consultation Document* (Hong Kong: Government Printer, 1993), p. 1.

Leung Man-fuk is a medical consultant in the United Christian Hospital.

The year 1992–1993 marks an important milestone in health care delivery in Hong Kong. The government's endeavour to revamp the system of health care delivery was evident. The Hospital Authority has come to its second year of operation. The Hong Kong Academy of Medicine is due to be officially established and, of course, the Green Paper *Towards Better Health* was published in July 1993.

Although the above developments can be regarded as satisfactory, we must admit that the system of health care delivery in Hong Kong still has a lot of problems. Besides, rising expectations and changing trends of the population have further subjected it to constant criticism. There are problems over the funding of public health care services, imbalance in funding between primary and tertiary care, differences in the level of funding and human resources among different hospitals, an overworked and frustrated health care workforce, and the lack of regulation and control of a vast private health care sector.

The aim of this chapter is not to review what the government has done in the past year but to highlight some major health care issues that will be faced by the Hong Kong community. As the centre for discussion, special reference will be made to the recipients of health care services. Lastly, an account on the constraints for a better health care system in Hong Kong will be made. It is hoped that through careful analysis a more thorough understanding of the problems of the present system could be achieved.

## ☐ Major Issues in the Current Year

### *Patients' Rights*

With the enactment of the Bill of Rights Ordinance and the arrival of the new Governor, Chris Patten, who advocated for the setting up of the citizens' charter, the issue of patients' rights was a centre of discussion in the past year. In fact, a number of factors have helped make the debate on patients' rights a lively one. They include frequent accusations of doctors' deliberate mystification of medical matters, overcharging by private medical practitioners and the increasing awareness of individual rights among a more educated public.

The issue of patients' rights was first brought forward in an adjournment debate of the Legislative Council on 8 July 1992 by Felice Lieh Mak. About ten Legislative Councillors spoke during the debate and all supported the pledge for patients' rights. Besides, Meeting Point, a political party, Leong Che-hung, a Legislative Councillor, and the Federation of Patients' Rights have all pushed for the making of legislation on patients' rights and the setting up of a Patients' Rights Committee. However, the Secretary for Health and Welfare was rather hesitant about the role of the government in the espousal of patients' rights. She insisted that patients themselves were the best safeguard of their own rights. Thus, so far, the government's response has been negative.

In the meantime, the Hospital Authority is drafting a Patients' Charter for those receiving services from the Authority. This charter is only restricted to those using the Authority's services. It is not targeted at the whole community. It is hoped that by promulgating a Patients' Charter by the biggest public medical care provider, there will be an impact on the whole medical community and the attitude of the medical profession will undergo some changes. Apart from the Hospital Authority, the Hong Kong Medical Association has also proposed some principles on patients' rights. Unfortunately, the principles of patients' rights supported by these two biggest organizations of the Hong Kong medical sector are rather limited in scope.

In fact, patients' rights should be fundamental rights guaranteed for all citizens who utilize medical care, irrespective of whether the care comes from the public or the private sector. The issue of patients' rights should be viewed from a wider perspective. It should examine the relationship between the health care professionals and patients, with the government as the mediator. Patients' rights should be an extension of basic human rights which implies equality of all human beings. In this sense, the traditional relationship between the medical practitioner in a superior position to their patients should be changed. Basic patients' rights should cover areas including: the right to know, the right to refuse, the right to be properly cared for, the right to make decision and the right to complain. Any person should have the right to make his or her own decision and this right should not be deprived simply because of sickness.

With an unregulated private medical sector in Hong Kong, the importance of a territory-wide charter for patients' rights that delineates the relationship between the provider and the receiver becomes more imminent. According to a study by the Hong Kong Baptist College on patients' rights, it was found that over 90 per cent of the citizens agree to formalizing patients' rights in Hong Kong. Commenting on patients' rights under the existing health care system in Hong Kong, only 40 per cent of interviewees showed satisfaction. This shows that protection of patients' rights in actual practice is still far from being acceptable. In light of this, improvement on patients' rights for Hong Kong citizens becomes necessary.

A number of steps can be taken to promote the proper guarantee of rights of patients. The most fundamental should be the proper education of both the health care providers and the community. In the present curriculum, health care professionals spend little time on ethics and patients' rights, leaving much scope to be covered. In reality, without the proper education, it is difficult to perceive how a medical practitioner can uphold his or her patients' rights. Moreover, looking from another angle, it is also difficult for the general public to safeguard their own rights if they do not have the necessary knowledge and information on their health care. So it is important to improve both the medical curriculum and community education for the public.

Secondly, the government should draft and eventually legislate a territory-wide patients' charter. With this, the relationship between health care providers and their clients can be properly delineated and the interest of patients can also be safeguarded. To seek further improvement, a special committee should be set up to oversee progress in this matter. Lastly, an independent complaints committee should be set up to look into all complaints which involve the infringement of patients' rights. To successfully realize patients' rights, a fundamental change in the values and attitudes of health care providers is needed and this change will certainly take time.

## Primary Health Care

The report submitted to the government by the Working Party on Primary Health Care in December 1990 made a total of 102 recommendations. One of the recommendations was to set up a District Health System in Kwun Tong. As a result, a Kwun Tong District Health System was set up in 1992. However, the move towards reforms in the district has been slow since then. One reason may be bureaucratic inertia which makes existing organizations unresponsive to change and innovative ideas. Therefore, under the present situation, structural reforms become necessary.

The primary health care working group has also recommended the establishment of a statutory primary health care authority to oversee the provision of primary health care in Hong Kong. However, up till the present moment, there is still no indication from the government that an organization of this sort will be established.

The working party has made yet another recommendation. It is the provision of health screening for the elderly and women. This recommendation was also stated in the Governor's address to the Legislative Council in 1992. However, it is still not known when and how the government will implement the elderly screening programme. In fact, some voluntary agencies have already set up preventive health programmes for elderly people for some years. To put this recommendation into reality the government can consider utilizing the existing services provided by these agencies. With their expertise and experience, the programmes provided are likely to be more cost-effective. Subsidizing and extending existing programmes is certainly more feasible than starting new programmes under a government department which has no past experience at all.

One limitation of the primary health care report is that it has only addressed the issue of providing primary health care in the public sector. As about 70 per cent of the Hong Kong population depends on private medical practitioners for the provision of primary care, a major segment of the population have been missed out. Unless we are able to address the issue of private medical care in Hong Kong, the goal for "Health for All in the Year 2000" as stated in the *Report of Working Party on Primary Health Care* will be unrealistic. Yet, we may hope that the level of primary care can see some improvement with the formation of the Hong Kong Academy of Medicine in the coming year because private general practitioners are more likely to practise more preventive care after being offered more guidelines.

## Hospital Authority

The establishment of the Hospital Authority is in line with the Public Sector Reform of the Hong Kong government. The concept of autonomy and management reform of the hospital system has received wide support from both the medical sector and the public. However, in its second year of operation, there is a nagging worry among the public that the Hospital Authority may put more emphasis on a cost-recovery type of approach to charges.

Management reform of the hospitals is now in the pipeline. Up to March 1993, 18 Hospital Chief Executives and 28 Hospital Governing Committees have been formed among the 39 institutions in the Hospital Authority. The Hospital Chief Executive has overall authority and responsibility over the running of the hospital. Each basic patient unit is composed of a Chief of Service, a Department Operations Manager and a

Hospital Administrator. To support the basic patient units, the hospital management structure is organized into five major divisions: Clinical Services, Central Nursing, Allied Health, Administration, and Finance. Each division is led by a General Manager accountable to a Hospital Chief Executive.

The implementation of these new management structures in the public hospitals have created new management positions. However, since most of these positions are occupied by people holding similar jobs before the management reform, many frontline staff show doubts over the possibility of real change from the management style of the past. It certainly takes time and effort for the Hospital Authority to ensure that managers at various levels uphold the culture promoted by the Hospital Authority. If the middle management is not able to take the lead, it would be difficult to expect the 38,000 staff from the 39 institutions to follow.

Apart from management reforms, the Hospital Authority also released its first business plan for 1992–1993 in the second half of 1992, the second business plan for 1993–1994 in 1993 and a five-year corporate plan from 1993 to 1998 in 1993.

Out of the 120 targets stated in the first business plan, 115 have been successfully achieved by the end of the 1992–1993 financial year. Three Regional Advisory Committees have been formed in 1993. As stated in the second business plan, 1,890 new hospital beds will be opened in the year 1993–1994. As in the corporate plan four major corporate strategies have been stated. They are: transforming the direct patient services; developing a strong partnership with the community; enforcing organizational development and management reforms; and providing challenging employment and development opportunities. One major change to the provision of hospital services in Hong Kong is the formation of eight hospital clusters in the whole territory of Hong Kong. The objective of forming these clusters is to make a whole range of care facilities available to patients admitted to the cluster hospitals and to ensure continuity of services. Another major initiative of the Hospital Authority is to establish a Patients' Charter this year.

The public is well aware that the Hospital Authority has the ambition to cure all the ills of the past hospital system in Hong Kong. No one will even doubt the sincerity of the Hospital Authority in motivating its staff, providing quality hospital care and giving efficient and responsive services. But owing to its inherent limitations, there are lots of worries over whether the Hospital Authority can achieve its goals.

Although the Hospital Authority is independent of the civil service, it is not as autonomous as one would think. It cannot determine the policy of health care delivery in Hong Kong. Determination of policy still rests in the hands of the Health and Welfare Branch. It must obtain approval from the government before making any adjustments. Also, there are restrictions in the setting up of revenue-generating projects. Thus, the Memorandum of Arrangement between the Hospital Authority and the government has yet to be drawn up.

While it may sound most generous that the Hospital Authority can enjoy the "flexibility" of a "one-line-vote" budget, this is, however, exactly where the flexibility ends. Apart from a fair percentage of money being saved by the Authority, all the revenues generated from fees and charges will be clawed back to the government. From the budget allocation, it may seem that the government has spent more on health care. However, as 81 per cent of the allocated budget go to staff emoluments, there is certainly not much room to manoeuvre. In fact, a big sum of the government's additional budget has been spent in bolstering the fringe benefits of the previous subvented hospital staff. That is why under the constraint in resources many hospitals encounter difficulties in making improvements.

Apart from the constraint in resources, there also exists gross imbalance of resource allocation among different hospitals. Since a historical budget is still in practice, those hospitals which used to have a bigger budget continue to enjoy more resources under the present system. The two largest teaching hospitals continue to take the biggest financial base of all hospitals. The ex-government hospitals still enjoy bigger funding. The ex-subvented hospitals still have less human and financial resources. Therefore, this uneven distribution of resources has been and is still causing much frustration among the hospital staff working in smaller or less well-off hospitals.

Although the Hospital Authority has emphasized a closer link with and a wider participation from the community, the Hospital Authority Board's make-up has reflected its insincerity. The composition of the Hospital Authority Board has been criticized for not being able to reflect the opinion of the community. Taking a closer look at its membership, one finds that the Board has a strong bias towards business people and professionals from the health care field. Unlike the Board of the Housing Authority, it neither has members from interest groups nor members from pressure groups. Out of the 18 directly elected Legislative Councillors, not one of them has been appointed to the Hospital Authority Board. The composition is certainly a conservative one and is surely not representative of the community. Thus, the Hospital Authority should put its words into practice. It must ensure that the community is properly represented on its Board. In that way, the Hospital Authority can become more responsive to the needs of the community and ultimately more open and accountable to the public.

### *The Chronically Sick*

A federation of patient self-help group, the Alliance of Patients' Mutual Help Organizations, was inaugurated in February 1993. It is a federation of 17 chronic illness self-help groups. According to patients' self-help organizations, there are 230,000 patients with chronic conditions in Hong Kong. Among them are patients suffering from various forms of physical and visceral disabilities like rheumatoid arthritis, systemic lupus erythematosus, stoma patients, silicosis, chronic renal failure, etc.

Although chronically sick patients are in huge numbers, their needs have been overlooked all along. Patients with visceral disabilities are not included in the eligibility for Disability Allowance. As most of these patients require long-term follow-up, they encounter great difficulties in attending medical care owing to their mobility and functional disabilities. Yet no special support have been developed for them. Besides, the provision of rehabilitation service for chronic patients has also long been neglected.

Hence, in the hope of improving the plight of the chronically sick, the federation made a number of recommendations to the government in 1992. They include the following provisions for the chronically sick:

1. Rehabilitation service should be provided for those with bodily dysfunction.
2. Those with chronic illnesses should be included in the entitlement for Disability Allowance.
3. Financial assistance should be provided to those with chronic illnesses.
4. Resource centres should be established for those with chronic illnesses.
5. Secondary and tertiary preventive care should be improved.

The lack of special care in the past has put the chronically sick under great difficulties. If chronically sick patients are to see improvement for themselves, they should unite and press for better services and support. If they are better organized they stand a better chance to obtain needed services.

## The Elderly

Elderly people are major clients in health care delivery everywhere. As shown by data from developed countries like the United States, approximately one-third of the health care expenditure is spent on the oldest 10 per cent of the population. This reflects the serious implication on the health care system in an ageing society. As Hong Kong is on the threshold of an ageing society, there is no way to escape from this inevitable trend (see Table 2). According to the latest Hospital Authority statistics, about 37 per cent of the bed days are taken up by persons aged 65 and above (8.8 per cent of the total population).

Elderly people's needs in health care are indeed many, comprising health promotion, general health care, acute medical care, rehabilitation, long-term care and terminal care. These should be met in a comprehensive manner. However, under the present system, only fragmented health care facilities are made available for them. Health education and health promotion activities for elderly people are essentially negligible since only 1.3 per cent of the Department of Health budget in 1988–1989 was spent on this item. The under-provision of health preventive activity for this age group has resulted in greater incidence of chronic illnesses and hospitalization. This not only affects the quality of life of the elderly people, but also brings a great burden to the hospitals.

Elderly people in Hong Kong can obtain public medical care either through attending the various general outpatient clinics run by the Department of Health or being admitted to the inpatient care of the public hospitals managed by the Hospital Authority. However, as a traditional trend, most hospitals are biased towards acute care. Since elderly people with multiple medical problems are slow to respond, they, therefore, have not been the focus of attention. Thus, many of these elderly patients with chronic illnesses fail to receive adequate assessment, rehabilitation, and aftercare. As a result, repeated admissions are the order of the day. Since their basic problems are not being adequately dealt with, readmission to hospitals becomes the only way out. According to the General Household Survey in 1991, readmissions into hospital are quite frequent (12 per cent of the respondents). Therefore, if we cannot provide a more organized aged care

Table 2.  The Projection of Elderly Population in Hong Kong
(in thousand)

| | Age group | | | | | | All ages | Total elderly population |
|---|---|---|---|---|---|---|---|---|
| | 60–64 | 65–69 | 70–74 | 75–79 | 80–84 | 85+ | | |
| Mid-1988 | 227.4 | 178.9 | 133.2 | 83.8 | 43.4 | 27.7 | 5,647.1 | 694.4 |
| | (4.0) | (3.2) | (2.4) | (1.5) | (0.7) | (0.5) | | (12.3) |
| Mid-1989 | 232.3 | 185.9 | 137.0 | 90.9 | 45.4 | 30.1 | 5,771.0 | 721.6 |
| | (4.1) | (3.2) | (2.4) | (1.6) | (0.8) | (0.5) | | (12.6) |
| Mid-1990 | 236.9 | 192.8 | 141.1 | 97.3 | 48.2 | 32.2 | 5,775.3 | 748.7 |
| | (4.1) | (3.3) | (2.4) | (1.7) | (0.8) | (0.6) | | (12.9) |
| Mid-1991 | 241.3 | 199.1 | 146.2 | 102.6 | 52.1 | 34.7 | 5,840.4 | 776.0 |
| | (4.1) | (3.4) | (2.5) | (1.8) | (0.9) | (0.6) | | (13.3) |
| Mid-1992 | 245.2 | 204.8 | 152.0 | 106.8 | 56.9 | 36.9 | 5,903.2 | 802.6 |
| | (4.2) | (3.5) | (2.6) | (1.8) | (0.9) | (0.6) | | (13.6) |
| Mid-1993 | 249.0 | 210.0 | 158.4 | 110.2 | 62.4 | 39.1 | 5,964.3 | 829.1 |
| | (4.2) | (3.5) | (2.7) | (1.8) | (1.0) | (0.7) | | (13.9) |
| Mid-1994 | 251.9 | 214.6 | 164.9 | 113.7 | 67.9 | 41.6 | 6,023.4 | 854.6 |
| | (4.2) | (3.6) | (2.7) | (1.9) | (1.1) | (0.7) | | (14.2) |
| Mid-1995 | 253.3 | 219.1 | 171.2 | 117.4 | 72.9 | 44.5 | 6,080.2 | 878.4 |
| | (4.2) | (3.6) | (2.8) | (1.9) | (1.2) | (0.7) | | (14.4) |
| Mid-1996 | 253.6 | 223.3 | 177.0 | 122.0 | 77.0 | 48.2 | 6,134.6 | 901.1 |
| | (4.1) | (3.6) | (2.9) | (2.0) | (1.3) | (0.8) | | (14.7) |
| Mid-1997 | 252.8 | 227.3 | 182.5 | 127.1 | 80.3 | 50.3 | 6,186.1 | 922.3 |
| | (4.1) | (3.7) | (3.0) | (2.0) | (1.3) | (0.8) | | (14.9) |

Note:   Figures in parentheses are percent shares.
Source:  Census and Statistics Department, *Hong Kong Population: A 20-Year Projection* (Hong Kong: Government Printer, 1987), Table B1, p. 16.

service for elderly people in the hospitals, the root of the problem will not be tackled with.

More seriously, the issue of long-term care for elderly people has long been neglected by the government. Besides, Hong Kong's system of care for elderly people who require long-term care is flawed in a fundamental way. It arbitrarily divides the patients who require institutional nursing care into two categories: (1) care and attention home, and (2) infirmary. The care and attention home is put under the jurisdiction of the welfare sector while the infirmary belongs to the hospital sector. This artificial division has created lots of problems which include coordination and referral problems.

Moreover, the provision of infirmary places is not without problem. The establishment of infirmary places in the then Hospital Services Department had always been inadequate. The number of infirmary places had remained static for a period of over ten years. Even at present, there is only a total of 1,300 infirmary beds in Hong Kong. Moreover, these infirmary beds cannot serve the real needs of many elderly people. Elderly people suffering from severe disabilities and requiring long-term nursing care are not welcomed in the infirmaries. They are often rejected upon referrals by hospitals. Therefore, elderly patients who are in acute hospitals cannot get access to infirmary hospitals even if they have such a need. In most instances, these patients will be discharged from the hospitals and admitted to profit-making private homes. Since the level of care available in the private homes is, in general, extremely poor, the health of the elderly will deteriorate rapidly. Many of them will soon be readmitted to hospitals because of bedsores, malnutrition and various sort of infections. We can see, therefore, that the existing care provided for our elderly population with long-term nursing need is extremely inadequate. In addition, their plight cannot be relieved by community-support services since the types of community-support facilities provided are far from sufficient to meet their needs.

There is no doubt that a skeleton of health care services is provided for Hong Kong's elderly people through general outpatient and hospital care. But in terms of quantity and quality, the provision is far from satisfactory. The upgrading in the provision depends very much on the real commitment of the government. If we really want to improve the care to the elderly, real resources need to be injected into the system. The areas of preventive and long-term care for elderly people have to be closely examined and the services provided have to be directed to their needs. Since elderly people have been serving the community for such a long time, the provision of care for them should be accorded high priority.

## □ Limitations on Better Health Care

We have seen in the previous discussion that the quality of health care in Hong Kong has been affected by many factors which in turn have been brought about by a number of fundamental defects which include health care policy formulation, health care financing, quality measures and attitudinal problems.

## *Issue of Health Care Policy*

One of the major drawbacks of the provision of health care in Hong Kong is the lack of a coherent health care policy. There is no overall direction on the development of health care in Hong Kong. The only policy directive claimed by the government in all official documents is that "no one should be denied adequate medical treatment through lack of means". Other than that, health care policy is an issue untouched on by the government.

The last health care policy White Paper dates back to 1974. But even after all these years most of the proposals made in that White Paper have not yet been achieved. Even if they have, the policy document is certainly out-of-date in the present context. Within these twenty years, Hong Kong has seen great change in its environmental, political, industrial, and population patterns.

The lack of a new health care policy has long been the major criticism of the government by academicians, professionals and politicians. What the government did in the past was only bits and pieces of review and reforms like the publication of the Scott report on Hospital Authority, the report on primary health care, Green Paper on rehabilitation and the consultation document *Towards Better Health*. They were not released under a central direction. Therefore, at most, they could only bring about incremental modifications to the existing structure.

The government has, in fact, placed the issue of policy-making in the hands of a few bureaucrats. It has been the sole decision of a few officials in the Health and Welfare Branch. No public participation is involved in the formulation and determination of health care policy. Informed public debate on health care for Hong Kong is also rare. Certainly, we need to define the value basis of our health care policy before we can devote the right and necessary resources for its development. Therefore, it is time for us to make a review of the overall aim and target of health care delivery in Hong Kong.

No doubt, there is the Health and Medical Development Advisory Committee (HMDAC). It is an advisory body on issues of health care delivery. However, the HMDAC only plays an advisory and consultative role. Its objectives are rather narrow. Its representation is again limited and it cannot initiate any policy review. If the HMDAC is to function more effectively, the government should consider appointing a representative group into the committee and enriching its power in health care evaluation and policy formulation.

## *Health Care Financing*

The financing of health care is another important area of concern. Every year, the health care budget takes up approximately 8 to 9 per cent of the total expenditure of the government. With the existing low-tax system, it is difficult for the government to increase its percentage of expenditure in health care even though it is facing a rising ageing population, a community with increasing expectations and a rapidly advancing medical technology. Without additional resources, the quality of health care services will be questionable. Therefore, it is expected that Hong Kong will face a serious problem of health care financing in the coming years. That is why a number of organizations which could foresee the problem have made repeated claims on the government to improve health care financing.

Upon constant request to do something to tackle the problem of health care financing, the government appointed a working group on health insurance in 1991. However, to the disappointment of many, the proposal worked out by the working group is merely to encourage voluntary health insurance with better government regulation.

In July 1993, the government produced a consultation document *Towards Better Health*. Despite its title, the content is disappointing to those who are looking for improvement in health care for Hong Kong. The main focus of the document is to find ways to increase the source of income through partial cost recovery of hospital care. Nothing has been mentioned on how the government is going to use the money generated to bring about improvement. Therefore, this document only elicited disappointment and criticism among the public.

However, with the commitment to a low tax rate on the one hand and the rapid pace of medical development and increasing demand for medical services on the other, the Hong Kong government has to find a way to help fund its future medical services. The medical and health care system in Hong Kong has long been a basically free one with equal access to all citizens. It is hard for the public to accept any major increase in the cost for public health care. With increasing politicization of the society, the option of reducing subsidy by the government as recommended in the consultation document will surely face severe opposition. It can never gain support from the grassroots-based Legislative Councillors. If the government has to push it through, it will surely face tremendous resistance. This is certainly not what one wishes to see in this transitional period. It will surely affect the stability and legitimacy of the government. Therefore, it may seem more reasonable and acceptable for the government to adopt some form of state-administered health insurance scheme. The scheme should cover the whole population and can help generate resources of health care financing.

### *Quality and Attitudinal Issues*

The problems of health care delivery in Hong Kong as discussed above are structural in nature. However, health care services serve to promote human well-being, and should require a humanistic approach in management. We need to be more sensitive to the individual's needs in the process of care provision. The issues of patients' rights, as well as care for the chronically sick and the elderly all help to demonstrate this aspect.

Disappointingly, it is easy to perceive that the health care system of Hong Kong has never progressed in this direction. The emphasis has always been on curative and high-technology medical care. The orientation of the health care system has been a hospital-based one and the focus of health care professionals has been high-technology types of remedial care. The caring perspective in health care delivery was not the focus of attention. Patients are often regarded as cases, not individuals.

In modern health care, the mere satisfaction of physical needs is not enough. The primary aim of an effective health care system should be the fulfilment of the needs of individuals. Therefore, there is a pressing need to refurbish the education and training of health care professionals in Hong Kong. More emphasis should be placed on preventive, community care and client-oriented approach in health care delivery. The multiplicity of the needs of the patients like psychological and social needs must be recognized by health care providers.

## ☐ Conclusion

With limited government budget and resources, the public health care system of Hong Kong has demonstrated a high degree of efficiency. However, this should not be the ultimate aim of health care delivery. Long life expectancy and low infant mortality rate are only quantitative measures. What the public now expects is not the same as what they did twenty years ago. The quality of care has become a major concern.

As health care provision is one of the main social services in Hong Kong, unavoidably it has a place on the political agenda. The government can no longer hide away from the important debate on how we are going to run and fund our health care services. The public should be well involved in discussions on any fundamental change on the mode of health care delivery in Hong Kong. Thus, there is a pressing need for the Hong Kong polity to determine the direction of our health care system.

To further advance Hong Kong's health care delivery, the government should in the coming years focus on adopting a more comprehensive review of health care policy, determining the goals and targets of health care provision and aiming at proper integration between private and public health care systems. There are still many questions on health care delivery to be addressed in the years to come.

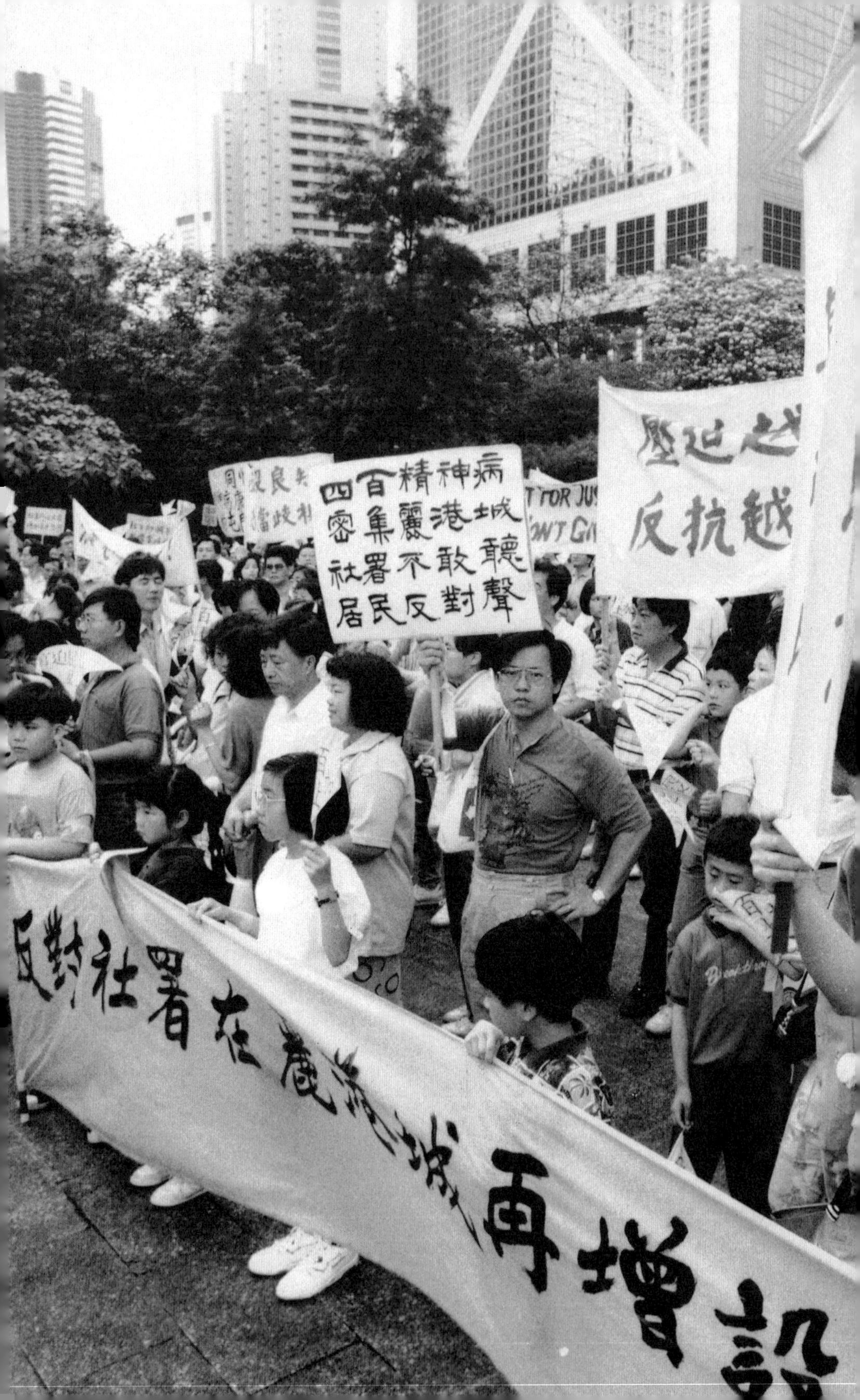
四百精神病
密集麗港城
社署不敢聽
居民反對聲
反抗越
反對社署在麗港城再增設

# 14

# Social Welfare

## Cecilia Chan

## ☐ Introduction

The year 1992–1993 marked a year of challenge, promise and some progress in the realm of social welfare. Promises of progress were indicated in the speech of the Governor, Chris Patten, in October 1992 and in that of the Director of Social Welfare, Ian Strachan, to a Rotary Club in May 1993.

In order to show that the government cares for its people, in his address to the Legislative Council (Legco) on 7 October 1992, the Governor gave a clear direction on the reorganization of the social security scheme to improve the livelihood of the poor, and promised an injection of $2.3 billion into the Lotteries Fund to finance the long-awaited expansion of services for the elderly and for mentally disabled persons, both of these groups having been neglected in the past. The Governor's first policy speech gave a reassuring message to the public that the Hong Kong government is committed to improving the well-being of the most needy groups in our society.

In preparation for the International Year of the Family in 1994, Strachan enthusiastically announced the family-focused strategies of the Social Welfare Department towards preventing family problems, giving support to families and helping families in need. Indeed, families are breaking down at a rapid rate and such matters as spouses physically separated due to emigration, and adjustment problems after divorce deserve greater public attention and policy concern.

Cecilia Chan is a lecturer in the Department of Social Work and Social Administration, The University of Hong Kong.

At the same time, there have been some controversial decisions concerning the planning and implementation of social welfare policy especially in the areas of rehabilitation, youth and family services, and welfare financing.

Two steadily emerging themes of the social welfare scene these days are the politicization of welfare and public participation influencing decision-making. Regarding the former, the government has, for instance, been criticized for handing out welfare to buy off the public for its political reform package for more democratic election. An example of the latter is the Alliance of Patients' Mutual Help Organizations, which was inaugurated in February 1993 as a self-help and advocacy group. These two themes will recur throughout this chapter in different contexts, sometimes with positive and sometimes less positive connotations, as will be seen.

## ☐ Major Issues Arising from Welfare Development 1992–1993

### *Policy Planning and Funding*

#### *Planning Objectives and Organizations*

The White Paper *Social Welfare into the 1990s and Beyond* described social welfare in Hong Kong thus: "Social welfare embraces laws, programmes, benefits and services which address social needs accepted as essential to the well-being of a society. It focuses on personal and social problems, both existing and potential. It also plays an important developmental role by providing an organized system of services and institutions which are designed to aid individuals and groups to achieve satisfying roles in life and personal relationships which permit them to develop their full capacities and to promote their well-being in harmony with the needs and aspirations of their families and the community." (White Paper, 1991, p. 13).

The Health and Welfare Branch in consultation with the Social Welfare Advisory Committee (SWAC) and the Rehabilitation Development Advisory Committee (RDAC) determines policies on social welfare and rehabilitation, which are implemented through the Social Welfare Department (SWD) and the Non-governmental Organizations (NGOs) in Hong Kong. Detailed planning of service implementation is conducted through the annual Five Year Plan Review exercise in which representatives from the SWD and the NGOs, through the Hong Kong Council of Social Service (HKCSS), work closely together. This partnership between the SWD and the NGOs is crucial for the effective implementation of social welfare policy and programmes.

There has been a major change in the membership of the SWAC in 1993 with more directly elected Legislative Councillors appointed to the committee. It is a big step forward for legislators to be involved in social welfare policy-making. It is also a good training for legislators to ensure a smooth transition to self-administration beyond 1997.

### Resource Allocation for Service Provision

Table 1 describes the resource allocation exercise on service and financial provision; it also provides a checklist of existing service provision as at 1 April 1993 and new developments in 1993–1994. From the table, it is obvious that there have been significant improvements in service provision in most aspects of social welfare services in Hong Kong. This sizeable increase in service should be seen in the light of the repressed expansion or zero growth in the previous three years, which was precipitated by the very tight control of public expenditure to prepare for the port and airport projects, sometimes dubbed the "rose garden" project.

The rapid increase in social welfare services was in part a result of strong pressure from various political and consumer groups, and in part a result of the need to reduce the embarrassingly huge governmental budget surplus of 1992–1993. Implementation of service improvements was speeded up by the injection of public money into the Lotteries Fund, which is designated for welfare services and is more flexible than the regular government subvention procedures. Despite these additional provisions, there are still huge shortfalls in relation to the projected demands for services. Moreover, as planned, the $2.3 billion injection into the Lotteries Fund will be exhausted by 1997. The future Special Administrative Region (SAR) government will have to incorporate these expenditure items into its general revenue account.

From Table 2, it can be seen that up to two-thirds of the total welfare expenditure is spent on social security. The second largest amount of welfare expenditure is on family and child care services, while the expenditure on youth, elderly and rehabilitation remains small. The present exercise of incremental planning will only cater for the development of existing provision. No allowance appears to have been made for newly emerging needs and increasing numbers within deprived groups.

Table 1. Resource Allocation Exercise: Service and Financial Provision, 1993–1994

| Objectives and services | Provision units | Provision 1.4.1993 | Additional provision 1993–94 | Total provision 1993–94 | Demand 1993–94 | Financial provision 1993–94 ($m) |
|---|---|---|---|---|---|---|
| *Offenders* | | | | | | |
| Aftercare service for ex-prisoners | Social worker | 23 | 7 | 30 | 36 | 0.612 |
| Community service orders scheme | Magistracy | 6 | 4 | 10 | — | 1.114 |
| Probation | Probation officer | 100 | 19 | 119 | 133 | 2.523 |
| Residential service | Place | 636 | — | 636 | — | 4.065 |
| Young offenders assessment panel | Social worker | 2 | 1 | 3 | — | 0.338 |
| *Young People* | | | | | | |
| Outreaching youth work | Team | 24 | 4 | 28 | 30 | 9.380 |
| School social work | Worker | 150 | 18 | 168 | 180 | 6.270 |
| Children centre | Centre | 217 | — | 217 | 237 | 3.450* |
| Youth centre | Centre | 217 | — | 217 | 237 | — |
| *Elderly* | | | | | | |
| Care & attention (C&A) homes | Place | 4,210 | 1,568 | 5,778 | 9,051 | 21.770 |
| C&A homes (infirmary unit) | Unit | 18 | 5 | 23 | — | — |
| Day-care centre | Centre | 12 | 6 | 18 | 32 | 1.370 |
| Holiday centre | Centre | — | 1 | 1 | — | 3.450 |
| Home for the aged | Place | 7,588 | 364 | 7,952 | 8,228 | — |
| Multi-service centre | Centre | 18 | 3 | 21 | 32 | 3.190 |
| Outreaching (elderly at risk) | Team | — | 2 | 2 | — | 0.580 |
| Social centre | Centre | 177 | 18 | 195 | 274 | 4.240 |
| *Family Welfare* | | | | | | |
| Clinical psychology | Clinical psychologist | 13 | 4 | 17 | 51 | 0.570 |
| Day crèches | Place | 977 | 273 | 1,250 | — | — |
| Day nurseries | Place | 22,079 | 1,400 | 23,479 | 29,631 | 1.110 |

| | | | | | | |
|---|---|---|---|---|---|---|
| Family aide | Worker | 4 | 16 | 20 | — | 1.846 |
| Family casework | Worker | 434 | 9 | 443 | 536 | 3.320 |
| Family life education | Worker | 59 | 8 | 67 | 78 | 3.090 |
| Foster care | Place | 320 | 160 | 480 | — | 3.420 |
| Home/halfway house for boys/girls | Place | 1,628 | 60 | 1,688 | — | 3.330 |
| Home help | Team | 72 | 12 | 84 | 119 | — |
| Medical social work | Social worker | 260 | 38 | 298 | 533 | 1.888 |
| Occasional child care | Unit | — | 75 | 75 | — | 5.990 |
| Small group home | Home | 23 | 24 | 47 | — | — |
| *Rehabilitation* | | | | | | |
| Activity centre for discharged MP | Place | 110 | — | 110 | — | 12.470 |
| Day-activity centre | Place | 2,293 | 440 | 2,733 | 3,800 | — |
| Halfway houses | Place | 809 | — | 809 | 1,149 | — |
| Home/C&A aged blind | Place | 339 | — | 339 | — | 2.020 |
| Hostel for MMH | Place | 1,046 | 100 | 1,146 | 1,596 | 3.350 |
| Hostel for PH | Place | 317 | 100 | 417 | 636 | 9.630 |
| Hostel for SMH | Place | 1,095 | 300 | 1,395 | 2,207 | 0.500 |
| Integrated child care centre | Place | 705 | 60 | 765 | — | 0.290 |
| Level 2 hostel | Place | — | 17 | 17 | — | 1.450 |
| Level 3 hostel | Place | — | 70 | 70 | — | — |
| Long stay care home | Place | 200 | — | 200 | 474 | 5.950 |
| Sheltered workshop | Place | 4,775 | 660 | 5,435 | 6,630 | 0.720 |
| Small group home | Place | 3 | 24 | 27 | — | 0.060 |

Notes: 1. MP: mental patient; MMH: moderately mentally handicapped; PH: physically handicapped; SMH: severely mentally handicapped.

2. The figure indicated by an asterisk (*) includes provision for youth centres and children centres.

3. A dash (—) means: no existing provision and additional provision, or data of demand and financial provision for 1993–94 not
available.

Sources: SWAC Paper No. 18/92; *Estimates for the Year Ending 31 March 1994*, Vol. I & II (Hong Kong government); Social Welfare
Department, *Five Year Plan Review 1991*.

Table 2.  The Share of Welfare Expenditure ($ million) on Different
Service Areas, 1989–1994

| Service Area | 1989–90 | 1990–91 | 1991–92 | 1992–93 | 1993–94 |
|---|---|---|---|---|---|
| Social Security | 2,783.4 | 3,320.9 | 3,892.3 | 4,620.4 | 4,948.3 |
| | (66.97) | (66.96) | (64.73) | (65.49) | (64.83) |
| Family | 416.7 | 515.8 | 612.1 | 708.0 | 781.4 |
| | (10.03) | (10.40) | (10.18) | (10.04) | (10.24) |
| Youth | 315.6 | 293.3 | 460.5 | 506.6 | 526.8 |
| | (7.59) | (5.92) | (7.66) | (7.18) | (6.90) |
| Elderly | 208.4 | 289.7 | 387.8 | 467.6 | 538.0 |
| | (5.01) | (5.84) | (6.45) | (6.63) | (7.05) |
| Rehabilitation | 259.9 | 329.4 | 419.0 | 481.2 | 556.7 |
| | (6.26) | (6.64) | (6.97) | (6.82) | (7.29) |
| Community | 89.8 | 110.9 | 128.6 | 143.5 | 144.2 |
| development | (2.16) | (2.24) | (2.14) | (2.03) | (1.89) |
| Ex-offenders | 82.1 | 99.3 | 112.7 | 127.8 | 137.6 |
| | (1.98) | (2.00) | (1.87) | (1.81) | (1.80) |
| Total | 4,155.9 | 4,959.3 | 6,013.0 | 7,055.1 | 7,633.0 |
| | (100) | (100) | (100) | (100) | (100) |

Note:    Figures in parentheses are percentage share of welfare expenditure.
Source:  *Five Year Plan Reviews* of Social Welfare Department, various years.

## Funding of Social Welfare

The government pays for most of the welfare services provided both by the
SWD and the NGOs ($7,055 million in 1992–1993). The Community Chest
($101 million in 1991–1992), the Lotteries Fund ($250 million in 1991–
1992), the Jockey Club Trust Fund ($1,124 million in 1991–1992) and other
private charities also contribute to the financing of social welfare programmes. The Jockey Club funds capital projects such as building schools
and hospitals as well as the premises for welfare agencies.

The NGOs which join the Community Chest as members surrender
their right to fund-raising from the public except for special circumstances.
Community Chest allocations tend to cover services which are only partially supported by the government, therefore resources left for research,
pilot projects and testing of innovative approaches are very small (see
Figure 1). The long-standing voluntary and pioneering spirit of welfare
organizations thus tends to diminish with time.

Figure 1. The Donation from Community Chest, 1989–1993

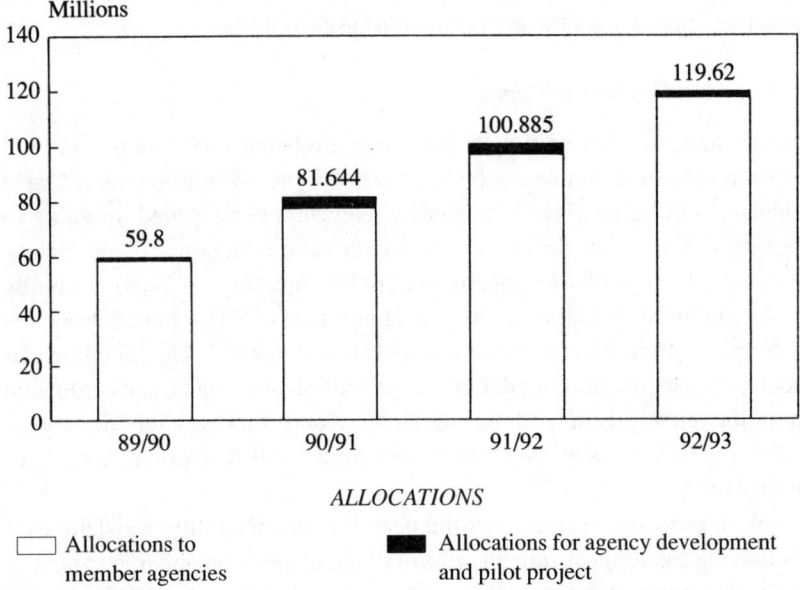

ALLOCATIONS

☐ Allocations to member agencies     ■ Allocations for agency development and pilot project

Source: *Social Welfare Statistics*, 1993 Edition, Hong Kong Council of Social Service.

## Non-government Funding

With increasing affluence and inflationary costs of service provision in Hong Kong, the pattern of non-government funding is changing. Some international welfare organizations such as Oxfam are retreating from direct service provision but are instead using Hong Kong as a fund-raising base. Owing to constitutional constraints, the Bradbury Trust Fund is planning to retreat from Hong Kong before 1997. Another charity, the Keswick Foundation, is funding experimental projects for three years with the expectation that the government or the Community Chest will pick up subsequent recurrent costs. Other volunteers and donors are shifting their interest to China. Fund-raising for local charities is becoming increasingly difficult in view of competition from Third World countries and China in particular.

The SAR government will have to establish new charity funds and re-establish local fund-raising mechanisms to support pilot and innovative projects to cater for the changing needs of Hong Kong. Meanwhile, one way to secure a sustained and regular source of funding for welfare would be to designate a larger percentage of the Mark Six turnover for the Lotteries Fund, which the government refuses to do so.

*Management of Charity Funds*

Donors have no idea how their donations are being used. Abuses are not uncommon; for example, only $214,000 of the $4 million raised in a popular 1993 Lunar New Year charity television show ended up going to the needy. The rest of the money went to cover production and administrative costs. The issue of management of public funding was brought vividly to the public's attention when the Hong Kong AIDS Foundation lost $1.6 million in its foreign exchange investment in 1993. The failed investment was part of the Foundation's $30 million seed money accumulated from the government and Royal Hong Kong Jockey Club donations. Following this incident, there were widespread calls for stricter control of charity funds.

With growing awareness of the need for accountability, legislators are demanding tighter government control of the disposition and investment of public donations. It is no mere coincidence that the SWD, the NGOs and the Community Chest are putting more emphasis on evaluative research in an effort to demonstrate effective use of their funds.

## Revisions of Social Security

*The New Comprehensive Social Security Assistance Scheme*

The Governor announced the revision of payment rates under the old Public Assistance (PA) and Special Needs Allowance (SNA) schemes as well as the implementation of the Comprehensive Social Security Assistance (CSSA) scheme and Social Security Allowance (SSA) scheme in his 1992 address to Legco. The renaming of the PA and SNA as CSSA and SSA was intended to provide the public with a clearer picture of the amount of financial assistance (a standard rate) that a person would get under the PA and SNA schemes. The amount of the standard rates for different categories of welfare recipients with effect from 1 July 1993 can be seen in Table 3.

The CSSA scheme describes the total amount each person is entitled to, including the non-means-tested cash allowance. In fact, the actual increase is only about 15 per cent. This new scheme has been criticized as a gimmicky tactic to reduce the pressure for a significant increase in the level

Table 3.  The Basic Rates of the Comprehensive Social Security Scheme
According to Different Categories of Clients Effective from
1 July 1993

| Categories of clients | Basic rates ($) | Other provisions/requirements |
|---|---|---|
| *Single person* (adult) | | Supplements of rent allowance, |
| Able-bodied | 1,035 | special and discretionary grants |
| Elderly/50% disabled | 1,550 | will be given. Maximum |
| 100% disabled | 1,935 | disregarded income of $775 per |
| In need of constant attendance | 2,835 | month. |
| | | |
| *Single person* (child) | | Permitted absence from Hong |
| Able-bodied | 1,260 | Kong for elderly and disabled |
| 50% disabled | 1,770 | recipients up to 180 days, able- |
| 100% disabled | 2,160 | bodied recipients up to 60 days |
| In need of constant attendance | 3,005 | over a 12-month period. |
| | | |
| *Family member* (adult) | | Value of cash, savings and |
| Able-bodied | 895 | investments: for a single person |
| Elderly/50% disabled | 1,285 | $22,800 maximum and for a |
| 100% disabled | 1,675 | family member $15,190 |
| In need of constant attendance | 2,470 | maximum. |
| | | |
| *Family member* (child) | | Monthly allowance for extra |
| Able-bodied | 995 | diet: $295 or $570. Monthly |
| 50% disabled | 1,510 | meal allowance for students |
| 100% disabled | 1,895 | attending full-day school: $154. |
| In need of constant attendance | 2,795 | |

Note:    The column for other provisions/requirements applies to all applicants.
Source:  Social Welfare Department.

of public assistance. The Welfare Panel of Legco has called for a review of
the level of public assistance. The result of this review will be available in
1994.

## Inequalities in Cash Allowance

The basic rates for different categories of clients under the new CSSA
scheme vary significantly. A single elderly person, for example, is entitled
to $1,550 a month while a child and an adult, such as a single parent, living
in the same family are only entitled to $995 and $895 a month respectively.
There seems to be little justification for the 60 per cent discrepancy between
the amount for subsistence for a single person and for a person living with
other family members. Although the cost of electricity, gas and water may

be shared by more than one person living in a household, the amount saved can hardly amount to $600 a month.

According to a study on the nutritional intake of elderly welfare recipients by The Chinese University of Hong Kong and the Tsuen Wan Ecumenical Social Service Centre in 1993, these elderly people spent an average of $789 per month on food. As active adults and growing children are likely to need more food than the elderly, the meagre amount of $895 and $995 respectively can hardly satisfy their needs, especially those of the younger welfare recipients.

There are 16,000 children living on welfare in Hong Kong. To have no toys, not enough clothing to keep themselves warm, no pocket money, no telephone at home, no money for extracurricular activities — these deprivations are all nailing the self-esteem of these children to the ground. Another anomaly is that young persons above the age of 18 are not eligible for the Public Assistance Scheme, even though they may still be receiving education and are not yet working.

Why has the social security system been so mean towards children? Children do not have votes while elderly persons do. Almost all candidates for District Boards, Urban and Regional Councils and Legco elections proclaimed their pledge to improve services for the elderly during their election campaign. Hardly any of them mentioned the needs of children in poverty.

### Nature of Cases on Public Assistance

From the analysis of the nature of cases on public assistance, it is obvious that the bulk of the actual increase of welfare recipients in the past 15 years was a result of the increase in the number of elderly persons and persons with permanent disabilities (see Table 4). The elderly and disabled persons have had absolutely no means of livelihood and therefore had no choice but to rely on public assistance. The chances of either group to move out of welfare dependency are also slim unless, regarding the permanently disabled persons, large-scale special employment training is provided for them and employment opportunities made available.

The proportions of single-parent families and low-income families dependent on public assistance are actually going down. Given the current low level of provision, persons with a capacity to work will definitely not rely on welfare. The percentage of elderly persons above the age of 60 will increase from 13.9 per cent in 1993 to 16.1 per cent in 2007 (see Table 5).

With our population ageing and the projected steady increase in the number of persons with permanent disabilities, the welfare expenditure on cash assistance for CSSA and SSA will increase significantly. It is essential for the Hong Kong government to plan ahead and consider a Central Provident Fund or some other form of retirement scheme to prepare for the reverse pyramid population distribution 20 to 30 years from now.

Table 4. Nature of Cases on Public Assistance

| Type of Cases | % share of the year | | | |
|---|---|---|---|---|
| | 1975–76 | 1980–81 | 1985–86 | 1990–91 |
| Old age (60+) | 53.20 | 63.87 | 64.30 | 67.20 |
| Temp. disabled/Ill health | 13.60 | 17.28 | 13.10 | 10.94 |
| Permanent disabled | 4.50 | 5.89 | 7.00 | 9.04 |
| Single-parent family | 4.80 | 6.06 | 5.90 | 5.85 |
| Economic circumstances | 22.80 | 4.78 | 5.90 | 4.01 |
| Others | 1.10 | 2.12 | 3.80 | 2.96 |
| Total | 100.00 | 100.00 | 100.00 | 100.00 |
| Total number of cases | 54,439 | 45,813 | 61,925 | 66,675 |

Source: *Five Year Plan Reviews* of Social Welfare Department, various years.

Table 5. The Projection of Elderly Population in Hong Kong
(in Thousand)

| Age group | Mid-1989 | | Mid-1993 | | Mid-1997 | | Mid-2003 | | Mid-2007 | |
|---|---|---|---|---|---|---|---|---|---|---|
| | No. | (%) | No. | (%) | No. | (%) | No. | (%) | No. | (%) |
| 60–64 | 232.3 | (4.1) | 249.0 | (4.2) | 252.8 | (4.1) | 224.3 | (3.5) | 239.7 | (3.7) |
| 65–69 | 185.9 | (3.2) | 210.0 | (3.5) | 227.3 | (3.7) | 233.5 | (3.6) | 222.0 | (3.4) |
| 70–74 | 137.0 | (2.4) | 158.4 | (2.7) | 182.5 | (3.0) | 206.8 | (3.2) | 211.4 | (3.2) |
| 75–79 | 90.9 | (1.6) | 110.2 | (1.8) | 127.1 | (2.0) | 157.9 | (2.5) | 168.8 | (2.6) |
| 80–84 | 45.4 | (0.8) | 62.4 | (1.0) | 80.3 | (1.3) | 101.2 | (1.6) | 114.0 | (1.7) |
| 85+ | 30.1 | (0.5) | 39.1 | (0.7) | 52.3 | (0.8) | 79.3 | (1.2) | 92.6 | (1.4) |
| All ages | 5,711.0 | | 5,964.3 | | 6,186.1 | | 6,433.9 | | 6,526.6 | |
| Total elderly population | 721.6 | (12.6) | 829.1 | (13.9) | 922.3 | (14.9) | 1,003.0 | (15.6) | 1,048.5 | (16.1) |

Source: Census and Statistics Department, *Hong Kong Population: A 20-Year Projection* (Hong Kong: Government Printer, 1987), Table B1, p. 16.

## Rehabilitation Services: Equal Opportunity and Full Participation

### The Green Paper on Rehabilitation Policies and Services

Since the White Paper *Integrating the Disabled into the Community: A United Effort* was published in 1977, rehabilitation services have developed steadily but very slowly. In view of the changing conditions in society, a thorough review was conducted by the Working Party on Rehabilitation Policies and Services under the chairmanship of the Secretary for Health and Welfare in January 1991. The Working Party produced a Green Paper on rehabilitation policies and services entitled *Equal Opportunity and Full Participation: A Better Tomorrow for All* in March 1992. The public consultation period ended in June 1992 but there is still no sign of the White Paper being released by mid-1993. This forthcoming White Paper is to provide a policy guideline on the development of rehabilitation services in the decade to come.

The overall policy objective for rehabilitation is: "To promote and provide such comprehensive and effective measures as are necessary for the prevention of disability, the development of the physical, mental and social capabilities of disabled persons, and the realization of a physical and social environment conducive to meeting the goals of their full participation in social life and development, and of equalization of opportunities" (Green Paper, 1992, p. 23). However, the shortfall of rehabilitation services is so large that full participation and equal opportunity will not be achievable in practice.

The major omissions of this Green Paper are:

1. New categories of disabled persons are ignored. The old classification which was developed two decades ago is still being used with no cognizance of newly emerging groups of persons with disabilities. Chronic patients who fall in the gaps in health and welfare policies and services are not included under existing categorization.
2. There is no mention of programmes to address the public's discrimination against disabled persons, yet this kind of discrimination is a major barrier to full participation and equal opportunity. The paper only pays lip service to offering mutual help, home care and community-based rehabilitation but it gives no firm resource commitment to strengthening community education and community rehabilitation.

Table 6. The Demand and Shortfall of Rehabilitation Service, 1992–1994

| Rehabilitation services | 1992–93 | 1993–94 |
|---|---|---|
| Day-activity centre | 3,154 | 3,326 |
| | (886) | (623) |
| Sheltered workshop | 6,804 | 7,161 |
| | (1,515) | (1,250) |
| Hostel for the severely mentally handicapped | 2,253 | 2,441 |
| | (1,258) | (1,146) |
| Hostel for the moderately mentally handicapped | 1,447 | 1,570 |
| | (378) | (372) |
| Half-way house | 1,693 | 1,810 |
| | (636) | (710) |
| Long stay care home | 671 | 852 |
| | (448) | (624) |
| Home for the aged blind | 371 | 406 |
| | (162) | (195) |
| Care & attention home for the blind | 484 | 566 |
| | (306) | (370) |

Note:    Figures in parentheses are the shortfall; figures other than these are the demand.

Source:  *Paper for Planning of Rehabilitation Services* provided by Social Welfare Department, 1993, Annex III.

## Omission of Persons with Chronic Illness (Visceral Disability)

Despite the call from patients' groups for the need for rehabilitation services of persons with chronic visceral disabilities, the Green Paper did not come up with a new category of visceral disability. The projection of persons with disabilities was still based on the old categories as listed in Table 7.

There are more than 200,000 hospital admissions a year for persons with diseases with chronic problems such as stroke, brain injury, rheumatoid arthritis, systemic lupus erythematosus, cancer, hemophilia, and chronic renal failure. Chronic patients need health education, training in home care, and emotional and social support. When their needs are not being served, they may relapse, deteriorate and be admitted into hospital again. The spouses, children and other family members of chronic patients also suffer from emotional and physical stress arising from the burden of caring for the patient and anxiety about the future. They need help too.

Table 7.  Estimated Number of Disabled Persons in Hong Kong,
1993–1999

| Type and degree of disability | 1993 | 1996 | 1999 |
|---|---|---|---|
| 1. Hearing impaired | 12,965 | 13,543 | 14,075 |
|    a. Profoundly deaf | 5,137 | 5,371 | 5,596 |
|    b. Severe | 3,130 | 3,275 | 3,387 |
|    c. Mild/moderate | 4,698 | 4,897 | 5,092 |
| 2. Visually impaired | 16,181 | 17,613 | 19,069 |
|    a. Totally blind | 7,417 | 8,128 | 8,855 |
|    b. Severe low vision | 3,184 | 3,491 | 3,802 |
|    c. Mild/moderate low vision | 5,580 | 5,994 | 6,412 |
| 3. Mentally ill (those requiring rehabilitation services) | 22,785 | 23,715 | 24,657 |
| 4. Autistic children | 1,046 | 1,035 | 999 |
| 5. Mentally handicapped | 117,244 | 120,417 | 123,049 |
|    a. Severe | 3,921 | 3,858 | 3,730 |
|    b. Moderate | 23,856 | 24,537 | 25,120 |
|    c. Mild | 89,467 | 92,022 | 94,199 |
| 6. Slow learner | 32,164 | 31,532 | 30,767 |
| 7. Maladjusted | 6,790 | 6,590 | 6,370 |
| 8. Physically disabled (including the cerebral palsied) | 70,871 | 75,099 | 79,248 |
| Total | 280,046 | 289,544 | 298,234 |

Source:  Extracts from the Estimated No. of Disabled Persons in Hong Kong 1990–
1999, *Rehabilitation Programme Plan Review 1991* (Hong Kong: Government Printer, 1991).

Medical social workers in hospitals are supposed to provide comprehensive psychosocial care for patients and their family members. Unfortunately, the planned ratio of medical social workers in hospitals is
disappointingly low (one medical social worker to 90 hospital beds). Social
workers are heavily involved in fee-waiving and dispensing of material
assistance which leaves very little time and energy for counselling, education, social and emotional support. Most hospitals do not have a clinical
psychologist. Chronic patients are often in despair, even to the point of
committing suicide as there is no one available to help. The long-standing
separation between medical care and psychosocial care must be rectified.

Seventeen mutual help groups for chronic patients formed themselves
into an Alliance of Patients' Mutual Help Organizations in February 1993.
These groups have been very active in mobilizing public support for the

inclusion of visceral disability into the White Paper on rehabilitation to come. The Alliance worked closely with the media to promote public awareness of the needs of chronic patients and health consciousness for all.

The Alliance and five other organizations jointly proposed to the government to set up five regional community rehabilitation networks to provide information, social and emotional support for chronic patients, who now suffer from the gaps in medical and social welfare provision. Besides the establishment of community-based rehabilitation networks, Queen Mary Hospital and Queen Elizabeth Hospital have set up Patients' Resource Centres which started operation in 1993. With increasing awareness among medical professionals of the psychosocial needs of chronic patients and their family members, hospitals can move towards providing comprehensive care to all concerned.

*Public Discrimination and Segregation*

The rush for service expansion for the mentally disabled as promised in the Governor's speech, regrettably, backfired. All available premises were used to accommodate new services for the elderly and disabled persons in an attempt to meet the targets laid down in the 1992 Governor's speech. New services for disabled persons were suddenly established in local communities without adequate preparation, planning and public consultation. These actions have resulted in some strongly negative public reactions such as the opposition to the proposed home for severely mentally handicapped adults in Tung Tau Estate and to the day-care centre for ex-mental patients in Laguna City. The extensive damage done to the Down Syndrome Association Parents' Resource Centre in August was an attempt to intimidate the clients from utilizing the facility in Tung Tau Estate. The issue of public acceptance of underprivileged groups must be addressed.

Unlike the services for the elderly, children and youth, rehabilitation services are not planned on a community level. Allocation of resources and placements are made through a central registry. As a result, disabled persons sometimes have to wait for a long time, for example for a place in a home for severely mentally handicapped persons, and have to travel a long distance to such facilities as sheltered workshops. With the increase in numbers of persons with disabilities and service expansion, rehabilitation services should now be planned on a regional if not district basis. Such localized planning will not only make services more accessible to consumers, but would have the advantage of educating the public about rehabilitation services being an integral part of community facilities.

The government is spending millions of dollars on AIDS education and prevention while only using $40,000 on public education for the acceptance of disabled persons in 1991–1992. Owing to the public pressure against the establishment of homes for severely mentally handicapped and ex-mental patients, an amount of $400,000 was allocated for public education in 1992–1993. However, half this amount was spent on a games day organized by the Health and Welfare Branch and the SWD. Unfortunately, *ad hoc* promotional programmes will not be very helpful. Promotion of community acceptance of persons with disabilities deserves greater government commitment and priority. Specialized community education teams with the knowledge and skills to educate the public and promote public acceptance of persons with various types of disabilities are needed.

*Politicization of Welfare*

Politicians of different persuasions volunteered their views on both the Tung Tau Estate and the Laguna City disputes. There were debates in the Health Panel, the Welfare Panel and Legco sessions on services for mentally disabled and mentally ill persons. Client groups, welfare agencies, parents' organizations together with the Joint Council for the Physically and Mentally Disabled lobbied for support while residents' groups expressed their opposition and solicited support from political groups. It will be disastrous if political groups, based on political rather than equitable principles, decide to adopt discriminatory positions against persons with disabilities. There is no representation of disabled persons in Legco. Despite the effort of the Rehabilitation Alliance in asking for a functional constituency seat for disabled persons in the coming 1995 Legco election, their views have not been heard.

*Separate Legislation for Mentally Handicapped Persons*

Persons with mental handicap constitute 41.8 per cent of the estimated 269,000 persons with disabilities (Green Paper on rehabilitation policies and services, p. 13). Under the existing Mental Health Ordinance, mental illness and mental handicap are served without distinction. Parents' organizations have been pushing for separate legislation for persons with mental handicap as they need to be protected by law in terms of guardianship, representation before the Court, and their rights to service. All the professional associations of lawyers, doctors and social workers support the idea of separate legislation to correct the existing anachronism.

*Transportation for Persons with Disabilities*

A special working group chaired by the Governor himself on transportation for disabled persons was formed in December 1992, as a result of a public consultation session on the Governor's speech when a member of the audience raised the issue of transportation difficulties for disabled persons in Hong Kong to the Governor. Operators of public transport and disabled persons discussed the issue of access to transportation services, but public transport operators refused to incorporate improvements to make their vehicles accessible to wheelchairs and urged the government to support the Rehabus service instead. The fact remains that even with a dramatic expansion of the Rehabus service, the needs of physically disabled persons could never be adequately served by an NGO. With the Governor taking a personal interest in rehabilitation services, the government officials and the NGOs concerned would have to work hard for solutions.

## Services for Young People

In order to foster healthy youth development and to help youths face life stress and emotional upheavals, youth work agencies are offering counselling services to provide young persons with personal guidance, supportive services to underprivileged young persons, socialization programmes to help young persons establish a sense of self-esteem, as well as participation in volunteer service to develop a sense of belonging and contribute to society.

*Service Integration*

There are children and youth centres, outreaching social work teams, school social work units and uniformed groups funded by the government in Hong Kong. A single children or youth centre-cum-reading/study room and a combined children and youth centre receive approximately $1.1 million and $1.5 million of government subvention each year respectively. During the review of children and youth centre services, it was found that the membership of some centres was very small, making the recurrent cost per head very high. The Working Party on the Review of Children and Youth Centre Services, in the *Draft Report on Review of Children and Youth*

*Centre Services* of June 1993, proposed an "Integrative Service Delivery Model" for youth service in which integrated teams would be set up for catchment areas with a youth population of 12,000. School social workers, outreaching youth workers and social workers in children and youth centres would work within an integrated team to provide comprehensive and, hopefully, more cost-effective youth services.

There are high-risk children and youths not being adequately served under the present system, for example children of parents in prison, survivors of child abuse, children in poverty, ethnic-minority children, children in divorced families, bereaved children, youths with disabilities, children with cancer and other chronic illnesses. The integrative model may offer solutions with, for instance, each integrative team experimenting on working with a particular group of children or youth.

## Youth Charter

The Youth Commission was formed in February 1990 to advise the Governor on matters pertaining to youth. The Commission issued a Youth Charter in 1993. The first section of the Charter stipulates the principles and ideals of youth development; the second section sets out the major rights of youth in the light of these principles and ideals; and the third section states the long-term social goals for youth development. Individuals and organizations are invited to subscribe to the Charter. However, it would be much more fruitful if the Youth Commission was given the authority to be actively involved in the coordination and resource allocation for programme implementation.

## Youth Suicide and Alienation

Public attention has been drawn largely by the media to the number of student suicide attempts and suicide cases which have increased quite significantly in the past five years. Suicide signifies the underlying ills of despair and alienation from society. It is the extreme of self-destructive behaviour. Besides suicide attempts, there are increasing numbers of drug addiction, smoking, triad involvement, recklessness and other self-destructive behaviour among the youth population.

The contributing factors are immensely complex and prevention must be directed at many levels. The SWAC endorsed a proposal to increase the number of school social workers to one social worker per secondary school in 1993. If this ratio can be implemented, the school social work service

Table 8. The Trend of Student Suicides from 1988–1993

| School year (Sept.–Aug.) | Number of attempted suicides | Number of suicides |
|---|---|---|
| 1988–89 | 25 | 2 |
| 1989–90 | 25 | 1 |
| 1990–91 | 32 | 3 |
| 1991–92 | 46 | 21 |
| 1992–93 (up to 31 March 1993) | 59 | 19 |

Source: Interview reports, data quoted from Education Department records.

will be an integral part of the school system in providing students with counselling and support services. Yet the increase of school social workers alone will not be a panacea to youth problems. Family and community support, and the system for child care and youth integration into society are vital in the prevention of youth crime and self-destruction. Unfortunately, one important service, the experimental afterschool care service for children of single-parent families, is to be terminated in August 1993. The NGOs and the SWD must explore a means to continue financing such services for children in high-risk families. Society can provide other opportunities for youth participation, such as lowering the voting age, establishing student unions in all secondary schools, and strengthening youth involvement in community affairs.

## Family and Child Care Services

The SWD and NGOs are providing families with family service centres, family life education, home help services, child care services, foster care, small group homes, as well as protection of juveniles, teenage or unwanted pregnancy and battered women through sheltered housing.

### Individuals and Families at Risk

Youth suicide attracted a lot of attention and publicity. However, in 1992–1993, more than 800 people of all ages killed themselves and the suicide rate per 100,000 population increases steadily with age. Five out of every 1,000 persons above the age of 70 kill themselves each year. It seems that old and chronically ill patients seldom seek help, with the result that some resort to killing themselves. The public seems not to care. It is essential for

Table 9. Number of Deaths from Suicide Per 100,000 Population

| Age | 1988 | 1989 | 1990 | 1991 |
|-----|------|------|------|------|
| 10–24 | 4.71 | 4.28 | 4.88 | 4.67 |
| 25–39 | 9.68 | 10.30 | 13.02 | 13.78 |
| 40–54 | 10.45 | 11.20 | 11.74 | 15.06 |
| 55–69 | 21.90 | 20.20 | 19.72 | 21.60 |
| 70+ | 40.73 | 44.32 | 45.99 | 51.05 |

Source: *The Samaritan Befrienders Hong Kong Annual Report 1991*, p. 24.

planners to develop a well-informed and rational strategy in the identification of individuals and families at risk so that appropriate services and intervention can be planned.

Families break down because of divorce, desertion, imprisonment as well as death due to accidents and industrial injury. Chronic illness, mental problems, physical disabilities and drug addiction make family life stressful. Marital disputes, communication problems, run-away children and domestic violence are destructive to family cohesion. The divorce rate in Hong Kong is increasing every year. Special services must be designed to better serve bereaved spouse, single parents, teenage mothers, survivors of sexual abuse, victims of rape and violence, children in divorced families, chronic patients, and families living on public assistance.

The Director of Social Welfare, Ian Strachan, has urged the public to take the family seriously and has proposed the expansion of various types of family services to support families. These include family activity and resource centres, increased numbers of family life education officers, improved child care facilities, increased family aide workers and home helpers to support families at risk, as well as improved quality of counselling in family service units and the Child Protective Services Unit, increased temporary residential care for children and the expansion of clinical psychologist services.

Unfortunately, there is no regular funding for research and programme evaluation. Much more research and more pilot projects should be encouraged in order to keep abreast of changing needs of society. New approaches such as mutual help groups and self-help organizations, social networking, helper-therapy should be further developed and tested as these can be cost-effective ways of bringing about change and helping people to help themselves.

Strachan also hinted that expansion in family services is only possible if cutbacks are made in other programme areas. However, when the government is determined to improve the quality of family life and to prevent family disaster, definite resource commitments are necessary instead of relying on cutbacks from other programmes.

Strategies to help families in trouble should also extend beyond the SWD. An obvious example is the case of housing for divorced women and their children, battered wives and abused children. It was a major improvement when the Housing Department designated conditional tenancies in public housing estates for divorced couples or victims of domestic violence.

Another example is children with special needs, such as the 16,000 children living on public assistance. Children and youth centres as well as family service units can join hands with the Social Security Field Units to provide services that will help these children through the most difficult and critical times.

### Women as Care-givers and Service Consumers

The burden of care and nurture falls mainly on the woman in the family. Life becomes particularly stressful for her if there is a chronic patient, a frail elderly person, a mentally handicapped child or a mentally ill family member at home. Women sometimes feel guilty for not being able to satisfy all the demands of home care while feeling inadequate in knowledge of specialized care and exhausted by the physical labour and emotional strain. Respite services, temporary residential care for disabled persons, training and support for home care-givers are essential to make it possible for elderly or disabled persons to stay at home.

Women are the key consumers of family services (70.1 per cent). Men are more reluctant to seek help for relationship problems and are generally not willing to take part in family enrichment programmes. Men usually approach family services for health and financial reasons while women usually for relationship and home management difficulties.

If women can be adequately mobilized in strengthening community support for each another, they can be effective in supporting life-enrichment programmes and the prevention of family disasters. Pilot projects such as the Hong Kong Women's Centre and Women's Development Project in Shau Kei Wan are not funded by the government. More policy recognition and effort must be invested in the welfare needs of women and in developing specific working approaches to cater for their needs.

*Community Care, Self-care and Family Care*

On policy, the government often stresses the traditional virtues of filial piety and home care among Chinese families and is reluctant to provide community care services. In practice, the size of Hong Kong families has decreased steadily in the past two decades. Owing to the diminishing capacity of the family to care for its members, elderly and disabled persons are particularly vulnerable when they lose the ability to take care of themselves. Formal service delivery should be designed to supplement family care and for those who do not have a family.

Elderly persons and disabled persons are the main consumers of home help services. The most popular services are meal delivery and personal care services. Tables 10 and 11 describe the reasons for requesting home help service and the type of services rendered.

Table 10. Percentage Distribution of Home Help Service by Reasons for Help by Type of Clients, Jan.–Dec. 1991

| Reasons | Type of clients | | | Total |
|---|---|---|---|---|
| | Elderly persons | Disabled persons | Social or family needs | |
| Sudden illness of family members/care-givers | 1.5 | 4.6 | 9.3 | 2.6 |
| Death of family members/care-givers | 0.3 | 0.3 | 4.2 | 0.6 |
| Hospitalization or confinement of family members/care-givers | 0.9 | 2.8 | 6.5 | 1.6 |
| Desertion of parents/family members | 0.6 | 2.2 | 5.6 | 1.2 |
| Loss and/or inadequate self-care ability | 96.0 | 88.6 | 55.6 | 92.2 |
| Others | 0.6 | 1.5 | 17.8 | 2.0 |
| Total no. of reasons | 2,293 | 325 | 214 | 2,827 |
| % | 100 | 100 | 100 | 100 |

Note: Rounding accounts for minor add-up discrepancies.

Source: Extracts from *Clientele Information System 1989–1992*, Hong Kong Council of Social Service.

Table 11. Percentage Distribution of Home Help Service by
Type of Client, Jan.–Dec. 1991

| Type of home help service rendered | Type of clients | | | Total |
| --- | --- | --- | --- | --- |
| | Elderly persons | Disabled persons | Social or family needs | |
| Personal care | 14.5 | 14.5 | 4.4 | 8.3 |
| General physical exercise | 1.0 | 0.9 | 0.5 | 0.6 |
| Household cleaning | 24.7 | 19.2 | 24.0 | 14.6 |
| Child care | — | 0.3 | 7.8 | 0.4 |
| Laundry service | 18.4 | 13.5 | 8.8 | 10.4 |
| Delivery/purchase of daily necessities | 6.9 | 9.4 | 13.2 | 4.1 |
| Escort service | 34.4 | 56.6 | 41.7 | 22.8 |
| Visiting | 0.2 | — | — | 0.1 |
| Meal delivery | 65.3 | 42.8 | 46.6 | 37.2 |
| Preparing of meals | 1.6 | 0.9 | 8.3 | 1.2 |
| Others | 0.6 | 0.3 | — | 0.3 |
| Total no. of services rendered* | 3,746 | 504 | 317 | 4,567 |

Notes: 1. Multiple services may be given to any client and therefore the percentage is more than 100%.
2. The item indicated by an asterisk stands for the total number of services given rather than number of clients receiving service.

Source: Extracts from *Clientele Information System 1989–1992*, Hong Kong Council of Social Service.

## Community Development

As at 1 April 1993, there are 51 Neighbourhood Level Community Development Projects (NLCDPs) and 26 Community Centres (CCs) in Hong Kong. The goal of community development is to facilitate mutual help, collective problem-solving and to cultivate a sense of community and sense of belonging to society.

### Underprivileged Groups

The NLCDPs mainly serve deprived areas such as squatter areas, temporary housing areas, old resettlement housing estates and urban slums. Most of the residents are new immigrants, single elderly persons, and low-income groups who know very little about community resources and do not have the capacity to help themselves. Problems such as addiction, gambling, single parenthood, running away of kids, crime, early school dropouts, accidents and family disputes prevail in these communities. The NLCDPs reach out to these underprivileged groups, provide them with services, and encourage them to participate in collective problem-solving. The NLCDPs could now move beyond their customary targets of residential neighbour-hoods and apply their expertise to serving underprivileged functional com-munities such as physically or mentally disabled persons.

*Social Action and Service Delivery*

The most controversial social action incident in 1992–1993 was the petitioning of the Housing Authority and the Governor on the double-rent policy of the Housing Department. A total of 2,000 residents was organized by residents' organizations to petition the Governor as part of a day-trip programme. The Hong Kong People's Council on Public Housing Policy and a few other community development projects also organized residents to petition the Housing Authority. As the Housing Authority decided to retain the double-rent policy, about 150 individuals marched to Govern-ment House. The demonstrators insisted on handing in their petition at the front gate of Government House, and the police blocked off the traffic in that region for more than six hours. Finally twenty-three demonstrators were arrested, of which eleven were social workers and one was a social work placement student. Although these demonstrators were not charged, this event has led to vigorous discussion on the role of community workers and their participation in civil disobedience.

## Elderly Persons as Assets or Liabilities

In thirty years' time, elderly persons above 60 years of age will be the largest population segment in Hong Kong (see Figure 2). Such growth in the elderly population will have important implications on welfare, social security, health and housing service planning.

Some of the "young-old", those of 60 to 69 years, may be able to contribute to caring for their grandchildren and participate in household chores or even take up open employment, if they are given the encourage-ment and opportunities. They might also serve as volunteers in community services, contributing to community betterment. But a growing number of "old-old", persons above 80 years old, face severe problems of personal

Figure 2.  Hong Kong Population Pyramid, mid-1986, mid-1996 and mid-2006

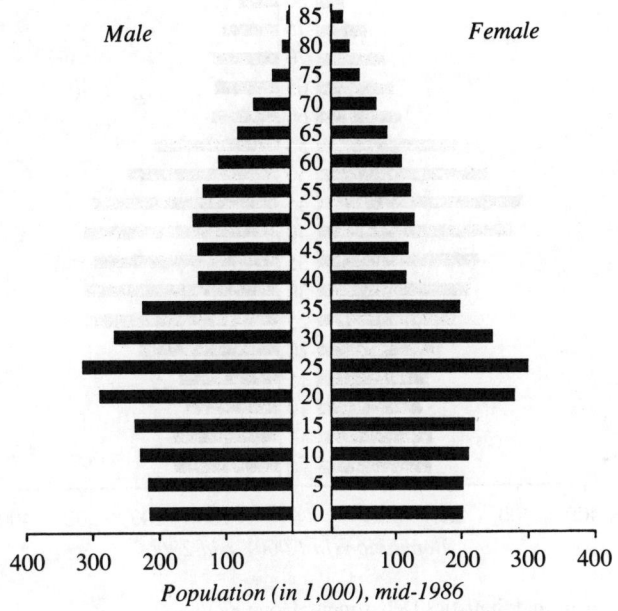

*Population (in 1,000), mid-1986*

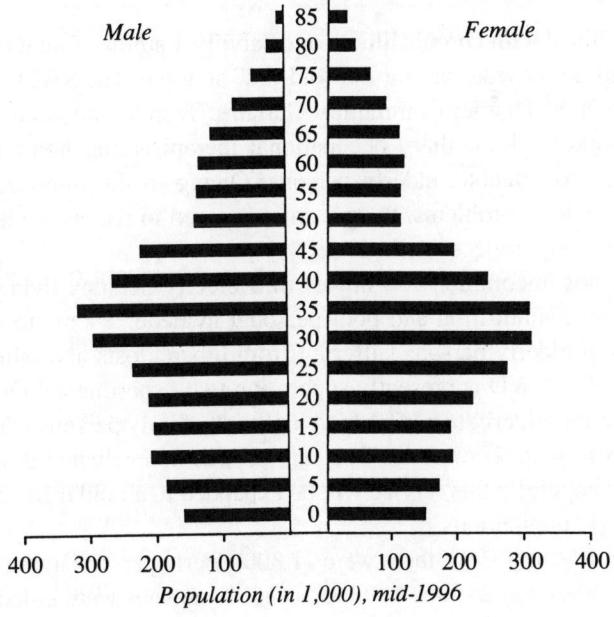

*Population (in 1,000), mid-1996*

Figure 2.  (Cont'd)

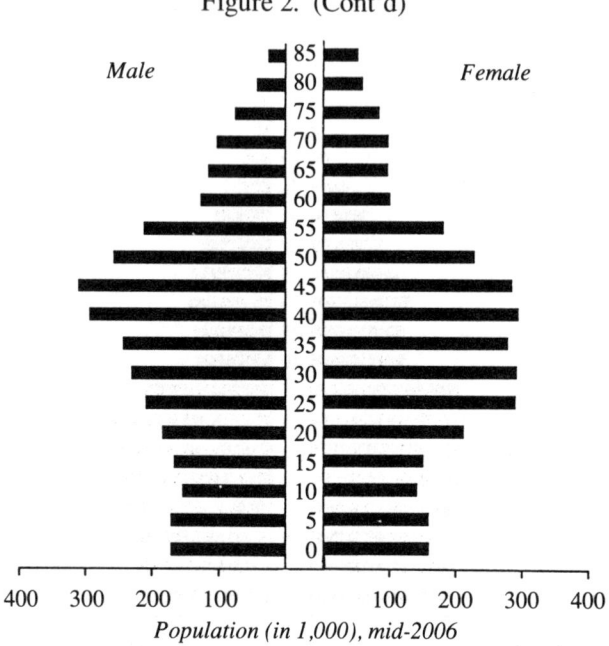

*Population (in 1,000), mid-2006*

Source:  Census and Statistics Department, Hong Kong.

care combined with chronic illness or disability. Families find it increasingly difficult to provide care for the "old-old" at home. The SWD is planning
to set up eight District Community Geriatric Teams with doctors, nurses,
social workers, domiciliary occupational therapists and home-helpers to
serve the more feeble, elderly persons. Owing to the multi-disciplinary
nature of elderly problems, the government need to reconvene the Central
Committee on Services for the Elderly.

It is not uncommon for single, frail elderly persons living alone to
suffer from malnutrition and poor personal hygiene. There are increasing
numbers of elderly persons suffering from tuberculosis and other chronic
illnesses. The SWD is presently supporting two experimental Outreaching
Teams for the Elderly to reach out to high-risk elderly persons who have no
resources to help themselves. The service will be evaluated at the end of
1993 and hopefully this service will be expanded to all old urban areas with
high elderly populations.

As at 1 March 1993, there were 11,800 elderly persons living in private
nursing homes. On 24 June 1993, two elderly persons were killed and over

twenty injured in a fire at a private old age home situated in an old tenement building. As the government cannot provide sufficient care and attention homes for the frail elderly, reliance on the supplementary services of private homes becomes inevitable. Legislation governing the standard of private homes for the aged becomes a public concern. Because of cost considerations, some homes are inadequately staffed and some are located in old buildings where the fire risk is high. In recognition of the demand for nursing homes for the elderly, private homes need to be controlled and the Housing Department and the Land Development Corporation should make available suitable space to private homes, so that standards can be maintained.

## □ Conclusion

Administrators and planners are faced with value choices in resource allocation. Mechanisms must be developed to encourage innovations and to establish regular monitors of changing needs and problems. Prioritization and resource allocation should take into consideration relative hardship, deprivation, social costs and economic consequences.

A lot of Hong Kong residents have to rely on public assistance and other welfare services because of the lack of overall social protection for people. Political will and administrative determination are required of government officials to move into the broader social policy issues of a central provident fund and retirement scheme.

A Hong Kong phenomenon causing much familial distress is the separation of family members in Hong Kong and China. Immigration policies need to be pursued to facilitate reunion of these divided families. The newly emerging problems of families with husbands and wives separated through emigration, sexual abuse, single-parent families, chronic patients, all require policy impetus for innovation, administrative encouragement for team work in medical and health settings with greater emphasis on psychosocial well-being, as well as long-term planning and resource commitments for welfare. The establishment of a Welfare Authority, similar to the Hospital Authority, to streamline service planning and coordination may be a viable alternative to ensure the best utilization of public funds.

# Housing

Leung Wai-tung

## ☐ Introduction

The year under review was an eventful one in the field of housing. It was another year of much progress and considerable achievement for the Hong Kong Housing Authority (HA), the major organization responsible for public housing. Nevertheless, much remains to be done as at least 219,000 households or roughly 13 per cent of the territory's total were still considered to be inadequately housed by the end of 1992 because their accommodation was of non-permanent construction, non self-contained or occupied on a shared basis. It was however another year of disappointment regarding the performance of the private housing sector with prices of domestic units continuing to be beyond the means of the vast majority of households.

In addition, the year under review was an extremely busy one for housing activists. Hardly a week elapsed without any demonstrations, protests, petitions, public rallies or press conferences in connection with housing issues. Quite a number of such events were organized by members of the District Boards, municipal councils, and the Legislative Council (Legco). Political organizations were also actively involved. The number of questions raised in Legco sittings, and of motion and adjournment debates moved in Legco on housing matters also reached a record high. Whether or

Leung Wai-tung is a lecturer in the Department of Geography and Geology, The University of Hong Kong. She is also a member of the Hong Kong Housing Authority.

not the issue of housing has been politicized, and if so, whether such a development is a blessing for society as a whole, are questions that have frequently been asked.

The year also witnessed the sudden departure of the first non-official chairman of the HA, Sir David Akers-Jones. Sir David took every one by surprise when he informed the Governor in mid-March 1993 of his intention to resign from the chair of the HA with effect from 1 April 1993, one year before the expiry of his term of appointment. According to media reports, the major reason given by Sir David for his resignation was that he could not tolerate any more the unjustified personal attacks and accusations made against him by some concern groups, public housing tenants, and legislators who were not in favour of some of the policies of the HA.

This chapter, while written with an aim to provide a critical review of major developments in the area of housing during the past year, nevertheless places an emphasis on public sector housing policies and practices. As Richard Y. C. Wong has presented in a similar chapter last year a very detailed analysis of rent control in the private housing sector and of the working mechanism and performance of the private residential property sector, the part on private housing in this chapter will be very brief. What the writer wishes to do is to discuss major public housing policies and practices so as to facilitate a better comprehension of the housing conditions of the mass of Hong Kong people and of government efforts in solving housing problems.

## ☐ Overall Housing Policy

The government has intervened considerably in the housing market in the postwar years particularly through the provision of subsidized public rental and ownership units, clearance of squatter areas, and the imposition of rent and other forms of control in the private housing sector. While housing has been one of the major issues of concern for the government and the construction of public housing has long been given high priority in the allocation of public funds, the government does not run any general housing subsidy scheme in the form of cash assistance, rent allowance, tax concessions or special mortgage arrangements to assist eligible members of the public to rent or buy homes. Exceptions are the Home Purchase Loan Scheme introduced under the Long Term Housing Strategy in 1988, and the interim loan scheme for middle-income families to be implemented at the end of August 1993. In both schemes, downpayment loans are given to a limited number of participating families for the purchase of private sector domestic units.

At the beginning of April 1993, it was estimated that there were some 121,000 households with monthly household incomes below the income limits eligible for public rental housing (PRH), which represented 38.3 per cent of all non-owner-occupier households in the private sector. There were also another 83,500 households, or 26.4 per cent of all non-owner-occupier households in the private sector, with incomes between the limits for PRH and the limit for the public ownership housing schemes including the loan scheme just mentioned. These two groups together constitute 12.3 per cent of all households in the territory.

## Long Term Housing Strategy

The Long Term Housing Strategy (LTHS) endorsed by the Executive Council (Exco) in 1987 provides a framework for Hong Kong's public housing programme and housing policies up to 2001. It resulted from a complete review conducted in 1986 of the government's housing policies, and of the demand for, and supply of, public and private housing between 1985 and 2001. There are two fundamental principles in the housing policy:

1. to promote an equitable and efficient use of scarce resources in satisfying the housing need of all income groups; and
2. to promote social stability and sense of belonging to Hong Kong by securing better living conditions for the needy and maximizing the opportunity for home purchase.

Based on these two principles, six objectives have been identified:

1. to ensure that adequate housing at an affordable price or rent is available to all households;
2. to promote and satisfy the growing demand for home purchase;
3. to ensure that the need for all types of housing is satisfied with minimum delay and in accordance with established priorities;
4. to improve residential living conditions by redeveloping older public housing estates and by encouraging redevelopment of older private housing;
5. to secure the most effective use of the resources of both the public and private sectors; and
6. to ensure that public resources spent on housing are used most

efficiently by ascertaining that a household's benefit from housing subsidy is in relation to its need.

The aim of the LTHS is to clear all identified outstanding demand by 2001, by which time adequate housing at affordable prices or rents will be available to all households.

The basis of the LTHS is demand-led, with increased emphasis on home ownership. The rental/ownership mix in the public housing sector was accordingly changed from a fixed ratio of 3:1 used since 1980–1981 to a flexible one based on forecast. The role of the private sector is emphasized and public housing programmes are to be designed in such a way as to satisfy demands that the private sector cannot satisfy. During the review, the production capacities of both the public and private housing sectors were examined. It was assumed that on average the annual production in the public sector would remain at around 40,000 housing units, while the private sector production would be around 30,000 units a year. Any shortfall in the private sector production was to be made up by increasing production in the public sector.

Three major changes were introduced in the LTHS. First, the public housing sector redevelopment programme referred to as the Comprehensive Redevelopment Programme (CRP) was to be enlarged to include Marks IV–VI Resettlement estates, and Former Government Low Cost Housing (FGLCH) estates with self-contained dwelling. In other words, all Resettlement and FGLCH estates would be redeveloped by 2001. Next, the opportunity for home purchase would be increased for sitting PRH tenants, prospective tenants and tenants affected by the CRP. Last, a loan scheme — the Home Purchase Loan Scheme — would be implemented from 1 April 1988 to assist those households eligible to purchase public sector home ownership scheme flats to buy flats in the private sector.

For the first time in Hong Kong, the government subsidized consumption in the housing market in the form of cash handouts. The scheme was conceived as a means to utilize more effectively the private sector's resources such as construction capacity, land holdings and financing. It was designed to utilize the forecast surplus production capacity of the private sector after the demand for home purchase from those who were not eligible for any form of government assistance had been met.

The public sector supply is basically provided by the HA with some contribution from the Hong Kong Housing Society. Implementation of the LTHS is monitored through reviews of the Public Housing Development

Programme. The HA conducts an annual reassessment of the demand and supply of housing up to 2001. Future public housing production figures are to be revised if necessary.

## ☐ Public Housing Programme

The public housing programme may be taken to embrace all housing assistance schemes intended for the general public according to eligibility which involve government subsidies. There are five government housing subsidy schemes, namely:

1. the public rental housing (PRH) programme,
2. the Home Ownership Scheme (HOS),
3. the Private Sector Participation Scheme (PSPS),
4. the Home Purchase Loan Scheme (HPLS), and
5. the housing scheme for the sandwich class to be implemented at the end of August 1993.

The first one is by far the most important of all and now houses about 40 per cent of Hong Kong's population. The other four schemes belong to the assisted home purchase sector providing participants with either an accommodation at a price below market value or cash assistance in buying a private sector domestic accommodation. It is also estimated that the HOS/PSPS flats house altogether 8.7 per cent of the total population. In other words, the public housing programme currently benefits nearly half of the territory's population.

### *Public Rental Housing*

By the end of March 1993, there were some 640,000 units in about 150 public housing estates managed by the HA accommodating 2.38 million people or 40.2 per cent of the territory's total population. As at the end of 1992, 49.9 per cent of the rental units were in the main urban areas, i.e. Hong Kong Island, Kowloon and New Kowloon; 29.2 per cent in the more conveniently located or closer by new towns of Tsuen Wan/Kwai Chung/ Tsing Yi, Sha Tin/Ma On Shan, and Tseung Kwan O; and 20.9 per cent in the less accessible or remoter new towns of Tai Po, Fanling/Sheung Shui, Tuen Mun, Yuen Long, and Tin Shui Wai, as well as in the outlying islands. In addition to the permanent stock, the HA provides dwellings built of non-permanent materials in Temporary Housing Areas (THAs) for people

rendered homeless by squatter clearances, fire etc., but who are not immediately eligible for permanent public housing. At the end of 1992, there
were 55 THAs housing 65,000 people and about 80 per cent of them will be
rehoused by 1997.

The objective of the PRH programme, which is now in its fortieth year
of development, has always been to provide subsidized accommodation to
selected groups of people on the basis of need. Rents have always been
maintained at low levels with tenants' affordability being the cornerstone of
the HA's domestic rent policy. As at the fourth quarter of 1992, the median
rent-to-income ratio (MRIR) for PRH tenants was 8.2 per cent while the
MRIR for tenants of private permanent living quarters was 19.7 per cent.

In addition to low housing costs, PRH tenants also enjoy among other
things security of tenure. It is no wonder that PRH is the most-favoured
housing tenure of many families, not necessarily restricted to lower-income
ones. PRH carries no social stigma in the Hong Kong context and is very
much sought-after. For most lower-income families, moving into PRH is
the only way for them to improve their living conditions and to cut down on
housing costs.

Broadly speaking, since the amalgamation of the earlier subsidized
rental housing schemes into a general PRH programme administered by the
new Housing Authority in 1973, households have been admitted into PRH
on account of either compliance with the Waiting List Income Limits and
other eligibility rules, or demonstration of a definite immediate housing
need, e.g. victims of natural disasters, or individuals displaced by government clearance programmes. The bulk of government clearances have been
the demolition of illegal structures built on Crown Land. In addition, a
special quota has been earmarked for junior civil servants every year.
Quotas are assigned to different eligible or rehousing categories on an
annual basis. Since the formation of the new HA, the broad eligible
categories have been more or less the same and the current categorization is
shown in Table 1. There are different eligibility criteria for different rehousing categories, each of which is assigned a different priority with particular
reference to the rehousing location selected.

*Allocation and Categories of Households Rehoused*

The annual allocation exercise is never a simple or easy task, as demand has
always far outstripped supply. While the HA has to carefully weigh the
competing claims of various rehousing groups, priorities have to be set.

Table 1. Allocation of Housing Authority Rental Flats, 1973–1994

| Rehousing category* | Quota for 1993–1994 | | Flats allocated, April 1974–March 1993# (%) | Persons rehoused, April 1973–March 1993 (%) |
|---|---|---|---|---|
| | No. of flats | % | | |
| Clearance | | | | |
| Squatter/cottage area clearance | 6,500 | 14.5 | 18.2@ | 17.3@ |
| THA clearance | 5,500 | 11.1 | 6.7 | 5.9 |
| Reuse of THA | 1,000 | 2.2 | | |
| Redevelopment | | | | |
| Comprehensive redevelopment | 13,000 | 28.9 | 21.1 | 20.7 |
| Major repairs | 1,000 | 2.2 | | |
| Waiting List | 14,000 | 31.1 | 35.9 | 35.3 |
| Compassionate | 1,500 | 3.3 | 2.8 | 2.1 |
| Transfer | 1,100 | 2.5 | 9.1 | 11.8 |
| Emergency | 500 | 1.1 | 1.8 | 2.1 |
| Civil servants | | | | |
| Junior civil servants & pensioners | 1,300 | 2.9 | 4.3 | 4.8 |
| Redemption of letters of assurance by estate assistants | 100 | 0.2 | | |
| Total | 45,500 | 100.0 | 100.0 (about 578,000 flats) | 100.0 (2.41 million people) |

Notes:  * Classification used for 1993–1994.
  # 1973–1974 figures are not available. The percentage figures in this column do not add up to 100 per cent due to rounding up.
  @ Includes all types of government clearance programmes such as the Kowloon Walled City clearance, clearances carried out in connection with the construction of the Mass Transit Railway, and the pilot urban renewal scheme.

Source:  *Hong Kong Annual Digest of Statistics*, various years; *Hong Kong Housing Authority Annual Report*, various years.

Higher priorities with better terms of rehousing inevitably have been given to public housing redevelopment, squatter clearance and other types of clearance categories.

Currently only prospective tenants from the Waiting List category are subject to a means test, and they are also the only group whose admittance is based mainly on the length they have registered on the Waiting List. As new PRH units and vacant units in existing estates in the main urban areas, the most sought-after residential locations, have to be reserved for allocation to households affected by the redevelopment of urban public rental estates and clearance of urban squatter areas and THAs, Waiting List applicants have to wait for a very long time before being allocated an urban flat. In recent years, it is not uncommon for Waiting List applicants to have waited for more than ten years before getting into PRH units in the main urban areas.

According to a study carried out by the writer regarding PRH allocation, a much greater proportion of households from the Waiting List category were allocated to housing estates in less popular locations as compared with any other group. While in the period between April 1975 and March 1985, the number of people rehoused from the Waiting List category constituted 35.56 per cent of the total number of people rehoused, only 17.3 per cent of them were able to get an urban flat, which represented only 15.26 per cent of the 468,566 people rehoused in the main urban areas in the same period by the HA.

The discrimination against Waiting List applicants went a step further when the Management and Operations Committee (MOC), the standing committee of the HA delegated with the responsibility regarding management issues of the PRH estates, decided at the end of 1990 not to allow new applicants who applied on or after 13 December 1990 to put down Hong Kong Island, Kowloon and New Kowloon as their districts of choice. The supply of flats in these locations had been forecast to be barely adequate to rehouse those affected by the CRP and the squatter and THA clearance programmes.

Even though overall speaking the Waiting List category has been the largest single category in terms of both the number of flats allocated and the number of persons rehoused since the inception of the HA in 1973, the overall ratio of households admitted through the Waiting List to all non-Waiting List categories combined was roughly 1:1.8. The Waiting List quota approved for 1993–1994 amounted to only 14,000 flats or 31.1 per cent of the flats available for letting.

It is apparent that as a result of administrative convenience the vast majority of households admitted through the Waiting List category have been given only flats in the New Territories, especially in the remoter parts in more recent years, or vacated units in existing estates in the urban area for the lucky ones. On the other hand, a lot of preferential treatments including no income test and favourable rehousing location have been given to households affected by PRH redevelopment or various clearance programmes to the extent that a lot of the privileges enjoyed by these households have now been taken for granted or considered as a matter of right.

The need to go through a means test, the need to join a queue, the long waiting time for an urban flat are some of the factors that have prompted people not to rely on the Waiting List but to resort to other means to gain access to PRH, in particular in the main urban areas. Some households imposed themselves as victims of fire or other natural disasters in order to be rehoused almost immediately while some posed as occupants of permanent buildings due for demolition by the government or of squatter structures earmarked for clearance. Besides, some households exploited the system by first becoming squatters on Crown Land, particularly in the urban area, in the hope of being rehoused by the HA within the same district on clearance. They can also escape income test as a result. Because of the above or some other similar tricks, families not eligible on grounds of income, for example, have got into public housing, while some families have "jumped the queue" and got rehoused in urban locations. The system is such that many undeserving families or families who can take care of their housing needs have been admitted into PRH, and having once got in, families would not be evicted on grounds of wealth or ownership of private sector domestic property.

## Waiting List Income Limits and the Waiting List

Income eligibility limits for households of each size are set in such a way that households with an income not sufficient to rent private domestic accommodation of a space standard applicable in the public sector are eligible for PRH. These however only apply to households admitted through the Waiting List as previously mentioned. These are so-called Waiting List Income Limits (WLILs).

After a substantial average increase of 28.6 per cent in the WLILs approved in the 1992 review, the higher space standards used for the assessment of housing expenditure for various household size categories with the exception of three-person and six-person households in the 1993 review has resulted in an average increase of 13.3 per cent in the WLILs. The increases in the WLILs for various household sizes ranged from 10.1 per cent for seven-person households to 21 per cent for one-person households.

With effect from 1 April 1993, the WLIL for four-person households is a monthly income of $11,400, representing an increase of 17.5 per cent over that of the previous year. The territory's overall median monthly household income was $11,000 in the fourth quarter of 1992. The PRH eligibility net in terms of income then expanded to cover a total of 121,000 non-owner-occupier households in the private sector or 38.3 per cent of all non-owner-occupier households in the private sector, which represented an increase of 6 per cent over the result of the March 1992 review.

In the general attempt to raise the WLILs so as to bring more households of higher and higher incomes into the eligibility net of PRH, we must not lose sight of the plight of those low-income families which have been queuing up patiently all these years for PRH. Any excessive increase in the WLILs has to be carefully considered as it will only lead to a longer waiting time for lower-income families currently eligible, i.e. families with greater financial hardship. Consideration should be given to accord priority to low-income families in the allocation of PRH.

The MOC at its meeting in April 1993 endorsed among other things that eligibility criteria regarding income and property ownership applies at the stage of registration. A review of the Waiting List is being carried out and is expected to be completed by the end of 1993. The Housing Department (HD) is also to take an active role to ensure that applicants who have waited for two years or more still wish to remain on the Waiting List. The HD has already started the validation exercise. These and other measures are taken to prevent people from applying before real need occurs and thus inflate the size of the Waiting List.

The Hong Kong People's Council on Public Housing Policy, a vocal interest group comprising public housing tenants and social workers, has condemned the HA for carrying out the review and contemplating changes to the Waiting List system as a means of suppressing the demand for PRH. To my mind, the review is long overdue. With the elimination of those ineligible from the Waiting List, applicants in real need can get rehoused more quickly. Furthermore, the size of the Waiting List will then become a better indicator of the demand for public housing.

*Domestic Rent Policies: Rent Setting and Review*

The current domestic rent policy is based on the recommendation of the *Ad Hoc* Committee to Review Domestic Rent Policy and Allocation Standards, which was endorsed by the HA in September 1991. The new policy guideline is that new rents set should not exceed the MRIR of 15 per cent and 18.5 per cent of the prospective tenants at the minimum space allocation of 5.5 square metres and 7 square metres internal floor area (IFA) per person respectively. Rents charged continue to include rates and management fee. While the affordability to tenants remains the principal criterion, new rent levels continue to reflect the comparative values of new estates in terms of location, estate facilities and environment, transportation and local services etc.

In general estates are grouped into "bands" according to their locations and within each band, the newer the estate the higher the rent level, with the rent of the newest estate referred to as the "Best Rent" of the relevant band. The highest "Best Rent" is currently that of the main urban areas in view of its popularity and convenience, whereas the lowest is that of Tin Shui Wai in view of its remoteness. Currently, the "Best Rents" are about one-third of their equivalent market levels.

Two rent setting exercises are conducted every year to determine the rents of new units due for occupation in four to twelve months' time. In every such exercise, in addition to setting rents for the new units coming on stream, a territory-wide revision of the "Best Rents" for all bands or districts is also attempted.

In the last few rent setting exercises prior to November 1992, a scale percentage increase was set for the various bands so as to widen the differential between rental levels of the urban area including the new towns of Sha Tin and Tsuen Wan/Kwai Chung and those of the remaining districts in the New Territories. In the two rent setting exercises in November 1992 and June 1993, an across-the-board percentage increase, however, was adopted instead of a sliding scale. It is of interest to note that the decision was taken after there was adverse reaction from concern groups and tenants to the new rent level for the main urban areas and the new town of Tsuen Wan/Kwai Chung set in May 1992. Moreover Tsuen Wan/Kwai Chung was removed together with the new town of Sha Tin from the highest rent band in November 1992. This leaves behind in the band of the highest "Best Rent" only districts in the main urban areas.

The guideline approved in September 1991 was first applied in the setting of rents in May 1992. Since then, two more new rent setting exercises have been carried out, one in November 1992 and one in June 1993 referred to earlier. Selected "Best Rents" and other relevant statistics for these three exercises are presented in Table 2. In interpreting the affordability or acceptability of these rent levels, we also have to bear in mind that the new rents will remain unchanged for about 30 months to three years before they are due for review for the first time.

All domestic rents of HA estates are reviewed biennially. In reviewing rents, the main consideration is once again the affordability of rents, namely that the MRIR should not exceed 15 per cent. Other factors taken into consideration include estate values, rate of inflation, rates, management and maintenance costs. The rent levels after review should not exceed the "Best Rent" for the same band. Table 3 presents some significant statistics in connection with the rent reviews that were carried out in the last three years for estates built by the new HA, i.e. post-1973 estates. It is obvious that the increases were reasonable with assessed MRIR ranging from 9.7 per cent to 10.5 per cent. At the time of review, the rents of the PRH units under consideration were only about 26 to 28 per cent of their market rents.

*Rent Assistance Scheme*

The Rent Assistance Scheme was introduced in September 1992 to grant temporary rent relief to those tenants who encounter difficulties in paying rents as a result of rent increase or change in family circumstances. When it was first formulated by the MOC in the middle of 1992, the details of the scheme were: (1) a six-month rent reduction of 25 per cent and 50 per cent are granted to tenants whose rent-to-income ratios (RIRs) exceed 25 per cent and 33 per cent respectively, renewable for another six months; (2) tenants receiving rent assistance are expected to apply to move to cheaper accommodation in the same district after twelve months. The implementation of the scheme was further examined by a committee set up by the HA in July 1992 to see to matters in connection with the allocation and standards of vacated flats, namely the Committee on the Allocation and Standards of Vacant Flats.

This new Committee came up with some more implementation details including *inter alia* (1) under special circumstances whereby the transfer of the tenant household to a cheaper one is undesirable or impracticable, the tenant will be allowed to stay in its present flat and continue to receive

Table 2. Information on New Rent Settings in 1992 and 1993 for Housing Authority Domestic Units and Related Statistics

| Time of rent setting | Anticipated occupation dates of units affected | Assessed median rent-to-income ratio (%) | | "Best Rent" ($/m²) (Figures in parentheses denote increase on the previous "Best Rent") | | | | Average cost rent ($/m²) | Rent of a typical unit of 34.76 m² in the highest "Best Rent" band ($) | Increase since last rent setting (%) | | |
| | | At 5.5 m² per IFA* per person | At 7 m² IFA per person | Urban | Tseung Kwan O | Yuen Long/ Tuen Mun | Tin Shui Wai | | | Consumer Price Index (A) | Nominal wage index | Rental index |
|---|---|---|---|---|---|---|---|---|---|---|---|---|
| May 1992 | September 1992–March 1993 | 13.6 | 17.0 | 41.8 (7.2) | 36.5 (4.9) | 26.0 (4.0) | 23.1 (0) | 49.1 | 1,450 | 5.4 | 4.6 | 6.6 |
| November 1992 | March–September 1993 | 13.0 | 16.5 | 43.5 (4.1) | 38.0 (4.1) | 27.0 (3.8) | 24.0 (3.9) | 60.4 | 1,510 | 4.5 | 4.6 | 6.5 |
| June 1993 | September 1993–April 1994 | 12.5 | 17.4 | 45.2 (3.9) | 39.5 (3.9) | 28.1 (4.1) | 25.0 (4.2) | 62.3 except urban flats# | 1,570 | 3.5 | 5.3 | 8.1 |

Notes: * IFA = Internal floor area
   # The average cost rent for flats in the urban area is $65.1/m².
   @ This is a typical "one-bedroom" flat in the Harmony block for allocation to three-person to four-person households.

Source: Hong Kong Housing Authority.

Table 3.  Summary of Rent Reviews for Post-1973 Housing Authority Estates, 1990–1993

| Implementation date of rent increase | No. of post-1973 estates affected | Rent increase | | | Assessed median rent-to-income ratio (%) | Comparison with market rent (%) | Movement of Consumer Price Index (A) (+ %) |
|---|---|---|---|---|---|---|---|
| | | $/m² | Average | | | | |
| | | | $ | % | | | |
| August 1990 | 68 | 2.8–4.2 | 122 | 19 | 10.0 | 26 | 18.7 |
| March 1992 | 69 | 2.5–6.0 | 165 | 24 | 10.5 | 28 | 22.0 |
| September 1992 | 77 | 2.5–6.0 | 163 | 22 | 9.9 | 26 | 22.5 |
| September 1993 | 81 | 2.5–6.0 | 166 | 20 | 9.7 | 27 | 20.8 |

Note:   The rent increase in March 1992 was originally scheduled to take effect from 1 September 1991. However, the Housing Authority decided to defer the implementation having regard to the moratorium on increases in department fees and charges imposed by the government as part of its efforts to curb inflation.

Source:   Hong Kong Housing Authority.

rental assistance after the 12-month limit; (2) in cases where the tenant's RIR still exceeds 25 per cent after moving to cheaper accommodation, the tenant will not be required to further move to an accommodation of lower rent but will be eligible for appropriate rent reduction.

The scheme has not attracted as many applicants as expected. As at the beginning of June 1993, of the some 260 applications received, 51 tenants have been granted 25 per cent reduction in their rent and 161 tenants received 50 per cent reduction. Most of those benefited are elderly one-person or two-person households.

Since implementation, the scheme has been criticized by concern groups. There have been calls to lower the qualifying RIR to 15 per cent or 20 per cent and increase the amount of rent reduction. The requirement of the recipient to move into cheaper accommodation has also been con-demned. A number of social workers, concern groups and tenants affected by CRP have insisted that tenants affected by redevelopment should be rehoused in new flats in the redeveloped estates or nearby estates, and not in vacated flats in existing estates or any cheaper accommodation. How-ever, there has been a general support for the scheme. Some have asked why the vacated units which will be completely refurbished before reletting are not good enough for living, as in the same block or estate there live hundreds or thousands of other families. The scheme will be reviewed in September 1993 after one year's implementation.

## Housing Subsidy Policy

The Housing Subsidy Policy has been quite controversial ever since its conceptualization. Starting in April 1987 the policy was implemented in five phases according to tenant's length of residence in PRH. The first batch of affected tenants began to pay double rent under the policy in 1988 and the policy was fully implemented in 1992–1993 when the last batch started to pay double rent.

The policy as endorsed in late 1986 required tenants who had been living in PRH for ten years or more with household incomes exceeding the Subsidy Income Limits set at twice the WLILs to pay double net rent in addition to rates. There were 62,500 households paying double rent in 1992–1993, representing some 24 per cent of all tenants covered by the policy, or about 10 per cent of all PRH tenants. As of September 1992, the average amount of additional rent paid by these better-off tenants was $550 a month and the MRIR among the double-rent payers was only 5 per cent.

In 1992–1993, the Subsidy Income Limits for a four-person household and a five-person household were $19,400 and $22,000 respectively.

The policy has to be reviewed on a regular basis according to the original package. After a review, the HA reaffirmed in July 1991 the basic principle of the policy. However, in view of criticisms by various concern groups and tenants, an *ad hoc* committee was set up to conduct a review of the policy and to make recommendations to the HA on any changes that should be made to improve the implementation of the policy. The *ad hoc* committee published a consultation document and launched a three-month public consultation in September 1992.

With the introduction of directly elected seats in Legco in October 1991 and the emergence of political groups in the last few years, housing issues have become more and more politicized. In the 1991–1992 Legco session there was an adjournment debate on the subject. In the 1992–1993 session, at the close of the consultation period, Legco had a motion to debate the policy. The motion "that the Government be urged to revoke the Housing Subsidy Policy (double rent policy) of the Housing Authority" was passed with 26 votes for and 22 votes against. This possibly incited or gave hope to those concern groups and tenants who were opposed to the policy. Demonstrations, protests, mass rallies etc. were held where participants made personal attacks on the then chairman and some members of the HA, and some members of the *ad hoc* committee, who were also burned in effigy. In a mass rally a Legco member belonging to the United Democrats of Hong Kong remarked that if the HA did not abolish the policy, he would move a motion in Legco urging the chairman of the HA to resign. His call was supported by another Legco member belonging to the same political party, as reported by the media. This contributed to the premature retirement of Sir David Akers-Jones from chairmanship, mentioned at the beginning of the chapter.

During the consultation period, the *ad hoc* committee commissioned an independent organization to conduct a territory-wide opinion survey to gauge public views on the policy. Well over half of the respondents (65.6 per cent) agreed that the HA should reduce subsidy to the high-income PRH tenants and even 51.4 per cent of PRH respondents held this view. About one-fifth of the respondents were of the opposite view.

After considering views expressed, the *ad hoc* committee recommended several changes to the policy which were subsequently approved in full by the HA in late March 1993. The HA's decision was endorsed by Exco in early May 1993. The amended policy was to be implemented with retrospective effect from 1 April 1993. The policy continues to apply only to those tenants who have been in PRH for ten years or more. For those tenants who have been required to move to another flat by the HA such as tenants affected by redevelopment, their length of residence in PRH for the purpose of the Housing Subsidy Policy counts only after the move. The important change is that tenants with incomes exceeding two to three times the WLILs are required to pay only 1.5 times net rent, instead of double rent, plus rates. Only those with incomes above three times the WLILs will need to pay double net rent plus rates.

It was estimated that about 80 per cent of the existing double-rent payers would pay 1.5 times instead. In addition, according to the HA's original decision, tenants who had been paying additional rent for five years or more were to be accorded priority in the purchase of HOS flats. In endorsing the HA's proposed amended policy, Exco requested the HA to consider reducing the qualifying period from five to three years. This was accepted subsequently.

Whether the changes introduced were concessions to pressure is a matter of opinion. However it is a fact that substantial concessions have been made, thus reducing the effectiveness of the policy. This writer has all along advocated reducing subsidy to public housing tenants who are better-off so that heavily subsidized PRH could be reserved for lower-income families.

## Refurbishment and Allocation of Vacant Flats

Another major initiative in the past year was the implementation of a refurbishment programme of vacated flats, renovating them to a reasonably good standard before reletting so as to provide better homes for those who cannot move into new PRH units.

Vacancies occur as a result of tenants' moving out upon the purchase of HOS/PSPS flats, voluntary surrender of tenancies or on rare occasions repossession. The HD also from time to time offers transfer opportunities to sitting tenants in the attempt to obtain units suitable in terms of size and location for allocation to tenants affected by redevelopment, households affected by THA and squatter area clearances etc. As these units are relet without any substantial renovation or repair, many families do not like moving into these units and some flats have been left vacant for a long time.

In the middle of 1992, the HA decided that vacated flats would be improved to a new enhanced standard before they were relet. The

Committee on the Allocation and Standards of Vacant Flats established in July 1992 as mentioned earlier was charged with the task. Vacant units with an expected life of over five years will be refurbished to a high standard including, where necessary, the plastering and repainting of walls and ceiling, provision of full sets of new sanitary fittings, and rewiring of electrical cables. When refurbished, vacant flats will be comparable in internal fittings and finishes to units in the Trident blocks. They naturally will be of a higher standard than the other flats in the same block, and a higher per capita space allocation standard applies as well. However, no additional rent is to be charged.

The refurbishment programme commenced in August 1992 when 10,250 flats were identified. By the end of March 1993, over 4,200 units had been refurbished and were available for reletting. The takeup rate in the reletting of these flats has improved and the feedback from tenants is very positive.

## *Assisted Home Ownership Schemes*

In addition to the ambitious PRH programme, the Hong Kong government has also implemented a number of schemes to assist public housing tenants and others who cannot afford to buy reasonable accommodation in the private sector to become home owners. With its origins in the HOS introduced in 1976, the assisted home purchase sector has expanded to include the PSPS in 1978, the HPLS in 1988 and the housing scheme for the sandwich class announced by the Governor in October 1992.

One of the major objectives of the LTHS is to promote and satisfy the growing demand for home ownership. In the original LTHS formulated in 1986, it was envisaged that between April 1985 and March 2001, some 354,000 additional households would be able to become home owners with the assistance of the first three schemes mentioned above.

### *Home Ownership Scheme (HOS) and Private Sector Participation Scheme (PSPS)*

The objective of the two earliest home ownership schemes, namely the HOS and the PSPS, is to assist existing and prospective PRH tenants and lower-middle-income families to become home owners by providing flats for sale at affordable prices below market value. Both schemes are administered by the HA.

The first batch of HOS flats (Phase 1) were offered for sale in February 1978 while PSPS units were first put on sale in November 1979. Thirty-six more sales exercises have been held ever since, with the latest exercise (Phase 15A) beginning in April 1993. It has been a practice in the last few years to launch three sales of pre-completion units every year, in April, August, and December.

Unlike PRH, a per capita space standard does not apply in the allocation of HOS/PSPS flats. Prospective purchasers are free to choose whatever size units they prefer subject to availability. Since Phase 10B (August 1988), in the pricing of HOS units, the discount from market value has been at least 30 per cent rising to 40 to 45 per cent in the last five sales exercises. While there was a five-year resale restriction period for buyers of HOS flats of Phases 1–3A, effective from Phase 3B purchasers must pay back to the HA the updated value of the discount at the time of purchase if they exercise their right to sell their HOS flats on the open market after the expiry of the ten-year period of sales restrictions. Participants also enjoy favourable mortgage terms, including a small downpayment which is only 5 per cent of the purchase price for green form applicants (prospective or sitting PRH tenants who have to surrender PRH accommodation if successful) and 10 per cent for white form applicants (all others). They also enjoy an interest rate below normal mortgage rates as the HA guarantees to indemnify the lending institutions' loss in case of default.

As at the end of 1992, there were more than 110 HOS and PSPS estates with 148,845 completed flats, of which 32.1 per cent were in the main urban areas, 28.6 per cent in the new towns of Tsuen Wan/Kwai Chung/Tsing Yi, Sha Tin/Ma On Shan, and Tseung Kwan O, and 39.3 per cent in the new towns of Tai Po, Fanling/Sheung Shui, Tuen Mun and Tin Shui Wai.

From the inception of the scheme to Phase 14C launched in December 1992, some 179,739 flats were sold. This figure was equivalent to 20 per cent of the total number of owner-occupied flats in the territory at the end of 1992.

The demand for HOS/PSPS flats has been very strong. A total of 1,889,700 applications were received during the same period, representing an overall over-subscription rate of 10.5. As the scheme is so popular and brings about much improved housing standards and living environment to participating households at very reasonable costs with the likelihood of substantial capital gains, it is of paramount importance that the flats are equitably allocated.

The eligibility rules are the same for the two schemes. Applicants can be broadly divided into green form applicants with a further distinction into priority green and ordinary green, and white form applicants. A general rule applies across the board, namely that the applicant should be at least 18 years old, and the applicant and one member of his or her household should be permanent residents and have lived in Hong Kong for the previous seven years.

White form applicants have to comply with a set of eligibility rules, for example, that they may not own domestic property and are subject to a prescribed household income limit which does not vary according to household size as in the case of the WLILs for the rental units. All green form applicants with the exception of prospective tenants from the Waiting List category are not subject to the HOS income limit, whereas the restriction on domestic property ownership does not apply to PRH estate tenants and residents of temporary housing areas and cottage areas managed by the HA.

In addition, green form applicants as a group enjoy two more privileges, even though as in the case of eligibility rules, there are still differential treatments within the group. Firstly, a larger quota was given to green form applicants in 25 out of the 38 sales held so far, while for the other 13 sales, a 50:50 quota arrangement was adopted. The overall quota allocated to white form applicants was 40.6 per cent of the total number of flats offered for sale, despite the fact that the number of white form applications was roughly twice that of green form applications. As a result, green form applicants had a much higher success rate. While the ordinary green form applicants as distinct from priority green form applicants had an overall success rate of 12.7 per cent, the overall success rate for the white form applicants was only 6.5 per cent.

Secondly, green form applicants also have an advantage in the selection of flats. Following receipt of applications for each sale, a ballot is held to decide the order in which applicants select their flats. PRH tenants who are affected by redevelopment and have been notified of the redevelopment details and Kowloon Walled City clearees are given first priority in flat selection. Tenants living in blocks due for redevelopment within three years under the CRP but not yet formally notified of the redevelopment details and prospective PRH tenants when their turns come for allocation of rental flats are given second priority. Afterwards, the selection sequence is in the form of three green form applicants without priority, i.e. the ordinary green form applicants, alternating with one white form applicant until the quota for the green status group is filled.

The order of flat selection means a lot because an earlier chance ensures a higher chance of getting a flat which meets one's expectations. As past sale records show, HOS flats in the urban areas were much more popular than those in the New Territories and the larger flats were also more popular than the smaller ones. Invariably it was the most expensive flats that were first snapped up. In other words, the larger flats in better locations especially in the urban areas in general went to green form applicants. As the amount of subsidy received by HOS purchasers is directly proportional to the price which has a close relationship with the size and location of the flat, those who are able to buy large flats in the main urban areas obviously enjoy a much higher amount of subsidy.

An analysis of the sales records for Phases 10A (April 1988) to 11A (April 1989) carried out by the HD reveals that while overall speaking green form applicants bought 60 per cent of the flats offered in these four phases, they managed to purchase as much as 91.2 per cent of the flats in the main urban areas and the new town of Tsuen Wan and 86.6 per cent of the flats in the new towns of Sha Tin and Tseung Kwan O. On the other hand, the white form applicants were left with 63.3 per cent of the flats in the New Territories outside the three new towns just mentioned and only managed to purchase 24.3 per cent of the units in the urban areas and Tsuen Wan, most of which were small flats.

Another point worth mentioning is that while the overall quota assigned to white form applicants was 40.7 per cent of the flats available in the last fifteen years from the inception of the scheme to Phase 14C (December 1992), they managed to have bought at the end 45.6 per cent of all the units sold. This happened because the green form applicants did not take up the full quota allocated to them and the flats not taken up were passed onto the white form applicants. As they do not have a genuine housing need and their housing expenditure as a PRH tenant is low, they are more likely to postpone the purchase of a HOS unit if they do not come across one of their desire.

The preferential treatment in the purchase of HOS/PSPS flats accorded to green form applicants, the vast majority of whom are PRH tenants, has often been criticized. To the general public, it is more equitable or makes more sense if a large share of the flats can be sold to lower-middle-income families living in the private sector which do not own domestic property. The argument in support of the sale of HOS flats to PRH tenants that may have some appeal to society at large is that the PRH units vacated as a result of the tenants' moving to HOS flats can be relet to families in need.

However, even if this argument can be accepted, it does not mean that all public housing tenants should be eligible for the HOS/PSPS. Restrictions on income and property ownership should be applied across the board.

## HOS/PSPS Sales in 1992–1993

A record sale of 20,792 flats was achieved in 1992–1993 in Phases 14A–C. Some 224,000 applications were received and the overall over-subscription rate was 10.8, which is very close to that of 11 for the year before. In line with the change in quota allocation effective from Phase 12A (April 1990) whereby green form applicants would be allocated two-thirds of the flats sold in each exercise, green form applicants purchased 65 per cent of the flats available in the three sales mounted in 1992–1993 with 9.4 per cent being bought by the applicants with priority green status. The success rates for the ordinary green and white applicants were 20.7 per cent and 4.4 per cent respectively reflecting the persistently high demand for HOS flats in particular from those living in the private sector.

## Quota Allocation

In September 1992, the HA endorsed the recommendation of the Working Group on the Sandwich Class that the split between the green and the white be changed to 50:50 for each phase. The priority green form applicants are to be guaranteed a place as before. The rationale behind the alteration was to improve the chances of white form applicants for HOS flats as they were in genuine need of help to achieve home ownership. The new quota allocation came into effect in Phase 15A (April 1993). The increase in quota was no doubt welcome to white form applicants. Nevertheless, the lower quota for green form applicants will lead to a smaller number of PRH units to be recovered or saved. Waiting List applicants may therefore have to wait longer for PRH allocation. An increase in PRH production should be considered.

## Home Ownership Scheme Income Limit

The Home Ownership Scheme Income Limit (HOSIL) had been based on the income required to afford a HOS flat from 1984. This gave rise to a problem as there would be households whose incomes were above the limit but who were still unable to buy a private sector flat. The Home Ownership Committee decided at the conclusion of an overall review of the HOS in

July 1991 to include this group of people by moving the limit towards the income required to afford a private sector flat. However, in order to avoid a dramatic increase in the limit the corresponding increase was introduced in two stages. The first step was to increase the limit to $18,000 a month, representing an increase of 28.6 per cent effective from 1 April 1992. It was raised again to a monthly household income of $20,000 with effect from 1 April 1993, representing another increase of 11.1 per cent.

Households with a monthly income of $20,000 or above would fall into the top 22 per cent income group in the territory; in other words, about 78 per cent of the households in the territory are now theoretically eligible for the HOS in terms of monthly household income, even though naturally those with low income can hardly afford an ownership unit. Back to the demand for HOS, it was estimated at the time of the latest HOSIL review in March 1993 that in the private sector there were 162,100 non-owner-occupier households of two or more persons with an income below the HOSIL. As mentioned at the beginning of this chapter, of these households 83,500 had incomes between the WLILs and HOSIL, representing some 26.4 per cent of all the non-owner-occupier households in private sector housing. The number of households which are eligible and in real need of HOS units is very large indeed.

## Sales of HOS/PSPS Flats After the Expiry of Resales Restriction

When the HOS was conceptualized in 1976, it was decided to impose a five-year restriction period on the disposal of a HOS flat whether by sale in the open market or letting. In 1981, the pricing formula was changed by replacing land premium (value) with the cost of site formation thus theoretically leading to larger discounts in prices. Resales restrictions were as a result tightened up with the period of sales restriction lengthened to ten years and requiring the payment of a premium of an amount equivalent to the updated value of the original discount at the time of purchase when the HOS unit is disposed of in the open market. The new restrictions became effective with flats sold in Phase 3B and have been applied ever since.

According to the HD's analysis of the transactions of HOS/PSPS flats of Phases 1–3A in the fourth quarter of 1991, which entered the post-five-year period between December 1979 and August 1987, the average price was about $26,300 per square metre. The highest average price was recorded for flats on Hong Kong Island ($30,000 per square metre) and the lowest in the New Territories ($26,000 per square metre). Flats in Kowloon and New Kowloon fetched an average price in between ($28,000 per square metre). In short, the appreciation of the prices of HOS/PSPS flats was quite substantial. The increases in flat prices ranged from 326 per cent for Yee Kok Court in Cheung Sha Wan from the most recent Phase 3A to 1,015 per cent for Shun Chi Court in Kwun Tong from the earliest Phase 1. The average annual rate of increase ranged from 14 per cent to 22 per cent, while the average annual rate of inflation for the same period was about 9 per cent.

With respect to HOS/PSPS flats subject to a ten-year resales restriction period, by the end of May 1993, some 7,972 flats had entered the post-restriction period, out of which a total of 284 owners had applied to pay the premium to the HA. Of those, 116 owners had settled the premium by the end of May 1993. A questionnaire survey conducted by the HD on these 116 owners with a response rate of 73 per cent reveals that the majority of owners (84 per cent) intended to sell their flats. In a follow-up survey on the latter group of owners, information on the sale of 54 such flats was gathered. The subsequent analysis shows that overall, net sales proceeds, i.e. sales price minus premium paid to the HA, ranged from 3.7 (Siu Hong Court, Tuen Mun) to 5.0 (Yuk Po Court, Sheung Shui) times the original purchase price on the basis of HOS courts. On the basis of individual units, the net proceeds ranged between 3.0 times the original purchase price for a unit in Siu Hong Court and 5.4 times for a unit in Yuk Po Court. The amount of net proceeds ranged from $497,928 for a flat in Siu Hong Court with an original price of $137,200 to $1,393,832 for a flat with an original price of $295,700 in On Kay Court in the urban district of Ngau Tau Kok. The average rate of capital gain was 14 per cent per annum.

As demonstrated in the above two analyses, a HOS owner is able to reap a substantial capital gain upon sale of his or her property after expiry of the restriction period in addition to the use of the accommodation before the resale. Relevant policy-makers in Hong Kong should take account of the potential capital gain in the formulation of policies of and measures to be adopted for any form of assisted home ownership scheme. A cap can be put on the amount of profit to be made.

*Home Purchase Loan Scheme (HPLS)*

The HPLS, which was implemented from April 1988, is to supplement the HOS/PSPS in assisting eligible families to buy flats in the private sector. This is achieved through providing either an interest-free loan to help with initial financing or a monthly contribution towards mortgage repayment for three years. The latter option started implementation in October 1991. Initially the scheme was restricted to green form applicants for HOS, but was extended to cover white form applicants in its second year of operation and has since followed eligibility rules including income limit used in the HOS/PSPS. The method of quota allocation also gives priority to green form applicants. The demand has so far fallen short of the provision allocated to the scheme, mainly because the loan amount has not been able to keep pace with the hefty increase in domestic property prices. That the benefit or subsidy to be derived from the HPLS is less than that from the HOS/PSPS is also another reason for the low demand.

When the HPLS was introduced, it was intended that the loan amount should be sufficient to cover the 10 per cent downpayment on a flat of 60 square metres gross area (48 square metres saleable), together with stamp duty and charges for conveyancing and the mortgage. This formula had not been strictly followed in all the previous adjustments on the loan amount for various reasons.

With the Home Ownership Committee's endorsement to use the price of a private sector flat of 40 square metres saleable area in the extended urban area in the calculation of the HOS, hence HPLS, income limit in March 1992, the Committee decided in March 1993 to make use of the price of a similar flat in the review of the HPLS loan amount. It settled for an increase of 33 per cent to $200,000 effective from 1 April 1993, with a quota of 1,000 for 1993–1994 as compared with 1,500 for 1992–1993 and 3,500 for 1991–1992. The monthly mortgage subsidy (MS) was increased at the same time in line with the revised amount of loan.

The original LTHS assumed the granting of 102,500 loans during the fourteen years from April 1987 to March 2001. However, the total takeup from inception to the end of January 1993 was only 7,786, with 7,659 loans and 127 monthly MS options. In the light of the likely takeup rate, the targeted number of HPLS loans has been substantially reduced. In the 1991 review of the LTHS the number of loans over the period from April 1990 to March 2001 was reduced from 92,500 to 66,000. The 1992 review reduced the quota further by 41,500 to 21,000. The quota of 1,000 approved for 1993–1994 as just mentioned was used as the assumption for the 1993 review, the result of which was that only 8,000 additional households would be assumed to benefit from the HPLS over the period from April 1992 to March 2001. Even if the quota of 8,000 can be fully taken up, the total number of HPLS loans granted over the entire period of the LTHS will only be 15,556 or 15.2 per cent of the original quota. It appears as a result necessary to increase the production of HOS/PSPS flats in order to meet the need for assisted home purchase.

## *The Option to Rent or Buy Scheme*

In a further attempt to promote home ownership, the Home Ownership Committee approved in July 1991 a trial scheme under which qualified PRH applicants are allowed the choice of renting or buying a flat in the same district when their turns come for allocation of a rental flat. Under this Option to Rent or Buy Scheme (ORBS), a rental type block in an estate due for rental allocation will be designated for sale and upgraded accordingly. Any flats unsold in the ORBS block will be included in the following main phase of HOS sales and it was decided in November 1992 that only green form applicants would be allowed to buy the unsold flats. The scheme can be considered as an extension of the HOS and is intended to offer a better chance to prospective PRH tenants to become home owners. Prices and conditions are similar to those of the HOS. The trial scheme was subsequently endorsed by the HA in April 1992.

The pilot exercise launched in December 1992 consisted of two Harmony blocks of 608 flats each, one in Tin Oi Court in Tin Shui Wai, a remote new town and one in Yu Ming Court in Tseung Kwan O, a new town close to the urban areas. The response on the whole has not been satisfactory. By the end of July 1993, only 1,543 applications had been received most of which opted for Tin Shui Wai. A total of 658 flats had been sold with 554 of those in Tin Shui Wai and only 104 in Tseung Kwan O.

One observation about the pilot sale is that the flats in Tin Shui Wai at an average price which was only 68.6 per cent of that in Tseung Kwan O were much more popular. What we have to bear in mind in the assessment of the ORBS is that for the pilot sale, qualified households no longer had a real housing need as they were already due for allocation of PRH units in the same district. It was much more expensive to buy than to rent: in addition to the initial monetary outlay required to buy a flat, the monthly mortgage repayment and associated housing costs would be at least four to five times the amount of inclusive rent payable for the same size unit. In short, there is not much incentive for these families not to take up PRH units and buy instead.

## The Sale of Flats to Sitting Tenants Scheme

As a result of the disappointing response to the invitation to buy from tenants in blocks selected for sale under the Sale of Flats to Sitting Tenants Scheme (SFSTS) launched in August 1991, the HA decided to carry out in November of the same year a thorough review of various schemes to promote home ownership, in particular the SFSTS with a view to relaunch it.

A report on the review was published in April 1992 and views from members of the public were invited. Eventually in October 1992, the HA taking account of views collected endorsed the amended SFSTS. Substantial changes were made to the conditions of sale, including lower prices at only 20 per cent of market value and guarantees on repairs. The amended scheme was then submitted to Exco which, however, did not endorse it. The SFSTS finally came to an end after more than three years' work since it was first approved in principle by the HA.

## Housing Scheme for Middle-income Families

The government eventually decided to embark on a housing scheme for middle-income families or the sandwich class in October 1992. The HA actually started work in this area by setting up a working group to study the problem in detail and produced a comprehensive report with recommendations. However no support was forthcoming from the government. It was not until being pushed by a few legislators in the 1991–1992 Legco session that the government's attitude began to change.

In his first policy address at the opening of the 1992–1993 Legco session on 7 October 1992, Chris Patten, the new Governor, announced the government's intention to introduce a new middle-income housing scheme for the sandwich class.

The scheme would be similar to the HOS and would benefit about 13,000 between now and 1997. As the first units of the new housing projects would not be available until 1995–1996, an interim measure would be implemented. The government would buy flats from the private sector to sell to the sandwich class at affordable prices, benefiting hopefully 1,000 in the first year of operation.

The Housing Society has been entrusted with the execution of this new housing scheme. The interim measure has eventually been changed to the form of a downpayment loan to help eligible families to buy private sector flats. A sum of $2 billion has been earmarked for the interim loan scheme, while 4.8 hectares of land has been allocated to the long-term scheme. Six sites have been reserved for 5,000 flats to be available in 1996 and 1997, mostly in the urban or extended urban areas under the 1993–1994 land disposal programme including Hung Hom, Tseung Kwan O, Tuen Mun, Sha Tin and Ma On Shan. Hopefully the first batch of flats will be available in 1996.

The scheme has been very controversial ever since its announcement. Members of the public have queried the equity of the scheme and argued that the money should be used for the needy instead, while some professional bodies have cast doubt on its effectiveness. There have been organized actions taken by some people in dreadful living conditions to demand for part of the $2 billion earmarked for the loan to be used to solve their severe housing problems.

Exco nevertheless approved the details of the interim loan scheme on 8 June 1993. Under the scheme, the loan will be 20 per cent of the flat price, up to $500,000 to help eligible families living in the private sector to buy private sector domestic units under ten years old up to $3 million worth. Applicants must have lived in Hong Kong for at least seven years with a monthly household income between $20,001 and $40,000. The minimum household size is three but priority will be given to couples with two or more children to be followed by single parents with two or more children. No one in the applicant's household may have owned property in the previous two years. Participants of the scheme who resell their flats within the first three years will have to repay the loan immediately. An interest of 2 per cent will be charged on the loan, but repayment is not required until the fourth year and then in the form of 120 monthly repayments. In addition 75 per cent of the 1,000 loans for the first batch will be given to families earning between $20,001 and $30,000, or the lower segment of the sandwich class, and 25 per cent to those earning between $30,001 and $40,000, i.e. the upper segment. Applications will be invited at the end of August 1993.

While there is not much argument that the lower segment of the so-defined sandwich class may experience difficulties in the purchase of private sector flats, there has been criticism that the upper income limit of $40,000 is too high. The upper segment of the so-defined sandwich class eligible for the scheme, which belongs to the top 10 per cent income group for the territory, should be able to take care of their own housing needs.

Another controversy concerns the long-term scheme. The homes to be built should not differ too much from the HOS/PSPS ones and should involve a lower level of subsidy. If a standard unit of 48 square metres saleable area is good enough for the HOS/PSPS which house a vast number of households, then it should be good enough for the sandwich class families if they are to be subsidized with public funds.

It has been said that higher-income households may tend to be more selective even when subsidized housing is offered, hence better locations should be allocated for sandwich class homes. The writer cannot subscribe to such a view because it contravenes the principle of equity used in public housing policies.

We must also bear in mind the undesirable socioeconomic consequences of concentrating a large number of low-income families in remote areas, such as in the case of the PRH estates in Tuen Mun, where a large proportion of the flats have been allocated to low-income families on the Waiting List.

## ☐ Private Housing Sector

Private sector flats are used here to refer to domestic units developed by the private sector (the PSPS flats are not counted as such) and include flats purchased with the assistance of the HPLS. In addition to permanent domestic quarters, there are accommodation units built of non-permanent materials such as squatter structures on Crown Land and on private, mainly agricultural, land in the New Territories. There are roof-top structures as well. As at 31 March 1992, it was estimated that some 2.62 million people or 45.5 per cent of the territory's total lived in private permanent housing units versus 39.1 per cent in PRH estates and 8.9 per cent in HOS/PSPS blocks. By the end of 1992 there were a total of 805,073 private permanent domestic quarters of which 69.0 per cent were in the main urban areas, 15.7 per cent in the districts of Tsuen Wan and Sai Kung, and 15.3 per cent in the remaining districts of the New Territories. At the same time 49,000 people lived in urban squatter structures and 228,000 in squatter huts in the New Territories. There were in addition a total of 3,086 roof-top structures at time of the 1991 Population Census.

According to the Rating and Valuation Department, the number of private sector flats completed in 1992 was only 26,220 as compared with the forecast production of 33,510, representing a decrease of 21.6 per cent from the 1991 figure. For the last two years, an overall vacancy rate of 4.2 per cent was recorded for the end of each year. According to forecast, the supply of new flats will be 37,300 units in 1993 and 38,400 in 1994.

## The Inadequately Housed

Living conditions vary tremendously within the private housing sector. In general low-income families are the worst-off in terms of housing conditions. Of the private sector households about one-third were owner-occupiers, representing some 80 per cent of all owner-occupiers in the territory according to the 1991 Census.

Between 1987 and 1992, a total of 78,000 households living in the private sector moved into PRH through the Waiting List. Nevertheless there were still some 105,000 households living in private permanent quarters which were considered to be inadequately housed, constituting some 46.9 per cent of all the households regarded as inadequately accommodated. A relatively higher concentration of such households was found in the older parts of main urban areas and the earlier developed areas of the oldest new town of Tsuen Wan. Nearly half lived in the three districts of Mong Kok, Shum Shui Po and Kowloon City.

A survey of the inadequately housed households in permanent private buildings and roof-top structures carried out by the HD in January and February 1992 revealed that the median living density among the survey households was only 4.6 square metres per person compared to 7.5 square metres for PRH. The median household income was $6,000 compared to $10,000 for PRH tenants. The MRIR was 16.9 per cent for the sampled households, compared to 7.5 per cent for PRH households. While the average RIR for four-person households of the inadequately housed was 20 per cent, 25.3 per cent of these households paid more than 30 per cent of their income on rent. Only 2.3 per cent of the sample occupied one whole unit, whereas 7.4 per cent were bedspace dwellers. The median rent was $1,000 compared to $680 for the PRH tenants as a whole and for four-person households the median rent was $1,500. For most of the inadequately housed, moving into PRH is the only way of getting a decent accommodation.

## The Property Market

The soaring of prices of private sector flats remains a major public concern in the year under review. According to the Rating and Valuation Department, in the year of 1992 prices for private domestic property were 42 per cent higher than in 1991, while the 1991 prices already represented an increase of 38 per cent over that of the previous year. Prices kept on increasing rapidly in the first half of 1992, notwithstanding the measures introduced by the government to curb speculation. The rate of increase slowed down and the property market was quiet in the third quarter of 1992. Falls in price levels of about 5 to 10 per cent were recorded for some transactions.

Moving into 1993, after a short period of consolidation, the market picked up again. A large number of flats were offered for sale and favourable mortgage arrangements including a lower downpayment and more "favourable" repayment terms were offered by some developers especially for those in the New Territories. Many of these flats were taken up within a fairly short period of time. There was a general increase by about 10 per cent in the second quarter or so of 1993. There were signs of speculation at the top end of the market. According to the July 1993 issue of the *Hang Seng Economic Monthly Journal*, prices of luxury flats had increased by 25 per cent while that of small and medium ones by 10 per cent in the first half of 1993. Lending institutions have become much more cautious in home mortgage financing and some have lowered in July the maximum loan for residential property worth over $5 million from 70 to 60 per cent of its valuation as a first step.

Against the background of hefty increases in property prices, increases in rent levels have only been moderate in the last couple of years. According to the Rating and Valuation Department, the increase in rent for fresh lettings of flats of 40–69.9 square metres saleable area was 13 per cent, 8 per cent, and 9 per cent in 1990, 1991, and 1992 respectively. Middle-income families are still able to rent an accommodation without undue hardship, even though at the end of last year the MRIR for sole tenants in private permanent accommodation was 27.2 per cent and for the co-tenants it was 16.7 per cent.

Excessively high domestic property prices have brought about serious socioeconomic repercussions. The large increases in property prices have no doubt brought to the public coffer handsome sums of money through the collection of stamp duties on property transactions, associated profits tax, land premium etc. However, the hopes of many to buy a home have been dashed at the same time. The government must be bold enough to undertake some more effective measures to ensure that prices of private sector flats are affordable to a larger section of the community rather than allocating public funds to help some of the lucky ones among the top 10 per cent income group under the housing scheme for middle-income families.

### *Rent Control: The Beginning of the End*

Any discussion on the developments in the private housing sector in 1993 will naturally include the issue of rent control, as a timetable for decontrol was passed by Legco in the middle of 1993. Rent control and related provisions has been the only policy measure implemented by the government to help renters in private housing by protecting them against excessive rent increases, unreasonable treatment or eviction by their landlords. The major relevant legislation is the Landlord and Tenant (Consolidation) Ordinance.

The Landlord and Tenant (Consolidation) (Amendment) Bill introduced into Legco on 3 June 1992 was finally passed after one year's lengthy scrutinization by legislators at the end of June 1993.

The new legislation in effect allows landlords of prewar tenancies to raise their rents to a minimum of 60 per cent of market value in 1993, going up to 70 per cent in 1994, 80 per cent in 1995 and 90 per cent in 1996. Postwar domestic tenancies created on or before 9 June 1983 for units completed on or before 18 June 1981 in premises with a rateable value of less than $30,000 in June 1983 may expect rents to increase to 75 per cent of the market rent in 1993 with a 5 percentage point increase every year thereafter until 1996. According to the current timetable, complete removal of rent control will be achieved by the end of 1996.

In addition, the amount of statutory compensation payable to tenants of postwar domestic premises on redevelopment by landlords is to be increased to 1.7 times the current rateable value of the premises versus the 1.3 times as originally proposed by the government. This represents a substantial increase over the previous provision.

The policy of rent control has been very controversial. It is undeniable that there are a lot of low-income families currently protected by the rent control policy, the relaxation of which will no doubt cause them hardship. However, it should be the responsibility of the government or society at large to help solve the housing problems of these families. It is not fair to dump the responsibility onto individual landlords for such a long time. It is also not uncommon for protected tenants to make money out of the rent control system through subletting in cases where sub-tenancies are not subject to control.

## ☐ Conclusion

As illustrated in the foregoing sections, much has happened in the past year.

No doubt there have been remarkable improvements in the housing conditions in the territory particularly in the last decade and its public housing programme has been widely acclaimed internationally. However, the housing conditions of many lower-income families which are not able to benefit from public housing, in particular recent immigrants from China or elderly singletons, are appalling. Much needs to be done.

Efforts should be made to reduce the waiting time for PRH especially for the most needy. The possibility of low-income families living in the private sector which are not eligible for public assistance to be given some form of temporary rent assistance should be explored.

In general, we need to devise a set of policies which are more equitable. Undeserving families should not be allowed to enjoy public housing benefits, and housing subsidy should be based on need. Bold measures should be undertaken such as withdrawing subsidy from households which are no longer in need, e.g. those owning private sector domestic property. Besides, as a matter of principle, HOS, PSPS, and HPLS participants should not be allowed to purchase private sector flats within a prescribed period of time. The above measures have the effect of lowering the demand for private sector flats and may as a result help reduce property speculation and contribute towards stabilizing prices.

A fairer way of distributing urban PRH flats should be contemplated. At the same time, the government should make every effort to turn remote new towns into more attractive residential locations. Insufficient or inappropriate job opportunities, inadequate transportation links with the urban area, high commuting costs, long commuting time are major factors that have rendered them unattractive. These and other problems have to be addressed by the government.

# 16

# Transportation

Stephen L. W. Tang

Since the publication of the last edition of *The Other Hong Kong Report*, a number of significant developments have taken place in the field of transportation. They include:

1. The new Governor, Chris Patten, while affirming the government's commitment to build the replacement airport and its purpose-built railway, made only minor concessions to China over the financing scheme of the Airport Core Programme (ACP) projects.
2. Patten also rejected China's demand to scrap his political reform package in exchange for her endorsement of the ACP projects.
3. In early July, China finally endorsed her support of the third harbour crossing construction project.
4. After close to five years of consideration, autopass for tunnel passages is finally adopted to reduce congestion.
5. Upon Patten's appeal, most public transport operators agree to cultivate a culture of service by forming passenger liaison groups to collate customers' views on service standards and quality.
6. Likewise, Patten has also gained support from the major public transport operators, such as Kowloon Motor Bus (KMB), Kowloon–Canton Railway Corporation (KCRC), Mass Transit

Stephen L. W. Tang is a public transport management strategist, a former member of the Transport Advisory Committee, and a lecturer in the Department of Sociology, The Chinese University of Hong Kong.

Railway Corporation (MTRC), etc. in his appeal for the introduction of performance pledge programmes.

7. Upon being chosen by the government as the new franchisee to run the 26 routes scrapped from China Motor Bus (CMB), the Citybus has been working hard to prepare for the introduction of Network 26 on the Island in September this year.

8. The government had released a *Taxi Policy Review*, and a *Railway Development Study* for public consultation in October 1992 and April 1993 respectively.

9. Most public transport operators started implementing some kind of fare concessions to facilitate the mobility of the aged after Patten proposed a new tax and rental exemption incentive scheme for them.

No doubt, each of these developments has its own significance, and fully justifies a close examination. Nonetheless, it is unrealistic to make a review of each of them within such a short essay. Hence, the author has decided to focus on just a few of them for a thorough review. There are a few good reasons for doing so. First of all, some of these developments are relatively new. It would be premature to make a meaningful and in-depth review of them. They include the commissioning of Network 26 on the Hong Kong Island by Citybus, the public's reception to the introduction of the new tunnel autopass and its actual effects on increasing tunnel through-put, and the value of performance pledges and practicality of passenger liaison group programmes in the improvement of quality of service in public transport. They deserve a close examination next year when the programmes will have been implemented for a year. Second, some of the developments, such as Patten's commitment to the ACP projects and his refusal to link the projects with his political reform package have already been dealt with extensively elsewhere, hence it would be redundant to repeat them here. To make the review more interesting, the author proposes to focus on just three of the developments, namely the *Taxi Policy Review*, the *Railway Development Study*, and the care of the aged. The reasons for choosing them will be self-explanatory in subsequent sections. The approach of this year's review will differ from those of earlier years as the review will focus more on the political aspects of these development. Such a bias is understandable as the author is a political sociologist by training, and a policy-adviser by experience. The subsequent sections will first deal with the *Taxi Policy Review*, followed by a brief review of the railway development, and the provision of care for the aged in public transport.

## ☐ Taxi Policy Review

Taxi has been one of the most important and controversial areas in public transport operation. The subject has always attracted an unusual amount of attention from transport policy-makers, the travelling public, and people involved in the trade. This is clearly reflected in the readiness of the Transport Advisory Committee (TAC) to set up either a subcommittee or a working group to look into the trade whenever there is a major turnover in their membership. This had taken place in 1986 and 1991 respectively. There are a number of good reasons for it.

First, taxis are playing a very significant role in the provision of public transport in Hong Kong as they account for roughly one-eighth of all daily public transport journeys. The daily patronage stood at 1.25 million passenger journeys in 1991. Given its importance, the travelling public are surely interested and concerned with their service quality, quantity, convenience, and fare level. Accommodating all these parameters have also been a major task for policy-makers. Secondly, the trade has always been a major source of employment. With close to 17,500 urban and New Territories taxis in operation, it is estimated that at any point in time, there are more than 40,000 self-employed or owner-drivers working either permanently or temporarily in the trade. In fact, they constitute the largest group of workers in the public transport field. Hence, any changes in government policy and working environment may have significant effects on their livelihood. Thirdly, the trade is fragmented organizationally and yet militant. Internal fights among factions have always characterized the trade. For years, a small number of factions among the taxi operators have claimed to represent the interests of the trade, but were constantly challenged by frontline drivers. In recent years, a faction of frontline drivers have made significant progress in positioning themselves as a powerful organized lobby.

In April 1991, the TAC once again experienced a major turnover of membership after a 1990 scandal about its Chairperson, Maria Tam, that had undermined public confidence in the Committee. In her stead, C. K. Leung, a professor at The University of Hong Kong and a long-serving member of the TAC, was appointed the new Chair. At the same time, a new batch of professionals with very limited exposure to public transport operation were appointed. Towards the end of 1991, the TAC set up a working group to look into the taxi trade. It was chaired by a member of the Committee with a strong academic link. The scope of the Working Group was less ambitious than that of the 1986 TAC Subcommittee on Taxi Policy Review. It was charged with the responsibility to undertake a fresh review of taxi policy with particular regard to (1) the licensing system, (2) fare policy, and (3) quality of taxi service. Interestingly enough, these issues had already been thoroughly covered and studied by the 1986 Sub-committee. Hence, its formation had attracted many wild speculations about its motives.

Similar to the 1986 Subcommittee, the Working Group was relatively small in size, and at the outset promised to conduct the review in con-sultation with the public and the trade. The Working Group consisted of three non-government members, the Commissioner of Transport, the Deputy Secretary for Transport, and a Principal Assistant Secretary for Transport who served as its secretary. Surely, the ranking of these officials spoke clearly of the government's perception of its importance. They started working in January 1992, and conducted consultation sessions with the public, District Boards, and the trade in subsequent months. These consultation exercises were completed by June 1992. By then, the Working Group had received a total of 45 submissions of comments, including 12 from District Boards, 12 from taxi associations, 20 from concerned groups and members of the public, and one from the Consumer Council. *Prima facie*, the reception to the consultation exercises appeared far from satisfac-tory. This was quite understandable as the public and the trade were quite surprised by the TAC's move when it was first formed, bearing in mind that the Administration's position on the role of taxi had just been reaffirmed in the January 1990 *White Paper on Transport Policy in Hong Kong*. Insiders suspected that while the formation of the Working Group and the consul-tation exercise might serve an important self-education function for the new members, it might also be connected with their scepticism of the independence of the 1986 TAC Subcommittee on Taxi Policy Review.

However, further speculation on the lukewarm public reception to the consultation may not be productive. Instead, we should proceed to analyse and discuss the core issues that were raised by the Working Group, and critically compare them with those recommended by the 1986 Subcom-mittee, and the respective policy in the 1990 White Paper. Two crucial questions need to be addressed before going further into the review. First of all, what was the position of the Working Group on the role of taxi? Were their views on the issue similar to or different from established policy? Second, did they encounter any problems in getting data on the trade? These will be dealt with in due course.

The 1988 *Taxi Policy Review* concluded that (1) taxi provides a personalized form of service complementary to other public transport modes; and (2) given that taxis are uneconomic road users, their number need to be restricted in order to balance the increasing demand for taxi service against what Hong Kong's roads can bear. This policy presumption was reaffirmed in the 1990 *White Paper on Transport Policy in Hong Kong*. Recognizing the persistent public support for this document, the Working Group reaffirmed their support of the established policy on the role of taxi. The reaffirmation implies that the fleet containment policy will hold. It clearly implies that subsequent recommendations of the Working Group need to comply with it.

The Working Group shared similar experiences with the 1986 Subcommittee in finding the roadside and taxi stand survey to be inadequate in providing them the needed information, and called upon the Administration to improve the quality and utility of these surveys in order to enhance the effectiveness of their assessment of the adequacy of the taxi fleet and its use of road space. Some hinted that as a remedy, the Administration should make good use of the expertise of the local academic community to improve the technical and conceptual quality of these surveys. Sharing their concerns, some former members of the TAC conceded that more sophisticated analytical tools and statistical methods should be applied to make sense out of the raw data. Simple cross tabulations might be too elementary and outdated for decision-making purpose. The common concerns of both the 1986 Subcommittee and 1991 Working Group over the quality and value of the taxi surveys should not be treated as purely coincidental, and deserve prompt action by the Administration. Their improvements are very crucial in enhancing the ability of policy-makers in identifying and solving the critical issues in the trade. The formation of an interdepartmental working group with participation from the academic community and the TAC in one form or another may be necessary.

## Taxi Licensing System

The subsequent section will deal with the three core issues the Working Group had reviewed in turn. It will begin with a brief description of the existing taxi licensing arrangement. Taxi licences have been issued by public tender at a premium since 1964. Starting from 1976, taxi licences are tendered out at regular intervals. At that time, the total registered taxi fleet was 4,754, but by the end of 1991, it stood at 14,750. The average tender premium in June 1985 when the government first imposed a quota on issuing no more than 200 licences a year was $219,771, but by the time the TAC set up a Subcommittee to look into the trade, the premium had already surged to $372,042. By July 1988 when the Subcommittee completed its review, the premium soared further to $694,443. Its upward movement had failed to stop. By the end of 1991 when the TAC set up a new Working Group to review the trade, the premium climbed further up to $1,512,055. Despite the government's constant denials, many attributed the skyrocketing premium to be closely associated with the imposed quota and the tender system.

Coincidentally, both the 1986 Subcommittee and the 1991 Working Group agreed that manipulative speculation was the major cause for the skyrocketing escalation of the premium, and were keen to adopt new measures to cope with it. Both had thoroughly re-examined the pros and cons of the tender system, and scrutinized those problems that were intimately associated with the tendering exercises. Having assessed other options, both groups concluded that (1) tendering is a fair and efficient way to allocate the limited number of licences; (2) it is consistent with the free market principle and there is no alternative which is demonstrably better. Similarly, both viewed the licence premium as a price paid for a capital investment, and advised that it should not be included as operation costs when assessing fare revisions. They all conceded that (1) the premium had risen beyond the profitability of taxi operation; (2) there was reason to believe that the taxi licences had become a commodity for profiteering for some speculators; (3) the tendering exercises had been dominated by a small number of companies. Such a domination was detrimental to the interest of individual bidders, and contrary to free market principles.

Convinced that something should be done to curb manipulative speculation and stabilize the licence premium, both went on to review the following options: (1) do-nothing approach; (2) taxi ownership scheme; (3) licence rental system; (4) franchised taxi companies; and (5) improving the existing system. Subsequently, they ruled out the first four options in favour of the fifth one. Despite this, there was a major difference between the positions of the 1986 Subcommittee and that of the 1991 Working Group. The 1986 Subcommittee acknowledged that the ability of the government to intervene in the market was severely curbed by its containment policy which restricts the annual licensing quota to a maximum of 200. Such a quota, in their view, only constituted less than 1.4 per cent of the total number of licences in the market. Furthermore, the government had practically no right to intervene in the circulation of those 17,500 licences that were in the market. So, whatever measures the Subcommittee recommended to deal with those 200 new annual licence quota, it could hardly be effective in affecting the operation of the market. Hence, the Subcommittee regarded it imprudent and inappropriate to make any substantive changes regarding the licensing system. Instead, they only managed to recommend a few face-saving administrative measures as follows: (1) transfer of newly issued licences during the six-month takeup period for a tender exercise should be prohibited; (2) the tender deposit should be increased from $25,000 to $50,000; and finally (3) the Transport Department should review the present tender procedure with a view to simplifying it and making it more easily understood to facilitate genuine operators to bid for the licences. In retrospect, none would see these measures as effective in curtailing manipulative speculation and stabilizing taxi licence premium.

The approach of the 1991 Working Group was grossly different. Instead of avoiding the issues, they made substantive efforts to assess the possibility of (1) issuing more licences; (2) repealing the preset quota system; (3) restricting the eligibility of the bidders; (4) controlling the free transfer of licences; (5) imposing transfer tax; and (6) reducing the mortgage level and period. Their views appear very interesting, and deserve a closer look in turn. Increasing uncertainty, such as issuing more licences or repealing the preset quota system, was judged by the Working Group as the most effective measure to cool manipulative speculation. The 1986 Subcommittee also shared a similar view. Nonetheless, they recognized that it might contradict the government's established taxi containment policy, and there were practically no signs that the government was even prepared to make any minor changes in the policy. Not surprisingly, the 1991 Working Group was also severely restrained by such an established policy.

Furthermore, the Working Group was quite critical of the existing licensing arrangement. They argued that the current licensing system is not conducive to discouraging speculation because setting the quota over a period of time would (1) enable the bidders to plan bids; and (2) reduce the risk for the speculators. They advocated a more flexible licensing policy to meet public demand for taxi services, and recommended that the preset quota system on taxi numbers over a relatively long fixed period should be repealed and the approval of the Governor in Council on the number of taxi licences to be issued should be sought as and when necessary. At first sight, such measures may further increase uncertainty, hence escalating the cost of speculation. Yet, for it to be effective, the policy of containment has to be lifted at the same time. This is to caution speculators that the government is willing to dump the market with a lot of licences. Without that, speculators can just ignore them as they can still anticipate the limited supply of licences, and calculate the short and long-term moving premium with similar level of precision. There was hardly any hint that the Working Group felt any confidence in convincing the government to change its containment policy. In addition, the Working Group also observed that the timing for tender should not follow a fixed schedule as corruption opportunities might arise related to privileged information on the tender exercise. This observation appears a bit out of line with the practice of the trade as the timing of the licence tendering exercise had lost its meaning due to the bidders' increasing ability to calculate the premium. Taking into account the government's established containment policy, the trade can generally forecast the expected premium months, and sometimes even by years ahead of any tendering exercise. Perhaps, with some in-depth knowledge of the trade, the Working Group might not have found it necessary to make this observation.

In furthering their pursuit, the Working Group had considered two additional strategies to mitigate speculation. The first involves restricting the maximum number of bids that each bidder is entitled to make, and the other requires the bidders to produce a pre-qualified mortgage statement. The first strategy was aimed at breaking the entrenched monopoly of the tendering exercises by a small group of taxi trading companies. Through this, chances for "genuine" individual taxi operators to obtain the licence may be increased. However, after careful review, they found such a strategy to be impractical as trading companies can easily resort to other tactics to handle the restrictions. Furthermore, it would be administratively difficult and costly to find out who the genuine operator is. Hence, they ruled out endorsement of this proposal. The second involves the requirement for bidders to produce a pre-qualified mortgage statement. They regarded this as a good measure to exclude "some unnecessary entrants". They further argued that the proposed measure would be far better than requiring the banks either to lower the mortgage cover/period. The observation was nonetheless regarded by bankers as totally naive. They argued that obtaining financing in Hong Kong was not as difficult as in other countries. So long as the applicants have established a good working relationship with the banks, and the risks are considered acceptable, banks in Hong Kong would generally provide them the needed financing. The same applies to home mortgage where the risks are significantly higher than those in the taxi trade. In other words, such a strategy is unlikely to have any effect on restricting "the unnecessary entrants" at all.

The Working Group further commented that free transfer and perpetual ownership of taxi licences are instrumental to speculation and the runaway licence premium. Against the objectives of stabilizing licence premium and deterring manipulative speculation, the Working Group did an elaborate academic exercise in assessing a number of alternative licensing conditions for new licences to be issued in the future. The options include: (1) non-transferable licences for a certain period after first registration before becoming freely transferable; (2) transferable fixed term non-renewable licences; (3) non-transferable fixed term non-renewable licences; (4) non-transferable fixed term renewable licences till the death of the holders; and (5) non-transferable licences valid for the life of the holders. The Working Group maintained that short-term tenancy and limited or non-transferability would reduce the attractiveness of taxi licences as a speculative instrument. Nonetheless, insiders of the trade had regarded these options as theoretical as they could accommodate neither the aspiration of the drivers to own a taxi permanently, nor the expenses incurred in operating a taxi for livelihood. Not surprisingly, when rumours that the Administration is actively considering issuing a new type of non-transferable, seven-year fixed term taxi licences were leaked, both drivers and traders immediately rejected the proposal as impracticable. Admitting its limited marketability, most contended that it serves neither the purpose of cooling the manipulative speculation nor stabilizing taxi licence premium. More importantly, some questioned the value of issuing a small batch of these non-transferable, fixed term licences if the government cannot tamper with the transactions of the existing 17,500 taxi licences.

To further enhance their argument for the introduction of the new type of licences, the Working Group observed that the government should seriously consider allowing the payment of these licence premium in annual instalment as the banks might be sceptical of the viability of their financing. Their intention is surely superb and bold but it runs completely against the government's basic policy that public funds would not be used to subsidize any public transport operation. In concluding their study on the licensing system, the Working Group hinted that the government should consider imposing either a capital gain tax or stamp duty on each transaction as a way to deter speculation. But on the other hand, they were also worried that the government might be criticized for imposing a new form of taxation. More importantly, the Working Group's observation may lead the public to question the propriety of government intervention into the marketplace. Hence, its political acceptability and practicability appear to be rather doubtful.

On the whole, the Working Group was right in their focus on the entrenched manipulative speculation in the trade of taxi licences and the skyrocketing of the licence premium. The 1986 Subcommittee had shared very similar concerns, but after very thorough review had refrained from intervening in the market. Perhaps, some might have been politically right in criticizing them for lack of innovative ideas. But the review so far has affirmed that they might not be too far from the mark. Undoubtedly, the Working Group had worked extremely hard to search for possible alternatives, and did come up with a few recommendations and proposals that the 1986 Subcommittee had already considered quite thoroughly, but had refrained to endorse them. Restrained by the government's taxi fleet containment policy, there are in fact very few practicable measures or strategies the TAC can adopt to balance out the demand and supply of taxis. Hence, one should never be surprised to find that the TAC may fail once again to bring forth any new and substantive proposals in its forthcoming taxi licensing policy.

## *Fare Policy and Structure*

The fare is certainly an important component of taxi policy, but compared with the licensing system, it is a less complicated issue. Undoubtedly, taxi fare is overwhelmingly dictated by the government's taxi containment policy. Nonetheless, in the actual decision-making on fare revision and fare scale, policy-makers have to make extra efforts in balancing the interests of all the key actors, e.g. the travelling public, taxi drivers, and operators/ owners. Moreover, it would be naive to assume that they are purely transport decisions. A crucial problem to be asked here is whether there has been a taxi fare policy. This surely was one of the key questions that led to the formation of the 1986 Subcommittee. At that time, the TAC was not so sure whether there was one. After an in-depth review, the Subcommittee came up with a solid package which contained the following recommendations that were endorsed and confirmed in 1988 by the TAC and the Executive Council respectively:

1. Given that taxis are uneconomic road users, a reasonable fare differential should be maintained between taxis and other public transport modes so as to regulate the growth in taxi demand.
2. The differential should be in the range of 5 to 7 times for urban taxis and 3 to 4 times for New Territories taxis.
3. Taxi licence premium should be excluded from the cost structure of taxi operation. The principle has since been well received and further reaffirmed by the 1990 *White Paper on Transport Policy in Hong Kong*. Hence, few would doubt that there is a taxi fare policy.

Despite the endorsement of earlier positions by the 1990 White Paper, the 1991 Working Group was keen on having a fresh look at the problem again. As expected, after the review, they came up with nothing new but reaffirmed the position of the 1986 Subcommittee. Moreover, the Working Group observed and agreed to the Subcommittee's unofficial views that fare revision should be justified mainly by the operating costs of the trade rather than for achieving a targeted differential. This reminder is important as it would impose some constraint on the government in case it wants to push the differential to its upper limit in order to achieve a maximum effect of its taxi containment policy.

The 1986 Subcommittee as well as the 1991 Working Group agreed that providing the drivers a fair income and sustaining the financial viability of the trade are of equal importance in securing a quality taxi service. Recognizing taxi as a labour-intensive industry, both groups agreed to the need for reviewing taxi fare scale on a regular basis. However, in doing so, they conceded that availability, affordability, and public acceptability should also be included as vital factors in the assessment scheme. Together they should form the yardsticks for fare revision.

Few would question the existence of the yardsticks, but the real problem is: Should the TAC openly consult any groups before making the fare revision decision? The conventional view was that after taking into account the interests of all parties concerned, there was no need for the TAC to conduct further consultation with the public or the trade. Instead, they should thoroughly review the proposals and forward their recommendation to the Governor in Council for final approval.

Though not addressing the issue directly, the Subcommittee acknowledged the need for a regular taxi conference organized by the Transport Department on a regular basis, and noted its importance as a useful communication channel for the trade and the Administration. However, the

Subcommittee was worried about the lack of representation of frontline drivers in the conference. At their insistence, the Administration promised to strengthen the representativeness of the conference. Subsequent to that, a taxi driver group was invited to join the conference. Since 1988, the group has made some significant progress in positioning itself as an authoritative voice of frontline drivers, and played a prominent role in shaping policies that affect the trade, particularly in fare revision exercises. The arrangement had appeared to be working fine. Up to 1991, the TAC had comfortably enjoyed its monopoly as the authority on fare revision.

In assessing whether the general public should be included in the consultation on fare revision, the Working Group shared a similar view with the Subcommittee that there was no need to do so. The reason is obvious as the extension of consultation will surely make the revision exercise even more politicized. But the two differed on a significant point. While affirming the role of the taxi conference as a body to be consulted, the Working Group hinted that the consultation with District Boards should be maintained. Such a position is very strange as the TAC had struggled hard for years not to make any concessions on this point, fearing that it might invite the Legislative Council to take over the power of fare determination in public transport provision.

A possible explanation for this position is that the Working Group is thinking of forming an alliance with District Boards to the exclusion of the Legislative Council. This is taken in view of increasing competition between the Legislative Council and the TAC over who should have greater say in transport policy and fare determination. Of course, if the position is correct, it may be welcomed by most members of District Boards as they have been struggling hard these days for gaining some new ground on public policy-making. Nonetheless, the move may provoke the legislature to step up its campaigns to take away the TAC's mandate in transport policy formulation. Besides, the Administration would hardly endorse such a move as it may open the floodgates for members of District Boards to take a similar role in the fare revision exercises of the franchised buses, MTRC, KCRC, etc. More important, in doing so, it will inevitably attract direct intervention from the legislature.

Like the 1986 Subcommittee, the Working Group made a serious study of the potential of using pricing to regulate the demand and supply of service. They conceded that the existing distance-based fare structure may be a major contributing factor to the hiring of taxis for short-distance trips. Increasing the first flagfall substantially may be a way to discourage short-distance trips, yet taxi is providing a vital feeder service in many areas of Hong Kong that are not adequately provided with alternative modes of public transport. Both points had been thoroughly noted by the Subcommittee when they took a serious look into using a similar kind of pricing strategy to regulate demand and supply. Having considered that it would be grossly inequitable to do so as the government had failed to provide alternative feeder services, they refrained from recommending to the TAC to endorse such a strategy. Moreover, the Subcommittee was very concerned with the potential of increasing malpractices. A substantial increase in the flagfall might induce drivers to concentrate on those who hire taxis for short-distance trips, and refuse hire for long-distance journeys. In the end, the Subcommittee recommended that no major changes should be made to the basic fare structure. In their assessment of a substantial increase in the flagfall, the Working Group seemed to have neglected this important point.

Despite the theoretical attractiveness of the financial returns of short-distance trips, the TAC noted hire refusal practices to be very rampant at the time. Having carefully studied the phenomenon, some members of the Subcommittee claimed that deteriorating road congestion in most urban corridors had made it impossible for drivers to make sufficient income even to cover their basic hourly cost such as the daily rental, fuel, a minimal labour rate, etc. The prevailing waiting time rate was obsolete as a means to compensate the basic cost of operation. Hence, to cope with the situation, they recommended a major revision in the waiting time charge which should truly reflect the cost incurred by the drivers.

The recommendation was well-received by the community and finally endorsed by the TAC. The trade welcomed the TAC's decision, and concurred that the new waiting time charge should be kept only to cover the basic hourly operating cost, but should not be intended to provide an incentive for drivers to profit from road congestion. In fact, even after the substantive increase in the charge, it could hardly beat even one-third of the potential income for the drivers if the hired journey was running smoothly. Most taxi drivers hailed the TAC's decision as a pragmatic strategy to solve the crux of hire refusals. The Working Group had also ventured into the same issue. They held that the prevailing waiting time charge should be upwardly adjusted. Their argument for it was slightly different from the concerns of the 1986 Subcommittee. They regarded the upward adjustment as an effective way to deter passengers from taking taxis to congested areas. But they were also concerned with its potential negative effects because it might encourage taxi drivers to go into congested areas deliberately. Their worry was nonetheless criticized by some frontline drivers as a failure to appreciate the drivers' practical concerns.

It would not be unfair to conclude our critical review of the Working Group's study on taxi policy and structure by asserting that they had failed to produce anything substantively different from the work of the 1986 Subcommittee. Such a conclusion is not surprising at all as the Subcommittee had spent close to two years in their study of the trade. Through that, they succeeded in putting together all the conventions and practices regarding taxi fares into a coherent framework. It would not be fair to adopt the same yardsticks to assess the Working Group. Besides, with the exception of the Maria Tam scandal, there were hardly any significant changes that had been taking place in the trade that deserved another fresh look into it. Hence, it is understandable why many insiders have regarded such a review as largely tautological.

### *Quality of Taxi Service*

Few would dare to say that taxi services are perfect in Hong Kong, but neither would it be fair to assert that services are deplorable. Official statistics may help to provide a fair confirmation of this. With the taxi fleet more or less constant at 17,500 and a daily passenger journey count at 1,220,000, the Transport Complaints Unit had received 1,666, 1,480, and 1,670 taxi complaint cases in 1989, 1990, and 1991 respectively. Over the period, the Unit had only registered less than five cases of complaints on taxis a day out of approximately 35,000 operating shifts, and approximately about four cases of complaints out of every 1,000,000 passenger trips. The official figures clearly confirm that malpractices in the taxi trade were not as rampant as most would assert. Despite this, it is generally presumed that malpractices are very pervasive. The Working Group appeared to have noted the fact, and yet, had to accommodate public demands for better taxi services. That was why they were quite cautious in admitting that there would still be room for improvement by both the government and the taxi trade without making any unnecessary overstatement.

Having thoroughly reviewed the quality of taxi services, the Subcommittee made the following recommendations to the TAC:

1. The Transport Department should maintain separate records for four-seater and five-seater taxis.

2. The Transport Department should review the criteria for issuing taxi driving licences and consider introducing a geographical road test in addition to a written test for taxi drivers' competence.

3. Consideration should be given to disqualifying or suspending the licences of those taxi drivers who are persistently guilty of malpractices.

4. Legislation should be enacted to require a fare plate specified by the Transport Department to be displayed on both the rear nearside door and the front dashboard on the passenger side or the front nearside door.

5. The Transport Department should discuss further with the taxi trade to consider ways to improve the present system of shift changing.

6. The Transport Department should assist the taxi associations in the production of an information pamphlet on taxi services.

7. No major restructuring of the existing taxi conferences was warranted.

8. Publicity should be organized to encourage taxi owners and drivers to join taxi associations and participate at taxi conferences.

Taxi associations should be encouraged to carry out activities to promote the quality of taxi services to the public. Since their endorsement by the TAC, the Administration had taken active steps to implement those recommendations that were within their control. So far, the Administration has made very little progress on the proposals (1) to disqualify repeated offenders of malpractices, and (2) to improve the system of shift changing. The main hurdle appears to be opposition from frontline drivers.

Following the steps of the Subcommittee, the Working Group had also come up with some interesting recommendations to upgrade the quality of taxi services. The major ones included:

1. simplifying the complaint procedures;
2. requiring taxi drivers to issue mandatory fare receipts;
3. introducing a demerit point system;
4. cooperating with the trade to educate drivers and the public of their rights and responsibilities for better-quality taxi services;
5. re-examining taxi drivers at regular intervals;
6. requiring compulsory medical examination for taxi drivers above a certain age;
7. exempting taxis from certain restricted zones; and

8. encouraging drivers/operators to form trade associations to enhance communication with the general public and the government.

These measures were intended to meet the Working Group's objectives to improve the quality of taxi services through deterrents, inducements and education. Of these eight observations, we expect that at least five of them would encounter little resistance from the trade, the public and the policymakers. They include: (1) simplification of complaint procedures; (2) education of the public and drivers for the provision of a quality taxi service; (3) compulsory medical examination for taxi drivers; (4) exemption from restricted zones; and (5) encouraging of drivers and operators to form associations. The Administration may be able to obtain substantive support from frontline drivers if public funds can be secured to cover those costs incurred by education and publicity programmes.

Overcharging has always been one of the major complaints about taxi malpractices. The Working Group was fully aware of this, and proposed the issuing of charge receipts as a preventive measure. The receipts will facilitate the work of the police in prosecuting those who overcharge. While recognizing the technical feasibility of the production of charge receipts, the Working Group agreed that the time-consuming aspect of the issuance of receipts should first be solved. Hence, they were prudent in not insisting on its immediate implementation. Furthermore, the proposal may encounter resistance from frontline drivers unless the Administration can ensure drivers and operators that the programme would not be too costly in both financial and administrative terms. Moreover, the Administration also needs to ensure the drivers that the Inland Revenue Department would not be allowed to gain access to the information for tax purposes.

In recent years, taxi drivers have put pressure on the Administration to set up cross-harbour taxi stands on both sides of the harbour. They argue that an increasing number of taxi drivers are not familiar with the routes and new locations in the territories. Consequently, many prefer to work only on one side of the harbour. The government has refused to endorse such an request as it contradicts the established policy that urban taxis should cover all areas except the outlying islands. Besides, an increasing number of drivers also use the same excuse to refuse hires. In view of this, the Working Group recommended that to ensure that drivers get familiar with new routes, locations, and regulations, drivers should be re-examined at regular intervals. The proposal has been regarded by many drivers as unnecessary as most veteran drivers should have a very clear idea of most new routes and locations. Besides, most of them are quite skilful in seeking directions if needed. If re-examination at regular intervals is designed mainly to deter malpractices, the Administration should instead increase the amount of penalty for hire refusal. Recognizing the need to update taxi regulation on a regular basis, drivers argue that the government should step up publicity on new legislation rather than taking additional efforts to re-examine drivers. Hence, few would support the re-examination proposal.

Of all the proposals, the adoption of a demerit point system has drawn the strongest objection from frontline drivers. But politically, this is one that is most well-received by the community. However, most drivers argue that a general demerit point system for driving offences has already been in place for years. If a purpose-designed demerit point system for taxi drivers is introduced, it would put additional stress on frontline drivers who are usually working on a 10 to 12-hour shift. Besides, they object to being discriminated as there are no similar penalties on drivers who work in other public transport modes, and as the amount of malpractices in the trade has been small even by world standards. If the Administration chooses to adopt the Working Group's recommendation without fully allaying drivers' anxiety, they should think carefully about the possible consequence of an ugly showdown with frontline drivers. Frontline drivers argue that they have no objection to dramatically increase the amount of fine for hire refusal offenders.

In sum, the Working Group has made some significant progress in their search for measures to improve the quality of taxi services. As discussed earlier, quite a few of their observations seem to be quite thoughtful and practicable. Perhaps, this is the most valuable part of their study, and also one that has the most potential support from the public, the regulators, and the taxi trade, particularly frontline workers. Still, they need to be cautious in pushing ahead with the demerit point system as it may impose a lot of stress on the majority while not necessarily be effective in penalizing an extremely tiny minority of repeated offenders. It may be prudent for them to take a fresh look at these two controversial proposals, namely re-examining drivers at regular intervals, and the introduction of a taxi-driver demerit point system. Failing to do so may jeopardize their good working relationship with frontline workers which has taken them years to build. Furthermore, the maintenance of a good working relationship with frontline workers may further enhance the government's efforts in improving other areas of taxi services.

## Concluding Remarks

The Maria Tam scandal in the 1990 had embarrassed many of those committed professionals who had been working under her leadership in the
Transport Advisory Committee of that time. It was particularly humiliating
for those who sit on the 1986 TAC Subcommittee on Taxi Policy Review
and who had devoted a large amount of their time at the expense of their
professional careers to work out a taxi policy. The Subcommittee's recommendations were taken by the TAC and the Administration as thoughtful,
and had been endorsed as Hong Kong's taxi policy since. As expected, their
policy was reaffirmed in the January 1990 *White Paper on Transport Policy
in Hong Kong*. Despite this reaffirmation, the integrity of the Subcommittee
was put under doubt when Tam and her family were found to be operating
a taxi firm while she was serving as the Chairman of the TAC whose
principal responsibility was to oversee public transport provision in Hong
Kong. It was undoubtedly a case of conflict of interests. It not only
surprised the public, but also those who had worked closely with her in the
TAC without any knowledge of it. The scandal had deeply distressed those
who retired together with her in April 1991. They had to risk their reputation being tainted by the scandal.

In 1991, some eight months after Tam's retirement, the TAC announced
the formation of a Working Group to look into the taxi trade. The terms of
reference of the Working Group mainly covered those critical issues that the
1986 Subcommittee had already studied. The move of the TAC was taken
by many as a surprising one as the Subcommittee's recommendations were
endorsed by the TAC only in 1988 and were reaffirmed in the 1990 White
Paper. As there were no signs of any significant change in the public
transport system that really deserved a new review, many suspected it to be
closely connected with the Maria Tam scandal. It might well be considered
as a political assessment of the work of the Subcommittee. The apparent
connection had raised suspicion among many observers that there might be
something crucially wrong with the 1986 Subcommittee, the integrity of
whose members had been cast into doubt.

After nearly a year of study, the Working Group finally came up
with a preliminary report that reaffirms nearly all the critical recommendations made by the 1986 Subcommittee. As presented earlier, the
Working Group had only succeeded in making some recommendations on
minor administrative improvements. Nonetheless, their findings served to
clear and restore the names and integrity of those involved in the 1986

Subcommittee. If it was not because of this, the Working Group's work might look extremely odd as they failed to come up with anything concrete and innovative. In other words, the work of the 1986 Subcommittee has stood the test of time.

## ☐ Railway Development Study

In January 1990, the government released a White Paper on Hong Kong's transport policy *Moving into the 21st Century*. Among others it reaffirmed the recommendations by the Second Comprehensive Transport Study (CTS2) and the Green Paper to build a third rail harbour crossing, the northwest New Territories urban rail link, and the Mass Transit Railway extension to Tseung Kwan O. Instead of giving a clear timetable for their construction, the White Paper stated that in light of the government's decision (1) to construct a purpose-built airport railway to serve the replacement airport in Chek Lap Kok, and (2) to advance the construction of Route 3 to tie in with the commissioning of the replacement airport, the government needed to commission a Airport Railway Feasibility Study to determine the alignment, capacity and financial viability of the airport railway. This would be followed by a Railway Development Study which would reassess the railway projects recommended by CTS2, and determine their priority, alignment and timing, taking full account of the airport railway.

The government's intention is crystal clear: the construction of the replacement airport and the purpose-built airport railway will have priority over other road and rail development projects. As controversies centring around the construction of the replacement airport have already been dealt with extensively elsewhere, there is no need to elaborate them further here. Upon their firm commitment to the construction of the replacement airport and the associated railway, the government commissioned a Railway Development Study as promised. The consultancy was completed early in 1993. Its findings and recommendations were briefly outlined in a public consultation document *Railway Development Study* which was released by the government in April. The document did not come up with any surprising conclusions as most of the recommendations had already been noted first in the 1989 Green Paper, and subsequently in the 1990 White Paper. Additional details had been revealed in the discussion of the airport and its rail projects. The following section will outline the role of railway in Hong Kong, clarify the evaluation criteria adopted by the study, summarize their main proposals, and briefly review the consultation exercises.

The consultation document is extremely brief. It emphasizes the dual role of railways in Hong Kong: serving internal movement, and linking with China. When reading between the lines, it is crystal clear that the government is trying to optimize future railway development projects to position Hong Kong strategically as a port centre for South China. Hence, those projects that can integrate Hong Kong's internal movement needs and her linkages with South China will logically top the government's priority. This policy presumption has been made even more explicit in the set of criteria which the consultants used in evaluating the priority of a wide variety of rail schemes. The list includes:

1. how well the project helps secure Hong Kong's strategic role as a port, trade and business centre in the region;
2. how it can enhance the development and economy of Hong Kong;
3. whether it could serve transport needs in an effective manner;
4. whether the benefits to the community arising from the project justify the cost of implementation;
5. whether it is financially viable; and
6. what its operational and environmental requirements and constraints are and how these can be satisfied.

The ordering of the items mentioned above, though not officially admitted, may well reflect the government's relative priority. If the same list was put forward in the mid-1980s, financial viability, cost-effectiveness, and internal development needs would probably have predominated the rest of the list.

### The Western Rail Corridor

In simple terms, the rail networks under the study of the consultancy can be differentiated as the Western Corridor, the Eastern Corridor, and the Island. According to the document, the proposed Western Corridor will provide a new arterial link to the border. Three services will share the corridor: a port rail line to the container port at Kwai Chung, a long-distance passenger service to China, and a sub-regional passenger rail link between the North West New Territories and the urban area. The government has forcefully argued that:

1. the construction of a new freight rail line from the border to Hong Kong's port is strategically vital in strengthening Hong Kong's role as a port;

2. it helps to move standard containers by rail direct to the port of Hong Kong for transfer to ocean-going vessels, with minimum intermediate handling;

3. it will also complement China's plan to develop a new north-south rail corridor and to expand the use of standard containers;

4. such a rail connection will reduce pressure on the road system caused by cross-border freight traffic; and

5. the construction of a new cross-border passenger service will ease the burden of the KCRC New Territories East corridor.

According to the document, over 37 million cross-border trips were recorded in 1992 and this is forecast to double by 2011. To cope with this demand, a new rail line to the border is recommended using the Western Corridor. The line would initially be connected to Lo Wu, and later to a second border crossing point proposed at Lok Ma Chau. To further convince the public of the benefits of this cross-border service, the government also points to (1) reducing travel time through faster train services in the Western Corridor; and (2) easier access to Huanggang and the Futian areas, and possible future connection with the proposed Shenzhen light rail system, as additional incentives.

Few would doubt the substantive and strategic benefits of the Western Corridor Rail Network to Hong Kong as a whole. Nonetheless, despite its obvious advantages to residents in Tin Shui Wai and Yuen Long, the proposed network fails to match the needs of residents in Tuen Mun who have continuously demanded for a direct urban rail link. Under the government's proposal, residents in Tuen Mun have to make a light rail detour to Yuen Long first before taking the Western Corridor Rail to the urban area. They regard such a detour to be both time-consuming and financially burdensome. In response to their critical comment, the Administration argues that the trip to the Central from Tuen Mun under the proposed option will only take an additional five minutes. While the argument may seem convincing, it fails to address their concerns over additional cost. This is quite understandable as residents only need to pay for a single work or home bound trip if there is a direct link to the urban areas. Under the government's proposal, residents in Tuen Mun will have to pay extra for both the Western Corridor Rail Network and the Mass Transit Railway. Should the issue of fare integration be properly addressed, the resistance would have been more easily ameliorated. This is the main weakness of the *Railway Development Study*. The study gave the impression that it was done by technocrats who failed to share ordinary residents' concern over the soaring transport cost which is a crucial item in their family budget. As customers are very concerned with cost, the government should fully address this problem. For the time being, most major public transport operators are working closely to assess the viability of using "smart card" as a common electronic payment system for all transport facilities. The government should take advantage of this development, and explore the possibility of introducing fare integration.

## *The Eastern Corridor*

The document appears to be very vague about the limits of peak loading capability of the KCRC domestic service in New Territories East. Instead, it has diverted the issue by calling upon the two railway corporations to improve the interchange facilities in Kowloon Tong. In recent days, some have suggested the introduction of double-deck trains to solve the problems of peak loading. However, there are practically no signs that the consultants have ever dreamed of this option. Some hint that the consultants and the government may be too obsessed with the technical difficulties of the existing tunnel arrangement whereas others claim that the further development of the KCRC network in New Territories East is not a priority in the government's plan. Indeed, the Western Corridor is the real focus. Obviously, this is why most of the observations about network developments in New Territories East appear to be relatively vague. Similarly, the rail development programmes in East Kowloon are equally ambiguous. In contrast, the development of the MTRC extension to Tseung Kwan O looks more concrete as the government had been quite sure of the need to have such an extension which was clearly spelt out in the CTS2 Report, the 1989 Green Paper, and the 1990 White Paper. In fact, most agree that the construction of an MTRC extension to Tseung Kwan O is really a matter of time. MTRC will find no difficulty in getting approval from the Administration in due course.

## *The Island*

Both CTS2 and the White Paper acknowledged the need to build a third rail harbour crossing towards the end of the decade. The issue had been resolved when the Administration decided to have a purpose-built airport railway linking the Chek Lap Kok replacement airport and the Central. It is clearly understood that the third cross-harbour rail link will share the same corridor with the airport railway. Although a few other potential railway projects were mentioned and outlined, such as the rail network along the north shore, and the southern connection on the Hong Kong Island, they were given extremely low priority.

## *Concluding Remarks*

The preceding analysis argues that the government might already have a clear decision on the priorities of future railway development projects. Top among the list are the airport railway and the Western Rail Corridor that combines a port link, a cross-border passenger service, and a regional urban rail connection. It is then followed by the MTRC Tseung Kwan O extension. The rest are absolutely peripheral. Strategically, the government is correct in giving top priority to the airport railway and the Western Rail Corridor because the benefits of both projects to the overall development of Hong Kong clearly outweigh any regional interest. If the government has already set its priorities then what is the point of having public consultation? Some suggest that the government has reckoned the strong resistance from residents in Tuen Mun. The consultation will serve its purpose to mobilize public opinion in support of the government's proposed Western Corridor Rail, and simultaneously neutralize the demands of the Tuen Mun residents. This explanation appears to be plausible.

Without disputing this conjecture, most would agree that (1) the study had failed to address the issue of rail integration; (2) the consultation has been poorly conducted. The first issue has been addressed earlier in our elaboration on Tuen Mun residents' opposition to the government's refusal to build a coastal link from Tuen Mun to the urban area. The consultation has been poorly received by the public and severely criticized by the Legislative Council and transport experts. The first criticism is quite clear as the brief public consultation document fails to provide anything more substantive than the CTS2 Report, the 1989 Green Paper and the 1990 White Paper. That in itself is frustrating enough. The second criticism is not difficult to understand either as the government has failed to provide sufficient technical data to the legislators, experts in the field, and the general public. Without that, it is impossible for one to make any seasoned assessment of the *Railway Development Study*. For this, the Administration has been severely criticized by the legislature after the publication of the consultation document.

## ☐ Care for the Aged

In most countries, governments have made substantive efforts to ensure that the aged would not be deprived of the opportunity to move around due to high public transport cost. Hence, most public transport operators would provide the aged with some kind of fare concessions. At times, for various policy reasons, there may be some reasonable restrictions. The situation in Hong Kong is quite deplorable as most public transport operators have only agreed to extend some kind of fare concession to those aged 65 and above in April this year. This was made only after the government has offered the exemption of licence fees and rental fee for temporary depots. To be fair, the operators should not bear the whole blame as the worry over who should pay for the cost of concession had been a main reason for its absence. Despite the government's concession, some critical problems centring around the issue have not yet been resolved. The following is a critical review of these issues.

Despite her affluence and economic prosperity, Hong Kong has been criticized for lagging far behind most nations with comparable income levels in terms of old age entitlement. The care of the aged should cover not only basic necessities like food, housing, medical care, but also transportation. For years, many regard the care of the aged as the responsibility of individual families. It is presumed to be part of the Chinese tradition. Nonetheless, this presumption has been under strong attack from all quarters. Sustained high inflation in recent years has further weakened the financial capability of the younger generation to support their aged parents. This has led to increasing pressure on the government to accommodate the needs of the aged. Though far from being adequate, the government has made some significant efforts to increase the amount of allowance steadily over the years. With transport costs soaring rapidly in recent years, groups who are working closely with the aged have stepped up their campaigns to lobby public transport operators to introduce concession fares for the aged. It has been argued that without those concessions, the mobility of the aged would be severely curtailed. Their campaign had nonetheless been rejected categorically. Operators argued that as public transport in Hong Kong is privately provided, they are required to run the services on prudent commercial principles. It is the government's established policy that no public fund would be used to subsidize the public transport operation. Operation costs and profits have to be generated through revenue. This is entirely different from most countries where public transport operations are heavily subsidized from the public purse. In Hong Kong, concessions to one group would have to be subsidized by another. It would be grossly unfair for the travelling public to shoulder the cost of social welfare. Such a view is widely shared by most public transport regulators. This policy presumption has nonetheless been rejected by the political community.

In recent years, politicians, community organizations, and political parties have been particularly keen on this issue. Instead of dragging on the welfare issue, many argue that public transport operators should commit themselves to corporate citizenship. They call upon the operators to use shareholders' profits to shoulder the cost of concession to the aged. Disagreeing with them, the operators insisted that they have already paid their share of tax. It would be unfair that they have to pay tax twice. Besides, no corporation should be compelled to make extra societal welfare commitment. Moreover, they claim that the profit margins of public transport operation have been relatively low as compared with other industries. Even if they are willing to do so, they may be incapable of shouldering the concessions to some 450,000 people age 65 and above financially. Instead, operators have advised them to lobby legislators for their support to shift the cost of mobility for the aged to the public purse. Having failed to convince the operators, campaigners have directed the focus to the legislature, and public transport regulatory agencies, such as the Transport Branch, the Transport Advisory Committee, and the Transport Department. Though sympathetic with their cause, the regulatory agencies had so far refrained from making any firm commitment. Instead, they argued that the Health and Welfare Branch should take a closer look into this policy area. Despite their enthusiasm and recognition of the potential political gains from the issue, none of the factions of the legislature was able to come up with a concrete proposal. Instead, they just kept on babbling.

In announcing his platform of governance for the next five years, Chris Patten brought forth his commitment to make Hong Kong a caring society. Improving the lot of the aged and the mobilization of the community to achieve this societal target was high on his agenda. Many had doubt whether such a promise was merely a political babble. His promise became partially realized in March this year when the Financial Secretary delivered his annual Budget Speech which outlined the government's proposal to exempt franchise bus operators from paying the vehicle licence fee and the rentals for the government-owned temporary depots if they are willing to introduce fare concessions to those aged 65 and above. The cost saving for KMB would amount to $45 million to $55 million a year, whereas it was estimated that CMB would get an exemption of some $5 million or more. The proposal was a great surprise to many because most would hardly imagine that the conservative Financial Secretary would make such an innovative policy move. Hence, most have regarded this as Patten's initiative. The proposal was important in two aspects. First, it has not changed the government's policy on limited provision of social welfare because the fund for it would not be taken from the welfare budget item. Second, it was presented in a way as a government-corporate partnership in the provision of concessions. It fits perfectly well with Patten's appeal for a societal partnership in the care of the aged who had contributed their share to Hong Kong's prosperity during their youthful days.

Patten's incentive scheme appears to be more effective than the threats of politicians and community groups. It helps to ease the financial burdens on franchise bus operators and the needs for compulsory contribution from the travelling public, hence making it more attractive for them to comply with the government's appeal. Responses from two major bus operators had been grossly different, however. KMB took a positive step in pledging its support, and started implementing the half-fare concession programme for those aged 65 and above without any time and route restrictions. On the other hand, CMB's reaction was quite disappointing. The company took a long time to make any commitment. After a lot of hard-selling persuasion from the government, the company finally came up with a half-hearted support of the scheme, imposing both time and route restrictions on the concessions. Not surprisingly, KMB have been praised for its generosity and good corporate citizenship, whereas CMB has been criticized severely as being mean. Before concluding this part, there are two additional observations to be made. First, the issue of "who should pay for the concessions" has yet to be solved. Despite its generous support, KMB has expressed its concerns over the limits of its ability to sustain the associated financial burden, and hinted that they may conduct a review on the programme in the foreseeable future. If the review proves that the burden has gone beyond the reasonable financial burden of the company, the Administration may have to find other solutions for it. The situation may similarly be applied to CMB. Second, the case has clearly shown that most of those in our political community seem to be short of imagination. Political babbling can never be a good substitute for imagination. Politicians have to learn how to make policy through a good mix of incentives. The good reception to Patten's fare concession proposal should have provided them a good political lesson.

# ☐ Conclusion

This year, we adopt an entirely different approach to handle the topic on transportation. Instead of providing a massive amount of descriptive statistics related to the field, we approach it with a critical review of a few selected issues, such as the *Taxi Policy Review*, the *Railway Development Study*, and the development of "care for the aged" in public transport provision. This may provide the readers an alternative to the government's Annual Report, which is surely the one for those who are interested in basic statistics. In previous editions of *The Other Hong Kong Report*, the areas being covered tend to be more comprehensive. They range from sea, air, cross-border, to land transport. This year, we decide to focus only on land public transport policy. They touch on the critical issues the community are facing with not only this year, but also in the years ahead. We think such an approach fits the nature of *The Other Hong Kong Report* well.

Instead of making a summary of the paper, we wish to single out a number of issues that may deserve a closer scrutiny in the years ahead. They include:

1. What are the effects of the government's new competition policy on limited deregulation in light of commissioning of Network 26 by the Citybus on the quality of public bus services, as well as the viability of other minor modes of public transport on the Hong Kong Island?
2. Should the government commission a study to assess the pros and cons of setting up a Rail Authority to coordinate and operate the highly fragmented rail networks, bearing in mind the need to alleviate the financial burdens of the passengers?
3. Is the existing policy to ensure the Swire-China monopoly over the airline industry the most optimal strategy to position Hong Kong as an air mega-city in the region and also to guarantee the travelling public a fair deal in air fare? Should the government or the legislature commission an independent study to assess the relative merits of having our air policy deregulated?

These are surely sensitive but important issues. They would be most welcomed by the majority of the public but would be resisted strongly by those with a strong vested interest.

# 17

# The Environment

Man Si-wai

## ☐ Old Problems and the Sea

Hong Kong has experienced another year of environmental management based on a strategy of "command and control" (alias bureaucratic control). Ironically, the approach, which is characterized by its sole reliance on the bureaucracy to initiate as well as implement pollution control ordinances, can again be held largely responsible for cases of gross negligence leading to serious environmental damage. The most dramatic and scandalous events last year were related to marine pollution. The formation of the "League for Saving Hong Kong Waters" comprising of protesting fishermen, divers, and marine conservationists in April epitomizes the dismal failure of the environmental strategy of Hong Kong. Let me briefly enumerate some major blunders that occurred last year to illustrate the point.

The sea waters of Hong Kong were muddied by a lot of dredging and dumping last year. This situation is expected to persist, unless there is a drastic change in the way it is currently (mis)handled. More precisely, in the current policy context, there is no requirement of nor quality control over "environmental impact assessments" (EIAs) (see Figure 1), nor is there proper enforcement of existing water pollution control laws. Hence, the water quality is well predicted to continue to deteriorate and the related social conflicts to escalate. The situation will not be helped by the perpetual reclamation work, demand for marine sand (which is obtained through

---

Man Si-wai is a lecturer in the Department of Educational Administration and Policy, The Chinese University of Hong Kong.

Figure 1.  The United Nations Environmental Programme Guide to
Assessment Procedures

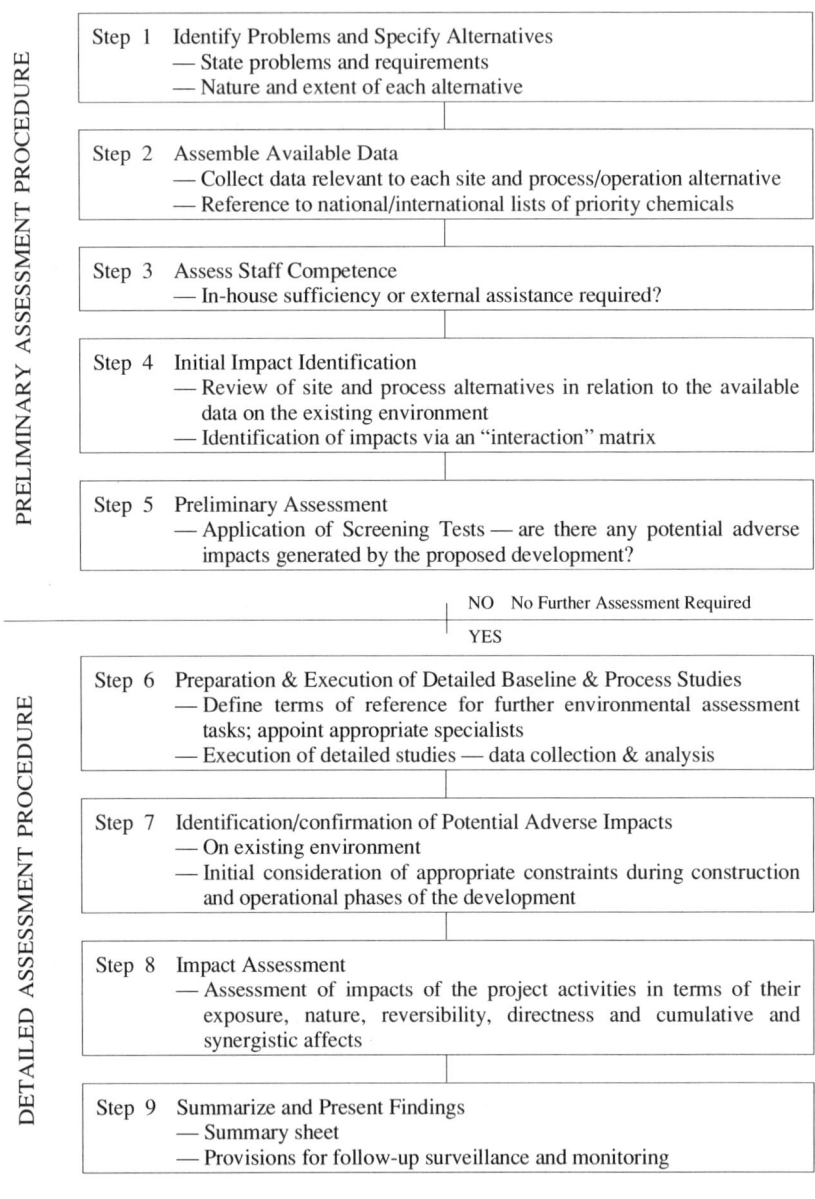

PRELIMINARY ASSESSMENT PROCEDURE

Step 1   Identify Problems and Specify Alternatives
— State problems and requirements
— Nature and extent of each alternative

Step 2   Assemble Available Data
— Collect data relevant to each site and process/operation alternative
— Reference to national/international lists of priority chemicals

Step 3   Assess Staff Competence
— In-house sufficiency or external assistance required?

Step 4   Initial Impact Identification
— Review of site and process alternatives in relation to the available data on the existing environment
— Identification of impacts via an "interaction" matrix

Step 5   Preliminary Assessment
— Application of Screening Tests — are there any potential adverse impacts generated by the proposed development?

NO   No Further Assessment Required

YES

DETAILED ASSESSMENT PROCEDURE

Step 6   Preparation & Execution of Detailed Baseline & Process Studies
— Define terms of reference for further environmental assessment tasks; appoint appropriate specialists
— Execution of detailed studies — data collection & analysis

Step 7   Identification/confirmation of Potential Adverse Impacts
— On existing environment
— Initial consideration of appropriate constraints during construction and operational phases of the development

Step 8   Impact Assessment
— Assessment of impacts of the project activities in terms of their exposure, nature, reversibility, directness and cumulative and synergistic affects

Step 9   Summarize and Present Findings
— Summary sheet
— Provisions for follow-up surveillance and monitoring

Source:  R.G.H. Turnbull, *Environmental and Health Impact Assessment of Development Projects: A Handbook for Practitioners* (London & New York: WHO &
CEMP, 1992), p. 239.

dredging), and used for dumping ground for contaminated and toxic mud dredged from the construction sites of the new airport and other projects.

## Enforcement of Laws

The shortcoming of the "command and control" approach requires further analysis. Let me begin with the implementation problem. Last year, cases of drastic deterioration of water quality occurred within the boundaries of water pollution control zones. For example, thousands of fish died in Tung Lung Chau waters due to dredging activity there. The water is, like that in Mirs Bay where dredging also took place last year, supposed to be protected by law. So is the water near Cheung Chau where dumping caused consider-able concern.[1] An even more striking instance of violation of existing ordinance occurred in the protected wildlife area in Inner Deep Sea, which is an important feeding ground for migrating birds. The shortage of man-power and lack of a sound government organizational structure can some-times explain the inertia (see Table 1), yet more often the unwillingness of the departments concerned to confront the very influential sectors of society explains the situation better.

Bureaucratic decisions are, according to Judith Rees, often "products of interdepartmental politics" too, with the regulators susceptible to manipula-tion and capture by different "key stakeholders". To complicate the scene, there is the influence by special interest groups on different departments.[2] As a result, the failure to check the overextended influence of some of these groups not only generates enforcement problems, but is also accountable for the shortage of potent laws to protect the environment. (I shall discuss this in greater detail under the next subheading.) One example is the lack of effective implementation of the part of the Town Planning Ordinance which governs rural land use (the law itself was passed in 1991 after undue delay). Now, much of western New Territories around Ha Tsuen–Lau Fau Shan is still on the road to ruin. Last year this trend of turning agricultural land into open land for storing containers has spread to the eastern part such as Sha Tau Kok. The ever-expanding ugly landscape powerfully tells of the government's impotence in enforcing environmental standard in the face of

---

[1] *Wah Kiu Yat Po*, 12 November 1992.

[2] Judith Rees, "Market — The Panacea for Environmental Regulation?" *Geoforum*, Vol. 23, No. 3 (1992), p. 386.

Table 1.  The Government Structure for Dealing with Environmental
          Protection Work

| | |
|---|---|
| POLICY | Secretary for Planning, Environment and Lands |
| | Environmental Division of Planning |
| | Planning, Environment and Lands Branch |
| POLICY ADVICE, PROGRAMME DEVELOPMENT & ENFORCEMENT | Environmental Protection Department |
| PROGRAMME IMPLEMENTATION | Civil Engineering Department |
| | Drainage Services Department |
| | Electrical & Mechanical Services Department |
| | Environmental Protection Department |
| | Marine Department |
| | Planning Department |
| | Regional Services Department |
| | Urban Services Department |
| SUPPORT SERVICES | Government Laboratory |
| | Royal Observatory |

Source:  Environmental Protection Department, Hong Kong, *Environment Hong Kong
         1992*, p. 21.

local interests. The official side of the story is that it is "too laborious and
too time-consuming" to stem the tide of unauthorized development.[3]

Another aspect of the implementation problem is the incredible light-
ness of the fine imposed by the courts for violation of environmental laws.
It seems that the legal profession too needs to update itself in environmental
topics and values in order to provide proper protection to our society.

## Scanty Laws and Watered-down Laws

Other significant defects of the "command and control" approach include
environmental laws which are scanty and often come too late. These
problems find their source in the over-representation of business and industrial interests in the Legislative Council, a phenomenon that has only
started to change recently. Even now the system is executive-led and the
decision-making process not at all open to public scrutiny. Defective
regulation has led to, among other things, the lack of compulsory EIA

---

[3] *South China Morning Post*, 29 May 1993.

rulings. As a result, dredging, reclamation, and dumping were launched without sound EIAs to appraise them. In October 1992, the Governor, in his policy speech *Our Next Five Years — The Agenda for Hong Kong*, proposed to take "with immediate effect" the policy that EIAs should be included in "papers on all policy proposals where there is likely to be a significant cost or benefit to the environment". However, there are two main drawbacks to this proposal:

1.  There is no requirement for the EIA reports to be released to the public and there is no channel for the public to know if there are environmentally friendlier ways to achieve the aim of the project.
2.  Assessments done in isolation on a project-by-project basis can fail badly to reveal the overall impact on the environment. The problem is pointedly depicted by a World Wide Fund for Nature (H.K.) spokesperson who said that while we are looking at environmental impact of different places, the "environment" will not be there when all the projects have got underway.[4]

Furthermore, laws passed in the existing socio-economic-political context are often too watered down to be effective in deterring polluters. In the past year, the allowance clauses in the Town Planning Ordinance and the Country Parks Ordinance granting right to use land in ways other than wildlife protection, beach and picnic areas continued to protect polluters rather than the environment. Even with this leniency, there were those who did not bother to file application for "developing" (polluting?) the protected areas. They just went ahead and predictably the government took no action. For example, villagers of Tang Yau Kung Tong who cultured oysters in a "Site of Special Scientific Interest" in Inner Deep Bay area simply started dredging the oyster beds at the end of 1992 and destroyed most of the mangrove trees there. Also, the government itself has been turning many hectares of country park land into rubbish dump. The list of uncontrolled destruction is expected to lengthen in future. The much-needed expansion of Mai Po Preserved Area, for example, is very likely to encounter opposition from local interests, whose representatives have already expressed reservation at a District Board meeting. In their view, the expansion plan poses potential threat to "development of the northwest of Hong Kong". Also, the more perennial issue of controlling the use of diesel fuel continues

---

[4] *South China Morning Post*, 13 May 1993.

to be at a deadlock, with the transport business refusing to budge. The air quality suffers persistently as a result.

## ☐ Market Approach in?

Only recently, the "polluter pays principle" which in theory works according to laws of the market through internalizing the external costs was introduced to the community as an attempt to salvage the environment. The market strategy is not put forth to replace the "command and control" approach, but to serve as a supplement. It is expected to bring in greater effectiveness (in solving the enforcement problem and discouraging excessive pollution) and fairness (since payment will be in proportion to extent of pollution).

Conceptual difficulties aside,[5] the practical task of implementing charges proportional to the extent of pollution is extremely arduous. How can we manage to measure the exact amount of pollutants discharged by every polluter? The other practical problem is to get the powerful industrial and business sector to endorse the principle. Right now, the government is still struggling to levy some charges on the chemical industry which is required by law since this year to deliver chemical waste to the newly opened chemical waste treatment plant at Tsing Yi Island. However, with the plant operating at a cost of about $350 million this year and rising by 50 per cent next year, it is disheartening to see the most recent proposal due for the Executive Council to endorse asking the industry to pay, initially, only 20 per cent of variable operating cost (VOC) for each waste stream, with the full VOC covered after ten years! This is but one typical example of how sound environmental strategies always fall foul of industrial opposition. As for charging a disposal fee for building rubble which is now quickly filling up our landfill sites, the effort was stymied by the construction business too this year. The government said it may try again next year.

In view of all this stalling, it seems that the sewage charge is going to be the first in the list to adopt the "polluter pays principle". The plan, however, has been conceived together with the "Long Term Sewage Treatment Plan" and that causes concern. As highlighted in the Governor's speech, the Long Term Sewage Treatment Plan is so important that most

---

[5] W. Sachs, "Environment and Development," *The Ecologist*, Vol. 21, No. 6 (November/December 1991), pp. 252–57.

funds earmarked for environmental cleanup will be apportioned to it. The government needs, approximately, $7.3 billion between now and 1997 and $17.86 billion for the coming ten years to complete the first stage of the clean-up project. The sewage charge is an important financial source. As the funds collected by this means will ease the financial burden of the government, it is unlikely that discouraging the production of excessive pollutants — which is one of the objectives of adopting the market approach — will be a priority.[6] Similarly, in order not to be too successful in deterring pollution by the industry, industrial effluents which are far more polluting than household discharge may at the end of the day be charged at a rate which fails to match with that required by the fairness principle.

The more fundamental cause for worry is therefore adequately expressed by the now almost platitudinous remark that markets do not operate in a power vacuum. How the decision-making process is overborne by industrial, business, and other sectoral interests has been demonstrated by numerous cases in the past and should be evident by now.

## ☐ Blueprint on a White Paper?

The difficulties faced by the control and command-cum-market approach in tackling environmental issues have affirmed the urgent need for a major transformation of the context and process of decision-making relating to the environment. That in turn calls for the articulation of a set of farsighted environmental goals as well as intermediate-term environmental target standards for the air, the water, noise level, energy conservation, chemical disposal, nature conservation, ... etc.[7] The environmental goals are to provide the framework for setting target standards while the standards are to serve as criteria for appraising the environmental attainment of Hong Kong. With the government ready to issue the *Second White Paper Review on the Environment* (whose release was originally due in June and now postponed to November, because of the delay in government departments' response to the first round of consultation), there is high hope that we can finally have a comprehensive document (see Table 2 for the list of subjects

---

[6] K. C. Ho and Y. H. Cheung, "On the Polluter Pays Principle," *Hong Kong Economic Journal*, 3 May 1993.

[7] Ministry of Housing, Physical Planning, and Environment, *National Environmental Policy Plan — To Choose or To Lose* (Government of Holland, 1989).

Table 2.  Table of Content in Consultative Paper Circulated for
Preparation of the *Second White Paper Review on
the Environment* (due in November 1993)

| Chapter | Subject |
|---------|---------|
| 1 | PREFACE |
| 2 | INTRODUCTION |
| | **STEP 1:  UNDERSTANDING OUR ENVIRONMENT** |
| 3 | AN OVERVIEW OF HONG KONG'S ENVIRONMENT |
| 4 | BASIC PRINCIPLES FOR PROTECTING THE ENVIRONMENT |
| | **STEP 2:  PROTECTING OUR ENVIRONMENT** |
| 5 | ECOLOGY/NATURAL ENVIRONMENT |
| | **STEP 3:  SUSTAINING OUR ENVIRONMENT** |
| 6 | PRE-EMPTING THE PROBLEMS |
| 7 | ENERGY EFFICIENCY |
| 8 | HONG KONG AND GLOBAL GOALS |
| 9 | THE ENVIRONMENTAL CHALLENGE — A SHARED RESPONSIBILITY |
| 10 | COSTING THE ENVIRONMENT |
| 11 | CONCLUSIONS |
| 12 | SUMMARY OF MAIN INITIATIVES |

in its Table of Content). Hopefully this document will provide future environmental strategies with a clear focus, as well as argue for a sound policy context in which there will no longer be social and economic policies staged to cancel out the positive effects of different environmental planning and management practices.

Unfortunately such hopes may be dashed. The 17-page summary of the draft document (distributed to legislators and Green Groups) is more like a fact sheet on government's past, present, and future undertakings in environmental protection than a reflective review of the current state and comprehensive plan for the future. No unifying themes for conceptualizing the environmental goals and formulating the target standards for various kinds of pollution control have been registered. The disappointment goes deeper when one finds that while the government asks the community to meet its obligations in environmental protection, no mention is made to inform the public of their environmental rights, especially with regard to monitoring the government's performance in fulfilling its environmental responsibilities. In the same vein of thought much emphasis has been put on the "educational and informative" aims in preparing the document while the preparatory process failed to involve different sectors of the society to participate in mapping out an environmental blueprint for the future. Such neglect of public consultation is underscored by the woeful result of a survey done by the "Green Groups United Front", which shows that by the end of the so-called consultation period, 83 per cent of those citizens interviewed have no knowledge of the consultation.[8]

Without a judicious and viable environmental blueprint to imprint environmental concerns on policies in the areas of industry, agriculture, housing, transport, energy, economic development, cultural, health, consumer protection, town planning, ... etc., environmental tragedies irking the past year are expected to recur and intensify. In August 1992, for example, thousands of fish at Stonecutters Island died when the reclamation work for Container Terminal No. 8 created an embayment which trapped sewage. While the blame could be laid on a certain individual party for not requiring the contractors to wait for a few weeks for nearby sewage works to complete, or on the lack of firm requirement for EIA, the more fundamental cause of this tragedy lies in the utter indifference at the policy level to the environmental imperative, so that the nature, priorities, and implementation process of development projects were defined with total disregard of this aspect.

In future, with the mushrooming of construction projects big and small and continuous pressure to sustain economic growth, environmental grievances are destined to perpetuate unless bold attempts to halt contradictions and inconsistencies among policies are effected. If the soon-to-be-released White Paper cannot serve the aim of providing an overarching environmental framework for different policies, it might as well be discarded as ineffectual and its assemblage of the wide-ranging topics haphazard. In that event we can anticipate contradictions among policies or questionable practices similar to those listed below to persist:

1. the objective of preserving the natural environment of the country parks running aground in the face of pressing need for dumping sites (there being no commitment to recycling or conservation strategies to release the tension);

---

[8] *Ming Pao*, 9 May 1993.

2. clean water and marine life being threatened by our indiscriminate dredging and dumping activities; and
3. the entrusting of the task of energy conservation to the monopolizing utility companies.

## ☐ Green Groups on the Long March

It is in this apparent impasse that the role of the environmental Non-governmental Organizations (NGOs) becomes discernible. After all, in different parts of the world NGOs of all kinds have demonstrated great effectiveness in countering bureaucratic inertia and restoring as much as possible the balance of power in decision-making. Overseas experience shows that environmental NGOs can affix policy inputs in many ways[9] and there is strong indication that local Green Groups have to move in the same direction if they are to find for themselves a niche to survive and thrive in. Let me first of all briefly describe some of the ways they can contribute to the environmental policy process:

1. liaising with the government and different social sectors over the articulation and review of long-term environmental goals and intermediate-term environmental target standards;
2. offering expert advice and disseminating information on alternative environmental strategies or policies so that the community can make educated choices;
3. monitoring the performance and behaviour of the government and various sectors and groups so that breach of environmental laws and any deviation from agreed policies and strategies can be detected and remedied at the earliest instance; and
4. enhancing citizens' awareness of their environmental rights and alerting them to their responsibilities regarding environmental matters.

In assuming an important role in the environmental policy process, local Green Groups will also be warranted an essential and unique place

---

[9] D. Scott, "Environmental Protection and Social Development: The Role of Non-Government Organizations" and N. A. Robinson, "Legal Techniques for Environmental Compliance: Alternatives to Command & Control" (Papers delivered at the ICSW Asia & Pacific Regional Conference, Hong Kong, 1991).

in the current trend of sociopolitical development. This is because with increasing openness brought to the system, Green Groups can no longer assume the task of pressurizing the government into scraping environmentally unsound projects or cleaning up heavily polluted areas by the old tactic of privately negotiating with the government and affected citizens (which was in the past very successful). On the other hand, their previously equally if not more successful role in environmental education is gradually being taken over by the quasi-governmental body of Environmental Campaign Committee (which gains an edge on them in fund-raising) and numerous district community groups (whose competitive advantage lies in their wider scope of contact, for unlike the Green Groups their members are not restricted to educated professionals and white-collar workers). The Environmental Protection Department (EPD) has created a Community Relations Section while the Education Department has pledged to promote and facilitate environmental education in schools. All in all, the ways that the Green Groups used to conduct business have either become obsolete or are steadily falling outside their capacity.

There are signs that the government and the business sector are also expecting the Green Groups to tender greater input and interest in policy planning at this stage. As we have mentioned, Green Groups were invited by the government to comment on the draft White Paper. As for business' seeking for closer cooperation with the Green Groups, the following example is quite revealing. Earlier this year Pioneer Quarries (H.K.) Limited, which had been awarded a contract to quarry nine hectares of country park land for ten years, invited the Green Groups to view the plan. This seems to be a marked departure from the secretive and exclusive approach which has, until recently, still been the hallmark of the way similar issues were handled. The successful High Court challenge launched by Friends of the Earth (H.K.) against the Shalotung golf course and housing complex planned to be built in the country park there in 1992 did set the stage for future close involvement of the Green Groups in environmental policy planning. Hence, unless these groups fail to sustain the willpower in asserting their influence over the environmental policy process, their profile in the policy realm is expected to rise in the future.

In sum, in order to play a serviceable part in improving the environment of Hong Kong and be recognized as such, the Green Groups have to empower themselves by reinforcing their legal, financial, academic, political, organizational, and operational resources for greater input in the policy process. In the course of executing their duties in the policy area it is likely that they will be empowering other citizens' groups including other NGOs, political parties, ... etc. With the support of these groups they will maintain a crucial position in the future development of the territory and the process of mutual empowerment will go on. With the government now in high profile and the business sector taking a proactive role in environmental matters, it is vital for the Green Groups to be able to consolidate their infrastructure which underpins their capacity to play an active part in the future policy process. Otherwise the government and the business sector which are far more resourceful will together monopolize the setting of future direction for environmental protection and nature conservation. Debates as well as checks and balances will be minimal if not non-existent. The government's recent increasingly prominent role in environmental education indicates how capable it is to extend its influence into an area previously dominated by the Green Groups. Also, business' creating of the "Private Sector Committee on the Environment" to set its own environmental agenda and the "Centre of Environmental Technology" to implement its own priorities shows how easy it is to have the Green Groups sidelined when it comes to matters of investment in environmental protection. It is therefore of crucial importance that these groups can, through active participation in the policy process, empower themselves so that at the end of the day, the whole community can be enriched by the multifariousness of perspectives on the future of the environment.

## ☐ Face the World

On the international front, in the past year Hong Kong has been very slow if not quiescent in bearing its share in protecting the environment. There is no government policy on tropical timber use and the Housing Authority continues to specify tropical hardwoods for interiors of buildings though it has ordered contractors of its projects to use steel in place of timber for the "moulds" used in concrete pouring. Moreover, there is no policy to develop a market for alternatives to use of timber woods so that the construction business will turn to other materials. Coupled with the lack of commitment in advancing the recycling of construction materials, Hong Kong continues to rank among the top importers of rainforest logs while rapidly using up its own landfill areas.

Even in the area where the government has pledged its obligations by signing the international protocol on control of chlorofluorocarbons (CFCs) the follow-up action has been sluggish. Though legislation to control the use of CFCs was enacted to ensure basic compliance with the Montreal Protocol signed in 1989, the legislative package that went to the Legislative Council early this year includes banning of some products which contain CFCs and which "vent" or release CFCs into the atmosphere while leaving out the CFCs tax proposal. The latter has been recommended by the EPD officials at an earlier stage as an effective measure to keep the price of new CFCs high so as to prevent venting and encourage recycling. In this case, industries' reluctance to switch to alternatives was again the main obstacle.

As for "Agenda 21" which represents the promise of the signatories of the 1992 Earth Summit to draw up enforcement plans for the summit agreements, it is still unclear when the Hong Kong government will take upon itself similar tasks. Though Hong Kong is not a signatory, the Legislative Council has in December 1992 passed a motion urging the government to formulate a comprehensive environmental policy in compliance with the concept of sustainable development which is the main theme underlying the summit agreements. However, in the meantime much precious time has been lost in the combat against global environmental pollution and resource depletion by the government's ambivalent response. In the draft White Paper, treaties signed at the Earth Summit are mentioned and endorsed. Yet in reality, there has been inadequate protection of our country parks, demonstrating a lack of devotion to upholding the spirit of the agreement on protecting biodiversity, which was pledged by nations attending the Earth Summit.

Hong Kong also stood alone among other Southeast Asian countries by being deliberately vague in its attitude and policy towards the Japanese plutonium shipment which took place in late 1992. Not even a contingency plan has been proffered. With the Japanese rapidly expanding its fast breeder programme we can anticipate that in the near future, similar situation will find Hong Kong equally ill-prepared.

## ☐ Joining Hands with China

The closest associate of Hong Kong in environmental protection and nature conservation is of course China. One cannot imagine Hong Kong taking any form of environmental initiative and be successful without concerted efforts on the part of China (or at least Guangdong). That proper management of the Mai Po Preserved Area requires complementary regulation of industrial activities in the nearby areas of China is the most palpable example. Another example is the imperative to obtain China's approval in order that the "Long Term Sewage Treatment Plan" which contrives to discharge effluents into the South China Sea can get going. Moreover, the plan is scheduled to complete after 1997. Without financial commitment of the government of the future Special Administrative Region (and China's blessing to guarantee this commitment) the launching of the project at this stage will be pointless. Regrettably, negotiation over the project did not start earlier and the Sino-British row at present may add a political dimension to the negotiation, which is unnecessary and most unfortunate. All in all, last year did not see any breakthrough in consolidating channels of communication between Hong Kong and China over environmental issues.

There were of course occasions when problems and queries were referred to the other side by the governments or interested parties. For example, officials for environmental protection from Guangdong's marine administration accused the dumping activity of Hong Kong near Outer Ling Ding of killing tonnes of fish. Also, members of the Democratic Alliance for Betterment of Hong Kong, a local pro-Chinese government political party, have expressed concern to the Guangdong officials during their visit to the province over pollution of the Pearl River which allegedly causes deterioration of the quality of the drinking water supplied to Hong Kong. There were also officials and academics from Hong Kong, Macau, Guangzhou, and Europe attending a meeting to deal with the contamination of the Pearl River by run-off sewage and livestock waste discharges, which has contributed in part to pollution in the Victoria Harbour. However, all of the above problems were perceived to be technical in nature and "politically innocuous" solutions were anticipated. The governments as well as citizens' groups on their mutual visits or in cross-border environmental campaign programmes were equally reluctant to confront these matters in a realistic, rigorous and open manner. In other words, there was a consistent refraining from tackling issues at dimensions other than the technical one, thus missing the boat in redressing difficulties originating in the decision-making contexts where different if not conflicting interests intersect. Consequently, some problems are not adequately dealt with, and others are consistently swept under the carpet. The most striking example of the latter is the evasion of environmental issues relating to the Daya Bay Nuclear Power Plant.

The power plant will have both reactors in operation by the end of 1993. However, by the middle of the year people in Hong Kong were still barely informed about warning arrangements in case of an accident. With both governments apparently not eager to pursue the matter any further, the citizens of Hong Kong can take as final decision on the issue that warning of an accident will come from the Guangdong authority. Apparently this authority is entitled to receive information about all accidents at the power plant in the first instance, and is bestowed the power to decide whether Hong Kong should be informed based on its knowledge of the extent of impact of the accident on Hong Kong.[10] As for contingency plans and various issues of environmental importance relating to the power plant, none has been satisfactorily and openly resolved so far. There is actually a general lack of enthusiasm over matters relating to the Daya Bay project which, from the early days of its conception in the mid-1980s, has been reckoned as politically very sensitive. With the project deemed as closely connected to national pride, economic sweetheart deals, and political frustration (of the Hong Kong people) there is little hope in the near future for a frank and open communication between the governments over it. To make the matter worse, the secretive aura in which nuclear technologies throughout the world has been shrouded has also tainted the Hong Kong government's way of handling matters relating to the Daya Bay power plant. In the final emergency drill (which involved 38 government departments) in Hong Kong before the switching on of the first reactor, no Chinese representative or citizens' group of Hong Kong was invited to participate. In short, so far little respect has been paid to local citizens' right to information about the safety standard and environmental and health impacts of the nuclear power plant.

Other pressing environmental issues that require joint efforts of Hong Kong and China include stemming the tide of wildlife smuggling from China to or via Hong Kong and the aggravation of contamination of the Pearl River. The former involves policies of the local authorities of different locations and the latter the development policies of the booming regions in Guangdong. It will take relentless effort to negotiate and persuade the parties concerned which include the business and industrial sectors, the local authorities, the state authority, and the local people. As such negotiations and persuasions are most likely to touch on different aspects of people's rights, public welfare, and state power, no solution will be in order

---

[10] The latest known arrangement from the time of writing is that the Guangdong authority has agreed to inform Hong Kong in the event of an emergency regardless of its chances of affecting Hong Kong. Yet the authority still enjoys a lot of discretionary power, since what kinds of irregularity count as emergency is not always very clear.

unless the issues are tackled on a multi-faceted basis. This supports my previous claim that the environmental NGOs have to assert their expertise in the environmental policy process by enhancing their competence in handling environmental issues from a wider perspective. Without such competence the good-will efforts to promote the Hong Kong–China joint endeavours in environmental protection is likely to result in marginal effects only. One regrettable incident is that when representatives of the Conservancy Association visited Beijing in June 1993 to express their environmental concerns, they were asked by Chinese officials to convey China's view on some aspects of the new airport project which has nothing to do with the environment. This demonstrates the lack of due respect for the group's expertise and the representatives' special status as environmental ambassadors.

## ☐ Conclusions and Prospects

The year 1993 sees Hong Kong at the juncture where various parties taking an interest in environmental protection and nature conservation have to resolve to define or redefine collectively the environmental goals and targets as well as their specific missions and responsibilities. In the absence of a coordinated strategy, increased resources devoted to the environmental cause will be wasted and efforts made in vain. The Dutch experience of drawing up long-term and intermediate-term plans may serve as an example of how efforts can be coordinated so that goals and targets can be met. In Hong Kong, to date it is still unclear whether the *Second White Paper Review on the Environment* will take steps in a similar direction. Hence, we may still be badly in want of a framework for proper assessment and revamping of the existing "command and control" approach and the budding "market" strategy for environmental protection and nature conservation.

The role of the Green Groups must be focused in light of the setting of environmental goals and targets too. Moreover, their potentially immense input in environmental and related policy processes (in form of articulation and monitoring of performance of policies as well as mobilizing support for better alternatives) makes them a force to be reckoned with in terms of development of the civil society. In other words, in assuming their policy roles competently, these NGOs will in fact be participating in and enhancing the democratization trend of Hong Kong. Yet in order to build up their competence, they do not only have to possess technical expertise. Skills and perspectives in the social, economic, political, and cultural dimensions have to be developed as well.

For Hong Kong to become a greener place, it also has to launch global and regional negotiations and make greater efforts at regional cooperation. The contribution of the Green Groups is also vital in these aspects, since related issues can never be properly debated and focused without their views and perspectives being seriously heeded. Furthermore, the Green Groups, the government, as well as various sectors of the society have to realize that given the multi-faceted and complex nature of environmental problems, no solution is in order without effective participation of all parties concerned. For that to happen, the unswerving opening up of the existing system is indispensable. Conversely, more extensive participation in environmental decision-making may serve to bolster the opening up of the existing system.

# 18

# Hong Kong Broadcasting

Simon Twiston Davies

## ☐ Introduction

The story of broadcasting in Hong Kong in 1992–1993 has sadly followed all too logically on that of previous years: a failure by the government to grasp the implications of new broadcast technologies and a general dithering as to what needs to be done next.

Even as the cable television franchise was finally carved up for the surviving players, Wharf Holdings and Hutchison Whampoa, there were huge gaps in the overall picture and it now seems that such vitally important projects as the corporatization of Radio Television Hong Kong (RTHK) and the introduction of a fully revamped Broadcasting Act have been shelved, seemingly forever.

This sad situation was only compounded by the consistent whittling away of what has often been referred to as one of Hong Kong's vital strengths: her international outlook.

The period saw yet further decline in English language radio after the false dawn of Metro News.

Terrestrial television services continued on a plateau, while the challenged purchase of a 22 per cent slice of the TVB (Television Broadcasts Limited) television network by the United States-based media mogul Rupert Murdoch and his News Corporation multinational created a worrying atmosphere of parochialism. Where the narrow interests that emerged

Simon Twiston Davies is a Hong Kong-based writer specializing in Asian broadcasting.

to oppose the input of Murdoch think they will leave Hong Kong after 1997 is for anyone to guess. It would seem that a media mix that is as various as possible (both international and local) after the imposition of Special Administrative Region (SAR) status is desirable for Hong Kong.

With the arrival of a regime that is generally opposed to freedom of speech, the further involvement of an international player who can bring both technical and financial resources to the local broadcasting industry should have been welcomed. One must not forget that while Murdoch would be more than happy to enjoy the profits of a 22 per cent stake in TVB, his final goal is to sell programming to viewers outside of Hong Kong: first in Taiwan and China, but ultimately to viewers right across the region from Berlin to Tokyo, from Ulan Bator to Darwin.

In the end Murdoch's advisers were so worried by the hostile reception given to the suggestion that he take a substantial stake in TVB, that the application to the Recreation and Culture Branch and the Broadcasting Authority for a waiver to maximum foreign holding rules was withdrawn. These rules were introduced after the Australian Alan Bond had paid US$271 million for 30.4 per cent of the TVB equity which he later was forced to sell when Bond Corporation ran into serious financial trouble.

Many people believe that not only should TVB have been enriched by the arrival of Murdoch's financial muscle in a regionally competitive market, but it would also have brought more solid advantages. The logic of the deal would have made the overseas distribution plans almost secondary to the goal of increasing the attraction of the golden egg of TVB's library.

The synergies between TVB and Murdoch's 20th Century Fox Studios in Hollywood, the Fox Broadcasting Company in Los Angeles plus the now profitable BSkyB satellite system in the United Kingdom (U.K.), are quite clear. Fox, for instance, has a worldwide video distribution network above and beyond the Asian, North American and European Chinatowns that TVB presently distributes through. And Fox, with its well-nurtured cable television connections in the United States (U.S.), can access a large market that was until now closed to TVB.

TVB executives said they would also like to create an ethnic Chinese channel for satellite distribution in Europe. BSkyB could help them find economic transponder space to do that as well, said the News Corporation representatives.

All of those facts would have increased the marketplace for TVB programming and that can only be good for Hong Kong as production quality inevitably improved.

"Certainly," said a News Corporation executive at the time of the 22 per cent bid, "we will be using Hong Kong as a base for TVB's new Chinese language productions for satellite. This is a commitment to production and training. We want to be far more than an uplinker of foreign programming." The argument was persuasive for some, but not enough for many.

Perhaps not as good for Hong Kong would have been the media cross ownership that would have occurred if Murdoch gained a substantial stake in TVB. Already News Corporation holds 51 per cent of the powerful and profitable English language *South China Morning Post* and also controls the less successful *Wah Kiu Yat Po*. That kind of clout can be destructive if misused, and Murdoch has a mixed reputation in that area, especially in Britain.

## ☐ Television (Amendment) Bill 1993

During the saga that led to Wharf Cable's tender to the government in September 1992, and its submission of a 2,000-page document, the Recreation and Culture Branch decided to review its complex broadcasting legislation once more to take into account the nuances of subscription cable television.

In the event parts of the results of that review were incorporated into the Television (Amendment) Bill 1993 which was passed into law by the Legislative Council in April.

The new legislation was introduced to fill in the gaps left by the original ordinance which had only covered Hong Kong's free-to-air television stations. Although STAR TV is a legal uplinker, it was given its licence under the Telecommunication Ordinance by order of the Governor in Council.

The new subscription television regulations also insist that at least three subscription channels by HutchVision and STAR TV are carried by the Hong Kong cable television franchise holder, Wharf Cable Limited. If there should be a dispute between the two parties about exactly how to cooperate the government is granted powers of enforceable arbitration.

The amendment also introduced technical standards for the microwave distribution system that Wharf Cable will be using before it introduces a full "hard wire" network over the next two to three years.

Another section of the amendment laid down the codes of practice for programming standards that are essentially the same as for the current terrestrials, TVB and ATV (Asia Television Limited). Even so the news and public service sections were less stringent than for the terrestrials.

The amendment also laid down the regulations that restrict Wharf Cable from carrying advertising for three years when there will be a review of the situation. The amendment also laid down the levels at which it will collect a percentage of the cable network's subscription revenues over the 12-year life time of the cable television licence.

Starting at one per cent the treasury take will eventually rise to a maximum of 7.5 per cent. A measure of the government's faith that it has at last got the cable television formula correct is one official's forecast that by the end of the life of the franchise, the government will have received "hundreds of millions of dollars" from its levy on the cable operator.

Away from subscription television the amended ordinance relaxes some of the rules that have allegedly prevented the terrestrial broadcasters TVB and ATV and their four channels from expanding their markets.

From now on the advertising codes on property and financial services have been relaxed and outward investment by the stations in overseas broadcasters was no longer inhibited. Until the new amendment there was a restriction to the 15 per cent level.

Hong Kong's broadcasters, TVB, ATV and Wharf Cable, may now invest in each other up to a 15 per cent threshold. Over that they need the permission of the Executive Council. Between 2 per cent and 10 per cent the permission of the Broadcasting Authority is required.

From October 1993 onwards HutchVision may broadcast in Cantonese as a regional operator, rather than in Mandarin.

According to government sources the restrictions were placed on STAR TV "in order to test their good faith as a regional broadcaster rather than being an organization that was trying to get into the local Cantonese market by the back door." From October onwards STAR TV may broadcast three channels — MTV Asia, Prime Sports and BBC World Service TV in Cantonese.

Because STAR TV will now be carrying Cantonese programming the government has given way to the terrestrials who will receive a "net abatement" of 2 per cent of advertising revenue taking it down from 12 per cent to 10 per cent. During the year of 1992 TVB contributed $148.3 million to the government's coffers, as compared to ATV's $19.8 million.

In fact there is continuing concern in official quarters concerning the quality and success of ATV's performance and increasing concern that the arrival of the non-terrestrial broadcasters could finally see the end of it after years of struggle for survival.

Another loosening of government shackles permitted by the new ordinance is the use of "other languages" on the English language channels, not necessarily with subtitles. The government's review apparently showed increased pressure on the English language channels.

The new broadcasting amendment also dealt with the implications of the 1992 Bill of Rights. Until the newly legislated Bill of Rights came into force the Governor in Council effectively had unlimited powers to control freedom of speech. Indeed, censorship of programming of any kind could have been imposed without explanation. Under the new legislation the Governor must apply for an order of the High Court and make a case that there has been or could be a breakdown of law and order, incitement to religious or racial hatred, or an adverse affect on public health or morals.

Finally the amendment declares that the licences of Hong Kong broadcasters can only be revoked after an open hearing by the Broadcasting Authority.

## ☐ Uplinking from Nowhere to Nowhere

The continued dithering — more than eight years after the now mouldering Broadcasting Review Board report by Justice Noel Power was tabled — was perhaps best illustrated by the decision of the responsible civil servant for broadcasting, the Secretary for Recreation and Culture, James So, to undertake yet another review of the territory's satellite uplinking policies and the methodology used for granting licences.

It would seem that the review was only prompted by a loosening of the regulatory atmosphere in rival Singapore, where there is now an established subscription television network and foreign broadcasters are being assiduously wooed for availing their state-of-the-art facilities. Of course, most Singaporean residents are almost completely cut off from the rash of international television broadcasters now taking to the airwaves, but that is another story.

Thus it was in recognition of the reluctance of foreign broadcasters to uplink from Hong Kong, despite its infrastructural advantages, that Mr. So announced yet another policy review to ease the "cumbersome nature" of its uplink licensing regime. The review has still not been completed by mid-1993 and probably will not be implemented until some time in 1994.

Currently the procedure for obtaining a licence takes up to six months and a decision is finally made by the Governor in Council, effectively the slow moving and secretive Executive Council. According to Mr. So, the intention is to have licences approved at an "administrative level" in order that the "disappointing number" of foreign broadcasters can be increased.

He added that the Hong Kong government is currently working with the holder of the international telecommunications monopoly, the Cable & Wireless-controlled Hong Kong Telecommunications Limited, to produce a new framework before the end of the year.

However, said Mr. So, Hong Kong has no intention of introducing tax holidays to encourage new programmers to move to Hong Kong. "Taxes are low enough already in Hong Kong," he said.

Meanwhile, the ESPN Asia network has begun uplinking its programming from Hong Kong via Hong Kong Telecom International's earth station at Stanley. ESPN is still the only foreign broadcaster to regularly use Hong Kong as an Asian base and will most likely remain so as other administrations look outward to the wider world.

One theory held by a number of legal figures who are closely involved with the regulatory process is that the Recreation and Culture Branch is working to the beat of a different drummer, i.e. that of China.

"Otherwise," said one of them, "it seems inexplicable that some apparently intelligent people are continuing to make such a hash of what is an apparently comparatively simple matter. Any other explanation escapes me as it does many other people."

## ☐ TVB

For all the talk of satellite and cable television broadcasts to, from and for Hong Kong, TVB continued to dominate the airwaves in much the same way it has for the past 25 years.

Consistently hitting about 80 per cent of the audience share, last year the company produced a net profit of $365.6 million, a massive 46 per cent up on 1991 and is forecast by the Mees Pierson Securities brokerage to come in with $433.2 million for this year, up 18.5 per cent on 1992. It is expected to offer shareholders $544.4 million in 1994.

Meanwhile, TVB International (TVBI), the station's overseas sales arm, was expanding its programming sales beyond the point of a $298.3 million turnover that gave them a profit of $152.7 million in 1991, which is the last year for figures to have been published. A continuing row with the Inland Revenue Department as to whether TVBI should be taxed on its overseas revenues has dogged the company for several years, and has yet to be resolved. That could become very important as the planned satellite ventures kick in.

In June 1993, the company's major shareholders, Sir Run Run Shaw and the Kerry Group of Robert Kuok, also cut a deal to sell 22 per cent of the company's equity to the Australian-born media mogul, Rupert Murdoch.

Besides signing the at least temporarily aborted deal to go into partnership with Murdoch's News Corporation, in late 1992 TVB also bought into a pair of Canadian cable television networks, ChinaVision in Toronto and Cathay TV in Vancouver, taking a 20 per cent of the equity — for regulatory reasons a Canadian conglomerate, Fairchild Communications, controls the rest — and supplying 100 per cent of the programming. TVBI already controls two cable television channels in the U.S., TVB USA in San Francisco and in Los Angeles, known as the Jade channels.

Even before Murdoch stepped in, TVB had announced plans to launch a Mandarin channel on a regional satellite, aimed primarily at the burgeoning Taiwanese cable television market. The station also signed a ten-year agreement to launch a new terrestrial station in Indonesia.

## ☐ ATV

While TVB continued to prosper, the strain on its main opposition, ATV, was much as before.

The station still has little hope of breaking the stranglehold of TVB on the Hong Kong market or even pushing far ahead in the face of the onslaughts of STAR TV and the now looming prospect of Wharf Cable. Both of the new broadcast technology operators have been heavily recruiting staff for their new ventures, and ATV, especially, would seem to have been hard hit by the losses in human resources.

The story of ATV is problematic, as the station has been almost sepulchrally silent on its latest moves and intentions, only creeping out of its shell to complain that its best staff are being poached by the new satellite and cable television operators.

The Lai Sun Group continues to control the station but would seem unlikely to see a return on its investment for some years to come, following substantial outgoings when the station was under the direction of Legislative Councillor Selina Chow some four years ago. A sign of the relative financial health of the station is the amount it paid the government in 1992 as a percentage of its advertising revenues: $19.8 million. Rival TVB, on the other hand, was levied $148.3 million for the same period.

## □ STAR TV

At STAR TV, the satellite network continued to hemorrhage cash to support its five free-to-air channels, even though advertising revenues have begun to pick up significantly across the station's 38 country footprint. The only problem is that the vast majority of the potential 45 million people able to view the network are in India, producing some 75 per cent of revenues, and the Indian broadcast market is expected to become fiercely competitive during 1994.

During the past 12 months the network was reported to have been in negotiations with several parties to sell as much as 40 per cent of its equity, in part because it is forecasting accumulated losses of US$200 million by the end of 1995. STAR TV, according to figures put out by the Goldman Sachs investment bank in London, is also forecasting profits US$500 million per annum by the year 2000. But the network would seem to be running out of time to launch an expensive digitally compressed "80 to 100"-channel subscription network and is in need of a cash injection before the profits begin to appear.

Indeed, now that STAR TV has decided on its subscription channels the total spending for the system could well hit more than US$700 million before the end of 1993. Maybe that was why Rupert Murdoch, when he was offered something close to just 40 per cent of the network for about US$250 million, turned it down and paid much the same money in a bid for just 22 per cent of TVB.

According to press reports, Murdoch and his advisers reviewed the STAR TV option and its assets, concluding that the entire five-channel, free-to-air satellite station "could be replaced for less than US$250 million." If a broadcaster has a strong programming base and US$24 million a year to lease transponders, "you just don't need that kind of investment [US$250 million] to set up a satellite network. It is the programming that is the key," said a New York-based executive attached to the Murdoch group.

Reportedly, the News Corporation's in-depth review concluded that outside of the MTV Asia music video channel the rest of the entertainment and sports programming was not suitable in a competitive satellite television market, a market that could have as many as 350 transponders covering it by 1995.

Certainly STAR TV's BBC World Service TV news service could be a liability, if you are keeping China in mind. As one analyst said: "If you want to keep the Chinese sweet so you can get a slice of the action, the last thing you need is to be seen transmitting contentious news reports."

But the clincher for the Murdoch decision not to buy into STAR TV was the strength of the TVB Chinese language entertainment library, with its 20-year backlog of programming, as compared to STAR TV's comparatively weak Chinese language, ATV-based stock of shows.

STAR TV's parent company, HutchVision Limited, also saw a change in top management with the apparent elevation of the combative and mercurial Richard Li Tzar-kai to the Hutchison Whampoa boardroom and the appointment of the former head of TV New Zealand, Julian Mounter, as President and Chief Executive Officer.

For a time there was a belief that Mounter could create a more conciliatory attitude towards competitors, such as Wharf Cable, TVB and the raft of programming sharks who have been trolling the Hong Kong's broadcasting waters in search of fast-rising Croesus-style Asian profits. In the event, even if Mounter himself is a gentle, though efficient, soul, the hard-nosed and uncompromising corporate culture of STAR TV was all-pervasive and the controlling hand of the 26-year-old Richard Li was still seen as calling the shots.

As far as programming is concerned, the planned expansion of STAR TV's channel roster has not only meant that the company now has some 500 employees, it is also investing millions of dollars in commissioned programming from independent Hong Kong and Chinese producers.

Wharf Cable has, of course, also been pressing ahead with its own plans to produce or dub or subtitle most of its launch-time channels in Cantonese.[1]

---

[1] Subsequent to the completion of this article in late July, Rupert Murdoch's Australian-based News Corporation purchased 63.3 per cent of HutchVision Limited (BVI), the holding company of STAR TV, from Hutchison Whampoa and Li Ka-shing and family for US$525 million. The Li family continues to hold 36.4 per cent of STAR TV.

In what initially appeared to be an unrelated transaction, in early September, Malaysian businessman Robert Kuok's Kerry Media Limited purchased 34.9 per cent of the *South China Morning Post* Publishers for US$349 million. News Corporation continues to hold 15.1 per cent of the paper.

At the time of the purchase of *South China Morning Post*, Mr. Kuok held just over 32 per cent of TVB. Whether, after this deal, News Corporation and STAR TV will now be able to access TVB's programming remained a question at time of editing.

## ☐ Cable Television

The year 1992–1993 was a year that Wharf Holdings finally was able to begin building a subscription television network — and, perhaps not so incidentally, a second telecommunications network. The final decision came after an unscheduled wait for China "to give the nod" and allow the now thoroughly lame-duck, British-run Hong Kong administration to make a positive announcement through the apparently still disorganized Recreation and Culture Branch.

It was only shortly before the Christmas holiday of 1992 that Wharf Cable was reassured it would be able to go ahead with its ambitious plan to build and operate the largest individual cable television network in the world. The long-awaited licence award to Wharf Cable was made following a positive announcement by the Sino-British Joint Liaison Group, the body that must endorse all Hong Kong franchises that straddle the change of territory's administration on 1 July 1997.

Up until the last minute, the licence bid was a close run affair for Wharf Cable, as HutchVision, the Li Ka-shing/Hutchison Whampoa group that controls STAR TV, had been threatening to produce a rival bid. However, on deadline day, humiliatingly for the government, Wharf Cable was the only bidder. Meanwhile, perhaps more than 25 other potential competitors had melted away during the confusion and accusations of broken promises that characterized the five years it took to grant a pay-television licence to a Hong Kong cable network at a cost of several million American dollars.

When Wharf Cable Limited officially took up its 12-year licence on 1 June 1993, managing director Stephen Ng reconfirmed the determination of his team of 350 engineers and programming executives to be "on-air" in October 1993. Others around the world have attempted similar ventures before but they have been less ambitious and have used internationally supplied programming as a backbone of the service, he said.

The main thrust of the Wharf Cable system will be locally made Cantonese productions, with additional international programming filling out the schedules for the 20-channel network that will be in place during 1996. Eventually, however, Wharf Cable plans to deliver more than 40 television channels of top-quality local and international programming to more than a million subscribers, making it the largest stand-alone cable television system in the world.

Wharf Cable, a wholly owned subsidiary of Wharf Communications Investments Limited, in turn a subsidiary of Wharf (Holdings) Limited, has committed more than $5 billion to creating the most effective structure available for a modern cable television system, having already started the complex work of "wiring" some 1.5 million homes throughout the territory. The initial system will be a microwave delivered network, but a "hard wire" fibre-optic cable television system will soon follow.

Spearheaded by an initial lineup of eight channels, Wharf Cable claims to be the first operator in the world to launch such a large home-grown, multi-channel pay-television service. The initial "Local Comprehensive Package" will be marketed at a flat monthly subscription fee of $198. Supposedly programmed and balanced for family viewing, almost all of the programming on the eight channels will be transmitted in Cantonese and subtitled.

The Wharf Cable plans revealed that each channel will consist of a 24-hour, non-stop cyclical "wheel" of programmes that will be repeated, so shift workers, for instance, will not miss out on prime-time segments of news or entertainment.

By far the most ambitious project is a 24-hour Cantonese language News Channel designed to track and analyse events throughout the territory while, where needed, placing them in an international perspective. The news facility alone will be bigger than the one at CNN's headquarters in Atlanta, Georgia in the U.S., claimed Wharf Cable.

The other "basic" services were announced as:

1. Entertainment Channel — A mass-appeal family entertainment service with input from local independent production houses.
2. Movie Channel — Chinese subtitled films selected from around the world.
3. Sports Channel — Voiced entirely in Cantonese and offering coverage of local and international sporting clashes.
4. English News and Finance Channel — A round-the-clock business news service for English-speaking viewers incorporating the U.S. network, CNN International, for about 22 hours a day with the remaining two hours programmed by a locally produced Wharf Cable feed.
5. Learning and Enrichment Channel — Distance learning and general interest programmes developed with local education experts.
6. Living in Hong Kong Channel — A service featuring programming from overseas in original languages, and aimed at foreign nationals.

The channel will offer everything from Peking Opera for Putonghua speakers, to popular shows in Tagalog for Filipinos, to dramas in Hindi for our Indian population.
7. Preview Channel — This will be a "barker" channel with an easy-to-follow display of what is happening at any time on the Wharf Cable television network.

In addition to the "basic" channels programmed by Wharf Cable, the system will also carry STAR TV's contracted networks, MTV Asia, Prime Sports and BBC World Service TV free of charge. These are the three channels that can be carried in Cantonese.

For an extra subscription fee, at launch time the Wharf Cable system intends to broadcast four "premium" channels supplied by the STAR TV network: a western movie channel, a mainly Chinese language Asian movie channel, a business channel and a family channel.

The deal for delivery of the STAR TV channels was part of a package agreed by Wharf Cable and STAR TV, that made the satellite broadcaster the "sole supplier" of "non-Chinese" international programming to the cable network. However that "sole supplier" agreement would seem to be less than comprehensive, since Wharf later announced deals with the U.S. CNN network and the ESPN Sports network.

While Wharf is under the obligation of a "Must Carry" clause for STAR TV's subscription channels, STAR TV in its turn is under a "Must Transmit" clause for the delivery of those channels in Hong Kong.

Also under the agreement is STAR TV's affiliated company, Fortress Satellite Services network. Approximately 300,000 households and hotel rooms were affected by the accord, all of which will be able to receive Wharf Cable subscription services eventually.

By the time of the launch of Wharf Cable in October 1993, the company will have erected eight of thirteen planned microwave transmitters set on hilltops across the territory. The Wharf Cable network had already forecast that it would have "passed" 250,000 dwellings by launch time and more than one million homes a year later. The total of 550,000 homes that are expected to be passed on "day one" is claimed to be a record.

While the wiring of thousands of apartments went ahead in concert with the building of the microwave transmitters, Wharf Cable's engineers are busy installing a state-of-the-art fibre-optic backbone that will have been "pulled" through the entire Mass Transit Railway tunnel system by September. The fibre-optic wire will eventually supersede the microwave system which will only carry a maximum of 20 channels. The fibre-optic network will allow the expansion of the Wharf Cable service to more than 40 channels, as well as offering subscribers access to a wide range of interactive and multimedia services.

## ☐ Radio Television Hong Kong

In 1992–1993 RTHK's status in the community remained steady despite cuts in funds in real dollar terms and yet more uncertainty about the role of English language broadcasting in the community. During this period it was confirmed, if confirmation was needed, that the government-controlled station would retain its status as a government mouthpiece and would not be "corporatized" and given life as a semi-autonomous body indirectly responsible to the government. The plan was originally to guarantee RTHK editorial independence after the 1997 handover. That was a forlorn hope once the Chinese government had voiced warnings over such a change.

In retrospect the dithering and delays since 1988 when the Broadcasting Authority was formed and corporatization was first considered are what killed the project. The inability of the government to come to an agreement with the station's 1,000 contract and non-contract employees only compounded the problem. Effectively the station is now in limbo, providing seven radio services (five in Cantonese, one bilingual and one English) and a small but effective television unit putting out programming deemed to be in the public interest.

## ☐ Non-government Radio

Over and above the continued operation of RTHK's seven radio networks, the most dramatic news of the period was the fall of Metro News, a 24-hour, English language all-news service, which had first gone on air in 1991.

Placed on the mediumwave band Metro had the heavy backing of a Hutchison Whampoa subsidiary, among others, and was expected to revolutionize Hong Kong's radio industry. For a time it did until poor ratings forced minor changes. By the spring of 1993, spokespersons for the station were complaining of a lack of support from the local advertising community which eventually led to the slashing of more than 20 jobs. The advertising stream outside of the "travel hours" just could not support the station.

Today a reconfigured Metro Plus still has six hours a day of prime-time news shows, but the majority of the broadcasting hours are given over to statistically programmed middle-of-the-road popular music.

However, it is still arguable that a 24-hour all-news station is a practical possibility. If some of the early problems at launch time could have been corrected, things could have gone differently.

Perhaps one of the reasons for the low audience figures and premature demise of the station was the inordinately "American" feel of its output and a failure from the very start to follow the original plans. Many of the senior managers at Metro News had worked in Taiwan and the American tone may have been more suitable for that market.

One plan for the channel that could have mitigated against the American tone was to utilize the BBC World Service radio as a source of regional news, despite the fact that RTHK Radio 3 also has agreements for re-transmission of the service. In the event, just days before launch, the BBC backed off its permission to allow Metro to carry its feed, allegedly because of Hong Kong government intervention.

A second, perhaps more important, failure was an inability to find a place on a subcarrier on the AsiaSat (Asia Satellite Telecommunications) satellite to broadcast the Metro signal regionally. Metro had allegedly held high hopes of regional advertising to support the Hong Kong revenues, but these never materialized.

The effective collapse of the Metro Radio news station was only highlighted by the almost unqualified success of the bilingual FM Select service, which features bland, rigidly middle-of-the-road popular music presented in a bright format suited to the Yuppie classes. While Metro News, FM Select and the all-Cantonese Hit Radio were making the running, Commercial Radio English (CRE) finally succumbed to the pressure of the arrival of FM Select. In the spring of 1993 Commercial Radio officials threw in the towel and changed the format to an all-music station, supposedly fulfilling its licence requirement to broadcast in English by playing English-language songs. Today there is no news, indeed no spoken word whatsoever. A mid-term review in 1995 of the CRE licence may well not look kindly on the present format.

## ☐ Other Players

Other broadcasting moves during the past 12 months saw the establishment of two new satellite television companies in the territory, to follow on the success of the AsiaSat project, which announced its long-planned second generation satellite, AsiaSat2, for television transmissions early in the year.

Hong Kong's AsiaSat is already well into profit, despite only launching AsiaSat1 just three years ago and has announced that it will launch AsiaSat2 in early 1995. There are also unconfirmed plans for a third satellite (Asia-Sat3) in late 1995 or early 1996. The shareholders in AsiaSat are Hutchison Telecommunications Limited of Hong Kong, Cable & Wireless plc of the U.K. and China International Trust and Investment Corporation of China, each holding 33.3 per cent of the equity.

Li Ka-shing and Hutchison's STAR TV currently utilizes eleven of twenty-four transponders on the AsiaSat1 satellite and holds a veto on any broadcaster joining it on the orbiter. The same situation will hold true for the larger and more powerful AsiaSat2. The AsiaSat1 signal already covers 38 countries, attracting to date 45 million viewers to STAR TV.

The onset of digital compression for satellite broadcasting has produced forecasts that up to 450 satellite television channels could be available in Hong Kong within two years: a staggering figure, but one not so unlikely in view of the dozen or so satellites that will be launched in that period and will have Hong Kong within their "footprints".

The serious challenger to the regional dominance of AsiaSat has been the establishment of the APT Satellite Company, a China–Thailand–Taiwan consortium which has signed a contract of over US$200 million to build and launch its first communications satellite, Apstar1 in late 1994.

Already the company has made a splash by announcing that it has cut a deal with STAR TV for the lease of 20 transponders on its second satellite due for launch in late 1994. A closer relationship between APT and STAR TV-associated company is expected before the end of 1993.

# 19

# Income Distribution

Tsang Shu-ki

It is not easy, if at all possible, to rigorously analyse the distribution of income and wealth in Hong Kong. The reason is simple: comprehensive data and information are lamentably scarce. The distribution of wealth is anyone's guess, there being no official, semi-official, or serious private surveys of any kind. Population census has been held every five years, but published household income statistics were too simple for more sophisticated treatment. A General Household Survey has been conducted on a quarterly basis since the first half of the 1980s. However, the format of the income data which are not published but are presumably available on request is such that not much systematic distributive diagnosis can be carried out. I do not know whether this state of informational paucity is a result of *laissez-faire* or deliberate policy, but all one can do now is to live with it and to write on the issue with as much objectivity as possible.

## ☐ A Long-term Trend of Widening Inequality

Table 1 lists the changes in the decile distribution of household incomes as well as the Gini Coefficient in Hong Kong since 1971. The former of course gives a more disaggregated picture of income distribution in the territory. Apparently, a long-term trend of widening inequality has emerged. The share of the lowest income group, the first decile, fell from 2.3 per cent in 1971 to 1.4 per cent in 1981, rebounded slightly in 1986, and then resumed

Tsang Shu-ki is a senior lecturer in the Department of Economics, Hong Kong Baptist College.

Table 1. Decile Distribution of Household Incomes in Hong Kong

Unit: % of total income

| Decile of households | 1971 | 1976 | 1981 | 1986 | 1991 |
|---|---|---|---|---|---|
| First (lowest income) | 2.3 | 1.9 | 1.4 | 1.6 | 1.3 |
| Second | 3.9 | 3.5 | 3.2 | 3.4 | 3.0 |
| Third | 5.1 | 4.6 | 4.4 | 4.4 | 4.0 |
| Fourth | 5.1 | 5.5 | 5.4 | 5.4 | 5.0 |
| Fifth | 7.0 | 6.8 | 6.5 | 6.4 | 6.1 |
| Sixth | 7.3 | 8.1 | 7.8 | 7.6 | 7.4 |
| Seventh | 9.0 | 8.8 | 9.4 | 9.1 | 9.0 |
| Eighth | 11.0 | 11.3 | 11.5 | 11.4 | 11.4 |
| Ninth | 14.7 | 15.9 | 15.2 | 15.2 | 15.5 |
| Tenth (highest income) | 34.6 | 33.6 | 35.2 | 35.5 | 37.3 |
| Official Gini Coefficient | 0.43 | 0.43 | 0.45 | n.a. | 0.48 |
| Derived Gini Coefficient | 0.408 | 0.417 | 0.437 | 0.435 | 0.462 |

Note:   The official Gini Coefficient for 1986 is not available. The derived Gini
        Coefficient is calculated on the basis of the decile distribution using the
        standard formula. The Gini Coefficient falls by definition within the range of
        0.0 to 1.0, with 0.0 representing absolute equality and 1.0 absolute inequality.
        Hence the larger the coefficient the more unequal is the distribution.

Sources: Hong Kong government, *Census Report*, various issues. The figures for 1991
        were released by the government in response to a question from a Legislative
        Council member in a meeting on 25 November 1992.

its slide to 1.3 per cent in 1991. The shares of the second and the third
deciles showed a similar pattern, falling by about 1 per cent over the same
time span. In contrast, the top 10 per cent of the households, i.e. the tenth
decile, took an increasing share of income, except for 1976, gaining 2.7 per
cent, while the ninth decile also chalked up a rise of 0.8 per cent. These
trends are confirmed by the rising Gini Coefficient.

    This is about the most detailed picture of income distribution in Hong
Kong in the past two decades that one can come up with. Any further
analysis is impeded by the lack (or, more accurately, by the non-
availability) of relevant data. One useful piece of data would have been
the average or median income of the deciles, per household or per capita,
none of which is released by the Hong Kong government. The Oshima
Index, for example, is defined as the ratio of the per capita income of the top
decile over that of the bottom decile — a popular indicator in the income

distribution literature. It can be and has been computed for China, at least for urban households.[1] A related index is the ratio of the average income of the top decile to the overall median income, which is regularly compiled in Western Europe and North America.[2] No such luck for Hong Kong.

## ☐ Some Recent Evidence

Table 2, on the other hand, is constructed on the basis of Table 207 of the quarterly *General Household Survey* conducted by Census and Statistics Department of the Hong Kong government. It shows the distribution of households under different monthly income groups in the first quarter of 1985, as well as that in the fourth quarter of 1992. The original table gives a 37-bracket breakdown, which has been simplified to make it easier for intertemporal comparison. In the period, nominal per capita GDP (gross domestic product) in Hong Kong went up by about 150 per cent. That extent of growth can be used as a proxy deflator to adjust the income brackets over time. The simplified brackets are indeed so determined: HK$1,499, the upper limit of the second income bracket, is about 250 per cent of the first, i.e. HK$599; HK$3,499 is roughly 250 per cent of HK$1,499, and so on. Such a simplification is of course constrained by the original income groupings in Table 207. There is for example no upper income limit of HK$3,747.50, which is exactly 250 per cent of HK$1,499. We are forced to choose the *nearest* limit in forming the brackets.

Table 3 standardizes the income limits into "1992 dollars", which have been adjusted for: (1) inflation between 1985 and 1992; and (2) the rise in average living standard in real terms. Hence a household which earned HK$600 a month in 1985 should be able to have earned HK$1,500 a month in 1992, if it could keep up with the improvement in nominal income of an

---

[1] See Li Roujian, "An Analysis of Differences in the Distribution of Income of People Living in China's Cities and Towns — With an Examination of Simon Kuznets' 'Inverse "U"' Hypothesis", *Hong Kong Journal of Social Sciences*, No. 1 (Spring 1993), pp. 19–34. The index for the urban households in China varied between 2.86 and 3.30 in 1985–1990.

[2] Figures are even disaggregated down to the individual level and broken down by sex. See for example Samuel Brittan, "Clues to Rising Unemployment", *Financial Times*, 22 July 1993. According to the article, the ratio of the earnings of the top tenth to median income for male was in the range of 1.6 to 2.2 for France, Germany, the United States and the United Kingdom in the past two decades.

Table 2. Household Income Distribution from General Household Survey

Unit: number of households

| Income group (HK$/month) | 1985 Q1 | | 1992 Q4 | |
|---|---|---|---|---|
| 0–599 | 22,624 | (1.61) | 14,926 | (0.90) |
| 600–1,499 | 64,322 | (4.59) | 17,439 | (1.05) |
| 1,500–3,499 | 327,898 | (23.37) | 65,318 | (3.93) |
| 3,500–9,499 | 724,887 | (51.67) | 558,015 | (33.55) |
| 9,500–24,999 | 243,184 | (17.33) | 763,431 | (45.90) |
| 25,000–59,999 | 19,072 | (1.36) | 223,590 | (13.44) |
| Above 60,000 | 913 | (0.07) | 20,541 | (1.23) |
| Total number | 1,402,900 (100.0) | | 1,663,260 (100.0) | |

Note:    Q1, Q4 represent the first and the fourth quarters respectively. Figures in parentheses are percentage points.

Source:  Census and Statistics Department, Hong Kong government, *General Household Survey*, Table 207. Data not published, but presumably available on request.

Table 3. Cumulative Comparison of Adjusted Household Income Distribution

Unit: % of households

| Household income (HK$/month) | 1985 Q1 | 1992 Q4 |
|---|---|---|
| Less than 600 | n.a. | 0.90 |
| Less than 1,500 | 1.61 | 1.95 |
| Less than 3,500 | 6.20 | 5.88 |
| Less than 9,500 | 29.57 | 39.43 |
| Less than 25,000 | 82.24 | 85.33 |
| Less than 60,000 | 98.57 | 98.77 |

Note:    n.a. — not applicable.
Source:  Same as Table 2.

average person in the territory. Even given its limitations because of the way that it is constructed within the confines of official information, the table reveals some disturbing evidence of widening income inequality. While about 30 per cent of households earned less than HK$9,500 (adjusted) a month in Q1 of 1985, nearly 40 per cent failed to rise above that income level in Q4 of 1992.

# ☐ International Comparison

Because of the scarcity of local data and information, comparative analysis of the income distribution patterns of Hong Kong and other countries is a difficult task. Table 4 simplifies the figures of Table 1 into quintile distribution, and Table 5 presents alongside Hong Kong's distribution those of a selected group of countries at various levels of economic development, as represented by per capita GDP. The income share of the top decile of

Table 4. Quintile Distribution of Household Incomes in Hong Kong

Unit: % of total income

| Quintile of households | 1971 | 1976 | 1981 | 1986 | 1991 |
|---|---|---|---|---|---|
| First (lowest income) | 6.2 | 5.4 | 4.6 | 5.0 | 4.3 |
| Second | 10.2 | 10.1 | 9.8 | 9.8 | 9.0 |
| Third | 14.3 | 14.9 | 14.3 | 14.0 | 13.5 |
| Fourth | 20.0 | 20.1 | 20.9 | 20.5 | 20.4 |
| Fifth (highest income) | 49.3 | 49.5 | 50.4 | 50.7 | 52.8 |

Source: Simplified from Table 1.

Table 5. International Comparison of Quintile Household Income Distribution

| Quintile | Hong Kong (1991) | Guatemala (1979–81) | Spain (1980–81) | Singapore (1982–83) | United Kingdom (1979) | Japan (1979) | U.S. (1985) |
|---|---|---|---|---|---|---|---|
| First | 4.3 | 5.5 | 6.9 | 5.1 | 5.8 | 8.7 | 4.7 |
| Second | 9.0 | 8.6 | 12.5 | 9.9 | 11.5 | 13.2 | 11.0 |
| Third | 13.5 | 12.2 | 17.3 | 14.6 | 18.2 | 17.5 | 17.4 |
| Fourth | 20.4 | 18.7 | 23.2 | 21.4 | 25.0 | 23.1 | 25.0 |
| Fifth | 52.8 | 55.0 | 40.0 | 48.9 | 39.5 | 37.5 | 41.9 |
| Top 10% | 37.3 | 40.8 | 24.5 | 33.5 | 23.3 | 22.4 | 25.0 |
| Per capita GDP 1990 | 16,230 | 2,920 | 10,840 | 14,920 | 14,960 | 16,950 | 21,360 |

Note: The 1990 figures of per capita GDP were estimates based on purchasing power parity adjustments provided by the World Bank. The numbers may not add up to 100 because of rounding.

Source: Data for Hong Kong from Table 4, and the rest from the World Bank, *The World Development Report 1992*, Table 30.

households is also listed for reference. The selection is admittedly subjective. It is nevertheless constrained by data availability as any reader of
*The World Development Report 1992* may testify. The GDP figures are
not the normal ones compiled, but the findings or derived numbers on the
basis of purchasing power parity adjustments, as provided by the World
Bank. Under such an analytical scheme, Hong Kong actually ranked
higher in terms of economic development than both Singapore and the
United Kingdom in 1990.

It is indeed worrying to observe that Hong Kong's household income
distribution in 1991 looked more like that of Guatemala in 1979–1981
rather than that of Spain, Singapore, or Britain, not to mention Japan and the
United States, at various time points in the late 1970s and the 1980s. Hong
Kong's degree of income inequality was worse than all of the latter five.
The shares of the first to the fourth quintiles were smaller than theirs, while
the percentage of the top (fifth) quintile was much higher. A noteworthy
point is that the share of the top 10 per cent of households was more than
4 per cent above that of Singapore and more than 10 per cent above the
other four countries!

Indeed, among the twenty-four "high-income economies" listed in
Table 30 of *The World Development Report 1992*, in which Hong Kong was
ranked the eighth, none of the economies' top quintile took more than 50
per cent of total income, with the exception of Hong Kong! In less than half
of the cases did the share go above 40 per cent. As for the top 10 per cent of
households, other than Hong Kong and Singapore, the share was invariably
below 30 per cent. It was 37.3 per cent for Hong Kong in 1991.

## ☐ Some Conjectures and a Plea

The standard theory defending non-intervention by the government in
the distribution of incomes and wealth hinges on the so-called "Kuznets
inverted-U", which hypothesizes that in the process of economic development inequality would worsen before it gets better. In "trickle-down
economics", it is also asserted that the rich should not be constrained in
their effort to create wealth, as economic benefits will eventually filter
down to the lower strata of the society. As far as Hong Kong is concerned,
there is no evidence that such a benign state of affairs is taking place, or is
about to take place, despite the fact that economic development in the
territory has already advanced to a very high level by any standard. Indeed,
the opposite seems to be occurring: a long-term trend of worsening income

gap is unfolding, as far as the very limited amount of available statistics can tell. Moreover, in the context of international comparison, Hong Kong's income distribution is strikingly unequal.

I have commented on the reasons behind such a phenomenon elsewhere.[3] Here I would only summarize the major considerations. In the 1950s and the 1960s, there appeared to have been a period of narrowing income gap due to the standard explanations: industrialization, increasing labour participation, etc. Local scholars have estimated that the Gini Coefficient in 1957 was 0.47.[4] It subsequently fell to 0.41 or 0.43 in 1971, as shown in Table 1 above. However, since then other countervailing factors have asserted themselves and the trend has been reversed.

First, the fall in the average size of households and the ageing of the population have been rather dramatic in Hong Kong. From the level of 4.5 in the late 1970s, the average number of family members dropped to only 3.4 in 1991, while the "old" population (those above 65) has been growing at an average annual rate of over 4 per cent. The overall labour participation rate, on the other hand, rose from 64.0 per cent in 1971 to 66.8 per cent in 1981, but then declined to 64.3 per cent in 1991. Hence the earning ability of the average household has in general been undermined. The incomes of the upper social strata are nevertheless more assets-generated (from all kinds of investments) than labour-generated, and should therefore have been less affected, compared with the middle and the lower classes.

Second, the very low level of unionization of workers, as well as the emergence of monopolies and corporations with market power in a number of fields, implies relatively weak bargaining power on the part of employees over their remunerations, and despite the tight labour market situation in recent years, there is little evidence that workers have unduly benefited.[5] The transformation of Hong Kong into a service-oriented economy would also tend to widen income gaps, as the salary structure in white-collar sectors usually shows a much wider spread than that in the manufacturing industries.

---

[3] Tsang Shu-ki, "Several Hypotheses on the Deterioration of Income Inequality in Hong Kong", *Ming Pao*, 31 January 1992 (in Chinese).

[4] Ibid.

[5] See Tsang Shu-ki, "Inflation", in *The Other Hong Kong Report 1992*, edited by Joseph Y. S. Cheng and Paul C. K. Kwong (Hong Kong: The Chinese University Press, 1992), pp. 425–45.

Finally, the relocation of plants and factories to the much cheaper processing zones in the Pearl River Delta has enabled many Hong Kong merchants to reap huge profits. Some of the money earned might not be repatriated but was reported in the census. The money repatriated might be spent or saved. In the former case, spending would generate a multiplier effect, benefiting also workers in the process through higher employment and wages, besides of course other employers and investors. In the latter case, no such effect would result. Overall, there is reason to believe that the China link might widen income inequality in Hong Kong, particularly if we take into account the inflationary impact of asset acquisition and conspicuous consumption by enriched local merchants and the increasing number of investors from the Mainland.

These factors seem to be long-term or structural in nature and it is unrealistic to expect any substantial improvement in income distribution in Hong Kong. The situation may indeed get worse in the foreseeable future. The Hong Kong government has of course not been totally non-interventionist. In the areas of housing, health care, education, and other public services, it has been subsidizing the less fortunate members of the society, and the *redistributive* effect could not be regarded as insignificant, although more can and should be done. In its eagerness to push forward the process of "corporatization" and "privatization", there is however a danger that redistributive objectives are brushed aside, exactly when the distribution pattern becomes worse. Taxation and expenditure policies need to be guided at least partly by these objectives, and as a start, much better data and information on income and wealth distribution should be collected and made available to the public. The present degree of data availability is bordering on the absurd.

# 20

# Women

Choi Po-king

## ☐ Introduction

Women's issues have begun to feature much more prominently in public discussion since mid to late 1980s, thanks to local voluntary efforts at organization and advocacy. Not surprisingly, such concern is far from being matched by government action, but even then, the bureaucracy found it necessary to conduct a related study in the spring of 1992, which resulted in a report by the Inter-departmental Working Group on Sex Discrimination in Employment (henceforth called the Report) in December. Apart from this, it has also compiled the *Green Paper on Equal Opportunities for Women and Men* (henceforth called the Green Paper), which was released in late August 1993. Such bureaucratic efforts, however, seem not to be well taken by advocates of gender equality, who, instead of being suitably grateful, denounced them as delaying tactics for stalling genuine legal and administrative changes in the right direction.

In this chapter, we shall examine the situation pertaining to local women in various spheres of life, and then proceed onto describing what could broadly be called the women's movement in recent years. My basic premise is that women's issues are essentially relational in character, so that while the focus of this chapter seems to be on women, it is in fact on women as they fare in the patriarchal structure. As such, this chapter might just as well be entitled "Gender Issues".

Choi Po-king is a lecturer in the Department of Educational Administration and Policy, The Chinese University of Hong Kong.

## □ **Employment**

Table 1 shows that among all employed persons in 1991, less than 40 per cent (38 per cent to be exact) were women, and they featured prominently in clerical jobs, taking up 69 per cent of this category. In two categories of occupations: managers and administrators, and craft and related workers, women were a minority, taking up only 20 per cent and 11 per cent respectively. There is clearly a formal or informal process of gender stratification at work in our employment structure. Indeed, various researchers and women's groups have identified specific recruitment policies which contribute to such segregation. It is common practice, for example, for private organizations to specify gender requirements for jobs. Very often, it is the more senior and responsible positions which are reserved for men, and junior, clerical ones for women. Even for jobs with the same title or placed at the same formal level, it is likely that men and women encounter diverse experiences and differential opportunities for further training. These discrepancies often lead to less favourable promotion prospects for women.

Even the Civil Service is not immune from discrimination. The official Report released in December 1992 admitted that a few departments "have traditionally not recruited women for certain grades". Happily, according to

Table 1. Gender Distribution within Occupations, 1991

| Occupation | Men | Women | Total |
| --- | --- | --- | --- |
| Managers & administrators | 198,857 (80%) | 50,390 (20%) | 249,247 (100%) |
| Professionals | 68,516 (69%) | 30,815 (31%) | 99,331 (100%) |
| Associate professionals | 164,121 (59%) | 115,788 (41%) | 279,909 (100%) |
| Clerks | 135,665 (31%) | 295,986 (69%) | 431,651 (100%) |
| Service workers and shop sales workers | 230,823 (64%) | 128,496 (36%) | 359,319 (100%) |
| Craft and related workers | 352,264 (89%) | 45,728 (11%) | 397,992 (100%) |
| Plant and machine operators and assemblers | 234,929 (64%) | 130,897 (36%) | 365,826 (100%) |
| Elementary occupations | 280,434 (56%) | 223,398 (44%) | 503,832 (100%) |
| Others | 20,757 (74%) | 7,239 (26%) | 27,996 (100%) |
| Total | 1,686,366 (62%) | 1,028,737 (38%) | 2,715,103 (100%) |

Source: Census and Statistics Department, *Hong Kong Annual Digest of Statistics*, 1992.

the same report, such departments have agreed to change their recruitment policies and offer equal opportunities to female applicants. However, because the identity of such departments is not disclosed, it is difficult for the public to judge when and how such discriminatory policies will be corrected.

Apart from discrimination in recruitment, women in general are also much more poorly remunerated. Table 2 shows the lower quartile, median

Table 2.  Women's Wages as a Percentage of Men's in Various
Economic Sectors, September 1992

| Economic sector/ Broad occupational group | Lower quartile | Median | Upper quartile |
|---|---|---|---|
| *Manufacturing* | | | |
| Craftsmen & other operatives | 69% | 71% | 69% |
| Supervisory, technical, clerical & miscellaneous non-production workers | 89% | 86% | 78% |
| *Wholesale, retail, import/export trades, restaurants & hotels* | | | |
| Supervisory, technical, clerical & miscellaneous non-production workers | 75% | 71% | 75% |
| *Transport services* | | | |
| Craftsmen & other operatives | * | * | * |
| Supervisory, technical, clerical & miscellaneous non-production workers | 99% | 93% | 73% |
| *Business services* | | | |
| Supervisory, technical, clerical & miscellaneous non-production workers | 98% | 89% | 84% |
| *Personal services* | | | |
| Craftsmen & other operatives | — | — | — |
| Supervisory, technical, clerical & miscellaneous non-production workers | 80% | 70% | 58% |
| *All Industries* | | | |
| Craftsmen & other operatives | 67% | 67% | 67% |
| Supervisory, technical, clerical & miscellaneous non-production workers | 74% | 77% | 78% |

Notes:    * Data suppressed for confidentiality reasons.
          — No figures supplied for this category.

Source:  Wages and Labour Costs Statistics Section, Census and Statistics Department, *Report on Half-yearly Survey of Wages, Salaries and Employee Benefits, September 1992*, Vol. I.

and upper quartile of women's earnings as percentages of men's for various industries as of September 1992. In all industries and at both the production and non-production levels, women's earnings are only around two-thirds to three quarters of men's. Furthermore, in four of the five economic sectors, the percentage of women's earnings decreases steadily as one proceeds to the upper quartile. In face of this evidence, one wonders how the Report arrives at its conclusion that the income differential between men and women is "relatively narrow". Similar statistics for executives are not available in the above government survey. In the Green Paper, however, it is disclosed that the ratios of median income of female to male employees in the occupational categories of "managers and administrators" and "professionals" in 1991 are both 0.83. For "associate professionals", the ratio is 0.94 (p. 14). The source of such figures is, however, not indicated.

The official Report argues that "judgemental" factors, such as different gender distribution in occupations and industries, might explain the discrepancies in fringe benefits and promotion aspects. The implication here is that the income differential might not be due to discrimination after all. Similarly, the Green Paper admits that "the above figures indicate that ... on average, the income of women is lower than that of men in most occupational categories." Yet, it goes on to state that "this however does not necessarily imply that women are earning less for the same job ..." (p. 15).

To see whether discrimination does exist, one would then have to compare men and women's incomes for jobs with the *same* titles (such as bookbinder, colour matcher) in the *same* industries (such as printing, bleaching and dyeing). Table 3 offers such a comparison.

It is clear from Table 3 that at the level of craftsmen and other operatives, women's income for all jobs are significantly lower than men's. The situation is slightly better for jobs at the non-production level, but even here, half of the jobs procure for women an income of no more than 90 per cent of that for men. In face of these findings, the Green Paper's explanation of pay differentials between the genders in terms of "differences in specific job requirements, physical or other capabilities, education attainment, and length of service and experience" (p. 17) rings very hollow indeed. By contrast, gender discrimination, an explanation which this official document tries to avoid, is most convincing.

Regrettably, Table 3 does not give us the complete picture concerning remuneration for women and men in various economic sectors. Apart from the absence of data concerning professionals, executives and administrators, the jobs that are included in Table 3 represent only a fraction of

Table 3. Ratio of Women's Income to Men's for Various Economic
         Sectors, September 1992

| Ratio of women's income to men's | Number of jobs | |
|---|---|---|
| | Craftsmen and other operatives | Supervisory, technical, clerical and miscellaneous non-production workers |
| 1.30–1.49 | 0 | 1 |
| 1.20–1.29 | 0 | 0 |
| 1.10–1.19 | 0 | 0 |
| 1.00–1.09 | 0 | 36 |
| 0.90–0.99 | 0 | 87 |
| 0.80–0.89 | 15 | 83 |
| 0.70–0.79 | 15 | 42 |
| 0.60–0.69 | 8 | 6 |
| 0.50–0.59 | 3 | 0 |
| 0.40–0.49 | 1 | 0 |
| Total | 42 | 255 |

Source:   Wages and Labour Costs Statistics Section, Census and Statistics Department,
          *Report on Half-yearly Survey of Wages, Salaries and Employee Benefits*,
          September 1992, Vol. II.

the total spectrum of jobs surveyed at relevant levels. Table 4 explains
why.

Table 4 shows that gender comparison can be made for only 25 per cent
and 41 per cent of the jobs at the production and non-production levels
respectively. The reason for this is that, for 53 per cent and 32 per cent
of jobs at the two respective levels, data has been suppressed for confidentiality reasons, usually for either one of the genders. Then, there is a
number of jobs which are single-sexed, with those exclusively for men
outnumbering those for women (35 to 1 for production, and 47 to 24 for
non-production level respectively). There is, then, clearly a process of
gender segregation at work at these levels. The highly optimistic statement
in the Green Paper that "generally, women enjoy the same rights as men do
to participate in the labour force and to take up the job of their choice"
(p. 11) is very misleading indeed.

The most significant difference between the two genders in employment is probably a structural one. While the requirements of marriage,
childbearing and childrearing significantly affect women's employment

Table 4. Data Regarding Income of Men and Women at Production
and Non-production Levels

|  | Craftsmen and other operatives | Supervisory, technical, clerical and miscellaneous non-production workers |
|---|---|---|
| Total number of jobs covered by survey | 165 | 628 |
| Number of jobs where gender comparison is possible | 42 (25%) | 255 (41%) |
| Data suppressed (usually for one gender only) | 88 (53%) | 199 (32%) |
| Jobs for men only | 35 (21%) | 47 (7%) |
| Jobs for women only | 1 (0.6%) | 24 (4%) |

Note: The percentage in parentheses represents that of the total number of jobs covered in the survey. The percentages of each column add up to more than 100 per cent because the categories overlap.

Source: Wages and Labour Costs Statistics Section, Census and Statistics Department, *Report on Half-yearly Survey of Wages, Salaries and Employee Benefits*, September 1992, Vol. II.

experience and pattern, they leave men totally unaffected. As shown in Figure 1, the respective labour force participation rates for the two genders differ only very slightly (less than 4 per cent) for young persons under the age of 20. These same rates for women, however, drop dramatically after this age, especially for the group aged 25–29, i.e. a period in life when women are most likely to bear their first or second child. At the age of 35–39, a time when men probably reach the peak of their earning power, the labour force participation rate for women is only about half of that for men.

Figure 2 shows the respective labour force participation rates in the first quarter of 1993 for women who have never married and for those who have. The significant discrepancy between these two groups of women calls further attention to the restraints marriage and the family place upon women in terms of labour participation.

Attention has indeed been drawn to this and other employment issues by local women's groups in the past few years. In fact, such issues have formed the most consistent focus of women's groups and their activities,

Figure 1. Gender Comparison for Labour Force Participation Rates
for Various Age Groups, 1991

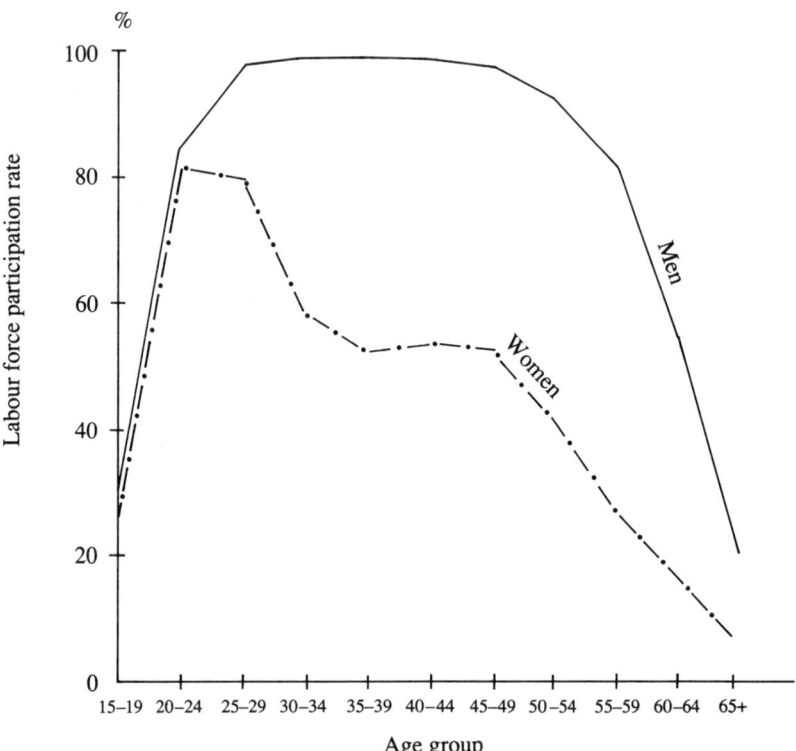

Source: Census and Statistics Department, *Hong Kong Annual Digest of Statistics*,
1992.

which were given a further impetus in the spring of 1992. In March of that
year, the government relented on its earlier refusal (in July 1991) to consider setting up a working group for women, and announced its plan to set
up an inter-departmental working group, chaired by the Secretary for
Education and Manpower, to examine the question of discrimination in
employment in Hong Kong. Soon after this announcement, a coalition of
18 women's groups, community groups and trade unions petitioned the
Governor (then Sir David Wilson) on 8 March (International Women's
Day) on the issue of job discrimination against women. They also put
pressure on the newly set up inter-departmental working group, asking it
to release its terms of reference and work schedule.

Figure 2. Labour Force Participation Rates for Various Age Groups
for Women, First Quarter of 1993

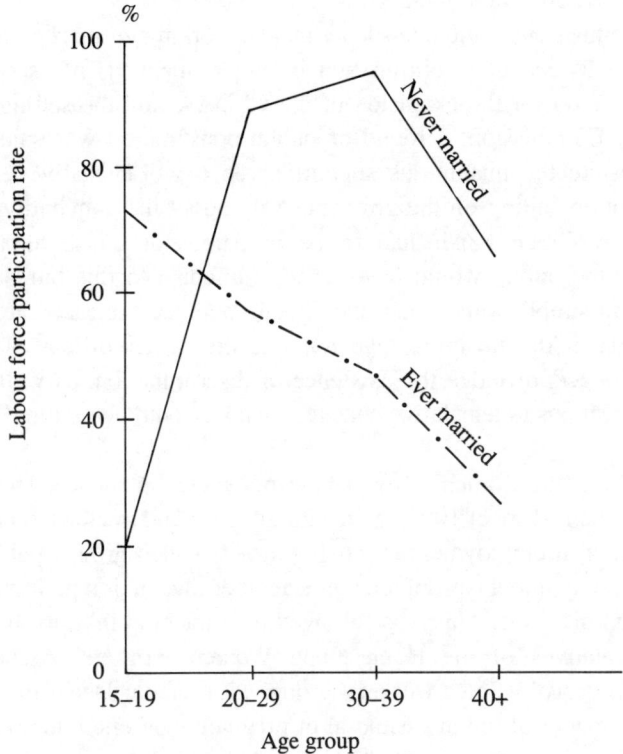

Source: Census and Statistics Department, *Quarterly Report on General Household
Survey*, Jan.–Mar. 1993.

Women's groups were adamant that the pressure on the government
would be kept up. On 29 July 1992, several months after the petition at the
Governor's House, a coalition of 12 groups representing a wide spectrum
of female employees met officials of the inter-departmental group. They
called for a thorough investigation into gender discrimination in employment, which the officials promptly dismissed as unnecessary. The coalition
also reiterated a demand put forward in the spring petition, namely, for the
government to adopt and implement an international agreement known as
the Convention on the Elimination of All Forms of Discrimination Against
Women (CEDAW), of which both the United Kingdom and the People's

Republic of China are signatories. Like the demand for investigation, the government's attitude towards the CEDAW was, and remains, one of extreme reservation and reluctance.

In December 1992, the inter-departmental working group reported that the problem of gender discrimination in employment "is not serious in Hong Kong". As for the extension of the CEDAW and the setting up of a Women's Commission, a round of public consultation was said to be needed, despite the unanimous support given to a Legislative Council (Legco) motion calling on the government to adopt the convention without delay. A Green Paper had to be prepared for consultation, and meanwhile, the public would have to accommodate to this bureaucratic schedule and simply wait. When the Green Paper was released at last in August 1993, it did no more than reiterate the earlier official stand of reluctance to acknowledge the existence of discrimination, as well as its strong reservations to legislative changes such as would be required by the CEDAW.

If anything, the women's groups have not waited in silence. The International Women's Day of 1993 again witnessed a round of attack on gender discrimination in employment. A coalition of ten such groups publicized results of a study into the problem, while another trade union petitioned the Governor on the issue. This was followed by a meeting in April between the representatives of the Hong Kong Women Workers' Association (HKWWA), a local women workers' group, with Labour Department officials on the matter of unfair dismissal of pregnant workers. Later, in May, the pro-Beijing Federation of Trade Unions organized a three-hour parade of floral floats on Mother's Day to publicize their request for retraining for women displaced by industrial relocation as well as by childbirth.

Official protestations of gender equality in employment notwithstanding, grievances voiced by women's groups have been consistent and clear. These include: the lack of equal opportunity in recruitment and promotion; discrepancies in pay and fringe benefits for the same jobs; earlier age of retirement for women required by individual institutions such as airline companies; unfair dismissal of pregnant workers; less than full pay (two-thirds) during the ten-week maternity leave for workers; restricted access of women to credit; and the lack of legal redress for victims of sexual harassment at work.

Two specific issues stand out in the protests of women's groups. The first of these concerns stringent age restrictions (18–22 for some, 30 for others) imposed by various organizations, such as hotels, retail chains, and even factories, on women job applicants. Such restrictions are very crippling indeed, in view of the fact that many women have to leave the workforce at the early stages of childrearing, re-entering only in their mid-thirties. Furthermore, this problem has been compounded by the massive relocation of industries across the border. Many workers in the manufacturing sector, a significant proportion of them being women, are seriously affected. And, to make matters worse, employers in the service sector are increasingly attracted to the option of imported labour, which is considerably cheaper.

The second issue concerns the introduction of legislative safeguards against gender discrimination, particularly in employment. Indeed, one of the major goals of women's groups for the past half decade is to work for the extension of the CEDAW to Hong Kong. In effect, this would require the government to formulate concrete strategies, including equal pay and anti-discrimination legislation, to eliminate gender inequality in various spheres. Up till now, the government's stand remains clearly negative, and it repeatedly cites high administrative costs, probable ineffectiveness of legislation, and, most importantly, adverse effect on the economy (sometimes curiously phrased as "social costs") as the major reasons. It remains to be seen whether and how the government could be persuaded (or pressurized) to acknowledge the social returns for official enactment of equality and human rights. As for the effect of equal rights legislation on the economy, meaningful discussion has not even begun.

## ☐ Education

The publication of official education statistics is such that it has become increasingly difficult to update on gender comparisons since the mid to late 1980s. Hence the gaps the reader would notice in some of the tables in this section.

Taking the overall enrolment of the two genders at various levels of education, one sees a general trend towards more equal gender participation throughout the past three decades. This is shown in Table 5. Although women's participation in university education was still below 50 per cent in 1990, there has been a steady improvement over the past decades at this and lower levels of the education hierarchy.

Despite the trend towards more equal participation at various levels, the process of "genderization" of subjects and curriculum has not abated. In other words, male and female students tend to concentrate in different

Table 5. Percentage of Female Students at Various Education Levels,
1961–1990

|      | Kinder-garten | Primary | Second-ary@ | Matricu-lation | Post-secondary (Non-degree) | University |
|------|------|------|------|------|------|------|
| 1961 | 43.5 | 44.5 | 40.1 | | 31.1 | 26.5 |
| 1971 | 45.8 | 47.7 | 42.7 | 35.1 | 26.8 | 31.8 |
| 1981 | 48.0 | 48.0 | 50.7 | 42.0 | 36.9 | 34.4 |
| 1986 | 48.5 | 47.7 | 50.2 | 44.4 | 50.1 | 39.3 |
| 1990 | 48.5 | 48.1 | 50.0 | 50.4 | * | 42.3 |

Notes:  @ Secondary education includes day and night certification courses.
        * Information not available.
Sources: *Education Department Annual Summary*, 1961, 1971; Census and Statistics
         Department, *Hong Kong Annual Digest of Statistics*, 1982, 1987, 1991; *Vice-Chancellor's Report, 1990/91*, The University of Hong Kong; student enrol-ment figures for The Chinese University of Hong Kong for the year 1990–1991, by courtesy of the Registration Section of the University.

streams or branches of study, which might ultimately lead to different job or career experience after they leave school.

Table 6 show that over the past twenty years or so, male students have increasingly avoided the arts faculty, as they do for the newly set up education faculty, where 90 per cent of the intake is female. By contrast, the architecture, science, medical and, particularly, the engineering faculties remain male-dominated.

Turning to technical and vocational education at the secondary level, one notices that girls concentrate in the commercial stream (over 90 per cent), while taking up only a small share in the technical and vocational streams (see Table 7). Data concerning gender share for post-secondary technical and vocational education is piteously scarce. From what one can muster, it seems that the same picture as at the secondary level holds (see Table 8).

From Table 9, we see that the pattern of increasing avoidance of the arts stream by male students at the university level repeats itself at the lower level of secondary grammar school. Meanwhile, there have been small increases in the proportion of girls taking science subjects, which are generally seen to be more prestigious, though the gender ratio for such subjects still remains skewed. What happens in school is probably similar to what goes on in society: while a small number of women are able to make inroads into formerly all-male territories, the ground rules of

Table 6. Percentage of Women Undergraduates in Various Faculties of
The University of Hong Kong and The Chinese University of
Hong Kong, 1971–1990

| Faculty | 1971 | 1976 | 1981 | 1986 | 1990 |
|---|---|---|---|---|---|
| *The University of Hong Kong* | | | | | |
| Architecture | 17.1 | 14.3 | 20.0 | 32.8 | 28.7 |
| Arts | 48.0 | 70.8 | 65.3 | 67.6 | 79.6 |
| Dental Studies | n.a. | n.a. | 14.1 | 14.9 | 31.5 |
| Education | n.a. | n.a. | n.a. | n.a. | 90.5 |
| Engineering | 2.2 | 0.8 | 2.4 | 1.4 | 6.2 |
| Law | 57.1 | 39.3 | 56.2 | 57.6 | 52.3 |
| Medicine | 20.0 | 17.2 | 16.1 | 14.6 | 27.8 |
| Science | 19.3 | 16.9 | 22.2 | 10.2 | 26.3 |
| Social Science | 34.2 | 49.5 | 42.3 | 48.1 | 52.5 |
| Overall | 28.4 | 33.5 | 34.0 | 33.1 | 41.2 |
| *The Chinese University of Hong Kong* | | | | | |
| Arts | 54.1 | 54.1 | 59.1 | 70.8 | 78.1 |
| Business Administration* | 42.1 | 25.0 | 29.0 | 47.8 | 62.0 |
| Engineering | n.a. | n.a. | n.a. | n.a. | 9.0 |
| Science | 19.2 | 14.5 | 11.5 | 20.6 | 31.6@ |
| Social Science | n.a. | 38.8 | 45.7 | 57.6 | 58.9 |
| Medicine | n.a. | n.a. | 11.7 | 19.8 | 31.2 |
| Overall | 38.7 | 33.2 | 35.6 | 44.5 | 51.3 |

Notes:   * For the year 1972, the faculty was not yet separated from the Commerce and
Social Science Faculty.
@ For the year 1990, the engineering programme was separated from the
science faculty and set up as the Faculty of Engineering
n.a. = Not applicable: faculty not yet established.

Sources: *Vice-Chancellor's Report*, The University of Hong Kong, relevant years; *The
Chinese University of Hong Kong Bulletin*, Winter 1976; *Vice-Chancellor's
Report*, The Chinese University of Hong Kong, 1978–1982, 1985–1987;
*Education Department Annual Summary 1971*; student enrolment figures for
The Chinese University of Hong Kong for the year 1990–1991, by courtesy of
the Registration Section of the University.

gender division and hierarchy remain unchanged. As a result, men tend
to avoid occupational and academic spheres which are seen to be associated
with women to a greater extent than before, probably because they have
better resources, educational and otherwise, to allow them to do so than
before. In fact, the fate of the subjects of biology and human biology
manifests this process of genderization very well. Biology used to be a
marginal science subject, having been popular among students in the arts

Table 7.  Percentage of Female Students in Full-time Secondary Level
Technical/Vocational (Including Commercial) Education,
1972–1990

|      | Technical/Vocational | Commercial | Overall |
|------|----------------------|------------|---------|
| 1972 | 24.0 | 99.5 | 31.7 |
| 1976 | 22.2 | 98.3 | 28.1 |
| 1982 | 28.9 | 95.5 | 32.6 |
| 1986 | 30.9 | 95.3 | 33.9 |
| 1990 | 34.2 | 93.3 | 36.8 |

Sources: *Education Department Annual Summary*, relevant years.

Table 8.  Percentage of Female Students in Full-time Post-secondary
Technical/Vocational Training, 1972–1990

|      | Polytechnic | Technical institutes | Overall |
|------|-------------|----------------------|---------|
| 1972 | 17.0 | 8.0 | 8.2 |
| 1976 | n.a. | 11.4 | n.a. |
| 1982 | 28.7 | 28.2 | 28.5 |
| 1986 | n.a. | n.a. | n.a. |
| 1990 | n.a. | n.a. | n.a. |

Note:    n.a. = Information not available.
Sources: *Education Department Annual Summary*, relevant years.

Table 9.  Gender Ratios for Subjects in the Arts Stream and the Science
Stream, Certificate of Education Examination, 1976–1992

|  | 1976 | 1982 | 1986 | 1992 |
|--|------|------|------|------|
| *Arts Stream* | | | | |
| History | 0.65 | 0.49 | 0.48 | 0.47 |
| Chinese Literature | 0.91 | 0.61 | 0.52 | 0.41 |
| Geography | 0.97 | 0.64 | 0.57 | 0.54 |
| *Science Stream* | | | | |
| Physics | 3.35 | 2.85 | 2.52 | 2.09 |
| Chemistry | 2.82 | 2.63 | 2.38 | 1.98 |
| Additional Mathematics | 3.41 | 2.83 | 2.40 | 1.95 |
| Biology | 1.10 | 1.10 | 1.41 | 1.58 |
| Human Biology | n.a. | n.a. | 0.31 | 0.27 |

Note:    Number of male candidates for every female candidate.
n.a. = Subject not yet introduced.
Sources: Hong Kong Examination Authority, *Hong Kong Certificate of Examination: Annual Report*, relevant years.

stream. In the mid-1980s, an even "softer" option, human biology, was introduced for arts students. Within the first half decade after it was introduced, one witnesses a "flight" of male students from human biology, perceived as an arts subject, and an increase in gender imbalance in biology, as it is "upgraded" to become a science subject proper.

The genderization of school subjects, besides acting to restrict the learning opportunities of boys and girls, also has a strong pedagogical effect. Children who grow up in the context of such gender divisions would most likely take these as "natural" and hence unalterable. Moreover, these divisions are further reinforced and expanded on by textbooks. Recent studies of textbooks used in local primary and secondary schools have found that girls and women are grossly under-represented, and if they do make an appearance, they are marked by passivity and restricted to domestic or very limited occupational roles.[1] Notwithstanding the bold pledges spelt out in the Green Paper (p. 24), there is as yet no evidence that serious attempts are being made to eliminate sexist contents from textbooks or the curriculum.

Besides curriculum and textbooks, children and young people also learn from daily life. Tables 10 and 11 show us the all too familiar picture of steadily decreasing participation of women as one goes up the organizational hierarchy. Thus the school, where children and young people spend most of their waking hours, unwittingly teaches them about male authority and female subordination.

## ☐ Violence

### *Rape and Indecent Assault*

Women suffer disproportionately from various forms of indignities and violence associated with sex, ranging from harassment, indecent assault to rape. A 1992 study made by the Coalition Against Sexual Abuse, a coalition of four women's groups, found out that 85.9 per cent of the adult women

---

[1] Yau-Lai, Betty Lai-ling and Luk Hung-kay, *A Study of Gender Roles in Junior Secondary Chinese History and Social Studies Textbooks in Hong Kong* (Hong Kong: Institute of Social Studies, The Chinese University of Hong Kong, 1988); and Au Kit-chun, *A Study of Gender Roles as Defined in Primary School Textbooks in Hong Kong* (Hong Kong Institute of Asia-Pacific Studies, The Chinese University of Hong Kong, 1993). Both are written in Chinese.

Table 10.  Percentage of Women Teachers in Primary Schools
by Rank, 1991

| Rank | % of Women Teachers |
|------|---------------------|
| Certificate Master/Mistress (CM) | 80.7 |
| Assistant Master/Mistress (AM) | 50.0 |
| Senior Assistant Master/Mistress (SAM) | 33.3 |
| Overall | 75.0 |

Source:  Statistics Section, Education Department, *Teacher Survey, 1991*, April 1992.

Table 11.  Percentage of Women Teachers (Including Principals)
in Secondary Schools by Rank, 1991

| Rank | % of Women Teachers |
|------|---------------------|
| Principals I & II | 28.9 |
| Graduate Teachers | |
| Principal Graduate Master/Mistress (PGM) and Senior Education Officer (SEO)* | 33.6 |
| Senior Graduate Master/Mistress (SGM) and Education Officer (EO) | 38.2 |
| Graduate Master/Mistress (GM) and Assistant Education Officer (AEO) | 49.6 |
| Non-graduate Teachers | |
| Principal Assistant Master/Mistress (PAM)[#] | 33.3 |
| Senior Assistant Master/Mistress (SAM) | 39.0 |
| Assistant Master/Mistress (AM) | 52.2 |
| Certificate Master/Mistress (CM) | 62.4 |
| Private School Head | 12.5 |
| Private School Teacher | 32.7 |
| Other Rank | 54.6 |
| Overall | 49.5 |

Note:     * The counterparts of PGM's, SGM's and GM's, who work in aided schools,
          are SEO's, EO's and AEO's in government schools respectively. While their
          nomenclature differ, their ranks are actually equivalent. The ranks of PGM's
          and SEO's were added as from 1991 onwards, and these take up the role of
          assistant principals in the schools.
          [#] PAM's, SAM's, AM's and CM's are equivalent in rank to the same working
          in primary schools. In secondary schools, they teach in the junior classes, i.e.
          up to Form 3, the third year. The rank of PAM was added as from 1991
          onwards.
Source:  By courtesy of M. L. Lau (for Director of Education), Education Department.

(aged over 21) interviewed had, in the previous two years, experienced some form of sexual harassment and abuse for at least once. This percentage seems unbelievably high, but is in fact comparable to findings in Western countries.

In the past year, violence against women was highlighted by the occurrence of six consecutive violent rape and murder cases, believed to be committed by a serial rapist, in several Tuen Mun housing estates.

Community reaction against the serial rapes in Tuen Mun was strongest in April 1993, one year after this rapist targeted his first victim. The body believed to be his first rape and murder victim had been discovered in February of that year, and emotions peaked when the body of the second victim was discovered on 14 April in Tai Hing Estate. Up till then, official figures indicated that he had claimed six victims altogether since April of the previous year. All had been raped, and among them, two were murdered and one left on the brink of death, who later died. In April, a "Concern Group for The Security of Tuen Mun Women" was formed, and, together with elected local District Board members, it campaigned actively for the improvement of security in housing estates, and the stepping up of police action in the area. Meanwhile, one District Board member, a gentleman by the name of Alfred Tso Shiu-wai, complained that too much fuss had been made over this matter. "I don't think the problem is that serious. It has happened in the past and will happen again in the future. It is a fact of life," he said. (*Sunday Morning Post*, 9 May 1993)

Tso's words, of course, brought little solace to women in Tuen Mun, and, indeed, to women anywhere. He is indisputable, however, on one point, which is that rape *is* a fact of life for women. According to official figures given in Table 12, cases of reported rape and indecent assault have increased steadily over the past decade. As of 1991, there was, on average, one case of rape reported in three days, and three cases of indecent assault in one single day.

The problem is, in all likelihood, even more serious than official statistics indicate. Judging from figures given by The Family Planning Association of Hong Kong (FPA) and the Women's Centre, which run a counselling service for rape victims and a Rape Crisis Line respectively, only between one quarter and a third of their rape cases are reported to the police. In 1992, for example, there were 301 calls to the hotline, but the police received only 116 reports of rape. In the first two months of 1993, the hotline received 165 calls, but only 11 cases were referred to the police. Meanwhile, the FPA counselled 22 rape victims in the same period, and

Table 12. Number of Sexual Offence Cases, 1982–1991

| Year | Rape | | Indecent assault | |
|------|----------|----------|----------|----------|
|      | Reported | Detected | Reported | Detected |
| 1982 | 79  | 49 | 784   | 542 |
| 1983 | 78  | 36 | 778   | 491 |
| 1984 | 87  | 46 | 768   | 444 |
| 1985 | 80  | 48 | 801   | 492 |
| 1986 | 72  | 41 | 808   | 500 |
| 1987 | 66  | 43 | 979   | 588 |
| 1988 | 97  | 61 | 922   | 580 |
| 1989 | 120 | 70 | 1,019 | 647 |
| 1990 | 111 | 66 | 1,078 | 731 |
| 1991 | 114 | 83 | 1,101 | 713 |

Source: Census and Statistics Department, *Hong Kong Annual Digest of Statistics*, 1992.

among them, only 11 reported to the police (*Hong Kong Standard*, 24 March 1993).

Social stigmatization of rape victims is a major inhibiting factor against reporting, a fact which has not been ameliorated by the police's way of handling rape cases. According to Acting Chief Staff Officer Jimmy Lee, it is standard practice for officers to deal with rape victims "like any other victim of crime". Except for initial interviews which are conducted by female officers, victims are usually interviewed by male officers in later investigations. It is said that police interrogations often leave victims feeling as if they were the criminals instead. Nor does the low rate of conviction help. In 1991, 86 people were charged with rape, but only 20 were convicted. In 1992, the figures were 17 out of 86 (*Hong Kong Standard*, 24 March 1993). This factor, together with the harrowing experience of reporting and testifying in court, easily explains the great discrepancy between the number of victims who seek help from the FPA and the Rape Crisis Line on the one hand, and the actual number of reports to the police on the other. With the possibility of the closure of the Rape Crisis Line due to financial difficulties, victims will be left with even less support than before.

To be fair, the police did offer their help in the wake of the Tuen Mun serial rapes. Immediately after the first murder-rape case in February 1993, police issued warning to women of that district against using the lifts late at night, and going out on their own. How women who work night shifts or attend evening classes could return home is left to anyone's guess, but at least, the police's warning underlined another sobering fact of life for women. This is, namely, severe restrictions on one's movement, and dependency on others who act as escorts.

After being accused by impatient Tuen Mun residents of inaction in a neighbourhood discussion held in Tai Hing Estate on 16 April 1993 (*South China Morning Post*, 17 April 1993), the police stepped up their public education endeavour by organizing a series of seminars for women on how to avoid becoming rape victims. On finding, with astonishment, that such talks in the past had been given by uniformed male officers to mixed audiences, staff officer Superintendent Graham Lander of the Crime Prevention Bureau decided that these seminars should be restricted to women and presented by women officers. In these seminars, women were advised to remain passive and not to attempt self-defence tactics in the misfortune of being attacked (*South China Morning Post*, 27 April 1993). Whether or not the absence of attempts to resist on the part of the victim might jeopardize the chance of conviction eventually was probably not discussed. And, in any case, it is highly debatable whether or not passivity might, as the police claims, reduce violence, or, on the contrary, induce it. It is probably impossible to judge the efficacy of these seminars and previous police warnings, except that they might have worked well as public relations tactics. On a more subtle level, they have certainly worked to reinforce the conventional belief in the weakness, dependency and passivity of women.

While the serial rapes in Tuen Mun convey terror of what might happen to women in dark corridors and stairwells of public housing estates, cases of indecent assault of primary school students by their teachers in two separate schools in July 1992 brought parents' attention to the presumably safe haven of the school. Calls for education of children in protecting themselves were reiterated, and some people suggested policies and guidelines with regard to sexual harassment and abuse in schools. Cheung Man-kwong, elected Legislative Councillor and chairman of the biggest teachers' union, the Hong Kong Professional Teachers' Union, however, reassured the public that those cases were mere aberrations. Local male teachers, to his mind, were all self-respecting people, and there was absolutely no need to establish any guidelines or policies. Instead, what these teachers must guard against, Cheung said, were "misunderstandings" on the part of teenage girls who might be "over-sensitive" to friendly touches and other such gestures of their mentors.

If, as Cheung said, the school is still a relatively safe place, then apparently the public transport system, particularly the Mass Transit Railway, is not. Luckily it seems that the situation has improved over the past few years. Reports of indecent assault on the Mass Transit Railway decreased from 218 offences reported in 1990, to 136 in 1991, and 58 up to the end of October in 1992. Again, there is much under-reporting, because victims either feel embarrassed or find it too troublesome to report. Nevertheless, a plain-clothes police team has been deployed to fight this form of crime, committed mostly to women but also to a small number of men. Judging from the decrease of cases mentioned above, their efforts seem to have paid off.

### *Domestic Violence*

Violence perhaps hurts deepest when it happens in the home, but unfortunately, it often passes unnoticed and, indeed, is sometimes unwittingly sanctioned by the public and even by frontline professionals such as the police, nurses and doctors, and social workers. Indeed, professionals working for the Harmony House, the only non-government refuge for battered wives (including co-inhabiting women), dub the family as a potential "special violence region", a place where the level of tolerance for violence is higher, and help or intervention from the outside is either withheld or resented.

At present, there are two refuge centres for battered women. One is the Wai On Home for Women run by the Social Welfare Department, with a capacity to shelter 40 women and their young children. Clients could only reach them through referrals by case workers, and publicity is minimal.

The other refuge is the Harmony House, set up under the aegis of the Hong Kong Council of Women in 1985. It was incorporated in April 1986, after which it became an independent organization with its own governing board and staff. Its present funds now come from private donations, the Community Chest of which it became a member since March 1988, and subvention from the Social Welfare Department since October 1989.

The Harmony House has a capacity similar to that of the Wai On Home. Unlike the Wai On Home, however, it runs active publicity campaigns, so that for the past six years or so, over half of their admitted clients have been "self-referrals" who approach them directly through their 24-hour hotline. Apart from easy access for women in need, the Harmony House also places

a high priority on follow-up, developmental services, including counselling, separate support groups for battered women and their children, as well
as tutorials and therapeutic art classes for children. Since 1990, two groups
are also set up for and by ex-residents: the Lai Kwan Women's Group,
which is a social and recreational network for abused women and their
children, and the Kwan Fuk Women's Concern Group, which is a pressure
group working for policy and other changes to ameliorate the plight of
battered women.

While Harmony House professionals reiterate continuously the need
for additional subvention for refuge of battered women and preventive
community education, the government insists that there is no such need and
that the problem of domestic violence has actually abated. In an adjournment debate in Legco on 10 March 1993, several councillors pointed to the
under-reporting of domestic violence, and asked for the convening of an
inter-departmental working group to address the issue. The Secretary for
Health and Welfare, Elizabeth Wong, however, dismissed the need for such
a review. She quoted figures collected by the Social Welfare Department to
the effect that the number of wife-battering cases had been on the decrease
in the past five years. She also mentioned husband battering, which, according to official figures, accounted for 1 out of 6 cases of domestic violence,
as well as child abuse. What she implied was clear: the problem of wife
battering had been exaggerated.

Harmony House professionals and the Kwan Fuk Women's Concern
Group, who petitioned outside Legco on the date of debate, however,
thought otherwise. The Harmony House had been stretched to its limits, and
sadly, within the past year, it had to turn away more than 50 women who
came to seek refuge. Considering the many-faceted follow-up services they
had to provide for abused women and their children, the Harmony House
also found it necessary to obtain more government subvention, which they
did not get.

Apparently, Wong has failed to convince Harmony House professionals that the problem has abated. First of all, they remain sceptical of the
official figures she offered, which do not square with their own experience
of increased demand (see Tables 13 and 14 for a comparison of official and
unofficial figures). In particular, they doubt whether or not the government
had access to accurate figures since they only relied on descriptions in
yearly reports sent by agencies. Judging from their experience working
with battered women, Harmony House professionals are also aware of the
fact that cases of domestic violence often appear in many guises, at least

Table 13. Number of Wife-battering Cases Made Known to
the Social Welfare Department, 1988–1992

| Year | 1988/1989 | 1989/1990 | 1990/1991 | 1991/1992 |
|---|---|---|---|---|
| No. of cases | 455 | 272 | 236 | 209 |

Source: *Oriental Daily News*, 11 March 1993.


Table 14. Services Rendered by the Harmony House, 1986–1992

| Year | 1986/ 1987 | 1987/ 1988 | 1988/ 1989 | 1989/ 1990 | 1990/ 1991 | 1991/ 1992 | 1992/ 1993 |
|---|---|---|---|---|---|---|---|
| Calls received | 365 | 498 | 379 | 1,652* | 1,575 | 1,620 | 2,544 |
| Self-referrals | 71 | 98 | 54 | 84 | 78 | 64 | 87 |
| Total admittance[@] | 182 (218) | 166 (175) | 105 (106) | 141 (150) | 164 (185) | 125[#] (145) | 142 (169) |

Notes:   * The first territory-wide publicity campaign was undertaken in this year. Hence the sharp rise in number of calls.
[@] The number without parentheses is that of women, and the one in parentheses is that of children admitted together with their mothers.
[#] Maintenance work between November 1991 and January 1992 forced the capacity to be greatly reduced for that year.
Source:   *Annual Report*, Hong Kong, Harmony House, various years; information by courtesy of Wong Mei-fung and Chan Po-ying, Family Ideal Community Education Project, Harmony House.


initially, and so may not appear on official record as such. Finally, there is the perennial problem of reluctance on the part of battered women to seek help due to stigmatization, and the fear of the consequences of separation, especially for those who have children.

Since May 1993, the Legal Aid Department provide immediate help to battered wives to obtain court injunctions against their husbands. The Department is also linked up with the police and the Social Welfare Department through a hotline, so that other services could be provided to women seeking help from them. These are welcome developments, but there is still a lot of room for improvement. This would not be made, however, until there is official recognition of the fact that wife battering involves a host of other problems besides the use of violence. These include:

1. emotional and psychological problems for both women and their

children, who are usually abused at the same time as their mothers are;

2. problem of schooling for affected children, some of whom fear interception by fathers at school;
3. financial difficulties (57.5 per cent of the women who sought refuge in the Harmony House between November 1992 and January 1993, for example, were full-time housewives with no income of their own); and
4. dire need for compassionate rehousing due to fear of husbands' or ex-husbands' threat in the premises of the home despite court injunction orders.

On recognition of the complexity of the problem, the government would do well to deploy resources, not only in adequate amounts, but also in a more integrated fashion so as to cater for the many-faceted needs of the troubled family. In view of the fact that wife battering also involves beliefs held about male authority and female submission, it is also essential that preventive community education is undertaken to facilitate changes in conventional perceptions of gender relationships. Indeed, this is what the Family Ideal Community Education Project, started by the Harmony House in 1992, is trying to do. Finally, education in the nature and complexity of wife battering is also important for different groups of frontline professionals. These include: the police, doctors and nurses, social workers, lawyers, as well as school principals and teachers. A receptive attitude towards victims of wife battering has to be nurtured among them, as is a realization that violation of one's right to live without fear and danger should not be condoned, even if it arises in the private sphere of the family.

## ☐ Women's Movement

### *Diversification and Politicization*

The 1980s saw an intensification of public discussion and collective action on various fronts in Hong Kong. In general, there has been a higher degree of politicization of social issues than before, coupled with a greater propensity for mobilization. The women's movement follows this trend, resulting in two interesting developments, namely diversification and politicization.

Up till 1992, there have been around 16 women's groups, among 200 or so, which are explicitly concerned with women's awareness and rights.[2] The history of such groups reveals the trend of localization as well as a widening of the social base of participants. The longest-standing women's group, the Hong Kong Council of Women (HKCW, established in 1947), for example, was founded by expatriate and local women of the upper social strata. Such social composition was also true of the women's welfare or *kaifong* women's associations, established mostly in the 1950s or 1960s. Then in the 1970s, professional women's groups, such as the Zonta Club, the Hong Kong Association of Business and Professional Women (HKABPW) and the Hong Kong Federation of Women Lawyers began to emerge, all of which have a distinctly elitist bent.

The 1980s, in turn, were marked by the establishment of groups more explicitly concerned with women at the grassroots level. Activists in such groups belong mostly to the so-called new middle classes that have emerged in Hong Kong in the 1980s. Typically, they were born to lower-middle or working class families in the 1950s or early 1960s, and, in the 1970s, experienced and contributed to the atmosphere of social concern and critique that characterized their college days. One example of these groups is the Association for the Advancement of Feminism (AAF, established in 1984), which distinguishes itself by explicitly declaring their ideological stand through incorporating the word "feminism" in their name, something which earlier groups have avoided. Along with the AAF, other groups such as the Hong Kong Women Christian Council (HKWCC, established in 1988) and the Hong Kong Women Workers' Association (HKWWA, established in 1989) have worked diligently to challenge gender inequality in various social and cultural spheres, especially for women of the working classes.

The 1980s also saw a tendency for women's groups to work in coalition, thus bringing together groups of different ethnic and social backgrounds, as well as orientations. The most notable coalition is the Campaign for a Women's Commission and for the CEDAW. Initially made up of nine groups in mid-1989, this Joint Committee of women's groups gradually

---

[2] Much of the information in this description of women's groups is drawn from B.L.L. Yau, K. C. Au and F. M. Cheung, *Women's Concern Groups in Hong Kong*, Occasional Paper No. 15 (Hong Kong Institute of Asia-Pacific Studies, The Chinese University of Hong Kong, September 1992).

gathered force through their various campaigning activities, and eventually the number rose to 18 by early 1993. The strength of coalitions such as this lies not in the number of participant groups, but rather, in the integration of different kinds of expertise. These include the legal perspectives on the part of the more elitist and expatriate groups, such as the HKCW, AWARE (Association of Women for Action and Research, a splinter group from the HKCW), the HKABPW and the Hong Kong Federation of Women Lawyers; as well as the mobilization skills and knowledge of grassroots experience such as those held by the AAF, the HKWCC, the HKWWA, and grassroots groups like the Eastern District New Women Association. In the past one or two years, there have been other smaller coalitions working for more specific issues. In general, the tendency is that of much broader-based participation and mobilization than before.

The opening up of 18 seats in Legco for direct elections in 1991 provided a further impetus for the women's movement. In the spring of 1991, five groups (the Women's Centre of the HKCW, the HKWWA, the AAF, the HKWCC and the Shaukeiwan Federation of Women, forerunner of the Eastern District New Women Association) worked together under the Coalition for the Education of Women Voters. In January, they issued a women's platform in which they detailed demands for gender equality in the legal, political, economic and social aspects, as well as the guaranteeing of women's rights and dignity. Throughout the year up to the elections, they monitored the political platform of candidates, and organized various education programmes for women at the community level. After the elections, their work is resumed in 1993 by the AAF in the form of a Women and Political Participation Programme, aimed at arousing the political consciousness of women at large, and pressurizing Legco members to respond to issues pertaining to gender equality.

Even before the direct elections of 1991, demands for a women's commission and anti-discrimination legislation have already been prompted by discussion about the drafting of the Bill of Rights. As observers have remarked,[3] the Bill as it was finally enacted in July 1991 represented a severe letdown to the movement for equal gender rights. The Bill as it now stands is only binding upon the government and public

---

[3] See, for example, Carole J. Peterson, "The Bill of Rights and Women: A Bate and Switch?", paper presented in the Faculty of Law Seminar of The University of Hong Kong, *Hong Kong's Bill of Rights: Two Years On*, 5 June 1993.

authorities, which means that private parties such as employers are not covered. The battle has clearly been won by business interests. These have lobbied hard against the earlier draft Bill published in March 1990, in which provisions were made for private parties.

With the women's groups continuing to put unrelenting pressure for anti-discrimination legislation and the CEDAW, however, the government responded by announcing in March 1992 that it would take some time to study the extent of discrimination in employment. As described in the earlier section on employment in this chapter, the result of the study, released in December 1992, was that discrimination was minimal. Pressure from Legislative Councillors and women's groups nevertheless succeeded to elicit from the government a promise of a Green Paper on gender equality for public consultation. This was released in August 1993.

Even before its release, we were already granted glimpses of what it is like through eminent sources such as the Chief Secretary Sir David Ford. In a newspaper article (*Sunday Morning Post*, 15 August 1993), he tells us that there is basically no problem of gender inequality in Hong Kong, that women in Hong Kong are extraordinarily privileged, and so on. One new, sobering warning, however, comes in the last sentence of Sir David's treatise: "Like many issues, applying the convention to Hong Kong would create international rights and obligations for the Government after 1997, and consultation with the Chinese Government would be necessary." This same reminder also appears in the Green Paper (p. 52).

Perhaps the government has taken the lesson of the Sino-British disputes in the past year very much to heart, and is now ready to consult the Chinese government on all matters big and small. Yet one is left with the uneasy feeling that this warning is, in effect, an apologia for having to preserve the status quo.

Sir David gave his treatise an uplifting title: "Government takes lead in upholding women's rights". But if he is really serious about consultation with the Chinese government, chances are that the government would have to beat a hasty retreat from its valiant campaign for women's rights. One major obstacle concerns the customary, exclusive male inheritance of property and entitlements to all proceeds from ancestral property, allowed to persist under the New Territories Ordinance. If there is to be anti-discrimination legislation, these controversial rights accrued to males, actively contested by women's groups and indigenous New Territories women in the past year or so, would certainly have to be repealed. This, however, is likely to be seen as incompatible with Article 40 of the Basic

Law, which states that: "The lawful traditional rights and interests of the indigenous inhabitants of the 'New Territories' shall be protected by the Hong Kong Special Administrative Region."

At present, the Heung Yee Kuk, a stronghold of established New Territories interests, has already made it clear that it would not budge on the issue of male inheritance and entitlement to ancestral property. Apart from Article 40 of the Basic Law, they could also count on their traditional amiable relationships with the Chinese government, which has stated in more than one occasion that the Basic Law cannot be changed, at least not before 1997.

Meanwhile, women's groups in the New Territories, many of which have a pro-Beijing background, choose to advise and help individual women to take matters to court, if and when property willed to them are taken away by their male kin. Education and bringing individual cases to the court, but not rapid legislative change, are the proper ways to improve the lot of women in the New Territories, these groups maintain.

Both the Heung Yee Kuk members and the government have stated unequivocally that the problem of inequity in inheritance can be resolved through the making of private wills. Yet, Carol Jones of The University of Hong Kong have argued that this is a misconception. She observes that a woman can still be ousted by the nearest male heir from property willed to her, because the 1971 Probate and Administration Ordinance specifically exempts the so-called Part 2 New Territories Land from its provisions.[4] At best, the legality of female inheritance has not been well established, and in any case, inequity lies in the fact that women have to be prepared to bear the high costs of litigation in order to gain their right to inherit what has been willed to them. In contrast, men's right of inheritance is automatic and unconditional.

The government would, in all likelihood, have preferred to let matters remain as they have been for almost a century, social inequity notwithstanding. The problem, however, is that anomalies arise with rapid social development. Apart from international and internal pressures for laying down formal provisions for social equity, such as the Bill of Rights, urbanization of the New Territories and massive migration into these areas mean that many residents of populous new towns find themselves subject to

---

[4] See Footnote 9 to Carole J. Peterson, *op. cit.*

customary law. Thus a highly inconvenient, not to say absurd, situation arises in which a woman resident in Sha Tin or Tsuen Wan finds herself barred from inheriting a flat in a modern estate.[5]

It is likely that such an administrative and legal anomaly rather than a true commitment to social equity has prompted the City and New Territories Administration officials to sound out the possibility of amendments to the New Territories Ordinance with the Heung Yee Kuk in April 1993. The Heung Yee Kuk rejected outright the idea of making any amendments to the Ordinance, fearing that deliberation over legislative changes in Legco might open the floodgates to even wider reform. As Albert Lam Kok-cheong, Kuk member and lawyer, put it: "We can only say if the legislation is put to Legco, there may be unforeseen things, anything can happen in Legco."

The Heung Yee Kuk put forth, instead, a counter proposal, namely, that the Governor used his powers to extend the land exempted from the New Territories Ordinance. In this way, the New Territories Ordinance itself would be left intact, and nothing would be changed, which is what the Heung Yee Kuk wants at the end of the day. The matter is left unresolved at the time of writing.

## The China Factor in the Women's Movement

Sir David's timely reminder about consulting the Chinese government serves to underline the centrality of the China factor in the area of gender issues, as it is in the political, economic and social spheres in general. Indeed, clear signs have emerged that pro-China forces are trying to co-opt the local women's movement and related activities.

---

[5] During the process of editing in mid-September, the Housing Authority suddenly issued a reminder that women would be barred from inheritance of Home Ownership Scheme (HOS) flats (Phase 1 to 14D) and Private Sector Participation Scheme (PSPS) flats located in the New Territories, unless these have been willed to them. Spokespersons of various political groups, however, pointed out that procedural difficulties would still prevent women from inheritance, even if there had been wills made in their favour. Subsequently, the Housing Authority indicated that they would consider retrospective administrative procedures to exempt lands on which HOS and PSPS estates stand from the New Territories Ordinance. How a similar problem for the numerous private buildings in the New Territories can be resolved has not been touched on, nor the absurdity of the prospect of having two separate legislation for residents, indigenous and immigrant, in the same location in the New Territories.

In late June 1993, a new women's group called the Hong Kong Federation of Women was officially registered, though its formal inauguration was not due until 31 October. Even at this early stage, however, its membership has already attracted much media attention. The roster of founding members and the executive committee is very impressive indeed: a delegate to the Chinese People's Political Consultative Conference (Peggy Lam, chairperson), members of the Beijing-appointed Preliminary Working Committee for the Special Administrative Region (Rita Fan Hsu Lai-tai, vice-chairperson, and Nellie Fong Wong Kut-man), Beijing-appointed Hong Kong Affairs Advisers (Nellie Fong Wong Kut-man, Chan Yuen-han, Elsie Leung Oi-sze), delegates to the local National People's Congress (Elsie Leung Oi-sze, Lisa Wang Ming-chuen), members of the pro-Beijing Democratic Alliance for Betterment of Hong Kong (Chan Yuen-han, Elsie Leung Oi-sze), as well as members of the past Basic Law Consultative Committee (Ng Siu-ching, vice-chairperson, Wong Yu-po, Fei Min, and Lau Hung Oi-kuk). The third vice-chairperson is Tsang Wong Lai-kwan, who has wide experience in organizing women's associations. Tsang's spouse is Tsang Hin-tze, a businessperson and member of the Preliminary Working Committee for the Special Administrative Region, delegate to the local National People's Congress, and Hong Kong Affairs Adviser.

In contrast to most of the other women's groups, making ends meet is the last worry of the nascent Hong Kong Federation of Women. Indeed, the Federation is extraordinarily well-endowed, having solicited generous donations from various individuals such as Tsang Hin-tze, who alone contributed HK$1 million (*Ming Pao*, 13 July 1993). Apart from individual donations, funds also came in through the awarding of the titles of Honorary Chairperson and Vice-Chairperson at stated prices: HK$200,000 and HK$100,000 respectively. By the end of July, it was estimated that the Federation has already received donations of up to HK$7 million (*Hong Kong Economic Journal*, 23 July 1993). With this strong financial base, the Federation can comfortably look to a spacious office with permanent staff, and an estimated yearly expenditure of HK$500,000.

At the time of writing in August 1993, the Federation has a membership of around 200, plus nine member groups, including pro-Beijing women's groups in various New Territories communities. With its distinctly pro-Beijing bent, as well as heavy reliance on entrenched business interests, the Federation is expected to be generally conservative in its political and social outlook. Not surprisingly, the "maintenance of the Sino-British Joint declaration and the Basic Law" tops the list of its eight objectives. As for the others on the list, they are relatively innocuous exhortations to educate women, to provide recreation and welfare for women and children, and to study women's issues, etc. To be fair, one of its objectives does demonstrate slightly greater resolution. This is, namely,

> To work for and maintain women's lawful rights, ensure equality between the sexes, encourage and support women in their concern for and participation in social development, and improve their political, economic, legal and social status.

Bearing in mind this objective of the Federation, one is interested in seeing how it will respond to the Green Paper on equal opportunities. Considering the pro-Beijing stance and business backing of the Federation, it seems likely that the issues of anti-discrimination legislation, the extension of the CEDAW, and exclusive male inheritance and entitlements in the New Territories will drive a wedge between the Federation on the one hand, and the other women's groups which have been working relentlessly for reform on the other.

Nor are these specific issues the only point of difference between the Federation and these other women's groups. There is also the political orientation and style of work to consider. Unlike groups with distinct feminist orientations, the Federation is expected to take up an accommodating rather than a confrontational stance, and to shy away from critical appraisals of the structural and cultural bases of gender inequity. Moreover, while feminist groups have gained strength from widened political representation, the Federation is likely to favour great restraint in the process of democratization. This is in order to "realize a smooth transition, and prosperity and stability in society", as stated in the first of its objectives. As anyone familiar with Chinese nomenclature used in the recent animated Sino-British exchange will know, "smooth transition" and "prosperity and stability" are terms meant to stand in opposition to a faster pace of democracy and wider political participation.

Finally, the upper-middle class initiative means that a top-down approach in the handling of gender issues is highly likely. This will be in great contrast to the grassroots orientation and mobilization manifested by women groups that have been active in the past decade.

Women's movement in the past decade has shown healthy signs of diversification and localization as the former elitist and expatriate hold gradually made room for initiatives arising from local and grassroots groups. Hopefully, the appearance of the high-profile and well-financed

Federation supported by pro-Beijing interests would not reverse this trend, though there is a real possibility that this might happen.

## Women's Movement at the Crossroads

I have mentioned earlier that the women's movement has received a great impetus from the opening up of Legco seats for direct elections. It remains to be seen, however, whether or not further democratization and more intensified political activities would benefit or, on the contrary, undermine the women's movement. One common experience of women's movement in various societies is that issues of gender inequality and women's suffrage often acquired prominence at the initial stage of social and political reforms. Yet, these same issues would soon be crowded out by other agendas (nation-strengthening, class redistribution, etc.) as the well-entrenched, patriarchal structure re-asserted itself in the wake of the high tides of social reform. In Hong Kong today, it will be up to women's groups and individual feminists not to allow their own agendas to meet the same fate.

At the present stage, the local women's movement could do with a still higher degree of pluralism, coupled with more dialogue among women of varying socioeconomic and ethnic groups. There is, in fact, still much to be done before newly emergent grassroots groups could make a significant impact on the movement. The Hong Kong Women Workers' Association, for example, is still having a hard time placing themselves among the well-established, elitist feminist groups and making known to them their interests and concerns. For instance, while professional women could quite logically argue for the abolition of limits on overtime hours specifically for women because these are inconsistent with the principle of gender equality,[6] women workers have been fighting hard to retain the valuable extra allowance paid for working beyond overtime limits.

Another area where dialogue is seriously lacking is that between middle-class, professional women on the one hand, and foreign-hired women domestic workers on the other. Some people like Sir David Ford might happily celebrate the success with which our society "helps women

---

[6] See Carole J. Petersen, "The Hong Kong Bill of Rights Ordinance: Its Potential Impact on Sex Discrimination in Employment", speech to Hong Kong Association of Business and Professional Women Seminar, 22 October 1991, p. 7.

participate in the workforce ... [by importing] over 100,000 foreign domestic helpers" (*Sunday Morning Post*, 15 August 1993). Yet the women's movement in Hong Kong would certainly suffer if it is confined within the narrow horizons of our territory, or, worse still, within those of the more vocal upper-middle and professional classes.

## ☐ Conclusion

Notwithstanding differentials in income and more job opportunities, gender segregation and stereotyping in formal education, as well as the ever-present threat of sex-related and domestic violence, the cliché saying in Hong Kong is that there cannot be a better place in this world for women.

One factor contributing to the perpetuation of this myth is the lack of gender-related statistics which are officially released and easily available. Earlier in this chapter, I have mentioned the difficulty of getting hold of figures for gender comparisons in the sphere of formal education, especially since mid to late 1980s. The same thing is true, in fact, for other areas such as employment, violence or health.

Of course, no government or institution is particularly keen to make available politically sensitive statistics, such as those facilitating comparison among different gender, social class or racial groups. And we have no reason to expect that our government and institutions would be any different. What we could expect, however, is a further opening up of information and discussion as the sense of local identity and citizenship strengthens within the society. The fact that the issue of gender equality begins to emerge on the public agenda is a good sign, however faint it is, that such processes are indeed making some headway.

# 21

# Public Opinion

Robert T. Y. Chung

In terms of public opinion, 1992–1993 was no doubt "the year of Chris Patten". The year under review for this *The Other Hong Kong Report*, namely July 1992 to June 1993, fits squarely into Patten's first year of office as Governor of Hong Kong. Patten arrived at Hong Kong on 9 July 1992, a year less two months after the first direct election of the Legislative Council (Legco) on 15 September 1991, which was a landmark in Hong Kong's political development. But if September 1991 was a landmark, July 1992 must have been a watershed — one which divides two very different forms of British governorship of Hong Kong.

Nobody ever doubted Patten as a political heavyweight. He who is the ex-Chairman of the Conservative Party in Britain has toppled Margaret Thatcher's eleven-year rule, and he who is a close friend of John Major is only at a distance of a telephone call from the Prime Minister. In fact, the row over his constitutional reform proposals has made him a hero in London, as even the opposition Labour Party is in stern support of him — a position which even Major himself could only envy.

Because Patten is such a heavyweight, he has caught the attention of practically every person in the street. His maiden policy speech, his walkabouts, and even the loss of his dog, all made headlines into almost every mass medium. Needless to say, a historical number of opinion polls were generated to gauge the public's reaction to his proposals, and other

Robert T. Y. Chung is a research officer at the Social Sciences Research Centre, The University of Hong Kong.

related issues. According to records kept at the Social Sciences Research Centre (SSRC) of The University of Hong Kong, out of the about 120 public opinion polls reported in the media between July 1992 and June 1993, over one-quarter were directly related to his constitutional proposals. Viewed from a different perspective, one can say that Patten has drawn so much public attention that opinion polls flourished because of him. Flourished because of him but not delivered by him, because opinion polls have already gained a foothold after the 1991 direct election, and has since become an accepted medium of expressing public sentiment. Patten has, nonetheless, accelerated the process.

The present chapter reviews the development of this medium from its genesis through its metamorphoses up to July 1993. Major findings from these polls in the year past are also described.

## □ Opinion Polls: Pre-1993 Development

While it is difficult to trace the beginning of opinion polls in Hong Kong, a rough survey of existing library records shows that opinion polls as we know them today probably have their beginning in the late 1970s. By early 1980s, records show that Survey Research Hongkong Limited conducted a series of polls for the Commercial Radio on a variety of issues like emigration, district administration, and governorship. In the mid-1980s, the same company also conducted a number of telephone surveys on the future of Hong Kong. A series of seasonal polls gauging the public's confidence in future development was also started, and the "confidence index" survey programme has been conducted regularly up to this date. Nonetheless, judging from both the frequency of opinion polls, and the amount of public attention drawn to them, the age of public opinion polls in Hong Kong really started in 1991, shortly before the first Legco direct election. This was the first metamorphosis.[1]

The 1991 election brought politics to the frontline. Driven by the urge to predict the outcome of the election, the media started to commission

---

[1] However, one must not forget that there are many other kinds of surveys other than opinion polls, examples being television audience surveys, government household surveys, market research surveys, and specific surveys commissioned by government committees and interested parties. These surveys have a long history in Hong Kong, but are not within the scope of this chapter.

opinion surveys as early as July 1991, immediately after electoral campaigns started. Readers, aroused by the new political setting, were eager to pick out information from these polls. Needless to say, candidates who participated in the election, and the political groups they belonged to, were more than eager to exploit the information. The whole society being sensitized and politicized, opinion polls became a tool of the horse-racing game.

In the two months leading to the direct election, practically every major newspaper commissioned some pre-election polls "to test the water". There was suddenly a flood of polls, but the public appeared to be more amused than annoyed. There was very little query on the methodology and reporting of these polls, with perhaps one exception: the exit polls.

Exit polls are in fact large-scale opinion polls conducted outside the polling stations on election days. The main purpose for conducting these polls is to capture the actual voters in order to study their reasons for voting in particular ways. From the media's perspective, exit polls also give early predictions of election results, and this sparked off the "exit poll controversy".[2] The particular event which triggered off the controversy was Asia Television Limited's (ATV) announcement that it intended to broadcast the results of the exit poll to be conducted on 15 September 1991 as they came in (and before the closing of the polling stations). The government was very concerned that such early disclosure of results might lead to chaos, as losing candidates are bound to file complaints against such reports. The government pressed hard for ATV to change the plan, and did not rule out the possibility of banning the programme altogether, but ATV stood firm in the name of freedom of the press. Subsequently, the Secretary for Constitutional Affairs appealed to voters for uncooperation, but promised he would leave the poll uninterfered. As it turned out, both television stations conducted the exit polls as planned and released preliminary findings in the evening news. Such findings, however, were restricted to time trends and reasons of candidate choice, and no information relating to particular candidates was released before the polling stations closed. This was due to self-restraint of the media upon advice offered by the polling organization.

---

[2] See the author's "Exit Polls: Controversies and Methodologies", in *Hong Kong Tried Democracy: The 1991 Elections in Hong Kong*, edited by Lau Siu-kai and Louie Kin-sheun (Hong Kong Institute of Asia-Pacific Studies, The Chinese University of Hong Kong, 1993), pp. 95–113.

Since then, the SSRC has conducted exit polls at every by-election, and exit polls have become a regular feature of media reporting. The exit poll controversy of 1991 has helped to raise the profile of opinion polls.

Throughout the world, opinion polls are most eye-catching during election periods for a very simple reason: information fuels the race, and public information is the best fuel to sensitize the public. How about off-election periods? In Britain and Japan, for example, opinion polls give signals to the opposition party when to move a non-confidence vote to dissolve the parliament. In other countries, the tide of public opinion can force a head of state into accepting, or refusing, certain moves initiated by members of the parliament, else they face rebellion even within their own party. In other words, opinion polls often have important bearings on political elections, even if they are not held in the immediate future.

In Hong Kong, quite on the contrary, direct election of the colonial Governor or the chief executive after 1997 is still beyond the imagination of any average person. Before the 1991 Legco election, direct election only occurred for the relatively unimportant district boards and municipal councils. Hong Kong was in fact a colonial society governed by elites; there was never any strong demand for public participation and, therefore, the collection of public opinion was not relevant until very recently. With the opening up of Legco for public participation, which gave birth to party politics, opinion polls became an important channel for capturing public reaction over particular issues, which in turn helped to modify government policies and party platforms. In a way, opinion polls have gradually become an indirect channel of public participation in Hong Kong. It was with this background that Hong Kong entered its "Patten year", at which time opinion polls underwent their second metamorphosis.

## ☐ Development of Opinion polls in 1992–1993

Chris Patten was designated Governor of Hong Kong in April 1992 to replace David Wilson, and was inaugurated on 9 July. Thereafter, the development of opinion polls entered a new phase.

Starting from April 1992, the author at the SSRC has been tracking Patten's popularity on a 0–100 point scale. The original idea was to measure people's receptiveness of the Governor on a regular basis at two-month intervals, much like the SSRC's tracking polls of political parties and Legco members. However, as it turned out, Patten was such an unprecedented personality in capturing public attention that bimonthly surveys were hardly sufficient to capture the details of the public's reaction. As a result, from October 1992 onwards, his popularity was tracked on a weekly basis. Thus, for the SSRC alone, during Patten's first year in office, over forty weekly polls were conducted to track his popularity alone,[3] however, not every one of these polls was released to the press.

Chris Patten's "contribution" to opinion poll development in Hong Kong was, however, not limited to their number. He also shaped their substance. Never before has any Governor of Hong Kong taken such a stiff stance against China, and never before has any Governor opened up the political arena so much to scrutiny of the public. As a result, about two-thirds of the media polls conducted within the period under review were concerned with political issues, the other one-third was mainly concerned with social issues.

In the following tables, public opinion polls reported in the media between July 1992 and June 1993 were counted and categorized. It should however be noted that the tables are only concerned with opinion polls which targeted the general population over issues of public concern and conducted by independent research organizations. Surveys conducted by government bodies, political parties, pressure groups, district boards, and the like, are not included. Moreover, casual street interviews conducted by reporters themselves are also not included. Very often, such casual surveys have very small sample sizes of only one to two hundred respondents.

Table 1 shows that out of the 120 or so separate polls recorded by the SSRC,[4] over three-quarters were conducted by two polling organizations, namely Hong Kong Polling and Business Research and the SSRC itself.

---

[3] In fact, during the period between 7 to 23 October, Patten's popularity was tracked on a daily basis for over half a month. There were therefore almost sixty data points for Patten's popularity in the year past.

[4] The author would not claim these figures to be exact, because although the SSRC has kept a very extensive record of all media reporting of opinion polls, there are bound to be some which escaped its notice. A request was also sent by the author in mid-July 1993 to all press companies for a listing of their polls, but the response was not satisfactory. Nevertheless, judging from the SSRC's daily routine of checking media polls, the figures reported should be accurate up to at least 90 per cent.

Table 1. Media Polls by Research Organizations, 1992–1993

|  | Percentage |
|---|---|
| Social Sciences Research Centre, HKU | 53.9 |
| Hong Kong Polling and Business Research | 24.3 |
| Asian Commercial Research Ltd. | 7.0 |
| Survey Research Hongkong Ltd. | 6.1 |
| Other academic institutions | 4.3 |
| Others | 4.3 |
| Total | 100.0 |

Source: Social Sciences Research Centre, The University of Hong Kong.

Out of the SSRC's 53.9 per cent share of polls,[5] more than half were published as weekly polls in the *Eastweek Magazine* since its first publication on 29 October 1992. Analysed across the topics of the polls, Table 2 shows that 65 per cent of these polls were concerned with political issues, out of which almost half revolved around Patten's policy speech and reform proposals. Sino-British talks also took up 7 per cent of the overall total.

These figures prove, beyond doubt, that the year under review was a year of politics, as far as opinion polls are concerned. The shift of attention from social issues like emigration, law and order, and general confidence to major political issues, and the resulting sudden flood of political polls, was another metamorphosis after 1991. This phenomenon was probably the result of three interactive factors: (1) the very special personality of Chris Patten; (2) the unprecedented tension generated by Patten's constitutional reform proposals between Britain and China; and (3) the continuing process of politicization after the Legco direct election of 1991. These factors have already been discussed, but would be looked at again along with specific poll findings.

---

[5] This should not be confused with market shares, which would take monetary turnovers into account. Moreover, it should be noted that most of the research companies listed in the table are heavily involved in market research, which generate the bulk of their income, and are usually taken on as private consultancy service. Table 1, therefore, is in no way a reflection of the different size and strength of the research organizations listed.

Table 2.  Media Polls by Broad Topics, 1992–1993

|  | Percentage |  |  |
|---|---|---|---|
| **Political issues** |  |  |  |
| Policy speech | 27.0 |  |  |
| Political figures | 19.1 |  |  |
| Sino-British relations | 7.0 |  |  |
| Other political issues | 12.2 | *Subtotal*: | 65.2 |
| **Non-political issues** |  |  |  |
| Social issues | 26.1 |  |  |
| Other topics | 7.0 | *Subtotal*: | 33.1 |
| **Electoral issues** |  |  |  |
| Exit polls | 1.7 | *Subtotal*: | 1.7 |
| Total |  |  | 100.0 |

Source:   Social Sciences Research Centre, The University of Hong Kong.


## ☐ Highlight of Poll Findings[6]

### *Patten's Popularity*

Table 3 tabulates Patten's popularity rating across 42 tracking polls conducted by the SSRC. Figure 1 presents the change graphically. One major
observation is that there was a steep rise in Patten's popularity in the first
three months after he arrived in Hong Kong. This is understandable because
of the tremendous effort he spent in meeting the media and the public. His
popularity rating culminated at 65.5 points on the day he delivered his
maiden policy speech, fluctuated at that level for five weeks, then plunged
to a record low of 53.3 in mid-December, after severe attacks from China

---

[6] Major findings discussed in this section are mainly derived from the SSRC's
Public Opinion Programme (POP) Polls, for the following reasons:
  1. There is no fear of infringement on others' copyright;
  2. Table 1 shows that POP Polls (excluding tracking polls) constitute 53.9 per
     cent of all polls reported by the media in the year past;
  3. High frequency tracking polls are only conducted by the SSRC;
  4. Methodologies adopted by other research organizations are often unknown
     and unreported.
Readers might like to consult the SSRC poll reports for methodological details, like
sampling method, response rates, and exact wordings of the questions.

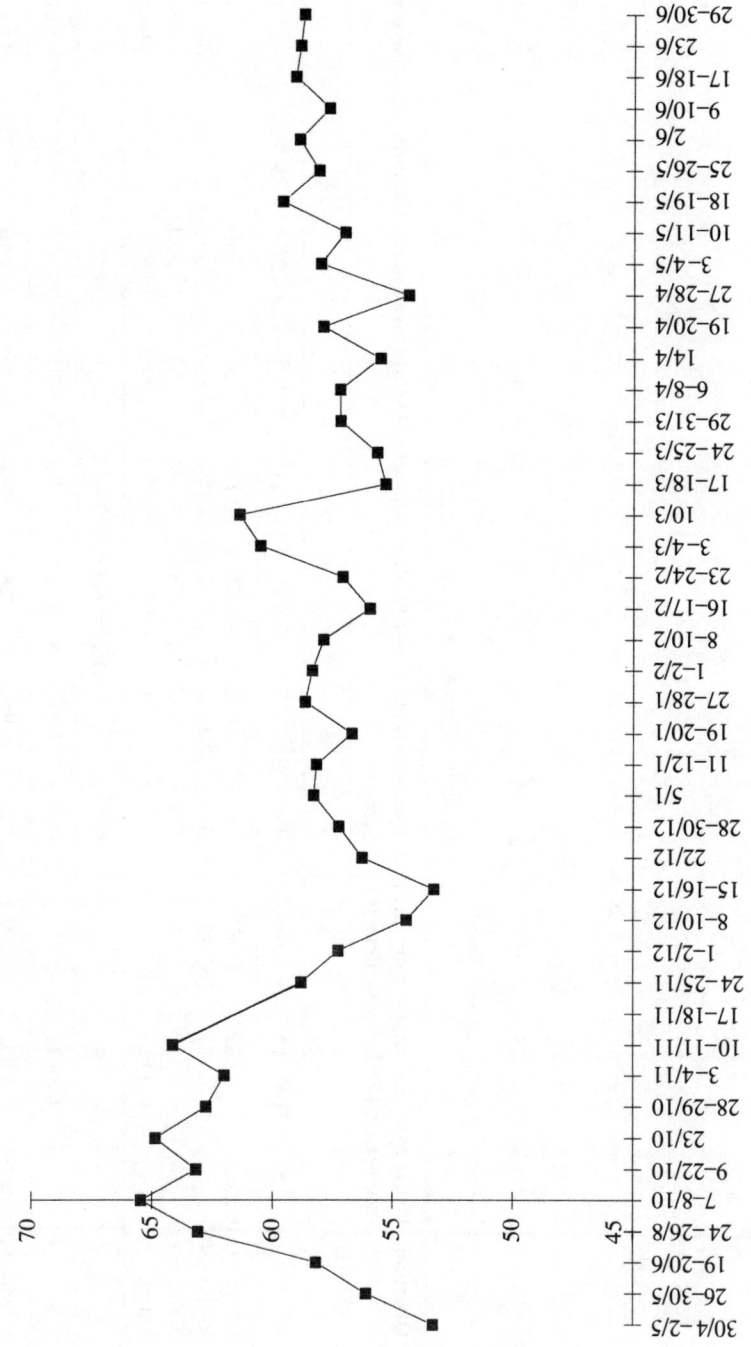

Figure 1. Ratings of Chris Patten

## Table 3. Ratings of Chris Patten

**Question:** Please rate your support for Mr. Patten using a scale of 0–100. Zero indicates absolute no support, 100 indicates absolute support, and 50 being neutral. (in Chinese)

### Date of poll, 1992

|  | 30/4–2/5 | 26–30/5 | 19–20/6 | 24–26/8 | 7–8/10 | 9–22/10 | 23/10 | 28–29/10 | 3–4/11 | 10–11/11 |
|---|---|---|---|---|---|---|---|---|---|---|
| Effective sample | 622 | 1,002 | 574 | 662 | 1,376 | 2,154 | 583 | 719 | 665 | 717 |
| Response % | 67.0% | 61.9% | 64.8% | 68.0% | 72.6% | 84.4% | 75.9% | 71.4% | 71.1% | 70.1% |
| No. of raters | 179 | 338 | 289 | 427 | 1,153 | 1,974 | 535 | 620 | 631 | 610 |
| Rating | 53.3 | 56.1 | 58.2 | 63.1 | 65.5 | 63.2 | 64.8 | 62.8 | 62.0 | 64.1 |

### Date of poll, 1992–93

|  | 17–18/11 | 24–25/11 | 1–2/12 | 8–10/12 | 15–16/12 | 22/12 | 28–30/12 | 5/1 | 11–12/1 | 19–20/1 |
|---|---|---|---|---|---|---|---|---|---|---|
| Effective sample | 1,833 | 749 | 726 | 954 | 728 | 606 | 1,165 | 550 | 731 | 1,017 |
| Response % | 75.5% | 64.3% | 66.8% | 64.8% | 63.3% | 65.9% | 63.9% | 65.4% | 60.2% | 66.1% |
| No. of raters | — | 667 | 659 | 583 | 658 | 538 | 1,114 | 520 | 679 | 626 |
| Rating | — | 58.8 | 57.3 | 54.4 | 53.3 | 56.2 | 57.2 | 58.3 | 58.2 | 56.7 |

Date of poll, 1993

| | 27–28/1 | 1–2/2 | 8–10/2 | 16–17/2 | 23–24/2 | 3–4/3 | 10/3 | 17–18/3 | 24–25/3 | 29–31/3 |
|---|---|---|---|---|---|---|---|---|---|---|
| Effective sample | 552 | 1,144 | 610 | 604 | 631 | 577 | 565 | 939 | 863 | 666 |
| Response % | 64.6% | 66.6% | 60.0% | 63.5% | 62.0% | 64.5% | 68.0% | 63.5% | 61.0% | 65.1% |
| No. of raters | 503 | 1,006 | 559 | 521 | 553 | 488 | 481 | 792 | 863 | 573 |
| Rating | 58.7 | 58.3 | 57.9 | 55.9 | 57.1 | 60.5 | 61.4 | 55.3 | 55.6 | 57.2 |

Date of poll, 1993

| | 6–8/4 | 14/4 | 19–20/4 | 27–28/4 | 3–4/5 | 10–11/5 | 18–19/5 | 25–26/5 | 2/6 | 9–10/6 |
|---|---|---|---|---|---|---|---|---|---|---|
| Effective sample | 746 | 541 | 526 | 622 | 657 | 573 | 568 | 699 | 593 | 509 |
| Response % | 62.5% | 62.6% | 67.9% | 59.6% | 55.4% | 57.7% | 58.5% | 60.5% | 60.8% | 52.7% |
| No. of raters | 632 | 461 | 453 | 453 | 602 | 533 | 527 | 624 | 514 | 468 |
| Rating | 57.2 | 55.5 | 57.9 | 54.4 | 58.0 | 57.0 | 59.6 | 58.1 | 58.9 | 57.7 |

Date of poll, 1993

| | 17–18/6 | 23/6 | 29–30/6 |
|---|---|---|---|
| Effective sample | 574 | 574 | 509 |
| Response % | 54.5% | 54.5% | 55.5% |
| No. of raters | 517 | 473 | 471 |
| Rating | 59.0 | 58.9 | 58.7 |

Source: Compiled by the author.

for his "confrontational" attitude. That plunge was almost as sharp as his rise in the first three months,[7] indicating that the support he has gained from the people was far from solid, probably because he has not spent enough time consolidating that support. Perhaps he has over-read people's outward enthusiasm; perhaps he has miscalculated China's reaction. All in all, he has not understood the Chinese way (both in Hong Kong and China) well enough.

Between late December 1992 and early July 1993, Patten's popularity fluctuated at a level slightly below 60 points, never fully recovering from the November plunge. In mid-March 1993, after deferring the gazetting of his proposals for a few times, he had the opportunity of breaking through the 60-point level, but that opportunity was spoilt when he finally gazetted his proposals on 12 March 1993. His popularity dropped 6 points (or 10 per cent) overnight. The message appeared to be that when Patten took a low profile at the Sino-British dispute, his popularity went up, otherwise it went down. How this reflects Hong Kong people's mentality would be the subject of other academic papers, but whether such phenomenon is desirable or not is a value judgement for everyone to make. To put Patten's rating in perspective, the reader should note that a rating at 60-point level is still far behind the ratings enjoyed by the most popular Legco members. The SSRC's record also shows that the rating of the former Governor, David Wilson, was 64.6 in December 1991 and 64.3 in March 1992. Patten's rating after his one year in office was not particularly high.

### Patten's Policy Speech

As over one-quarter of all media polls published in the year past (excluding the SSRC's unpublished tracking polls) was concerned with people's reaction to Patten's policy speech, his proposals were no doubt the centre of public attention. Tables 4 to 6 summarize the result of the SSRC's three tracking questions concerning Patten's proposals.

Question 1 is a weekly tracking question on people's general satisfaction over Patten's policy speech, while Questions 2 and 3 are biweekly tracking questions on people's support of his constitutional proposals in

---

[7] The reader is cautioned that the scale of the time axis before and after the policy speech are different, but this does not affect the general observation.

particular. From Figure 2, it can be seen that answers to the three questions are very consistent, and the structure of opinion is very stable.[8] From Question 1, it can be seen that the most favourable replies (over 40 per cent satisfaction) occurred in October, then dropped to below 30 per cent in late December, and then fluctuated at that level from mid-January to July.

On the level of support for Patten's constitutional reforms, the trend of change was very similar to that for his policy speech. Naturally, the fluctuations of answers to Questions 2 and 3 are remarkably consistent. Question 2 asked respondents to rate their support for Patten's reform proposals on a five-point scale, and the level of support fluctuated around 35 per cent. Question 3 further pressed the respondents to say "yes" or "no" to the proposals, and the result was that the "yes" level became 40 per cent. Looking at the raw data, it can be seen that normally 40 to 50 per cent of the respondents hesitated to give an opinion. The conclusion seems to be that although Patten's proposals have a regular support ratio of about 2:1, he could not claim majority support because of the existence of a silent majority. A corollary of this finding is that Patten is not in safe waters, because the tide could easily turn against him when (some of) the silent majority is swayed.

## Ratings of Legco Members

With increasing politicization after the 1991 direct election, members of Legco were placed under unprecedented surveillance of the general public. Since July 1991, the SSRC has been keeping constant watch over the popularity of various Legco members by measuring people's recognition of, and support for, them on a 0–100 point scale. Table 7 summarizes the findings obtained during the year under review.

The Legco members included in Table 7 are in fact the top ten members in terms of recognition by the public, ranked by the degree of support expressed by the public. It can be seen that the list is very stable across the

---

[8] Questions 2 and 3 were tracked on a regular basis from mid-November 1992, instead of from Day 1 of the policy speech, because the issue of political reform only began to overshadow other issues in Patten's policy speech as time went by. The two questions were tracked biweekly in order to conserve resources.

Table 4. General Satisfaction of Hong Kong People over Chris Patten's Policy Speech

**Question 1: How satisfied are you with the Governor's policy speech? (in Chinese)**

Date of poll, 1992

| Raw data | 7–8 Oct. | 9–22 Oct. | 23 Oct. | 28–29 Oct. | 3–4 Nov. | 10–11 Nov. | 17–18 Nov. | 24–25 Nov. | 1–2 Dec. | 8–10 Dec. | 15–16 Dec. | 22–23 Dec. | 28–30 Dec. |
|---|---|---|---|---|---|---|---|---|---|---|---|---|---|
| Very satisfied | 8.1% | 4.7% | 6.2% | 4.7% | 4.8% | 6.3% | 6.6% | 5.6% | 3.8% | 4.8% | 3.4% | 3.6% | 4.9% |
| Just satisfied | 25.4% | 36.8% | 29.8% | 29.2% | 36.9% | 33.5% | 30.5% | 30.2% | 30.9% | 28.6% | 27.1% | 24.9% | 28.6% |
| Neutral | 6.2% | 10.3% | 10.8% | 10.9% | 12.3% | 6.0% | 12.9% | 12.9% | 14.7% | 14.8% | 9.6% | 13.2% | 14.8% |
| Just dissatisfied | 2.7% | 2.7% | 4.8% | 10.1% | 6.8% | 5.7% | 7.1% | 7.4% | 10.1% | 12.6% | 13.0% | 13.9% | 12.6% |
| Very dissatisfied | 1.2% | 0.9% | 2.4% | 3.2% | 2.9% | 3.1% | 4.6% | 3.3% | 4.4% | 5.3% | 7.8% | 5.3% | 5.1% |
| Don't know | 56.4% | 44.5% | 46.0% | 42.0% | 36.3% | 45.44% | 39.3% | 40.4% | 36.0% | 33.9% | 39.1% | 39.1% | 34.0% |
| Total | 100.0% | 100.0% | 100.0% | 100.0% | 100.0% | 100.0% | 100.0% | 100.0% | 100.0% | 100.0% | 100.0% | 100.0% | 100.0% |

Date of poll, 1993

| Raw data | 5 Jan. | 11–12 Jan. | 19–20 Jan. | 27–28 Jan. | 1–2 Feb. | 8–10 Feb. | 16–17 Feb. | 23–24 Feb. | 3–4 Mar. | 10 Mar. | 17–18 Mar. | 24–25 Mar. | 29–31 Mar. |
|---|---|---|---|---|---|---|---|---|---|---|---|---|---|
| Very satisfied | 4.2% | 4.5% | 5.9% | 2.8% | 3.5% | 3.5% | 3.6% | 3.1% | 2.4% | 3.0% | 3.8% | 4.4% | 4.1% |
| Just satisfied | 35.7% | 21.9% | 24.0% | 30.4% | 27.6% | 23.8% | 23.2% | 24.2% | 27.7% | 29.2% | 23.4% | 21.7% | 22.9% |
| Neutral | 14.4% | 11.1% | 9.6% | 14.0% | 10.0% | 9.8% | 10.0% | 10.1% | 9.2% | 8.3% | 7.2% | 7.3% | 8.9% |
| Just dissatisfied | 12.8% | 9.4% | 10.3% | 8.5% | 9.5% | 8.4% | 10.1% | 7.7% | 6.9% | 7.6% | 10.4% | 8.8% | 10.4% |
| Very dissatisfied | 4.2% | 4.5% | 4.8% | 2.6% | 3.6% | 3.8% | 5.2% | 3.1% | 1.5% | 2.1% | 5.1% | 5.0% | 3.8% |
| Don't know | 28.7% | 48.5% | 45.4% | 41.7% | 45.9% | 50.6% | 47.9% | 51.8% | 52.3% | 49.8% | 50.1% | 52.7% | 49.9% |
| Total | 100.0% | 100.0% | 100.0% | 100.0% | 100.0% | 100.0% | 100.0% | 100.0% | 100.0% | 100.0% | 100.0% | 100.0% | 100.0% |

Date of poll, 1993

| Raw data | 6–8 Apr. | 14 Apr. | 19–20 Apr. | 27–28 Apr. | 3–4 May | 10–11 May | 18–19 May | 25–26 May | 2 June | 9–10 June | 17–18 June | 23 June | 29–30 June |
|---|---|---|---|---|---|---|---|---|---|---|---|---|---|
| Very satisfied | 5.9% | 2.7% | 2.4% | 3.2% | 2.9% | 1.5% | 2.4% | 3.1% | 4.4% | 5.2% | 3.3% | 4.2% | 4.7% |
| Just satisfied | 23.5% | 25.0% | 27.7% | 23.6% | 27.2% | 27.8% | 25.1% | 22.1% | 23.5% | 25.0% | 23.2% | 20.3% | 23.1% |
| Neutral | 6.7% | 9.3% | 14.2% | 13.6% | 9.8% | 13.8% | 8.2% | 10.3% | 9.5% | 6.7% | 7.3% | 4.7% | 6.7% |
| Just dissatisfied | 8.1% | 11.6% | 8.8% | 10.4% | 7.4% | 9.5% | 5.6% | 5.9% | 5.4% | 6.6% | 7.0% | 9.0% | 6.5% |
| Very dissatisfied | 4.5% | 2.8% | 2.6% | 2.1% | 1.5% | 1.4% | 2.4% | 2.2% | 3.0% | 4.4% | 1.9% | 2.6% | 3.3% |
| Don't know | 51.2% | 48.7% | 44.3% | 47.2% | 51.2% | 46.0% | 56.4% | 56.4% | 54.3% | 52.0% | 57.4% | 59.3% | 55.8% |
| Total | 100.0% | 100.0% | 100.0% | 100.0% | 100.0% | 100.0% | 100.0% | 100.0% | 100.0% | 100.0% | 100.0% | 100.0% | 100.0% |

Note:   Please refer to Table 3 for sample size and response rates of the polls. Add-up discrepancies are due to rounding.

Source:  Compiled by the author.

## Table 5. Hong Kong People's Degree of Support for Chris Patten's Reform Proposals

### Question 2: Do you support or oppose Mr. Patten's reform proposals? (in Chinese)

| | Date of poll, 1992–93 | | | | | | | |
|---|---|---|---|---|---|---|---|---|
| | 8–10/12 | 15–16/12 | 28–30/12 | 11–12/1 | 27–28/1 | 8–10/2 | 23–24/2 | 10/3 |
| Support very much | 10.4% | 8.7% | 8.0% | 6.7% | 7.2% | 7.0% | 6.0% | 7.8% |
| Just support | 25.5% | 27.7% | 28.0% | 22.7% | 31.3% | 26.2% | 27.3% | 30.0% |
| Neutral | 16.5% | 11.1% | 15.1% | 11.8% | 14.7% | 16.7% | 12.3% | 10.8% |
| Just oppose | 14.1% | 16.7% | 13.5% | 12.0% | 12.0% | 11.5% | 13.0% | 11.7% |
| Oppose very much | 6.8% | 7.7% | 6.5% | 5.9% | 2.4% | 4.1% | 3.9% | 3.2% |
| Don't know | 26.7% | 28.2% | 28.9% | 40.9% | 32.4% | 34.5% | 37.5% | 36.6% |
| Total | 100.0% | 100.0% | 100.0% | 100.0% | 100.0% | 100.0% | 100.0% | 100.0% |

| | Date of poll, 1993 | | | | | | | |
|---|---|---|---|---|---|---|---|---|
| | 24–25/3 | 6–8/4 | 19–20/4 | 3–4/5 | 18–19/5 | 2/6 | 17–18/6 | 29–30/6 |
| Support very much | 6.7% | 7.4% | 4.2% | 5.0% | 4.0% | 11.3% | 9.9% | 9.8% |
| Just support | 19.9% | 27.7% | 28.8% | 32.3% | 25.8% | 26.0% | 27.1% | 21.6% |
| Neutral | 14.6% | 8.4% | 15.7% | 11.5% | 11.9% | 8.7% | 9.1% | 8.1% |
| Just oppose | 13.1% | 10.7% | 13.8% | 11.0% | 9.4% | 8.8% | 10.1% | 8.6% |
| Oppose very much | 5.2% | 6.2% | 2.1% | 2.1% | 2.0% | 3.5% | 3.3% | 3.7% |
| Don't know | 40.5% | 39.6% | 35.4% | 38.1% | 46.9% | 41.8% | 40.6% | 48.1% |
| Total | 100.0% | 100.0% | 100.0% | 100.0% | 100.0% | 100.0% | 100.0% | 100.0% |

Note: Please refer to Table 3 for sample size and response rates of the polls. Add-up discrepancies are due to rounding.

Table 6. Hong Kong People's Attitude towards a Referendum on Chris Patten's Reform Proposals

**Question 3: Were there a referendum on Mr. Patten's political reform proposals, would you vote for or against them? (in Chinese)**

Date of poll, 1992–93

|  | 17–18/11 | 1–2/12 | 8–10/12 | 15–16/12 | 28–30/12 | 11–12/1 | 27–28/1 | 8–10/2 | 23–24/2 |
|---|---|---|---|---|---|---|---|---|---|
| For | 43.0% | 38.5% | 47.0% | 39.4% | 42.2% | 36.3% | 43.4% | 41.9% | 39.6% |
| Against | 17.1% | 23.7% | 24.7% | 29.9% | 26.9% | 25.3% | 23.0% | 23.4% | 20.9% |
| Abstain | 39.9% | 37.8% | 28.3% | 30.7% | 31.0% | 38.4% | 33.6% | 34.7% | 39.5% |
| Total | 100.0% | 100.0% | 100.0% | 100.0% | 100.0% | 100.0% | 100.0% | 100.0% | 100.0% |

Date of poll, 1993

|  | 10/3 | 24–25/3 | 6–8/4 | 19–20/4 | 3–4/5 | 18–19/5 | 2/6 | 17–18/6 | 29–30/6 |
|---|---|---|---|---|---|---|---|---|---|
| For | 43.8% | 30.3% | 40.9% | 34.8% | 46.0% | 37.3% | 41.6% | 44.6% | 40.4% |
| Against | 19.3% | 20.5% | 19.9% | 18.6% | 16.9% | 15.7% | 17.4% | 17.0% | 18.8% |
| Abstain | 36.9% | 48.7% | 39.2% | 46.6% | 37.1% | 47.1% | 41.0% | 38.3% | 40.8% |
| Total | 100.0% | 99.5% | 100.0% | 100.0% | 100.0% | 100.0% | 100.0% | 100.0% | 100.0% |

Note: Please refer to Table 3 for sample size and response rates of the polls. Add-up discrepancies are due to rounding.

Figure 2. Policy Speech and Political Reform Proposals Tracking Questions

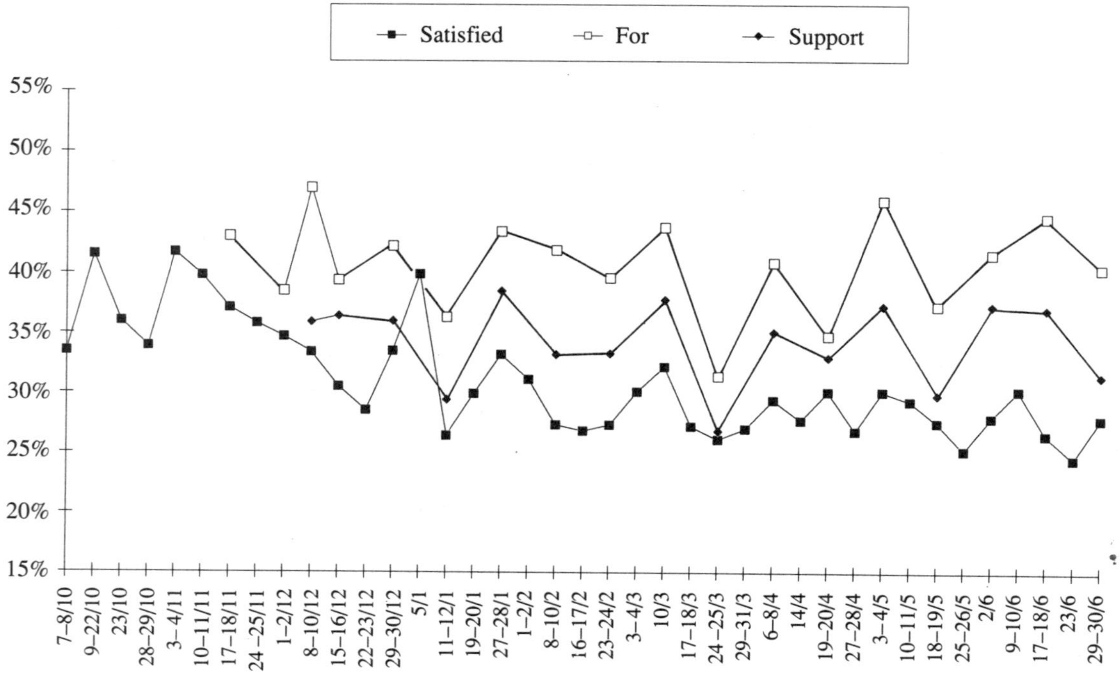

## Table 7. Popularity Ratings of Top Ten Legco Members

| | | Support | Std. Err. | Total sample | Raters | Recognition |
|---|---|---|---|---|---|---|
| **POP POLL 17–18 JUNE 1993** | | | | | | |
| 杜葉錫恩 | Elsie Tu | 70.3 | 0.8 | 574 | 428 | 74.6% |
| 劉慧卿 | Emily Lau | 67.4 | 0.9 | 574 | 469 | 81.7% |
| 李柱銘 | Martin Lee | 65.0 | 1.0 | 574 | 506 | 88.2% |
| 劉千石 | Lau Chin-shek | 64.0 | 0.9 | 574 | 462 | 80.5% |
| 楊森 | Yeung Sum | 62.4 | 1.0 | 574 | 372 | 64.8% |
| 司徒華 | Szeto Wah | 61.3 | 1.0 | 574 | 507 | 88.3% |
| 李鵬飛 | Allen Lee | 60.1 | 0.9 | 574 | 493 | 85.9% |
| 黃宏發 | Andrew Wong | 60.0 | 0.8 | 574 | 413 | 72.0% |
| 周梁淑怡 | Selina Chow | 56.6 | 0.8 | 574 | 449 | 78.2% |
| 劉皇發 | Lau Wong-fat | 54.5 | 1.0 | 574 | 388 | 67.6% |
| **POP POLL 15–16 APR. 1993** | | | | | | |
| 杜葉錫恩 | Elsie Tu | 66.9 | 1.0 | 548 | 408 | 74.5% |
| 劉慧卿 | Emily Lau | 65.8 | 1.1 | 548 | 413 | 75.4% |
| 李柱銘 | Martin Lee | 63.6 | 1.1 | 548 | 457 | 83.4% |
| 劉千石 | Lau Chin-shek | 62.8 | 1.0 | 548 | 410 | 74.8% |
| 楊森 | Yeung Sum | 60.7 | 1.1 | 548 | 340 | 62.0% |
| 司徒華 | Szeto Wah | 59.6 | 1.1 | 548 | 452 | 82.5% |
| 馮檢基 | Fung Kin-kee | 59.2 | 1.0 | 548 | 359 | 65.5% |
| 黃宏發 | Andrew Wong | 56.9 | 1.0 | 548 | 385 | 70.3% |
| 李鵬飛 | Allen Lee | 52.6 | 1.1 | 548 | 434 | 79.2% |
| 周梁淑怡 | Selina Chow | 51.1 | 1.0 | 548 | 424 | 77.4% |
| **POP POLL 8–10 FEB. 1993** | | | | | | |
| 杜葉錫恩 | Elsie Tu | 65.7 | 0.8 | 610 | 502 | 82.3% |
| 劉慧卿 | Emily Lau | 62.0 | 0.9 | 610 | 479 | 78.5% |
| 劉千石 | Lau Chin-shek | 60.8 | 0.9 | 610 | 505 | 82.8% |
| 馮檢基 | Fung Kin-kee | 58.7 | 0.8 | 610 | 406 | 66.6% |
| 李柱銘 | Martin Lee | 58.1 | 1.0 | 610 | 545 | 89.3% |
| 司徒華 | Szeto Wah | 56.2 | 1.0 | 610 | 537 | 88.0% |
| 黃宏發 | Andrew Wong | 56.0 | 0.8 | 610 | 455 | 74.6% |
| 譚耀宗 | Tam Yiu-chung | 54.4 | 0.9 | 610 | 403 | 66.1% |
| 周梁淑怡 | Selina Chow | 54.0 | 0.8 | 610 | 486 | 79.7% |
| 李鵬飛 | Allen Lee | 52.3 | 0.8 | 610 | 521 | 85.4% |
| **POP POLL 3–4 NOV. 1992** | | | | | | |
| 杜葉錫恩 | Elsie Tu | 65.7 | 0.7 | 665 | 485 | 72.9% |
| 劉慧卿 | Emily Lau | 62.8 | 0.8 | 665 | 484 | 72.8% |
| 劉千石 | Lau Chin-shek | 58.7 | 0.8 | 665 | 506 | 76.1% |
| 李柱銘 | Martin Lee | 58.7 | 0.8 | 665 | 564 | 84.8% |
| 馮檢基 | Fung Kin-kee | 58.4 | 0.8 | 665 | 409 | 61.5% |
| 黃宏發 | Andrew Wong | 55.4 | 0.7 | 665 | 465 | 69.9% |
| 周梁淑怡 | Selina Chow | 54.6 | 0.8 | 665 | 508 | 76.4% |
| 司徒華 | Szeto Wah | 54.4 | 0.9 | 665 | 550 | 82.7% |
| 張鑑泉 | Stephen Cheong | 51.5 | 0.8 | 665 | 448 | 67.4% |
| 李鵬飛 | Allen Lee | 50.3 | 0.8 | 665 | 547 | 82.3% |

Remarks: Support = 支持度     Recognition = 認識度

Note:    All data are weighted by sex of valid raters.
Source:  Social Sciences Research Centre, The University of Hong Kong.

four surveys, especially for the first four positions. In terms of recognition, Szeto Wah, Martin Lee, and Allen Lee are the most popular councillors, with recognition rates[9] above 80 per cent. Lau Chin-shek, Emily Lau, Selina Chow, Elsie Tu and Andrew Wong occupy the second tier, with recognition rates of over 70 per cent. In terms of support, however, Elsie Tu is indisputably at the top of the list, followed somewhat closely by Emily Lau. Martin Lee and Lau Chin-shek are slightly behind. The fact that both Elsie Tu and Emily Lau are female councillors without party background seems to point out that there is still plenty of room for non-affiliation and female politicians in Hong Kong. The two councillors are of very different personality and political outlook; the fact that they continued to occupy the top two positions of the list throughout the year shows that Hong Kong people readily accept divergent views over political issues.

### *Ratings of Political Groups*

The year 1992–1993 was a period of intensive development on the part of political parties. Strictly speaking, since there is no general election in Hong Kong, and no political group could ever come to power, political parties simply could not exist. Nevertheless, with the opening up of Legco to public participation, in the form of direct and indirect elections, many pressure groups which existed in Hong Kong before September 1991 have claimed to change themselves into political parties. The most notable example was the Cooperative Resources Centre, which turned itself into the Liberal Party in June 1993. Other groups, like the Meeting Point, the Democratic Alliance for Betterment of Hong Kong, have all proclaimed their intention to become political parties. "Political party" is thus used in a very loose sense to refer to any organized group which aims to exert its influence through its members' coming to office in various councils. Although this definition is far from satisfactory, the term has already found its footage in the media and people's daily usage. For this reason, the SSRC has deliberately not made a distinction between political parties and political groups in its studies.

---

[9] "Recognition" is used here to mean more than mere identification. A subject may know the existence of a group, but could not give a meaningful score to that group because of unfamiliarity. That person is taken not to have recognized the group in this instance.

Table 8 summarizes the result of the SSRC's regular study of the various political groups in the year past. It is an abstraction from a vast amount of data on party development collected since 1991. From these figures, it can be seen that people's recognition of political parties fall far behind that of individual councillors (compared with Table 7). Even when we concentrate on the five most well-known political groups, not all of them received a recognition rate of over 50 per cent as late as June 1993.[10] Both in terms of recognition and support, the United Democrats of Hong Kong has topped the list, while the Liberal Party trails behind in terms of recognition. Other groups are not readily recognizable. In terms of popular support, it seems that the Hong Kong Association for Democracy and People's Livelihood and Meeting Point have often occupied the second and third positions, but their degree of recognition seldom reached the benchmark of 50 per cent. All in all, however, the list of the top five political groups appears to be very stable over the year, and the difference between people's support for each of them has been relatively small. These point to the conclusion that party development in Hong Kong is still at a infancy stage. Whether this infant would ever grow into an adult or not is another matter.

## ☐ Conclusion: The Way Ahead

After the "metamorphoses" of public opinion polls in 1991 due to the maiden Legco direct election, and then 1992 due to the arrival of Chris Patten, opinion polls have become a regular feature of daily life. Whenever crises arise, people wait for polls, and whenever there are elections, people want predictions. Opinion polls have in fact undergone a silent revolution in the two years past.

In 1991, the emergence of polls was mainly stimulated by the crave for information related to the Legco elections. They produced snapshots of people's mentality over various social and political issues. From 1992, tracking polls emerged to display trends rather than frozen pictures. In the

---

[10] According to the SSRC's standard, support ratings of any political figures or groups with recognition rate below 50 per cent are not worth comparing. They could at best be used as points of interest. Nevertheless, to illustrate the development (or underdevelopment, to be exact) of political parties in Hong Kong, such figures are still included in Table 8.

## Table 8. Popularity Ratings of Top Five Political Groups

|  |  | Support | Std. Err. | Total sample | Raters | Recognition |
|---|---|---|---|---|---|---|
| **POP POLL 29–30 JUNE 1993** | | | | | | |
| 港同盟 | UDHK | 56.1 | 1.1 | 509 | 411 | 80.7% |
| 民協 | ADPL | 53.9 | 1.2 | 509 | 212 | 41.7% |
| 匯點 | MP | 53.4 | 1.1 | 509 | 266 | 52.3% |
| 自由黨 | LP | 51.0 | 1.1 | 509 | 330 | 64.8% |
| 民建聯 | DABHK | 46.2 | 1.3 | 509 | 263 | 51.7% |
| **POP POLL 27–28 APR. 1993** | | | | | | |
| 港同盟 | UDHK | 55.0 | 0.8 | 622 | 444 | 71.4% |
| 工聯會 | FTU | 51.2 | 0.9 | 622 | 339 | 54.5% |
| 匯點 | MP | 50.0 | 0.8 | 622 | 294 | 47.3% |
| 啓聯 | CRC | 49.5 | 0.8 | 622 | 415 | 66.7% |
| 民建聯 | DABHK | 47.3 | 0.9 | 622 | 278 | 44.7% |
| **POP POLL 23–24 FEB. 1993** | | | | | | |
| 港同盟 | UDHK | 55.8 | 0.9 | 631 | 491 | 77.8% |
| 民協 | ADPL | 51.4 | 1.1 | 631 | 269 | 42.6% |
| 匯點 | MP | 51.2 | 1.1 | 631 | 305 | 48.3% |
| 啓聯 | CRC | 49.6 | 0.9 | 631 | 442 | 70.0% |
| 民建聯 | DABHK | 45.9 | 1.2 | 631 | 289 | 45.8% |
| **POP POLL 24–25 NOV. 1992** | | | | | | |
| 港同盟 | UDHK | 54.0 | 0.9 | 681 | 503 | 73.9% |
| 民協 | ADPL | 50.9 | 1.2 | 681 | 218 | 32.0% |
| 匯點 | MP | 50.8 | 1.0 | 681 | 285 | 41.9% |
| 啓聯 | CRC | 48.3 | 0.8 | 681 | 448 | 65.8% |
| 民建聯 | DABHK | 43.4 | 1.4 | 681 | 215 | 31.6% |

Remarks:      Support      = 支持度
              Recognition = 認識度

Abbreviations: ADPL    = HK Assn. for Democracy & People's Livelihood
               CRC     = Cooperative Resources Centre
               DABHK   = Democratic Alliance for Betterment of Hong Kong
               FTU     = HK Federation of Trade Union
               LP      = Liberal Party
               MP      = Meeting Point
               UDHK    = United Democrats of Hong Kong

Note:     All data are weighted by sex of valid raters.

Source:   Social Sciences Research Centre, The University of Hong Kong.

years ahead, it can be predicted that more and more tracking polls would appear, and more effort would be spent on studying the hidden factors, by many more academics.[11]

As society becomes more open, and the voice of the people needs more often to be heard, opinion polls will have an increasingly important role to play. In terms of historical development, compared to most countries, opinion polls in Hong Kong have developed overnight and they have flourished. This, of course, is an advantage for latecomers, which early-players could only envy. Nevertheless, one must not forget that as newcomers, we are prone to many defects, both in the methodology and reporting of opinion polls. There is as yet no professional body of pollsters, and no professional standard for conducting and reporting polls. These, of course, take time to develop, and there is no hurry for 1997. The most important point to bear in mind, however, is that we should never let poll findings dictate our development, because poll findings, as much as data obtained from any social studies, could at best represent objective reflections of people's subjective feelings. They tell you what is, but not what ought to be.

---

[11] The SSRC's plan is to set up a data archive to collect and document all POP Polls, and make the datasets available to all academic researchers in Hong Kong. When that happens, it is anticipated that research activities across institutions would be greatly stimulated, and people would have a much better understanding of our society during the period of political transition.

# 22

# China's Investment in Hong Kong

| George Shen |

## ☐ Introduction

Ever since the launching of China's open door policy in the late 1970s, there has been a lot of capital flow into China from the outside world, particularly from Hong Kong. At the same time, China also started to invest overseas, especially in Hong Kong.

China's investment overseas has a long history. In the case of Hong Kong, many Chinese enterprises, such as the Bank of China, China Merchants Steam Navigation Company, China Travel Service, China National Aviation Corporation, the Commercial Press, China Products Company, etc. which existed in the pre-1949 or even pre-World War II days, are still operating in Hong Kong. Some of them have been reorganized since 1949 and are now operating under new names. Today, it is estimated that there are over 1,000 China-funded enterprises operating in Hong Kong, covering a wide range of economic activities.

Till the late 1970s, China's business interests in Hong Kong were represented mainly by four large conglomerates, namely the Bank of China and its 12 sister banks, China Resources Company, China Merchants Company and China Travel Service. Except for the Bank of China Group, the other three were all reorganized into holding companies incorporated in Hong Kong. In addition, there were many small enterprises engaged in the selling of Chinese products, including daily necessities and various types of services provided for local businesses and residents.

---

George Shen is Editor-in-chief, *Hong Kong Economic Journal.*

Since China's economic reform, many companies which are wholly or partially owned by central (mostly ministerial), provincial and municipal/local authorities have been established in Hong Kong. While some of them are listed on the Stock Exchange of Hong Kong and are readily visible, the activities of many of these enterprises are only vaguely known to the local business community. Also, China has invested quite extensively in the local equity market in recent years. But as stocks and shares change hands freely on the market, and many such transactions may be conducted through proxies, it is virtually impossible to have even a rough estimate of the total amount involved.

In 1991, it was estimated that China's investment in Hong Kong had reached US$10 billion, or $78 billion in Hong Kong dollars. It was also reported in local newspapers that between December 1990 and May 1993, China had spent about $17 billion to acquire listed companies in Hong Kong. Since May 1993, several acquisition deals have been reported, some of them nearing completion. It is estimated that by early June, China's investment in Hong Kong's listed companies, including the holding of shares through subsidiaries, amounts to about $57 billion. This figure, plus property holdings estimated at more than $13 billion, puts China's investment in Hong Kong at over $70 billion, not including many unlisted companies and over $530 billion worth of bank assets.

In late 1992, it was announced that nine state enterprises in China would seek to be listed on the Stock Exchange of Hong Kong and were having their books audited by international auditing firms to meet listing requirements. Since these enterprises are located in China, their listing in Hong Kong would provide channels for Hong Kong capital to invest in China rather than for China to invest in Hong Kong.

Apart from seeking listing on the Stock Exchange, Chinese enterprises started, in early 1993, to take over local listed companies to acquire *de facto* listed status. This started in October 1992 when the majority share of Tung Wing Steel Holdings Limited was acquired by Shougang (Holdings), the largest steel conglomerate in China. In early 1993, the market was abound with takeover rumours which made the stock market very volatile as speculators snatched at shares of potential takeover targets. The fact that China-based companies could become listed companies in Hong Kong "through the back door" at a much quicker pace than the nine Chinese state corporations which had been preparing themselves for listing on the Stock Exchange of Hong Kong through proper procedures and channels has since caused some concern both in China and in Hong Kong. However, as long as capital movements from China and share acquisition procedures in Hong Kong adhere to laws and regulations, such moves should be welcomed.

It may be said that China's investment in Hong Kong took a new turn in recent years, especially during the year under review, when three significant changes took place. First, China became the largest investor in Hong Kong, overtaking Britain, the United States and Japan, and her share is likely to increase further as the economies of China and Hong Kong become more interdependent. Second, China started to utilize the local equity and capital markets to avail herself of funds necessary for economic development. Third, Chinese enterprises in Hong Kong became "foreign" companies which could go to China to invest as a foreign entity. While these changes have resulted in a vigorous interflow of capital between China and Hong Kong, they have also made Hong Kong more indispensable to China as a source of profit as well as a channel of foreign capital supply. In the meantime, the increasing number of Chinese enterprises operating in Hong Kong and their dealings with the local business community have exposed them to modern business practices and know-how, the transfer and assimilation of which are of significant value to China.

## ☐ Sectoral Review

China-funded companies in Hong Kong are engaged in a wide range of activities, covering almost all walks of life. A typical Hong Kong resident lives in a building built by materials imported from China or supplied by China-funded companies, wears clothes made partly or wholly in China, eats food supplied by farmers across the border who produce the food under contract with Hong Kong-based Chinese companies, invests in the stock market by buying some China-related shares, rides in a city bus operated by a company with Chinese capital and fuelled by Chinese petroleum, deposits money in one of the Bank of China Group banks, reads a China-run newspaper, goes to a movie produced in China and distributed by a China-funded local distributor, and takes a holiday by utilizing the services of the China Travel Service or flies Cathay Pacific airlines. China's investment has virtually become part and parcel of Hong Kong's daily life. In terms of economic activities, China's investment is present in every sector of Hong Kong's economy.

The best way to assess the scope of China's investment in Hong Kong is to look at the activities of the Hong Kong Chinese Enterprises Association, which was incorporated in Hong Kong on 8 March 1991. The

Association's establishment was initiated by the chief executives of the Hong Kong–Macau Regional Office of the Bank of China, China Resources (Holdings) Limited, China Merchants Holdings Company (CMH) and China Travel Service (Holdings) Hong Kong Limited, and seconded by several other China-funded enterprises in Hong Kong, such as Guangdong Enterprises (Holdings) Limited, Fujian Enterprises (Holdings) Limited, China Everbright Holdings Company, China International Trust and Investment Hong Kong (Holdings) Limited, which is the Hong Kong arm of the Beijing-based China International Trust and Investment Corporation (CITIC) and hence usually referred to as CITIC Hong Kong, Shanghai Industrial Investment Company, China Overseas Building Development Company, Scriven Trading Limited, etc. At the end of 1991, membership stood at 952, including 922 company members and 30 individual members. Today, it is estimated that members of the Association employ over 100,000 people, among whom about 10 per cent are assigned by their principals in China to work in Hong Kong.

According to the Association, its members are engaged in the following types of business:

| | |
|---|---|
| Manufacturing and related investment | 11.5% |
| Construction and real estate management | 6.9% |
| Import and export | 38.8% |
| Tourism | 3.5% |
| Transportation and storage | 8.5% |
| Finance and insurance | 10.4% |

The above businesses embrace about 80 per cent of the Association members' activities. The remaining members are so-called comprehensive companies operated by central or local governments. These are holding companies or non-business administrative organizations.

It is difficult to have an accurate account of the total investment involved in the above types of business, for a number of reasons. First, only a small percentage of the Chinese enterprises are public companies and hence it is next to impossible to know about the capital of the companies operating in Hong Kong. Second, even in the case of public companies listed on the Stock Exchange of Hong Kong, many of the major shareholders, though they came from China, have now become local residents. Third, there are companies which are not members of the Association but may actually be China-funded, though officially they may not be so. Last but not least, it is not necessary to hold a majority stake in a public company to be the controlling shareholder, and China may either have invested in or have control over many large companies by local proxies. With such limitations, the following paragraphs only serve as a general description of China-funded enterprises in Hong Kong, rather than a statistical survey of the amount of capital invested by China in Hong Kong.

## *Manufacturing and Related Investment*

One of the most visible manufacturing companies in Hong Kong with Chinese capital are members of the Conic Group, engaged mainly in the manufacture of electronic products. Established in 1965, this local enterprise was first acquired by the Bank of China and China Resources, later by the China Aerospace Industry Corporation. Other China Resources-related companies include the Hong Kong Toy Centre International Limited and M.C. Packaging (Hong Kong) Limited. More recently, as already mentioned, Tung Wing Steel has been acquired by Shougang of China.

There are long-time establishments in the manufacturing sector, such as the Tien Chu Ve-Tsin Chemical Industries (H.K.) Limited, which originated in Shanghai in the 1930s as the largest producer of monosodium glutamate in China. It now comes under the aegis of Shanghai Industrial Investment Company. Tien Chu has several subsidiaries engaged in the manufacture of chemicals, dyestuff, etc. Another old manufacturing house under Shanghai Industrial Investment is the Nanyang Brothers Tobacco Company, one of the largest tobacco companies formerly owned by overseas Chinese and Hong Kong merchants.

Many other local manufacturing concerns have Chinese interest in one way or another. Since they are not public companies, it is difficult to go into detail.

The Sil-Metropole Organization Limited, a motion pictures production and distribution company, could be counted as one of the few enjoying considerable popularity. It consists of former left-wing motion picture producing companies in Hong Kong, including Great Wall, Feng Huang and others, plus Hong Kong-based distributor of Chinese movies, Southern Film Company.

Another prominent group consists of well-established book publishers, including the Commercial Press, Chung Hwa Book Store, Joint Publishing (Hong Kong) Company. They also operate retail outlets in Hong Kong.

Then there are the pro-China printed media, namely *Ta Kung Pao*, *Wen Wei Po*, the *Hong Kong Commercial Daily* and the weekly *Economic Information and Agency*. News agencies include the editorial operations of Xinhua News Agency, China News Service (Hong Kong Branch) and Hong Kong China News Agency.

There are also many prominent establishments in the retail trade, many of them subsidiaries of the China Resources Group. For example, China Arts and Crafts is well-known for its antiques, precious stones, handicrafts and so on and also operates department stores. The China Products Company (H.K.) is an old establishment dating from pre-war days, and there are many department stores formerly selling mainly Chinese products but in recent years have included non-Chinese goods on their shelves.

Last but not least, Southeast Economic Information Centre, a research organization, has been quite active in Hong Kong for some time. It is headed by Yang Zhenhan, brother of Nobel Laureate Yang Chen-ning.

## *Construction and Real Estate Management*

Many state, ministerial and provincial-level organizations have established subsidiaries in Hong Kong to engage in construction-related business. They include: the China State Construction Engineering Corporation, whose Hong Kong arm is China Overseas Building Development Company and its group of companies; the Ministry of Railways, which established CCECC (H.K.) Limited; the Ministry of Communications, which formed China Harbour Engineering Company; the Ministry of Metallurgical Industry, which formed Nan Hua International Engineering Company; Guangdong International Economic and Technical Corporation and China Guangdong Construction Development, whose subsidiary Licon Construction Company engages in building and piling work; and Guangdong Enterprises (Holdings) Limited, whose subsidiary Guangdong Investment Limited, a listed company, has real estate development as its main line of business and which also has a group of other subsidiary companies engaged in construction and property management.

It is also a well-known fact that such companies as China Resources (Holdings), China Everbright Holdings Company, CITIC Hong Kong, China Merchants Holdings Company and China Travel Service (Holdings) Hong Kong Limited all engage actively in real estate development and management.

China-funded companies also engage in property development and investment in real estate, involving millions of dollars. These will be dealt with in a later section on property investment.

## *Import and Export*

China-funded companies are engaged in all aspects of import and export trade, and the handling of merchandise ranging from machinery, petrochemical products, metals and minerals to textiles and garments. China has many state-owned and provincial-level import/export corporations handling specific products, and many of them have subsidiaries or agents in Hong Kong. For example, China National Textile Import and Export Corporation and a number of provincial textile import and export corporations have subsidiaries in Hong Kong handling textile products.

Again, large conglomerates like China Resources, CITIC Hong Kong, Guangdong Enterprises (Holdings), etc. have subsidiaries engaged in the trading of all kinds of goods. For instance, China Resources Petroleum & Chemicals Company is a general agent in Hong Kong for China National Chemicals Import and Export Corporation. It operates a network of retail outlets for petroleum and petroleum products, including gasoline stations, and has about 20 per cent of the local market share. Also, Ng Fung Hong, a long-established importer of cereals and foodstuffs, is a subsidiary of China Resources, whereas CITIC Hong Kong's trading arm is CITIC Multi-Trading Limited.

In view of its close relationship with Hong Kong, the Shenzhen Municipal Government operates a holdings company in Hong Kong under the name of Shum Yip Holdings Company to handle import and export trade. The company also handles labour export, contractual engineering, China visas for foreigners, consulting service and insurance. Similarly, the Zhuhai Municipal Government also has an import/export arm in Hong Kong, namely Zhuhai International Limited, which serves as a general agent for the Zhuhai Special Economic Zone in Hong Kong in economic and trade affairs.

Import and export business is closely related to the everyday life of Hong Kong residents. The business of Shum Kong Vegetables Trading Company is a good example. It is a subsidiary of the municipality of Shenzhen and handles all vegetables, fruits and other foodstuffs transported by land from Shenzhen to Hong Kong.

## *Transport and Tourism*

In the transport sector, China-funded companies are most visible in passenger and merchant shipping services between Hong Kong and China. China Merchants Steam Navigation Company, one of the wholly owned subsidiaries of China Merchants Holdings (CMH), was established in 1872 as a national maritime shipping business. Since the 1970s CMH has diversified into related areas of business, with over 400 subsidiaries operating both within and outside China. Its ocean-going fleet handles over 10 per cent of Hong Kong's maritime trade, and it has taken a 15 per cent stake worth of $202 million in Modern Terminals Limited, providing it with container feeder service between Hong Kong and most major ports in China. CMH now operates a large fleet of ocean-going vessels totalling over four million tons dead-weight. Another subsidiary, Hong Kong Ming Wah Shipping Company, operates not only coastal and worldwide cargo service but also long-term and short-term chartering business. CMH also manages, through its subsidiary China Merchants Godown, Wharf and Transportation Company, the China Merchants Wharf. Another subsidiary, China Merchants Lighterage and Transportation Company, operates the biggest barge fleet in Hong Kong. CMH also owns several dockyards in Hong Kong for repairing ships as well as ship-building.

CMH also operates several big projects in China, such as the Shekou Industrial Zone with its own container port in Guangdong and development projects in Pudong, Shanghai. It is estimated that CMH's total fixed assets is worth more than $10 billion.

In the field of air transport, CITIC Pacific, a local public company with CITIC Hong Kong holding a 46 per cent share, holds 12.5 per cent of Cathay Pacific Airways and 46.2 per cent of Dragonair, both Hong Kong-based international airlines.

China also invests in local city transport through the Guangdong Holdings Company.

The largest among tourist enterprises in Hong Kong is China Travel Service (Holdings) Company. It was incorporated on 29 October 1985 and now comprises a group of 20 companies. The company was first founded in Shanghai in 1927 by private businessmen and was closely related with the Shanghai Commercial Bank. The Hong Kong branch was founded on 1 April 1928, acting as a travel agent organizing group and individual tours. It was reorganized in 1946 when its business was taken over by China Travel Service (Hong Kong) Limited, a locally incorporated company.

Over the years, China Travel Service gradually expanded its business to include the handling of cargo, shipping, warehousing, trading, forwarding, air freight, advertising, etc. In 1967, it became the sole company in charge of cargo handling by rail from Shenzhen to Kowloon, later expanding into forwarding rail freight from Hong Kong to China. China Travel Service (Holdings) Hong Kong Limited was established as the holding company of the group and China Travel Service became its wholly owned subsidiary specializing in providing passenger travel services, and other companies were formed to handle businesses such as cargo, hotels, etc. For example, the group's operations include four hotels in the territory, with over 1,300 rooms.

In November 1992, China Travel International Investment Hong Kong Limited was formed and became listed on the Stock Exchange of Hong Kong, with China Travel Service (Holdings) Hong Kong Limited as its ultimate owner. Today, the China Travel Services group handles a substantial portion of passenger travel and almost all rail cargo between Hong Kong and China. It also operates the Overseas Chinese Town in Shenzhen, a tourist attraction with the Splendid China Miniature Scenic Spot and China Folk Culture Villages. It is one of the pillars of China's investment in Hong Kong.

Another major tourist enterprise is Guangdong (H.K.) Tours, formed in May 1981. It is a subsidiary of Guangdong Enterprises Company, the local business arm of Guangdong province. The company engages in travel, hotel management and related services, and operates three hotels and two guest houses in Hong Kong with over 1,000 rooms.

## Finance and Insurance

The most visible investment in the financial sector by China is the Bank of China Group, which is the second largest financial institution in Hong Kong. It has 13 member banks, namely the Hong Kong branches of Bank of China, Bank of Communications, Sin Hua Bank Limited, South Seas Bank Limited, Kincheng Banking Corporation, The China State Bank Limited, National Commercial Bank Limited, Yien Yieh Bank Limited, Po Sang Bank Limited, Chiyu Banking Corporation, Hua Chiao Commercial Bank Limited, the Hong Kong incorporated Nanyang Commercial Bank Limited and the China Development Finance Company (H.K.) Limited.

In addition, there are two other local banks, i.e. the Ka Wah Bank Limited, of which CITIC Hong Kong has a 60.6 per cent stake, with another 6.25 per cent held by the China Development Bank; and the Union Bank, of which New Concept Company, a company controlled by the China Merchants Holdings Company, has a 51.1 per cent share. Many of these banks have their own subsidiaries in the form of finance companies and nominees to handle deposit-taking and other financial services. As at the end of 1992, the Bank of China Group and the two banks jointly held over 22 per cent of total deposits in Hong Kong.

The Bank of China Group comes under the control of the Hong Kong–Macau Regional Office which is directly accountable to the Bank of China's head office in China. The Bank of China itself is one of the settlement banks and is to join the Hongkong and Shanghai Banking Corporation and the Standard Chartered Bank as the third note-issuing bank in Hong Kong in May 1994. The total amount of bank notes to be issued is likely to be around HK$6 billion, or 10 per cent of the total of bank notes in circulation. Acquiring the new status of a note-issuing bank will no doubt increase the influence of the Bank of China Group on Hong Kong's economy.

The Group has been continuously expanding its business in recent years. Apart from retail banking through its 300 branches and more, it also has a considerable share of the corporate finance and real estate market. Loans and advances to customers have been on the increase in recent years. At the end of 1992, the Group's Hong Kong dollar loans and advances amounted to $151 billion or 18.6 per cent of the total bank loans. Out of this total, $147 billion were for use in Hong Kong.

Table 1 lists the Group's assets, deposits and loans for the period 1988 to 1992. Its assets are mainly in Hong Kong dollars, and the share of deposits has been on the increase, though lagging behind in terms of foreign currency loans.

In February 1993, the banks within the Group agreed to centralize part of their foreign exchange trading as a step towards further consolidating their position in a bid to expand their influence on the local financial and exchange markets.

The Hong Kong Chinese Enterprises Association formed a Finance Committee in September 1992 with 67 members. Its present members include the Bank of China Group, the Ka Wah Bank and the Union Bank, and other companies engaged in finance-related services. It is a well-known fact that China also invests in Hong Kong's banking and finance sector by acquiring shares in local public and private companies, or by entering into joint ventures with local or foreign companies. For instance, there is a number of finance companies engaged in investment banking and syndicate

Table 1. Bank of China Group — Assets, Deposits and Loans

(HK$ billion)

|  | Assets | Deposits | Loans |
|---|---|---|---|
| **1988** | | | |
| HK$ | 150(21.25) | 88(22.50) | 79(19.51) |
| Foreign currency | 149( 5.98) | 90(19.78) | 24( 4.30) |
| Total | 299( 8.09) | 178(21.04) | 103(10.71) |
| **1989** | | | |
| HK$ | 169(18.25) | 96(21.28) | 83(15.81) |
| Foreign currency | 160( 4.74) | 100(17.95) | 25( 3.35) |
| Total | 329( 7.74) | 196(19.44) | 108( 8.57) |
| **1990** | | | |
| HK$ | 202(20.20) | 115(22.11) | 96(15.82) |
| Foreign currency | 195( 4.61) | 139(19.55) | 27( 2.28) |
| Total | 397( 7.59) | 254(20.63) | 123( 6.88) |
| **1991** | | | |
| HK$ | 261(22.23) | 139(23.61) | 126(17.40) |
| Foreign currency | 208( 4.68) | 152(19.74) | 33( 2.17) |
| Total | 469( 8.35) | 291(21.16) | 159( 7.09) |
| **1992** | | | |
| HK$ | 289(22.32) | 172(25.15) | 151(18.60) |
| Foreign currency | 241( 5.43) | 169(20.63) | 44( 2.66) |
| Total | 530( 9.25) | 341(22.69) | 195( 7.89) |

Notes:  1. Loans include advances to customers.
2. Figures in parentheses denote percentage shares in Hong Kong's total.
Source:  Office of the Commissioner of Banking.

loans, such as Royeast (a joint venture between CITIC Hong Kong and Royal Bank of Canada), and CCIC Finance Limited (a joint venture between Bank of China, the First National Bank of Chicago, Japan Industrial Bank and China Resources). One of the Bank of China Group, the China Development Finance Company (H.K.) Limited, is among Hong Kong's top ten merchant bankers. In December 1992, The Bank of China Group Securities Limited was formed, with China Development Investment Company (H.K.) Limited and the 13 members of the Group as shareholders. Chinese capital also took up equity shares in such Hong Kong companies as China Assets, Evergo International Holdings, First Pacific Bank and Hong Kong Chinese Bank, among others.

Apart from banking, China also operates a number of well-established insurance companies in Hong Kong. The China Insurance Group Hong Kong and Macau Regional Office, an arm of the People's Insurance Company of China, manages and supervises all China-funded insurance companies in Hong Kong and Macau. Companies within the Group include the Hong Kong branches of China Insurance Company, Tai Ping Insurance Company, China Life Insurance Company, China Reinsurance Company and Ming An Insurance Company. The People's Insurance Company of China has a separate subsidiary in Hong Kong, China Bao Lian Investment Company, which is engaged in investment.

In addition, provincial and local enterprises such as Guangdong Enterprises (Holdings) and the Shenzhen Municipal Government also run subsidiary insurance companies in Hong Kong, namely Guangdong Asia Insurance Company and Shum Yip Insurance Management and Agents Company.

In November 1992, 15 insurance companies formed the Insurance Committee of the Hong Kong Chinese Enterprises Association.

All in all, a conservative estimate of China's investment in Hong Kong's finance sector is more than $15 billion.

## □ Property Investment

In 1950, the tallest building in Hong Kong, the then Hongkong and Shanghai Banking Corporation headquarters, was dwarfed by a neighbouring skyscraper under construction. The skyscraper turned out to be the Bank of China Building, the first visible major property investment by the People's Republic of China in Hong Kong. Today, more than forty years later, China-owned properties are everywhere, and the new Bank of China Tower by the famous American architect I. M. Pei towers over the old Bank of China Building across Queen's Road.

It was in the early 1980s that China-funded enterprises started to invest heavily in local property. China Resources was among the first to build its 50-storey headquarters at an estimated cost of $1 billion and to build godowns and wharfs. This was followed by the CMH group's purchase of the Union Bank Building, a couple of 3-star hotels, wharfs and godowns, also at an estimated cost of $1 billion. Between 1983 and 1987, many central and provincial government-backed enterprises came to Hong Kong to do business, many of which also invested in property. For example, China State Construction Engineering Corporation's Hong Kong arm, China Overseas Building Development Company, started to invest in residential buildings in 1983 and made considerable profit in selling completed flats. Guangdong Enterprises, Fujian Investment Enterprises and Yue Xiu all invested in office buildings, hotels and residential buildings. These enterprises later also built their own headquarters. Today, most major China-funded enterprises own their own buildings.

By 1987, Hong Kong's property market saw the beginning of a new boom era, and China's investment in residential and commercial properties, including hotels, became very active. Some of them even went into short-term property investment, i.e. acquiring properties and selling them shortly afterwards at a profit, although such practices were prohibited by Chinese authorities.

Total Chinese investment in Hong Kong property at the end of 1991 was estimated at $7,337 million, which was the total of purchase prices paid by China-funded enterprises between 1988 and 1991. The estimated total invested in local property by China-funded enterprises in 1992 was $850 million. This brings the total amount at the end of 1992 to $8,187 million. After a brief lull in early 1993, property acquisition by China again became active with many large-scale purchases. By the end of May 1993, properties purchased by China-funded companies during 1993 amounted to about $5,015 million, with another $480 million purchased by Guangdong (H.K.) Tours and $100 million by four different companies. However, as figures before 1988 were not included, and as some properties were sold after their purchase at a profit, it is difficult to arrive at a figure that reflects the actual situation.

Apart from property investment, China-funded enterprises often participate in government land auctions. Between 1988 and 1992, China's total investment in crown land amounted to $4,518.5 million, some of them in joint venture with Hong Kong property developers. It may be noted that till the end of 1991, the total figure was only $1,253.5 million, and the sharp increase in 1992 was due to the acquisition by CITIC Pacific of two lots, one for godown in which it had a one-third share out of the total $415 million, the other for residential flats for $2,850 million in a 50/50 partnership with the Swire Group.

## ☐ Market Value of China-owned Shares in Public Companies

While it is difficult to obtain the total amount of China's investment in Hong Kong, annual reports and other related documents issued by public companies listed on the Stock Exchange of Hong Kong provide information on their substantial shareholders, thus making it possible to gauge China's share in these companies. This section gives a brief account of China-funded listed companies in Hong Kong to give an indication of China's investment in these companies.

## *Central Government / Ministerial-level Companies*

### *CITIC Group*

China International Trust and Investment Corporation (CITIC) has its head-quarters in Beijing and is under the direct supervision of the State Council. Its Hong Kong arm, CITIC Hong Kong, owns 43 per cent of CITIC Pacific, a listed company whose local investment includes a 12 per cent share in Hong Kong Telecommunications acquired in 1992 at $11,400 million, a 12.5 per cent share in Cathay Pacific Airways, and a 46.2 per cent share in Dragonair. CITIC Hong Kong is also the 100 per cent owner of Hang Chong Investment, acquired in June 1992 at the cost of $3,006,585,530, which in turn owns Dah Chong Hong, which engages in motor vehicle distribution and servicing, import and export and food and food items distribution. CITIC also invests in property and owns 20 per cent of Companhia de Telecomunicacoes de Macau S.A.R.L.

Through its wholly owned domestic subsidiary, CITIC Industrial Bank, CITIC has a 60.6 per cent share in the Ka Wah Bank Limited, Hong Kong. Also through a wholly owned affiliated company, the China Poly Group and its Hong Kong arm Poly Technologies, it owns 61 per cent of Continental Mariner Investment Company, a listed company.

CITIC Hong Kong, through its chairman Larry Rong, has a 15 per cent interest in Seapower International Holdings Limited, a listed company which, before the takeover of Seabase International Holdings Limited by China-funded Top Spring Development Limited on 30 April 1993, had a 64 per cent share in Seabase International Holdings Limited, which in turn held a 50.6 per cent share of Seapower Resources International Limited. On 15 May 1993, Seapower International Holdings agreed to acquire 440 million shares of Summa Promet Energy Limited at par value of US$0.01 for each share or US$4,400,000 in total.

It may be noted that the Seapower deal also gave option to China Offshore Oil Corporation to purchase not more than 330 million shares thereof. China Offshore Oil was established in 1982 in China as a state enterprise, hence this deal signified another China state enterprise's direct investment in Hong Kong.

On 10 June 1993, when Manhattan Card Company, the Hong Kong credit card issuing subsidiary of the Chase Manhattan Bank, floated its shares, CITIC Pacific subscribed to 298,512,000 shares or about 20 per cent of the total at $1.87 per share, or $558,217,440 in total.

It is estimated that CITIC's investment portfolio in Hong Kong is worth over $34 billion. This not only makes it one of the major players in Hong Kong's investment market but also China's flagship in expanding investments overseas.

## The China Merchants Holdings Group

China Merchants Holdings Company (CMH) is an enterprise directly under the Ministry of Communications of China's State Council and acts as the Ministry's representative in Hong Kong. Apart from its shipping and related business, CMH also owns major interests in two listed companies, namely Hai Hong Holdings Company and the Union Bank of Hong Kong.

Hai Hong is engaged mainly in the manufacture and sale (through subsidiaries) of paint products, comprising marine paints, container paints, industrial paints, construction paints and road-marking paints, in China and Hong Kong. China Merchants, through its wholly owned subsidiary Hoi Tung Marine Machinery Suppliers Limited of Hong Kong, held 75 per cent of Hai Hong when the latter was listed in 1992. Hoi Tung changed its name to Hoi Tung (BVI) Limited thereafter and at the end of 1992, it held 183,750,000 shares or about 75 per cent of Hai Hong.

The Union Bank of Hong Kong was established in 1964 and became listed on the Stock Exchange of Hong Kong in 1973. Today it has 18 branches in Hong Kong. The bank was reorganized in 1986 with Modern Concepts Limited becoming its major shareholder, holding 51.1 per cent of its shares. Modern Concepts is a Hong Kong company 68 and 32 per cent owned by China Merchants Steam Navigation Company and Search International Limited respectively. Hence the actual percentage of shares of the bank controlled by China Merchants is 34.748 per cent.

## China Resources Group

China Resources (Holdings) Company is under the Ministry of Foreign Relations and Trade, now renamed Ministry of Foreign Economic Relations and Cooperation. It became the parent company of a listed company in

September 1992 when Winland Investment Limited changed its name to China Resources Enterprises, Limited. This resulted from China Resources (Holdings) increasing its share in Winland from 32.6 per cent to 51 per cent and from Winland acquiring from China Resources a godown and a cold storage in Sha Tin and the entire issued ordinary share capital of the property company owning the godown and cold storage for $800 million. Since the changing of name, China Resources Enterprises has been engaged in property investment both in Hong Kong and in China.

China Resources (Holdings) holds 4.65 per cent of Lippo Limited and 1.26 per cent of HKCB Bank Holding Company, which in turn holds 85 per cent of the Hong Kong Chinese Bank. China Resources also holds 15 per cent of the Hong Kong Chinese Bank.

Ng Fung Hong, a wholly owned subsidiary of China Resources (Holdings), became a substantial shareholder in M.C. Packaging (Hong Kong) Limited, two years after its establishment in Hong Kong as a manufacturer of three-piece tin containers for Lam Soong (Hong Kong) Limited, Mobil and various other customers. M.C. Packaging became a listed company in September 1992. At that time, a 58/42 joint venture between Lam Soong and Ng Fung Hong held 336 million shares representing 60 per cent of the issued share capital of the company. In addition, Ng Fung Hong was directly or indirectly beneficially interested in 5.2 per cent of the company's shares. Hence Ng Fung Hong's net share is 30.4 per cent.

China Resources Enterprises acquired 23,333,333 shares or 7 per cent of Hong Kong Toy Centre International Limited in February 1993 at $1.04 per share, totalling $24,266,666.

In March 1993, it acquired from the Hong Kong Chinese Bank 1,277,760 shares or 10 per cent of Hong Kong Building & Loan Agency Limited at $19.00 per share, totalling $24,277,440.

*The China Travel Services Group*

China Travel International Investment Hong Kong Limited (CTII) is a subsidiary of China Travel Service (Holdings) Hong Kong Limited (CTS). Following its incorporation in 1992, CTII acquired all the equity interest of China Travel Service (Cargo) Hong Kong Limited and a 51 per cent interest in Shenzhen Splendid China Development Company. CTS (Cargo) and its subsidiaries handle freight forwarding and transportation services, while tourist attraction operations are handled by Shenzhen Splendid China.

As at 21 December 1992, CTS (Holdings) had an interest in 1,200 million ordinary shares of the company. The total issued shares according to the record of the Stock Exchange of Hong Kong at the end of March 1993 amounted to 1,600,004,400. At the end of March 1993, the total worth of the China Travel Service group, including unlisted subsidiaries, was well over $4 billion.

*Shougang (Holdings) Company*

Shougang, short for Shoudu (Capital) Gangtie (steel), is one of China's largest state enterprises. Through its 100 per cent owned Hong Kong subsidiary Shougang (Holdings) Company, it started to invest in Hong Kong public companies in October 1992, when it acquired 63.37 per cent of shares of Tung Wing Steel Holdings Limited. This was followed by the acquisition of 25.12 per cent of Eastern Century Holdings Limited in March 1993 and 67.80 per cent of Santai Manufacturing Limited the following month. In May 1993, Shougang and Cheung Kong (Holdings) Limited formed a joint company and announced plans to acquire more companies locally.

On 18 May 1993, Essential Assets Corporation, a company owned 50/50 by Shougang (Holdings) and Kotech Investment Limited, a Hong Kong-incorporated company, joined hands with Botany Limited (primarily owned by Cheung Kong: 87.5 per cent), Kaberry Holdings Limited (controlled by Hong Kong businessman Martin Kwok), and Tung Tai Finance & Investment Limited (a member of Leo Lee's Tung Tai group), to acquire 74 per cent of Kader Investment Company. The total amounted to $582,484,000, comprising 76,473,244 shares at $7.02 per share and 14,867,057 warrants at $3.07 per warrant. Essential Assets Corporation's share was 68 per cent or $396,089,120.

It should be noted that Kotech Investment is 60 per cent owned by Grand Development Company of Shanghai, Shenzhen and Guangzhou, with Deng Zhifang, son of Deng Xiaoping, as Chairman.

*China National Nonferrous Metal Industry Corporation*

China National Nonferrous Metal Industry Corporation is another large state-owned enterprise in China, whose Vice-President, Wu Jianchang, is Deng Xiaoping's son-in-law. Through its wholly owned subsidiary, Jinchuang Nonferrous Metals Corporation, one of China's most successful enterprises engaged in mining, metal fabrication and trading, it acquired 130 million shares or 30.1 per cent of Paladin Limited, a company whose majority share was formally held by Taiwan interests. Another move was to increase its share in Jinhui Holdings Company from 13 per cent to about 18 per cent. Also, through its wholly owned subsidiary Oriental Metals (Holdings) Company, which has an 80 per cent share in Haka International Limited and in which Jinhui Holdings has a 20 per cent share, it holds 68 per cent of Laws Property Holdings Limited, which has since been quite active in acquiring both commercial and residential properties in Hong Kong. Moreover, Oriental Metals holds 7 per cent of Tem Fat Hing Feng (Holdings) Limited, which is engaged in precious metal mining with sites in Malaysia and in base metal trading through a joint venture with China Nonferrous Metal of Shenzhen.

On 13 May 1993, China National Nonferrous Metal Industry Corporation further acquired 68.31 per cent or 20,710,000 shares of International Industries Limited, a listed company, at $11.78 per share or a total of $243,963,800.

## China Everbright Group

China Everbright was founded in Hong Kong in May 1983 with Wang Guangying, brother of Wang Guangmei, widow of former State President Liu Shaoqi, as chairman. Directly under the State Council of the central government, it was very active in local business circles, entering into property development as well as manufacturing. However, its efforts did not attain expected results and the top management was subsequently reshuffled. It is now headed by Qiu Qing, former assistant manager of the People's Bank of China.

In March 1993, it acquired through a subsidiary a majority share of Newfoundland International Company, a listed company since February 1973 mainly engaged in property investment, trading, stockbrokerage and securities trading. In May 1993, the name of Newfoundland was changed to Everbright International Investments Limited. The group has subsidiaries operating in Hong Kong, China, Malaysia and Australia.

## China State Construction Engineering Corporation

China State Construction Engineering Corporation (CSCEC), a large state-owned group of construction enterprises in China, established its Hong Kong subsidiary China Overseas Building Development Company in 1979. CSCEC has been a List II public works contractor in Hong Kong since 1981 and has done a large number of piling and mechanized construction projects locally. Since 1988, China Overseas Building Development has been functioning as a company with subsidiaries engaged in building, civil construction, property development, finance, investment, trading, etc. In August 1992, following group reorganization, China Overseas Holdings Limited became the holding company of China Overseas Land and Investment Limited and of China Overseas Construction Limited. At the same time, China Overseas Building Development was renamed China Overseas Land and Investment Limited and became the holding company of the property development and investment operations of the group, and China Overseas Construction Limited became the holding company of the construction, trading and project management operations of the group. China Overseas Land and Investment was listed on the Stock Exchange of Hong Kong in August 1992. At the end of 1992, the company had an after-tax profit of about $414 million.

## China Aerospace Industry Corporation

China Aerospace Industry Corporation (formerly Ministry of Aerospace Industry) announced in April 1993 that it had, through its wholly owned British Virgin Islands-registered subsidiary company Jetcote Investments Limited, purchased 158,168,800 shares or 51 per cent of the issued shares of Conic Investment Company for a total of HK$238,108,113. Conic was established in 1965 by a local entrepreneur, and its ownership was transferred to a China-funded company which was registered in Hong Kong and is now owned jointly by the Bank of China and China Resources (Holdings) Company. The company had sustained losses since then till 1991 when it registered its first profitable year. This was China Aerospace Industry's first involvement in a local company.

Conic Investment has a group of subsidiary companies engaged in a variety of businesses, including electronics manufacturing, printed circuit board manufacturing, plastic manufacturing and property investment. Conic's main products include colour television monitors, liquid crystal displays and telecommunication equipment. This ties in with China Aerospace Industry's line of business which, apart from satellite launching rockets, also includes electronic and telecommunication products for civilian use. China Aerospace Industry's after-tax profit in 1992 was about RMB 1 billion. After acquiring Conic, it plans to develop its present line of business as well as to diversify its products.

*CEROILFOOD*

On 30 April 1993, China National Cereals, Oils and Foodstuffs Import and Export Corporation (CEROILFOOD), through Top Spring Development Limited, a company with 70 per cent of its shares owned by CEROILFOOD's Hong Kong subsidiary, Top Glory Company, purchased 55 per cent of Seabase International Holdings Limited at $2.60 per share for $381.75 million. Meanwhile, Seabase would hold 15.1 per cent of Seapower Resources International Limited, another listed company. Top Spring would also purchase the rest of Seabase International Holdings's shares, making the latter a wholly owned subsidiary of the former. This makes CEROILFOOD a 70 per cent controlling owner of Seabase International Holdings and a 10.57 per cent owner of Seapower Resources.

On 10 June 1993, CEROILFOOD, through its subsidiary Top Glory, acquired from Tomson Pacific Limited 640 million shares or 34.98 per cent of the World Trade Centre Group Limited at $1.88 per share. Top Glory also agreed to acquire all the remaining shares and warrants of the World Trade Centre Group at an estimated total of $3,683 million.

*China Venturetech*

China Venturetech was established in Beijing in 1986 as a financial institution specializing in venture capital, with the Ministry of Finance and the State Science & Technology Commission as main shareholders. It is directly under the supervision of the People's Bank of China, and its Chairman is Chen Weili, daughter of Chen Yun. In 1988, it established in Hong Kong a wholly owned subsidiary, China Venturetechno International Company (CVIC).

CVIC owns 20.43 per cent of China Assets (Holdings) Limited, whose principal business is to make equity and equity-related investments in small and medium-sized companies in China. Together with Shanghai International Securities Company, CVIC also controls about 51 per cent of Public International Investment Limited, a listed company in Hong Kong. In April 1993, Forma Property Investments Limited, of which Public International Investment owns 17.9 per cent, purchased the controlling share of Ong Holdings (H.K.) Limited, a company with a group of subsidiaries dealing in investment and securities trading, subsequently making Ong a wholly owned subsidiary in May 1993. Forma's other shareholders include 40 per cent share by Venture-Some Investments Limited (70 per cent owned by Shanghai International Securities (Hong Kong) Company), and 15 per cent share by Makeway Management Limited, a Taiwan-based securities merchant.

*Petroleum-related Companies*

In early May 1993, China Petroleum and Natural Gas Corporation, another China state-owned enterprise, acquired 36 per cent of Paragon Holdings Limited, a Hong Kong company engaged in business related to natural resources and energy. Soon afterwards, the Corporation, through its sub-sidiary Sun World Limited, proposed to acquire the remaining shares of Paragon, which will remain a listed company. This was followed by the acquisition of a 10 per cent share in Asia Standard International Group Limited by Sinopec (Hong Kong) Limited, the Hong Kong arm of China's petrochemical giant, marking its first entry into Hong Kong. On 19 May 1993, it was announced that China Offshore Oil Corporation had plans to acquire 21.6 per cent of Summa Promet Energy Limited. When realized, such a move would enable China to have access to oilfields outside China to supplement its energy requirements.

## Provincial/Municipal-level Companies

### Guangdong Enterprises (Holdings) Limited/Yue Xiu Group

Guangdong Enterprises (Holdings) Limited, founded in early 1981, is the Hong Kong agent for various economic organizations and enterprises of Guangdong province. It is engaged in trade, investment, engineering, computers, etc. Its subsidiary, Guangdong Investment Limited, is engaged in industrial investment, transportation, real estate, hotel as well as environ-mental protection. It was listed in 1991.

Guangdong Investment's annual report dated 27 April 1993 stated that, as at 31 December 1992, Guangdong Enterprises (Holdings) held 608,974,740 issued share of the company. It further stated that following a number of acquisitions and investments in 1992, the company operations consisted of three main categories, namely industrial investment, property development and investment, and travel services and hotel operation.

While most subsidiaries engaged in industrial investment are located in China, the company has a 20 per cent share of Citybus Limited, a local company engaged in public transport. In property development, the com-pany has a wholly owned subsidiary which owns the Cameron Commercial Centre. In travel services and hotel operations, the company owns the

Guangdong (H.K.) Tours Company which in turn owns the New Cathay Hotel, among others.

Yue Xiu Group was established in Hong Kong in 1985 as a trading and investment vehicle of the Guangzhou Municipal Government in Hong Kong. The companies comprising the Group are engaged principally in property development and investment in Hong Kong, Macau and China. It also provides management services to properties developed by the Group as well as consultancy services to certain property development projects undertaken by the Group.

In November 1992, Yue Xiu's subsidiary, Guangzhou Investment Company became a listed company and shares offered to the public were over-subscribed 230 times. Guangdong Investment has since engaged in numerous property investment projects in Guangzhou, including property development along the proposed subway line. At the time Guangzhou Investment was being listed, Yue Xiu had participated in 39 property development projects in Hong Kong, Macau and China, and was involved in five projects in Hong Kong. As Cheung Kong holds a 7.5 per cent share in the company, it has been actively engaged in property development and related projects in Hong Kong.

In February 1993, Denway Investment Limited, of which Yue Xiu has a 17.4 per cent equity share, issued new shares in Hong Kong which were over-subscribed 658 times, an all time high, involving a total of $241 million. The attraction lies here: Denway owns 95 per cent of Weida Machinery Enterprise Limited, a Guangzhou-based company which in turn comprises 11 companies engaged in the manufacture, assembling, maintenance and trading of automobiles, including the Guangzhou Peugeot Automobile Company, a joint venture with the French automaker.

### Fujian Investment & Enterprise Corporation

Fujian Investment & Enterprise Corporation is a state-owned enterprise based in Fujian province. In 1987, it became the single largest shareholder of Min Xin Holdings Limited through Vigour Fine Company, a wholly owned subsidiary in Hong Kong. Subsequently, in May 1991, its Chairman, Chen Yuankui, became Chairman of Min Xin Holdings Limited.

Min Xin's predecessor was Panin Holdings Limited, a holding company of a deposit-taking company in Hong Kong and a commercial bank in Macau which was listed on the Stock Exchange of Hong Kong in June 1982. In 1985, it formed a 60 per cent joint venture, Xiamen International

Bank, with three China-backed organizations in Xiamen. The name of the company was changed to Min Xin in 1987.

In November 1991, Asian Development Bank, the Long-Term Credit Bank of Japan Limited, and Sino Finance Group Limited joined Min Xin and took up 10 per cent, 15 per cent and 5 per cent respectively of the shares of Xiamen International Bank, the first foreign capital bank in China. Min Xin's share in the Bank was thus reduced to 36.75 per cent.

Min Xin's subsidiaries include over 10 property investment companies in Hong Kong and also the Min Xin Insurance Company. It has also acquired a 10 per cent share in each of the following three local listed companies, namely Evergo International Holdings Company, Allied Group and Indesen Industries Company.

Table 2 lists shares held by the above China-funded groups in Hong Kong's listed companies as at 31 March 1993, unless otherwise noted. Table 3 summarizes the total market value of shares of these companies.

Table 2.  Market Value of Shares Held as at 31 March 1993

| Company | Shares issued | % held | @$ | Market value |
|---|---|---|---|---|
| **1. CITIC Group** | | | | |
| *CITIC Pacific Ltd.* | 1,809,024,580 | 43.00 | 17.80 | $13,846,274,135 |
| *(Hong Kong Telecom-munications Ltd.* | 11,152,785,865 | 12.00 | 9.95 | $13,316,426,322) |
| *(Cathay Pacific Airways Ltd.* | 2,864,511,540 | 12.50 | 9.50 | $3,401,607,453) |
| *(Manhattan Card Co., Ltd.* | | 20.00 | 1.87 | $558,217,440) |
| *The Ka Wah Bank, Ltd.* | 774,563,647 | 60.60 | 4.05 | $1,901,011,558 |
| *Continental Mariner Investment Co., Ltd.* | 88,000,000 | 61.00 | 9.75 | $523,380,000 |
| *Seapower International Holdings Ltd.* | 293,869,180 | 15.00 | 2.375 | $104,690,895 |
| *(Seabase International Holdings Ltd.* | 266,631,474 | 64.00 | 3.425 | $584,456,191) |
| *[Seapower Resources International Ltd.* | 1,016,314,695 | 50.60 | 1.15 | $591,393,521] |
| *[Summa Promet Energy Ltd.* 440,000,000 shares acquired on 15 May 1993 at US$4,400,000 at HK$7.8 = | | | | $34,320,000] |

N.B.  Seabase International Holdings Ltd. taken over by CEROILFOOD's subsidiary on 30 April 1993. See Section 9 of this table.
  CITIC Pacific subscribed to 298,512,000 shares of Manhattan Card Co., Ltd. when the latter floated its shares in June 1993.

## Table 2. (Cont'd)

| Company | Shares issued | % held | @$ | Market value |
|---|---|---|---|---|
| **2. China Merchant Holdings Group** | | | | |
| *Hai Hong Holdings Co., Ltd.* | 245,003,200 | 75.00 | 2.225 | $408,843,750 |
| *Union Bank of Hong Kong Ltd.* | 229,795,096 | 34.748 | 5.90 | $471,110,279 |
| **3. China Resources Group** | | | | |
| *China Resources Enterprises, Ltd.* | 420,000,000 | 51.00 | 3.50 | $749,700,000 |
| *Lippo Ltd.* | 1,225,955,948 | 4.65 | 2.425 | $138,241,857 |
| *The HKCB Holding Co., Ltd.* | 500,002,797 | 1.26 | 2.65 | $16,695,093 |
| *M.C. Packaging (Hong Kong) Ltd.* | 560,220,000 | 30.40 | 3.95 | $672,712,176 |
| *Hong Kong Toy Centre International Ltd.* | 300,000,000 | 7.00 | 1.23 | $28,700,000 |
| *Hong Kong Building Loan & Agency Ltd.* | 12,777,600 | 10.00 | 18.70 | $23,894,112 |

N.B. M.C. Packaging shares held through wholly owned Ng Fung Hong; 23,333,333 shares of Hong Kong Toy Centre purchased at $1.04 per share or $24,266,666 in total.

| Company | Shares issued | % held | @$ | Market value |
|---|---|---|---|---|
| **4. China Travel Services Group** | | | | |
| *China Travel International Investment Hong Kong Ltd.* | 1,600,004,400 | 75.00 | 2.376 | $2,850,000,000 |
| **5. Shougang (Holdings) Co., Ltd.** | | | | |
| *Tung Wing Steel Holdings Ltd.* | 336,682,100 | 63.37 | 3.625 | $773,413,494 |
| *Eastern Century Holdings Ltd.* | 380,001,600 | 25.12 | 2.025 | $142,604,813 |
| *Santai Manufacturing Ltd.* | 272,989,790 | 67.80 | 2.075 | $384,055,686 |
| *Kader Investment Co., Ltd.* | 481,644,749 | — | — | $198,044,560 |

N.B. Kader was acquired in May 1993 at $585,484,000, of which Shougang's share was 50% of $396,089,120.

| Company | Shares issued | % held | @$ | Market value |
|---|---|---|---|---|
| **6. China National Nonferrous Metal Industry Corporation** | | | | |
| *Paladin Ltd.* | 432,270,594 | 30.10 | 1.240 | $161,340,676 |
| *Jinhui Holdings Co., Ltd.* | 423,561,142 | 18.00 | 1.670 | $127,322,479 |

Table 2. (Cont'd)

| Company | Shares issued | % held | @$ | Market value |
|---|---|---|---|---|
| *Laws Property Holdings Ltd.* | 274,297,493 | 68.00 | 3.375 | $629,512,746 |
| *Tem Fat Hing Fung (Holdings) Ltd.* | 913,676,597 | 7.00 | 1.570 | $100,413,058 |
| *International Industries Ltd.* | 30,312,500 | 68.31 | 11.78 | $243,963,800 |

N.B. Acquisition of International Industries Ltd. took place on May 12 by taking up 20,710,000 shares at $11.78 per share.

**7. China Everbright Group**

| | | | | |
|---|---|---|---|---|
| *Newfoundland International Co., Ltd.* | 260,000,000 | 51.00 | 1.730 | $229,398,000 |

N.B. Name of Newfoundland changed to Everbright International Investments Ltd. in May 1993.

**8. China State Construction Engineering Corporation (CSCEC)**

| | | | | |
|---|---|---|---|---|
| *China Overseas Land & Investment Ltd.* | 3,280,020,000 | 75.00 | 1.290 | $3,173,419,350 |

**9. China Aerospace Industry Corporation**

| | | | | |
|---|---|---|---|---|
| *Conic Investment Co., Ltd.* | 310,084,800 | 51.00 | 1.450 | $229,207,709 |

N.B. Amount shown is acquisition cost in April 1993.

**10. CEROILFOOD**

| | | | | |
|---|---|---|---|---|
| *Seabase International Holdings Ltd.* | 266,631,474 | 70.00 | 3.475 | $648,581,060 |
| *(Seapower Resources International Ltd.* | 1,016,314,695 | 10.57 | 1.150 | $123,538,132) |
| *World Trade Centre Group Ltd.* | 1,831,238,290 | 100.00 | 1.880 | $3,683,000,000 |

N.B. All acquisition took place after 31 March 1993.

**11. China Venturetech**

| | | | | |
|---|---|---|---|---|
| *China Assets (Holdings) Ltd.* | 74,263,160 | 20.43 | 6.950 | $105,445,146 |
| *Public International Investments Ltd.* | 365,501,477 | 51.00 | 2.150 | $400,772,369 |
| *(Ong Holdings (Hong Kong) Ltd.* | 95,187,414 | 100.00 | 1.550 | $147,540,491) |

## Table 2. (Cont'd)

| Company | Shares issued | % held | @$ | Market value |
|---|---|---|---|---|

N.B.  Public International acquired after 31 March 1993 although shares prices shown are of that date. Controlling shares of Public International held together with Shanghai International Securities Co., Ltd.

### 12. Petroleum-related companies

| Company | Shares issued | % held | @$ | Market value |
|---|---|---|---|---|
| *Paragon Holdings Ltd.* | 2,223,966,170 | 100.00 | 0.051 | $113,422,274 |
| *Asia Standard International Group Ltd.* | 607,458,221 | 10.00 | 1.480 | $329,146,993 |
| *Summa Promet Energy Ltd.* | 3,270,169,566 | 21.60 | 0.078 | $255,073,226 |

N.B.  China Petroleum & Natural Gas Corporation acquired Paragon through Sun World Ltd. in May 1993 with new shares at an estimated cost of $144,000,000. Figure listed above represents market value at the end of March 1993.
China National Petrochemicals Corporation acquired Asia Standard through Sinopec (Hong Kong) Ltd.
China Offshore Oil Corporation announced the intention to acquire 21.60% of Summa Promet in June 1993 and amount shown is based on assumption of acquiring issued shares at par value of US$0.01 each.

### 13. Guangdong Enterprises (Holdings) Ltd.

| Company | Shares issued | % held | @$ | Market value |
|---|---|---|---|---|
| *Guangdong Investment Ltd.* | 1,395,843,875 | 43.63 | 2.725 | $1,659,456,166 |

### 14. Yue Xiu Group

| Company | Shares issued | % held | @$ | Market value |
|---|---|---|---|---|
| *Guangzhou Investment Co., Ltd.* | 1,700,001,200 | 67.50 | 1.420 | $1,629,451,150 |
| *Denway Investment Ltd.* | 1,320,000,000 | 17.74 | 1.880 | $440,235,840 |

### 15. Fujian Investment & Enterprise Corporation

| Company | Shares issued | % held | @$ | Market value |
|---|---|---|---|---|
| *Min Xin Holdings Ltd.* | 243,000,000 | 64.00 | 2.325 | $361,584,000 |
| *(Evergo International Holdings Co., Ltd.* | 816,954,873 | 10.00 | 3.675 | $300,230,915) |
| *(Allies Group* | 2,537,271,952 | | 0.650 | $149,500,000) |
| *(Indesen Industries Co., Ltd.* | 250,000,000 | 10.00 | 1.420 | $35,500,000) |

N.B.  Min Xin holds 230,000,000 or approximate 10% share of Allied Group.

Notes:   Shares of companies in parentheses are held by the company preceding them; shares of companies in brackets are held by the company in parentheses preceding it.

Sources: *Hong Kong Economic Journal*; Stock Exchange of Hong Kong; annual reports issued by concerned listed companies.

Table 3. Summary of China's Investment in Hong Kong's
Listed Companies

| | |
|---|---|
| 1. CITIC | $34,861,777,515 |
| 2. China Merchant Holdings Group | $879,954,029 |
| 3. China Resources Group | $1,629,943,238 |
| 4. China Travel Services Group | $2,850,000,000 |
| 5. Shougang (Holdings) Co., Ltd. | $1,498,118,553 |
| 6. China National Nonferrous Metal Industry Corporation | $1,262,552,759 |
| 7. China Everbright Group | $229,389,000 |
| 8. China State Construction Engineering Corporation | $3,173,419,350 |
| 9. China Aerospace Industry Corporation | $229,207,709 |
| 10. CEROILFOOD | $4,455,119,192 |
| 11. China Venturetech | $653,758,006 |
| 12. Petroleum-related Companies | $697,642,493 |
| 13. Guangdong Enterprises (Holdings) Ltd. | $1,659,456,166 |
| 14. Yue Xiu Group | $2,069,686,990 |
| 15. Fujian Investment & Enterprise Corporation | $846,814,915 |
| Total | $56,996,839,915 |

Note: The above figures include acquisitions after 31 March 1993.

## ☐ Outlook

With the economic reform in China going full speed, Hong Kong's economy is becoming more and more closely knit with that of its northern neighbour, which will become its master on 1 July 1997. In fact, Hong Kong and South China have already become economically so closely integrated that many people refer to these two places as having a borderless economy. Hong Kong operates thousands of manufacturing concerns in China, mostly in Guangdong, and it invests in a wide range of projects, including property development, hotels and tourism and infrastructure such as roads, energy and communications. China's investment in Hong Kong is believed to be of the same magnitude as that of Hong Kong's in China, if not greater. With the recent pace of acquisition of listed companies in Hong Kong, China's cumulative direct investment in Hong Kong, including property, may have reached hundreds of billions.

The positive side of China's investment in Hong Kong is that it helps to build up the investors' confidence in the future of the territory. The more China invests in Hong Kong, the more interdependent the two economies become. As mentioned earlier, nine state-owned enterprises in China have sought to be listed on the Stock Exchange of Hong Kong. They are:

|  | *Estimated New Issue* |
|---|---|
| Shanghai Petrochemicals | $2,500 million |
| Tsingtao Brewery | 600 million |
| Guangzhou Shipyard | 300 million |
| Beiren Printing Machinery | 100 million |
| Maanshan Iron and Steel | 1,000 million |
| Dongfang Electric Co. | 100 million |
| Tianjin Bohai Chemicals | 400 million |
| Jiangsu Yizheng Chemical Fibre | 1,500 million |
| Kunming Machine Tool | 100 million |

On 19 June 1993, a Memorandum of Regulatory Cooperation was signed in Beijing by five parties, namely, China Securities Regulatory Commission, Shanghai Securities Exchange, Shenzhen Stock Exchange, Hong Kong's Securities and Futures Commission and the Stock Exchange of Hong Kong Limited, paving the way for Chinese companies to be listed in Hong Kong. The Memorandum aimed at making Chinese firms listed on the Hong Kong exchange subject to the rules and regulations of the territory, thus protecting investors' interests and enhancing the ability of the stock markets in Shanghai and Shenzhen to raise capital.

Owing to the rapid devaluation of the Chinese currency, especially during May and June 1993, whether Hong Kong investors would be as eager to subscribe to share issues of these companies as before would only be known when shares are actually floated. The Memorandum would hopefully serve to allay such fears. The first two Chinese companies to be listed are likely to be Shanghai Petrochemicals and Tsingtao Brewery.

Should all the nine companies be listed on the Stock Exchange of Hong Kong, an estimated $30 billion or 1.7 per cent of the total capitalization would be added to the stock market.

Integration of the economies of Hong Kong and the southern part of China, as well as mutual investment between China and Hong Kong, has the advantage of helping a smooth economic convergence in 1997. In addition to seeking listings on the Stock Exchange of Hong Kong, many Chinese companies are acquiring shares in Hong Kong's public companies in order to gain listing on the Stock Exchange "through the back door". Such moves by enterprises in China are mutually beneficial to both China and Hong Kong because they provide more choice to investors while at the same time open up Hong Kong's capital market to China. As the trend continues, it will eventually help China's modernization as well as its market economy.

Moreover, such moves by China's state-owned enterprises and/or central government-level agencies also imply a new strategy in China's investment in Hong Kong. First, China aims at the induction of capital through Hong Kong-based companies to help restructure its industries. This can be achieved by either listing state-owned enterprises on the Stock Exchange of Hong Kong or by acquiring local companies, or both. For example, China National Nonferrous Metal Industry Corporation, through its Hong Kong subsidiary Oriental Metals, plans to buy up to 15 companies in Hong Kong and turn it into a large listed company which will take on substantial industrial investment in China.

Second, China intends to establish key companies in various sectors of Hong Kong's economy to extend its influence. For example, the acquisition of a controlling share in Public International Investments Limited and Ong Holdings jointly by China Venturetech and Shanghai International Securities has led to the reorganization of Ong Holdings into the securities trading vehicle of its Shanghai principal, and the acquisition of Kader Investment signifies Shougang's entrance into the property investment and development market. China National Nonferrous Metal Industry Corporation is also going into property development through the reorganizing of Laws Property into Onfem Holdings.

Third, Chinese corporations can extend their operations to other parts of the world for the ultimate benefit of the parent companies. This is manifested by the three petroleum-related state corporations acquiring local companies having interests in energy extraction in the third countries.

The induction of capital is perhaps of greatest significance to China. Since the start of economic reform, there has been a huge inflow of foreign capital into China. However, during the early stages, such capital mostly went into labour-intensive processing industries which depended heavily upon raw and semi-processed materials imported from abroad. While this helped provide employment and earn some foreign exchange, it did not help alleviate China's serious economic bottlenecks in energy, transportation, raw materials and low productivity of state-owned enterprises. With Chinese companies raising capital through their Hong Kong-listed companies, it is expected that the capital thus raised would be directed to the most needed sectors.

However, as mentioned earlier, increased Chinese investment in Hong Kong has made the territory more dependent on China and any economic instability in China would affect Hong Kong. For example, when Japan's economy faced difficulties, many Japanese companies liquidated their investments overseas to help support their domestic operations. China-funded companies in Hong Kong may face similar pressures to liquidate their assets in Hong Kong in the event of requests from their parent companies. In view of the large amount involved, the impact of such moves would have important ramifications on Hong Kong's economy. Despite the fact that the Chinese government has recently made statements that such actions would not take place, the possibility cannot be discarded. Moreover, the devaluation of the Chinese currency has had a mixed effect on Hong Kong's investments in China. Some may have benefited from cheaper local costs, whereas those in the tertiary sector have suffered. There is the view that any losses sustained on the part of Hong Kong investors due to exchange rate fluctuations may be a price paid for the benefits gained by Hong Kong through China's increased investment in the territory.

It is a well-known fact that corruption is rampant in China and there is concern that it is already spreading to Hong Kong through China-based and China-funded enterprises. There is as yet no substantial evidence that such is the case, but it is certainly something worth bearing in mind.

# 23

# History

Chan Kai-cheung

While there are an increasing number of quality works regarding specific topics on Hong Kong's history since British colonization, works claiming to be the general history of Hong Kong are on the whole disappointing. They have yet to liberate themselves from the colonial paradigm which dismisses pre-colonial history as either non-existent or irrelevant, and presents British colonization as a fundamental break in the continuity of history for Hong Kong.

The purpose of this review is to provide a brief narrative, from a critical perspective, of Hong Kong's pre-colonial history. A narrative of colonial history from a similar perspective is certainly also badly needed, but this has to wait for another occasion.

## ☐ The "Barren Island" Myth

### *Origin of the Myth*

In January 1841, British Plenipotentiary Charles Elliot agreed to end the First Opium War in return for, *inter alia*, China's cession of Hong Kong Island to Britain. Lord Palmerston, British Foreign Secretary, furious at Elliot's not getting the cessation of the better-known Zhoushan 舟山 islands with its estimated population of some 100,000 persons, dismissed the acquisition of Hong Kong as that of "a barren Island with hardly a House upon it."

---

Chan Kai-cheung is Chief Editor, *Huanan Jingji Journal*.

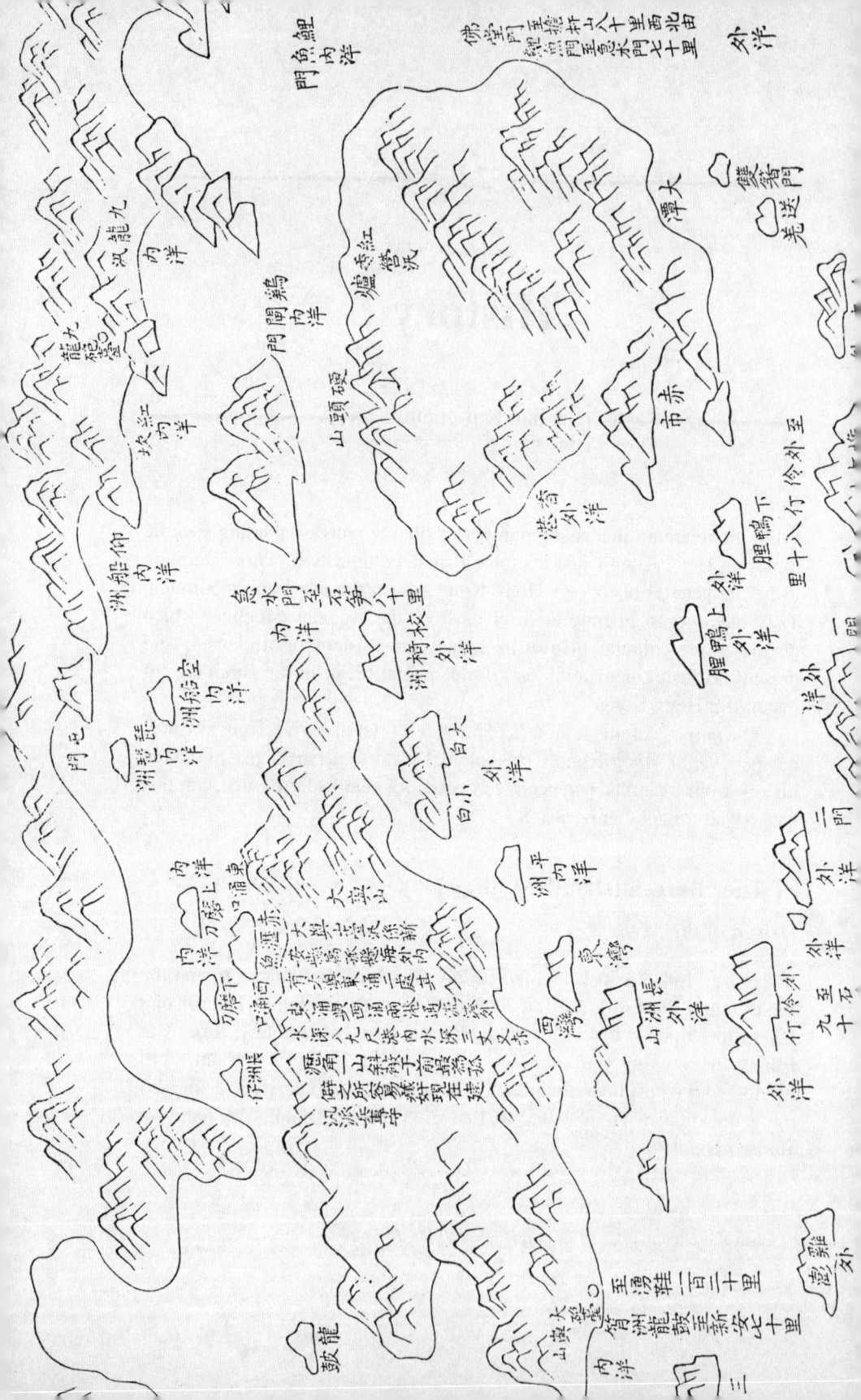

Palmerston's "barren island" remark, made in the context of a tirade against Elliot in order to justify the resumption of hostilities against China, was a hyperbole with no pretension to full factual veracity. Yet every British official and semi-official narration of Hong Kong history in the past century and a half has repeated one or another version of the "barren island" remark.

The semi-official *Hong Kong Guide 1893* went as far as claiming, "For ages prior to the year 1841, [Hong Kong] existed only as a plutonic island of uninviting sterility, apparently capable only of supporting the lowest form of organisms." The official British booklet *Britain and Japan*, published in 1944 as part of the propaganda campaign against American support of retrocession of Hong Kong to China, stated: "When the Island of Hong Kong was ceded to Britain one hundred years ago, it was almost uninhabited. Since then Britain has built ... a trading centre and a port for commercial shipping which had enriched the communities all around it." A virtually identical claim is made in the latest official British booklet on Hong Kong: "Hong Kong remained sparsely populated up to the nineteenth century" (HMSO, *Britain and Hong Kong*, 1992, p. 12).

By treating the "barren island" remark as historical truth, the impression is given that Hong Kong owes everything to British colonization. Sometimes the further impression is given that Britain, because she has created Hong Kong out of a deserted wilderness, has more claim to Hong Kong than that based on her treaty rights. One is reminded of the official historiography of South Africa during the apartheid era, with its insistence on the "fact" that South Africa at the time of occidental colonization was empty space virtually uninhabited.

Historians of modern Chinese history have also tended to uncritically repeat the "barren island" thesis. A recent example is Jonathan Spence's description of what happened after Charles Elliot was expelled by Lin Zexu in 1839 from Guangzhou and Macau because of the illicit opium trade: "Elliot inaugurated a new phase in east Asian history by settling his group on the almost deserted rocky island of Hong Kong" (*The Search for Modern China*, 1990, p. 154).

## Elaborated Version of the Myth

Mainstream accounts of Hong Kong's past, wittingly or unwittingly, have adopted the same colonial paradigm. Indeed, recognizing that the "barren island" remark is not literally true, these accounts have qualified and elaborated the remark to arrive at the same conclusion.

The elaborated version of the "barren island" thesis can be summarized as follows:

1.  Hong Kong Island at the time of British colonization, while not exactly houseless or uninhabited, was "sparsely populated", "virtually uninhabited", "uninviting", merely a "fishing village".

2.  Pre-colonial Hong Kong, while it was not exactly slumbering for ages in "uninviting sterility", "had little part in the main current of Chinese history" (G. B. Endacott, *A History of Hong Kong*, 1973, p. 3); it "was barely more than a geographical expression to Chinese government and foreign visitors alike" (Hong Kong History Society, *Forts and Pirates — A History of Hong Kong*, 1990, p. 1); it was "not a very important corner of the Empire ... remote and inconsequential" (Jan Morris, *Hong Kong, Epilogue to an Empire*, 1988, p. 18); it "was an altogether insignificant place" (Nigel Cameron, *An Illustrated History of Hong Kong*, 1991, p. 4). Pre-colonial history is relegated to the status of "archaeological background" (Hong Kong government, *Hong Kong 1993*).

3.  Hence the "history of Hong Kong really begins with the coming of the British in 1841" (Endacott, p. 4), such that "the territory grew from what was then a fishing village to what is now a leading industrial, trading and financial centre" (Ng Lun Ngai-ha, "History", *The Other Hong Kong Report*, 1989, p. 381). The two recent very substantial works claiming to be the history of Hong Kong, by respectively Nigel Cameron (*An Illustrated History of Hong Kong*, 1991, 362 pages) and Frank Welsh (*A History of Hong Kong*, 1993, 624 pages), both emulated Endacott's dismissal of pre-colonial history without even bothering to state any reason.

## *Logical Fallacy*

Ng Lun Ngai-ha's "fishing village to megapolis" inference, also adopted implicitly in the chapter on history in the Hong Kong government's *Hong Kong 1993*, contains a fatal logical fallacy. The megapolis that is today's Hong Kong consists of Hong Kong Island, Kowloon and the New Territories, with Hong Kong Island taking up less than 10 per cent of the colony's land mass. It is fallacious to assert that Hong Kong has grown out of a fishing village on the evidence that Hong Kong Island *alone* was a fishing village in 1841. To be cogent, the inference has to start from a demonstration that Kowloon and the New Territories were *also* mere fishing villages in 1841.

It may be argued that the "fishing village to megapolis" inference can still make sense in that Hong Kong Island has been the oldest and most important part of the colony. Against this line of reasoning, let us be reminded of how Edward Youde persuaded Margaret Thatcher in 1982 to give up any thought of maintaining a viable colony consisting of Hong Kong Island and Kowloon once the lease of the New Territories expired in 1997 — Hong Kong's prosperity depended so much on the industries, facilities and population located in the New Territories, that "Hong Kong would stand or fall with the New Territories" (Robert Cottrell, *The End of Hong Kong*, 1993, p. 71). It was Hong Kong including the New Territories and Kowloon, not Hong Kong Island alone, that has grown into a megapolis.

One way out of Ng Lun Ngai-ha's logical fallacy is of course to assert that the *entirety* of Hong Kong in 1841 consisted of sparsely populated fishing villages. This was exactly the stance adopted by many publications, such as HMSO's *Britain and Hong Kong*, cited above. However, no attempt has been made to adduce any proof. There is a strong suspicion that the assertion is no more than a sleight-of-hand extrapolation from the claim that Hong Kong *Island* was almost uninhabited in 1841.

### Hong Kong in the 1810s

The claim that Hong Kong as a whole was sparsely populated in the nineteenth century could only be a lie. Xinan 新安 county, parts of which became the colony of Hong Kong, in the eighteenth and nineteenth century was listed in various directories and gazetteers as an average (*zhong*) county in Guangdong province. Xinan had a population of around 150,000 persons some time in the eighteenth century, making it the seventh most populous county among the fourteen counties of Guangzhou prefecture, itself the most populous prefecture of Guangdong province.

By the time the 1819 version of *Xinan Gazetteer* was compiled, the population of the county had grown to some 240,000 persons. Guangdong in the 1810s had 82 counties or similar administrative units with a total population of 19.2 million, giving an average of 230,000 persons per county. The eighteen provinces in China proper in 1812 had a population of 350 million living in some 1,500 counties, giving an average of again 230,000 persons per county. That is, Xinan was slightly more densely populated than an average county in both Guangdong and nationwide. Xinan was in many other aspects an average county in Guangdong — besides being moderately well-peopled, the quota for land tax (10,284 taels per annum) and that for the number of scholars passing the imperial examinations (eight licentiate degrees per year for Punti, two for Hakka) were also about average, indicating that the county was moderately affluent and civilized.

As to the pre-colonial population of those parts of Xinan that became the colony of Hong Kong, very little research has been done on the subject. We know, nonetheless, that British traders in the 1830s found Lantau Island to be "in some parts well peopled" (G. B. Sayer, *Hong Kong 1841–1862*, 1937, p. 32). We also know that the 1819 *Xinan Gazetteer* recorded a total of some 850 villages in the whole of the county, of which around 340 were in what became the colony of Hong Kong. On a crude *pro rata* basis, the pre-colonial population of Hong Kong could be estimated as to be in the region of 100,000. This compares well with the official estimation of the New Territories having a population of over 100,000 when the British took over in 1898 (when there had been very active emigration overseas, not to mention population shift to urban Hong Kong, it would not be surprising that the net population growth since 1819 had not been phenomenal).

### Hong Kong Island just before Colonization

Even the veracity of the assertion that Hong Kong *Island* was an "almost uninhabited" "fishing village" is subject to serious doubt.

Since at least the early nineteenth century the British had frequently used Hong Kong Island as a watering place. An account in 1817 stated that water from Hong Kong Island was considered "uncontaminated by any vegetable matter, for few places present a more barren aspect than these islands" (Sayer, pp. 26–27). The barren nature of Hong Kong Island is interesting. This is because from what we know of the fuel requirement for the rice-based cuisine of Punti Chinese settlers, a treeless topography indicated not the lack of population. On the contrary, it was a symptom of population pressure on the ecology.

Indeed, in 1817 a British visitor to Hong Kong Island found the place fairly well-populated and vibrant: "At night the number of fishing-boats, each with a light, presented the appearance of a London street well-lighted" (Sayer, p. 25).

The first enumeration of population by the British authorities, published in May 1841, estimated the Chinese population on Hong Kong Island to be around 7,500 persons, including 800 traders and 300 temporary labourers. E. J. Eitel, one of the first historians on Hong Kong, asserted that the pre-colonial population "probably never exceeded, at any one time, a total of 2,000 people" (Eitel, *Europe in China*, 1895, p. 134).

Eitel did not provide any grounds at all for his assertion. There are good reasons to think that he was wrong, that the population on Hong Kong Island immediately prior to colonization was *significantly larger* than that in 1841.

One consideration is that, from 1839 onwards, Hong Kong Island, the harbour and Kowloon were the sites of frequent Sino-British hostilities in the First Opium War: "The British who had retreated to Hong Kong were harried by the local Chinese, who poisoned many wells and refused to sell the foreigners food. Armed clashes between British and Chinese war junks in Hong Kong harbour ... occurred in September and October 1839 ... Lin [Zexu] even encouraged mobilization of local 'braves' against the British, who had grown even more unpopular since a group of drunken seamen had killed a Chinese villager on Kowloon ... and Elliot had refused to hand the accused over ..." (Spence, p. 155).

It is reasonable to assume that, with war, foreign occupation, general lawlessness, and repeated proclamations from Commissioner Lin Zexu threatening dire consequences for collaborators, many residents on Hong Kong Island had left for safer refuge until peace (a very uncertain one, for that matter) was proclaimed in January 1841. By the time the first population enumeration was carried out in early 1841, it would be unlikely that many refugees had the time or the confidence to return.

Another consideration is that the British occupation of Hong Kong Island from 1839 onwards had upset the local balance of power between the originally dominant, more numerous Punti group and the underprivileged, less numerous Hakka and Tanka groups: "from the first advent of the British and all through the wars with China, the Puntis as a rule were the enemies and the Hakkas the friends, purveyors, commissariat and transport coolies of the foreigners, whilst the fishing population provided boatmen and pilots for the foreign trade" (Eitel, p. 132).

The Puntis, being classified as "enemies", would have to live in fear of reprisal from the British invaders and of revenge from the formerly oppressed Hakkas and Tankas. It would only be rational for many Puntis, particularly the more respectable ones, to leave the place. Even after peace was proclaimed, they would be hesitant to return, as the Hakkas and Tankas, now in the good books of the foreigners, might turn the table on their former oppressors. Indeed, the upsetting of the local balance of power may well be one of the reasons why during the first few decades after 1841, there were few respectable Chinese resident in the colony.

Given the above considerations, it may be safely assumed that the pre-colonial population on Hong Kong Island was significantly higher than the count of 7,500 persons in 1841. Further research may well show that the Island was moderately affluent like the rest of Xinan county. Suffice it to say that the Island, just like the rest of Xinan county, was neither "almost uninhabited" nor a mere uncivilized "fishing village".

## ☐ Pre-colonial Hong Kong

Now we can deal with the other premise of the colonial paradigm, namely that pre-colonial Hong Kong was so "remote and inconsequential" that it was "barely more than a geographical expression" that "had little part in the main current of Chinese history".

The influence of the colonial paradigm has meant that scant attention has been given to pre-colonial history. The only monograph (apart from picture books) on prehistoric Hong Kong is William Meacham's *Archaeology in Hong Kong*. This was published over a decade ago and has long been out of print.

The standard reference on pre-colonial history based on historical documents, written by Lo Hsiang-lin 羅香林, was written some thirty years back (*Hong Kong and Its External Communications Before 1842*, 1963). Lo's work, apart from being outdated, was handicapped by its narrow focus (confined to external communications), its restrictive methodology (a conventional Chinese-style historiography resulting in a rather disjointed narrative), and the lack of thoroughness in sourcing and analysing available Chinese materials (not to mention the lack of reference to materials in languages other than Chinese). Publications by Lin Tianwei 林天蔚, Xiao Guojian 蕭國健, Xiao Guojun 蕭國鈞 and others in Chinese in recent years have filled in some gaps, but sadly these works were again mainly pieces of disjointed narratives on quite narrow topics, based on a less than exhaustive use of sources.

The semi-official works representing the view on Hong Kong history of the People's Republic of China, such as *Xianggang shilüe* 香港史略 (Outline History of Hong Kong, 1988) by Yuan Bangjian 元邦建, are quite indifferent pieces of scholarship. The main concern of these works is to score polemical points that are politically relevant to China (such as that Hong Kong has always been Chinese territory, and that the events leading to its colonization constituted an injustice to China), but are of less use in enlightening us on historically relevant matters.

The following narrative of Hong Kong's pre-colonial past is therefore based mainly on this author's own research and interpretation. Admittedly many points in my reconstruction of historical reality are based only on circumstantial evidence or rather speculative reasoning. However, it would serve my purpose if this narrative could be considered as a provocative agenda for future research. (To make the narration flow smoothly, citation of sources has been dispensed with as far as possible.)

## The Stone and Bronze Ages

Prior to the end of the last Ice Age, the sea level in the South China Sea was 80–100 metres lower than it is today, exposing a vast plain, called by geologists the Sundae Shelf, that linked continental China, Taiwan, Hainan and the present-day ASEAN (Association of Southeast Asian Nations) countries into one continuous land mass.

Around 4000 BC, the rising sea level submerged the Sundae Shelf, converting Hong Kong from mountainous uplands into a collection of peninsulas, islands and harbours. The alluvial plains that make up today's Pearl River Delta had not risen from the sea. Immediately south of Guangzhou, stretching all the way to present-day Macau, was a collection of small islands among turbulent seas. (Refer to Tan Qirang 譚其驤 [ed.], *Zhongguo lishi ditu ji* 中國歷史地圖集 [Chinese Historical Maps], Vol. 1, 1993).

In contrast, Hong Kong, both the solid, fertile mainland and the islands with well-sheltered harbours and an abundance of marine produce, was much more inviting to the refugees driven back from the Sundae Shelf. These refugees, including those driven inland into the Pearl River Basin, still maintained an active intercourse with their former kins in what remained of the Sundae Shelf — up north to eastern China and Taiwan, and down south to Southeast Asia. Before the Pearl River Delta emerged, Hong Kong was the last landfall in the Pearl Estuary before the open seas were reached, and the monsoon could be caught to go across the South China Sea. Hong Kong was the gateway to and from China, thousands of years before the British came.

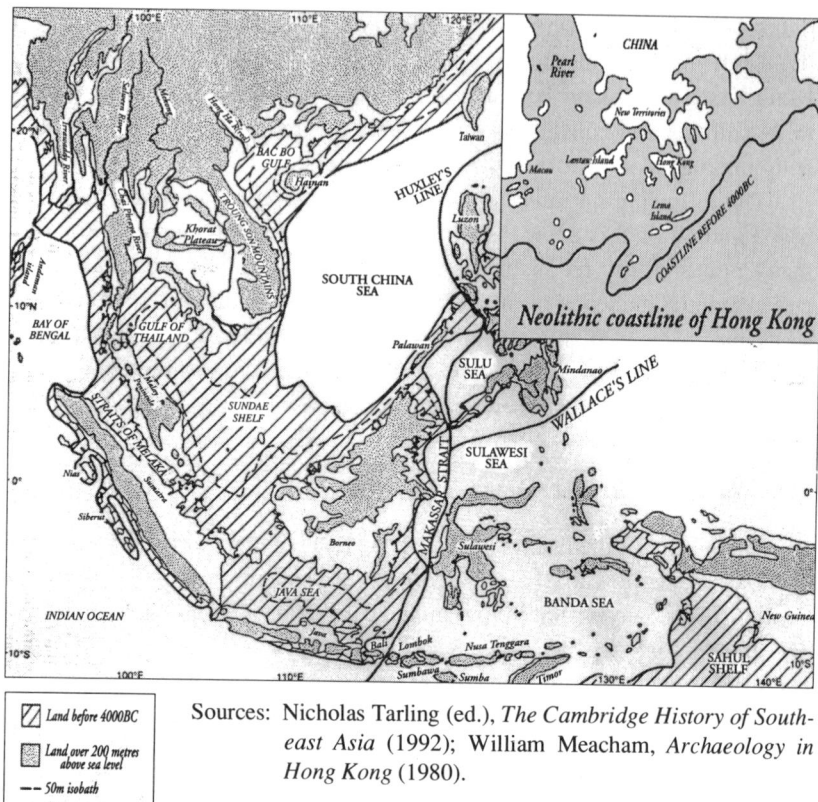

Neolithic coastline of Hong Kong

Land before 4000BC
Land over 200 metres
above sea level
— — 50m isobath
—— 200m isobath

Sources: Nicholas Tarling (ed.), *The Cambridge History of South-east Asia* (1992); William Meacham, *Archaeology in Hong Kong* (1980).

South China and Southeast Asia before 4000 BC

Archaeological excavation has located over a dozen neolithic settlements on Hong Kong Island, Lantau, Lamma and Tuen Mun, with clear evidence in those sites on northern Lantau of the existence of fortification and well-organized series of permanent buildings. The most exciting discovery was made recently in Tuen Mun of "a densely populated settlement between the middle and the late neolithic period (between 4000 BC and 2500 BC)" which was probably a centre for commerce as it yielded the "most refined stone artifacts and earthenware found in southern China", as well as jade ceremonial artifacts indicative of the influence of mainstream Chinese culture (*South China Morning Post* and *Oriental Daily*, 21 July 1993).

There are hundreds of Bronze Age sites in Hong Kong. The findings from these sites and similar ones in China have tended to confirm the view of the archaeologist Walter Schofield, active in the 1930s, that "the Hong Kong area was a meeting-place of cultures and probably of races; it had trading relations with other lands, and formed part of a cultural province extending a considerable distance along the China coast" (Sally Rodwell, *Historic Hong Kong*, 1991, p. 17).

The Bronze Age also leaves a legacy of many beautiful, intriguing rock carvings all over Hong Kong. These pre-historic works of art were referred to in dozens of ancient Chinese texts (the earliest I have come across so far dated back to the Song Dynasty). Daxi Shan 大奚山 , the ancient name of Lantau, was known in ancient Chinese folklore as a magical land, because of its rock carvings that were supposed to reveal either supernatural secrets or potent medical formulae, as well as the mermaids that frequented the seas (the breed of white dolphins native to Hong Kong waters now sadly facing extinction because of the construction of the new airport on Lantau).

## Sinicization

Maritime southern and eastern China was inhabited by a race known as Yue 越 , speaking a multi-syllabic, non-tonal language. A song in the Yue language of the fifth century BC, sung to entertain an official of the Chu 楚 kingdom which was extending its suzerainty over the region, was recorded in transliteration and translation into the mono-syllabic, tonal Chinese language. From this, modern scholars have shown that the Yue tongue was probably an earlier version of the language of the present-day Zhuang 壯 race in Guangdong and Guangxi provinces (Chen Guoqiang 陳國強 , *et al.*, *Baiyue minzu shi* 百越民族史 [History of the Hundred Yue Races], 1988, pp. 369–71.)

Sinicization of the Yue people in Guangdong — that is, assimilation of them into mainstream Chinese culture (subsequently known as Han Chinese culture) to form the Cantonese subculture — did not start with military conquest by the Qin Dynasty in the second century BC as Lo Hsiang-lin, Ng Lun Ngai-ha and others have suggested. It had started much earlier, at first probably through cultural influence (such as the adoption as early as 2500 BC of mainstream Chinese ceremonial format by the local nobility, as indicated by the jade ceremonial artifacts excavated at the neolithic site at Tuen Mun). Later on, mainstream Chinese influence came by means of the stationing of officials and troops as the Chu kingdom extended its suzerainty from the middle Spring and Autumn Period (sixth century BC onwards) over strategic points in the region. This may well explain why a third century BC tomb in Lamma Island contained a jade *yazhang* 牙璋 , an insignia of high military command in mainstream Chinese culture.

Guangdong and Guangxi were conquered by the Qin Dynasty in 214 BC, "in order to serve as settlements for exiles" (*Shiji* 史記 , *Juan* 6). As many as half a million settlers were reportedly sent to the newly established counties. After the fall of the Qin in 207 BC, the military governor, Zhao Tuo 趙陀 , founded the Kingdom of Nanyue 南越 (Southern Yue) with its capital in Panyu 番禺 (present-day Guangzhou and the Pearl Estuary including Hong Kong). Trade with Southeast Asian countries and perhaps land even farther away was quite active, as the artifacts from overseas discovered in the tomb of one of the Nanyue kings indicated. Hong Kong's role in the land-hugging, peddling international trade during this period has not yet been established, but it is reasonable to assume that it continued to play the same role since neolithic times, as the gateway to China.

The Han Dynasty at first accepted Nanyue as a vassal but conquered it in AD 111 using a 200,000-strong force. By that time, the Qin colonists had been so well-assimilated into the local community that the Nanyue ruling class considered themselves different from people from the "middle kingdom" (*Zhongguo*).

Thus it was not surprising to find that although the "newly founded prefectures (*jun* 郡 )", according to *Shiji* (*Juan* 30), were "ruled according to local native customs with no taxation levied ... small-scale rebellions frequently occurred. Officials were murdered. Han authorities sent officials and soldiers from the south to suppress the rebels. Some 10,000 soldiers had to be sent even during a relatively quiet year."

The economic backdrop to the Han conquest was the rich endowment of the region with exotic produces as well as with more mundane natural resources such as sea salt, the monopoly of which provided a substantial part of central government revenue. A *yanguan* 鹽官 , the official in charge of the imperial salt monopoly, was stationed in Panyu soon after the conquest to oversee salt production in the Pearl Estuary.

The most productive salt pans in the Pearl Estuary were located on the eastern coast, from Nantou 南頭 and Huangtian 黃田 in present-day Shenzhen to Tai O on Lantau, and Kowloon Tong and Lam Tin on Kowloon. The elaborate brick-built tomb of a first century Panyu official, discovered in the 1950s at Li Cheng Uk right under one of the world's busiest flight path into Kai Tak Airport, was most probably what remained of a fairly sizeable imperial outpost for the salt monopoly.

The salt pans on the eastern coast were sufficiently important for them to be consolidated in AD 265 by the Wei Dynasty into the *Dongguan yanchang* 東官鹽場, or Eastern Government Salt Administration. By the early years of the East Jin Dynasty, in AD 331, the area became a prefecture, and it was named after the salt pans administration as Dongguan prefecture. Under the new prefecture were a number of counties, one of which was Baoan 寶安 with apparently the same boundaries as Xinan county in 1841, stretching from present-day Shenzhen to Hong Kong.

## Lu Xun Uprising and Decline of the East Jin Dynasty

Endacott's allegation that Hong Kong "had little part in the main current of Chinese history" cannot be farther from the truth. The Hong Kong region made its first appointment with China's dynastic cycles in the first decade of the fifth century, during the last years of the East Jin Dynasty. It was by all standards an amazing story, of cross-cultural religious influence and long-distance maritime warfare. This author's preliminary research can hardly begin to do justice to it.

The East Jin was a period of almost frenzied religious and philosophical activities. Confucianism was subject to continuous re-evaluation. Missionaries for Buddhism, as well as for Christianity, Zoroastrianism and other middle eastern religions, arrived in large number and their doctrines were assimilated into Chinese culture. Taoism, based on native Chinese shamanism, also began to be organized with scriptures and rites in the way Buddhism and the other foreign religions were.

Some of the foreign missionaries used the overland route via central Asia into north China. However, they were not always allowed by the non-Han rulers of north China to go south. Thus many missionaries used the alternative route by sea to Guangzhou and then by land to the capital in present-day Nanjing. The trade routes to Southeast Asia, India and the Persian Gulf were by this time well-developed. Shi Chong 石崇, reputedly the richest man in the empire, amassed a fortune beyond one's wildest dream during his tenure of the governorship of Guangzhou.

After crossing the South China Sea, Tuen Mun, as it had been since neolithic times, was the first port of call for the mercantile fleets. A stop at the Tuen Mun area (which, admittedly, could mean anywhere from Lantau to today's Tuen Mun to Nantou in present-day Shenzhen) after the turbulent journey across the South China Sea, for re-fitting and re-supply, was a necessity to the coast-hugging crafts of the time. After all, Guangzhou, over

100 kilometres to the north through shallow waters, could take a journey of two to three days. It was apparently also an administrative requirement to stop at Tuen Mun for assessment of customs duties and other procedural matters.

With the arrival of foreign missionaries, Tuen Mun developed in the fourth century into a religious centre as well. The most famous missionary using Tuen Mun as his base was an Indian Buddhist monk known by his Chinese name Beidu 杯渡 around whom many legends have gathered and were commemorated by subsequent literary works. An alternative name for Tuen Mun Shan (Castle Peak as it was called by the British) was Beidu Shan. It is interesting to note that today Tuen Mun and Lantau on the opposite shore are still renowned for their Buddhist, Taoist and Catholic monasteries. It is a 1,600-year-old tradition.

By the late fourth century, a Taoist sect known as *wudoumi dao* 五斗米道 was becoming very fashionable, because it was preaching a more direct form of salvation. True believers were required to donate five *dou* of rice (hence the name of the sect) to the church, and salvation would follow. A large following from the gentry class was attracted. One of them, Sun Tai 孫泰, a descendant of the royal family of the defunct Wu Dynasty, apparently started to popularize the sect by means of magical practices. His fellow gentry believers ostracized him to the Guangzhou region. There, he got the inspiration, probably from the various foreign religions active in south China, for preaching millenarian doctrines to the underprivileged. He and his south China disciples returned to east China in the closing years of the fourth century and soon built up a large following, especially among the seafaring population.

Sun Tai was executed around AD 399 for plotting a rebellion. His nephew, Sun En 孫恩, gathered a seaborne force to stage the uprising nonetheless. It took the imperial court many years to quell the rebellion. Sun En committed suicide after his defeat.

In the winter of AD 404, Sun's brother-in-law, Lu Xun 盧循, re-grouped what was left of the rebel fleet and took it to conquer the Guangzhou region. The winter monsoon allowed Lu's fleet to accomplish a surprise attack. Disciples recruited during Sun Tai's sojourn in the region could also have provided assistance.

After ruling Guangzhou for several years, Lu marched north in the spring of AD 411 using the inland waterways to launch a surprise attack on Nanjing (the winter monsoon was still blowing, making it impossible for the rebel forces to go by sea). Liu Yu 劉裕, the commander of the loyalist forces, made use of the monsoon blowing in his favour to sent his fleet south to attack Guangzhou. Tuen Mun was unguarded and easily captured. After a short battle, Guangzhou capitulated.

Lu, his base lost, retreated by sea. He was unable to recapture Guangzhou. After a series of futile sea battles off Hainan and Vietnam, Lu committed suicide in AD 412. Liu Yu's victories turned him into the *de facto* ruler of the East Jin court, and in AD 420 he replaced the East Jin with his own dynasty.

We do not know the extent to which rebels recruited from the Hong Kong region had taken part in these amazing maritime manoeuvres. However, we do know that Lu Xun's sailors, who were apparently of non-Han race subject to some degree of sinicization, were sent after they surrendered to work the salt pans in the thirty-six islands around Daxi Shan, present-day Lantau. These ex-rebels, said to be 20,000-strong according to some accounts, became known as Lu Yu 盧餘 (Lu's remnants) or Lu Ting 盧亭 (Lu's bond labourers for the salt pans), indicating that they were probably sent in semi-servile status to Lantau and nearby islands. Hong Kong did not have to wait for the nineteenth and twentieth centuries to be a haven for ex-rebels and political refugees.

The Lu Yu came to a tragic end many centuries later. We shall deal with this in due course.

## The Founding of the Chen Dynasty

The rising importance of the area around Tuen Mun was probably one of the reasons why during the Taihe years 太和 (AD 336–371) of East Jin, a Xinan prefecture was created in the region. No details on boundaries were given in official records. However, there are circumstantial evidence to support the belief that Baoan county, including Tuen Mun, was part of the new prefecture.The traditional belief in the connection between Baoan and Xinan was sufficiently strong that, when Baoan county was re-established in the sixteenth century, the Ming government chose to name it Xinan.

It was as Xinan that the Hong Kong region made another impact on China's dynastic cycles. The Chen Dynasty (AD 557–589) was founded by Chen Baxian 陳霸先 who started his career as an army officer in Guangdong during the Liang Dynasty. In AD 535, Chen quelled a minor rebellion in the Guangzhou area and was made into Xinan *Zi* 新安子 (Viscount of Xinan), with a fief consisting of 300 households.

It was not until AD 548 that Chen moved from the provincial to the national political arena by responding to a call for help against usurpers who had captured the imperial capital at Nanjing and whose sympathizers were threatening Guangdong. Chen's troops crushed an enemy army at Nanye 南野 county just to the north of Guangdong in AD 550. Chen was promoted to Nanye *Bo* 南野伯 (Count of Nanye). Chen proceeded to relieve Nanjing, installed himself as the *de facto* ruler and eventually founded his dynasty.

One reasonable interpretation, admittedly based on circumstantial evidence, of the above narration is that Chen, as Viscount of Xinan, may be regarded as the first-ever Lord of Hong Kong. (There was another Xinan in the sixth century, a populous prefecture in Zhejiang; Chen would not have been given this as his fief for quelling a minor rebellion in a far-away province; if he had, the rank would have to be higher than a viscount, as the conquest of Nanye, a moderately affluent county, already merited the elevation to the rank of a count.) Subsequently, Chen founded his dynasty with the help of an army partly recruited from Xinan.

### Tuen Mun Garrison and Guanfu Chang

Tuen Mun continued its role as port, naval base and cultural centre during the Tang and Song Dynasties (as well as the interregnum of the Nan Han Dynasty). Foreign trade was of immense importance to the financial health of these dynasties. A nationwide market had been developed. Yet the central government had insufficient organizational means, and the copper-based currency of insufficient physical availability, to extract sufficient revenue from inland taxes to provide the necessary liquidity to effectively operate the economy.

Customs duties from foreign trade to a certain extent filled the gap, and hence it was not surprising to find in Guangzhou, which monopolized foreign trade during Tang, a colony of foreign traders reportedly over 100,000 strong. Other ports for legal foreign trade were opened during Song times, but Guangzhou continued to have a sizeable "foreign city", affluent enough to build and maintain a fine mosque and light house.

The importance of revenue from foreign trade was most keenly felt when a dynasty was on decline. The provinces, always ready to assume a semi-autonomous status under warlords when the influence of the imperial court began to wane, became reluctant to remit taxes to the centre. Thus by the ninth and tenth centuries, the Tang court, having lost effective control of even the regions close to the capital at Loyang, survived partly through its control of Guangzhou's customs duties. Indeed, the governorship of Guangzhou was at times the only provincial-ranking post the emperor could freely appoint, and only officials of a prime ministerial rank could get this coveted position.

The role of Tuen Mun during these centuries continued to be that of the outer port for Guangzhou, a naval base, a centre for religion, and a production centre for salt and other produces. As the outer port, the importance of Tuen Mun was underlined in contemporary record of the main sea route from China to Southeast Asia, India, Arabia and East Africa.

The Tang route started at Guangzhou, with the last landfall after 100 kilometres at Tuen Mun, and then it was sailing across the seas. For the Song trade route, the compendium on south China, *Lingwai daida* 嶺外代答, recorded that "to get to Guangzhou, go through Tuen Mun; to get to Quanzhou [the trading centre next in importance to Guangzhou], go through Jiazimen 甲子門 ". Tuen Mun Mountain was the byword for adventurous travel by sea in Tang literary tradition, as exemplified by two well-known poems by Han Yu 韓愈 and Liu Yuxi 劉禹錫 on the subject.

As a naval base, Tuen Mun Garrison (*zhen* 鎮 ) was founded in AD 736, probably absorbing Baoan county which was abolished. Maps of the Tang and Song period eminently indicated Tuen Mun on the south China coast (refer to Maps 97 and 196 in Cao Wanru 曹婉如 , *et al.* [ed.], *Zhongguo gudai ditu ji* 中國古代地圖集 [An Atlas of Ancient Maps in China], 1990). The garrison was said to be 2,000-strong. It was from here that a fleet was sent north in AD 744 to successfully eradicate piracy in east China. The garrison during the Song Dynasty acquired the exalted title of *Cuifeng jun* 摧鋒軍 (Destructive Vanguards). As we shall see, it had its glorious and inglorious moments in the service of the empire.

As a religious centre, Tuen Mun continued to play host to Buddhist monks and Islamic mullahs. During the Nan Han Dynasty (AD 917–971), Tuen Mun Shan was accredited with supernatural powers, and renamed Ruiying Shan 瑞應山 (Response to Auspicious Sign Mountain), and monasteries were founded by imperial decree.

The region continued to be a major production centre for the salt monopoly in the Tang and Song Dynasties. During the North Song Dynasty, when there was a dramatic increase in salt production to pay for war expenses, the salt administration in the area was separately constituted and named Guanfu Chang 官富場 . It was located at present-day Kowloon City, next to Kai Tak Airport.

Guanfu's foundation could be traced to some time before 1012, when an outpost of Guanfu Chang for customs inspection was established on Fat Tong Island 佛堂州 , the western entrance to the Hong Kong harbour. A stone carving by an official from Guanfu Chang dated 1274 is still extant outside the Tin Hau Temple opposite Fat Tong. Stone tablets indicating that the Fat Tong outpost was also used for collecting customs duties from ships from Vietnam have been found on Fat Tong.

Lime production was very active in the Hong Kong region from the Tang Dynasty onwards, as the almost ubiquitous remains of elegant Tang kilns scattered throughout the colony today testifies. The Nan Han Dynasty turned Tolo Harbour into a pearl-diving centre and a quota for pearl was not finally relieved until the Ming Dynasty.

### The Lu Ting Massacre

The Lu Ting, since they were sent to Lantau and the islands in the fifth century to work the salt pans, had developed their own dialect, a dragon-worshipping religion, and an idyllic lifestyle based on a barter economy. They were said to be good-natured, easily satisfied people wearing scanty costumes made from local material and thriving on marine produce procured by means of their fishing boats. Their Taoist religious practices gave credence to legends that they had descended from, or had inter-married with, dragons and mermaids, such that they possessed superhuman prowess, being able to swim across the Pearl Estuary unaided. They may have been partly sinicized when serving under Lu Xun centuries back, but now they could claim to be, and were regarded by Han observers as a race apart and a culture unto themselves.

Meanwhile, the Song Dynasty had lost north China to invaders in the late 1120s. The newly established South Song court had difficulty in protecting itself from the invaders, not to mention enforcing law and order in the provinces. Song officials in the Hong Kong region resorted to recruiting young Lu Ting into the Pearl Estuary navy (*Shui jun* 水軍 ) and the crack troop formation *Cuifeng jun*. In return, the salt monopoly was relaxed, allowing the Lu Ting to produce and sell a certain amount of tax-free salt on their own. At the time, Baoan county had yet to be resurrected and Lantau was under the jurisdiction of Panyu county, while the rest of Hong Kong was part of Dongguan county.

By the 1190s, South Song was in the grips of an economic recession, partly due to over-production of monopoly produces such as salt, and partly due to heavy government expenditure. Imperial edicts were sent to eradicate illegal salt production. The quota of tax-free salt granted to the Lu Ting was revoked, and soldiers were sent to Lantau to confiscate the salt.

The Lu Ting considered themselves being unfairly treated, and disturbances started. Incompetence and bickering among the officials at Guangzhou led to exacerbation of the unrest, resulting in full-scale rebellion in 1197. Led by a leader called Gao Deng 高登 , they took their fishing boats to attack Guangzhou but was defeated in a naval engagement. The Prefect of Guangzhou thereupon sent his forces in summer 1197 to slaughter Lantau. Reportedly not a single soul was left alive.

Such was the tragic end of the Lu Ting people and their culture, after nearly eight hundred years living on Lantau and surrounding islands. It is interesting to note that the year 1997, when Hong Kong (once more with its own cultural identity based on the Cantonese dialect) reverts to China, is exactly the eight-hundredth anniversary of the Lu Ting Massacre.

For some years, the only human beings on Lantau and surrounding islands were the small contingent of *Cuifeng jun* on guard duty there. The agricultural mainland parts of Hong Kong, on the other hand, continued to be well-populated, with sinicization being carried out by both cultural influence on the indigenous people and immigration of Han people to the region. An island further south of Hong Kong Island, called the Laowan 老萬 , or Ladrones, continued to be populated by a race similar to the Lu Ting. They were exterminated by Ming officials in 1580 for committing piracy.

In 1235, the *Cuifeng jun*, having been sent away from the Hong Kong region to serve outside Guangdong for a number of years, staged a mutiny and moved south to threaten Guangzhou. The governor of Guangdong assigned a respected scholar, Li Maoying 李昴英, to successfully negotiate the surrender of the rebels. Li's family had migrated some years back to Panyu, the jurisdiction of which at that time included Lantau. After many more years of distinguished service to the imperial court, Li was made the Founding Baron (*kaiguo nan* 開國男 ) of Panyu, with a fief consisting of 300 households located on Lantau.

At least two boundary stones of the Li fief are still extant on Lantau. The Li family's claim to the land constituting the fief on Lantau was still recognized by officials of the Qing Dynasty. A stone tablet, dated 1777, recording such recognition is still in display in a temple in Tung Chung, Lantau. After Chen Baxian, Li Maoying was the second "Lord of Hong Kong" in Chinese history.

### *The Last Emperors of the South Song*

It is a sad indication of the low standards of historiography on Hong Kong that even the well-known story of the sojourn in the region of the last emperors of the South Song has not been well told. The conventional narration was hardly titillating — the last South Song emperors took refuge from the Mongol invaders in various places in the Hong Kong region in 1277; one died, and the other left, to be defeated and drowned on the other side of the Pearl Estuary in 1279.

The real story was more interesting.

After the South Song capital Linan was captured by the Mongols in April 1276, the two boy emperors, Shi 昰 and Bing 昺 , sought refuge in Quanzhou, a seaport in Fujian province that had developed in the Song Dynasty to be as affluent as Guangzhou. Unfortunately, court officials alienated the military governor, a sinicized Arab merchant who proceeded to collaborate with the Mongols.

The next refuge was Guangzhou. The Song court arrived there some-time in the twelfth month (lunar calendar) of 1276, but it had already fallen to the Mongols. The loyalist forces tried to land, but was repelled. After briefly retreating west to Jiazimen on the west Guangdong coast, the Song court moved east to the Hong Kong region in the second month of 1277, wandering around Lantau, Guanfu Chang (where a "travelling palace" was built), Guta 古塔 (present-day Fat Tong) and Qianwan 淺灣 (present-day Tsuen Wan).

Contrary to what many historians have alleged, the Song court was *not* seeking refuge in the Hong Kong area. Historical records, when pieced together, show the court using Hong Kong as a base for rallying support for its cause. Zhang Zhensun 張鎮孫, a senior ex-official, was contacted at his home near Guangzhou and ordered to raise an army. Guangzhou was taken by Song loyalists in the fourth month of 1277, at the same time as the arrival of the Song court at Guanfu.

Guanfu, though not a big city, was a sizeable imperial outpost next to the populous Tugua 土瓜 (present-day To Kwa Wan), one of the five major townships in Dongguan county. Sufficient supplies would be stocked for the substantial forces protecting the court. Expertise for re-fitting the ships would be available. Communication with the various loyalist forces scattered along the coast would also be easier from Guanfu than Guangzhou.

The Mongols counter-attacked from the ninth month of 1277 onwards. The instruction to their naval forces was that they should move south from

Quanzhou to capture the various strategic points on the coast, before converging on Guanfu for a rendezvous with the land forces for a coordinated attack on Guangzhou. By the eleventh month of 1277, all the above objectives, with the exception of reducing Chaozhou, had been accomplished. Guangzhou was attacked and Zhang Zhensun soon surrendered.

The *Cuifeng jun* and the *Shui jun*, made up of recruits from the Hong Kong and nearby regions, came to a tragic but glorious end. They were annihilated in defence of the provincial capital.

Details are not available on the capture of Guanfu by the Mongol fleet during these manoeuvres. Anyway, the Song court evacuated Guanfu in the eleventh month of 1277. An engagement was fought with the Mongols in Qianwan. Thereafter the Song court took refuge on various islands in the South China Sea.

In the third month of 1278, the loyalists had apparently re-conquered the Hong Kong region. The Song court moved to Lantau. Zhang Zhensun was contacted and persuaded to support the loyalist cause once more. He raised an army to take Guangzhou the next month, but was somehow forced to surrender shortly afterwards. Two of his generals, Wang Daofu 王道夫 and Ling Zhen 凌震, however, soon recaptured Guangzhou. Guanfu, it seemed, was also in Song hands once more.

Emperor Shi died and was buried in Lantau in the fourth month of 1278. Emperor Bing and his court moved in the sixth month to Yashan 崖山 on the other side of the Pearl Estuary. In the eleventh leap month, the Mongols, now well-reinforced, destroyed both loyalist armies at Guangzhou and Chaozhou.

The situation was desperate. It could well have been otherwise had Wen Tianxiang 文天祥, the titular prime minister of the loyalists, heeded the advice of one of his generals, Du Hu 杜滸, before his forces were destroyed at Chaozhou. Du's advice was to abandon Chaozhou, take to the sea, and join forces with the Song court. Du's advice was not accepted. Nonetheless, the loyalist fleet at Chaozhou was asked to turn over a few boats to Du as reinforcement for Guanfu. This request may or may not be one of the causes of unrest among the naval commanders. Wen proceeded to use strong arm tactics to bring the situation under control. His efforts backfired, leading to the defection of the loyalist fleet to the Mongol cause.

Du did take his small squadron to relieve Guanfu. It proved to be no match for the invading Mongols, and Guanfu had to be evacuated.

Wen Tianxiang lived to regret his decisions. After his capture at Chaozhou, he was taken aboard the Mongol fleet (partly consisting of the former loyalist fleet at Chaozhou) which arrived at Guanfu in the first month of 1279. There, the ships stayed for six days, to be re-fitted and re-supplied, before they sailed to Yashan. It is ironic that Wen is often remembered for his heart-rending poems declaring his loyalty to the Song cause written while on board Mongol ships, when these crafts were made sea-worthy and battle-ready at Guanfu which fell into Mongol hands precisely because of Wen's incompetence.

In the second month of 1279, the Mongol forces, sailing in favourable winds from the winter monsoon, attacked and destroyed the Song fleet at Yashan. Emperor Bing reportedly drowned. Thus ended another of Hong Kong's involvement in China's dynastic cycles.

### Decline of Tuen Mun and Guanfu Chang

The 1277–1279 war against the Mongols caused widespread destruction in Guangdong. Tuen Mun and Guanfu were so badly affected that they were unable to recover. A lot of those from the region who joined the loyalist forces were among the 100,000 reportedly killed at Yashan. Those who joined the Mongols were subsequently pressed into service against Japan. Indeed, former South Song generals headed the disastrous expeditions, during which almost all either perished or were sold into slavery.

It was during the Yuan Dynasty that the Tuen Mun Garrison was abolished. Guanfu was downgraded from *chang* 場 , an administration, to *zhai* 寨 , a mere fortification. Lime production and pearl diving went into decline and eventually stopped.

Worse still, by the time Guangzhou's foreign trade had recovered in the 1290s, the customs points had been moved north to Huangpu. There was no more need for Tuen Mun or Guanfu except as anchorage and landmark.

The only consolation was the development during this period of the cultivation and preparation of incense wood, which was not a particularly labour-intensive activity. It suited a depopulated region short on labour but with plenty of uncultivated fields. The industry disappeared in the eighteenth century, when the region became well-peopled.

There was even less need for Tuen Mun when the Ming Dynasty was founded in 1368. The first Ming emperor, Zhu Yuanzhang, knew all about the tragic journeys of the last Song emperors through Quanzhou, Guanfu and Yashan. His maternal grandfather was a loyalist soldier who survived the defeat at Yashan, and who constantly exhorted his grandson to avenge the death of the boy emperors.

The Arab merchants, who betrayed the Song court and who defended the Yuan Dynasty, did not endear themselves to Zhu Yuanzhang. Moreover, with the introduction of a silver-based currency backed up by efficient collection of land rent, the imperial government no longer had to rely on customs duties as a main source of revenue. The irony was that the abundance of silver was due to the existence of a very active illicit trade with silver-rich Japan.

Thus Zhu Yuanzhang banned all foreign trade except the very restrictive form of tribute trade — in the name of bearing tribute to the imperial court, traders from a country can bring in a small quota of goods to be bought and sold by officials. Customs duties were abolished altogether.

Zhu Yuanzhang's son, Emperor Yongle (1403–1424), did build what was by the standard of the early fifteenth century the world's finest and largest fleet. His ambassadors travelled as far as East Africa, but the purpose was to show off imperial prowess, not to encourage trade. The last landfall in China for the fleet was recorded as Tuen Mun which, sadly, had long been reduced to a mere anchorage.

## Portuguese Colonization of Hong Kong

The British were not the first Europeans to colonize Hong Kong. The Portuguese had proclaimed themselves colonial masters of Hong Kong as early as the sixteenth century. The ensuing Sino-Portuguese war precipitated a prolonged closure of China to foreign trade, ushering in the well-known era of "Japanese piracy".

Conventional historical accounts tend to portray the rest of Ming and the succeeding Qing Dynasty as totally introvert, intolerant of trading and other relationship with foreign countries. Lo Hsiang-lin, in accepting such a generalized view of Chinese history, attributed the apparent decline of Tuen Mun and Guanfu to the prohibition of foreign trade.

As we have already seen, the decline had come much earlier, from Yuan times onwards. However, the ban on foreign trade started to lose its grip by the late fifteenth century.

By the reign of Emperor Hongzhi (1488–1505), the ban on illicit trade was becoming less and less observed, certainly because the lure of silver from Japan was too great. Tuen Mun and Lantau certainly profited from such trading activities. It was during this period that Tai O, Lantau, became sufficiently affluent to commission a fine dual temple, for the worship of both the Goddess of the Sea and the Martial God.

The easy-going Emperor Zhengde (1506–1521) even relaxed the restrictions on trade and reintroduced customs duties. Thus in 1513, when the first Portuguese to reach China, Jorge Alvares, did so on a Burmese tribute craft, he was allowed to conduct a highly profitable trade at Nantou. Thereafter, Portuguese traders came on an annual basis from Goa (colonized in 1510) and Malacca (colonized in 1512).

The first European embassy to China arrived off Tuen Mun in 1517. It was led by Tomes Pires, representing the Portuguese court. Pires was sent to Nanjing where he befriended Emperor Zhengde and was then sent to Beijing, where the untimely death of the emperor in early 1521 put an abrupt end to the embassy.

Meanwhile, the Portuguese, headed by Frenao Perez D'Andrade who commanded the squadron carrying the Pires embassy, were allowed to trade at Nantou and Tuen Mun. In 1518, another squadron arrived under the command of D'Andrade's brother Simao, a brutal, insensitive man who soon fell foul of the officials at Nantou by erecting fortifications and obelisks bearing the Portuguese national emblem at Tuen Mun and Lantau. For the next three years, the western part of present-day Hong Kong was a *de facto* Portuguese colony where taxes were levied and cases were tried according to Portuguese law.

Requests to the imperial court for instruction on how to handle these interlopers were unanswered by Emperor Zhengde, who was on a round-the-country tour and who took a liking to Pires and his entourage. The death of Zhengde, together with the intolerable attempt by the Portuguese at Tuen Mun to collect protection money from Southeast Asian tribute traders, gave the imperial court the impetus to act.

The new Emperor Jiajing (1522–1566), of a fundamentalist inclination, in any case did not look kindly on foreign trade. He ordered the eviction of the Portuguese by force. In the winter of 1521, the Chinese attacked and captured the Portuguese position at Kau King Shan 九徑山 overlooking Tuen Mun. Further naval action forced the Portuguese fleet to evacuate Lantau.

The Portuguese authorities at Goa, reacting exactly like Lord Palmerston did three hundred years later, decided to send a large squadron to teach the Chinese a lesson and to impose upon them a treaty of "peace and trade". The squadron arrived at Tuen Mun in 1522. The Chinese were well prepared for the arrival of the invaders. A naval battle took place off Chek Lap Kok, the site of Hong Kong's new airport. Chinese fire rafts destroyed two Portuguese ships, killing over seventy enemies. The rest of the squadron had a hard time making to the open sea. Pires and his entourage, under confinement after hostilities started in 1521, were either executed or died in prison.

## *Illicit Trade and Macau*

The Sino-Portuguese war led not only to a ban on trade with Portuguese merchants. It reinforced Emperor Jiajing's determination to eradicate all non-tribute trade. During the next thirty years, China's coast, including the Hong Kong region, was ravaged by pirates as well as soldiers sent after them. Piracy was caused partly by illicit traders taking up arms against the authorities to defend their livelihood, partly by ex-illicit traders being forced into a life of plundering because their former gainful employment was no more, and partly by Japanese marauders. Though the majority of the pirates were Chinese, they were known to the fearful population as "Japanese pirates".

The Portuguese returned to the China coast to join the illicit trade in 1540. A decade later, after the governor of Fujian was forced to commit suicide when the imperial court disapproved of the brutal manner in the destruction of an island settlement servicing Sino-Portuguese illicit trade, the Portuguese were allowed to trade on a semi-legal basis. In 1555, trade with the Portuguese was formally legalized and their fleet (as well as missionaries) could proceed to Guangzhou during the summer months.

Macau, on the opposite shore of the Pearl Estuary from Lantau, was rented at around the same time to the Portuguese as a depot and wintering station. Macau thrived during the next eighty years on the very profitable entrepôt trade between Japan and China (Japanese being banned from direct trade with China because of past records of war and piracy).

Soon after Emperor Jiajing died in 1566, the court under the new Emperor Longqing (1567–1572), after a lengthy debate among officials and scholars up and down the country, decided to legalize the formerly illicit overseas trade. Until the Ming Dynasty was toppled in 1644, foreign trade, while subject to a certain amount of regulation, was no longer prohibited. The *Yue daji* 粵大記 (Grand Guide to Guangdong), published during the Wanli years (1573–1620), contained a map of the sea route from Guangdong to both the various ports farther up the China coast and to the ports in Japan.

It was against a background of greatly increased overseas trade that the Hong Kong and Shenzhen region was reconstituted in 1572 or 1573 into a county, named Xinan. The military command was also upgraded to the senior level of a full general (*zongbing* 總兵 ), with six sub-command positions (three of which being located in present-day Hong Kong).

The population of the county then was 33,971. Ten years later, it had expanded marginally to 34,520. A map of the coastal part of Xinan in *Yue daji* showed that "Hong Kong" had already existed then as the name for present-day Hong Kong Island. Over seventy present-day place names in Hong Kong can be identified in the same map. The Hong Kong region was certainly not "barely more than a geographical expression", as the Hong Kong History Society has alleged. Indeed, a petition to the imperial court at that time pointed out that, although trade had gravitated to Macau, Tuen Mun and Nantou still commanded the only waterway in the Pearl Estuary deep enough for ocean-going vessels travelling between Macau to Guangzhou.

High hopes were clearly entertained for Xinan when it was reconstituted. These hopes were dashed. The county not only failed to reclaim its former glory as port and naval base. Its population declined by over 60 per cent in the late sixteenth century, to only 13,202 in 1593. There were a few incidents of piracy (a good indicator of the level of trading activities and general affluence), but these were not sufficiently serious to merit the continuation of the posting of a senior military officer to the region. The command was downgraded in 1590 to that of a junior general (*canjiang* 參將 ), commanding a garrison and navy consisting of 3,000 soldiers and sailors.

Insufficient research has been carried out to enlighten us on why Xinan failed to grow and prosper. Indeed, this key question on Hong Kong history has yet to be properly formulated and put on the agenda by historians.

## *Desolation*

The first forty years of the Qing Dynasty saw Xinan county reduced to a desolate wilderness. After establishing itself in Beijing in 1644, the Qing court took some six years of incessant warfare before it could firmly control Guangzhou. In the meantime, in 1647, one group of Ming loyalists, led by Li Wanrong 李萬榮 , set themselves up in Xinan. One of their bases was in the Dapeng 大鵬 walled city, located to the north of the present-day boundaries of Hong Kong. Another base was in the Tai Mo Shan area, right in the heart of the New Territories. An outpost was established on a foothill near Tsuen Wan. The site of the fortress came to be known as Shing Mun, or castle gate. Some three hundred years later, the British would build a fortress at Shing Mun to defend Hong Kong against Japanese invaders, in vain.

The loyalists in Xinan and Qing forces sent to quell them battled one another for nearly a decade, until Li Wanrong surrendered in 1656. By that time, reportedly half of the buildings in the area had been reduced to ashes and tens of thousands of residents killed. The population was down to 6,851 persons.

Worse was to come. The most powerful of Ming loyalists, Zheng Chenggong 鄭成功 (known in Western literature as Koxinga, a corruption of his honorific title Guoxing Ye 國姓爺 ), had been harassing the China coast for many years. In 1662, despite the fact that Zheng's forces had retreated to Taiwan, the imperial court adopted the policy of *qianjie* 遷界, moving the territories. All land within 50 *li* (25 kilometres) of the sea coast was abandoned. Every person had to leave and all buildings destroyed, so that no food or assistance would be available to the loyalists.

Studies on the adoption of the *qianjie* policy have tended to view it as the result of petitions from local officials. It would be closer to the truth to look at it in the light of the sudden death in 1661 of Emperor Shunzhi (1644–1661). The new Emperor Kangxi (1662–1722) was only eight years old. A group of ultra-conservative Manchu aristocrats dominated the court for four years, and the scorch earth policy was one of the many imprudent decisions made.

The *qianjie* order was re-confirmed in 1663 and 1664. Almost all of present-day Hong Kong was included in the area to be evacuated. Soldiers were sent into the doomed area and all had to leave within three days. Many of those who left died of starvation and disease. Those who refused to leave were considered rebels and mercilessly killed. Xinan county was abolished in 1667 when the population was down to less than 4,000.

The *qianjie* policy was abolished in 1669, and Xinan county was reconstituted. However, for the islands of Hong Kong, *qianjie* was reintroduced in 1678, and re-population was not allowed until 1683 when Taiwan surrendered to Qing forces. The population for Xinan at that time was only around 7,000.

## *Regeneration*

Re-population proceeded steadily, partly by means of attracting Hakka migrants from north Guangdong. By 1772, the population had reached

32,000, around the same level two hundred years ago when Xinan was first reconstituted. The next forty years saw a population boom in the county, with population rising nearly eight-fold to around 240,000 by the 1810s.

Before the Ming loyalists in Taiwan had been subdued, the Qing court prohibited all maritime commerce (though very restricted trade through Macau was exempted). Two years after the conquest of Taiwan, in 1685, the policy of *kaihai* 開海 (open sea) was adopted. Foreign ships were allowed to trade at Guangzhou and three other ports farther up the coast.

However, Tuen Mun and Guanfu, just as in Yuan and Ming times, no longer served as the outer harbour for Guangzhou. It is interesting to note that, after Guangzhou had been declared the only port of call for foreign trade in 1757, the Guangdong Maritime Customs set up six additional key ports and 69 minor ports along the Guangdong coast to handle business spilled over from Guangzhou. Both Tuen Mun and Guanfu could not achieve the status of even a minor port.

Instead, Tuen Mun and Guanfu became lairds for pirates. More research would have to be carried out to untangle cause and effect. Did these fine harbours become desolate because they were frequented by pirates, or did the pirates come because these harbours had been inactive in the first place?

The pirates were in fact remnants of Ming loyalists still clinging, or paying lip service, to the ideal of restoration of the defunct empire. Rather like members of triad societies that sprang up around the same time bearing the same ideal, these pirates rarely earned their keep by plundering. Instead, they collected protection money from the coastal population and maritime traders in return for maintaining some sort of peace and order. The most active of the pirates were led by a legendary woman known as Zheng Yisao 鄭一嫂 and her common law husband Zhang Bao 張保 (Cheung Po Tsai 張保仔). They had some 20,000 to 30,000 followers and their field of operation stretched from Vietnam to Fujian. The Hong Kong waters were their base.

By the early years of the nineteenth century, Xinan was well-peopled. Foreign trade on the Pearl Estuary was also thriving due to the opium and tea trade by British and American vessels, with over ninety vessels arriving every year. The pirates had become intolerable. After a lengthy engagement off Chek Lap Kok against the Chinese navy assisted by Portuguese vessels from Macau, Zheng Yisao and Zhang Bao surrendered in 1810.

There is circumstantial evidence to suggest that trading activities, and the infrastructure to support them, started to be developed in the Hong

Kong region after the eradication of the pirates. By the mid-1830s, the British opium traders were regularly mooring their supply ships in Hong Kong waters, and they were also buying supplies from the region. The suggestion that Hong Kong Island be chosen as a British trading station was made by these opium traders.

The British colonization of Hong Kong, seen against the background of previous Portuguese colonization in the 1510s and prolonged usage of the harbours by British traders in the 1830s, was no accident. What was fortuitous was that the British, unwittingly, had chosen a site that, for most of the past 6,000 years with the exception of recent centuries, had been a busy crossroads of world trade and cultural intercourse.

Since British colonization, Tuen Mun and Guanfu have reclaimed more than their share of past glories, to become a megapolis with a per capita national income higher than that of Britain herself, as of the 1990s.

It would be simplistic to attribute, as most authors on the colonial history of Hong Kong have done, Hong Kong's phenomenal growth mainly to British administration. It would take another critical study to delineate the multifarious factors, mostly external to British administration, that have contributed to the colony's rise to greatness. The colony of Hong Kong, as Edgar Snow observed in the 1930s and still is the case today, is "England's own little corner of China, which refuses to become anglicized" (*Journey South of the Clouds*, 1991). In that Hong Kong is a *very* Chinese city even today, its pre-colonial past is as relevant as its colonial history.

# Index

Legend:  † place names